WOMEN
AND THE
VOTE

A WORLD HISTORY

JAD ADAMS

OXFORD
UNIVERSITY PRESS

OXFORD
UNIVERSITY PRESS

Great Clarendon Street, Oxford, ox2 6DP,
United Kingdom

Oxford University Press is a department of the University of Oxford.
It furthers the University's objective of excellence in research, scholarship,
and education by publishing worldwide. Oxford is a registered trade mark of
Oxford University Press in the UK and in certain other countries

© Jad Adams 2014

The moral rights of the author have been asserted

First published 2014
First published in paperback 2016

Impression: 1

Published in the United States of America by Oxford University Press
198 Madison Avenue, New York, NY 10016, United States of America

British Library Cataloguing in Publication Data
Data available

Library of Congress Cataloging in Publication Data
Data available

ISBN 978–0–19–870684–7 (Hbk.)
ISBN 978–0–19–870685–4 (Pbk.)

Printed in Great Britain by
Clays Ltd, St Ives plc

For Julie

Acknowledgements

I was the grateful recipient of a grant from the Scouloudi Foundation that allowed me to undertake research in the United States. An Authors' Foundation grant allowed me to devote myself to this book and eschew other commitments, my thanks to Sir Michael Holroyd and the selection panel.

My thanks to Warwick Gould and my colleagues at the Institute of English, School of Advanced Study, University of London, where I have perched as a historian in the English Department, working on a long term project called 'Decadent Women: Lives of the Lost Generation'. This has enjoyed the support of a travelling scholarship from the British Academy; some work gleaned in those travels has found its way into this book.

The Indian section of this book was written at the home of Narendra Singh Sarila in Sarila; the New Jersey section was written at the home of Serge and Christine Angiel in New Jersey, my heartfelt thanks for all the hospitality I have enjoyed.

My thanks to Cindy Brown at the Wyoming State Archives and Carol Bowers at the American Heritage Centre. The work on Wyoming was written in the Great Plains Hotel, Cheyenne where the staff made me welcome, as did Paula Taylor, Larry Sprague, and Dan Lyon at the Warren Air Force Base Museum. I am also grateful to Bette Epstein at the New Jersey State Archives.

I undertook archive and other research at the John Rylands University Library, University of Manchester; the Women's Library; the Parliamentary Archives; Butler Library, Columbia University; New York Public Library; Senate House Library, University of London; and I am most grateful to the British Library, which I inhabited for such extended periods that the staff pay me the compliment of knowing my name, and I have Reader Enquiries as my 'best friend' on my telephone dialling system.

This book has undergone revisions under the thoughtful guidance of my constant companion, Julie Peakman. I have also received practical help and in some cases advice on revisions from many sources around the world, notably from Margot Badran, Mineke Bosch, Joanna Bourke, Sean Brady, Laurel Brake, Louise Edwards, Geraldine Forbes, June Hannam, James House, Stacey Hynd, Harriet Jones, Asunción Lavrin, Neil MacMaster, Marie Mulvey-Roberts, Marianna Muravyeva, Lucy Riall, Mina Roces, Rochelle Ruthchild, and Arlette Strijland.

I also received research assistance from Keith Barltrop, Emily Carter, Catherine Dolphin, David Goldfrank, Sheila Gopaulen, Ray L.Hanna, John Hodgson, Gary Kelly, James Lees, Jess Mookherjee, Aviel Roshwald, Dianne Shepherd, Mari Takayanagi, and Tony Williams; and have had correspondence with Ellen DuBois, Richard J. Evans, Karen Offen, Polly O'Hanlan, and Martin Pugh. I am grateful to everyone for their kind attention to my sometimes abstruse questions. Thanks also to computer expert Kevin Vuong of Cymar Electronics who saved the manuscript when I feared it eaten by a computer; to Matthew Cotton and Luciana O'Flaherty at OUP; and to Fiona Burrows and Diana Tyler at MBA Literary Agents, who had faith in this book.

Contents

List of Illustrations

Abbreviations

Attempts have been made to keep abbreviations to a minimum, but those saving lengthy repetition are:

HWS   Susan B. Anthony, Elizabeth Cady Stanton, and Ida Husted Harper, *The History of Woman Suffrage*, 6 vols. New York: Fowler Wells 1881–1922

IWSA   International Woman Suffrage Alliance

NAWSA   National American Woman Suffrage Association—a product of the union in 1890 of the American Woman Suffrage Association (AWSA) and the National Woman Suffrage Association (NWSA)

NUWSS   National Union of Women's Suffrage Societies

PRO   Public Record Office

WCTU   Woman's Christian Temperance Union

WSPU   Women's Social and Political Union

Most national legislatures are bicameral, and in most cases the chambers have names such as, in the US and UK, House of Representatives or House of Commons for the lower houses, and Senate and House of Lords for upper houses. Excepting these, which are internationally known, in this text the specific names are generally ignored in order not to burden the text with unfamiliar terms, and chambers are referred to as 'upper house' and 'lower house'.

Introduction

The history of democracy is enormously indebted to the creativity of places that historians have hardly studied.[1]

Going back to Wyoming

My involvement with this story began in the 1970s when as a student I decided to travel across the United States. I did it the romantic, if impoverished, way on a Greyhound bus; I had the smart idea that I could see more and cut down on hotel bills by using overnight buses, visiting cities during the day. What I did not take into account was that when the coach stopped to refuel, passengers would receive the instruction to 'de-bus' and so would climb out in the small hours of the morning at a chilly coach stop to hang around until the Greyhound was ready to move again. Thus it was that after hours of rolling over the monotonous flat prairie of the West, I found myself in Cheyenne with its wide, windswept streets devoid of decoration, and shops selling saddles and other cowboy goods.

With half an hour to kill, I walked towards the only interesting sight I could see, the golden-domed capitol building, wondering whatever I had done to find myself at three a.m. here in this awful outback place where nothing had ever happened except cattle rearing and violence.

I was not, therefore, in the most receptive frame of mind, so I was startled to see, directly in front of the state government building, a huge statue of a woman in a flowing dress. The monument had an inscription saying it was Esther Hobart Morris who in 1869 had promoted legislation that made Wyoming the first place in the world where women had equal rights. This bemused me, for progress was not supposed to be made in the outback. This did not fit in with any world view I had, where the great centres of

Figure 1. The statue of Esther Hobart Morris in front of the State Capitol building, noting Wyoming as the first government in the world to grant women equal rights, in 1869.

population and learning were supposed to make advances in human rights, and the hicks followed at a respectful distance.

What was happening here in the middle of the nineteenth century with these frontier people who had nothing in common with the sophisticated women I knew in feminist politics back home at Sussex University? How come an out of the way place like Wyoming could accomplish a great democratic advance which then took more than half a century for the most complex political cultures to achieve?

That question irritated me through years of writing books and making television programmes about radicals in public life. It has become one of the themes of this book looking at women's enfranchisement around the world, the writing of which permitted me, among other pleasures, a return to Wyoming.

The role of individuals

There is a deliberate focus on biography in this narrative, as a means of humanizing what can be dry constitutional matters, and supporting the truism that history is collective biography. There is also the joy of discovery in learning of the engagement of these women with a hostile world, such as Funmilayo Ransome-Kuti and her market women challenging the king's fearsome bodyguard; and the revolutionary Chinese suffragists invading the new provisional assembly.

While it was not my intention to seek out biographical themes, the occurrence of the same relationships through different centuries and cultures is inescapable. A recurring theme is the indulgent father who encourages the daughter against tradition as with Tching Soumay in China; Aletta Jacobs in Holland; Elizabeth Cady Stanton in the US and Sarojini Naidu in India. Another theme running through the lives gathered here is of the tyrannical father in such lives as that of Mary Wollstonecraft in eighteenth-century Britain and Ichikawa Fusae in twentieth-century Japan. Older brothers often played a prominent part as in the lives of Matilde Hidalgo de Procel, the pioneer of women's suffrage in Latin America, and Rokeya Sakhawat Hossain in India. It is striking too to note the recurrence of couples in this story, whose relationship gave them a greater strength than merely the sum of their individual powers: people such as Marquis de Condorcet and Sophie de Grouchy; John Stuart Mill and Harriet Taylor; Aletta Jacobs and Carel Gerritsen.

Very often the suffrage pioneer was the first doctor in their country, the first to go to university (or both); but while the story of women and the vote contains such tales of academic courage against the odds, it also has soap opera actress Eva Perón in Argentina and beauty queen Pura Villanueva in the Philippines, both offering very different models of women's achievement from that of the earnest suffragist.

The individuals studied here were part of collective suffrage movements, sometimes vast, sometimes containing only a handful of people. These movements are taken as a starting point as, of necessity, suffrage movements analysed the women's suffrage situation in the nations where they operated. This does not mean that suffrage organizations 'won the vote' in any particular nation, though they always liked to claim they did.

My approach is always to look first at accounts of events written by the participants themselves. In this case there is in some ways an embarrassment of riches brought about by the tendency of participants to write their own histories of the movement before it had fully run its course, and therefore to frame the interpretation of its development and of its controversies. Thus, one objective of the six-volume *History of Woman Suffrage*, that began publication in 1881, was to demonstrate that the experiences of the leaders of the National Woman Suffrage Association 'entitled them to priority in the women's movement', as a commentator remarked.[2] It was a priority enjoyed by Elizabeth Cady Stanton and Susan B. Anthony rather than their third author for the first three volumes; one writer has been moved to remark on these two women's 'historical betrayal' of Matilda Joslyn Gage and her ideas.[3] Despite its bulk the *History of Woman Suffrage* is a partial history and it is entirely deliberate that, for example, Victoria Woodhull, the first woman presidential candidate, is absent from the index.

It is highly questionable whether the women who wrote the histories were actually the people who did most for women's suffrage. It is a paradox that the old, established areas of political activism contributed more talk than achievement to suffrage battles, while hitherto neglected areas were triumphant. Thus the sophisticated eastern parts of the United States, the radical areas of England, and the literary centres of Scandinavia urged women's suffrage in the second half of the nineteenth century and the first part of the twentieth. But the practical achievements, as historian Ross Evans Paulson remarks, 'occurred on the frontiers of the Anglo-American and Scandinavian cultures: Australia, New Zealand, the American West, and Finland'.[4]

Sylvia Pankhurst wrote *The Suffragette* in 1910 when the Women's Social and Political Union still had its most violent episodes ahead of it; her later book, *The Suffragette Movement*, with its detailed description of the shortcomings of her sister Christabel, demonstrated how Sylvia with her working-class movement won the vote in the UK. Her account may be counterposed with Christabel Pankhurst's *Unshackled: The Story of How We Won the Vote* with its failure to mention events others might think significant—such as the expulsion of Sylvia and her East London women's group from the Women's Social and Political Union.

The non-militant suffragists, demonstrating how in fact it was they who won the vote, reflected their own divisions in the official history '*The Cause': A Short History of the Women's Movement in Great Britain*. This was written by Ray Strachey who had worked with Millicent Fawcett to expel the 'poisonous pacifists' from the National Union of Women's Suffrage Societies at the beginning of the First World War. In keeping with this approach, the names of pacifists were omitted from Strachey's history, though in 1915 pacifists had been in the majority on the NUWSS executive.[5] Historian Kathryn Dodd argues not only that *The Suffragette Movement* and *'The Cause'* were written from 'two conflicting political positions', but that Sylvia Pankhurst's book was a socialist response to the earlier work, which had constructed a history that favoured conservative constitutionalism over radical direct action, in the service of the political landscape when the book was being written in the late 1920s.[6] Brief but reliable guides to the complex events of the 1860s to 1928 have been written by Paula Bartley and Harold Smith.[7]

An account which is contemporaneous or near-contemporaneous might be thought to be particularly reliable but the opposite is often the case: Alice Zimmern's benign 1909 account in *Women's Suffrage in Many Lands* of the Russian Congress of 1908 omits any mention of its disruption by Alexandra Kollontai and her Social Democrat 'labour women' or the bitter division between the socialists and the feminists. This may merely be diplomatic, Zimmern's wishing not to embarrass fellow suffragists still involved in the struggle, but volume six of the *History of Woman Suffrage*, printed in 1922, after universal suffrage had been granted, merely remarked that the conference was addressed by eminent people and speeches were 'favourably received'.[8] There seemed an unwillingness to admit that women disagreed about the means to achieve shared goals—or that they actually engaged in the recognizable conflicts of politics.

If works by participants in suffrage movements tend to overplay their importance, the fewer works by parliamentarians commensurately stress their own. William Pember Reeves, a cabinet minister in the 1893 New Zealand government that gave women the vote, and therefore both a commentator and a participant, wrote two volumes of *State Experiments in Australia and New Zealand* in 1902. He argued that the franchise was 'given freely and spontaneously, in the easiest and most unexpected manner in the world' by high-minded statesmen with little opposition or debate and without public agitation.[9] The matter had in fact been in public debate for twenty-five years and had been coming before parliament for fifteen years; the last suffrage petition was signed by one in four of the adult female population and was organized by a national franchise league.

A vast secondary literature has been produced on women's suffrage in some nations, notably in Britain and the US. The pioneers of women's suffrage, in New Zealand and Finland (enfranchising in 1906) have had nothing like so much attention. Women's suffrage in southern hemisphere countries has been academically neglected, even in works that make the leap from considering suffrage in one country to looking at it internationally.

International studies of women's suffrage before the 1990s were few, particularly in the period after the publications by participants in first two decades of the twentieth century. Three books of the 1970s took a view of women's movements including the suffrage issue: Richard Evans' *The Feminists: Women's Emancipation Movements in Europe, America and Australasia 1840–1920* (1977); Ross Evans Paulson's *Women's Suffrage and Prohibition: A Comparative Study of Equality and Social Control* (1973); both of whose titles explain their contents; and Trevor Lloyd's short, illustrated *Suffragettes International: The World-wide Campaign for Women's Rights* (1971) which, like the present work, focuses on women and the vote globally. Lloyd in fact pays scant attention to any except the European and Anglophone nations. Kumari Jayawardena's classic *Feminism and Nationalism in the Third World* (1986), again from the point of view of feminism in general rather than electoral rights in particular, has drawn the valuable conclusion that feminism was an essential and integral part of national resistance movements.[10]

Limited areas of women's suffrage history have been extensively studied, notably England from 1903 to 1914. Global history on the subject, however, was so neglected it was possible for Carole Pateman to remark to the 'Suffrage and Beyond' conference in New Zealand in 1993, 'We know remarkably little about how women won the vote around the world'; and for Ellen DuBois to lament, 'Why have woman suffrage movements so little history?'[11] The publication resulting from that conference, a collection of essays, *Suffrage and Beyond: International Feminist Perspectives* went a considerable way towards addressing questions of comparative study of women's enfranchisement.

The twenty-first century in its first years made major contributions to international women's suffrage scholarship. *The International Encyclopaedia of Women's Suffrage* (2000) by June Hannam and collaborators, fulfils its mission to demonstrate the international dimensions of women's enfranchisement with entries on countries and individuals in all five continents.[12] Karen Offen's *European Feminisms 1700–1950: A Political History* (2000) covers suffrage issues where relevant. Two collections of essays, Louise

Edwards and Mina Roces' *Asia: Gender, Nationalism and Democracy* (2004) and Ian Fletcher and collaborators' *Women's Suffrage in the British Empire: Citizenship, Nation and Race* (2000) map out the intellectual terrain and take our understanding further in the areas they cover.[13] Edwards and Roces' introductory essay, 'Orienting the Global Women's Suffrage Movement' is particularly valuable in terms of the current book. Essays on global women's suffrage history have been written by John Markoff (2003) and by June Hannam (2005). Markoff emphasizes suffrage being won away from the centres of power; Hannam writes of international themes in suffrage movements and the necessity of viewing the world from other than a western perspective. Francisco O. Ramirez and collaborators (1997) bring in a notion of 'field pressure' on nations moving towards an inclusive, global concept of citizenhood.[14]

What has been lacking is a book which addresses the subject of women's suffrage chronologically, globally, and with attention to the major themes and questions that women's suffrage throws up. This book is intended to contribute in that area. I have drawn on individual studies of nations by noted scholars, but I bear responsibility for the regional approach giving Catholic Europe, sub-Saharan Africa, Latin America, the East, and the Muslim world a separate chapter each. This is a matter of emphasis (rather than dogma); a right–left or liberal–conservative political division is acknowledged, but a far more important categorization over this issue of gender and the constitution is of the majority religion of a nation. There was a significantly similar attitude towards women's suffrage within Protestant or secular nations; within European Catholic nations and in Latin America. The influence of Muslim culture was so strong that the former Ottoman territory of Greece, even though profoundly Christian, followed the path to women's enfranchisement of 'first wave' Muslim nations. Arabian peninsular countries ('second wave' Muslim nations in terms of women's franchise) resisted women's suffrage up to the point of the massive international pressure expended on them in the twenty-first century. More than 40 per cent of the world's population of women, in the immensely populous nations of China, India, and Indonesia were enfranchised within a year of each other in the middle of the twentieth century.[15] This can be taken as a clue that there are similarities that would benefit from collective examination. A partiality in the point of view has to be acknowledged (even the term 'East' implies a standpoint half a world away) but it is hoped that awareness of potential bias provides some inoculation.

The advantages of such an approach over a book with individual chapters written by experts are the unified stylistic and theoretical framework. The disadvantage is the author's linguistic limitation leading to a clear bias towards Anglophone evidence and a consequent neglect of, say, Francophone and Lusophone enfranchisements in Africa and the Far East, not to mention the doubtless rich sources in native languages that of necessity have been neglected. It is hoped that others will follow this work.

This book is not a history of feminism or women's movements. Such scholars as Olwyn Hufton, Barbara Taylor, and Karen Offen have made great contributions in this field and their work has illuminated this study. Others have engaged in a discourse about 'feminisms' and the highly selective histories that exclude women because of their race, class, ethnicity, or creed, or because of ideological divisions.[16] This is a history of the achievement of a single, clear, and measurable objective: the right to appear on an electoral register which either was or was not present at different times in a nation's history.

Themes

Before 1893 no women had the right to vote for a national parliament; within a century, almost every nation in the world had women voters; more than 100 countries enfranchised women after the Second World War. The exceptions were (and are) countries in which men had or have little democratic influence.

The franchise for women in western countries was the great challenge, it was an assault on the citadel, the heart of male power. Early battles—for example, for married women to have the right to their own property or for the right to practise in the professions—hard fought though they might have been, were on a smaller scale: they were advances on the personal stage, about individual lives and careers. The right to take part in directing the country in issues of the economy or foreign policy in peace and in war was a gender advance on an altogether different scale.

The franchise for women was not the creeping march of progress sometimes presented, a victorious army slowly taking all in its stride. It was more like a guerrilla war where a few courageous souls would dash out and fire a fusillade and be driven back to gather support. Sometimes ground won was then snatched back and women were subsequently disenfranchised as they were in New Jersey in 1808 and as they almost were in Wyoming in 1871, as they were in Spain in 1939.

Developing countries such as New Zealand and Australia, remote from the centres of power, found it easier to enfranchise women than sophisticated metropolitan societies. The existence of an organized feminist movement was a generally helpful but not essential factor in enfranchisement; in some countries vigorous feminist organizations deterred erstwhile supporters by militancy or by unrealistic proposals as to what the vote would achieve in such fields as sex regulation and alcohol prohibition. In some countries the women's vote was granted with no major feminist agitation—the territory of Utah enfranchised women with no suffrage movement at all; in Norway the suffrage movement was feeble—though the women's vote was still granted there earlier than in Holland with its massive suffrage movement. This is not to say suffrage movements were uninfluential, but other factors were more important; American women's suffrage leader Carrie Chapman Catt lamented that it seemed 'the better the campaign, the more certain that suffrage would be defeated'.[17]

While organizations and individuals made real contributions, particularly in setting the terms for enfranchisement and keeping the issue in the public mind, supra-national issues played a greater part. The most important factors making for women's suffrage were national crises such as war or nationalist uprisings (often, of course, happening at the same time). The first great tranche of countries enfranchised women during or after the First World War regardless of whether they were on the winning or losing side, or even combatants. A struggle for national self-determination such as that undertaken by Finland and India made for an ultimately painless enfranchisement for women. Invasion and civil war had the same effect in China.

Internationally, the speed at which women obtained the vote in different countries related more closely to local conditions than to any argument about the justice of their political claim. Women's enfranchisement was bitterly resisted in some places, in others it was taken as a matter of course. In keeping with the complexity of this subject, this book uses a multi-factoral model. Factors promoting this legislative change, but not all essential to it, were: a national crisis such as war, an independence movement or revolution; the presence of educated and unarguably capable women; an established notion of 'rights' of the citizen if not, necessarily, 'human rights'; movements such as socialism or feminism that had (respectively) universal suffrage or women's suffrage as part of their programme. Finally, for late enfranchising countries, the 'field pressure' of neighbouring or influential nations exerted a shaming effect on those that had not enfranchised women: a deficiency that was, by the last third of the twentieth century, seen as a symbol of national backwardness.

The factors against women's suffrage were: conservatism, by which is meant the resistance to anything new, whatever the political constitution of the legislature; a contradictory fear from radicals that if enfranchised, women would vote for conservative candidates; the Catholic and Muslim religions, that gave a higher authority to arguments about women's fixed role on earth than the merely political; the under-education of women; and mere misogyny that resented any increase in women's influence.

Across these broad factors pushing for or against women's suffrage were fault lines involving race and class which recur in narratives of women's suffrage. These were significant for notions of solidarity since they could cut across collective action based on gender.

The complicating factor of race is most starkly shown up in the US situation where, though the women's suffrage movement had its roots in anti-slavery agitation, in 1869 black men and suffragist women (with some exceptions) refused to support each other's enfranchisement; and by the end of the century the notion of women's suffrage was being promoted to southern states as a means to keep black people under subjection. After enfranchisement, black women were disenfranchised—just as black men had been after the amendment granting them the vote. Frequently women's suffrage was promoted as a means to enhance the political power of a dominant race, as in South Africa in 1930.

Suffragist women also exerted a racial superiority over immigrants, particularly marking out illiterate immigrant men who had the vote when educated white women did not. A similar complaint was made about labourers and others of lowly occupation, who might have the vote when women who considered themselves socially superior did not.

The fault line of class was much more important in Europe than in the US and Australasia. In Norway the enfranchisement of women property owners in 1907 resulted in middle-class women abandoning their former gender-based position and voting with their class, which elected a government that refused to give the vote to working-class women. A parliamentary majority existed for the principle of women's suffrage for more than twenty years before limited suffrage was granted in the UK, but it meant nothing while political parties looked to the comparative political advantage of enfranchising propertied women or working-class women.

In places as far apart as Italy, Russia, and Japan, wealthy women were able to vote prior to the establishment of some semblance of modern democracy: if they had property or fulfilled other voting requirements, they were considered the equal of men in this respect, because of the status conferred by nobility. By the end of the nineteenth century an increase in notions of democracy had overwritten the feudal attitude that rank alone conferred political benefits; now it was masculinity that did so. Increasingly, manhood suffrage was awarded, with only Finland awarding men and women the vote equally from the start.

The clue to the venom with which 'bourgeois feminists' were treated by socialist women such as Alexandra Kollontai is that the bourgeois feminists seemed to be asking for the return of a system in which money was the measure of the right to political participation—posh ladies or educated ladies (who were very often the same) laid claim to a gender solidarity, but it was their wealth that guaranteed the vote. This was not the system that progressive thinkers wanted to see restored.

There were, in addition to race and class, more minor complicating factors involved in many nations where influential movements became involved in women's suffrage issues: campaigns for temperance, 'moral purity', socialism, and pacifism.

Many of those who promoted women's suffrage saw the measure as part of a 'progressive' improvement of society and the prohibition of alcohol (which had quickly taken over from temperate use as the goal of the movement) was thought in the Anglophone world to belong to the same sphere. Campaigners from the Women's Christian Temperance Union contributed to the setting up of suffrage organizations in New Zealand, Australia, and Japan. In state-wide referendums in the US, however, the temperance connection was felt to impede women's suffrage. The success of temperance mirrored that of women's suffrage: severe licensing restrictions were imposed in Britain from 1914; prohibition was imposed in the US in 1919—both of these developments showing a close temporal proximity to the achievement of women's suffrage in those nations.

Though temperance campaigners wanted the women's vote in order to deliver prohibition, this was reciprocal: suffragists would enjoy the campaigning abilities of temperance agitators, who could be jettisoned when the vote was won—not every suffragist believed in prohibition by any means.

The campaign for 'moral purity' was another movement of ambivalent utility for women's suffrage. Suffragists in most countries, including those in Latin America and the East, moved in an environment in which there were two sometimes conflicting trends: for equal rights and for moral reform. That is, for the right of women to be treated as equal to men in terms of citizenship; and an objective of ending prostitution, venereal disease, and other manifestations of 'social evil'. Often suffragists decided they had to abandon the social reform part of their agenda to attract the widest range of supporters. More frequently they lost focus on the achievable goal of suffrage, by listing it as one of a number of social objectives and dissipating their efforts.

The belief that, given the franchise, women would raise the tone of public morality was endorsed even by John Stuart Mill, but by the end of the nineteenth century such women as Eliza Lynn Linton were able to mock the pretensions of those who felt the introduction of drawing room proprieties into political life would be a boon. In Sweden writer Ellen Key thought some feminists' preoccupation with prostitution showed a dubious morality. Arguments about the moral superiority of women tended to be made to audiences outside the parliamentary forum, as they did not play well in national assemblies of men, who were more likely to be swayed by the view that the franchise for women was fair and just than that the legislature needed to be morally reinvigorated.

In Latin America and the East suffragists generally promoted the positive, home-making and nurturing aspects of women's roles rather than denigrating men. Women's contribution to notions of free, healthy nationhood were also brought to the fore in newly independent countries.

The ideas of socialism developed alongside feminism in the last quarter of the nineteenth century in Europe and North America, along with other manifestations of the 'modern' such as spiritualism and vegetarianism. In the Edwardian period in Britain socialism and feminism became solidified as separate ideologies, particularly after the founding of the Labour party in 1900 and the WSPU ('suffragettes') in 1903. At least by 1900, and long before that in many places, socialists 'viewed feminism as a rival enterprise and attempted to counter its attractiveness by smear and counterclaim' as Karen Offen has said.[18] Most if not all socialists were supporters of women's suffrage to the extent that they believed in universal suffrage—men and women being enfranchised equally. Socialism derided the women's movement's claim to represent both the duchess and her housemaid, while accepting a claim (that both socialism and feminism had derived from revolutionary Liberalism with its roots in the Enlightenment) of the equality of the sexes and the right of universal access to political power. Most women's movements argued, effectively, that the political structure should reflect the class structure so that if the vote came with the ownership of property, then wealthy women should have the vote as did wealthy men. The interests of other, unenfranchised women would be protected by the inclusion of some women in the democratic fold.

Ultimate victory, in Europe at least, tended to come with the working out of the democratic idea, with the enfranchisement of all. Conservative elites had found that there was no danger but considerable legitimizing strength in being more inclusive and taking all people into newly formed democratic systems. Long-standing arguments from both feminists and socialists made it imperative that this extension of democracy would encompass women as well as men.

The argument from women's supposed innate pacifism played an important part in the story of women's enfranchisement, not least in the terms of the current work that seeks to situate winning the vote in the context of national crisis. It had been feared that women not only could not understand war, but would be a pacifist or a defeatist force in the body politic, and the nation would be at risk from aggressors. In nations with conscript armies women were not called up and so theoretically deserved a lower level of citizenship, but this argument fell into desuetude as modern armies required a vast hinterland of people in supporting roles, most of which could be done by women, and no one suggested that men who could not bear arms should be disenfranchised.

Still, there remained the argument of many suffragists themselves that women's engagement in politics would eliminate war as a means of settling differences. One suffragist angrily denounced 'the two most dangerous rivals and foes of feminism—Peace and the Social Reformers' as these distracted from the struggle for the vote.[19] Pacifism should have been more of a problem for gaining women's suffrage, in fact it became a problem for the suffrage organizations, causing divisions in the US and UK movements. As soon as danger threatened their nation, nationalism became stronger than any idealism most suffragists felt for pacifism. Carrie Chapman Catt became a supporter of the war against her previous convictions; Emmeline Pankhurst and Millicent Fawcett likewise became vociferous supporters of the war effort. Those such as Aletta Jacobs in Holland and Rosika Schwimmer in Hungary who maintained their pacifist beliefs, did so at no cost to the enfranchisement of women.

Framework

The first chapter of this book is a brief survey of some of the prevailing attitudes towards women in the period before suffrage was considered, with a glance at fledgling democracies and women's position in them.

Chapter 2 looks at the development of the concept of the 'rights of man' with particular reference to the political rights of women in the age of revolutions. Chapter 3 follows the development of radical thought in Britain in the first half of the nineteenth century; Chapter 4 narrates the rise of the middle class in campaigning and formulating arguments over women's position in society.

Chapters 5 and 6 describe advances in women's suffrage in outlying, agricultural, and mining areas in the US, Australia, and New Zealand. The seventh covers enfranchisement in Scandinavia and the eighth the development of 'militancy' in Britain.

Chapters 9 and 10 review the enfranchisements taking place at the end of the First World War in the US and Europe. Chapter 11 examines the European Catholic countries, whose rate of enfranchisement of women proceeded at a different pace from that of their Protestant neighbours.

Chapter 12 covers the continent of Latin America, Chapter 13 the vast enfranchisements in India and the East. With India, China, and Indonesia enfranchising almost half the world's population of women in or close to 1949, this year at the middle of the century was numerically the high point of women's political emancipation.

The subject of Chapter 14 is sub-Saharan Africa with enfranchisements coming from the dismantling of colonial empires and the drawing of new constitutions, in the political climate of the Cold War where women's suffrage was not an issue disputed between the main combatants.

Chapter 15 looks at a specifically Muslim approach to women's suffrage, where women's service of the state became an honourable route to public life. It also covers those eastern countries which are predominantly Muslim, and the late enfranchisements of Arabian peninsular countries.

An appendix shows the dates of women's suffrage in different countries, with some explanation of the difficulty and the pitfalls of producing such a list. Plotted as a graph, the world picture of women's suffrage shows rises and falls in alignment with the great wars of the twentieth century: a close relationship exists between the end of the First and Second World Wars and the number of enfranchisements of women in different nations.

There is a pronounced but less clear relationship with the height of the Cold War in the late 1950s and early 1960s when a large number of new nations enfranchised women. In the last phase, the relationship of the global 'War on Terror' with late enfranchisements of women in Arab states is inescapable.

It is unwise to over-stress the relationship with the Cold War for two main reasons: though the number of countries had increased, there was not an unlimited number that could gain voting rights, so extrapolating from the increasing numbers enfranchising in the 1955–65 period could be very misleading—there were few countries left to enfranchise by 1965. Secondly, there could be different interpretations of the boundaries of the Cold War which began in 1948 with the Berlin Blockade and ended in 1989 with the fall of the Berlin Wall. I place its high point in 1962 with the Cuban missile crisis, after which the major players found it more expedient to fight wars by proxy in such places as Vietnam and Afghanistan, rather than confronting each other. Alternative interpretations would discount the Cold War and associate the enfranchisements of the late 1950s and early 1960s with the retreat of European colonial power, particularly in Africa. In either case, the relationship of women's suffrage is primarily to catastrophic or revolutionary national events, not to 'movements'; this book undertakes to understand that phenomenon.

I

Democracy before democracy

'What will you tell your wives and daughters?'

In the reign of Athens' legendary first king, Cecrops, men and women had
the vote equally, and sexual relationships were promiscuous to the extent
that children did not know who their fathers were. This lifestyle was undermined when the goddess Athene and the god Poseidon competed for
the position of patron of the city. The men voted for Poseidon while the
women, who were more numerous, voted for Athene, so she received the
honour. In revenge for being thwarted, the men took away the vote from
women and broke with matrilinear succession: in future children would no
longer be known by their mother's name, but that of the father. Thus, the
myth explains, was monogamous marriage introduced into Greek society:
women lost sexual freedom and political freedom as a consequence of
opposing men.[1]

The creation of monogamy was seen as one of the civilizing innovations
of Cecrops' rule; others were the creation of writing, burial of the dead, the
abolition of certain bloody sacrifices in favour of barley-cake offerings, the
division of Athens into twelve administrative units, and the building of tem-
ples to Athene.[2]

Characteristically, a myth of Greece illuminates a timeless question. In this
case it is the relationship of political rights to gender and to sexual behaviour, a recurring theme in the story of women and the vote. There is also,
from a pragmatic point of view, the relationship of the development of civilization to the control of women by monogamy and, by implication, the
sequestering of women in the home with a restriction of their opportunity
to play a part in public affairs.

Some kind of *ekklesiai* (assemblies) existed in the Greek city-states for
as far back as there are any references to political organization, but they

tended to be infrequently called and decided only major questions such as war and alliances. By the sixth century with the development of the culture of what is referred to as classical Greece there was a clearly defined Athenian assembly controlling legislation, administration, and justice that consisted of citizens: men over 18 who were not slaves or foreigners. Women did not vote, speak at, or even attend meetings of the assembly in Athens, nor did any other Greek state enfranchise women. They could not own property and they could not conduct legal business.

Plato's utopian *Republic* included women among the ruling Guardians; this would have them ruling over both men and women of the lower classes (though the very highest class of guardians was exclusively male). This classical precedent at least admitted women's political rights for discussion in later centuries where references to Greek philosophy carried weight in debate. As nineteenth-century radical Catherine Barmby wrote in *The Demand for the Emancipation of Women* in 1843, 'That woman is not the equal of man, who can assert?... Plato in his Commonwealth has thought it reasonable to admit women into an equal share of the dignities and offices with man.'[3] Plato admitted only a difference in physical strength between men and women.

Regardless of the absence of formal political power, it is worth dwelling on the position of women in Athenian democracy as many of the arguments concerning them can be related to the position of women up to the modern period. The question of whether women were despised and held in contempt, or were honoured and cherished members of Athenian society has been discussed since the 1920s.[4] Women were certainly kept indoors except for attendance at women's festivals. The question is whether women were behind the bolts and bars of the 'women's rooms' of a wealthy Athenian house because they were entrapped, or because they were treasured and therefore protected.

Discussion of the position of women is confused by the fact that twentieth-century woman-friendly western academics saw in classical antiquity a reflection of their own values. Classicist Sarah Pomeroy specifically relates the interpretation of women's position in the case of one writer to 'the wave of feminism which culminated in the passage of the Nineteenth Amendment' (which granted women the vote in the US).[5] That is: in an age influenced by feminism, F. A. Wright wrote *Feminism in Greek Literature* in 1923 where he deprecated the 'low ideal of womanhood' and the 'degradation of women'. Other urbane scholars, starting with A. W. Gomme in 1925, have pointed up the more positive aspects of ancient Greek life, emphasizing home life and sociability rather than such manifestations of the Greek spirit as the massacre or enslavement of their enemies. Sarah Pomeroy comments that 'they were reluctant to believe that the Athenians might not have treated their wives the way cultivated gentlemen in the twentieth century treat theirs'.[6]

Regardless of whether they were captive or treasured, the fact remains that the notion that women might take part in the political process would have seemed outrageously strange—the subject of comedies such as Aristophanes' *Lysistrata* and *Ekklesiazusai* where women intervene in the state. For example, in *Ekklesiazusai* ('women at the assembly') the women succeed in taking over the assembly by pretending to be men. Now in the majority, they vote to transfer the control of affairs from men to women. The women set up a socialist system of community of property and extend this to a kind of sexual communism where everyone has a right to sex with anyone else. This leads to such ribald events as three old hags claiming the right to a youth with whom they each want to copulate.

There is clearly a notion in these entertainments that women *could* have such thoughts of deciding policy. In such a way the very concept of democracy is subversive: if one group can share power equally, why not another? Both these plays were written during the second half of the Peloponnesian War (431–404 BC) when the numbers of men had been depleted by warfare, both from death and absence on campaigns. Women were presumably, as is customary in wartime, performing public tasks otherwise reserved for men. The plays show the anxiety about the changes such gender imbalance and role reversal wrought in Athenian society. This theme, of gender imbalance affecting the political rights of women, was to recur throughout the history of women and the vote. It is hardly coincidence that the only classical text the Woman's Press of the Women's Social and Political Union ('suffragettes') offered to its readers was Laurence Housman's translation of the *Lysistrata*.

A speech attributed to Demosthenes, the greatest orator of classical Greece, described how things should work: 'Mistresses [*hetairai*] we keep for the sake of pleasure, concubines [*pallakai*] for the daily care of our persons (meaning bodily needs), but wives [*gynaikes*] to bear us legitimate children and to be the faithful guardians of our households.'[7] Thus the gradations of respect and the position of women are carefully established, as are their roles in life. Women have roles that do not include, for example, bearing arms or taking part in government. How many women resented this is not a question it is possible to answer, but probably it was accepted as a part of life, as resistant to change as the seasons of the year. Men too had different roles, but they were less well defined. A farmer was also a soldier when the city was threatened, and because of this dual role he was also able to talk in the assembly, to make laws, and to sit in judgement on others as a juryman. This was an important part of part of his citizenship, while a woman's contribution was to bear children and bring them up as citizens.

In another play, Euripides' tragedy *Medea*, the eponymous heroine is challenging Jason, her husband, who has abandoned her for another woman, after she has made immense sacrifices for him and put her scheming brilliance at his service. 'Men say that we live a life free from danger at home while they fight with the spear. How wrong they are! I would rather stand three times with a shield in battle than give birth once.'[8]

This is perhaps the first surviving example in history of the argument for equivalence: that women did not do exactly the same as men, but did equivalent things and therefore should enjoy the same rights. This argument was to change through the centuries, particularly as machines took over much of what had previously been manual labour in the modern period. It could be argued in the twentieth century that in most of everyday life and work women and men did exactly the same thing, and differences were minimal. The question of quite how much innate difference there is between men and women has continued to be the central question of women's rights and, latterly, men's rights in relation to women (as men have demanded the right of access to their children).

It should not be thought that, because women had no power to vote in Athens, they did not take part in the discourse of government. In the same court case from which the speech of Demosthenes quoted above comes, the orator warns the jurymen of the trouble they will have at home if they acquit a villain: 'What will you say to your wives and daughters when you go home? They will ask you where you have been. You will say "In the courts". They will say "What was the case?"... You will tell them the details of the case and you will tell them how carefully and completely the case was proved. When you have finished they will say, "And what did you do?" And you will reply "We acquitted her" and then the fat will be in the fire.'[9]

The speaker is playing this for comic effect but he unintentionally is presenting later centuries with what was to him a familiar scene of women discussing and challenging decisions made on their behalf by the head of the household. Tellingly, he is calling on this scene of the home life of

Athenians because he knows the image will help the prosecution as the conjectured wives and daughters will be sure to be vindictive. He is prosecuting a woman, Neaira, alleged to be an alien and a prostitute living as a Greek citizen. Such virtuous women as jurymen's wives, he asserts without fear of contradiction, would be angry if a woman like Neaira were to go unpunished.

An inevitable modern consideration is that, if women were well versed in the subjects of public debate, why did they not demand a more public say, for there is no evidence that they did so? This is to apply a later mindset to the subject; doubtless they did not do so because they did not question the role of the man as the person within the family who performed in the public arena. A woman could be a private disputant in the house, it would be unseemly for her to make public pronouncements.

No less say in the household

Another early democracy worth attention for female participation is that of Iceland, perhaps the Thule mentioned by the ancients. Their assembly, the Althing, was set up around 930 (the date is as close as can reasonably be established for an event in the tenth century).[10] Certainly, it was a forerunner of modern democracy for a national assembly to be founded as a state without kings, as a self-government of settlers.

At midsummer, ensuring uninterrupted daylight and mild weather, a meeting would take place at Thingvellir, about 49 kilometres from Reykjavik in an active volcanic area, in a natural amphitheatre formed by a cliff wall. Delegates would travel from their own part of the island to the assembly to stay in shelters; remains found at Thingvellir include fragments of around fifty attendees' booths built of turf or stone which would have had canvas roofs. The meeting stretched over fourteen days and dealt with all matters relating to justice, trade, marriages, and disputes. The assembly consisted of a law council, to make and amend laws, and a system of courts of justice. Decisions would be made by chiefs, who would be accompanied by some of their followers and their households. Women and workers, both free and slaves, were excluded from decision making or legal judgements (and women could not even bear witness in courts) but it is obvious from the records of the sagas that women were far from being without influence.

The great and enduring myth of Iceland, based on indubitable fact, is of how Scandinavians arrived and settled the uninhabited island. The tenth-century settlements are recounted in the *Íslendingabók*, The Book of the Icelanders, written by Ari Thorgilson in the 1120s. He lists the four most important settlers, one for each quarter of the island, one of whom is a woman: Aud, the daughter of Ketil Flatnose, a Norwegian chieftain. Aud became a heroine mythologized in the *Laxdaela Saga* where one learns that according to early Icelandic law it was grounds for divorce if a husband wore effeminate clothing such as a low necked shirt—women's dresses had low bust lines to emphasize femininity. Similarly, it was grounds for divorce if a woman wore masculine costume. Thus Gudrun, who was eager to marry Aud's husband Thord Ingunnarson, undermines his wife by telling him she is known as 'Breeches-Aud' because she wears breeches shaped like a man's.

At the next Althing, Thord spends a great deal of time talking to Gudrun in her family's booth. He asks her (though he of course knows the answer and is only desiring encouragement) what the penalty is for a woman who always wears breeches like a man's. Gudrun replies, 'The same penalty applies to a woman in a case like this as to a man who wears a neck-opening so wide that his nipples are exposed: both are grounds for divorce.'[11] She goads him into going there and then to the Law Rock ('Only idlers wait till the evening') and declaring himself divorced on the grounds of Aud's masculine attire. Later Aud rides to Thord's home in her man's breeches carrying a sword and wounds him severely, across his right arm and both nipples, an injury from which he never fully recovers.

The *Íslendingabók* tells how Aud sailed from Norway with twenty free men (and a large retinue of others) and went adventuring in the British Isles before settling in Iceland. Other sources show that large numbers of women were among the settlers, not just as part of a man's following, but as primary settlers in their own right. Women had the right to own property independently and when acting as heads of households after Christianity had been introduced, they were required to pay tithes to the church and were subject to the 'masculine' penalties of outlawry for wounding or killing.[12] A woman could own and run a farm and even own a chieftancy but she had to commission a man to act as chieftain on her behalf.[13]

This was a violent and male-dominated age but, if the sagas are any guide to thinking, women would often start and would benefit from feuds, and they knew their influence very well. It is the beautiful and wilful Hallgerd, for example, in the thirteenth-century *Njal's Saga*, who takes offence at the seating arrangements at a feast, who sends slaves to kill servants of a rival household, who arranges for food to be stolen and the store-house burned, setting off a feud. When her husband Gunnar is fighting this feud she refuses him her aid (which leads to his death) in retribution because he once struck her. The point is not whether she existed or behaved in exactly that way, but that for the audience for the sagas this was a perfectly comprehensible way for a woman to behave. As Njal's wife Bergthora says to someone who comes looking for work, 'I am Njal's wife...and I have no less say in the household than he does.'[14]

If the sagas can be taken as evidence, they are suggestive of a society in which rigid gender divisions were subtly manipulated for personal gain. The model of separate spheres of influence for men and women, with women commanding the household and hospitality, seems to fit with Icelandic life, but the literature shows how gender boundaries were permeable. Engagement with the Althing was a male activity though women would be present as onlookers and women can hardly have been expected to remain silent outside the assembly on matters under discussion.

Equality before God

Other societies, where some form of democracy existed, such as Rome under the republic (510–30 BC), give further examples of states where women were excluded from political power but were often able to exert influence on political discourse in different ways according to their class and family.

Historically the call for the rights of man had a slow gestation; and the rights of woman was not necessarily thought to follow. Even at its most radical, rebellious thinking in medieval society did not challenge notions of gender. The revolutionary preacher John Ball, one of the leaders of the Peasants' Revolt of 1381, taught of equality before the Almighty: God did not ordain that there should be lords and ladies and yeomen and serfs, this was a construction by society on God's handiwork. Ball was in the habit of preaching outside churches on Sundays after the mass, saying 'Good people, things cannot go right in England and never will, until goods are held in common and there are no more villains and gentlefolk, but we are all one and the same. In what was are those whom we call lords greater masters than ourselves? How have they deserved it? Why do they hold us in bondage? If we all sprang from a single father and mother, Adam and Eve, how can they claim or prove that they are lords more than us, except by making us produce and grow the wealth which they spend?'[15] The principle was reduced to a rhyme:

> When Adam delved [dug] and Eve span
> Who was then the gentleman?

The challenge is to a hierarchy imposed on society, the gender division is not challenged: it is the men's job to labour on the land and woman's to work in the home on the spinning wheel.

Religion, a primary factor in early English radical thinking, was a double-edged weapon as far as women were concerned: religion offered radical ideas of equality before God, but also deeply entrenched gender divisions.[16] The English Revolution and the subsequent Commonwealth saw the predominance of Puritan notions of greater rights for wives (though still under the husband's control) and the development of notions of love and monogamy within marriage. Such groups as the Ranters argued for sexual freedom which, as historian Christopher Hill noted, 'tended to be freedom for men only, so long as there was no effective birth control'.[17]

Some sects allowed women to participate in church government and some to preach. Such radicals as Mary Cary announced that the time of New Jerusalem was coming when 'not only men but women shall prophesy' but this was a share in spiritual, not political rights.[18] This focus on spiritual freedom ensured that the courageous and politically engaged women of the Leveller sect in the Civil War did not argue for women's political rights but for spiritual equality. As historian Olwyn Hufton wrote, 'the most pernicious of the many inequalities which they perceived to exist between the sexes was religious inequality. In an age of faith it was essential to confront God on equal terms.'[19]

The Leveller women were active in support of their menfolk whose aim was democracy for men, arguing for universal manhood suffrage and annual or biennial parliaments. Agitating within the parliamentary army, they forced their generals to accept an army council made up of ordinary soldiers as well as officers. In October 1647 a Leveller proposal for a republican constitution called the Agreement of the People was discussed but it was rejected, army discipline was forcibly restored and mutinies of Leveller troops suppressed. Leaders such as John Lilburne were later imprisoned and their wives, notably Elizabeth Lilburne, printed pamphlets and organized mass demonstrations before parliament for their release. In the use of petition, the press, and political demonstration these women appear entirely modern, but they did not seek power for themselves, accepting representation of their home and family through the male head of the household. The radical potential of Christianity did not extend to female emancipation.

The Renaissance rediscovered the greatness of classical antiquity but this was a mixed blessing for women's political rights as there was no precedent in classical Greece or Rome for women's engagement in politics. The Reformation gave more hope but its character as a primarily religious movement at grass roots level (princes of course manipulated its political potential for their own ends) meant that spiritual equality with men was the realizable goal. This was, however, also a mixed blessing: if everything contained in the Bible had absolute value as revealed spiritual truth, then St Paul's statements such as injunctions to women to stay in their place had a negative effect on political emancipation. A radicalism based on religious notions alone would therefore only go so far to give women political equality.

When almost no men had any political rights, a discussion of extending rights to women was fanciful but the mere discussion of the extension of rights from the landowning class down the scale opened up the possibility of change. It was eighteenth-century Enlightenment thinking, with its notions of universal human rights, and the break between religion and advanced thought that gave women the opportunity for a case to be heard.

Island democracies

Island communities frequently have idiosyncratic systems of government, and in some cases this led to more inclusive forms of government, long before they were embraced in mainland communities.

The Pitcairn Islands can claim to be the place where women first voted on the same basis as men. Following the 1789 mutiny of the crew of the HMS *Bounty* on Tahiti, the mutineers and their Tahitian companions took the ship to the uninhabited Pitcairn Island. Their descendants and occasional new arrivals continued to live there with, presumably, no form of government until a British captain stopped by in the HMS *Fly* in 1838 and the captain claimed the island for the Crown and provided them with 'a few hasty regulations'. The islanders had urged Captain Russel Elliott to impose some kind of order as they were subject to marauding crews of whaling ships who would come ashore and threaten to rape Pitcairn women, which obliged the men to neglect their crops so they could act as protectors. They felt the solution was the protection of the British Crown for the ninety-nine natives. Elliott thought they could best be protected 'by conferring the stamps of authority on their election of a magistrate or elder, to be periodically chosen from among themselves, and answerable for his proceedings to Her Majesty's Government'.[20]

Captain Elliott's feeling was to 'least involve my own government', and the best way to achieve this was to prescribe self-government for the islanders. He therefore said the island was to be governed by a magistrate 'to be elected by the free votes of every native born on the island, male or female, who shall have attained the age of eighteen years; or, of persons who have resided five years on the island.'[21] Thus suffrage was universal, and based on residency alone, making it an advanced form of democracy. It had come about at a time of crisis for the community, and had been granted by a superior power which had nothing to lose and some slight gain by doing so. While there is no reference to the reasons why women were equally enfranchised, it was doubtless because they were already playing some part in community life; and there had to be sufficient numbers to make the fledgling democracy work.

The South Seas were considerable forerunners in democracy. New Zealand's pioneering of women's suffrage in 1893 will be covered in detail, but the Cook Islands deserve mention here. In the 1880s the Cook Islands were attracting the interest of several European imperial powers and of Maoris. They were subject to attacks by Peruvian slavers and incursions by New Zealand merchants and missionaries. It is a testimony to the importance of women in the islands that in 1890 four of Rarotonga's five chiefs were women and they appreciated that the British Navy served a queen. The historian of the Cook Islands, Dick Scott, reported how they had already adopted the title of queen themselves, called their houses palaces: 'the flummery of the court was carefully followed and a succession of impressionable tourists and travel writers regaled the folk at home with accounts of how they had been received in royal chambers.'[22] The monarchy was not, however, a hollow ornament—in playing the imperialists at their own game the Rarotongan chiefs obliged the foreign power to respect their precedence along with their royal flag; a visit to New Zealand by the leading chief Makea Takau in 1885 was treated by ministers as a state visit.

The islands became part of the British Empire, with a British Resident, Frederick Moss, a former Auckland member of parliament appointed from New Zealand. A contemporary remarked that 'He held advanced views and the fact that the island was not big enough to contain them in no ways damped his ardour.'[23] Among other reforms, Moss established an elected parliament which enfranchised women. Moss wrote proudly that 'The Cook Islands' parliament is the only free Maori parliament ever attempted.'[24] Universal suffrage was officially granted three days after New Zealand's Election Act but Rarotongan women voted before New Zealand women, on 14 October 1893.

These enfranchisements were part of a tradition of power for women of prestigious families in the South Seas; they were communities in which it was not unusual for women to be performing in the public sphere. The principle that politics, or community organization, was a male sphere and the home a female one that cursed female suffrage in northern counties simply did not exist on Rarotonga (and probably many other South Sea islands). The cultural activity which was specifically male, however, was fighting. This of necessity reduced the male population and left a commensurately larger number of females to bear the burden of community life.[25] The paucity of information about early government in the South Seas is evidence of the truth of John Markoff's comment, 'The history of democracy is enormously indebted to the creativity of places that historians have hardly studied.'[26]

The Isle of Man also played its part in the story of women's enfranchisement in island communities. In the 1880s a debate about the low proportion of the population who could vote on the island led to a proposal to extend the vote among men. Members of the Manchester National Society for Women's Suffrage thought this would be an opportunity for their issue to be debated and they organized a series of meetings on the island. Their restrained campaign was focused on the usual principle that women should not be taxed without representation, and suggested the technical expedient of simply removing the word 'male' from the Election Bill. The parliament, the House of Keys, discussed the bill on 5 November 1880 and agreed by sixteen votes to three to extend the vote to unmarried women and widows who owned property. As a result 700 women received the vote, making them 10 per cent of the electorate (who were property-owning men).

Perhaps these island stories tell only of local conditions; certainly island enfranchisement of women was related to immediate problems, particularly those of low population; and innovations were of course limited to the boundaries of the island, these decisions could not affect greater powers outside. They were seen as unimportant quirks at the time, merely quaint local customs with no implications for others.

The wider meaning, however, is the recognition that it was rural (or fishing-based) and conservative, traditional societies that first gave women the vote on the same basis as men. This is a pointer to the relative importance of different factors when large nations began to discuss women's suffrage: perhaps the refinement and sophistication of argument in the great centres of population was not the key to women's suffrage; perhaps what was needed was not greater complexity, but more simplicity.

2

The Rights of Man

Election bill met better fate,
On every hand defended,
To check confusion through the State,
The female voting's ended.[1]

Women in the Age of Revolutions

The 'Age of Reason', with its scepticism about previous knowledge and willingness to challenge every accepted norm on the basis of philosophical analysis, allowed for the first flowering of applicable concepts of equal or comparable rights between men and women. The Enlightenment was the intellectual revolution that finally allowed thinkers to pursue the notion of women's political rights on a level with those of men. A revolution in thinking that had as one of its forebears Bernard de Fontanelle who declared 'Everything is possible; and everyone is right' at least opened the door for alternative approaches.

The ideas of the Enlightenment were not an unalloyed blessing, however; the movement's sensuality reinforced women's role of providing sexual pleasure for men, whose restraints were relieved by the prevailing notion of liberty. The dual meaning of liberty—both an unbridled search for pleasure as an individual, and freedom from arbitrary despotism, offered both a personal and political message. The men of the Enlightenment no longer wished to obey laws imposed externally, they wanted to respect only the law of their own desires. This return to 'natural' laws gave primacy to woman's role as sexual partner and child-bearer rather than her rational faculties.

Jean-Jacques Rousseau, to whose novel *Emile* much of the passion for the 'natural' can be traced, was notorious for saying he had left his five children at the foundling home, shucking off his responsibility for them. It is probable, however, that there were no children and he invented the story to conceal his impotence: he would rather be thought a bad father than an impotent lover. Such were the attitudes that a thoughtful woman would encounter in the eighteenth century.

The intellectual development of a democratic framework largely bypassed women. Rousseau might preach that man had been born free and equal, but this was no boon for women. A belief in the 'natural' militated against the primacy of reason: if men's and women's roles were ordained by their nature, no exercise of the will could change them, just as a snake would not fly since it was not in its nature to do so. Rousseau's image of the ideal woman was as Republican Mother.

Philosophers were prepared to deny the existence of God, to propose reform in the age-old institutions of agriculture and land taxation, and the very system of government. Voltaire's epitaph is 'He taught us to be free' but he had no great interest in political science. What Voltaire thought of as freedom was the state of affairs in England where a man could not be thrown into prison on the whim of the monarch for writing a satirical epigram, as he could (and Voltaire was) in France. England certainly had a measure of freedom, but Mary Wollstonecraft was to rage at a notion of freedom that was all about private property and not at all about public rights.

The respect for the mind in Enlightenment circles meant that brilliant women such as Madame de Staël and Madame Roland could have influence; but this was a personal freedom to participate in political discourse—it did not constitute rights of women, but of men to have clever women as decorous accompaniments. Where the great philosophers discussed women, it was generally to dismiss them; Diderot, for example, acknowledged the constraints on women of poor education and an unfair legal system but considered women's nature and destiny was so linked with reproduction that this was the natural way of things.

Political thinkers, however, were addressing questions of rights and responsibilities in a way that would lead directly to women's active involvement in the political process. The English–American activist Thomas Paine's arguments against a hereditary aristocracy opened to question other age-old and irrefutable positions, about the inviolability of private property and the hegemony of men over women.

Montesquieu was prepared to discuss different forms of government; he considered every form carried the possibility of despotism, but it was other protections such as the rule of law that genuinely preserved liberty. He was not therefore strongly arguing for democracy as even a democracy could deny freedom to members of a minority. However, Montesquieu's ideas inspired the French Declaration of the Rights of Man in 1789 and 1793 and suggested many of the main principles of the Constitution of the United States.

The ideas of the Enlightenment were first put into practical effect in the American Revolution, usually dated from the Declaration of Independence of 1776. This included the idea of nationhood; of the rights of man; and the obligation of taxation by government coming with a corresponding right of self-representation. These notions were gender-neutral, unlike ideas of kingship and primogeniture which assumed a pre-eminent masculinity where women might rule or inherit only in default of an appropriate man.

For example, the right to bear arms (the famous second amendment to the US constitution) became a major women's issue in the French Revolution—if women bore arms in defence of their country or their revolution, did that not entitle them to the same civic rights as men? If not, what was it that disqualified them? Once this Pandora's box of liberty had been opened the notion of rights would not be contained within a single social group or gender.

The French, perhaps decisively, supported the secessionist American colonists against their old rivals the British with the consequence of French exposure to practical concepts of political liberty. International propagandists such as Thomas Paine were active in Britain, in America, and in France over the period of revolutions. Paine was in America from 1774 to 1781, where he coined the phrase 'the United States' and he was the first propagandist to advocate complete separation from Britain. In France from 1781, he vigorously engaged in political debate to define the terms of the revolution that was underway. He was well known to the Marquis de Condorcet and Mary Wollstonecraft, both major names in the history of women's political emancipation.

Paine wrote one of the central doctrines of democracy, *The Rights of Man*, in 1791. Here he said man is born equal and free with rights that are divinely ordained. The civil power (the government) has no power to invade those rights. The exercise of those rights had to be reliant on the naturally social instincts of mankind, based on reason. It was a literally revolutionary mode of thought that, while it excluded women, presented a conceptual frame-work that would make the argument for their admission ultimately irrefut-able. This line of thinking reached its apogee during the age of revolutions in the French constitution of 1793 in which every man had a vote—though this was later suspended, it was an important staging post in the move towards modern democracy.

Condorcet and the French Revolution

The legal position of women before the French Revolution gave them few rights—a woman remained under her father's authority until she married and she was transferred to her husband's rule. Once married she had almost no control over her person or her property until her husband died and she had some measure of autonomy.[2]

The most significant advance in the enfranchisement of women during the revolutionary period came with the work of the Marquis de Condorcet and his wife Sophie. The Marquis, whose full name was Marie-Jean-Antoine-Nicolas de Caritat, is remembered for his ideas of the notion of human progress and the inevitable perfectibility of humanity. It was a doctrine of progress and optimism that made him an early and enthusiastic supporter of the French Revolution. Born in Picardy in 1743, he was raised by his pious mother without education until the age of 9, then went to a Jesuit school and finally to the College of Navarre where, at the age of 15, he was first introduced to mathematics at which he immediately excelled. He first came to prominence as a mathematician, opening new fields for calculus and becoming a member of the Academy of Sciences when he was only 26. His first prominent work was on probability theory, though he was also a biog-rapher (of his friend Voltaire among others) and took an active part in the production of the *Encyclopaedia*, the greatest representation of the thought of the Enlightenment. He argued for tax reform and free trade, promoting 'social mathematics' that applied the great truths of mathematics to the organization of society. In his first foray into human rights he considered the situation of slaves, and wrote 'Reflections on Negro Slavery' in 1781; seven years later he was to found the Society of Friends of the Negro.

In common with many male pioneers of women's emancipation, Condorcet had a strong partner in Sophie, née de Grouchy, though his path towards love had not run smoothly. Condorcet was shy and physically weak and given to nervous habits such as biting his fingernails in public. He had passionate attachments to his friends and to scientific truth, but kept his expression of them under control; he was later described as being 'a volcano covered with snow' and 'a rabid sheep'.[3] His acute sensitivity to suffering led him to pondering even the suffering of animals, declaring: 'I gave up hunting, which I had enjoyed, and would not even kill an insect unless it was very harmful.'[4]

In a characteristic of brilliant people, Condorcet had difficulty in appreciating the nuances of commonplace human behaviour and fell obsessively in love. In 1771–2 he fell for the wife of a Paris tax collector who had been polite but had not reciprocated his feelings. In 1782 he eloped with the 18-year-old niece of his friends the Suards who had the police find the runaways and the incident was smoothed over. Some four years later he was supporting a radical magistrate, Charles Dupaty, in his campaign to save three peasants from torture and execution. During the campaign Condorcet met Dupaty's niece Sophie de Grouchy and fell in love at first sight; she was 22 and he 43. Mercifully for him, this time his feelings were reciprocated.

Sophie had been self-taught, listening to the tutors of her brothers and having read the *Enyclopaedia* during her stay at a convent (though she was an atheist). They married in 1786 after which one of Sophie's first acts was to take on the son of one of the condemned peasants as a servant. Their only child, Eliza, was born in 1790.

Sophie, nicknamed Grouchette, after her maiden name of de Grouchy, became established at the centre of a salon held at the Hôtel des Monnaies, Quai de Conti, where Condorcet was inspector-general of the mint. As Sophie spoke fluent English the salon attracted a number of foreigners; notable among them were the Scottish philosopher David Hume, whose work she translated; the future US president Thomas Jefferson; and Thomas Paine.

Condorcet's political work included advocating the freedom of French-owned slaves and urging the obligation on the state to provide universal education. As Condorcet's political views became increasingly radical, his friends blamed the change on Sophie, and some pieces published under his name were attributed to her, such as the letter 'from a young engineer' about how he had built a robot king that could carry out all the ceremonial and religious functions of royalty.

Condorcet wrote essays addressed to US colonists in Virginia in 1787 advising on the ideal form of government and briefly advocating the vote for women—probably the first time such a proposal was made in serious discourse at a time when it could have had an effect. He considered political rights to be 'natural' because they derive from the nature of human beings, capable of rational thought and moral judgement. 'We consider that the right to vote on matters of common interest, whether in person or through freely elected representatives, is one such right.'

'If we agree,' he continued, 'that men have rights simply by virtue of being capable of reason and moral ideas, then women should have precisely the same rights... we are discussing the rights of half of the human race which have been neglected by all legislators.'[5]

He returned to the theme in July 1790 in a pamphlet called 'On Giving Women the Right of Citizenship'. It began,

> Habit can so familiarize men with violations of their natural rights that those who have lost them neither think of protesting nor believe they are unjustly treated. Some of these violations even escaped the notice of the philosophers and legislators who enthusiastically established the rights common to all members of the human race, and made these the sole basis of political institutions. Surely they were all violating the principle of equal rights by debarring women from citizenship rights, and thereby calmly depriving half of the human race of the right to participate in the formation of the laws. Could there be any stronger evidence of the power of habit over enlightened men, than the picture of them invoking the principle of equal rights for three or four hundred men who have been deprived of equal rights by an absurd prejudice, and yet forgetting it with regard to twelve million women?[6]

Why are women denied these rights? Condorcet asks, is it because they are incapable? Condorcet addresses the question of women's innate differences: 'Why should people who experience pregnancies and monthly indispositions be unable to exercise rights we would never refuse to men who have gout every winter or who catch cold easily?' There was an argument that women were naturally less intelligent than men, but this was hard to establish when women had no formal education. So how was such a claim made? It was said that no woman had ever made an important scientific discovery or shown signs of genius in the arts, but neither had most men, so this argument, followed to its conclusion, would limit the vote to men of genius.

Against the argument that there are natural 'qualities in a woman's mind or heart' which should disbar her from political judgement, he presents the cases of such women as England's Elizabeth I and Russia's Catherine the Great who were thrust into positions of power by accident of birth but showed themselves to be leaders of courage and strength of mind. He skilfully uses an argument that could appeal to the most conservative monarchists—that a woman could be considered incapable of any public function yet worthy of the monarchy, 'that a woman could rule France and yet, before 1776, she could not become a dressmaker in Paris'.

Condorcet diverges from an argument from equality and deals with assumed gender differences with the statement that 'Women are more gentle and more domestic than men' which is assumed to need no qualification. He thinks women are simply 'better' than men, 'gentler, more sensitive and less subject to the vices of egoism and hard-heartedness'.

He concedes to his imagined opposition that men and women think differently—women 'may never have behaved according to the reason of men; but they do behave according to their own reason'. Condorcet here enters into a subtle argument considering that laws which have restricted women and guided them into particular roles have forced them to base their conduct on different principles and set themselves different aims, 'education and society [which] accustom women not to the idea of justice, but to that of decency'. If they were permitted to act in the world of business or the law, they would develop the capacities to do so: 'It is quite unfair to justify continuing to refuse women the enjoyment of their natural rights on grounds which are plausible precisely because they do not enjoy these rights.'

Moreover, to say the vote should be available only to those with wide knowledge and an appreciation of the law would mean the creation of a new aristocracy which is hardly a revolutionary goal. Condorcet then addresses the question of women's influence behind the scenes in politics: that this form of feminine influence would be a threat to good government. He says the threat is greater from secret influence than public participation, that women would not be distracted wholesale from their domestic role, because only a small number of people would ever be engaged full time in public affairs. 'There is no need to fear that, just because women could be members of the National Assembly, they would immediately abandon their children, their homes and their needlework.' If women should stay at home, that was a reason not to elect them, but not a reason to deny them the vote.

Condorcet realized that he would receive little support from women as they were so entranced by Jean-Jacques Rousseau with his feelings and sensibility that they would not be interested in an appeal to reason. Education needed to accompany political liberation; accordingly, in 1792 he put forward a scheme for a system of universal state education, the same year he drew up the declaration justifying the suspension of the king and summoning the National Convention.

The Marquis had run unsuccessfully as a candidate for the National Assembly in 1789, and was finally elected (to what was now the National Convention) in 1792. He was one of the nine-member team (Paine was another) who drew up the constitution that allowed for universal manhood suffrage—for all men who were over 21 and self-supporting. The constitution was overwhelmingly Condorcet's work, and in the wrangles with Jacobins about it, Condorcet's prestige was in decline and his safety in question. One women's club, that of Besançon, considered urging the Convention to extend the suffrage to women but backed down in the face of the mockery of local Jacobins (members of the most influential political club). The Convention adopted an amended constitution on 25 June 1793 but it was almost immediately 'suspended'.

Condorcet was on the run soon after the trial of Louis XVI when he bravely voted against the death sentence (presumably because of his opposition to the death penalty rather than for any more political motive). For some time he lived in hiding in the house of Mme Vernet, a Paris landlady. Sophie, now working on a translation of Adam Smith's work, visited him when she could.

It was while in hiding that he wrote his posthumously published *Sketch for a Historical Picture of the Progress of the Human Mind* of 1795, a profoundly influential work outlining an ascent of man from animalistic savagery to reason, equality, and freedom. He also wrote the touching 'Advice to My Daughter', on the flyleaf of a book as it was all the paper he had to hand, addressed to 4-year-old Eliza whom he was never to see again. By the time he wrote it, most of his friends in politics had been guillotined.

In March 1794 he was declared an outlaw, meaning anyone harbouring him would be guillotined without trial. He therefore left Mme Vernet's so as not to bring her into danger, and went to his former friends the Suards, but they refused him sanctuary. Condorcet lived in the open for three days until he entered the village of Bourg Egalité. He turned up in disguise at the village inn where he was captured and imprisoned while they tried to establish his identity. After only two days in captivity he was found dead, whether from suicide, exhaustion, or poisoning is not known.

Condorcet's central importance in the context of the franchise is that he formed a realistic argument for the vote for women, two years before Wollstonecraft's *Vindication of the Rights of Women* (1792) though obviously both were influenced by the same currents of thought, and notably the work of Thomas Paine.

Olympe de Gouges

The Declaration of the Rights of Man and of the Citizen had been signed in August 1789; it declared the 'natural and inalienable' rights of man that included freedom, property, security and resistance to oppression. The 1791 constitution (which preceded that on which Condorcet worked) was based on the Declaration and on laws passed since 1789; it had given the right to vote to men over 25 who had an income of over 250 francs a year.

In the month this was enacted, the actress and would-be dramatist Olympe de Gouges produced the 'Declaration of the Rights of Woman and Citizen'. The first principle stated the natural right to freedom and equality: 'Woman is born free and lives equal to man in her rights.' Specifically female rights included the right to own property in marriage, protection against seducers, and the regulation of prostitution; equal rights with men included the obligations of citizenship, including the right to fight in defence of the state.

This was a compilation of rights and obligations identical with those of men and of rights that women supposedly should have in addition to those of men (because women have different needs). The declaration thus fore-shadows feminist debates of the late twentieth century about equality and difference. The right to vote was related to the making of laws: 'The law must be the expression of the general will; all female and male citizens must contribute either personally or through their representatives to it; it must be the same for all: male and female citizens, being equal in the eyes of the law, must be equally admitted to all honours, positions, and public employment according to their capacity and without other distinctions besides those of their virtues and talents.'[7]

Olympe de Gouges, whose real name was Marie Gouze, was a tall, beautiful, eloquent woman who had more success with her pamphlets than her plays (though some were, apparently, accepted by the Comédie Français). She was ostensibly the daughter of a butcher in Montauban, she was married at 16 to Louis Aubry, who was much older than her and who died early in the marriage. She refused to take the designation Widow Aubry but instead took her mother's middle name, added 'de', and changed her second name

Figure 2. The influence of Olympe de Gouges in a radical Russian drawing
of 1905 headed 'National Representation in Russia without Distinction of Sex'.
De Gouges is quoted as saying 'If a woman is eligible to mount the scaffold,
she is worthy of entering parliament.' The suffragist woman indicates how Sofia
Perovskaya had been hanged.

to Gouges. In line with the aristocratic pretensions of this name, she let it
be known that the butcher had not been her father, but she had been born
as a result of a liaison between her mother and a local aristocrat.

The Revolution saw her throwing herself into a number of causes:
freedom for slaves, a national theatre, street cleaning, divorce reform, and the

rights of illegitimate children and unmarried mothers. Her proclamations covered the city walls but they were said to be regarded with disdain by the public, as yet more outpourings from a garrulous woman. She would attack women for being frivolous and called on them to behave responsibly to deserve citizenship, but also called on the legislature to protect women because of their special position as mothers. It was an argument of contradictions but at least it was a public argument.

One solution to the 'problem' of women's rights would simply be to add 'woman' where the Declaration of the Rights of Man had 'man'.[8] But de Gouges wanted to refer to specifically female complaints, thus on the right of free speech she says, 'The free communication of ideas and opinions is one of the most precious rights of woman, since this liberty guarantees that fathers will recognise their children. Any female citizen can thus say freely: "I am the mother of your child" without being forced by barbarous prejudice to hide the truth.'[9] The argument is cleverer than it seems on first appearance, for the very reason why men would deny women rights as citizens, their capacity for maternity, is used as a reason why they *should* have those rights. De Gouges insists on placing maternity at the forefront of her argument—not saying (as does Condorcet) that it is a relatively minor inconvenience to political participation, but that it is a mainspring of the argument. As she says in the Preamble: 'the sex that is as superior in beauty as it is in courage during the sufferings of maternity recognises and declares in the presence and under the auspices of the Supreme Being, the following Rights of Woman and Female Citizens.'[10]

De Gouges was hampered by the fact that she was a fervent monarchist at a time when the king was under suspicion as being opposed to the constitutional monarchy that was the political solution to the problems of the early part of the Revolution. She even addressed her 'Declaration' to the queen, Marie-Antoinette. Before the king's trial in December 1792 she offered her services as a lawyer, to speak in his defence. She had also left her husband to live a life of literature in Paris, making her both suspect and the butt of jokes such as a comic song on her Declaration that finishes, 'Swap husband twenty times a year / With Women's Rights she's free.'[11] Women's civic rights were therefore, as soon as they were expressed, immediately compounded with notions of sexual liberty.

A foray into the principles of representative democracy was made in an anonymous pamphlet (by Mme B——— B———) circulating around this time. In 'Grievances and Claims of Women' the author asked why men should continue to make women the victims of injustice when the common people were entering into political rights and even slaves were gaining their freedom. She insisted that just as a noble could not represent a commoner, a man could not represent a woman.[12] Both of these issues—the relationship between women's right and the rights of slaves, and the question of gender representation—were to become important in the suffrage battles to come. Other feminist proposals at the time included appeals for the education of women and for laws forbidding men to enter trades commonly performed by women, so as to assure women a way of making their living.

National Amazons

Women had played a leading part in the events of the 1789 revolution including the iconic march of the women of Paris to Versailles in October 1789. On this fateful day women had gathered in Paris, many from outlying districts, demanding bread and arms. They led a march to Versailles where the demonstrators, now effectively a mob accompanied by the National Guard, insisted the king and queen return with them to Paris and brought the royal couple back.

The participation of women in war and national liberation was to be a running theme through the history of the franchise. Such groups as the National Amazons, a woman's militia, fuelled the climate in which the demand for women to have the right to bear arms was made of the Assembly in June 1790. A similar demand, in the form of a petition signed by 315 women of the Fraternal Society of Mimimes called for pistols, sabres, and rifles. It is unwise to overestimate the influence of these forays into the public arena, as historian Olwyn Hufton remarks, 'Such initiatives had no official encouragement and, as far as one can tell, next to no popular base.'[13]

Women took up arms as revolutionary France entangled itself in wars with Austria, Britain, Holland, and Spain in 1792–3, conflicts which saw dozens of women fighting beside men. The Fernig sisters Félicité and Théophile notably distinguished themselves against Austrian forces fighting at Jemmapes. Eighteen-year-old Théophile led a unit of cavalrymen which routed a battalion of Hungarians and captured its commander. Despite such heroism, and the obvious willingness of some women to fight, the Convention permanently dismissed women from the army in April 1793, part of a backlash against women in public life. The constitution on which

Condorcet had worked, enshrining universal manhood suffrage, was almost immediately suspended. The provisions of the constitution are known to have been criticized at the women's Républicaines Révolutionarie club, but so much political activity was underway that there appears to have been no public discussion of the constitution as it affected women—despite the fact that the systemization of the law actually eliminated some electoral idiosyncrasies that had permitted women to vote in some cases.[14]

A more public battle was of the right of women to take the oath as citizens—a means of demonstrating their revolutionary commitment. Issues under discussion were whether women could take the oath at all, or whether only women with children could do so as they had by giving birth 'contributed' to the nation. This was reduced to a men's power struggle—one faction would welcome women and another would refuse them, thus the National Guard invited women to the oath-taking ceremony in Beaune in 1790 but the municipal authorities refused to allow them to take it.

The manifestations of women's assertiveness were not greeted with favour by the Jacobins who were increasingly dominating an assembly where the Girondins, who tended to be idealist and liberal, had previously been dominant. As part of the repression engendered by the Jacobin faction in its ascendancy, the Convention on 30 October 1793 closed the women's political clubs, and banned women from forming political associations. In acts of suppression against *clubistes* they used as a pretext the discontent of the market women of La Halle, who were resentful over political activists harassing them over the cost of food and political issues. Republican women had gone to the market brandishing pistols, they had wanted the market women to wear the revolutionary cockade as citizens, but the market women saw a conflict in their role as women: citizens would bear arms and fight; their primary duty was as mothers.[15] Thus perhaps for the first time, but certainly not the last, educated activist women had tried to bully their less politicized sisters into taking the radical path, and the less educated women sided with men who were taking a conservative line on women's rights.

While much can be said of women taking part in revolutionary activity such as demonstrations and bread riots, more spontaneous women's uprisings took place locally against the suppression of the Catholic religion, with mobs of women occupying churches and freeing imprisoned priests during the period of Jacobin rule in 1793–4. A radical assumption that the popular will would be leftist (a term that came into use during the French Revolution) was thwarted: the popular will can also express a militant conservatism. This was an early sign of radicals' failure to appreciate the endurance of conservatism which would be a consistent theme in the story of women's political emancipation.

The legal pretext for closing the clubs was a report from the Committee of General Security that had met to deliberate on whether women should exercise political rights, and whether they should be permitted to meet. The occasion allowed André Amar as representative of the committee to declare that women should not engage in political activity, since for them to do so would be immoral: 'Does the honesty of a woman allow her to display herself in public and to struggle against men?'[16] A woman's honour, he argued, confines her to the private sphere. Thus 'honour', a concept related to sexual restraint, is what confines women.

'Should they take an active part in discussions the passion of which is incompatible with the softness and moderation which are the charms of their sex?' he asked rhetorically. He argued that the political education of men was in its infancy: 'how much more reasonable it is for women, whose moral education is almost nil, to be less enlightened concerning principle.' The state would be open to hysteria, 'interests of state would soon be sacrificed to everything which ardour in passions can generate in the way of error and disorder'. This implicitly offers the glimmer of hope that with sufficient political education, women could be in a position to exercise political rights. However, women did not have the strength of character necessary to govern, and politics took them away

> from the more important concerns to which nature calls them. The private functions for which women are destined by their very nature are related to the general order of society; this social order results from the differences between man and women. Each sex is called to the kind of occupation which is fitting for it; its action is circumscribed within this circle which it cannot break through, because nature, which imposed these limits on man, commands imperiously and receives no law.

Thus he made a call to the primacy of nature after the model prescribed by Rousseau.

A further measure, of 20 May 1795, forbade women from even attending meetings of the Convention; they would be allowed to watch from the visitor's gallery only if they were accompanied by a man who was a citizen. Women had fewer political rights at the end of the French Revolution than at the beginning, as the revolutionary debates established and the later

Napoleonic Code codified their inferior position. Women were barred from political rights, then granted divorce and some property rights, which were then restricted under Napoleon, and then revoked by the Restoration.[17]

Olympe de Gouges was imprisoned and eventually sentenced to death by a revolutionary tribunal. She pathetically attempted to evade (or merely delay) execution by claiming she was pregnant, a claim which was not believed.

She was guillotined on 3 November 1793 with the words, 'Children of France, you will avenge my death.'[18] Pierre Chaumette, who prosecuted the enemies of the Jacobins gloated, 'She wished to be a politician and it seems the law has punished this conspirator for having forgotten the virtues appropriate to her sex.'[19]

One of the leaders of early French feminism, Théroigne de Mérincourt, who had participated in revolutionary action on the streets of Paris and promoted a women's militia, was badly beaten up by a group of Jacobin women in 1793, who stripped her and beat her about the head with stones, an event from which she never seems to have fully recovered.[20]

Sophie, the Marquise de Condorcet, lived in poverty after her husband's death but recovered some of her property at the end of the century and worked on a first edition of her husband's works that was published from 1801 to 1804. She reopened her salon and continued political discussions, now with those opposed to the emperor Napoleon Bonaparte. She died at the age of 58, and her daughter Eliza continued editing her father's works.

In terms of electoral democracy, a new constitution of September 1795 swept away previous constitutional clauses that had granted universal manhood suffrage. Now the vote was granted to men over 25 who were French citizens and had an income equal to 200 work days. This tax-based voting system remained in effect for half a century.

Some themes that were to persist are clearly emerging in the French experience—of women in a separate sphere, that of motherhood and home, while men were in the public arena. Part of this was the contention, going back to fifth-century Greek society at least, that citizens bore arms and protected the land from enemies. As women did not do this, they could not be citizens. This was already a failing argument before even a single woman had a vote, as vocational specialization and the development of professional armies meant very few men in the general population bore arms until the great wars of the twentieth century.

The rights of slaves or of non-whites were compared to those of women, as they would be later, and these rights suffered similar changes on the tides of revolution: 'men of colour' were excluded and then included as citizens; slaves were denied, then granted rights, which were then lost again under Napoleon.

Another theme was the investment in property of the right to vote—the people who should have a say in the running of the country were the people who owned the country. Another was education—women did not know enough to act responsibly in the political arena. These two hurdles, of equal property rights and the right to education, were barriers on the way to political equality that would have to be broken down before electoral progress could be made in most cases.

The distinction introduced in the debates around the Revolution were those of active women themselves: were women who engaged in the political arena doing so in order to assure their rights as wives and mothers to feed their families at reasonable prices? Or were they committed to full legal equality with men in every aspect of life? The underlying question was whether there was a fundamental difference between women and men that suited them for different roles, or whether such anatomical differences as existed were immaterial to political life?

Mary Wollstonecraft and the wrongs of woman

Despite the fact that French Enlightenment thinking had largely inspired modern democratic theory, the seeds of political emancipation for women were more strongly apparent in Anglo-Saxon than in French culture. It was in the events following the American Revolution and in the emergence of Mary Wollstonecraft, that women's emancipation saw its most vigorous flowering.

At the end of the eighteenth century, British democracy, such as it was, was a lower chamber, the House of Commons, largely nominated by the great landowners and then elected. The number of electors in constituencies was in the hundreds or less: thirty constituencies returned Members of Parliament on the basis of fewer than forty voters each. The upper house was made up of peers sitting by hereditary right.

People who did not vote still had a tradition of participating in elections, so the Duchess of Devonshire in supporting the radical member of parliament

Charles Fox in the election of 1784 in theory had only as much political power as an artisan, as neither of them had the vote and would simply be attempting to influence those who did. Political thinkers paid no great heed to women. The essayist Joseph Addison considered that women should refrain from showing an interest in politics,

> which of late Years is very much crept into their Conversation. This is, in its Nature, a Male Vice, and made up of many angry and cruel Passions that are altogether repugnant to the Softness, the Modesty, and those other endearing Qualities which are natural to the Fair Sex. Women were formed to temper Mankind, and soothe them into Tenderness and Compassion, not to set an Edge upon their Minds, and blow up in them those Passions which are too apt to rise of their own Accord.[21]

Thus Addison expresses a view that is to become more prominent in later centuries: that women should be excluded not because of their lack of qualities that might render them fit for political service—decisiveness, debating ability, and so on—but because of their positive qualities which fitted them for another purpose. The mere fact that he needs to comment on women's involvement or non-involvement in politics in the early eighteenth century, however, shows there was discussion of the subject.

When Mary Wollstonecraft was born in Spitalfields, London in 1759 her family was moderately prosperous: her grandfathers were both in business, in the silk and the wine trades; but she was less fortunate in her father, Edward Wollstonecraft, who was described as a drunken bully, and whom she despised. She was no more fortunate in her mother Elizabeth, however, whom she described as doting on her son to the neglect of her daughters. Wollstonecraft was largely self-taught and always argued for better educational opportunities for women. 'Strengthen the female mind by enlarging it, and there will be an end to blind obedience,' she wrote.[22]

Her first book, written when she was twenty-seven, was *Thoughts on the Education of Daughters.* It was published by a radical, Joseph Johnson, who was to remain a lifelong friend and publisher. She began to earn her living by her pen, writing articles, translations, and stories, and to adopt a romantic bohemian posture with her hair hanging down her shoulders and clothes of coarse cloth with blue worsted stockings, demonstrating how little she cared for the world of the conventional lady.

Not everyone felt fully able to participate in Wollstonecraft's unconventional private life. She was captivated by the artist Henry Fuseli whom she met in 1788. He encouraged her and they were close for three years (whether lovers or not is not known) but when she proposed to Fuseli's wife Sophia that the three of them should cohabit and Wollstonecraft would be recognized as Fuseli's spiritual spouse, Sophia threw her out.

When the French Revolution began Wollstonecraft was in an ideal situation to comment in support, and to refute the work of conservatives such as Edmund Burke who attacked revolutionary ideals. 'Reason has, at last, shown her captivating face,' she wrote.[23] Calling together the ideas she had been juggling with for years, she wrote *Vindication of the Rights of Women* in about three months. It was entirely self-generated, and written without any special reading or research on the subject. She was later apologetic for the speed with which it had been set down, but its breathless pace gives an authentic flavour of the woman herself. *Vindication* declares that women are human beings before they are sexual beings and that the mind has no sex. Much of the book's criticism of women's estate comes across as a criticism of women who are presented as silly, empty-headed and capricious. They were so, however, because they were expected to be so by society, and were not educated to be any better. Educated to the same level as man, woman would be his equal. Unfortunately for the historian of women's suffrage, Wollstonecraft conceived *Vindication* as a first volume, the second of which was to be about laws concerning women, so the book is short on conventional politics and does not mention suffrage except to say tantalizingly that 'I cannot help lamenting that women of a superior caste have not a road open by which they can pursue more extensive plans of usefulness and independence. I may excite laughter, by dropping a hint, which I mean to pursue, some future time, for I really think women ought to have representatives, instead of being arbitrarily governed without having any direct share allowed them in the deliberations of government.'

As always in *Vindication*, Wollstonecraft compares the degradation of women to the degradation of humanity in a pernicious class-based system. Women suffer from an absence of democracy only as much as do the working poor who are producing the wealth of the nation:

> as the whole system of representation is now, in this country, only a convenient handle for despotism, they [women] need not complain, for they are as well represented as a numerous class of hard-working mechanics, who pay for the support of royalty when they can scarcely stop their children's mouths with bread. How are they represented whose very sweat supports the splendid stud of an heir-apparent, or varnishes the chariot of some female favourite who looks down on shame?[24]

Wollstonecraft is more interested in the relation between the sexes and in women's marital state. She was the first person to apply the phrase 'legal prostitution' to marriage.[25] Society had obliged women to become fixated on marriage alone, to the disgust of Wollstonecraft, who felt that the romantic fantasies and fickle manoeuvres of conventional courtship degraded women and denied them the full use of their mental resources. She was calling for a 'revolution in female manners.' She seemed to treat sex as a necessary evil, largely imposed by men on women, and thought it better for marriage to exclude passionate love—'a master and mistress of a family ought not to continue to love each other with passion'—though these views would change as she matured as a person.[26] Her later development of thinking on the institution of marriage led her to disapprove of a fixed marriage bond, feeling young people should not make binding contracts for life in ignorance of what might come to pass in future. A man and woman need not be married to love and parties need not feel bound to each other after the death of love.

The book was an immediate best-seller, was published in the US and widely translated. Whether she had become, as William Godwin claimed in his *Memoirs* of her, the most famous woman in Europe, she was certainly one of a handful whose name everyone knew. Lady Palmerston joked to her statesman husband: 'I have been reading the *Rights of Woman* so you must in future expect me to be very tenacious of my rights and privileges.' Writer Horace Walpole famously called her 'a hyena in petticoats' and she stimulated satires on her position such as *The Rights of Boys and Girls*—taken to be a self-evidently absurd notion—and the *Vindication of the Rights of Brutes*, facetiously suggesting animal rights.[27]

Wollstonecraft welcomed the French Revolution and, when arrangements with others to travel to France fell through, she went alone to revolutionary Paris in 1792 where she was welcomed by the expatriate community that had gathered to be part of the most exciting adventure taking place in the world. One of the adventurers she met was Captain Gilbert Imlay, an American revolutionary soldier engaged in various commercial schemes in France in an attempt to make fast money from such deals as buying at auction luxury goods seized from aristocrats by the state, with the intention of selling them abroad. Wollstonecraft and Imlay became lovers and he left her alone and pregnant. Paris became a dangerous place for foreigners and anyone else suspected of disloyalty to the regime in the period leading up to the Grande Terreur; Wollstonecraft is reported as having to restrain her disgust at having to step through puddles of blood on the street, for fear that any expression of revulsion would be considered unpatriotic.

Wollstonecraft followed Imlay to Le Havre where her daughter, Fanny, was born, and on to London. She hoped they would set up as a family but Imlay had no intention of remaining faithful. Wollstonecraft attempted suicide with opium, but she was resuscitated and bidden to look at her child and stay alive for her sake. She and Imlay were briefly reconciled, but she was reduced to the pathetic expedient of asking servants about Imlay's affairs with women; it was hardly an elevated foray into the new world of equal relationships between men and women. When Imlay established himself with a new mistress, and Wollstonecraft went to see the furnished house he had provided for this woman, the author again attempted suicide, this time by throwing herself in the Thames. Imlay was called and tried to be as sympathetic as possible, but would not leave his actress girlfriend. Wollstonecraft for the second time suggested that one of her lovers live with her and another woman. 'If we are ever to live together again, it must be now,' she wrote, 'I consent then, for the present, to live with you, and the woman to whom you have associated yourself.'[28] She thus presented the offer imperiously as if it were his last chance rather than *her* last attempt at reconciliation; it was obviously no solution.

Wollstonecraft finally broke with Imlay and in July 1796 called at the house of William Godwin, a leading radical philosopher, whom she had met at a dinner party given by her publisher Joseph Johnson for Thomas Paine. Godwin was 41, three years older than Wollstonecraft, and had his own great success at roughly the same time as hers, with his *Enquiry Concerning Political Justice* in 1793 and his novel *The Adventures of Caleb Williams* the next year.

The two radicals, who had quarrelled when they had first met at that dinner party, became lovers in August 1796. On the evidence of her letters, they had a few months of happiness in a relationship that was sometimes fretful and intense but always displayed an equality between them. She soon found herself pregnant. Wollstonecraft was horrified at her condition, doubtless because she expected Godwin to behave as Imlay had done, which indicates her poor judgement of men (if this were not already abundantly clear). Godwin was an altogether better man, willing to keep faith with her, and with her young daughter and unborn child.

The theoretical opposition to marriage he entertained could not resist the social pressure of gossip that isolated Wollstonecraft and they married on

29 March 1797. They moved into a new house, finding domestic life surprisingly congenial to them both. Wollstonecraft had intended to have as
'natural' a childbirth as possible and refused the services of a doctor, she
intended to be an example to other women. In the event, after giving birth
to Mary, she suffered from a retained placenta and succumbed to septi-
caemia on 11 September 1797. She died a death, as clergyman poet Richard
Polewhele remarked, 'that strongly marked the distinction of the sexes'.[29]

Godwin wrote his *Memoirs* of her life in 1798, with a thorough account
of her sexual history which damned her in the eyes of several succeeding
generations of feminists who were striving for an image of respectability.
Wollstonecraft had deliberately challenged conventional morality by living
with a man not her husband and bearing an illegitimate child. This was hardly
uncommon behaviour in the eighteenth century, her offence (and that of
Godwin, who did not suppress information about her relationship with Imlay)
was a failure to behave with sufficient hypocrisy, to have no shame over it.

The emotional adventures of Wollstonecraft's descendants also counted
against her in the minds of later commentators. Added to her two suicide
attempts were her daughter Fanny Imlay's suicide at 22 and the suicide of
the poet Shelley's first wife Harriet Westbrook, after he had run off with
Godwin and Wollstonecraft's daughter Mary. 'One is sickened for ever,'
wrote Millicent Garrett Fawcett in her introduction to a centenary edition
of *A Vindication of the Rights of Woman* in 1891, 'in unravelling the curious
tangle of relationships, intrigues, suicides and attempted suicides of the
remarkable group of personalities to whom Mary Wollstonecraft belonged.'[30]
The refusal of many later feminists to confront conventional sexual morality
was to have divisive effects on women's emancipation generally, but would
have particularly deleterious effects on the claim for women's suffrage.

Wollstonecraft's approach was defined by scholar Miriam Brody as one
'which considers all aspects of women's condition, economic, psychological,
cultural as inter-related, with economic reform dependent on basic social
changes in the distribution of political and economic power'. Brody considered that the women of the later suffrage movement lost sight of these
insights, prizing respectability too highly.[31]

It was not until second wave feminism of the 1970s that Wollstonecraft
was given her rightful place at the bosom of the movement, once some
measure of sexual liberation had loosened the chains of morality that had
fettered the nineteenth- and early twentieth-century suffragists. A twenty-first-
century biographer, Lyndall Gordon, wrote that 'To see Mary as shifting and

rash would be to scale her down. Dimly, through the glare of celebrity and slander, it's possible to make out the shape of a new genus reading, testing, growing, but still uncategorized.'[32]

The *Vindication*'s publication has been taken not just as a landmark but as a foundation stone. For example, Ray Strachey in her history of the women's movement writes 'the real date for the beginning of the movement is 1792'. She then remarks that 'After the appearance of this book the subject seemed to die away.'[33] In fact this was only true for the respectable middle class. The position of women was one of the many strands of radical working class thinking. Through the agitations following Waterloo, over the Great Reform Bill and the Chartists, voices were heard calling for women's suffrage amid the clamour of demands for universal manhood suffrage.

The Garden State

In only one place did the ideas of the Enlightenment meet lasting, practical success; on the continent of America. Manhood suffrage was an obvious corollary of the demand for self-government, making women's suffrage a possibility.

The correspondence of the first vice-president of the Unites States (later the president) John Adams with his wife Abigail shows the level of political discourse that could take place amid discussion of commonplace matters. Writing to her husband on 27 November 1775, while discoursing on the weather ('great and incessant rains') and her health ('I yesterday took a puke which has relieved me') Abigail shows envy as to her husband's exciting political tasks in these revolutionary times:

> I wish I knew what mighty things were fabricating. If a form of Government is to be established here what one will be assumed?... I am more and more convinced that Man is a dangerous creature, and that power whether vested in many or a few is ever grasping, and like the grave cries give, give. The great fish swallow up the small, and he who is most strenuous for the Rights of the people, when vested with power, is eager after the prerogatives of Government.[34]

Adams read Thomas Paine's pamphlet 'Common Sense', advocating separation from Britain, in New York early in 1776, weeks after it had been published, and sent it to Abigail to read, so he was not reluctant to see her engaging in politics. On 31 March 1776 she wrote,

I long to hear you have delivered an independency—and by the way in the new Code of Laws which I suppose it will be necessary for you to make I desire you would Remember the Ladies and be more generous and favourable to them than your ancestors. Do not put such unlimited power into the hands of the Husbands. Remember all Men would be tyrants if they could. If particular care and attention is not paid to the Ladies we are determined to foment a Rebellion, and will not hold ourselves bound by any Laws in which we have no voice, or Representation.[35]

He replied mockingly, but referred to the contaminating power of democratic ideas, 'As to your extraordinary Code of Laws, I cannot but laugh. We have been told that our Struggle has loosened the bands of Government every where. That Children and Apprentices were disobedient—that schools and colleges were grown turbulent—that Indians slighted their Guardians and Negroes grew insolent to their Masters.'

His reply that American freedoms had fomented disobedience among Negroes and Indians is not exclusively a rejection of women, but additionally links the women's issue with that of race which, far more than class as in Britain, was a barrier to limit women's suffrage in the US; or was used as a barrier when none other existed. He further commented that, 'your Letter was the first Intimation that other Tribes more numerous and powerful than all the rest were grown discontented. This is rather too coarse a compliment but you are so saucy, I won't blot it out.'[36] He went on to chide that men were the subjects and women in control, 'Masculine systems' were 'little more than theory.' Abigail could not resist a retort: 'I cannot say that I think you very generous to the Ladies, for whilst you are proclaiming peace and good will to Men, Emancipating all Nations, you insist upon retaining absolute power over Wives. But you must remember that Arbitrary power is like most other things which are very hard, very liable to be broken.'[37]

Reflecting this revolutionary discourse, the most successful case of early women's suffrage was the state of New Jersey where women were enfranchised as of right, in a simple application of the rights of man. In colonial America women had shared with men the hazards of pioneer life, and were often engaged in enterprises on their own account and were the main support of their families. Under the Grants and Concessions of 1664 the right to vote was given to 'inhabitants being freemen' but some free men may well have been women, as land was offered to a 'free man', 'free woman', 'master' and 'mistress' as long as they came armed, so freedom and the willingness to seize and defend it with arms was a quality in itself, separate from gender. Some women do seem to have exercised rights, as a woman signed the document which yielded up the right to govern to Queen Anne in 1702.[38]

During the revolution against the British, women had carried on a large part of the work otherwise done by men when they were away, which doubtless was the reason for the goodwill felt towards them in the immediate post-revolutionary period. The New Jersey Constitution, framed in 1776, gave the franchise to 'all inhabitants of this Colony, of full Age, who are worth fifty pounds, Proclamation Money, clear Estate in the same, and have resided within the county in which they claim a Vote for twelve Months immediately preceding the Election'. Thus there were qualifications of property (to own outright at least £50 worth of property or other goods), of age (21), and of residency, but none as to race or sex.

Some certainly did vote: on 9 October 1787, Burlington County records attest, there was an election for members of the council and assembly where the names of Iona Curtis and Selvenia Lilvey appear on the poll list.[39] The law was revised in 1790 to specify that a 'free' inhabitant of New Jersey (therefore specifically excluding slaves) with a specific amount of property was legally entitled to vote in a township where 'he or she' resided. Women were therefore explicitly included, though they must have been 'femmes soles' (widows or spinsters) as married women could not own property. The enfranchisement of women was thought to be due to the influence of Joseph Cooper, a prominent Burlington County Quaker who was said to have persuaded the legislators to incorporate 'he or she' but he was not on the legislative committee when another act regulating elections was enacted, in 1797. That retained 'he or she', so his ideas about the enfranchisement of women were not the views of a lone enthusiast but must have been generally held. New England Quakers tended to be ahead of contemporary thinking as regards women, allowing both unmarried and married women to preach and to have an influence in religious matters that extended into secular affairs. The legislature of 1790 passed the election law with generous support: thirty-three to four.

It is probable that this was a deliberate maintenance of the existing franchise system as it was understood, rather than a revolutionary alteration, though there was certainly will behind it. Neighbouring Massachusetts, faced with the same decision when writing a new state constitution agreed to introduce the word 'male' for the first time. The suspicion is that such prohibitions had to be introduced because women were using their voting rights, probably first at local township level.[40]

The first occasion on which women voted in any numbers was at Elizabethtown in 1797, where a contest for a seat on the legislature was bitterly fought between two men and the supporters of one, Federal aristocratic candidate William Crane, appeared near the close of the polls with a number of suitably qualified women, who duly voted for their candidate (in all seventy-five women did so). He did not win, losing by ninety-three votes to the Republican candidate John Condict, but the involvement of women in such a shabby manoeuvre was noted with disgust. The *Newark Sentinel of Freedom* wrote ironically, 'too much credit cannot be given to the Federal Ladies of Elizabeth for the heroic virtue displayed on Wednesday last in advancing in a body to the polls.'[41] The same newspaper satirized the event:

> Let Democrats with senseless prate,
>   maintain the softer sex, Sir
> Should ne'er with politics of state
>   Their gentle minds perplex, Sir:
> Such vulgar prejudice we scorn;
>   Their sex is no objection.
> New trophies shall our brows adorn,
>   By *Freedom of Election*!
>
> Why tho' we read, in days of yore,
>   the woman's occupation
> Was to direct the wheel and loom,
>   not to direct the nation.
> This narrow minded policy
>   by us hath met detection;
> While woman's bound man can't be free,
>   nor have a *fair Election*.

In the presidential election between Adams and Jefferson in 1800 women voted generally throughout New Jersey. When Jefferson's victory was celebrated, women were specifically mentioned in the toasts, as at Liberty Corner, 'The fair daughters of America particularly those who stepped forward to show their patriotism in the cause of republicanism at the late election.'[42]

The law was first construed to admit single women only, but as the practice of female voting extended, a commentator in the next century noted, 'the construction of the privilege became broader and was made to include females eighteen years old, married or single; and even women of colour.'[43]

Petitions to the legislative council relating to women voting complain of the judge and inspectors of the election of 1802 permitting illegal voting, mentioning 'persons under age, persons who had not resided in that township the time prescribed by law, and a numerous body of Negroes,... they admitted married women to vote' with the implication that no complaint was made about unmarried or widowed women voting.[44]

Burlington lawyer, and later a member of the legislature, William Griffith (1766–1826) wrote a case for constitutional reform in which he attacked the property qualification. 'Every citizen', he wrote, 'has (besides property) his liberty, his life, and his just rights in society to be protected; and these are equally important and common to all members of the community.' He proposed a qualification based on whether or not a man was liable to pay tax. He was not willing to consider that these rights could be equally applied to women, however. 'To my mind (without going into an historical, or philosophical deduction of particulars on the subject) it is evident, that women, generally, are neither, by nature, nor habit, nor by education, nor by their necessary condition in society, fitted to perform this duty with credit to themselves, or advantage to the public.' Rather, women had been party to electoral fraud: 'It is perfectly disgusting to witness the manner in which women are polled at our elections. Nothing can be a greater mockery of this invaluable and sacred right, than to suffer it to be exercised by persons who do not even pretend to any judgement on the subject.'[45]

More detail was given in the *True American* of the 'privileged fair' being taken to register their vote by carriage. Women are described as a body as being, 'Timid and pliant, unskilled in politics, unacquainted with all the real merits of the several candidates, and almost always placed under the dependence or care of a father, uncle or brother &c, they will of course be directed or persuaded by them; and the man who brings his two daughters his mother and his aunt to the elections, really gives five votes instead of one.'[46]

In 1806 a new court house and jail were to be erected in the county of Essex, but the county was divided, with an intense political and economic rivalry between North and South. The northerners wanted Newark and the southerners Elizabethtown as the location for the new buildings. The legislature passed an act by which qualified electors in the county should choose the location of the buildings by referendum. The election that took place in February 1807 was marked by bad behaviour and multiple voting for which women were blamed. As a commentator said, 'as the conflict proceeded and the blood of the combatants waxed warmer, the number of female voters increased, and it was soon found that *every* single and *every* married woman in the county was not only "of full age" but also "worth fifty pounds proclamation money, clear estate'", and as such entitled to vote if they chose. 'And not only once, but as often as by change of dress or complicity of the inspectors they might be able to repeat the process.'[47] The *New-Jersey Journal* of 3 March 1807 mocked,

> For they called in bog trotters, and Negroes I'm told,
> And young boys and girls of a dozen years old –
> And wives they admitted to give in their votes,
> And a great many changed both their hats and their coats
> And voted five times, yes, six, eight and ten,
> And from Bergen they called over two hundred men.[48]

The election was so scandalously corrupt that the legislature set it aside as illegal and saw to it that the buildings were erected in Newark. Now John Condict, still a member of the legislature, saw a way to withdraw voting rights from the women who had almost denied him his place ten years before. It seemed his sense of propriety had been offended (he had after all been elected so had not suffered materially). Condict, sponsoring the bill, made the chief speech in favour of the new law that was widely supported by both parties. He forbore from attacking women directly but, knowing the sensibilities of his audience, called attention to the vote of a Negro slave, himself the property of another slave, who had the deciding vote in a contest that elected one of the members of the legislature which (after that election) was evenly balanced and unable to come to serious decisions. Clearly this was a chance occurrence and no argument for or against the voting rights of any group, but the notion that political outcomes might hang on the vote of a Negro slave was abhorrent to the legislature, an early example of the way in which the race issue was to bedevil women's franchise in the US.

An Act was passed on 16 November 1807 noting 'great diversities in practice.... in regard to the admission of aliens, females and persons of colour or negroes' to vote while it was 'highly necessary to the safety, quiet good order and dignity of the state to clear up the said doubts by an act... declaratory of the true sense and meaning of the constitution'. The true sense was then said to be to restrict the suffrage to 'free white male citizens' of 21 worth fifty pounds but stipulated that mere appearance on the tax lists was to be considered evidence that a man was worth that much, so effectively the measure extended manhood suffrage by enfranchising every adult man who was subject to paying taxes.[49]

Women voters were thus disenfranchised after being blamed for a chaotic electoral contest in which it was obvious that at least some of the officials were corrupt. Women (and Negroes, it was claimed) voted not as a matter of customary right but rather when they were whipped up to tip the balance of a hotly contested campaign. It has been described as 'a holocaust of political morals in which every kind of abuse was exploited with festive extravagance'.[50]

The underlying problem, concealed by corruption and bad political behaviour, was that there was insufficient intellectual justification or understanding of the franchise for women. It was not sought by women in any organized way or made consistent use of once conferred. It would be another half-century before political thought, organization, and willpower would combine in a pressure group that would seriously demand voting rights for women.

3
Early British radicals

'Very clever, but awfully revolutionary'

In the early nineteenth century, after the Napoleonic wars, real wages fell to half their previous level in England. Illegal liquor shops hummed to talk of how to obtain weapons for the coming revolution; bread riots broke out in major cities; revolutionaries drilled on the moors by night. The working poor were unrepresented politically and bitterly resentful at their shabby treatment in the post-war depression. Workers met in large out-door meetings to hear orators enunciate their woes. Women were present with a sense of shared danger—justifiably, for at St Peter's Fields ('Peterloo') both men and women were attacked indiscriminately by the Manchester Yeomanry and equally suffered death or sabre cuts to the bone.

There is an account of women at a meeting of mill and other industrial workers at Lydgate in the Saddleworth district, on the border of Lancashire and Yorkshire. The radical weaver turned poet Samuel Bamford was making a speech. As he described it,

> I, in the course of an address, insisted on the right, and the propriety also, of females who were present at such assemblages voting by a show of hands for or against the resolutions. This was a new idea; and the women, who attended numerously on that bleak ridge, were mightily pleased with it. The men being nothing dissentient, when the resolution was put the women held up their hands amid much laughter; and ever from that time females voted with the men at the Radical meetings.

The hesitancy and nervous laughter that Bamford describes certainly has the ring of truth about it, and it tells of an underlying trend repeated every time women's suffrage was discussed: before converting the wider world, in which there were many enemies, women first had to have the confidence of the men in their own beds and around their own hearthsides; it was not enough for people with the interests of women at heart to call for change—the change had to happen in their own groupings. If women were going to have political rights in the wider world, they must first have them in their own organizations. The other, linked development was paradoxically the opposite, not unity but difference: women setting up their own single-sex groups, mirroring the women's clubs of the French Revolution. Bamford, improbably, claims responsibility:

> I was not then aware that the new impulse thus given to political movement would in a short time be applied to charitable and religious purposes. But it was so; our females voted at every subsequent meeting; it became the practice, female political unions were formed, with their chairwomen, committees and other officials; and from us the practice was soon borrowed, very judiciously no doubt, and applied in a greater or a less degree to the promotion of religious and charitable institutions.[1]

Bamford was writing his reminiscences of this period after 1839, from a position of comfortable respectability, about his time as a radical leader during the turbulent years of 1816 to 1821. The radicalism of his experiences was softened for his Victorian audience and his later circumstances, but he still wanted to mention this innovation. Bamford had led the Middleton contingent to St Peter's Fields on 16 August 1819 where he had witnessed the Perterloo massacre. Although his behaviour and that of his contingent was orderly, he was later charged with treason and sentenced to a year in Lincoln gaol for inciting a riot. The experience of massacre and brutal injustice did not incline him to political violence, but filled him with a horror of it; and in later life he parted company with radicals when the electoral reformers were prepared to embrace 'physical force' to achieve their ends. He always considered that Britain was able to make peaceful progress towards political reform and this put him firmly in the tradition of the majority of campaigners for women's suffrage.

Women's employment, particularly in the textile industries, was altering the economic status of women, giving them the self confidence to act within their own groups. E. P. Thompson in his classic history *The Making of the English Working Class* notes that the period from 1815 to 1835 saw the first indications of independent trade union action among women workers, but observes that the Female Reform Societies did not raise the demand for women's suffrage.[2] It was, however, through the work of such radicals as Robert Carlile and Eliza Sharples; Anna Wheeler and William Thompson; and Catherine and Goodwyn Barmby that the idea of a vote for women was maintained in activist circles. It was in this atmosphere that the discussion of women's suffrage became widespread for the first time as a focus for a political group, and not the preserve of a small coterie of intellectuals. As historian Kathryn Gleadle has shown, it is too simple to see women as rigidly confined to a domestic and apolitical sphere; women were involved in political debate and action, though usually more as spectators and supporters than leaders. The parochial was, moreover, an area where women could make an impact, even if they were 'borderline citizens'.[3]

When mentioned at all, women's suffrage had been raised in the House of Commons in order to be dismissed, so that even the radical Charles Fox in 1797 in a debate on parliamentary reform asked rhetorically why it had never been imagined that women should have the right to vote. The answers were that the laws of the nation and of nature had made 'that sex dependent on ours'; that women would only use the vote as directed by their husbands or father, and that 'in all the theories and projects of the most absurd speculation, it has never been suggested that it would be advisable to extend the elective suffrage to the female sex'.[4] This is an odd remark, implying that Fox did not know that Condorcet had suggested just this seven years before. It may be that he did not consider one of many revolutionary statements in France to be worthy of comment (Wollstonecraft's hint is too vague to be considered a real suggestion, it was an indication of a recommendation to come). This, then, was the starting point, where even the most radical of parliamentarians was unable to countenance women's suffrage.

Hoisting the black flag

It was individuals, not parties or organizations, who were to take the issue of women's enfranchisement further, linking it to other radical causes. Their personal behaviour was very much part of the radicalism. 'Early feminism was closely identified with a new definition of sexual morality,' remarked historian Constance Rover, 'perhaps even more closely than with the demand for an improved legal and civil status for women.'[5] Two such pioneers were Richard Carlile and his 'moral wife' Eliza Sharples ('Isis') who produced the first journal in English supporting women's emancipation.

Carlile, who was born in Ashburton, Devon in 1790, received elementary education and worked in shops and as a tin worker, he married Jane (whose maiden name is not known), moved to London in 1813 and became caught

up in the radical zeal that swept through the artisan class. Carlile's biographer Guy Aldred remarked that Jane and Richard had married in 1813
after only two months' courtship and then, 'Finding that their tempera-
ments were incompatible, they wisely agreed to separate in the year 1819,
but postponed putting this resolution into effect owing to their common
determination to resist the Government's attempt to suppress Paine's writings and other radical literature.' He noted that Jane's capacity for organization far exceeded that of her husband and that 'he was bent on propagandism
and paid no heed to business details', but that they were incompatible too
for other reasons, 'she was hot tempered whereas he was cool but resolute,
which, in domestic life, means obstinate. Hence they tolerated rather than
loved each other.'[6]

He first became a distributor of political pamphlets and then a writer of
them. In 1817 he became publisher of fiery pamphleteer William Cobbett's
newspaper, the *Weekly Political Register*, and rapidly developed into a prolific
journalist and publisher supporting the abolition of the monarchy, secular
education, birth control, and the emancipation of women. He spent his first
jail terms for publishing the political parodies of William Hone (he was
released after four months on Hone's acquittal).

After 1819 radicalism was focused on the 'gag acts' that aimed at the suppression of dissent, including the undermining of political discussion by
the imposition of a tax on printed material. In E. P. Thompson's spirited
description, unlike other publishers who modified their tone to accommodate the six acts, 'Carlile hoisted the black ensign of unqualified defiance
and, like a pirate cock-boat, sailed straight into the middle of the combined
fleets of the State and Church.'[7] In February 1819 he took over a shop in
Fleet Street and sold the *Political Register* and the *Black Dwarf*. He published
the *Rights of Man* then commenced the publication of all Thomas Paine's
works serially in the *Weekly Political Register* then in book form, culminating
in 1818 with *The Age of Reason* which had been banned since 1797. He was
repeatedly prosecuted and imprisoned, notably in October 1819 when he
was sentenced to six years.

So many shop workers were arrested and imprisoned that they began to
edit *Newgate Monthly Magazine* in 1824. His wife Jane, and other family and
friends kept the publishing work going until Jane and his sister Mary-Anne
were also imprisoned, as were shop men and women who volunteered to
serve, knowing they were likely to be imprisoned for period of up to four
and a half years. In all, 150 people were imprisoned for acting as Carlile's

agents. The government eventually gave up and in 1825 Carlile was released unconditionally despite having refused to pay his fines. 'I have accomplished the liberty of the Press in England,' he declared.[8]

In 1826 he published *Every Woman's Book*, the first book for the public giving contraceptive advice (chiefly the use of the vaginal sponge) and contesting traditional views about women, calling for 'equality between the sexes' and arguing that women were not 'mere breeding machines'.[9] In a later publication, the *Prompter* of 9 April 1831, he asserted that 'a constitution cannot be founded on equal rights that excludes the woman from all share of power and influence'.

Carlile was increasingly interested in religion and consequently joined up with the Revd Robert Taylor, an Anglican priest who now defined himself as a deist and preached anti-clerical sermons. They leased the Rotunda in Blackfriars Road, which became an important centre for radical and free-thought meetings and working-class discussion. Among those using it was the National Union of the Working Classes which demanded universal manhood suffrage, though its confused aims and poor leadership prevented development of this theme and the Union did not thrive. Carlile was soon incarcerated again (he spent some nine years in total in prison) and the Rotunda closed.

When in prison in 1831, at the age of 41, he was approached by Eliza Sharples who had seen him on a lecture tour. They wrote to each other and she visited him in his cell. It is not clear whether his final parting from his wife was related to the appearance of 29-year old Eliza in his life, or whether the marriage was already over, but Jane Carlile separated from him in 1832 and set up her own book shop, after they had undergone a 'moral divorce' in which she received an annuity, their furniture and part of the stock from the bookshop.

Sharples was the daughter of a counterpane manufacturer from Bolton, Lancashire. She had a religious, boarding school education and did not question her faith until the deaths of her sister, father, and brother shook the foundations of her world. She had first encountered Carlile through his published work, and took to writing to him. She arrived in London and began visiting him in prison where he obviously enjoyed privileges appropriate to his renown and the wealth his publications were producing, as they conceived their first child while Carlile was incarcerated.

She reopened the Rotunda, and gave lectures on women's emancipation and free thought under the name Isis, which was also the title of the feminist free-thought journal she edited. It promised that sooner or later female emancipation would come, 'and no other reason is to be offered against the equality of the sexes, than that which tyranny has to offer on every occasion—its will and power'.[10] She appeared in the role of the Egyptian goddess Isis, with the floor before her strewn with white thorn and laurel. Her lectures on mystical religion and women's rights captivated audiences but only for a short period—she was unable to keep their attention past the point of spectacle. 'I,' she said, 'who, six months ago, was absolutely without prospect, without purpose in life, should now be waving the magic wand of intellect over the darkness of this land, this real Egyptian darkness...and be successfully introducing new love, new light, into this people.'[11] Many early feminists were radicals and/or socialists and not a few were mystics. It was as if, once the mental fetters that tied women to strict gender roles were released, anything was possible and they could, spiritually, reach for the skies.

When Carlile was released he and Eliza began to live together in a 'moral marriage' with their children. Carlile later disappointed his radical followers by converting to a mystical Christianity. He was no longer in step with the most advanced thinking that moved towards socialist ideas and Chartism. The Carliles were now limited to the world of mystical sects, supported by such rich eccentrics as Sophie Chichester who relieved the couple's poverty.

Carlile died of a bronchial infection aged 53 in 1843 and Chichester sent the penurious Eliza and her children to Alcott House, 'the Concordium', an ideal community run by the 'spiritual socialist' James Pierrepont Grieves. Eliza managed six months in the atmosphere of abstinence and vegetarianism, then left. She was last engaging in public discourse from a coffee and discussion room she ran in the Hackney Road where she promoted radical free thought and women's rights, before her death at 49 in 1852.

An appeal of one half of the human race

The most advanced thought arguing for women's suffrage in the first half of the nineteenth century came from another couple, an eccentric landlord and an embittered wife, both deeply imbued with the spirit of esoteric socialism.

William Thompson was born into a middle-class family in Cork in 1775; his father, a merchant, became mayor of the town and later high sheriff of the county so Thompson's background was entrenched in the values of the Protestant ascendancy. From an early age he took an interest in social questions, influenced by the work of Godwin and Bentham and new ideas emanating from revolutionary France which he discussed in the Cork Philosophical and Literary Society. He became estranged from his family over his radicalism which extended to supporting Catholic emancipation and popular education.

After the death of his father in 1814, Thompson took over the family's estates in Glandore in the West of Ireland where he was able to put some of his principles into practice: acting as a fair landlord, creating a model farm and introducing advanced agricultural techniques. Thompson became the prototype eccentric socialist who lived frugally, was a non-smoker, a vegetarian, and a teetotaller and attracted attention to himself by behaviour such as walking about the Irish countryside with a revolutionary tricolour tied to his walking stick. He was popular with the locals because of his fair behaviour as a landlord, despite his atheism. He was said to live on potatoes, turnips, and honey (to which he was said to have had a fondness bordering on addiction).

Thompson first visited Jeremy Bentham in London in 1819, meeting James Mill (J. S. Mill's father) and other leading radicals. Thompson was also being influenced by the ideas of Robert Owen, the first person to use the term 'socialist' to describe his co-operative ventures, including his factory at New Lanarck which treated workers fairly, provided schooling for workers' children and a co-operative shop. Owen, a close contemporary of Thompson (he was born in 1771) provided platforms for the discussion of the status of women and the reformation of marriage. Under the Owenite banner meetings were taking place such as that described in the newspaper *New Moral World* for 12 June 1841 where a 'grand annual festival of the universal community society' is reported. Here 'Prosperity and emancipation to the female portion of the human race' was a toast proposed by a Mr G. A. Fleming, who criticized the Chartists for promoting male suffrage but not recognizing 'one half of the human race', which was not, he could confidently say, an error which would entrap true socialists.[12]

Some felt the Owenites had a way to go, however. 'A Female Socialist' writing from Edgbaston complained that socialists were following the priesthood and practising one thing while preaching another, meaning that women were not apparent in sitting on Owenite councils. She advanced, 'If they really and truly desire to see the females intelligent and useful members of community, why not establish a rule throughout the branches to have an equal number of females with the males on their councils, and introduce them into their private meeting, and, if they feel them ignorant, endeavour to imbue their minds with useful knowledge.'[13] This early excursion into the concept of gender quotas was not met with fulsome welcome (or any response, it seems).

Thompson's thought created a bridge between the idealistic socialism of the Owenites and the hard-headed liberalism of the political economists. Moved by the practical application of Bentham's principle of providing the greatest happiness for the greatest number, Thompson wrote *An Inquiry into the Principles of the Distribution of Wealth*, published in 1824, describing the inequality of the contemporary economic system and laying down the main principles of the co-operative movement.

In this and his subsequent *Labour Rewarded: the Claims of Labour and Capital Conciliated* Thompson attacked the subjugation of women which was inevitable under the existing system of private property. This engaged him in a literary debate with James Mill who had written an article 'On Government' for the 1824 supplement to the *Encyclopaedia Britannica*. In it he argued that women had no need of the franchise because their interests were subsumed under or contained within those of men. The dismissive passage was,

> One thing is pretty clear, that all those individuals whose interests are indisputably included in those of other individuals may be struck off from political rights without inconvenience. In this light may be viewed all children up to a certain age, whose interests are involved in those of their parents. In this light also women may be regarded, the interest of almost all of whom is involved either in that of their fathers or in that of their husbands.[14]

In his fierce opposition to this piece of reasoning Thompson's ally was Anna Wheeler (née Doyle), another member of the Protestant ascendancy, the daughter of an Anglican archdeacon, who probably met Thompson at one of Bentham's gatherings at Queen Square Place, Westminster, or at the Co-operative Society in Chancery Lane, perhaps in 1824. As a girl Anna had been a 'reigning beauty of the Irish countryside' she was not formally educated but self-taught. Against the wishes of her mother, she married Francis Massy-Wheeler in 1800 after he had seen her at the races and conceived a passion for her. She married him in order to escape from her mother's clutches but as he was a wealthy Irish squire whose interests did not extend beyond the hunting field and the bottle, this was not the escape she had hoped for. She had six children of whom two daughters survived, Henriette and Rosina (who was to become Lady Bulwer Lytton). During her unhappy marriage Anna Wheeler read the French philosophers and Mary Wollstonecraft. Rosina described her mother as 'stretched out on a sofa, deep in the perusal of some French or German philosophical work that had reached her via London'.[15] She was described as being beautiful with chestnut hair, grey-blue eyes, a chiselled aquiline nose and a slightly curling upper lip, though her daughter said she cared nothing for physical beauty.

Finally, after twelve years of a miserable marriage, Anna left her husband and his dilapidated house, with her daughters, then aged 10 and 11, and joined her uncle General Sir John Doyle on Guernsey where he was governor. They stayed with him for four years until his resignation from his post. She went on to London, then to Caen in France in 1816 where she met followers of Henri Saint-Simon, founder of French socialism, and Charles Fourier, a French utopian socialist and sexual radical, whose work she translated for Owen's journal *The Crisis*.

After her estranged husband's death in 1820 she was able to move more freely in British society and she went to London where she formed relationships with Jeremy Bentham and Robert Owen. Intellectually, what Anna Wheeler brought to the dining tables of London was a link between the British co-operative movement and the Saint-Simonians with their criticism of Christianity and the family. In her movement between radical groups in England, France, and Ireland she was able to take ideas from one group and transplant them to another. She wrote for Owenite newspapers and spoke on radical platforms, where one lecture is recorded as beginning, 'Having learned only to serve and suffer, in my capacity as slave and woman...'[16] She was referred to as the 'Goddess of reason' and 'the most gifted woman of the age'.[17]

After Rosina's marriage to the novelist Bulwer Lytton, in 1827 Anna was to meet many of his literary circle, including the young Disraeli who, having once met her at dinner in 1833 described her as 'not so pleasant, something between Jeremy Bentham and Meg Merrilies, very clever but awfully revolutionary. She poured forth all her systems upon my novitiate ear.'[18]

In discussion of their opposition to James Mill's notions of female inequality (or 'identity of interests' between men and women) Wheeler and Thompson conceived their joint work, *An appeal of one half of the human race, Women against the pretensions of the other half, Men, to retain them in political and thence in civil and domestic slavery: In reply to a paragraph of Mr Mill's celebrated Article on Government.*

They addressed the moral deficiencies of the utilitarian argument which pretended to offer the greatest happiness to the greatest number but ignored women, half the race. The work was produced under Thompson's name but it opened with an introductory 'Letter to Mrs Wheeler': 'Honored with your acquaintance, ambitious of your friendship, I have endeavoured to arrange the expression of those feelings, sentiments and reasonings which have emanated from your mind. In the following pages you will find discussed on paper, what you have so often discussed in conversation.'[19]

Thompson considered most of the *Appeal* their 'joint property' excepting a few pages that were 'the exclusive produce of your mind and pen, and written with your own hand'. He declared they were 'Weary of waiting, the protest of at least one man and one woman is here put forward against doctrines which disgrace the principle of utility.'[20] They were not, he wrote, committed to 'equality with such creatures as men now are' but would 'equally elevate both sexes'.[21]

Thompson devotes attention first to the question of whether James Mill was right to exclude women because their interests were supposedly identical with those of the men of their household. 'Does the identity of interest between men and women, in point of fact, and of necessity, exist?' he asks.[22] What about women without husbands or fathers; adult daughters within their fathers' establishments; illegitimate daughters and wives? Even within their fathers' establishments, daughters have more community of interests with their mothers.

The writers' greatest invective was retained for the doctrine that the interests of married women were subsumed under those of their husbands. Clearly informed by Wheeler's personal experiences, the *Appeal* declared, wives are 'the slaves of husbands by law'.[23] In a mixture of forensic argument and rant it continued:

> As little as slaves have had to do in any part of the world in the enacting of slave-codes, have women in any part of the world had to do with the partial codes of selfishness and ignorance which every where dispose of their right over their own actions and all their other enjoyments, in favour of those who made the regulations; particularly that most unequal and debasing code, absurdly called the *contract* of marriage... From regulating the terms of this pretended contract, women have been as completely excluded as bullocks, or sheep, or any other animals subjugated to man, have been from determining the regulations of commons or slaughter-houses.[24]

Then, anticipating that opponents of women's franchise would shift the ground of their opposition to say women were not fit to vote, they turn their attention to the fitness of women to exercise political judgement. Denying women the vote on grounds of lesser physical strength was specious: if strength were the qualification, why not award the franchise on the basis of a weight-lifting competition?

Thompson and Wheeler demolish the argument that men were any more fitted for the exercise of the vote than women, and pose a counter-argument that women could reasonably be considered the superior political being. Ultimately they attributed the degraded position of women to the economic system and felt the solution was socialism. Under socialism there would be a communality and no dependence of women on men, a removal of oppression and the 'vile trade of prostitution', men and women would live as equals.[25] The liberation of women would reward man 'with knowledge, with freedom and with happiness'.[26]

Richard Pankhurst declared the *Appeal* was 'a major landmark in the history of both the women's movement and of socialist thought. This work was the first voice of a nineteenth-century man against the subjection of women, and the first with a direct bearing on women's suffrage.' Pankhurst considered it was the most significant document relating to women in the three-quarters of a century between Mary Wollstonecraft's *Vindication of the Rights of Women* of 1792 and John Stuart Mill's *Subjection of Women* of 1869.[27]

Thompson and Wheeler were close but how intimate they were is not clear; they never lived together. Marriage was out of the question, if only because Thompson refused to marry within the unequal legal provisions constraining married women. Wheeler used to attack the ideal of romantic love which she felt concentrated women's thoughts on pleasing male sensuality; they were not the sort of couple to have left a trove of love letters.

Wheeler became a frequent writer in the co-operative and socialist journals, complaining, for example, at 'the hateful and unjust policy' of denying women education on the basis that 'to keep women our slaves we must keep them in ignorance'.[28] She argued for equal education, an equal right for women to acquire and possess property, and against the 'absurd system of sexual morality'.[29] Something of her sharp temper and fighting spirit are apparent in her harangues but as Dolores Dooley wrote, 'Wheeler decried the social conditioning of men by corrupt institutions, but she aimed always to promote harmony between the sexes rather than adversarial rancour, to plead the cause of men in advocating the rights of women.'[30] Wheeler proposed co-operative communal living under which, she maintained, gender justice would be possible.

Thompson died of inflammation of the chest on 28 March 1833 at the age of 58, after which he was buried, despite his atheism, in a churchyard according to Anglican rites. After the reading of his will made his wishes known, that no priest 'is to meddle with my remains', he was exhumed and dissected in the cause of medical science. The will caused further complications as his relatives contested its terms, which left almost everything to the co-operative movement. After a battle of some twenty-five years in the Irish court of chancery, reminiscent of Jarndyce v. Jarndyce in Charles Dickens' *Bleak House*, the relatives won, but the greater part of the estate had been eaten up in legal fees.

Wheeler, stricken with neuralgia and suffering money problems, had the deaths of other friends as well as Thompson to endure in a short period: Jeremy Bentham had died the year before Thompson; her uncle General Sir John Doyle died in 1834; and Charles Fourier in 1837. During the French Revolution of 1848 a friend wrote that she should come to France, 'The moral atmosphere would give you life.'[31] But it was too late, Wheeler died in 1848; both her work and that of 'Philosopher Thompson' became harder to obtain, but its influence was still apparent: J. S. Mill records his discussions with Thompson, 'a very estimable man, with whom I was well acquainted' and cites the *Appeal*;[32] *The Woman's Signal* ('A weekly record and review for ladies') republished the whole *Appeal* in weekly instalments from 13 October 1898.

In the twentieth century an interest in the roots of socialist thought developed, following the rise of national regimes based on Marxism. The extent to which Karl Marx himself was influenced by his predecessor in economic philosophy is open to question. Richard Pankhurst, Sylvia Pankhurst's son and the third generation of his family to make a contribution to women's suffrage, wrote a biography of Thompson that was published in 1954, and his edited version of the *Appeal* appeared in 1983.

Reform for some

From early in 1831 working-class energy was channelled into reform of the corrupt electoral system; tens of thousands joined demonstrations, many wearing the white scarves which had come to represent manhood suffrage.

John Wade, the editor of the *Black Book*, the mouthpiece of discontent, put forward a claim for the vote for rate-paying householders. In justifying the exclusion of women he wrote 'why disenfranchise women in preference to men, or minors to majors; why we would allow a person to vote at the precise age of twenty-one, and not at twenty or eighteen; we confess in answer to these inquiries, we can only give one reply, namely, that EXPEDIENCY, and not strict justice, dictates the exclusion.'[33]

In the event, the effect of the reform of 1832 was to enfranchise the middle classes in accordance with property qualifications. Wheeler complained 'there was not a word about justice to women in the Reform Bill. Else these poor creatures [male politicians] would have opposed it with more animosity than they did...'[34] The 1832 Act, if anything, made the situation even worse for women in that it, for the first time in a piece of British legislation, put the word 'male' in front of the world 'person' in the Act to specifically exclude women even if they had fulfilled every other qualification to vote.

This shows an increasing understanding of the importance of gender; there had been quite enough discourse over the previous forty years to give parliamentary draftsmen a clear impression that the gender of the person who would be voting was an issue. There was an ambiguity which would allow women to assert their right to vote in the courts. There was perhaps also some knowledge of the situation in New Jersey where women had been enfranchised by a constitution that was not gender-specific. There is no evidence for this, but specialists in the field, writing what was effectively Britain's electoral constitution, were doubtless professionally aware of the work of previous constitution writers. The 1832 specific exclusion of women reflects the same procedure in France where the advanced manhood suffrage constitution of 1793 excluded women for the first time in a process of codification and a recognition of contemporary debate.

The issue had also been tested in a contested election 100 years previously in 1733 when Sarah Bly had stood as a sexton at St Bartolph Without Bishopsgate church in the City of London. She received 169 votes from men and 40 from women parishioners while her male opponent received 174 male and 22 female votes. The defeated man therefore brought a case to dispute that women voters should have been excluded (not that Sarah Bly had no right to stand, she clearly had). The case reached Lord Chief Justice Lee who sat with three other judges and, after deferring the case twice, eventually concluded that the women's votes should stand as parish sexton's duty was by way of a private trust rather than a state-endorsed election, 'and not a thing of public consideration in which I incline to think women have not a right of voting, though they are not positively excluded'.[35] It was the loophole of this lack of positive exclusion that the legislators wanted to close. Clearly the judges could not be relied upon, and when the opportunity came in 1832 the law was firmed up to exclude any possibility of female suffrage. For good measure, the same procedure was followed for local elections in 1835 for the Municipal Reform Act, which made provision for specifically 'male' voting, where previously women had voted in local affairs.

Some champions of reform tried to keep up the momentum of change, and on 3 August 1832 the radical MP Henry 'Orator' Hunt presented a petition to parliament 'giving the Elective Franchise to every unmarried woman' possessing the necessary pecuniary qualification. Thus it enshrined the principle that married women were 'covered' by their husband's rights, but made a submission of fairness, that in the absence of a husband a woman fulfilling the appropriate residency and tax qualifications should be treated as an equal. The petition was drafted by Mary Smith, a rich spinster of Stanmore, Yorkshire, who felt that since the vote was granted on the basis of property taxation, as she had property, as had many other spinsters and widows, they should have the vote to go with it. She said that 'women were liable to all the punishments of the law, not excepting death, and ought to have a voice in the making of them.'[36] The plea was received with gales of laughter: it would be almost a hundred years before this case which was unanswerable except in terms of ribaldry, would receive the unqualified support of the House.

The Great Reform Act did less than nothing for the working poor, indeed, it even swept away some anomalous franchises whereby artisans in particular constituencies had had the right to vote. 'They threw their hearts into the contest,' ran a plaintive Address to the Reformers in 1838, 'and would have risked their lives to obtain that which they were led to believe would give *to all* the blessings of LIBERTY. Alas! Their hopes were excited by promises which have not been kept, and their expectations of freedom have been bitterly disappointed...'[37]

Thenceforward, the thrust of working-class movements was towards Chartism, agitation for the fulfilment of the People's Charter which was unsuccessfully presented to parliament in 1839, 1842 and 1848. The reforms being demanded were for the right of every male over the age of 18 to vote;

annual parliaments; a removal of the property qualification for MPs and payment of MPs; and equal electoral districts. All these were ultimately achieved, (voting at 18 not until 1969) excepting annual parliaments, a notion that was gradually abandoned as an objective of reform.

When the People's Charter was first drafted by cabinet-maker William Lovett he had included a clause making provision for extending the franchise to women, but when it was published on 8 May 1838 'it was unfortunately left out' Lovett remarks, on the urging of 'several members' who 'thought its adoption in the Bill might retard the suffrage of men'.[38]

Several sporadic attempts to reintroduce the clause and to raise the issue were made but were rejected. The arguments put forward were like those of the Manchester Chartist James Leach who, when the issue was proposed by a debating opponent, said, 'he did not think that such a wide difference existed between a man and woman as to make it necessary for women to enjoy the suffrage: he thought men, as fathers, husbands and bothers, would secure the best interests of women'.[39] This is a paternalistic argument which is, in terms of the status of women, an advance on a more conservative position that women are constitutionally incapable of engaging rationally in politics. It moreover leads back to the line of argument that if the only reason women were denied the vote was because they were under the protection of their husbands and fathers, how could the denial of the vote to widows and spinsters be justified?

Women's suffrage was a subject that was freely addressed along with universal manhood suffrage. For example, an address on the subject of free education issued by the Working Men's Association of London in 1837 said without the anticipation of any disagreement: 'the selection of teachers, the choice of books, and the whole management and superintendence of schools in each locality should be confined to a SCHOOL COMMITTEE of twenty or more persons elected by *universal suffrage* of all the adult population, male and female.'[40]

Engaging in these debates were many colourful characters that lived on the fringes of Owenite millenarian socialism, believing in a unity of socialism and Christianity, and often living in experimental communities. Among them were Catherine and Goodwyn Barmby; he was a Chartist and writer for the Owenites' journal the *New Moral World*, he claimed to have originated the word 'communism'. He was the son of a Suffolk solicitor, who had been destined for the church but had moved to more radical pursuits. Catherine, née Watkins, was also a contributor to the *New Moral World*, under the pseudonym Kate. The daughter of a government officer, her first articles were about such matters as women's restricted employment opportunities; in 1836 she wrote 'The religion of the millennium' offering a vision of socialist faith founded on 'moral purity and moral liberty'.

In 1841 Watkins married Barmby and in the same year, when she was 24 or 25 and he 21, Barmby founded the Central Communist Propaganda Society which soon became the Communist Church, its name indicating the close connection between religion and politics in these radical movements. Historian Barbara Taylor describes the Communists as cerebral and intensely romantic, vigorously experimental in their approach to everyday life that included enthusiasms ranging from vegetarianism and hydrotherapy to meditation. Taylor remarked, 'Goodwyn himself became an increasingly Shelleyan figure over the years, with blond hair flowing down to his shoulders (to the joyful amazement of the crowds he addressed, who occasionally demanded locks as souvenirs).'[41]

Catherine published poems in his praise and seems to have acted as his faithful co-worker but clearly had considerable political abilities of her own. The couple travelled the streets of London with a hooded cart from which they distributed communist tracts and harangued passers-by. Among their tracts, also in the eventful year of 1841 (that Barmby had designated Year 1 of the new communist calendar) was a *Declaration of Electoral Reform* which demanded that the People's Charter be amended to include the vote for women. This may well have been the first time that an organization supported women's suffrage.

The atmosphere created by Chartism allowed the wide dissemination of ideas of democracy, making further progress easier to contemplate. It was in the atmosphere of heated debate that in 1843 Catherine Barmby produced a leaflet in a series entitled 'New Tracts for the Times' with a mystical symbol on the front page of a triangle with God in the middle and woman, man, and child around the outside. The tract dared 'assist woman from her political serfdom to the freedom of the electoral vote'. Woman should be the teacher and the priestess, 'the sharer of equal rights'. Barmby demanded the emancipation of woman '1st Politically, 2nd Ecclesiastically, 3rd Domestically'.[42]

In terms of politics, Barmby presents the demand as one of absolute equality with men, 'That woman is not the equal of man, who can assert?' she asks defiantly. She is not claiming that women have a superior moral contribution to make, any more than she is conceding women's inferiority in any field: 'We demand the political emancipation of woman because it is her right, possessing as she does with man, a three-fold being, sentimental, intellectual and physical, because she is subject to like wants, expected to pay the same taxes, taxation without representation being tyranny, and because all other laws act as severely, and many more severely upon her than upon man.'

Barmby also argues for 'the emancipation of the hand of woman from mere household drudgery' and independence to work in any area she might 'which alone can be her security from the tyranny of her husband, and her preservation from the oppressions of society'. Thus an independent income was supposed to bring domestic and social freedom.

Her images are all drawn from the arena of class warfare. Just as the wealthy are opposed to the advancement of the working class, so men are opposed to the advancement of women, but this is mere prejudice. Barmby considers suffrage the essential and original claim, 'The demand for woman's religious and social emancipation cannot be brought forward until primarily the right of suffrage has been claimed by her. And this demand my faith is that she will soon make.' Her appeal to justice from men is also one of self interest, she says—'for without woman is free, man cannot obtain his own liberation'—but does not expand on this.

Ultimately she makes an appeal for women internationally to resist customs ranging from Chinese foot-binding to 'ridiculous' fashions in Europe. 'The equality of woman and man must be our rallying cry. Women's slavery under Muhummedism [sic] and her subaltern situation under Christianity, must be repealed, and her equality with man be acknowledged under Communism.'

As part of a development of her millennialist beliefs Catherine Barmby in other writings evoked the figure of a female Messiah who would come to free all humanity from the chains of sex-based oppression. Barbara Taylor traces the influences for this figure to the Devon 'female Christ' Joanna Southcott and the doctrines of the French Saint Simonians who awaited the arrival of a woman Messiah, La mère; and finally to Goodwyn Barmby himself who evolved a concept of woman-man-power, a divinity foreshadowed by all earlier female prophets, whose arrival 'will socialise our planet and establish true communism amid our globe'.[43]

The couple attempted an ideal community in 1843, the Moreville Communatorium at Hanwell, Middlesex, but it folded after less than a year; others who had joined all left, unable to maintain the standards set by the

Barmbys. By 1848 with the decline of Chartism, together with its monster meetings and threat of revolution, the communist faith was also crumbling and the Communist Church closed.

Catherine Barmby continued working as a journalist but died at the age of 37 or 38 in 1853 of asthma and consumption. Goodwyn Barmby became a Unitarian minister and, with his second wife Ada Shepherd, was to see a revival of interest in women's suffrage; he was a member of the National Association for Women's Suffrage in the 1860s. He died in 1881 at the age of 61.

A voice from quiet house

Any hopes for women's franchise in the short term were swept away in the disappointment at the failure of working-class radicalism. If the working class could not obtain their major demand, of manhood suffrage, the more radical measures that had been voiced affecting women were not even worth discussing. It was clear in the intensely class-conscious 1840s that the middle class had won their battles of the last two decades—for electoral reform in 1832 and the abolition of the Corn Laws in 1846. Their orators had stirred up the working class and used the threat of working-class unrest if their demands were not met, but the net gain had been for the middle class. Weak leadership, internal divisions, and poor co-ordination had bedevilled the Chartists. Their impetus had run out with their ignominious failure to achieve either revolution or reform in 1848. Now working-class attention turned increasingly towards trade unionism as an area in which they could exert direct power.

The agitation for a vote for women was to pass from the radical working class to the middle class around the middle of the nineteenth century, through the medium of those such as Anne Knight who, as historian Marian Ramelson said, 'for years carried the torch left by Mary Wollstonecraft practically alone'.[44] Knight, daughter of a prosperous grocer, lived at Quiet House, Chelmsford, Essex. She was not only a Quaker, as were many social reformers, but was observant, dressing in their traditional simple black garb and speaking in the antiquated form of address used by devout Quakers.

Her early work had been in the long Quaker tradition of opposition to slavery, which was the training ground for many suffragists. She came from a family of fervent abolitionists and she was a mainstay of the Chelmsford

Ladies' Anti-Slavery Society. She was present at the World Anti-Slavery Convention held in London in 1840 where the exclusion of women from taking part in the proceedings made many women turn their attention towards their own emancipation. At this meeting Anne Knight met the American anti-slavery campaigner Lucretia Mott who described her as 'a singular-looking woman—very pleasant and polite', and gives some idea of her conversation, 'Anne Knight enlarged on the importance of belief in the Atonement.'[45]

The movement for women's suffrage has been dated from the exclusion of American women delegates from the floor of this conference as it drew attention to woman's marginal status within the anti-slavery campaign. But although the American women's movement might well be dated to this event, in Britain it was more than a quarter of a century before a national women's suffrage campaign was set up.

So far as is known, Anne Knight did not do a great deal of platform speaking, but influenced others in meetings and wrote a prodigious number of letters, as well as a leaflet on Women's Suffrage in 1847. She was prepared to draw on working-class support, asking Isaac Ironside, a Chartist, Owenite, and radical Sheffield councillor to help her locate Chartist women who were interested in revising the Charter. Ironside sent her the names of seven women who were politically involved. Knight was arguing, as an extant letter shows, for the Charter to be extended to women as it was 'calling that universal which is only half of it. It will now dishonour them to go on repeating their demand for only men when it is so widely spread and acknowledged that every adult member of the human family bearing the same burdens has the same right to a vote.'[46] It is impossible not to be in awe of her courage, for after the Charter had failed for asking too much of the political process, she was proposing to revive it and demand more. This radical spirit led to a meeting of the first women's suffrage society, the Sheffield Association for Female Franchise on 26 February 1851 at the Democratic Temperance Hotel. A declaration was issued calling on 'beloved sisters' to take up 'this holy work' of franchise campaigning.[47] They organized a petition which was presented by Lord Carlisle, a former Viceroy of Ireland and an advanced thinker, to the House of Lords, 'to take into their serious consideration the propriety of enacting an Electoral Law which will include adult females'.[48]

This agitation was stillborn, however, probably because of its prime mover's absence from the scene. Anne Knight was living in Paris from 1847 or

1848, a supporter of the British and French utopian socialist movements. She was an enthusiastic observer of the year of revolutions and a contributor to *La Voix des Femmes* which called for women to be recognized as citizens. She attended the international peace conference in 1849 and asked, but was refused, permission to attend the 1851 conference as a delegate (with a right to speak). She was to live in France until her death in 1862.

Anne Knight's quiet Christianity was an anomaly in the suffrage arguments of the first half of the nineteenth century which were more marked by a strong strain of mysticism. The image of the woman priestess in the feminist agitation of 'Isis' Sharples and Catherine Barmby was not to re-emerge until Annie Besant pursued her dreams of Theosophy to India. Women's suffrage in the early nineteenth century was presented as part of a millennarian vision, a belief in the approaching time of peace on earth where woman would come into her own—a notion that again rises to prominence with the Pankhursts in the early twentieth century.

By the middle of the nineteenth century the working-class, radical edge to women's suffrage was gone. For the next half-century middle-class campaigners were to take the lead, as the country became more prosperous and self-satisfied.

4
The rise of the middle-class campaigner

'Every woman is personally incapable'

'Give women the vote, and there will be no more bribery among the electors, no more drunkenness on election days, no more roués among the elected,' mocked Eliza Lynn Linton, scorning the 'New Morality' pretensions of those who said that the admission of women to the polling-booths would sanitize politics. She disparaged 'the hard, unfeminine, and yet not manly Shrieking Sisterhood'.[1]

She poured scorn on the Victorian notion of female virtue,

> The good women's tendency to hold sobriety and chastity as of more importance than statesmanlike qualities even in a ruler—to believe that man can be made moral by Act of Parliament and to insist on 'something being done' no matter how delicate the task of interference; how dangerous the elements interfered with—would make this oft-repeated promise to look into the private lives of the elected, and have them judged according to a moral standard only, a national peril if kept.

Linton urged that 'wise diplomacy has nothing to do with domestic virtues; and we want a brave soldier and good strategist as the leader of our armies without reference to moral austerity.'[2]

How had a revolutionary cry for equal rights, rooted in the militancy of English radicalism become so entrenched in the values of the comfortable middle class that by the end of the century votes for women could be attacked by a character such as Linton? Eliza Lynn Linton was a novelist born in 1822, the first woman on the staff of a newspaper, who as much as any other of that century typified the values of the sexually advanced, irreligious, emancipated women, only too willing to shock society. She was showing herself at the end of the century to be vociferously anti-women's suffrage. This was not only a matter merely for the dismay of contemporary feminists, modern scholars have also questioned 'why women themselves, in large numbers, opposed the suffrage'.[3]

Rise of the organizers

The ascendancy of the middle class in the wake of the Reform Act, consolidated by the Anti-Corn Law agitation, was clearly a benefit for that class in terms of material wealth and power, though it was more of a boon for men than it was for women. Every strengthening of a man's prestige seemed to be accompanied by a weakening of women who were characterized as delicate flowers, to be sequestered at home and protected from any hint of controversy. Reinforced by absurdly restrictive clothing and silly social rules expecting women to absent themselves when men talked after dinner, for they could have no possible contribution to make, middle-class women were suffocating in comfort. They were also protected from work within the home, that role being taken by the standing army of domestic servants drawn from the working class. This was no doubt an attractive role for women who were temperamentally disposed to that sort of life, and many lived and died in comfortable gentility with no notion that they were in fact suffering the enslavement of marriage, as feminists would later inform them.

The elevation of women as repositories of love and domestic harmony reached its apogee in the success of Coventry Patmore's poem 'The Angel in the House', lauding the 'honourable and womanly' middle-class spouse in the second half of the nineteenth century. There was, however, always a counter-culture—the flagellation-loving poet Swinburne for example, mocked Patmore in his 'The Person of the House' where the wife and mother is so ignorant of the world she cannot even tell the sex of her own baby. The impression that the Victorian period was all strait-laced gentility is false, though a narrow puritanical faction dominated.

There had been a tendency in representations of gender prior to the nineteenth century to focus on the inherent wickedness of women, who were tempters of man. The Victorian period, reinforced by the presence of Victoria herself, and her moral example to the middle class of wifehood and family life, elevated woman. There was no doubt of women's moral ascendancy; 'the general superiority of women over men is, I think, unquestionable' writes William Lecky in his two-volume *History of European Morals* published in 1869. Both in spontaneous virtue and in obedience to a sense of duty, 'women are superior to men. Their sensibility is greater, they are more chaste both in thought and act, more tender to the erring, more compassionate to the suffering, more affectionate to all about them.' Men are superior in intellect and 'active courage' and are more judicious, Lecky asserts, making assumed gender roles into biological constants; 'Men excel in energy, self-reliance, perseverance and magnanimity; women in humility, gentleness, modesty and endurance.'[4] This was not merely the view of the conservative elite, the radical Harriet Taylor concurred, remarking that 'the common opinion is, whatever may be the case with the intellectual, the moral influence of women over men is almost always salutary.'[5] The conservative Prime Minister Lord Salisbury agreed, and in supporting the vote for women remarked: 'their influence is likely to weigh in a direction which, in an age so material, is exceedingly valuable in the direction of morality and religion.'[6]

The limited amount of work middle-class women could do outside the home—such as charitable activities, promoting missionary work, and condemning slavery—showed them the ills of society and gave them an impetus to gain political influence, though this rarely led to a criticism of the underlying beliefs of society—of laissez-faire economics and the primacy of the family as a social unit.

Many chafed against their domestic circumstances and a number rebelled. For those of a mind to change their situation, with the many disabilities faced by women, the question was where to start. Any excursions outside the home, and the example of their well-educated brothers, showed up the lack of education of Victorian girls. Many leading Victorian women, including the novelist George Eliot, felt that women must educate themselves before they were fit to accept responsibility. Early campaigners, such as Anna Wheeler, raged at their poor education which had fitted them so ill for public life, and a good deal of the effort of early suffrage campaigners such as Lydia Becker, Elizabeth Wolstenholme Elmy, and Emily Davies was expended on the enriching but unglamorous work of improving education for girls.

There is an apocryphal story of a time in the 1850s when Emily Davies went to stay with her friend Elizabeth Garrett at her family home at Aldburgh. One night they sat in front of the fire discussing the possibilities before them, with Elizabeth's younger sister listening to the conversation.

Davies finally summed up that in the future she would secure higher education for women, Elizabeth would open up the medical profession for them, and they allotted the task of securing the vote to Millie. Whatever the basis in fact of the tale, which has doubtless improved in the telling over the years, it gives a realistic picture of the high sense of purpose of these women, all of whom were to see their ambitions realized: Elizabeth Garrett Anderson was indeed the pioneer of medicine as a profession for women; Emily Davies opened up higher education; and Millicent Fawcett did see women given the vote on the same basis as men.

The Ladies' College in Bedford Square was founded in 1849; the North London Collegiate School for Ladies was opened by Frances Mary Buss in 1850; Cheltenham Ladies' College in 1853 by Dorothea Beale. In higher education, the College for Women (later Girton College) was founded by Emily Davies in 1869. Education was followed by the right to train for the professions and then (once trained) the right to enter formerly exclusively male professions. The background to the suffrage movement of the late nineteenth century was of how education was slowly but cumulatively producing a body of educated middle-class women who could argue their case. It was a half century of 'The Cause' in which women were increasingly taking on new roles and, like Florence Nightingale as an administrative nurse, and Elizabeth Garrett as a doctor, representing role models for others.

In the wider national debate, there were two strands affecting women that appeared to be progressive: improving the rights of women in marriage and in education; and preventing their exploitation at work. Thus the Infants' Custody Act of 1839, the Matrimonial Causes Act of 1857, and the Married Women's Property Act of 1870 represented greater rights within marriage, even if they enshrined contemporary opinions (men could divorce after 1857 simply on the ground of a wife's adultery, for women a husband's adultery was insufficient). Such leading lights of women's suffrage as Lydia Becker, Elizabeth Wolstenholme Elmy, Jacob Bright, and Richard Pankhurst were all to campaign together over the Married Women's Property Act.

Over the same mid-Victorian period the dreadful working conditions in mines and factories had been brought to the attention of public and parliament by campaigners. In the Mining Act of 1842 women and children were forbidden to be employed in mines; and in 1847 the Ten Hours Act restricted the working hours of women and children in factories. The restriction of women's work alone, however, reinforced a view of women as vulnerable and dependent, while linking their interests with those of children compounded this picture. There were obvious short-term benefits, but in the long term such philanthropic advances categorized women as inferior. A more caring society was being constructed but one in which, as historian Carolyn Steedman says, 'individual and collective progress in civilisation is expressed by being kind to groups of the weak, feeble and disenfranchised in society—women, slaves, the insane and...children'.[7]

There were therefore different currents of activity involving women converging in the suffrage campaign: women were showing themselves able to take rights and positions previously held by men; but women were also being protected at home and increasingly protected in the workplace. Their assumed moral superiority was a challenge to male behaviour, but when they moved into the public sphere their sequestered lives and ignorance of the world left them without clear direction amid the complexities of party politics.

'A brief summary...'

The issue of women's rights was up for discussion in the mid-nineteenth century largely because of a pamphlet by Barbara Leigh Smith (later Bodichon), with assistance from progressive lawyer Matthew Davenport Hill, published in 1854, 'A Brief Summary, in Plain Language, of the Most Important Laws Concerning Women'. The first law noted was that though a single woman had the same rights to property and protection from the law and the same obligation to pay taxes as did a man, 'A woman over the age of twenty-one, having the requisite property qualifications, cannot vote in elections for members of Parliament' (though she could vote in parish elections). Leigh Smith drew attention to the iniquity of the law, particularly as it affected married women.

Leigh Smith successfully urged the Law Amendment Society in 1855 to introduce a Married Women's Property Bill that allowed married women the same right to hold property and make wills as unmarried women. This was not successful (it was not until 1870 that the Married Women's Property Act was passed, giving married women the right to their own earnings) but the network of women formed to promote it went on to sponsor subsequent campaigns including those involving the women's suffrage movement. Leigh Smith and her circle became known as the Langham Place Group from the address, at 19 Langham Place, of *The English Woman's Journal* which she founded.

Barbara Leigh Smith, a writer and painter, was a Unitarian, therefore a religious dissenter as were many of the early feminists, both male and female. She was the illegitimate daughter of a radical Liberal MP, Benjamin Leigh Smith, and Anne Longden with whom he lived, in a house that was frequently used as a meeting place for abolitionists and political refugees from the continent of Europe.

Her mother died when she was young and she assumed the duties of hostess. She was described as being 'tall, handsome, generous and quite unselfconscious, she swept along, distracted only by the too great abundance of her interests and talents, and the too great outflowing of her sympathies'.[8] Barbara Leigh Smith was a friend of George Eliot (herself involved in an unconventional living arrangement with a married man) and of Bessie Rayner Parkes who became the editor of the *English Woman's Journal*. She attended the newly formed Ladies' College in Bedford Square and later set up a school, the Portman Hall School where children from different classes and religious backgrounds were educated together.

The unconventional family in which Leigh Smith had grown up led to their ostracization from other branches of the family. This did not dissuade Leigh Smith herself from being prepared to enter into an unconventional partnership. In 1855 she had considered making her affair with John Chapman, editor of the *Westminster Review*, into a more permanent arrangement, though she decided against it when her father refused to countenance the proposed arrangements and the affair ended.

Those feminist campaigners who had unconventional sex lives were careful to conceal them in order not to blemish their standing in the eyes of the conservative middle-class public. The dread hand of bourgeois respectability led them to disdain their heritage in public and disparage the memory of Mary Wollstonecraft while admiring her in private correspondence.[9] Their fear of sexual scandal derailing the campaign was probably not mistaken. Even the close female friendships in the Langham Place Circle such as that between Leigh Smith and Parkes were subject to criticism as a threat to 'normal' heterosexual relationships. With sexual scandals constantly threatening to emerge to break through the veneer of respectability, the atmosphere of Langham Place must have sometimes resembled that of a French farce, but the fear of a word out of place or an embarrassing disclosure did not hinder campaigns to expand secondary and higher education for women, and the establishment of a women's employment agency.

After the failure of her relationship with John Chapman, Leigh Smith suffered a breakdown and went to Algeria to recover while she explored and painted. There she met a French doctor, Eugene Bodichon, whom she married in 1857. Together they toured America where they encountered prominent abolitionists and proponents of women's rights including Lucretia Mott.

Many suffrage campaigners came to the fore after having early experience in charitable and political campaigning work in such organizations as the Ladies Society for the Relief of Negro Slaves founded in 1825 (more than forty years before the national societies for women's suffrage set up in various cities). The most successful campaign, running from the 1860s and so coexistent with the suffrage campaign, with which it had a difficult relationship, was the Ladies National Association for the Repeal of the Contagious Diseases Acts. This was in opposition to the Acts passed in 1864 and extended in 1866 as a pragmatic treatment for the level of venereal disease in the army and navy. They were pushed through with scant debate, their proponents doubtless hoping that there would be little discussion of this unsavoury subject.

However, Josephine Butler, though a supporter of women's suffrage, felt here was an abuse about which she had to protest; indeed, it was so serious it would not wait until women had the vote, but must be tackled immediately. This had the markings of a successful campaign: brutally salacious subject matter in descriptions of medical examination; an obvious gender-based unfairness; and the image of righteous campaigners battling for downtrodden victims (the prostitutes). The objection to the law from the campaigners' point of view was that it allowed only women to be forcibly treated, not men, so endorsed and gave legal embodiment to the sexual double standard that women must be chaste while men could have sexual licence.

Prostitutes themselves doubtless saw the whole matter differently; forced examination and incarceration for treatment was clearly undesirable, but the campaign's avowed aim of ending prostitution was merely the threatened removal of a source of income. As historian Barbara Caine remarked, 'Butler's powerful campaign drew very strongly on its use and manipulation of a number of particular views and stereotypes of women, all of which served both to empower her and her supporters and to make it unnecessary even to ask whether any women might choose to enter prostitution as a career.'[10] Doubtless free choice was not an issue for most women in this line of work. As historian Constance Rover points out, prostitution was an integral part of the economy; to have removed it would have been like abstracting a whole trade or occupation, such as factory work, from the trades followed by women.[11] And, while destitution was undoubtedly associated with prostitution, there would be more without it. The demand for prostitutes was fed by the need for men to wait before marriage until they had secured sufficient income to keep a house, and an assumption that men would have some experience to bring to the marriage bed (and that respectable women would have none).

In the history of the suffrage movement in Britain the importance of the Contagious Diseases campaign was that it was the first high-level campaign organized by women alone, and that it emphasized in a very public way the supposed moral superiority of women over men who nevertheless 'enslaved' them. This was both its positive and its negative side: for the simplistic presentation of 'vice' and 'morality' led men who otherwise might well have supported women's suffrage to feel that women's approach to public affairs was too facile to justify their having voting rights. As women's suffrage campaigner Frederick Pethick-Lawrence was to say, 'The principal motive of men's opposition to woman suffrage was undoubtedly fear of the use to which women would put the vote if they got it.' It was said 'that on sex matters women were narrower and harder than men; and that if they were given power they would impose impossibly strict codes of morality, and endeavour to enforce them by penalties for non-observance'.[12] The association of suffragists with narrow puritans was particularly unhelpful, as the most important people who had to be convinced were male parliamentarians whose attitudes to morality ranged across a wide spectrum.

'You know that I have done my work'

The next great exponents of women's suffrage, after Barbara Leigh Smith Bodichon, were Harriet Taylor (née Hardy and second married name Mill) and John Stuart Mill. Taylor also had an unconventional personal life, a common thread running through the lives of many suffrage campaigners. She was born in 1807 in Walworth, South London, the daughter of a surgeon. At the age of 18 she married John Taylor, a wholesale druggist, and lived in Finsbury, near the Unitarian chapel they attended at South Place. This was a gathering with a strongly radical and feminist tone; Anna Wheeler occasionally lectured there. It included the writer Harriet Martineau and was led by the spellbinding preacher William Johnson Fox. Fox ran a magazine called the *Monthly Repository* which, under his editorship, gradually lost its theological bias and became mainly a literary magazine, though with significant contributions on political reform.

Harriet in her twenties was described as having a unique beauty, 'Tall and slight, with a slightly drooping figure, the movements of undulating grace. A small head, a swan-like throat, and a complexion like a pearl. Large eyes, not soft or sleepy, but with a look of quiet command in them.'[13] She began to have problems communicating with her decent but dull husband and she turned to her minister, William Fox, for advice. Harriet's problem was that she was so much cleverer than her husband that she could not discuss intellectual problems with him and felt stultified. Fox, who had his own marital problems (and was to leave his wife for another member of the congregation) contrived a novel solution: introducing Harriet to another man. He is said to have replied to her expression of her problem that 'John Mill was the man among the human race to relieve in a competent manner her dubieties and difficulties' and he had her arrange a dinner party at her house to which he and Mill and others, such as Harriet Martineau were invited.[14]

John Stuart Mill was already at the age of 24 a considerable intellect, though he had a head start. The son of Benthamite philosopher James Mill, he was brought up in a severe, loveless household where he bore the brunt of his father's educational theories. James Mill became obsessed with the idea that he could give 'the highest order of intellectual education' to his children.[15] Consequently John could write in his *Autobiography* 'I have no reminiscences of the time when I began to learn Greek, I have been told that it was when I was three years old'; history, Euclid, and algebra followed, but he conceded 'learned no Latin until my eighth year'. Advanced study of philosophy began at the age of 12. As Mill remarked in his *Autobiography*, 'My father, in all his teaching, demanded of me not only the utmost that I could do, but much that I could by no possibility have done.' Mill was also expected to instruct his younger siblings and was held responsible for their progress, and was early introduced to such characters as the utilitarian philosopher and reformer Jeremy Bentham, economist David Ricardo, and the radical artisan Francis Place.

Mill senior refused to allow John to go to university but retained him as a tutor for his siblings and as amanuensis for himself, in 1823 taking him in as a clerk in his own department in the India Office (where John was to work for the whole of his professional career). John was a curious mix of domestic obedience to his father and external radicalism: he spent two nights in jail for distributing birth-control literature in the servants' basements of large houses. In the radical maelstrom of 1820s London, John became well acquainted with William Thompson and his ideas, debating on the side of the 'political economists' against Thompson and the Owenites at the Co-operation Society; he mentions Thompson's *Appeal* on behalf of women in his autobiography.

Over 1826 to 1827 John Mill suffered a breakdown but recovered with an approach to life now more influenced by Romantic thought and that of the Saint-Simonians and less by his father. It was this young man who was invited to meet Harriet Taylor at that fateful dinner party in autumn 1830, to make up the intellectual deficiencies in her life. Thomas Carlyle mockingly referred to Mill, 'who up to that time, had never so much as looked at a female creature, not even a cow, in the face, found himself opposite those great dark eyes, that were flashing unutterable things while he was discoursin' the unutterable concernin' all sorts o' high topics'.[16] The young philosopher was smitten, she was 'the most admirable person I have ever known'; his relationship with her was to be 'the honour and chief blessing of my existence, as well as the source of a great part of all that I have attempted to do...for human improvement'.[17] Most obviously they found common cause in their agreement over the removal of legal disabilities imposed on women. In 1832 they both wrote each other an essay on the condition of women, as a rarefied intellectual courtship ritual. Mill certainly said that he had strong convictions in favour of sexual equality and that: 'the strength with which I held them was, as I believe, more than anything else, the originating cause of the interest she felt in me.'[18]

Taylor was liberally minded but his wife's passionate engagement with Mill and the world of the mind must have caused him anxiety. Mill explicitly denies that they had sex: 'our relation to each other at that time was one of strong affection and confidential intimacy only' though clearly there was a temptation for her to leave her husband. In 1833 Harriet arranged a trial separation from her husband during which she and Mill travelled to Paris together but after six weeks away she must have decided not to make an irreconcilable break and they returned. She tried to give up Mill but felt her companionship was essential to his creativity which was suffering without her, thus convincing herself that seeing Mill again was a contribution to the greater good, not just her peace of mind. John Taylor eventually, in the late

1830s, provided his wife with a house in Bromley where she could stay and entertain Mill. She had her daughter with her, one son travelled between them and the other stayed with John Taylor. Harriet went to the marital home during school holidays to be with her sons. Harriet Taylor and Mill would go out together, until public comment on their relationship caused them to be more reclusive. They travelled abroad under assumed names.

Mill suffered a nervous collapse after his father's death in 1836, which left him for the rest of his life with severe facial twitching and recurrent depression. In 1849, when John Taylor was diagnosed with cancer, Harriet returned to nurse him until the long-suffering man's death that year. After a respectable interval Harriet and Mill married, on 21 April 1851, and lived together in Blackheath. Prior to the marriage Mill made a formal declaration that he renounced any 'rights' he was assumed by law to have acquired over Harriet. At this time, and stimulated by the Convention of Women held in Ohio in spring 1850, Harriet wrote an essay, 'The Enfranchisement of Women', arguing for completely equal political and social rights between men and women. It was published under John Stuart Mill's name in the *Westminster Review*. Why she used his name is not certain; doubtless the arguments were those they worked on together, and perhaps she felt Mill's name would give greater weight to the work than would that of an unknown woman. She may simply have been shy, shrinking from pushing herself forward in the world and thinking that as a woman no one would pay attention to her.

She asserted that the political movement for the enfranchisement of women was not merely the creation of philosophically minded men, while women, 'those who are professedly to be benefited' remained 'either indifferent or ostensibly hostile' but 'it is a movement not merely *for* women but *by* them.' It could be no argument that women had not excelled in the field of politics previously, 'Women have shown fitness for the highest social functions, exactly as they have been admitted to them,' she noted, where women had been queens they had been able and firm. Of the contention that maternity might unfit women for politics she said, 'It is neither necessary nor just to make imperative on women that they shall be either mothers or nothing; and that if they have been mothers once, they shall be nothing else during the whole remainder of their lives.'

In what was to be a common complaint, the lack of any qualification of men excepting maleness for their legal control was disparaged: 'Wretches unfit to have the smallest authority over any living thing have a helpless woman for their household slave.' The contention that women have asked for no change in their condition was countered that this was the same point: 'that has been argued, times out of mind, against the proposal of abolishing any social evil—"there is no complaint;" which is generally not true, and when true, only so because there is not that hope of success, without which complaint seldom makes itself audible to unwilling ears.'[19] The article finished in referring to the petition of Anna Knight's, in favour of women's suffrage, presented by the Earl of Carlisle on 13 February 1851, clearly a sign of future change.

Mill attributed many of his works such as *Principles of Political Economy* of 1843 and *On Liberty* of 1859 to their joint intellectual endeavours; and though later judgement has questioned this attribution, it is psychologically true that her mental and spiritual support allowed Mill the creative freedom that had been denied him under his father's jurisdiction.

Under Harriet's influence Mill moved away from an extreme Benthamism in which private property was supreme, and was looking towards the social problem of the future which was felt to be individual liberty and 'common ownership of the globe'.[20] In practical terms this meant an extension of the franchise and a socialist method of political organization. Bentham and utilitarianism with its principle of the greatest happiness for the greatest number was not abandoned, but extended, to insist that this had to include women or the equation could not add up, if half the population were kept in ignorance and denied rights because of their sex.

The couple travelled a great deal to alleviate the tuberculosis from which Harriet was suffering and worked on their great endeavour, *The Subjection of Women*. Harriet died at Avignon on her way to winter in the south of France in 1858. 'The spring of my life is broken,' he said.[21] Mill bought a house overlooking Harriet's grave in Avignon where he and her daughter Helen Taylor stood watching as a hugely expensive Carrera marble tomb was erected, inscribed with a fulsome dedication to Harriet's heart, soul, and intellect. Mill and Helen lived for half the year in France, Harriet's daughter working as Mill's amanuensis and housekeeper both at Blackheath and at Avignon.

Mill completed *The Subjection of Women* in 1861 though it was not published until eight years later. It was to become (with Marx's *Das Kapital*) one of the two most influential political books of the nineteenth century, to be widely translated and quoted. Its strident tone is set in the first paragraph: 'the principle which regulates the existing social relations between the two sexes—the legal subordination of one sex to another—is wrong in itself, and now one of the chief hindrances to human improvement; and that it ought to be replaced by a principle of perfect equality, admitting no power or privilege on the one side, nor disability on the other.'[22]

He argues that under whatever conditions men are admitted, 'there is not a shadow of justification for not admitting women under the same'. Remarking prophetically: 'The majority of the women of any class are not likely to differ in political opinion from the majority of the men of the same class.'[23] In other words, expanding the franchise on gender grounds is not likely to change the balance of power, as women were not likely to vote on gender grounds but according to their class or party loyalty. This prescient observation was overlooked by campaigners for the next fifty years who argued (as did their opponents) that the enfranchisement of women would bring about major political changes.

In *The Subjection of Women* Mill was not particularly concerned about the single women who lived alone or with parents—the situation of many feminist campaigners. He has been criticized for this but it is merely the expression of the utilitarian philosophy of Jeremy Bentham: the greatest happiness for the greatest number could be achieved by arguing for the enfranchisement of married women, who were in the majority among adults. Moreover, the anti-suffrage argument was always on weak ground when confronted by women who were not 'covered' under the doctrine of coverture by husband or under the protection of a father; women who were spinsters or widows who paid taxes and owned property. Mill felt there was no great merit in an argument about them which was easily conceded. An argument should, he believed, be defeated at its strongest point. There is also more than a hint of son–father rivalry in this, in that his father had so publicly declared in the *Encyclopaedia Britannica* that married women should *not* have the vote (thus inciting William Thomson and Anna Wheeler to action); if the philosopher son were to overthrow his philosopher father, this was the stage on which to do it.

He cited, as a demonstration of women's fitness to govern, the example of famous queens of the past (always a politic thing to do in the age of Queen Victoria) and the evidence of Indian women ruling principalities judiciously as regents, which his work at the India office allowed him to understand. While supporting complete equality and fitness in women, Mill also suggested women were superior in intuition, 'With equality of experience and of general faculties, a woman usually sees much more than a man of what is immediately before her.... A woman seldom runs wild after an abstraction.'[24] He did, however, concede: 'it cannot now be known how much of the existing mental differences between men and women is natural, and how much artificial; where there are any natural differences at all; or, supposing all artificial causes of difference to be withdrawn, what natural character would be revealed.'[25]

When Mill was invited to stand as Liberal candidate for Westminster in 1865, he declared that he would not bear any election expenses and would not canvass, and he attended few meetings, though he did issue an election address in which he supported votes for women on the same basis as men. Rather than gender or property, at this stage he was interested in an educational requirement and self-reliance as qualification for the franchise. 'All grown persons, both men and women, who can read, write, and perform a sum in the rule of three, and who have not, within some small number of years, received parish relief should be allowed to vote.' He believed women in politics would 'strengthen the influences opposed to violence and bloodshed' and prevent 'the expulsion of all beauty from common life'.[26] He argued that the introduction of women in public life 'raises the tone of public morality' so he had a higher view of women than Wollstonecraft who berated women for their superficiality and for having so little to contribute.[27] He was elected with a majority of 700 over his Conservative opponent, considerably advancing the women's suffrage argument by demonstrating that the principle was clearly not a vote-loser. He remarked: 'The use of my being in parliament was to do work which others were not able or not willing to do.'[28]

The first suffrage societies

A Ladies' Discussion Society was set up in Kensington in 1865 which was mainly composed of educational pioneers such as Emily Davies, Elizabeth Wolstenholme (later Wolstenholme Elmy), Elizabeth Garrett, Dorothea Beale, and Frances Buss. Barbara Leigh Smith Bodichon took a leading part in discussions on suffrage and she was moved to form a Women's Suffrage Committee despite the opposition of Emily Davies who felt vigorous political activity would injure the education movement.

Barbara Leigh Smith Bodichon approached Mill, at this stage an MP, and asked if he would present a petition for women's suffrage. Mill agreed on condition that she obtained at least 100 signatures. She formed the first Women's Suffrage Committee and sought her signatures. Emily Davies, perennially conservative, was unhappy about requesting the vote for married women, but Mill would not have a petition that compromised the position of equality for all women, so it was ambiguously worded to admit of either interpretation. Mill presented the women's first multiple-signatory petition for the vote in 1866 with almost 1,500 signatures. Petitioning was a parliamentary procedure to bring attention to a subject, and was not expected to make any changes of itself. The most important effect it had was to bring together the women who had worked on the Petition Committee and to expand its work.

Suffrage reform was much in the air in the mid-1860s, with both Liberal and Tory parties vying for the support of the working class who were emerging as a force to be reckoned with. Liberal Chancellor Gladstone's Reform Bill failed in 1866, leaving the field open for the Tory Disraeli's Bill, which was fundamentally a men's household franchise measure. On 20 May 1867 Mill moved an amendment which was heard with respectful attention—not always the case when subjects relating to women were heard in the House of Commons—asking: 'is it good for a man to live in complete communion of thoughts and feelings with one who is studiously kept inferior to himself, whose earthly interests are forcibly confined within four walls, and who cultivates, as a grace of character, ignorance and indifference about the most inspiring of subjects, those among which his highest duties are cast?'[29]

He asked the House to recognize the changes that were taking place: 'We talk of political revolutions, but we do not sufficiently attend to the fact that there has taken place around us a silent domestic revolution: women and men are, for the first time in history, really each other's companions.' His principal argument was that the obligation of taxation necessarily carried a right of parliamentary representation. For the first time in public (*Subjection of Women* had been written but not yet been published) he used the perceptive, if unglamorous argument, that there was no justice in denying women the vote, and giving it to them would make no difference anyway: 'is it feared that if they were admitted to the suffrage they would revolutionise the State—would deprive us of any of our valued institutions, or that we should have worse laws, or be in any way whatever worse governed through the effect of their suffrages? No one, Sir, believes anything of the kind.'

The mechanism by which women's suffrage was to be achieved was merely the substitution of 'person' for 'man'. The motion was defeated by

196 votes to 73 (if pairs and tellers are included, more than eighty MPs supported it). The fact that more than a third of those voting gave support was a considerable encouragement to women's campaigners. There was, indeed, excessive optimism, as if progress would continue unabated as more were converted to the cause at the same rate that the first supporters had been. As Ray Strachey in her history of the women's movement says, 'They had never before done any political work, and, being intelligent and disinterested themselves, they assumed that if a cause was just, and demonstrably just, as this was, it must quickly prevail.'[30] Mill and the other men with political experience knew this to be untrue, but for a time the women's committees hummed to the hopes of franchise supporters, bolstered up by their contact with others who thought as they did.

Mill was defeated in the election of 1868; few backbench MPs and few indeed who have been in parliament for so short a time have made their mark so distinctively. He now spent much of his time in Avignon, revising earlier works. In 1869 he published *The Subjection of Women* that was bitterly denounced by those who saw it as subversive of the family and therefore of social stability, but adored by campaigners for women's suffrage for whom it consolidated Mill's heroic status as the person who had done most for their cause.

Helen Taylor played a leading role in setting up the London National Society for Women's Suffrage in July 1867 (and similar societies were founded in Manchester in 1866, Edinburgh in 1867, and in Birmingham and Bristol in 1868). The organizers were divided over the name of the organization and also over the usual question of whether married women or all women should have the vote. Emily Davies supported an expedient measure to exclude married women from the franchise and declined to be part of the Society. At the first public meeting the motion was passed that voting rights should be granted to women 'on the same terms as it is or may be granted to men'. It is indicative of the influence of men in the movement that, though the motion was moved by Lydia Becker, it was seconded and supported by three men: Archdeacon Sandford, F. B. Potter MP, and Richard Pankhurst.[31] Mill put himself on the side of those suffrage campaigners who said that no women should be disbarred, as against those who felt that 'females' could be subdivided into categories of married or not.

The situation of married versus single women continued to be contested, though any scheme based on the principle of female interests being subsumed into those of males under the doctrine of 'coverture' was against the trend of thinking, which was moving towards greater independence for women and for their living and marital arrangements to be their own affair. Nor would married women's suffrage be practical to administer—an adult spinster might live with her father, then be an independent householder, then marry, then be widowed, progressing from voteless to voting to voteless to voting in what could be a short number of years. Was the voting register to be amended each time there was a change in every woman's life circumstances? In response to this criticism, it was argued by Millicent Fawcett that 'a constant passing to and fro, from the ranks of the represented and the unrepresented... would become the indirect representation of all women.'[32] The ponderous Victorian joke 'Women's Rights are Men's Lefts' meant that only women who could not get a man were interested in emancipation. It is a contemptuous quip but it demonstrates an attitude that in some way helped the cause of unmarried women: if the vote were given only to poor creatures who had missed out on the big prize in life, it could hardly matter and could therefore be more easily conceded. On the positive side for such thinking, therefore, the notion of an unmarried women's vote appealed to a largely conservative nation, as it was in keeping with previous ideas of the relationship between men and women and the dependent position of married women. It formed the basis of a significant advance in 1869, when Manchester MP Jacob Bright successfully amended the Municipal Franchise Act to permit unmarried women and widows to vote for town councils; the amendment was drafted by Richard Pankhurst and was supported by the Liberal government (though women could not stand for election as councillors until 1907).

Lydia Becker wrote to Leigh Smith Bodichon, 'The question passed through the House without a dissentient word, causing surprise and excitement of a quiet sort and much pleasure to real friends of the Cause.'[33] Women were empowered to vote for and sit on school boards in 1870. Women sitting on Poor Law boards of guardians and school boards received valuable training in public affairs: suffrage campaigners Lydia Becker, Emily Davies, and Elizabeth Garrett were all successful candidates at the first elections. Lydia Becker calculated that over 14,000 women voted in the municipal elections of 1871, putting the lie to the notion that women were not interested in politics.

Jacob Bright, a Quaker as were so many radical campaigners, was a Manchester MP from 1867 to 1895 (excepting two years, after 1874). He was one of a large and active family of a Rochdale cotton manufacturer. His more charismatic elder brother John Bright was also a Liberal MP. Women's suffrage was Jacob's obsession, as a newspaper remarked: 'He brought it into all his speeches, much to the annoyance and even dismay of some of his staunchest supporters. "Jacob is at it again!" some really affectionate friend would whisper; and it was true. He was always "at it".'[34] His wife, Ursula, was also a leading suffragist and Liberal committee-woman; her other causes included vegetarianism and opposition to the Contagious Diseases Acts and to compulsory vaccination; in later life she became a Theosophist.

A division existed between campaigners who wanted women's suffrage committees to enjoy the support of prominent men, and those such as Mill who felt the committees should be exclusively female. He wrote to the London National Society warning of 'anything tending to keep up the vulgar idea that women cannot manage any important matter without a man to help them. You know how utterly false this supposition would be in the case of the present movement'.[35]

Another division was over whether to support other campaigns such as that against the Contagious Diseases Acts, or whether the suffrage campaign would be tainted by association with a pressure group concentrating on sex acts. As Mill believed, these social issues could be dealt with more easily after the vote was won. Later feminists have stressed the educative and emancipatory function of participating in campaigns around social issues— that women who had not previously spoken in public or even attended a meeting were introduced to public work through campaigning.

One of Mill's last public appearances was before the Royal Commission on the Contagious Diseases Acts where he argued that, whether the Acts were retained or repealed, the overwhelmingly important point was to be fair to both sexes, not to single one out. When Mill died in 1873, his last words to Helen Taylor were 'you know that I have done my work'. He was buried in the marble tomb beside his wife.[36]

The Contagious Diseases Acts were later to split the movement, in 1871, when a number of principally Manchester members who were also active lobbyists over the Acts pressed for more active lobbying of parliament. Further splits and divisions occurred over affiliation and political strategy.

Uphill campaigning

Despite their divisions, the campaigners' willingness to act creatively and take advantage of circumstances is shown in the case of Manchester housewife and suffrage supporter Lily Maxwell. A clerical error had slipped her name onto the parliamentary electoral register. When there was a by-election, she went to the poll accompanied by Lydia Becker and recorded her vote in favour of Jacob Bright (who in fact won the election). There was no opposition or official obstruction, Maxwell was even cheered by the men at the polling station. With this test case to work on, Lydia Becker arranged a house-to-house canvass of female householders, to sign them up as wishing to have the same right to vote as Mrs Maxwell. In all, 5,346 women householders petitioned in a case that went to court on 7 November 1868.

Richard Pankhurst, who prepared the case as one of the counsel, was the first of three generations of the Pankhurst family to make a lasting contribution to women's suffrage. The Pankhursts were based in a house in Old Trafford, Manchester, described as being 'a centre of earnest and passionate striving'. Sylvia Pankhurst described her father as 'vilified and boycotted, yet beloved by a multitude of people . . . a standard-bearer of every forlorn hope, every unpopular yet worthy cause then conceived for the uplifting of oppressed and suffering humanity'.[37]

Pankhurst was born into a radical dissenting family in Manchester in 1835; he doted on his own parents and lived with them until their deaths when he was past 40. He attended the University of London where he received a doctorate of law, practised as a solicitor, and was called to the bar by Lincoln's Inn in 1867. He thenceforth was armed to put himself at the service of every radical cause, of which he had many—he was a republican, supported the nationalization of land, anti-imperialism, and was not afraid to challenge authority: in 1878 on a platform with Gladstone he urged the Grand Old Man to support universal suffrage, for women as well as men, and the democratic reform of the Liberal Party itself.

Manchester became a centre of activity, notably for the work of Lydia Becker, who had previously devoted her energies to botany, and who had been inspired by a lecture from Leigh Smith Bodichon to turn towards women's suffrage. The case of the Manchester householders went to court on 7 November 1868 where judgement was awarded against the women because 'every woman is personally incapable' in legal terms, of exercising a vote.[38] Before the decision was taken, Lydia Becker, with the gift for timing of the instinctive campaigner, had made arrangements that every electoral candidate in England and Wales had been written a letter calling on them to support a Bill to give parliamentary votes to women. As soon as judgement had been given in London, Becker telegraphed her committee 'Post your letters' and so the first note of parliamentary agitation started when news of the legal defeat was under discussion in the newspapers.[39]

Becker had been busy summoning support. An extant letter shows both her earnest resolution and the connection through history and across nations that these pioneers managed with means no more sophisticated than the postal service. She asked for help from Goodwyn Barmby, he who with Catherine Barmby when both were young had harangued passers-by on women's suffrage from their covered wagon. Barmby gave her the names of other pioneers and she wrote to the great Anne Knight who had called on the first women's franchise organization to perform 'this holy work'. Lydia Becker wrote to Knight in France, 'I send you a circular of our Society and hope you will be willing to join us on the terms indicated'; but Knight was already dead by the time the letter was written and the agitation had passed to the hands of a new generation.[40]

Jacob Bright in 1870 moved the Women's Disabilities Removal Bill, drafted by Richard Pankhurst, extending the parliamentary franchise to women householders. The Bill passed its second reading by 124 to 91 on 4 May but was defeated in the committee stage when Gladstone showed his formidable opposition, saying 'it would be a very great mistake to proceed with this Bill' but gave no reasons why.[41] The majority in favour was reversed and it was lost in committee by 220 to 94. Jacob Bright again introduced the Bill the following year; in 1872 a women's suffrage Bill had received fewer votes than Mill's amendment did five years before.[42]

Bright lost his seat in 1874 and Lydia Becker passed the suffrage bill to a Conservative MP, who insisted on adding a clause specifically excluding married women from the vote. Lydia Becker acceded to this, thereby splitting the movement as such radicals as Jacob Bright, Richard Pankhurst, and Elizabeth Elmy would not countenance provisions which reinforced the most negative aspects of marriage. The bill was voted down both in 1875 and in 1876; its concession to conservatism had won no new friends for women's suffrage.[43] As Sylvia Pankhurst wrote, 'The women's movement, in short, passed from timidity to timidity.'[44] They were still, however, in the late 1870s when the Bill was being presented minus the married women's exclusion, holding more than 1,000 public meetings a year.

Ray Strachey, an early historian of the movement, described the curious responses of audiences to that novelty, a woman speaker: 'They frequently referred to the "heroism" of the speakers, and were sometimes extended to include the husbands who had been so good as to spare their wives to come away and speak on this occasion!' Great efforts of tact were required to ensure that women's suffrage was represented by pretty women and not those who were 'not only plain, but positively uncouth to the outward eye'.[45] Sometimes facing ridicule and abuse, the suffrage organizers built up a national network of societies. Imbued with the Victorian belief in slow progress, they felt the patient earnestness that had eliminated slavery and spread Christianity through the world would prevail.

In parliamentary terms, the Liberals were more likely to support women's suffrage out of principle or because the support of women in the constituency associations was essential for running the party machine and getting the vote out. Unfortunately the leaders and prime ministers at the end of the nineteenth and beginning of the twentieth century, William Gladstone and Herbert Asquith, were both opposed to women's suffrage on any terms. The first of these formidable opponents, Gladstone, was the most extreme kind of conservative, very difficult to move from whatever position he occupied at any particular time, though when he did move, he held his new principles with all the tenacity that had attached him to the old. He was too imbued with all the Victorian notions of family life and the position of women to support any measure that would alter their status. He told a colleague he had too much respect for the 'permanent and vast difference of type [that] has been impressed upon women and men respectively by the Maker of both' to invite woman 'to trespass upon the delicacy, the purity, the refinement, the elevation of her own nature, which are the present sources of its power'.[46]

By contrast, the Tory Disraeli voted in favour of women's suffrage, when he troubled to be in the House for the votes. He had, in a debate on parliamentary reform in 1848, remarked that in a country governed by a woman, where women could sit in the House of Lords (if they were peeresses in their own right) and various other positions such as churchwarden were open to women, 'I do not see, when she has so much to do with State and Church, on what reasons, if you come to right, she has not a right to vote.'[47] In his 1867 Act Disraeli had added more electors to the register than any previous premier so he was no stranger to electoral reform, and as a man who appealed to women, he might have been thought of as the politician most likely to benefit from a female electorate. But although he both spoke and voted for Jacob Bright's 1871 Bill, Disraeli was no enthusiast for points of principle, and he was no great friend to women's suffrage when he was prime minister from 1874 to 1880.

Thus the early optimism of feminists was to be disappointed. It was not merely that there were opponents to women's suffrage: the argument could swing to and fro and those previously in favour could reverse their position. The great herald of working-class manhood suffrage, John Bright, voted in favour of Mill's amendment, and found 'no valid argument' against women's suffrage in principle but had opposed the inclusion of a women's franchise measure in the general proposals because it would 'in the present state of opinion do more harm than good to the cause of improved representation'. Invited to think further about it, he put forward the idea that it would help the Tory Party and that it would 'add to the power of Priestcraft' because of the presumed influence vicars had over women.[48] Perhaps for this reason, when the issue was raised again in April 1876 he spoke and voted against women's suffrage. This was not the only case in which opinions could be swayed against women's suffrage; it was clearly not to be a path of steady progress.

By the 1880s new reforms were on the horizon with discussion of the Third Reform Act, intended to enfranchise male agricultural labourers, which was being proposed by Gladstone's administration. A meeting of 2,000 delegates from Liberal Associations and the National Reform Union met in Leeds in October 1883; John Bright presided over this meeting at which his daughter, Helen Bright Clark, spoke in favour of giving women the franchise on the same basis as men. The American suffragist Susan B. Anthony was in the hall and her friend Elizabeth Cady Stanton described the effect of the woman being heard in hushed silence: 'For a daughter to speak thus in that great representative convention, in opposition to her loved and honoured father, the acknowledged leader of that party, was an act of heroism and fidelity to her own highest conviction almost without a parallel in English history.'[49] The vote was carried by an overwhelming majority with only thirty delegates voting against. Thus stimulated, the Liberal Associations bombarded the government with resolutions and meetings of women were held through the country—an enthusiasm in marked contrast to the attitude of the agricultural labourers, who were largely indifferent to the vote.

Elizabeth Wolstenholme Elmy, Lydia Becker, and her colleagues did the parliamentary arithmetic and found a small majority of MPs for the women's franchise—249 'known friends' as against 236 'known opponents'.[50] Liberal MP for Stoke-on-Trent William Woodall sponsored an amendment to give unmarried women the vote. On a free vote the amendment would have a very good chance but Gladstone refused this, saying he would rather lose the Reform Bill than keep it with the amendment in: 'I offer it the strongest opposition that is in my power.'[51] The intransigent attitude of their leader caused distress among suffrage-supporting members of the government and three ministers were admonished for refusing to vote against the measure: Henry Fawcett, Sir Charles Dilke, and Leonard Courtney.

The eventual legislation would leave two out of every three adult males able to vote, a UK electorate of 5,600,000. This was still, however, less than 29 per cent of the adult population, with women making up the bulk of those unrepresented, and a large number of them better educated and owning more property than those who were now entitled to vote. Thus every advance in manhood suffrage left more glaring the disabilities of women. Large-scale immigration in the 1890s added a racial dimension to the debate, as middle-class women were appalled that 'alien' men who might not even speak the language were given the franchise when pure-bred English women were not.

Despite this defeat, which could clearly be laid at the door of the 75-year-old prime minister, the situation in the House of Commons looked hopeful. Conservatives were inclined to support enfranchisement of some women property holders to offset the labourers, colliers, and Irish peasants enfranchised, who were expected to vote with the Liberals. This is doubtless the solution that Disraeli would have chosen (had he still been alive to manipulate the levers of power): either to increase the Conservative share of the voting population, or to split the Liberals on the issue; both would have been equally attractive to him. It is the absence of this kind of thinking in the words of the suffrage campaigners that strikes a modern campaigner— all their talk of fairness and rights were as nothing compared to the hard facts of politics. As the trend was towards greater enfranchisement of men, and as there were more working-class than middle-class men, Tories had two options: to attract more working-class voters, or to enfranchise Tory women. In the end conservatism won and they decided on the least radical measure: to make their policies more populist and attractive to the working class. In 1885 it became obvious the Conservative Party could do without women, when a minority Tory administration was formed under Lord Salisbury, so the idea of enfranchising women went into abeyance, though Salisbury himself was positive about women's suffrage.

In addressing the Primrose League, formed in memory of Disraeli, and extensively engaging women workers for the party, Salisbury said on

30 November 1888,'I earnestly hope that the day is not too far distant when women, also will bear their share in voting for members in the political world, and in determining the policy of this country. I can conceive no argument by which they are excluded. It is obvious that they are abundantly as fit as many who now possess the suffrage.'[52] Paradoxically, the leaders of the Conservative Party tended to support women's suffrage, while their membership generally did not, the opposite of the situation in the Liberal Party. A preponderance of Liberals in the leadership of the suffrage movement tended to give the unhelpful impression that it was a Liberal cause.

Anti-suffrage

As the campaign gained speed and suffrage campaigners honed their arguments, a corresponding form of the debate was taking shape. Anti-suffrage opinion had not required any organization as their victories in the House of Commons had been simple; Bills had been talked out or fallen victim to parliamentary machinery. In the late 1880s anti-suffrage thinkers, noting the advances made in organization and influence by the suffrage campaigners, started their own campaign.

Middle-class women who supported higher education, who were actively engaged in philanthropic work, became politically vocal in writing to the press against women's suffrage.[53] Principal among them was Mrs Humphry Ward (née Mary Augusta Arnold) who wrote novels preoccupied with political and social conflict and religious doubt, informed by conservative values. The publication of her most successful novel *Robert Elsmere*, of 1888, gave her considerable social standing which was augmented by the review of the book by Gladstone in *The Nineteenth Century*. She was also active in promoting higher education for women and education for the poor and for handicapped children.

The fame bestowed by the novel allowed her the impetus to suggest a petition to the editor of *The Nineteenth Century*, James Knowles, when she met him at a reception at the French Embassy and bearded him on the evils of women's suffrage in January 1889. Thus the timing of the petition was related to the level of fame of its prime mover, not the chance of a particular franchise Bill's success.

The Bill of 1889, one of the many regularly put to parliament, was allocated a date in the parliamentary timetable after the Easter recess was due to begin so it had no chance, but its early promise stimulated correspondence in journals. In common with others at the time it excluded married women so as not to offend conservative sympathies. The Suffrage Bill failed in April and was withdrawn in June, but the suffrage and anti-suffrage discourse had its own resilience and in June 1889 *The Nineteenth Century* carried an article and petition titled 'An Appeal Against Female Suffrage'.

It was a significant challenge to the notion the suffragists wished to give of their cause as being progressive, modern, and female, opposed by backward, conservative men. The signatories went out of their way to show they were advanced: 'We, the undersigned, wish to appeal to the common sense and the educated thought of the men and women of England, against the proposed extension of the Parliamentary suffrage to women.' The introduction emphasizes that women are not opposed to women's rights, they support 'the fullest possible development of the powers, energies, and education of women'. But they believed that the work of women for the state 'must always differ essentially from those of men . . . To men belong the struggle of debate and legislation in Parliament, the hard and exhausting labour implied in the administration of the national resources and powers'—to which can be added the army and navy, industry, commerce, financial management, and merchant shipping. It was inconceivable that women could contribute: 'In all these spheres women's direct participation is made impossible either by the disabilities of sex, or by strong formations of custom and habits resting ultimately on physical difference, against which it is useless to contend.'[54]

The practical application of the franchise to women would be beset with grave difficulties: 'If votes be given to unmarried women on the same terms as they are given to men, large numbers of women leading immoral lives will be enfranchised on the one hand, while married women . . . will be excluded.' A more cutting remark was that 'A social change of momentous gravity has been proposed; the mass of those immediately concurred in it are notoriously indifferent; there has been no serious and general demand for it, as is always the case if a grievance is real and reform necessary.'[55] It opined that pledges to support female suffrage had been hastily given by politicians in the hopes of strengthening their parties by the female vote.

The petition itself was loosely ranked in terms of social hierarchy: first ladies such as Lady Randolph Churchill and Viscountess Halifax, then celebrities. Historian Laurel Brake comments in her extensive analysis of the anti-suffrage petitions, 'Almost all of these women included in this first foray would be recognisable to the male readers of the journal, bearing as these women do the names of some of the most famous men of the day.' The signatories against female suffrage included Mrs Leslie Stephen, Mrs Huxley, Mrs Alma Tadema, Mrs Matthew Arnold; another signatory was Miss Beatrice Potter (later to be the Fabian leader Beatrice Webb). Some of the women were distinguished by their common location: twenty-three were students from Oxford and Cambridge who had therefore benefited from the campaign by Emily Davies and others to allow women higher education on the same basis as men.

The Nineteenth Century published petition forms for women to fill in and send up, and in August 1889 printed an appendix of over twenty-nine pages listing more than 2,000 names. The petition formed part of a debate in serious journals; the April number of the *Fortnightly Review* had two articles, 'The Enfranchisement of Women' versus 'The Proposed Subjection of Men'.

Millicent Garrett Fawcett's rejoinder to the petition in the July issue of *The Nineteenth Century* was surprisingly tepid, accusing the female opponents of suffrage of leading comfortable lives and wanting nothing for themselves and therefore denying others further advance; they were 'ladies to whom the lines of life have fallen in pleasant places'.[56] Fawcett pointed out that women property owners and employers let premises to and employed men who could vote while they could not. Against an argument that women should not be obliged to enter the hurly-burly of politics, there was the defence that merely voting did not oblige women to be involved in hustings and other election machinery, yet women were more and more invited to be involved in the running of political parties and political machinery, without having the vote. She was drawing attention to a relatively new situation that had come about as a result of the Corrupt and Illegal Practices Act in 1883 that had forbidden the payment of canvassers and other election workers. This work was now done on a voluntary basis, and for the large part by women who thus made themselves indispensable to their party machines in such organizations as the Primrose League founded in 1884 and the Women's Liberal Federation of 1886 (though an anti-suffrage Women's Liberal Association was set up in 1892).

'The Proposed Subjection of Men' remarked that if women were given the same voting rights as men, as was proposed (not by Woodall's Bill, that endorsed coverture, but by one by fellow Liberal Walter McLaren that proposed gender-neutral political equality), it 'would mean quite literally the political subjection of men by a preponderant female vote of half a million'.[57] Equality of adult suffrage would mean, because of a higher population of women, an effective transfer of power to the gender that had no previous national political responsibility at all. This was not a question that was effectively addressed until 1918, when it was done by enfranchising only women over 30.

Mrs Humphry Ward was later (in 1908) prominent in the founding of the Anti-Suffrage Association, disappointing many of her friends, family members, and colleagues with whom she did charitable work. She was to exhaust herself in speech making and writing articles for the anti-suffrage cause. Her fiction deteriorated with her declining health and the burden of this work, and the anti-suffrage novels *Daphne* of 1909 and *Delia Blanchflower* of 1915 were not well regarded. Her activities encapsulated a paradox, for she was daily showing in her own person how well women performed in the political arena from which she wished to deny them formal access.

Fawcett to the fore

As Becker advanced in age, with no victory in sight, leadership of the movement passed to a younger contingent, and after Becker's death in 1890 Millicent Garrett Fawcett emerged as the nation's leading suffragist. The Garretts of Suffolk were a Liberal family, keenly interested in politics, and in 1865 the 18-year-old Millicent Garrett had gone to hear John Stuart Mill address one of his few election meetings. She was already mixing in radical circles and had already met the man she would marry two years later, the Liberal MP for Brighton, Henry Fawcett, who had previously unsuccessfully proposed to Bessie Rayner Parkes and to Millicent's sister Elizabeth Garrett. Fawcett's blindness (a result of a shooting accident) did not impede him from being both professor of political economy at Cambridge and an active politician—he seconded Mill on the women's suffrage amendment in 1866. Millicent Garrett Fawcett was to play a leading part in suffrage campaigning for the next sixty years, though Henry Fawcett, who was fourteen years her senior, was to accompany her for only some of them, as he died suddenly in 1884 after seventeen years of marriage.

As her most pressing task after Becker's death, Fawcett worked towards uniting the suffrage societies that had been divided by differences of opinion and strategy. That led in 1897 to the setting up of the National Union of

Women's Suffrage Societies of which she was always a leading member, taking various positions including president after 1907.

Notwithstanding the now vigorous opposition, in the last decade of the nineteenth century winning the right to vote seemed more likely than ever, particularly as advances had been made in the 1890s in other English-speaking countries: New Zealand, Australia, and the United States. In 1892 those in favour of women's suffrage were beaten in the Commons by a majority of only three. A quarter of a million women signed a petition calling for the vote in 1894. After 1895 more than half of the new parliament was committed to women's suffrage; the argument had clearly been won. When a favourable majority was secured in 1897 of 71, the Conservative leader in the House of Commons, Arthur Balfour, said that any further electoral reform measure would have to include women's suffrage.[58]

The form which the suffrage would take was, moreover, now clear. Decades of bending to a supposed conservative bias against enfranchising married women had made no gains. In consequence the Women's Franchise League was set up in 1889 by Elizabeth Wolstenholme Elmy, Richard and Emmeline Pankhurst, and others, in disgust at the unceasing proffering of bills that excluded married women, leading to the verbal pirouettes Millicent Fawcett had to employ to justify their exclusion. Fawcett seemed to her critics to be partially agreeing with her opponents, arguing that if married women got the vote, 'changes will be introduced into home life which have not been adequately considered. For my own part, it has always seemed for many reasons right to recognise this, and therefore to support the measures which would enfranchise single women and widows, and not wives during the lifetime of their husbands.' She then proceeded to what was effectively an anti-suffrage argument: If wives were enfranchised, 'the effect in ninety-nine cases out of a hundred would be to give two votes to the husband. Wives are bound in law to obey their husbands.'[59] It is easy to see how young women might yearn for a more radical leadership. In fairness to Fawcett, it was no easy task to make strategic contributions in a movement that was so divided, her moderate nature led her to support any degree of women's franchise as it would concede the principle of votes for women, and further progress could follow. For this willingness to compromise, the Women's Franchise League criticized Fawcett's supporters as the 'spinster suffrage party'.[60]

Women had consolidated their progress in removing barriers to the professions and, very importantly in view of labour's emergence as a political force (with the Independent Labour Party being founded in 1893) in the trade union movement. The work of the educational reformers in the middle of the century now paid off with increased female vigour: a new wave of young women educated at Girton were taking to smoking, to bicycling (a use of new technology to develop individual freedom), and were not afraid to express their views.

The Women's Franchise League was run along non-party lines with an objective 'to establish for all women equal civil and political rights with men' irrespective of marital status. It owed much to the League's efforts that in 1894 that year's Local Government Act placed married women on an equal footing electorally and, as Sylvia Pankhurst said, 'gave the death-blow to attempts to exclude married women from any political rights which might at any time be extended to widows and spinsters'.[61] Now all women were enfranchised locally excepting lodgers; as Ursula Bright wrote to Emmeline Pankhurst: 'The House of Commons has an insane dread of women lodgers. It believes they are all prostitutes.'[62] The Women's Franchise League, having done its work in eliminating the divisive issue of married women's votes, joined in Fawcett's amalgamation of the National Union of Women's Suffrage Societies in 1897.

The success of the high-profile campaign in suspending the Contagious Diseases Acts in 1886 (to which Lydia Becker had never referred in her *Women's Suffrage Journal* except in euphemistic terms) did the women's movement some good in that it showed that vigorous campaigning could produce results. Fawcett was not involved in the Contagious Diseases Acts campaign, partly because her husband and John Stuart Mill had both been against diversion from the goal of women's suffrage, partly because her sister, Doctor Elizabeth Garrett Anderson, supported the Acts as the only contemporary means of protecting women and children from infection.

Such influences no longer held sway over Fawcett by the end of the century and she zealously took to 'moral purity' causes involving prostitution, incest, and children. As her biographer Jane Howarth remarks, 'Historians have found it particularly hard to sympathise with her censoriousness towards individuals.'[63] Private immorality should, she believed, be incompatible with public influence, for men as it was for women. Sexual transgressors who were suffrage supporters but who fell foul of Fawcett's code included Elizabeth Wolstenholme Elmy who had lived with a man and become pregnant before being persuaded to marry (at Fawcett's urgings that her behaviour 'has been and is a great injury to the cause of women'[64]);

Sir Charles Dilke MP for a messy divorce and libel case involving three-in-a-bed sex; and the Ulster Unionist MP Harry Cust for his seduction of a woman whom he proposed to abandon after she became pregnant, but whom he was then persuaded to marry. By her moralistic interventions Fawcett thus alienated many influential allies without advancing the cause. Some, such as Lady Frances Balfour, one of the most aristocratic leaders of the suffrage movement, felt Fawcett was harming the suffrage cause by her puritan hounding of Cust, and if she 'persisted in this course, our suffrage would suffer, not because anyone identifies themselves with Cust, and would resent your action against him as an individual, but your action involves a policy about morals with relation to public life, and I have heard it more than once said by those who have supported us "if women are going to take this line they are not fit to have the suffrage"'.[65] Her brother-in-law and future prime minister, A. J. Balfour, was said to have never forgiven Fawcett.

By the end of the nineteenth century the women's suffrage movement contained both free-thinking new women, and old-guard Victorians who coexisted in an uneasy alliance.[66] Opposing them in the anti-suffrage campaign was a rearguard of solidly based conservative 'new women' active in public life but determined to retain perceived differences between the sexes. The anti-suffragists addressed a genuine fear that had been formulated by the suffragists themselves: that gender difference was both important, and that it would be reflected in major changes in the political process when women were given the vote. The early twentieth century was to see the apotheosis of these notions in the Women's Social and Political Union.

What Britain lacked, after almost a century of peace and (from 1850) growing prosperity, was the national crisis or international upheaval that was to contribute to women's suffrage in the new century.

5

New-found rights in new-found lands

'Woke up and found themselves enfranchised'

Writing in secret so her husband would not know, 50-year-old Mary Muller of Blenheim penned a strident call to action in 1869. In 'An Appeal to the Men of New Zealand' she asked: '*Why has a woman no power to vote*, no right to vote, when she happens to possess all the requisites which legally qualify a man for that right?' In 3,000 words she argued not only that women should be allowed to vote (a proposition that had only recently been publicly aired in Britain) but that New Zealand should take the lead in enfranchising women: 'Our women are brave and strong, with an amount of self-reliance, courage, and freedom from conventionalities eminently calculated to form a great nation. Give them the scope... The change is coming but why is New Zealand only to follow? Why not take the initiative?'[1]

Muller, née Wilson, was born in London in 1819 or 1820 and emigrated to New Zealand in 1850 with her two small children after the death of her first husband. In 1851 she married Dr Stephen Lunn Muller, a surgeon whom she had met on the crossing from Britain. The marriage seems to have been far from happy—'how I have suffered under man's unjust laws', she was to write, saying she had 'been called upon to endure heavy domestic afflictions', but details are not known.[2] Her husband became a member of the Nelson Provincial Council and resident magistrate, which allowed her to become familiar with some of the influential men of the day, and to discuss women's rights with them, a subject she had been pondering before she came to New Zealand. She was able to see some of her ideas represented in the Married Woman's Property Protection Acts of 1860 and 1870.[3]

She could not make her views public, because of the strong disapproval of her husband which must have arisen partly out of his own entrenched attitudes but also because his public position would be compromised by his wife's forthright views. Mary Muller found an ally in Charles Elliott, editor of the *Nelson Examiner*, who encouraged her to publish anonymously in his newspaper, under the name Femina. In 1869 she had 'An Appeal to the Men of New Zealand' published as a pamphlet, arousing considerable attention in New Zealand and abroad, including that of John Stuart Mill, who corresponded with her and sent her a copy of *The Subjection of Women* in 1870.

Thanks largely to the educational work of an early feminist campaigner, Learmonth Dalrymple, women's education had grown up in the colony along with that of men, so by 1893 half the student population was female. Women were in consequence increasingly taking on professional and other roles in the work-place.[4] Women rapidly gained local voting rights— municipal suffrage for some women ratepayers in 1867, consolidated for the whole country in 1875; school board suffrage in 1877 (for 'women householders' which was interpreted to mean all adult women); and liquor licensing board elections in 1881.[5] Thus in terms of local suffrage, which normally preceded the national vote, New Zealand was close to Britain which had introduced municipal suffrage for women in 1869 and for school boards in 1870. The New Zealand liberals included women's suffrage in their successful campaign of 1877 and the subject was debated in 1878 and 1879.

Some influential politicians were already on the side of suffrage campaigners before they had even held a meeting, indicating the openness of New Zealand political society to new ideas. The story of the first independently governing nation to enfranchise women is connected to three major leaders in New Zealand political life: Julius Vogel, journalist and businessman who was prime minister from 1873 to 1875 and in 1876; former lawyer Robert Stout who was prime minister from 1884 to 1877; and John Ballance, a former journalist who held important ministerial posts in the 1870s and 1880s before becoming prime minister in 1891. All might be described as liberal though before the foundation of the Liberal Party in 1891, such labels should be used cautiously. All were committed to the cause of women's suffrage; Robert Stout attributed his views to the influence of *The Subjection of Women* and their ministerial colleague William Pember Reeves (also a women's suffrage supporter, and a historian) specifically remarked on the ideas of Mill working through them. They were among six past or future prime ministers who argued on the side of women's suffrage in parliament.[6]

Stout introduced the Electoral Bill in August 1878 which proposed universal manhood suffrage in which women ratepayers were enfranchised for parliamentary elections. He went further than the franchise and boldly announced his as the first government in the world to introduce the principle of the eligibility of women to stand for parliament. Stout's evident pride was appealing to the instinct for radicalism—or perhaps merely novelty—that he knew was present in his parliamentary colleagues. Introducing eligibility to stand at this stage was probably a step too far too early, and it was defeated (though only by twelve votes) but the main principle of votes for female ratepayers was passed by 41 to 23. The bill then passed the upper house, the Legislative Council, but fell because of a dispute over a different part of it, concerning Maori voting rights. Questions of race and party advantage were jostling with women's suffrage in the corridors of Parliament House.

The extension of men's franchise was based on arguments about the rights of man; women's suffrage advocates were irritated to have their argument presented in terms of tax and property rights rather than citizenship. For this reason radicals voted with the conservatives, the latter wanting to defeat measures on women's suffrage because they went too far, the radicals because they did not go far enough. Historian Patricia Grimshaw questions the radicals' complete sincerity, however, asking why radicals did not bring forward women's suffrage bills in subsequent years if they were so committed to the principle. It is at this point that she feels the women's suffrage campaigners played an important part in persuading society, and legislators, of the importance of women's suffrage.[7]

After political philosophy, as presented for the New Zealand setting by Muller, Stout, and others, the next leading influence on women's suffrage in New Zealand was the world temperance campaign. The men who had originally settled New Zealand were a hard-drinking community of whalers, miners, and farmers and they carried a drinking culture to the towns as urbanization proceeded. A depression in the 1880s increased social distress and attention turned to temperance campaigners who believed society's ills could be addressed by the prohibition of alcohol. As in Britain and the US, in New Zealand many women learned the skills of organization through the temperance movement; it was a small step for women who were already acting in the public sphere in a campaign to change society to call for the vote.

The start of temperance campaigning for suffrage is often taken to be a lecture by the US Woman's Christian Temperance Union representative Mary Clement Leavitt, who talked in Christchurch in May 1885 on 'Woman, her duties and responsibilities', arguing for full political rights. The first national women's society was formed that year along the lines of the American WCTU so New Zealand, though a colony of Britain, was already looking for its leadership not to the mother country but to the more similar and also young United States.

With the hyperbole common to the temperance movement, the well-structured WCTU was described as 'not only one of the grandest philanthropic and religious movements, but the most perfect organisation the world has known'.[8] The leaders of the New Zealand WCTU, who were all female, tended to be already prominent such as Learmonth Dalrymple who had good personal contacts with leading politicians because of her educational work; women active in the non-conformist churches; or wives of well-connected individuals such as Margaret Home Sievwright, whose barrister husband was a friend of Stout. Most activists had already made contributions in such fields as prison visiting, caring for the homeless and pre-school child care. They were not, therefore, middle-class campaigners with no real understanding of society who were telling the poor that all their problems could be ascribed to their drinking habits—a charge that could easily be laid at the door of temperance activists in Britain.

Kate Sheppard

The leading figure in suffrage campaigning was Kate Sheppard who was born in Liverpool in 1847 to Scottish parents. Her father died when she was 15 and she was sent to an uncle, a Free Church minister, who ensured her education. In 1869 her mother took Kate and her siblings to New Zealand where the family settled in Christchurch and in 1871 Kate married Walter Sheppard, a businessman and councillor. She had not been afraid to promote her views publicly, attracting attention as one of the first women cyclists and as an advocate of equal status within marriage. Already a moderate supporter of temperance, she was one of the founding members of the New Zealand Woman's Christian Temperance Union and in 1887 became national superintendent of the franchises, putting her in charge of the NZWCTU's suffrage campaign.

Sheppard had every branch appoint a member for suffrage agitation; women were urged to attend political meetings and vote in institutions where they had the ballot. The American example was called upon with a request for leaflets on women voting in Wyoming. Sheppard herself in 1888 wrote a hugely influential leaflet, 'Ten Reasons Why the Women of New Zealand Should Vote', which is a mixture of the practical and the principled that Sheppard felt would appeal to her compatriots. She first remarked that New Zealand as a democracy 'already admits the great principle that every adult person, not convicted of crime, nor suspected of lunacy, has an inherent right to a voice in the constructions of laws which all must obey'.[9] This was far from admitted by the opponents of women's suffrage, except in terms of the municipal and related franchises, but stating it was a smart debating move as it set the opponents of the principle on the defensive.

Sheppard's argument then turned to what women could bring to the political process, emphasizing that women's position in the home was a positive attribute. For example, women were less accessible than men to 'debasing influences now brought to bear upon elections' and by doubling the number of electors, corruption would be less effective and more difficult.

Women's function in child-rearing, far from disqualifying them or limiting them to the home, gave them 'a more far-reaching concern for something beyond the present moment'. The admitted physical weakness of women was not a disbarment, but a spur to the exercise of caution and an interest in the preservation of 'peace, law, and order, and especially in the supremacy of right over might'.

Thus Sheppard's ten points emphasized, first, common humanity, and then women's difference, and finally reconciled the two in saying that: 'women naturally view each question from a somewhat different standpoint to men, so that whilst their interests, aims and objects would be very generally the same, they would often see what men had overlooked, and thus add a new security against any partial or one-sided legislation.' This seminal tract was notably lacking in jibes against men for their supposedly intemperate and corrupt behaviour, appeals to Christianity, or an endorsement of prohibition.

On the national stage, in a coalition called the Stout–Vogel ministry, Julius Vogel who was then colonial treasurer, introduced his Women's Suffrage Bill in April 1887 to enfranchise women on the same basis as men. Vogel had emigrated to New Zealand from England at 17; he was a former businessman known for his bold project to regenerate New Zealand's economy in the 1870s through large-scale public works including the building of transport and communication facilities. He had a tendency to be cautious and said he was 'in general opposed to exceptional reforms' but in the case of women's suffrage he was indefatigable.[10] It may be that as a Jew and therefore a member of a marginalized group, he felt particular sympathy with those denied their rights. More cynically, it has been thought that he believed he would gain party advantage; or in a simply nationalist ploy he wanted to attract progressive women from England to the under-populated colony. Most probably no motivating force was required beyond his conviction that women's suffrage was a just measure which would do good.

His colleague Pember Reeves described him in his final parliamentary battle: 'Physically, Vogel was never a strong man, and, tortured by gout for many years, he had by this time almost lost the use of his lower limbs. Out of doors, he was wheeled about in a bath-chair; indoors, if he walked across a room, it was on crutches. Unable to stand when addressing the House, he was too deaf to hear the speeches of his antagonists in debate... he spoke sitting—a man not past middle age, yet with his beard and the hair of his curiously-shaped head heavily streaked with grey, and with deep lines of suffering marking a face from which large, dark, gentle eyes gazed out patiently. So looked Vogel when, with his last political stake on the table, and with the game going against him, he calmly turned aside to move the Women's Franchise Bill.'[11] Vogel spoke eloquently and won the day; his bill, supported by 41 members to 22, was sent to committee. The bill outfaced a challenge from opponents to make it apply only to property holders, and some supporters then left the house, while three opponents entered. A sudden vote was then forced on a critical clause that the opposition won by 21 votes to 19, rendering the bill useless and Vogel was forced to withdraw it. The Stout–Vogel ministry was defeated later that year and Vogel soon retired from politics. After his retirement, in 1889 Vogel wrote a novel, *Anno Domini 2000, or Woman's Destiny*, about the year 2000 when women would rule in a world of airships, hydroelectricity, air conditioning, instant communication, and world banking.

The new prime minister was in favour of women's suffrage though not sufficiently to introduce a government measure: he said he would support a private bill or an amendment. The house was engaged with pressing economic matters and no one took up the challenge until 1890 when a motion was passed in theory but failed when the crucial decision was taken. John Hall, the suffragist's parliamentary spokesman, and the New Zealand

Woman's Christian Temperance Union leadership were reduced to discussing methods of amending their proposals to attract the half-hearted: for a property franchise or one based on education.

Parliamentary support, and the existing power of the NZWCTU as a middle-class pressure group was obviously inadequate. By the end of 1890 the NZWCTU began appealing to women workers who were, as in other rapidly industrializing countries, seeking to improve their position through unionism. The local NZWCTU branch in Dunedin published an appeal to the working class in 1890: 'No man can be a friend of labour and against the women's franchise. Women's franchise will do more for the working class than any combination of unions will ever manage. Let working men instruct their wives to work for the women's franchise; let every working man's wife come to our next public meeting.'[12] The thinking behind this address is revealing: the natural assumption that women were seen first as wives rather than individuals, and that they were available to be commanded politically by men. It is also telling that earlier that year the NZWCTU conference had voted for a property franchise which would have enfranchised few working women, calling their sincerity into question.

To increase the base of their support, Kate Sheppard determined on a petition to parliament which could be signed by every adult woman. The NZWCTU thus began seeking support nationally from working-class women, and they also now sought the support for suffrage from women who were not in sympathy with their temperance goals, but who were generally feminist; and of rural women in isolated communities. For the first time the organization was genuinely attempting to reach all New Zealand women; canvassers called at homes throughout the country, ensuring they reached 'housewives', as well as those in the workplace; the signature rate was 90 or 95 per cent.[13]

Petitions were presented in 1891, 1892, and 1893, the last of them signed by 32,000 women, a third of the adult population. This wore away the parliamentary opposition that suffrage was desired only by a few temperance activists. In response to the changing mood, in 1892 Women's Franchise Leagues were set up in all the major centres in New Zealand for women (men could not be full members) who supported suffrage but not necessarily the NZWCTU programme, thus attracting a number of hitherto unrecruited advanced feminists. Anti-suffragists fought back with their own petition, collected in public houses, organized by members of parliament and liquor industry spokesmen, but it was discredited when it was found that some signatures had been obtained fraudulently—from women asked by paid canvassers to sign the 'suffrage petition' who thought they were signing in favour of women's suffrage.

The government of prime minister John Ballance took office in 1891 with a majority committed to women's suffrage. His grouping of parliamentary colleagues as Liberals was the start of the consolidation of New Zealand interest groups into party politics. The opposition was not necessarily conservative, and included John Hall, who had been the suffragists' spokesman. There was less party opposition to women's suffrage than was to be found in other national parliaments though there were those of conservative views who feared activist women as radicals bent on reform programmes. A leading cabinet member, Dick Seddon was a bitter opponent of 'petticoat government', and had contributed to the defeat of earlier measures, calling on colleagues to 'look well to our laurels and assert our prerogative as the Lords of Creation'. He believed women were best suited to home life, performing their duties as 'ministering angels', declaring that 'if you give too much power you unsex women'.[14]

Women's suffrage was supported by the prohibitionists, which lost it some liberal support where there were jobs in the liquor trade and issues of personal freedom at stake; but the opposition backed it in the hope of strengthening their own hand. They felt their defeat in the election of 1890 had been caused by universal manhood suffrage and adding women to the mix would get the Liberals out. Liberals were not deaf to these arguments, and wondered, since they had gained a large majority without voting women, what they needed them for.

In 1891 a woman's suffrage bill introduced by John Hall passed the lower house but failed by two votes in the conservative-dominated upper house. The following year the proposal was included in a government Electoral Bill, which was more difficult to undermine, as even if members of the government did not privately support it, they were publicly expected to back it; this led to underhand dealing and spurious objections among those attempting to kill the bill.

Ballance was still dedicated to women's franchise (even if committed to achieving it at the best possible party advantage) but he was unwell and his deputy Seddon was charged with attempting to get it through. Seddon was a conceited and bullying character whose ultimately successful manoeuvres for sinking the bill, ostensibly over the issue of postal votes, were deeply resented.

Robert Stout, Ballance's friend and a keen advocate of women's suffrage, had lost his seat and retired from parliamentary politics in 1887. Ballance urged him to return and take over the leadership of the party but before he could be re-elected, in June 1893, Ballance died and Seddon took over as caretaker prime minister on the understanding that a caucus would be held to elect a new leader. In the event, no such vote was held and Stout and Seddon's other enemies failed in their attempt to insist on one. Whatever the wider political ramifications, from the point of view of women's suffrage, New Zealand had lost a powerful friend in Ballance and gained as premier in Seddon an autocratic enemy.

As prime minister, Seddon came to be referred to as King Dick. He was to accrue six ministerial posts to himself, and talked of favouring a presidential system of government, ruling without a cabinet. Despite his undoubted progressive successes, such as the introduction of old age pension, Seddon was at heart a right-wing conservative. An additional problem was that the suffragists' long term spokesman, John Hall, intended to retire after the 1893 session. Kate Sheppard and other campaigners felt that with a government nominally committed to women's suffrage, in its last parliament, they must seize the day or their time would run out. Hall duly introduced his own Suffrage Bill, presenting the most recent women's petition during the second reading on three hundred yards of paper containing the signatures of a quarter of the adult female population. In the subsequent division, only two members voted against, all other opponents being absent—but the absentees, significantly, included the entire cabinet.

The government's Electoral Bill with its suffrage clauses also passed its stages in the house—having Hall's private bill as well as a government bill gave the suffragists a lever: if the government did not proceed with its own legislation, they could forge ahead with theirs. The government bill passed the lower house easily, but now faced the upper house where other bills had been defeated. Members of the upper house were appointed, supposedly by the Governor but in fact on the advice of the prime minister; seven were Seddon's recent appointees. Seddon refused to order these members of the upper house to support the issue.

Amendments were added to the bill with the intention of overloading it, including one to allow women to become members of parliament (which would have opened up a new range of debates). With the liquor interest and suffrage campaigners holding meetings, public attention was focused on the parliamentary processes of the passage of the bill to a far greater extent than usual. Seddon assured MPs supported by the liquor interest that three members of the upper house would vote against the government bill if necessary at the last minute. Even this did not seem enough, and Seddon sent a telegram to one member who was absent and paired, telling him to change his position and vote against. This was one manipulation too far for two opposition councillors, William Reynolds and Edward Stevens, who had previously voted against the bill, now voted in favour in order to deny Seddon his triumph of trickery. On 8 September 1893, the bill that enfranchised women in New Zealand was passed by 18 votes to 20. 'It is hardly too much to say that the enfranchisement of women has been accomplished by her enemies,' said the *New Zealand Herald*.[15]

There were still means to stop the bill, however: it had to pass the Governor who had to give his assent; it could be sent to Britain for the Queen's assent; it could be returned to the lower house because of a technical error. Various ruses were tried and the bill's opponents lobbied to urge the Governor to withhold his assent but in the end further machinations would be worse for Seddon, and he sent the bill to the Governor on 19 September.

Why the vote was won

'So, one fine morning of September 1893, the women of New Zealand woke up and found themselves enfranchised. The privilege was theirs— given freely and spontaneously, in the easiest and most spontaneous manner in the world by male politicians.'[16] This was a dubious judgement by Pember Reeves who downplayed the influence of the NZWCTU and the Franchise Leagues in gathering support and focusing political pressure on legislators.

The most comprehensive modern writer on New Zealand suffrage, Patricia Grimshaw, argues that the concession of the vote was the outcome of the work of the New Zealand feminist movement. She acknowledges the work of the NZWCTU but says their 'motives in campaigning for the vote were basically feminist'.[17]

The actions of Stout (and Vogel and Balance in their efforts before him) were certainly underwritten by high-minded sentiments and they had doubtless, as Pember Reeves put it, 'been converted to faith in the experiment by reading the English arguments so gallantly and unavailingly used by Mill',[18] but they still needed a political atmosphere in which such sentiments could flourish, and it was the NZWCTU supporters with their public social work (rather than merely temperance work) who created that atmosphere along with the non-temperance feminist women brought late into the fray in the Franchise Leagues. The final votes in the upper house (though not the more representative votes in the lower house) were obtained by the subversion of political chicanery, but the reason for the chicanery was that the bill was going to go through and its opponents wished to prevent it. The franchise was not granted by political sleight of hand; the democratic impetus to pass the bill was *almost* subverted by its enemies.

Paradoxically, while Pember Reeves is at pains to point out how little any organized campaign had to do with the eventual granting of women's suffrage, putting his view that the idealistic proposals of politicians were paramount, in fact he demonstrates the reverse. The flow of parliamentary debates and the voting pattern, particularly in the years 1890 to 1893, show that the dedicated work even of cabinet members and prime ministers was not enough, the attention of the nation had to be focused on them by campaigners; parliamentarians had to be shamed into voting along with their expressed principles. A party leader's being committed merely in principle did not of itself guarantee success for women's suffrage, as is apparent from the British scene, where Disraeli, Salisbury, and Balfour all spoke in favour of the cause to no practical effect.

It was of importance to have a movement calling for the vote, at the very least to forestall conservative gibes that women did not want to be enfranchised. A powerful argument was knocked out of the opposition's armoury by the collection and presentation of well-supported petitions. The New Zealand case was a rare occasion on which the somewhat sterile practice of presenting petitions before parliament actually benefited the cause.

There was also a merely nationalistic pride in New Zealand in being the 'experiment station' of advanced legislation as governments enacted a wide array of programmes that interested progressive thinkers in distant countries who used such terms as 'the political brain of the modern world' and 'a genuine Democracy' to describe the tiny colony.[19] This was not always well received abroad: contemporary author Norwood Young in the *Westminster Review* berated parliamentarians who wished to be in the vanguard: 'A good many were in favour of the change merely because they thought other countries were tending in the same direction, from the shallow vanity of men who wish to make a sensation by being the first to inaugurate what they believe to be a coming revolution.'[20]

Figure 3. A section of the Women's Suffrage Memorial in Auckland's Khartoum Place by Jan Morrison and Claudia Pond Eyley, commemorating suffragist pioneers who helped make New Zealand the first nation to enfranchise women, in 1893.

There were some three reasons for New Zealand's early enfranchisement of women that related not to what New Zealand was, but what it was not. Firstly there were less rigid party divisions; the first real political party, the Liberals, had been founded only in 1891 by Ballance, and prior to this politics had been a matter of interest groups and individuals anxious to present their ideas in parliament. Seddon's machinations over the women's vote were early attempts to impose party discipline on legislators who had hitherto considered themselves their own men. There was therefore a more genuinely free vote on the women's franchise than there would have been in a whipped and rigidly divided parliament. Once a proposition was won intellectually, it had a real chance in such a parliament; unlike in Britain where, though the argument was clearly won in the 1890s, women's franchise continued as a political toy passed between the parties.

Secondly, the major fault line of class, which continually derailed suffrage campaigns in other countries, hardly existed in New Zealand where, by the

1890s, society was dominated by people who had self-evidently received no benefit of birth or rank but had arrived thirty years previously to seek their fortune. Of the major players in the suffrage battle, for example, Seddon, Stout, and Vogel had arrived in New Zealand from Britain as teenagers; Ballance, Sheppard, and Hall in their twenties, their skills and determination being their only advantages. Proposals to enfranchise only property-owning women, the cry of a militant middle class, never took root in New Zealand, despite attempts at the policy in 1890.

Thirdly, there was no racial divide over this issue, there was no dissent when votes for women was assumed to include Maori women (though they were thought to be less interested in voting than white women). New Zealand's 'state experiments' had already extended to developments on race and democracy. Maori men were all enfranchised some ten years before, with white men receiving manhood suffrage; with the qualification that they could vote only for their own quota of members of parliament. Maori women's enfranchisement appalled imperialists in Britain. Millicent Fawcett addressing a meeting in 1909 fulminated at the comparatively inferior position imposed on her compatriots compared to 'that of the Maori women of New Zealand who have more power in developing and moulding the future of the Empire than we have in England. Why should the Maori women be in a superior position to that held by the women of England?'[21]

The work of Kate Sheppard and the suffragists was now to get as many women as possible on the electoral rolls before they were closed for the next election; the liquor interest also began enrolling women who could be relied upon to support their trade; politicians encouraged women voters, assuring them they had been in favour of suffrage all along. With such enthusiasm, more than 100,000 women registered, a large proportion of the 140,000 adult woman population (there were 180,000 males, a majority but not an overwhelming one).[22] The election of November 1893 resulted in a landslide for the Liberals—something of a lesson for the party machine men who so confidently argued that women's votes would mean defeat for them and victory for the conservative opposition. In fact the Liberals were in power for the next twenty years, thirteen of them under Dick Seddon who enjoyed five consecutive election victories.

Kate Sheppard was pleased to receive a letter from the aged Mary Muller in October 1893. Muller had done what she could in her covert work; she wrote to Sheppard, 'I am an old woman now, but I thank God I have been able to register myself an Elector and I now look forward with hope.'[23]

Now her husband was dead she could be revealed, in *The Prohibitionist* of 4 November 1893, as the author of the many articles and pamphlets published under the name Femina. She died in 1901. Kate Sheppard went on a triumphal tour of Britain in 1894–5; she died in 1934 at the age of 86.

As far as the objectives of the New Zealand Woman's Christian Temperance Union were concerned, though there was a short-term increase in the total vote in liquor referendums in favour of prohibition, at the end of the century prohibitionist proposals were overwhelmingly defeated in favour of continuing with the system of liquor licensing then in place.[24] If obtaining votes for women was a ploy to impose prohibition, in New Zealand it failed.

Votes in the outback

As in New Zealand, in Australia there was no entrenched aristocracy. The egalitarian ideal was that a can-do attitude in a hostile climate saw people judged by their abilities, not their origins. Tough 'frontier' life favoured women who were prepared to undergo its hardships, investing them with respect and authority. The origins of the settlement of parts of Australia as penal colonies also gave a rugged, masculine atmosphere to the nation (though some of the convicts were women, men vastly outnumbered them).

Idealists eager to found a new form of society had later come to settle in Australia, including people who had experience in temperance movements. In keeping with this profile, the first feminist organizations were concentrated on philanthropic work with prostitutes and destitute women. Temperance formed a strong part of this work because of the contribution of alcohol to general lawlessness, to family poverty and to marital violence.

Benevolent work promoting schools and university entrance followed, so by the last quarter of the nineteenth century all women were educated, some to degree level, and a select group of activists was accustomed to working in the public sphere for social change. The requisites for a women's suffrage movement—education and social activism—were therefore already present, but awaiting a political catalyst.

Of the six states of Australia, manhood suffrage was achieved by the 1860s in South Australia, New South Wales, Victoria and Queensland; in Western Australia in 1893 and in Tasmania in 1900. However, plural voting by landowners in most states meant the wealthy had commensurately more votes than the poor. Labour politicians therefore considered plural voting the primary evil of their electoral set-up and declined to support women's suffrage as a principal goal. Women's suffrage advocates were themselves divided, with some arguing for the vote as it was given to men (meaning women too would have the right to plural votes) and others campaigning for universal suffrage.

As in New Zealand, a visit from Mary Clement Leavett of the American Woman's Christian Temperance Union in 1885 motivated already committed women and within a decade Australian WCTUs were set up in all six states. Another American 'missionary', Jessie Ackermann, extended the Union's work and set up tight structures with different departments, each responsible to a superintendent, so there would be a different person in each state responsible for temperance education, for 'moral purity', for suffrage, and for other priorities.

For the Union, women's suffrage was on the agenda immediately, though only as a means to control the liquor trade. In 1891 the Victoria WCTU collected 30,000 signatures for a woman's suffrage petition though as historian Richard J. Evans observed, the WCTU never desired votes for women as anything more than a means to an end, namely liquor prohibition, evidenced by the Victoria WCTU's continued opposition to the idea that women should be allowed to stand as candidates in elections.[25] The WCTU was contradictory in being protective of woman's traditional role in the home, even while they were calling for her action in the public sphere.

The WCTU set up suffrage leagues in four states: Tasmania did not have one, and in New South Wales radical women suffragists refused to accept temperance leadership, feeling this would compromise the clear message of votes for women (whatever their views on liquor). A Women's Suffrage League was therefore formed in Sydney in 1891 without temperance leadership. Populous Sydney had the numbers to maintain a separate organization; it may well have been that there were women in other WCTUs who were unhappy with the temperance aspect of the organization (as opposed to suffrage or philanthropic work) but had no other feminist grouping to attend.

Fair do's in South Australia

South Australia was demonstrably a fairer place than most in the world in the second half of the nineteenth century. It had been settled not by convicts but industrious folk who had been brought over specifically under the scheme put forward by a former convict, Edward Wakefield, who proposed the sale of crown lands in Australia at a fixed, reasonable price. The proceeds paid for sending emigrants from Britain, who were to be equally divided by sex and to represent a cross-section of English society. This gave South Australians what has been called a 'deep-seated belief in the superiority of their own society. Founded as it was by hard-working non-conformists, the community had long cherished the conviction that their social order was pre-eminent among the Australian colonies and that it transcended British society because of its freedom from traditional barriers and bigotry.'[26]

There were therefore none of the problems of criminality of Western Australia, or the large disparities in income caused by the awarding of vast tracts of land to individuals. The colony's commitment to religious toleration attracted a large number of people, who tended to be open to social experiment. In 1856 South Australia instituted advanced forms of government including manhood suffrage with no property qualification for the lower house, three-year parliaments, and secret ballots. There was no plural voting as there was in other Australian colonies.

By 1885 the progressive momentum had stagnated, though social advances had taken place regarding the education and property rights of women. Edward Stirling, a professor of medicine at Adelaide University, had promoted the admission of women to degrees. He, like so many in the history of women's suffrage, was influenced by Mill's *Subjection of Women*. When he became a member of parliament he introduced a motion that single women should have the vote.

Stirling grandly proclaimed, 'So long as half the human race was unrepresented our boasted representative government was a hollow mockery of an idea which it did not even approach.'[27] The motion (which was a declaration of principle and did not commit the house to anything) was passed amid cheering. In 1886 he gave notice of a bill that he intended to bring forward, and now the proposal was more closely scrutinized. Though he had offered compelling arguments why *all* women should have the vote, there were serious flaws in Stirling's proposal in that his bill did not propose enfranchising all women. It suggested enfranchising only single women, in deference to the doctrine of coverture, and proposed that the franchise should be on the property qualification by which members of the upper house were elected.

There had not been a property franchise in South Australia for the lower house and in women's suffrage on this basis the Trades and Labour Council suspected the introduction of a class-based franchise just at the time when they were finding a political voice. A property franchise would benefit the middle class; accordingly the Council presented a petition, supporting women's suffrage but saying the property qualification should be dropped, 'and that the franchise should be extended to women irrespective of property or wealth'.[28] The bill was fully debated, and finally received nineteen votes from a possible thirty-six which, though a majority, was insufficient to bind the whole legislature on a constitutional amendment.

Though flawed, Stirling's bill at least put the principle in the open and after Stirling lost his seat in the election the following year, a supporter, Robert Caldwell, proposed a bill to give all women over 25 the vote. It gained one vote less than the previous year's bill—though in a more polarized and more right-wing house. In 1889 a weakened Bill again failed.

Mary Lee

The leading extra-parliamentary activist working on women's suffrage was a diminutive matron, Mary Lee, who had been born in Ireland in 1821 and had emigrated to Australia in 1879 with some of her seven children after being widowed. She was therefore over 60 when she took up public work. In 1883 she was noted as secretary to the ladies' committee of the Social Purity Society that worked to change the law relating to the legal and social status of young women who were often working from the age of 10 or 12. Among other reforms, they successfully lobbied for a raised age of consent, from 13 to 16.

Feeling that this work could be better advanced if women had the vote, the Social Purity League called a meeting of interested parties at the YWCA building in Adelaide on the afternoon of 21 July 1888. Stirling chaired the meeting, whose audience was mainly women but also included several members of parliament and ministers of religion, giving an indication of the seriousness with which the issue was already viewed. A comparison with the situation in many European countries, where suffrage campaigners had not a single friend in parliament, shows the advanced state of political thought.

The meeting set up a Women's Suffrage League with Stirling as president and Mary Lee as secretary; she called on the men of Australia to be 'chariot-eers in the brave reform'. They put out a statement of principles that called for all women to have the vote on the same basis as men, but explicitly stated that no claim was put forward for women to stand for parliament.[29] The only area on which there was disagreement was the age for voting, which was originally proposed at 25 then set at 21.

Lee, initially a hesitant speaker, was to become the mainspring of the League's presentation because of her skill, commitment, and ability to cover a range of interests. Concerned at the low pay and miserable conditions of women workers, she proposed the formation of a women's trade union. It was set up in 1890 with support from the Trades and Labour Council, with Lee as secretary. She had now become a valuable cross-over into the world of organized labour, as she attended meetings of the Trades and Labour Council which endorsed Liberal candidates who shared their views. The WCTU and the Women's Suffrage League were also active on the hustings, calling on candidates to declare their views. By the 1890 election a subject which had been written on to the political agenda only five years earlier, was centre stage.

Caldwell reintroduced his bill in 1890 for a vote for propertied women (married and unmarried) for the upper house. The Women's Suffrage League supported the bill as an acceptable compromise measure on the way to full enfranchisement. An amendment to give all women the vote was defeated, but the bill was passed and sent to the upper house where it failed by one vote.

Mary Lee fulminated on the slow rate of progress,

> in our own Parliament the Dog Licence Bill, the Sparrows Destruction Bill, a road or railway, a bridge or well, anything and everything is allowed prece-dence of the Women's Suffrage Bill and the women's petitions for suffrage. The suffrage is the right of all women, just as it is the right of all men, and although the immediate need may not be felt by the happy and prosperous— by women with kind husbands and comfortable homes—we insist on it on behalf of the solitary, the hard-pressed and the wronged; we insist on liberty that all may share the blessings of liberty.[30]

By the following year, the Women's Suffrage League, emboldened by the promise of help from the Trades and Labour Council, declared there would be no more support for half-measures, and only complete women's suffrage would do. A large public demonstration of March 1893 supported by the

Women's Suffrage League, the WCTU and the Working Women's Trade Union rounded on supporters of the propertied vote and pledged to support only full women's suffrage.

This was something of a stand-off politically: Labour and the radical Liberals supported complete women's suffrage; moderate Liberals supported limited women's suffrage and the Conservatives opposed it. Slow progress began to be made after the first three Labour members were elected to the upper house, all committed to women's suffrage; then in 1893 eight Labour members were elected to the lower house, in support of the strong Liberal government of Charles Kingston. He had previously opposed women's suffrage so it was a surprise when he assured a Women's Suffrage League deputation that he would not only introduce a women's suffrage bill, it would be provisional on a referendum of all the men and all the women in the colony (effectively, therefore, giving women the vote on whether women should have the vote). This was perhaps a conservative expedient, ensuring that Kingston would not be considered responsible for the leap in the dark of enfranchising women—no country had yet done so, New Zealand was still to take the step. On the other hand, it may have been the intention of Kingston to placate the radical Liberal and Labour members with a measure that had little chance.

Mary Lee and the suffrage campaigners were angry at this additional hurdle for women to jump; no referendum had been held to confirm manhood suffrage. The WCTU protested, in a condescending remark characteristic of the stance of the organization, that a referendum would 'give thoughtless men and women who would not value a vote the power to deprive others of a right'.[31] This was not a wise position to adopt, as it implied they feared losing the vote because they were lacking in popular support. In the event, the bill had a majority but not a sufficient majority for a constitutional matter, and it fell.

The most important changes in South Australia were in demographics, where the increase in population and therefore of electoral strength of Adelaide left the conservatives (tellingly called the Country Party) at a disadvantage. Early in 1894 in elections for a third of the upper house Labour and Liberal representation was increased, resulting in the unusual situation of an upper house which was not conservative. The conservatives' best option would have been to have backed a property franchise that would have enfranchised property-owning country women but the time for such expedients was passed.

The numbers were now stacking up in favour of women's suffrage, with the additional encouragement of success in New Zealand the previous year. A bill was introduced in the upper house early in 1894 proposing only to give women the vote on the same basis as men and to forbid them from standing for elections. When the bill was near its close, a die-hard conservative, Ebenezer Ward, moved a wrecking amendment to strike out the clause forbidding women to stand, in the belief that it would kill the bill as no one would pass such an extensive measure. Supporters of the bill were irritated by the trick and so were not deterred from passing the legislation. The right to be elected, the first time women were so empowered in the world, became an unsought boon. 'The right of candidature had been given to South Australian women by its opponents,' as historian Audrey Oldfield comments.[32]

Voting had been close, at one point down to one member in the lower house (which in a reversal of the usual procedure considered the bill after it had been introduced and passed the upper house). This man, an elderly and infirm supporter of the measure, regularly went home to bed at eleven o'clock. Those against the bill therefore simply kept talking until after eleven, and the house could be adjourned with no decision taken. Finally the old gentleman was detained in the lobby by an emissary sent for the purpose, 'who beguiled him with pleasant converse for the needful few minutes' then bundled him into the voting lobby.[33] The bill was finally carried and passed its third reading (confirmation) on 18 December 1894 with royal assent received the following year.

Mary Lee declined requests that she stand for parliament though she accepted an unpaid position as official visitor to the Lunatic Asylums. A public subscription for her raised fifty pounds on her 75th birthday in 1896. She was later to fall on hard times, and had to sell her library; she wrote to a fellow suffragist that she was threatened with homelessness.[34] She died at the age of 89.

Western Australia

The sparsely populated mass of Western Australia was granted a constitution by the British Crown only in 1887. Election was by manhood suffrage with a property qualification, and there was plural voting. As in New Zealand, the issue of women's suffrage was raised by Jessie Ackermann, the Woman's

Christian Temperance Union 'missionary', who visited the state to form branches in 1892.

Prime Minister John Forrest, a civil engineer by profession, had concentrated on building up the roads and other infrastructure of the colony but by 1892 with a population of 60,000, there was pressure to increase democratic representation. A gold rush in 1893 had brought a flood of gold-hungry prospectors or Outlanders to newly discovered gold fields. The miners tended to be politically radical and insisted that their interests should be addressed in such things as government infrastructure to support the gold fields where great wealth was being produced for the colony in civically primitive conditions.

In response to calls for greater democracy, in July 1893, a bill was introduced to give men the franchise on a simple residency qualification. A couple of conservatives, J. Cookworthy and R. Sholl, immediately proposed the enfranchisement of unmarried women, in order to rebalance the electorate which would alter from being property-based (and therefore a wealthier population, more likely to be right-wing) to the more politically volatile general population. In defence of the proposal, women were said to be 'the most conservative class in the world' and though the debate ranged to the usual facetious remarks that women, like cats, were best left at home, the proposal was lost by only one vote.[35]

The conservatives were obviously motivated by the need to protect their own party interests; the significant aspect of this ploy was that they had realized faster than legislators in the northern democracies that women could be a safeguard of conservative values. The smaller proportion of women in the proposal was also a factor: they would contribute, it was hoped, to a conservative administration, but could not overwhelm the legislature, particularly as the proposal was to enfranchise only the unmarried.

The agitation and debates over Electoral Bills in New Zealand were influential (the debate in Western Australia took place two months before enfranchisement in New Zealand). The willingness of legislators to embrace a radical solution to their problems showed what was very much a New World approach. Forrest was too traditional in his thinking to support votes for women immediately, and he gave no hope to delegations of suffrage activists who visited him; but women's suffrage as a solution to political problems was making an early appearance in the political mix.

After the 1894 election the seeds of political parties became apparent in that the prime minister and his cabinet formed one block, while all those opposed (who did not necessarily agree with one another and had no leader) formed another. Members newly elected for the goldfields complained that a residency qualification was insufficient for miners who often moved around. A liberal member, Walter James, proposed women's suffrage without giving details and a deal between James and the miners' representatives to democratize the assembly seemed likely. The miners' representative, Frederick Illingworth, baulked at women's suffrage, however. There were few women in the goldfields and therefore few votes in it for him; he was committed to increasing representation for miners; and votes for women would increase the power of the towns, where most women lived. The miners themselves were by no means united against women's suffrage, and for many of them any measures that would make the hinterland of Western Australia more attractive to women were desirable.

The parliamentary groupings were in an unusual situation: there was no labour or socialist party as such but Illingworth and his miners' representatives occupied that position on the radical end of political thought, and in all other countries such politicians were in favour of women's suffrage. Those who could be called the liberals supported Walter James who genuinely upheld women's suffrage as a matter of principle. The conservative wing, of Forrest and his cabinet, were in the position of having the most to gain by supporting women's suffrage, if they could only overcome their distaste for the measure.

Elections in 1897 reinforced the strength of the miners' representatives. James introduced a motion for women's suffrage later that year, again to opposition from Forrest and Illingworth. He tried again in 1898, it was a far from hopeless task; James saw how the political wind was blowing when he observed the strength of Forrest's opposition decline as the prime minister's arguments became more abstruse and ambiguous. 'I feel almost inclined to give a sigh, and say that on the next occasion the Premier will be found voting for it,' he said, 'On each occasion his opposition has become less and less.'[36]

Similarly to the situation in New Zealand, the WCTU thought it wise to promote a Women's Franchise League to bring in those who were repelled by the message of total abstinence. From spring they launched a series of public meetings, writing to the press and gathering support. A meeting at York on 16 June 1899 forwarded a resolution to the prime minister calling for women's suffrage; Forrest took the opportunity of replying that his government was prepared to introduce a bill. This was a low-key way of backing down from his previous position, which he justified by saying there had been a change in opinion in the nation over the issue. In fact it was simply his only means of increasing his own support in the next elections where Illingworth and the mining newcomers were close to being able to take political power from the established landowners.

The decision, said Pember Reeves, 'sprang from the division of the community into two classes—the old and the new, the landowners and the gold-seekers, the settled, governing element and the immigrant out-landers'.[37] By enfranchising women the voting strength of the farming and grazing districts and of the seaports would be increased, and the influence of the Outlanders to some extent neutralized.

Under the Constitution Acts Amendment Act of 1899 full suffrage was extended to women. It was not an elevated session of parliament: as Pember Reeves observed, 'Of all the hopelessly uninspired and uninspiring discussions on the subject, that at Perth was perhaps the flattest and most meanly commonplace.'[38] Giving more political power to the older, settled areas was not enough to save Forrest: his ministry was voted out in 1901 and Walter James as the next prime minister formed a liberal ministry. Forrest was too smart a politician to be manoeuvred out of power, however, and he had already signalled his intention of going into the Federal Parliament. He served in several ministries and in the coalition wartime ministry and became the first person born in Australia to enter the British peerage.

Australian Federation

On one midwinter day in 1889 as the story was told, the weekly executive council meeting was over and the governor Lord Carrington and Sir Henry Parkes, prime minister of New South Wales, sat talking. 'I could confederate these colonies in twelve months,' said Parkes, who was serving his fifth term as prime minister of the colony.

'Then why don't you do it, it would be a glorious finish to your life,' said Carrington.[39]

Sir Henry was no longer the gaunt young Chartist he had been as a member of the Birmingham Political Union before leaving Britain; or the fierce spokesman of the Sydney mob from his early years in Australia. Now he was caricatured as 'Sir 'Enery', the sophisticates mocking his accent. It was not twelve months but twelve years before federation was achieved, yet the democratic objectives of the his early years were maintained and extended.

Figure 4. The winsome debutant 'White Australia' is crowned with suffrage by her doting maid the Labour Party. She holds the bouquets of promised 'reform' and 'progress' while prime minister Edmund Barton is represented as her mother. Aboriginals of either sex were not given the national vote unless they had already been granted a state franchise.

Over the second half of the nineteenth century technological change had gone some way to bridging the three million square miles of the continent. Railways and telegraphs had been bringing the six colonies into closer touch, and they had had been gradually growing closer in trade and defence matters.

A convention on confederation opened in Sydney on 2 March 1891 with Parkes as president. The franchise options discussed were between universal manhood suffrage and an electorate identical to that of the house of parliament in each state. The organizing committee received a petition from the Woman's Christian Temperance Union asking for universal suffrage but declined to consider the proposition.

New Zealand was party to these talks, though eventually it became an independent nation, choosing against confederation. Its presence meant, however, that when the next convention was held, in 1897 two of the participants, South Australia and New Zealand, had already enfranchised women so now women would have to be either disenfranchised (if manhood suffrage were chosen) or given a federal vote in accordance with the practice in individual states.

Throughout Australia interest groups were pushing for the question of women to be addressed: liberals, the developing labour movement, suffrage societies where they existed and of course the WCTU all made sure that female suffrage was raised at meetings. The WCTU, as usual both a spur to women's aspirations and a drag on them, was at the same time calling for prohibition to be written into the constitution.[40] Delegates to the 1897 Convention were elected by popular ballot in South Australia and one woman, Catherine Helen Spence stood, winning a respectable 7,000 votes but failing to be elected: early evidence that was to be repeated wherever newly enfranchised women stood that women candidates could not rely on a gender vote alone.

When the convention met in Adelaide petitions from supporters of women's suffrage gave the familiar arguments that women would have to obey the laws of the new Commonwealth, pay taxes towards it, and would contribute socially to the nation, so they should have equality in electing its representatives. An early proposal from South Australia, for universal suffrage at 21 was lost by twenty-three votes to twelve, amid fears that if women's suffrage were imposed, several states would refuse to join the federation. The convention went for the existing states' parliamentary arrangements as those for the new Commonwealth Parliament; the only concession for South Australia was that their women would not be disenfranchised.

The new parliament opened in Melbourne on 9 May 1901. It very soon applied itself to resolving the anomalies of its own composition, working towards a measure for the grant of a uniform suffrage in federal elections. South Australian and Western Australian women by now had the franchise, which meant the electorate for those states was much larger than in the other four. They would not consent to disenfranchise their women so the only way to balance the electorates was to enfranchise women in the other states.

It was fortuitous (or perhaps a matter of his own design) that the prime minister, Edmund Barton, was away in Britain when the matter came up, as he had never been supportive of women's suffrage; his place was taken by a supporter, William Lyne. The four colonies that had not enfranchised women made their objections but it was clear which direction the debate would take, and the bill was passed without a division. It completed all its stages on 12 June 1902, and all white Australian women got the vote, making Australia the second nation in the world where women were enfranchised. The measure was adopted quietly; as Pember Reeves said, 'Its use in three colonies had at least shown that it was harmless. That its most sarcastic opponents admitted.'[41]

Race in Australia

The race fault line running through women's suffrage surfaced over the Aboriginal vote. The unamended enfranchisement would give the vote to all Aboriginals, male and female, by virtue of their being adult British subjects. This was going too far for delegates from Western Australia and Queensland who objected to votes being given to 'savages' and were rewarded with exemptions so no Aboriginals were given the vote there. In South Australia Aboriginal males and females had the vote, both federally and in state elections.

There was discussion whether 'half-bloods' should have the vote, but none about Maoris who were automatically accepted if they were citizens. When the prime minister introduced the point a member countered 'An aboriginal is not as intelligent as a Maori. There is no scientific evidence that he is a human being at all.'[42]

The Commonwealth Parliament discussed the ignorance of Aboriginal women, and the slight on white wives and daughters if the vote were given to these native Australians. In order to exclude them, the parliament reverted to its earlier formula in relation to Aboriginal women—not the federal enfranchisement of all, but the enfranchisement of Aboriginal women *only* when all women in the state in question had the franchise.

The result was that in New South Wales, Tasmania, and Victoria all white women could vote for the Commonwealth Parliament though could not vote in their state elections. When the remaining women were admitted to the state franchise in the six years after 1902, Aboriginal women were also admitted to both the state and federal franchise in these three states. An Act of 1962 gave Commonwealth voting rights to male and female Aboriginals in Queensland and Western Australia, who then conferred state voting rights.

Between the federal enfranchisement and the enfranchisement of women in the last four states, suffrage activists shamed their legislators in places where women did not have the state vote but Aboriginal males did, by pointing out that they had put wholesome white womanhood in an inferior position to 'blackfellows'. A cartoon on the front page of *The Australian Woman's Sphere* in October 1900 shows an Aboriginal with a boomerang in one hand and a bottle in the other saying: 'I have a vote.'[43] The state right to vote remained an urgent priority even after Federation as it was not merely a 'local' franchise, most of the issues which concerned women remained state responsibilities.[44]

Why Australasia?

Australia and New Zealand had in a short period made dramatic advances that startled the rest of the democratic world. To a large extent this was because of the stock from which the settlers had come; the colonies had attracted radicals and those interested in social experiment.

It is not the case that John Stuart Mill enfranchised women in New Zealand and Australia, as William Pember Reeves would have it; but Mill created the intellectual underpinning in which the proposition could realistically be introduced into parliaments and debated. Suffrage activism played an enabling but not essential role: the WCTU acted to put the solution before a wide public and make it acceptable to them. When the WCTU realized that its *raison d'être* was damaging to the suffrage cause, it pushed ahead with suffrage, leaving prohibition behind, suggesting that prohibition may not have been the main attraction of the temperance unions. Perhaps they were just the only feminist organization in most towns, where an intelligent woman went for serious conversation, regardless of her views on alcohol. In some places there was a variety of organizations to choose from:

Victoria had an anti-Christian Victorian Women's Suffrage Society which blamed many of women's ills on the church; another organization in the state additionally promoted birth control.[45] Regardless of their make-up, none of the suffrage organizations held real power; they could, at best, have impeded women's suffrage by embarrassing pronouncements.

In terms of the great 'fault lines' which were impediments to women's suffrage elsewhere: class divisions were not sufficient to derail the measure; and race was a matter of little consequence (a formula had to be found to make the race issue go away). These enfranchisements do not support the theory that national crisis is necessary for women's enfranchisement, but they certainly took place at the time of the development of new nations, and the making of new constitutions.

The passage of equalizing legislation was eased by the fact that it would not in fact bring electoral equality because of the vast population disparity between men and women in the first states to enfranchise women. Attracted by mining and other male pursuits, there were simply more men than women; in South Australia there were 78,972 males as against 59,044 females on the electoral roll in 1896. In Western Australia in 1899 out of 171,000 less than 59,000 were females.[46] The gender disparity was closer in the other four states but nowhere did women outnumber men as they did in Britain. Anyone perusing the England and Wales census report for 1891 could reflect that throughout the whole of the century the female population had been greater than the male.[47] In nations where there was a preponderance of women, enfranchising them equally gave them the majority power; this was not the case in places of early enfranchisement such as the Antipodes and the western United States.

Part of the objective of enfranchising women was to introduce supposedly feminine values to rugged pioneer lands and therefore to aid settlement, family life, and an increase in population, so it was obvious that gender disparity would not last. But if a high preponderance of women in politics was going to prove a problem it would be a problem delayed, causing no difficulties for the generation that enfranchised them, so it was not a disincentive.

Ultimately, the winning argument was political expediency. In New Zealand, South Australia, and Western Australia the vote was awarded to ease established politicians out of a tight corner. This alone would not be sufficient in every country, or it would have been adopted by the Tories in Britain after 1884, but their conservatism precluded it. In the politically fluid assemblies of Australasia, where political boundaries were less clearly drawn, it was easier to adopt flexible solutions.

The political result, in the first national elections where women voted, were what was to be found elsewhere: those women who took an interest in politics found themselves divided from other women over matters of principle in the same way that men were divided; there was no solidarity of gender. Other women, those who showed no great interest in political issues 'are content to vote with their mankind or their class' according to Pember Reeves.[48]

6

'In with our women' in the Western US

'Why, Lizzie, thee will make us ridiculous'

Two women were sitting talking in the entrance to the British Museum on a June day in 1840; the younger, Elizabeth Cady Stanton, was 25 with black ringlets. The other, Lucretia Mott aged 47, was a petite matron wearing a white cap and plain, sober dress, with a white kerchief across her shoulders that identified her as a Quaker. They had just walked arm-in-arm down Great Queen Street and now they sat talking for hours about the curtailed rights of women, about which they had just received a sharp lesson.

Mott was born in Nantucket and educated at a Quaker school. She learned early the lessons of gender inequality when as a young teacher she was paid half the salary male teachers were receiving. She married James Mott in 1811; he was another high-minded Quaker who had been a cotton merchant but left this profitable trade as he did not wish to benefit from the products of slavery. The couple settled in Pennsylvania where, in keeping with the commitment to anti-slavery, their home became a sanctuary for runaway slaves. Lucretia became an official Quaker minister in 1821; she and her husband later allied themselves with the liberal 'Hicksite' branch of the Quakers, against the more fundamentalist and evangelical wing of the sect. When in London at the World's Anti-Slavery Convention she was described as 'the lioness of the Convention... thin, petite, dark-complexioned woman, about fifty years of age. She has striking intellectual features and bright, vivacious eyes.'[1]

Elizabeth Cady Stanton had a grander background, as the daughter of a US congressman (later a high court judge). It was said that the death of her brother drove her to excel in every area in which he had done, in an attempt to compensate her father for his loss. She was sent to school, receiving a

good education for the 1830s, studied law in her father's office and determined to reverse discriminatory legislation against women. Earlier in 1840,
the year of the London anti-slavery convention at which she met Lucretia
Mott for the first time, she married fervent anti-slavery orator and lawyer
Henry Brewster Stanton. Her behaviour at the time of the convention was
described as 'prankish and immature', she was 'a plump young bride' who
was told not to bother the saintly Mrs Mott.[2]

Mott was a delegate to (and Cady Stanton an attender at) the convention
in London, called to discuss slavery, seven years after abolition in British overseas territories. The leader of the delegation, William Lloyd Garrison, was
delayed and was not there when seven of his colleagues turned up, of whom
four were women. The British organizers had no conception that women
might be involved in a cause to the extent of having full speaking and voting
rights. Before the convention, emissaries of the arrangements committee were
sent to the American women to persuade them not to attend. Samuel Prescod,
who was a Jamaican, said it would lower the dignity of the convention and
bring ridicule on the whole thing if ladies were admitted. He was tartly told,
'that similar reasons were urged in Pennsylvania for the exclusion of coloured
people from our meetings'.[3]

Lucretia Mott argued that the delegates had no discretionary powers, they
had been elected to represent certain societies and it was their duty to submit
their credentials. The responsibility of rejection must fall to the convention.
The women therefore knew what to expect and were duly refused admission
as delegates when they appeared at the gathering in Freemason's Hall in
Great Queen Street on 12 June 1840. They were obliged to sit 'behind the
bar' in the ladies' section and politely escorted to their seats curtained off
from participating delegates. The first day was taken up with debate on the
'women question' which the proponents of women's rights lost to opponents who considered that for women to be publicly involved was 'not only a
violation of the customs of England, but of the ordinance of Almighty God'.[4]

The matter had therefore already been put to a vote and decided upon
when William Lloyd Garrison, the prophet of immediate and unconditional
abolition of slavery (as against those who believed in gradual emancipation)
arrived, delayed on his voyage from America by a becalmed ship. Garrison
had previously attempted to insist on the rights of women in the American
Anti-Slavery Society, which eventually split the organization, so he was no
stranger to this controversy. Garrison could not re-address a motion which
had already been decided by the convention, so he took his place with the

women. He explained, 'It was said that the London meeting resolved from the beginning to keep out other questions—to discuss nothing but Anti-slavery. Then I turn to that convention and tell them that, in excluding women, they *did* undertake to settle another great question.'[5] Garrison wrote to his wife, 'In what assembly, however august or select, is that almost peerless woman Lucretia Mott, not qualified to take an equal part?'[6]

Fortified by such lively proceedings, Lucretia Mott and her young friend Elizabeth Cady Stanton discussed the need for a campaign based solely on women's rights. Stanton would later declare: 'the movement for women's suffrage, both in England and America, may be dated from this World's Anti-Slavery Convention.'[7] She is extending her remit when she dates the British movement from this point, though doubtless such a British pioneer as Anne Knight was stimulated to continued action by both the exclusion of women, and the vigorous response thus evoked, from some of the men present as well as the women.

Mott and Stanton did not meet as a matter of course, as they were of different wings of the anti-slavery movement that did not hold conventions together in the US. They corresponded and mentioned an intention to hold a woman's convention, but Mott was deeply involved in abolition work and Stanton had turned to the law to redress the wrongs of women; in the 1840s she managed to secure the passage of a statute in New York ensuring property rights for married women.

Stanton and her husband settled in upstate New York in 1847. She was visited the following year by Lucretia and James Mott who were travelling to see settlements of escaped slaves. Over tea with Lucretia's sister Martha and two other Quakers, they determined to put into effect the resolution that they had taken previously to hold a women's rights convention, and picked Seneca Falls as a convenient location. They placed an advertisement in the county newspaper, the *Seneca County Courier*, and contacted others. Those who attended were generally supporters of abolitionism and temperance and belonged to liberal theological sects—the sort of middle-class, reform-minded people who featured prominently in upstate New York culture. Roughly a quarter were Quakers and the meeting was chaired by their co-religionist James Mott.

Stanton wrote the Seneca Falls Declaration of Sentiments that begins: 'We hold these truths to be self-evident: that all men and woman are created equal . . .' Thus the declaration was a challenge to the US Declaration of Independence, just as Olympe de Gouges' *Declaration* and Mary Woolstonecraft's *Vindication* had been challenges to the 'rights of man', putting the Seneca Falls in a defiantly democratic tradition. It declared that 'the history of mankind is a history of repeated injuries and usurpations on the part of man toward woman.' The first of these, in a list including marriage, employment, and property rights, is: 'He has never permitted her to exercise her inalienable right to the elective franchise.'[8]

Lucretia Mott had been against putting a demand for the franchise in the declaration, thinking it unrealizable: 'Why, Lizzie, thee will make us ridiculous,' she said to Stanton.[9] Stanton's keynote speech, in the Seneca Falls Wesleyan Chapel on 19 July 1848, set out the current situation as regards the ballot: 'All white men in this country have the same rights, however they may differ in mind, body or estate.' Gender should therefore be no bar, nor any other qualification as, in an expression of racial and class superiority that was to recur in the movement, she said, 'We need not prove ourselves equal to [the great nationalist] Daniel Webster to enjoy this privilege, for the ignorant Irishman in the ditch has all the civil rights he has. We need not prove our muscular power equal to this same Irishman to enjoy this privilege, for the most tiny, weak, ill-shaped stripling of twenty-one has all the civil rights of the Irishman.'[10]

The Declaration of Sentiments was accepted unanimously by those present though only a third of them, sixty-eight women and thirty-two men, were prepared to put their names to it. A series of declarations relating to equality and property rights were approved unanimously; the only one which was not was the resolution for the vote for women, 'That it is the duty of the women of this country to secure to themselves their sacred right to the elective franchise.' This was won by only a narrow margin with the active endorsement of Frederick Douglass, a black abolitionist of high standing. The struggle for the principle of the vote, even in such a high-minded gathering, showed how far women suffragists would have to travel in the US.[11] It is also indicative of future divisions that the suffrage resolution specifically called upon *women* to fight for their rights, while others called for the efforts of both men and women to, for example (in a resolution of Lucretia Mott's), secure equal participation with men in the ministry, trades, professions and commerce.

Stanton and Mott therefore had a difference of opinion over men and women, Stanton noting approvingly that man 'does accord to woman moral superiority', while Mott said to a later convention that she 'did not believe in holding up women as superior to man' as, given the temptations of power, women could be as tyrannical as men.[12] The notion of women as superior

moral beings was to have positive and negative effects on the suffrage movement in the US.

Another meeting was held in Rochester, New York the following month,
and a convention took place in Salem, Ohio in 1850 (at which men were
not permitted to speak). Douglass secured the support of various Negro
conventions in 1848 and a national convention at Worcester, Massachusetts
followed in October 1850 that adopted the resolution that 'political rights
acknowledge no sex and that therefore the word "male" should be stricken
from every state constitution.' So the franchise was early seen as a state
measure which would ultimately be a national policy. Further conventions
were held throughout the decade; Lucretia Mott was elected president of
the 1852 convention at Syracuse, New York.

The reaction from the press to these meetings was dismissive. The *Rochester
Advertiser* said they were 'extremely dull and uninteresting and, aside from
the novelty, hardly worth notice'. The *Mechanics Advocate* in Albany directly
attacked the Declaration, saying, 'Every truehearted female will instantly
feel that this is unwomanly, and that to be practically carried out, the males
must change their position in society to the same extent in an opposite direction, in order to enable them to discharge an equal share of the domestic
duties which now appertain to females, and which must be neglected to a
great extent, if women are allowed to exercise all the "rights" that are
claimed by these Convention-holders.'[13]

The essential objection that underpinned male opposition to women's
taking an independent role in society was enshrined in law as the doctrine of
coverture that had been exported to the British colonies as part of William
Blackstone's *Commentaries on the Laws of England*. This work, based on English
common law and Blackstone's interpretation of a model society, had been
taken up enthusiastically by such legally-minded founding fathers of the new
nation as John Adams and was frequently cited in Supreme Court decisions.
'Husband and wife are one person in law,' Blackstone averred, and that pro-
nouncement weighed heavily on nineteenth-century suffrage campaigners in
the US, giving a legal justification to political opposition to women's rights.

'No, sister, no.'

Elizabeth Cady Stanton was to form an important and enduring partnership with another Quaker, Susan B. Anthony, who was born in Adams,

Massachusetts, in 1820 into a mill and factory-owning family; they were later to move to Rochester, New York. Anthony was brought up in a tradition of active Quaker women and received as good an education as any of the boys of her family. She taught for ten years then, from 1848, became a temperance activist, joining the Daughters of Temperance and rising to be a state leader of the movement. When she met Elizabeth Cady Stanton in March 1851 it was the start of a long emotional and political relationship. They became close friends and allies who planned, wrote, shared platforms and drew up resolutions together. Stanton said that the two of them worked like a married couple, freely indulging in criticism of each other in private but with 'the feeling that we must have no differences in public'. Stanton was confined at home by motherhood (she gave birth to her seventh and last child in 1859), so Anthony would visit her at Seneca Falls: 'Night after night by an old-fashioned fireplace, we plotted and planned the coming agitation; how, when, and where each entering wedge could be driven, by which women might be recognised and their rights secured.'[14]

They worked together in the New York State temperance movement then, after 1854, to reform the 1848 Married Women's property law, thereby widely increasing the activities in which a married woman could legally engage; after 1860 women were able to own their own property, engage in business, and to sue (and be sued) in a court of law. Other states followed suit, and so rights in marriage and property preceded concerted demands for the national franchise, so the vote in America would consolidate gains already made in the position of women.

The work of Stanton and Anthony on the law in New York set a template for later activity: Stanton, who was the better theorist, researched, wrote, and planned at home; while Anthony, who was single and without family demands, was the travelling activist. Anthony worked as agent of the American Anti-Slavery Society in New York State from 1856 until the outbreak of the war, thus she embodied as an activist the preoccupations of socially committed women of the second half of the nineteenth century: anti-slavery, temperance, and suffrage.

'Temperance' was a misnomer for what had been a movement to promote the temperate use of alcohol (one presumes on the model of Jesus and the disciples). By the time Anthony was active the temperance movement was anything but temperate, having moved away from the pledge of abstinence from distilled spirits towards the more extreme position of total abstinence. The objective of the movement was transmuted over time from the encouragement of abstinence as a personal choice to an intention to impose the prohibition of alcohol on the nation, temperate and intemperate drinkers alike. Historians take differing views of prohibitionists, some seeing them as puritans seeking to impose a narrow rural mentality on sophisticated and burgeoning urbanites; and others who see both prohibition and women's suffrage as progressive forces attempting to cleanse the moral and political life of the nation.[15] This also reflects contemporary regional differences: eastern states tended to see women as narrow bigots, messing with matters beyond their understanding; in the west, women were a civilizing force.

Women had been deeply involved in the anti-slavery movement and notions of women's rights owed much to discourse in the anti-slavery debates. As US historian Ross Evans Paulson points out, even the word 'emancipation' was borrowed from the lexicon of abolitionism.[16] Comparisons with a literal condition of slavery were the standard fare, such as the first words of the *History of Woman Suffrage*, 'The prolonged slavery of woman is the darkest page in human history.'[17]

The weight of tradition was against both women's suffrage and the end of slavery. As a Special Committee to the New Jersey Assembly reported in 1857, 'We find that from the beginning of the World to the present day, women, whether under the laws of the Creator—the Patriarchal government, the Mosical and Levitical law, or the more benign influence of the Christian designation, has ever, in the affairs of government, been assigned a position subordinate to that of man.'[18] The same, of course, could be said of slavery, and of drinking alcohol, all were long sanctified by precedent, by the Bible and classical literature. In opposing any one of them reformers were challenging fundamental beliefs that had the validation of holy writ; they were asserting the primacy of their own conscience over traditional values. Crusaders for any of these need not be informed by the practices of the past, they were truly modern and revolutionary in their outlook.

Even in the early days of the movement, there were those who wished to separate abolitionism from women's suffrage. Frances D. Gage, chairing her first public meeting at the Akron Conference in Ohio in May 1851 described the convention as being dominated by ministers of different sects, variously talking about the superior intellect of man, the manhood of Christ, and the 'sin of the first mother'. Few women spoke and when they did it was uncertainly and with a hum of tittering and barracking from members of the public who had come to the convention for a novel entertainment. In Gage's account the meeting was getting out of hand on the second day. A tall, gaunt black woman attended the convention, perhaps the only black woman there. Sojourner Truth, well known as a freed slave who was an evangelical preacher, had quietly sat through most of the convention, during the intermissions selling copies of her autobiography *The Narrative of Sojourner Truth*, a work she had dictated to a supporter as she was illiterate.

Gage wrote how people had approached her during the convention, asking her to keep Sojourner Truth from speaking. As she paraphrased their concerns, 'Don't let her speak, Mrs Gage, it will ruin us. Every newspaper in the land will have our cause mixed up with abolition and niggers, and we shall be utterly denounced.' Gage refused to give assurances that she would not let the black woman speak, and when Truth rose she called the meeting to order. Truth was a commanding presence, standing almost six foot tall with a powerful speaking voice and an idiosyncratic delivery. As Gage described it, 'At her first word there was a profound hush. She spoke in deep tones, which though not loud, reached every ear in the house, and away through the throng at the doors and windows.'[19]

Truth said, 'I think that 'twixt the niggers of the South and the women of the North all talking about rights, the white man will be in a fix pretty soon. But what's all this about? That man over there says that women need to be helped into carriages and lifted over ditches, and to have the best place everywhere. Nobody helps me into carriages or over mud puddles, or gives me any best place. Ar'n't I a woman?' She described her work in the fields and the birth of her children who were sold into slavery. 'If my cup won't hold but a pint and yours holds a quart, wouldn't you be mean not to let me have my half-measure full?'[20]

This was a much mythologized speech and consequently has been picked over by scholars who question, for example, whether Truth actually said the precise words 'Ar'n't I a woman?' as it was only in Gage's account, written some twelve years later, that this precise phrase occurs, not in three contemporary newspaper accounts.[21] The general tenor, however, is uncontested: Sojourner Truth challenged the underlying principle of the convention's claim to represent women at all if it did not represent poor working women; furthermore she embodied the truth they wished to avoid: that if they were radical abolitionists calling for the vote for women, that meant black women too.

Sojourner Truth was born a slave in New York State in 1797 with the name Isabella Baumfree; she had several masters and five children by a fellow slave. She was distressed when a son was sold off to a plantation owner in Alabama but, after New York abolished slavery in 1827, Quaker friends helped her to win her son back through the courts. She moved to New York City and worked as a servant, there coming into contact with evangelical religion. She had had visions and heard voices since childhood, and in New York City she became associated with a charismatic, evangelical sect and began preaching in the streets. Obeying what she believed to be a call to travel and preach throughout the land, she left New York in 1843 and became an itinerant preacher, now taking the name Sojourner Truth. In the same year she was introduced to abolitionism at a utopian community in Massachusetts, starting a lifelong association with the movement. She supported herself by selling copies of her autobiography to which William Lloyd Garrison had contributed a preface, so she was already involved with the people who would contribute to the women's rights movement before it had started in earnest. She was associated with the cause of women's suffrage from that first meeting in 1851, encouraged by suffrage leaders who recognized that her magnetic attraction and bold speaking style added much-needed zest to their presentations.

Some anti-slavery campaigners were also dubious about the merits of going in with feminists. The popular anti-slavery poet Lydia Sigourney questioned if it was proper

> For women's rights to clamour loud,
> And dare the throng, and face the crowd?
> Or wrapped in wild desire to roam
> Forfeit those charities of home,
> That pain can soothe, and grief control,
> And lull to harmony the soul? –
>   No, sister, no.[22]

As so often happened in suffrage movements, war hastened the pace. In the Civil War of 1861–5 some women fought and women in general made well-appreciated contributions to the cause in which their state was involved. Sojourner Truth helped to recruit black men to help the war effort; and she and Stanton worked in the Women's Loyal National League to gather signatures to persuade Congress to emancipate slaves. Stanton and Anthony had founded the League, the first organization to petition Congress to make emancipation permanent and universal in a constitutional amendment. The Thirteenth Amendment to the Constitution

abolished slavery, a long-awaited victory for the abolitionists who num-
bered so many women among their ranks.

After Lincoln's assassination in April 1865, his successor President Andrew
Johnson welcomed the readmission of Confederate states to the union and
during the period of reconstruction in 1865–6 they passed laws restricting
the rights of Negroes, the so-called 'Black Codes' that virtually reproduced
slavery. The war seemed to have been fought and won for nothing. The solution was to give the vote to black men, with a Fourteenth Amendment, which
would shore up the Republican Party, against the southern Democrats.

It was an obvious move to link the two issues of rights for black people
and for women, given the close association between abolitionists and wom-
en's campaigners. In keeping with this, Stanton and Anthony converted
their organization into the American Equal Rights Association in May 1866
with Lucretia Mott as president and Frederick Douglass as one of the vice
presidents.

There were tensions from the start over the Fourteenth Amendment to
enfranchise all men; an amendment which Stanton opposed. President
Johnson and the Republicans would not give white women the vote: in
the South such women would probably be Democrats, which would again
imbalance the polls against Republicans, so women's suffrage was not on
their agenda. The mood was altering between white women who were dif-
fident about fighting for the rights of mainly uneducated black men; and
black men who showed no enthusiasm for the rights of white ladies who
seemed to have comfort enough, compared with their own lives.

Kansas and equal rights

The empowering effect of the women's rights meetings that were held in
the 1850s was realized for the first time in Kansas where the territory was
fast approaching the level of social order and organization necessary for
statehood. Once the argument was won within their boundaries, the next
step was to frame a constitution acceptable to Congress.

Kansas became a focus for national attention as the first state to vote on
women's suffrage in 1867. The legislature submitted two constitutional
amendments to the electorate, supported by the two main parties. The
Republicans proposed enfranchising black men, and so proposed eliminating the word 'white' from the constitution. The Democrats therefore,

taking a step further in order to turn a possibly winning amendment into a losing one, proposed additionally to strike out the word 'male' and thus enfranchise women, even though they had previously declared their opposition to women's suffrage. Finally the Republicans accepted this smart piece of political manoeuvring and gave the comprehensive amendment lip-service. Thus the democrats were not, as a party, in favour of their own comprehensive amendment that was going before the voters and neither were the Republicans. Having superior moral values did suffrage campaigners no good; when confronted with real political jousting of this nature, their only recourse was to get involved with politics in the world where it was really practised.

Activist women gravitated towards Kansas, starting with Lucy Stone and her husband Henry Blackwell who travelled across the state by open wagon, addressing suffrage and town meetings. She believed the measure for black and women's suffrage would be sure to pass, they just had to keep it before the voters through the summer until the vote. Lucy Stone had been assured by the Republican leadership that they would furnish means of transport and other facilities for women's suffrage speakers, and would make all the appointments and open meetings for them. She urged Reverend Olympia Brown, the first woman ordained as a Universalist (Unitarian) minister and a keen suffragist, to go to Leavenworth to begin a tour. Arriving at Leavenworth, Brown found that the Republican organization knew nothing of any arrangement with Lucy Stone but a couple of meetings were hastily arranged; at Lawrence she found the same situation, and she had to use her own resources and hold a meeting at the Universalist church. The Revd Brown's campaign proceeded in the same way from town to town: the Republicans did not feel obliged to put themselves out, though there was often local support.

The conditions in the state were not conducive to what were seen to be largely arguments of principle: many men had been killed in the war and in conflicts with lawless elements; the crops had been destroyed by grasshoppers that season; malaria and other diseases were taking their toll on the pioneers; there was little public transport and the roads were so bad as to be in some cases non-existent. Olympia Brown described the experiences of women on the suffrage circuit:

> There were good men in Kansas in those days, and although securing conveyances by chance, sometimes riding with rough men, Indians or Negroes—anybody that would go there—there was not one instance on the part of

these men of rudeness or discourtesy or anything but the utmost kindness and apparent interest in the success of the campaign. Often men would leave their work, sorghum boiling in the kettle or the ploughing of the field, and borrow a horse or a wagon to take the speaker on. The interest that these men took in the cause was most encouraging and inspiring.[23]

In autumn 1867 the early stalwarts were joined by Elizabeth Cady Stanton and Susan B. Anthony. Their main ally in Kansas was George Francis Train, a man who had become rich dealing in shipping and railways and who hoped to become United States president. Train, who advocated votes for women but not for 'low-down nigger men', became their friend and financial supporter.[24] Train's unsophisticated message was presented in an epigram:

> My mission to Kansas breaks the white women's chains
> Three cheers for virtue and beauty and brains.[25]

Other activists, including Lucy Stone, would not deal with him. In the end, both Negro suffrage and women's suffrage were defeated in Kansas, where experiences had laid bare an already existing racial fault-line in the suffrage movement. These came to a head at meetings of the Equal Rights Association such as that in New York City in May 1867. Anthony had asked Truth to come and Stanton had her as a houseguest.

The Fourteenth Amendment had recently introduced the world 'male' into the constitution for the first time, and was due to be ratified. Sojourner Truth said, 'here is a great stir about coloured men getting their rights, but not a word about the coloured women.' Truth shrewdly said she wanted to keep arguing for women's suffrage before the political climate changed. White women needed the vote, but black women needed it more, having less education and a more limited choice of jobs. She depicted black men as idlers, living off their womenfolk. The most important right she could have, she insisted, was merely the right to equal pay, not to be paid half what a man received: women's suffrage was about making changes to the whole economy to make life fairer for women. 'If coloured men get their rights, and not coloured women theirs, you will see the coloured man will be masters over the women, and it will be just as bad as it was before.'[26]

Later in the conference George T. Downing took the floor and asked Stanton if she opposed the enfranchisement of black man if women did not get the vote at the same time. Stanton said she would not trust black men to make laws for her because 'degraded, oppressed himself, he would be more despotic with the governing power than even our Saxon rulers are'. In default of universal suffrage, she preferred an educational franchise so 'this incoming tide of ignorance, poverty and vice' would be outweighed by the 'virtue, wealth and education of the women of the country'.[27]

The black woman was now truly outcast: as a woman, as a Negro, and as uneducated. Negroes and women currently had no vote; but even if Stanton's principle were accepted so that educated men and women, black and white, *were* enfranchised, then poor, illiterate Sojourner Truth would still be excluded, notwithstanding that she had served so well as a symbolic black woman at Stanton's meetings.

Despite a reaffirmation of the call for the enfranchisement of all women and black men, the meeting ended with its uncomfortable questions still unanswered: were women's suffragists in favour of black male suffrage or not? As Sojourner Truth's biographer Nell Irvin Painter wrote of Stanton and Anthony, 'As they pulled farther away from the ideals of universal suffrage, their language became increasingly nativist, racist and classbound.'[28] Railing against the waves of immigrants who were entering America from Ireland, Africa, Germany, and China, Stanton expressed her disgust at an 1869 conference held in Washington DC that 'Patrick and Sambo and Hans and Yung Tung, who do not know the difference between a monarchy and a republic' should make laws for women who were excluded from the ballot. How could American politicians 'make their wives and mothers the political inferiors of unlettered and unwashed ditch-diggers, boot-blacks, butchers and barbers, fresh from the slave plantations of the South and the effete civilisations of the Old World?'[29]

Her old ally and supporter of women's suffrage, the black leader Frederick Douglass, at a later meeting was to deplore the bigotry, but he defended the woman: 'Let me tell you that when there were few houses in which the black man could have put his head, this woolly head of mine found a refuge in the house of Mrs Elizabeth Cady Stanton, and if I had been blacker than sixteen midnights, without a single star, it would have been the same.' Susan Anthony, defending the proposition of women first, argued from education: 'We say, if you will not give the whole loaf of suffrage to the entire people, give it to the most intelligent first. If intelligence, justice and morality are to have precedence in the Government, let the question of the woman be brought up first and that of the Negro last.' Striking a gender blow at Douglass, and picking up his theme of regard for Stanton, she jibed, 'Mr Douglass talks about the wrongs of the Negro; but with all the outrages that he today suffers, he would not exchange his sex and take the place of Elizabeth Cady Stanton.'[30]

Some, such as Lucy Stone, applauded the Amendment to enfranchise black men, as a genuine if partial democratic advance, but the mood was divided. White female suffragists such as Stanton and Anthony blamed male abolitionists for betraying the women suffrage cause; black and white abolitionists felt betrayed by the women who they felt should have been united in applauding an abolitionist victory for black men; black women had been betrayed by both: women who would no longer support the black cause and abolitionists who would no longer support the women's cause. Frances Harper, a black woman, expressed her disappointment: 'When it was a question of race, [I] let the lesser question of sex go. But the white women all go for sex, letting race occupy a minor position.'[31]

Once the alliance between abolitionists and women's rights was destroyed, the forces of women's suffrage were further divided by a split between suffrage leaders in 1869. The National Woman Suffrage Association was New York based and run by Stanton and Anthony and was supposedly 'all-woman', Democrat in politics, and not interested in black male suffrage. 'I protest', said Stanton, 'against the enfranchisement of another man of any race or clime until the daughters of Jefferson, Hancock and Adams are crowned with all their rights.'[32] It attracted the young, radical, and educated and was prepared to challenge marriage legislation, supporting reform of the divorce laws, and was critical of the church. Their strategy was to have Congress enact national legislation to enfranchise women. Stanton was the writer and editor of their newspaper uncompromisingly titled *The Revolution*, started in 1868 and devoted to suffrage and other progressive causes. Anthony was the publisher and business manager and it was financially backed by George Francis Train. The paper folded after three years but it had produced a valuable forum for Stanton and Anthony.

In retaliation, Lucy Stone and Henry Blackwell set up the American Woman Suffrage Association in 1869. Representing the Boston elite, it supported black male suffrage, the Republican Party and the church, but it concentrated on the vote and paid no attention to such issues as the working conditions of lower-class women. Strategically it believed in a state-by-state cumulative achievement of the vote. Overall, the AWSA was more respectable and gradualist than its rival; their paper was the *Woman's Journal*, supporting the sanctity of family life. Sojourner Truth tried to stay out of the conflict and attended the National Woman Suffrage Association but settled with the AWSA eventually; Frances Harper also went with the AWSA.

It was customary to have male presidents of ladies associations, so despite their supposedly all-female membership, the American Woman Suffrage Association invited the Reverend Henry Ward Beecher head of the fashionable and very successful Plymouth Church, to be its president. The titular head of the National Woman Suffrage Association was Theodore Tilton, a journalist and disciple of Beecher's; and the reverend had, in fact, married Theodore Tilton to his wife Elizabeth, usually known as Lib, in 1855. However, roughly a year before he became titular head of one of the two leading women's organizations in the US, the Revd Beecher started having sex with Lib Tilton, a relationship that was to enliven the subsequent decade of women's suffrage history.

Despite these two organizations, it was more localized activities that led to the first enfranchisements of women in the US in the nineteenth century, the first of which was in Wyoming.

Pioneers in Wyoming

One chill winter morning in 1963 the civic dignitaries of Wyoming gathered in front of the Capitol building in Cheyenne, to honour Esther Morris, a pioneer settler and suffragist. They unveiled a statue of her bearing a copy of the Bill of Rights in one hand and a bouquet of sage brush flowers in the other. The speeches were cut short because of the bitterly cold weather but the point was made: the statue confirmed in a solid medium what every Wyoming schoolchild knew: that Esther Morris had gained the vote for women. For the first time in the world, women were equal citizens, in 1869 in the territory of Wyoming.

Wyoming in the late 1860s had a population of around 8,000 but it was a territory crossed by many more people on their way further west, seeking the riches of California or freedom from religious persecution. The 1860s saw the advance of the railroad with its accompanying 'hell on wheels': the railroad workers, land speculators, and their camp followers offering liquor, sex, and gambling. Hordes of adventurers arrived in Wyoming to dig or sift for gold and had no need of complex forms of government that would provide for schools and a centralized administration; they were there to strike it rich and move on, they had no interest in the viability of settled communities.

To bring some kind of order to this chaos, a territorial government was set up with a governor and council secretary sent from Washington DC, with a territorial legislature of nine elected members. One of the more surprising events in the legislature's first term was that council president William H. Bright, a mine and saloon owner, introduced a women's suffrage amendment on 27 November 1869 and it was later passed by a vote of six in favour, two against (with one absentee). The members of the upper house then passed it by a vote of seven to four.[33] It became law on 10 December 1869.

Such dissent as there was had the air of jocularity, such as an unsuccessful wrecking amendment making the bill apply only to 'coloured women and squaws'.[34] In fact, finally, the only difference from Bright's original proposal was that where he had recommended the vote at 18, a successful amendment increased it to 21. The bill enfranchised women on a simple residency qualification. This was thus not only an advanced piece of legislation in its conception, but also in its mechanism, at a time when most men in the world were enfranchised on a property or tax qualification. It would be sixty years before, for example, the UK enfranchised men and women equally on a residency qualification.

Many ascribed Bright's action in bringing forward the bill to the influence of his wife, Betty; he 'venerated his wife, and submitted to her judgement and influence more willingly than one could have supposed', according to one source. Another politician characterizes Bright as saying to his wife, who at 25 was twenty years younger than him, 'Betty, it's a shame that I should be a member of the legislature and make laws for such a woman as you. You are a great deal better than I am; you know a good deal more, and you would make a better member of the Assembly than I, and you know it.'[35]

Bright, who was 46 in 1869, had no formal education, a matter which always gave him a sense of inferiority and a desire to excel. In later years he wrote for the press and was always well informed, but he said of himself, 'I have never been to school a day in my life, and where I learned to read and write I do not know.'[36] He was from Virginia and had travelled to the west seeking opportunities which could not be found in the South which was recovering from the civil war; he settled in the gold rush town of South Pass. It is claimed that Bright, as president of the council, went in to see Edward M. Lee, the council secretary, and asked what he could do to secure his place in history. Lee told him to carry through a women's suffrage bill 'for you can thus distinguish yourself. The act will give you a lasting place in history, advertise the territory and promote immigration of people with capital.'[37] Lee certainly helped draft and carry through the legislation, of which he had previous experience: he had as a legislator in Connecticut put forward a women's suffrage bill that had failed. However, this account of his suggesting the issue to Bright (written by Lee's sister forty years later) has too much of an eye for historical outcomes to be trusted as an accurate record.

Other accounts favour the influence of Esther Morris who is said to have had recently heard Susan B. Anthony speak in Illinois; though another suffragist, Anne Dickinson, had lectured in Cheyenne in September 1869 and might have been thought of as more directly influential.[38] Esther Hobart Morris, née McQuigg, was born in 1814 in New York State. She was left an orphan at an early age (both 11 and 14 are recorded) and relied on her own resources. She was active in the anti-slavery cause as were so many suffragists; at one time an anti-slavery meeting was held in a Baptist church which pro-slavery thugs threatened to destroy. Esther, described as not yet 20, stood up in her pew and declared: 'This church belongs to the Baptist people and no one has the right to destroy it. If it is proposed to burn it down, I will stay here and see who does it.'[39]

The next time she is mentioned in the record she was carrying on a successful millinery business; at 28 she married a railway engineer. His death several years later gave her an education in the iniquities of the law of property regarding women, as her husband had left a large tract of land in Illinois and she, now with an infant son, had to struggle to gain her inheritance. She married a merchant, John Morris, and joined him in the town of South Pass in 1869.[40] She was said to have been a commanding presence; a big woman standing six foot tall, she was described as 'heroic in size, masculine in mind' and to have been a firm disciplinarian to her three sons.[41]

There is an apocryphal story that Esther Morris had a tea party at which she asked the two opposing candidates for the legislature to pledge themselves to work for women's suffrage, so that whoever won, women's suffrage would be passed.[42] An alternative story is of a dinner party of all candidates to the territorial legislature, at which she bound the two leaders.[43] Doubtless she had been involved in lobbying, but she had nothing to offer candidates in return for their support, and she always downplayed her contribution, three years later stating publicly, 'So far as woman suffrage has progressed in this Territory we are entirely indebted to men. To William H. Bright belongs the honour of presenting the woman suffrage bill.'[44] The tea party story can be traced to Bright's Republican opponent Herman G. Nickerson, writing fifty years later, after the death of Morris, Bright, and Lee, in an attempt to establish that Republicans secured the vote for women. After telling the tea-party story he wrote, 'Mrs Morris was an ardent Republican...the Republicans—the real authors of woman suffrage in Wyoming...woman suffrage in Wyoming, the state of its inception, thanks to the Republican party, is irrevocably established.'[45]

There are several answers to the question of why Bright proposed women's suffrage. He was a smart enough legislator to listen to the territory's experienced secretary Lee; and he also had a strong woman as a wife and respected other strong women including his South Pass neighbour Esther Morris. Robert Morris described how he and his mother visited the Brights and discussed women's suffrage, about which the politician was pleased to have their support.[46] Race also played a part, with the ballot having recently been given to black men. Bright was a Southerner who was said to have 'cherished a deep prejudice against giving the Negroes full rights of citizenship, maintaining that his mother and wife were far more capable of exercising such privileges than ignorant men'.[47] There was, as in most examples of the enfranchisement of women, a time of constitutional change after a period of national upheaval.

Bright was said to have secured the passage of the bill by the usual process of political bribery and power dealing: the legislature was entirely Democrat, the governor was Republican; Bright urged his more conservative colleagues to support an ultra-liberal measure with which they did not agree because the governor would be sure to veto it and this would show him up to be against progressive measures. While this has a certain cynical appeal, it is obvious that this was an extremely progressive legislature. The same body passed a bill protecting married women's property, allowing married women to make wills, enforcing equal pay for women teachers and forbidding inter-racial marriage (then considered to be a progressive and civilizing decision, in keeping with modern eugenics). There is every reason to think the Wyoming legislature was fully aware of its liberal objectives and set out to achieve them. Governor John A. Campbell, moreover, approved the measure after some consideration, so he was clearly not a die-hard conservative who was going to veto every progressive measure, and his political colleagues must have known this.

Another powerful argument was that it was an advertisement for the new territory of Wyoming that was so sparsely settled, despite the fact that thousands crossed it. Something was needed to make Wyoming more attractive so travellers would stay, and to make it more attractive to women was a long-term solution to the population problem.

The most important effect was that women's suffrage doubled the political power of the settled, married population (though absolute voting numbers were down, not up, when the first post-women's suffrage ballot took place).[48] Polling took place in a controlled and dignified manner, particularly compared to the previous election, putting the lie to the notion that the rough and tumble of election day would sully women's dignity. It may be that the presence of women made men behave with more decorum; or the desire to have women as voters at all was a desire to have a more restrained society.

Women were permitted to occupy public office by the same legislation and in 1870 Esther Morris was appointed justice of the peace by Edward M. Lee in South Pass City, making her the first female government official, and she is often referred to as the first woman judge. Her first case was to bring the justice of the peace she had replaced to trial for refusing to give up to her papers and items relating to the office she now occupied. Women were also eligible for jury service and they quickly distinguished themselves, particularly after an excessive number of women were called in Laramie by officials who deliberately selected women in the expectation that they would make fools of themselves. In fact the Grand Jury at Albany court, two-fifths of whom were women, improved court behaviour and made a visible change in the town, creating a frontier legend: the tough-minded women jurors who cleaned up Laramie. The attitude of women themselves is demonstrated by a letter from Amalia Post, wife of a Cheyenne businessman, to her sister in Vermont: 'I suppose you are aware that Women can hold any office in this territory I was put on the Grand Jury. I am intending to vote this next election makes Mr Post very indignant as he thinks a Woman has no rights.'[49]

Women's emancipation in Wyoming then started going into reverse: women served on juries in 1870 and 1871 until a new judge declared that jury service was not an adjunct to suffrage and Wyoming women did not serve on juries again until 1950.

Esther Morris was not reappointed when her term came to an end; she had been a justice for less than a year. Edward M. Lee, a friend to women's suffrage and to women in office, was removed on 18 February 1870 after a campaign by his enemies alleging moral misconduct. In 1871 the Democrats in a new legislature and upper house (who believed that woman voters had supported the Republicans) passed a bill to repeal women's suffrage, but Governor Campbell vetoed it. His veto was almost overridden (the upper house voted 5 to 4 to override, when 6 to 3 was needed).

Wyoming finally approached statehood in 1889. A state convention in Wyoming wrote women's suffrage into its draft constitution and sent the document to be ratified by Congress. Congress Democrats, wishing to resist the entry of what had become a Republican state, attempted to block entry on the basis of the women's suffrage clause. The response came back from Wyoming, 'We will remain out of the Union a hundred years rather than come in without woman suffrage.' Eventually Congress gave way and statehood was ratified in June 1890.[50] Wyoming came to revel in its celebrity over women's suffrage, taking the nickname 'The equality state' and adopting a seal depicting a lightly clad woman with the motto 'Equal Rights' behind her head, supported by a miner and a cowboy.

William H. Bright went bankrupt in 1870 and left Wyoming with his family the following year for Denver where he played a prominent role in the unsuccessful attempt to secure women's suffrage in 1877. He died in Washington DC in a rented house in 1912 and was buried in an unmarked grave. Esther Morris began to be heralded as the 'mother of women's suffrage' in the 1890s when her son Archibald Slack started using the term in his newspaper the *Cheyenne Sun*.[51] She died in Cheyenne on 2 April 1902 at the age of 87.

Morris thus had already begun her elevation to the hall of fame, a process considerably accelerated by Grace Hebard, an academic at the University of Wyoming who originally trained as a surveyor but became the university librarian and collected a vast amount of material on the history of the state. Unfortunately, her methods were far from objective; she was known for her manipulation of facts and she was said to have browbeaten people into agreeing with her theories.[52]

Hebard was in close contact with Herman Nickerson (who told the original of the tea party story) as he was president and she secretary of a commission to set up monuments on the Oregon trail. Her extant correspondence file with Nickerson is extensive, from 1915 to 1923, but is surprisingly silent on his account of the 'suffrage tea party', excepting a typescript of his letter to the newspaper in which he told the story. It seems unlikely that there would be no record of their exchanges over information so important to both of them, and more probable that correspondence showing Hebard's coaxing of Nickerson was removed by her from the record because it compromised the story.[53]

In her *How Woman Suffrage Came to Wyoming* of 1920 Hebard simply reported Nickerson's account of the tea party, as in his *Wyoming State Journal* account of 1919, without comment. By May 1928, the year after Nickerson's death, she was telling the story of Morris, inspired by hearing Susan B. Anthony, holding a dinner for forty people including Bright and Nickerson and causing them to pledge themselves for women's suffrage.[54] Over time Morris's unsought pre-eminence in securing the vote for women was assured

Figure 5. The seal of Wyoming after it became the 44th state of the US in 1890. A cowboy and a miner, representing the major industries, support the idealized image of a woman under the banner 'Equal Rights'. Wyoming is known as 'the Equality State'.

by constant repetition in popular form and such sources as Grace Hebard's standard school textbook history of Wyoming, which mentions Morris but not Bright.[55]

Morris was chosen in 1955 as Wyoming's outstanding deceased citizen and identical statues were subsequently erected of her in Statuary Hall in Washington DC and later in front of the state capitol. The inscription simply says she was 'proponent of the legislative act in 1869' which gave women equal rights in Wyoming.

Latter-day saints

Votes for women was tied up in Utah with the venerable tradition of polygamy, an established practice of the Church of the Latter Days Saints, otherwise known as the Mormons, who had settled in Utah in 1847 after fleeing persecution in the East. Far more than in other frontier communities, the Mormon families had faced hardships together. In most frontier regions there was a disproportionate number of men to women; in Utah family groups and caravans of families had made the trek west, giving them more numerical gender equality. Moreover, out of their previous persecution and a sense of shared values, they took a strong community to Utah, they did not have to build one. They were a 'chosen people'—they termed those not of the faith 'gentiles'—with a common outlook and style of life.[56] Polygamy, blessed by the Old Testament, was a practical solution to the problems of low population, in a society where women tended to outlive men and might live and die without marrying or having children if they had to wait for a single man.

When the Cullom Bill outlawing polygamy was introduced in Congress in 1869, it was intended to break the power of the Mormon elders. This was cloaked in language offensive to the Mormon idea of family life, comparing polygamy to slavery and prostitution. One way to respond to this rebuke was to demonstrate that Mormon women were among the most politically free in America. Brigham Young and the elders conceived women's suffrage during the time the Cullom Bill was under discussion. A negative report said of Young, 'The wily deceiver then evolved from his narrow soul the magnanimous scheme of enfranchising the women...Every Mormon citizen thus had his civil powers extended in correspondence with his numerous alliances,' the assumption being that women would vote as their husbands told them.[57] The law enfranchised women and men who had lived in the state for six months, though men additionally had to be taxpayers so it was in fact easier for women to qualify for the vote than men under the Mormons.

The territorial legislature in Utah therefore adopted women's suffrage on 12 February 1870 without, apparently, public discussion.[58] In Washington DC, the Cullom Bill passed on 23 March 1870 but Senate did not act on it. The tussle continued with a law passed by Congress in 1882 against polygamy, and a law in 1887, the Edmunds–Tucker Act, revoking women's suffrage in the Utah territory (Congress had control over territories). This was the only federal legislation on women's suffrage in the nineteenth century, and it was to disenfranchise women. The battle for Utah then included the US government's taking control of the property of the Mormon Church. Polygamy was finally abandoned in 1890 and when the power of the church had been capped, and Utah was allowed into the Union with a constitution enfranchising women, in 1896.

A women's suffrage proposal in the Dakota Territory legislature in 1872 lost by one vote; fourteen popular referendums were to be held in states west of the Mississippi on women's suffrage before the end of 1910. Such interest in the subject gives further evidence that it was the west that was the homeland of women's suffrage, not only reflecting local conditions in isolated states, but as a geographical entity.[59] Various reasons have been advanced for this phenomenon; Walter Prescott Webb in *The Great Plains* put forward what has been called 'the western thesis', that the geography itself of the west with its vast distances imposed a new pattern of settlement and living, while the scarcity of women meant they 'were very dear and were much sought after, prized, and protected by every man'.[60] This would not, however, of itself ensure the franchise for women—women in middle-class society in Boston were considered as precious as drawing room ornaments, but that did not secure them the vote.

One factor was the lack of social distinctions in frontier society: with the tough practical demands of daily living, practical abilities were admired, and the endurance of women equalled that of men. Secondary factors include the fact that in most frontier territories (Utah is an exception) there was a much lower population of women than men so their enfranchisement did not affect the balance of power in a place such as Wyoming where men outnumbered women by six to one: there were 6,650 males over the age of

10 in Wyoming in 1870, and 1,409 females.[61] The apparent lack of political ambition of women also came to endear them to political bosses; it was very early realized that women were not office seekers and therefore not in competition with the men who could give or deny them the vote.[62] Women were in one way the perfect electors for the party bosses: they cast their ballots but did not want to actually run the government or take any political jobs.

Alan Grimes, who wrote a classic work on women's suffrage, considers the imposition of the puritan ethic of order, religion, family cohesion, and temperate behaviour in the west was the key to the issue there. Women's influence was associated with the traditional puritan values which were being threatened by mid-European immigrants and by lawless adventurers. 'Though men conquered the wilderness, women made it inhabitable,' Grimes says.[63] Women were looked upon as the guardians of civilization; the demands of frontier life led men to hand over the field of culture and the work of civilizing their communities to women; these views were represented publicly by such women-friendly groupings as the Populist Party.

This is very plausible, though looking at Wyoming and Utah, it is more accurate to think of male power brokers enlisting women into the battle to civilize the frontier, with (usually) the involvement of active women who aspired to make a social contribution. There was also a need to populate the new-found territories, a need that could only be supplied by the introduction of more women who could be attracted to progressive states. Introducing women's suffrage was a way of saying that the west was not now the wild land it had been, but a place for families.

The eastern women's organizations made little of the battle for women's suffrage in Utah, feeling that a defence of the Mormons would be interpreted as a defence of their scandalous polygamous behaviour, a choice irony considering events that were already unfolding in their heartland.

Scandal in the East

The achievements of women's suffrage in the west should have inaugurated a period of steady advance for suffragists in the US. In fact the period following the 1869 enfranchisement in Wyoming on the supposedly progressive east coast was dominated by 'Mrs Satan', the notoriously libertine

Victoria Woodhull, and the adultery scandal involving the top leadership of both the American and National Associations.

In the 1870s Stanton and Anthony and their National Woman Suffrage Association needed a new strategy. Their 'New Departure' reasoned that advances in democracy with the fourteenth and fifteenth amendments guaranteeing citizenship and equality before the law, meant that there was no specific ban on women's citizenship and no state could deny women's right to vote. The principle was, then, that women already had the right to vote, they just had to exercise it.

In this policy they found themselves with a new hero: Victoria Claflin Woodhull, the first woman to stand as president of the United States. Woodhull was an old-style feminist committed to free love, communal living, and spiritualism, she did not really belong to the earnest world of women's campaigners of the mid-Victorian period, but as their high-minded commitments had not produced results they needed some excitement. 'All this talk of woman's rights is moonshine,' she declared, 'women have every right. They only have to exercise them.'[64]

Victoria was born in Homer, Ohio, on 23 September 1838 into the large and raucous Claflin family who at that time ran a mill. Deeply imbued with spiritualist and revivalist notions, she and her sister Tennessee, who was born in 1846, used to give demonstrations of clairvoyance and such events as tipping tables, summoning spirit music, and conducting séances. Victoria was described as a beautiful girl, and at 15 her parents consented to an offer of marriage from Canning Woodhull, a doctor from a wealthy family. After the wedding she found he was a drinker who had a habit of visiting brothels. When he decamped to live with a mistress, leaving Victoria with their first child, she went to the boarding house where they were staying and upbraided him in front of all the boarders who were gathered for dinner, shaming the mistress into leaving and Woodhull into returning with her. It was the first time she clearly took charge of her life; she then took various jobs as a cigar girl in a bar, a seamstress, and an actress.

Eventually she returned to live with her family who took to running a travelling medicine and fortune-telling show, then a quack cancer clinic, and she also set up as a spiritualist physician. She formed a relationship with a Colonel James Blood, another spiritualist with whom she travelled and worked and who told her of the new doctrine of women's rights. Victoria was poorly educated, but had a retentive mind and an active imagination so that anything she learned she could interpret and reissue in the light of her own experience. In keeping with the tradition of messy personal arrangements for leading feminists, Victoria divorced her husband, though she continued using his name; Blood divorced his wife, and though he and Victoria Woodhull were said to have married, no record of the marriage has been found.

As she told the story later, her spirit guide appeared and told her to go to New York City so she did so, with the family in tow, settling at 15, East 38th street, soon to be known as the site of a salon of radical thinkers presided over by Victoria. In 1868 she met Cornelius Vanderbilt, probably the richest man in America and an inveterate attender at séances and spiritualist gatherings. His introduction to the Claflin family was probably via Tennessee Claflin, formerly the clairvoyant wonder child, now in her twenties. It took little time for Victoria and Tennessee to captivate the 76-year-old widower; Tennessee went to bed with him and Victoria impressed him with spirit advice about the stock market. In return, Vanderbilt was generous to the sisters and gave them stock market tips for investments that Colonel Blood placed for them, making a fortune for the family, as Victoria discovered a natural talent for dealing in stocks and shares. With Vanderbilt's backing, Victoria and Tennessee (who now styled herself Tennie C.) set up the first brokerage office run by women in the US in 1870, Woodhull, Claflin & Co. Victoria, who had developed her connections with free-love advocates and political radicals, said 'We are doing daily more for women's rights, by practically exercising the right to carry on our own business, than the diatribes of papers and platform speeches will do in ten years.'[65]

In keeping with her radical ambitions, Victoria sent a letter to the *New York Herald*, published on 2 April 1870 and titled 'First Pronunciamento'. Victoria described herself as 'the most prominent representative of the only unrepresented class in the Republic'. Victoria Woodhull was not ignorant of the work of Susan B. Anthony, Elizabeth Cady Stanton, and Lucy Stone, she 'simply relegated them to second place' as her biographer Joanna Johnstone wrote. 'I now', she declared, with her talent for grandstanding, 'announce myself as candidate for the presidency.' In an editorial the *Herald* mocked 'suffrage tea parties' of the old guard of the movement and endorsed 'the merits of novelty, entertainment, courage and determination'.[66]

Victoria had her supporter Stephen Pearl Andrews write an intellectual underpinning of her campaign with the title 'The Tendencies of Government' over her signature. Victoria cultivated positive contacts with the press and had an instinctive understanding of how to make a truly American appeal of her can-do fighting spirit that impressed even her opponents. Journalists could not be relied upon to remain tame, however, and she needed her own mouthpiece, so Victoria and Tennie launched a newspaper, *Woodhull and Claflin's Weekly*, in May 1870.

The newspaper was prepared to be more intellectually daring than other publications, including in its pages Stephen Pearl Andrews' proposal for 'A United States of the World' and the equally improbable *Communist Manifesto* by Karl Marx and Frederick Engels, the first English edition of which was published by Victoria Woodhull in 1871. The content of the paper had at first been somewhat restrained: as well as news about Woodhull there had been articles on women in history, theatre reviews, spiritualism, fashion, and finance. As time went on, the paper was prepared to be more daring, including articles on 'The Social Evil' of prostitution that dwelt on the profits made in the trade and the exploitation of women. It recommended licensing brothels and ensuring the trade was fairer to its practitioners.

The leaders of the women's suffrage movement had exhausted themselves over the issue of black male suffrage; they were shocked at this outrageous self-publicist, but could not deny that her message was getting across. Woodhull had transcended the struggle between the conservatives and liberals by ignoring the issue of the black vote, for her the big question was women's rights as embodied in the person of Victoria Woodhull.

In an attempt to engage Victoria Woodhull with the established suffrage movement, Stanton wrote to her asking if her spirit guide could give any new arguments on the fourteenth and fifteenth amendments for their forthcoming convention. As the chief strategist of the women's suffrage movement, she had realized that Woodhull was saying just what the National Woman Suffrage Association said about the state of the constitution: that the fourteenth and fifteenth amendments could be interpreted as giving full citizenship rights, including the franchise, to women. They gave rights to 'persons' and women were persons.

Woodhull did not need the help of the suffrage associations for her next step, which was plotted with the advice of a new friend, Benjamin Butler, a former Civil War general and now representative to Congress from Massachusetts. She travelled to Washington DC and had a petition on the citizenship of women presented to the Senate and the House of Representatives on 22 December 1870. There had been no advance warning, opponents of women's suffrage were taken unawares and not organized to oppose progress of the petition to the Committee of the Judiciary. Victoria Woodhull was announced, on 10 January 1871, to address the House Judiciary Committee the following day on the subject of her petition.

The National Woman Suffrage Association was having some difficulty raising interest in its convention, to begin on 11 January 1871; the previous year's conference had been virtually ignored by the press; but their immediate thoughts were to distance themselves from Woodhull. Anthony described the confusion they felt: 'we had been preceded... a poor lone woman, without consultation even with any of those who had laboured for years in the great cause of female suffrage had already presented her petition to Congress'.[67]

Morally also she was questionable. Woodhull's main offence was association with her sister Tennessee, who had had an affair with Vanderbilt; her belief in free love; and the fact that she had invited her ex-husband Canning Woodhull to live with her and her family. This was in fact an act of charity towards an alcohol- and opium-addicted wreck of a man, but her detractors thought that living under the same roof with two men with whom she had had marital relations was tantamount to holding a public orgy.

However, sensible counsel prevailed and the ladies of the National Association postponed their convention to the afternoon and attended the Congressional Committee for the first personal appearance by a woman. Starting slowly and quietly, but then warming to a lucid argument, Woodhull presented the view that sex has nothing to do with the right to vote and begged the committee to recommend to Congress that the law be clarified in women's favour. The committee members listened politely and agreed to consider the petition. The matter had been refined to a simple case of justice before the law which was currently unclear.

The ladies who had previously been dubious about Woodhull now applauded her as the heroine of the hour and escorted her to the Lincoln Hall where they held their convention in the afternoon. They urged her to repeat her argument for the public platform. Again, she started unsteadily but her voice gained strength as she spoke and she won the enthusiasm of the hall. The rest of conference business was swept aside in emergency motions to adopt the Woodhull petition and urge clarification on Congress of the fourteenth and fifteenth amendments. The conference made it 'the duty of American woman... to apply for registration'.[68] After years of torpor, the suffrage argument was racing forward. The Judiciary Committee's report in late January merely said that Congress did not have the power to clarify the amendments as requested. A minority report, however, by

Benjamin Butler and William Loughridge, strongly argued in favour of women's suffrage.

Woodhull found new friends and supporters, but her higher profile now attracted criticism both from opponents of women's suffrage and from its conservative supporters such as Lucy Stone's American Woman Suffrage Association (still with the Revd Henry Ward Beecher as its president). Elizabeth Cady Stanton, to her credit, made a public defence of Victoria Woodhull:

> When the men who make laws for us in Washington can stand forth and declare themselves pure and unspotted from all the sins mentioned in the Decalogue, then we will demand that every woman who makes a Constitutional argument on our platform shall be as chaste as Diana...We have had enough women sacrificed to this sentimental, hypocritical prating about purity...This is one of man's most effective engines for our division and subjugation.'[69]

Meanwhile Theodore Tilton, titular head of the National Woman Suffrage Association, had been travelling on the lecture circuit to raise his professional reputation and he had urged his minister and friend Revd Henry Ward Beecher, head of the American Woman Suffrage Association, to visit Lib Tilton (also a women's suffrage activist) in order to comfort her in her loneliness. Beecher did so, and explained that the sexual expression of their divine love was as proper as a kiss or a handshake, and thus reassured by her spiritual mentor she went ahead and had an affair with him. An honest woman, Lib felt it was right to tell her husband of her divine love for their family friend, which he did not take well. Tilton was to find that Beecher had comforted other young wives from the church in a similar manner. Tilton told Elizabeth Cady Stanton of Beecher's infidelity with Lib, and by coincidence, on returning home from speaking with Stanton about it, found Susan B. Anthony with Lib. In a scene of some domestic consternation he upbraided Lib, so now most of the leaders of women's suffrage movement knew the story. Discussing the scenario together, Stanton and Anthony decided discretion was the best path and advised Tilton to keep quiet about this practice of a variety of 'free love' while Beecher was thundering from the pulpit about the sanctity of marriage and the sinfulness of sex outside of it. Lib Tilton wrote to her enraged husband, 'I feel that you are not in a condition of mind to lead the women's suffrage movement.'[70]

Stanton and Anthony had distanced themselves from the free-love doctrines of Victoria Woodhull and embraced a Victorian concept of the moral superiority of women and the sanctity of marriage. Now, with their failure either to condemn Beecher or to tolerate extra-marital sex, their only recourse was hypocrisy; Woodhull saw this clearly and chose to act.

Woodhull had been attacked in the person of a New Woman, Audacia Dangyereyes, in a novel, *My Wife and I* by Harriet Beecher Stowe, sister of Henry Ward Beecher. Woodhull was not able to take mockery and the caricature unnerved her. Stowe was also on the conservative side of the women's suffrage movement, along with her brother who was increasingly vulnerable as a growing number of people knew about his affairs with attractive parishioners. When another Beecher sister, Catherine, took it upon herself to lecture Victoria Woodhull on the sanctity of marriage life and the wickedness of her stand on free love and divorce, Woodhull could bear it no longer and informed an outraged Catherine Beecher that given her brother's conduct, her sentiments about marriage were unfortunate.

Victoria Woodhull was invited to address the National Association at their May meeting, though many members were disturbed at her sudden prominence and her reputation for outrage. Lucretia Mott was also unhappy about giving Woodhull pride of place, but Stanton intervened and on the day Woodhull sat between Stanton and the saintly Lucretia Mott on the stage. Woodhull did not disappoint; if Congress refused women electoral rights, she declaimed, 'We mean treason, we mean secession, and on a thousand times grander scale than was that of the South. We are plotting a revolution; we will overthrow this bogus republic and plant a government of righteousness in its stead.'[71] Amid the euphoria of the conference a number of resolutions were passed including one that called for the repeal of laws that restricted the legitimate adult search for happiness, a resolution that effectively pledged the convention to a defence of free love.

Subsequently a messy court case involving members of her family exposed the conflicts within Victoria's home life in New York, where she and Tennessee continued to support the entire extended family. Woodhull thought it time to respond to her critics, so she wrote a letter to the *New York Times* accusing them of hypocrisy: 'I know of one man, a public teacher of eminence, who lives in concubinage with the wife of another teacher of almost equal eminence. All three concur in denouncing offences against morality.'[72] This letter brought Theodore Tilton to her door, urging her to publish no more for fear of injuring the innocents: his children, Beecher's family, and the congregation. Before long he too had been captivated by Woodhull and he became her lover through the summer of 1871. Colonel

Blood, true to his free love principles, made no objection and Tilton made a lively addition to the radical circle meeting at 38th Street. Tilton wrote praising Woodhull in the magazine he now edited, *The Golden Age*, and wrote a biography of her.

Ever eager to go on the offensive, Woodhull hired the Steinway Hall to explain to her detractors exactly what her principles were regarding free love, marriage, divorce, and prostitution. She asked Henry Ward Beecher to introduce her to the audience—they had become friendly since she had been seeing Tilton, and may even have had sex. Beecher earned her enmity by refusing and Tilton presided over the meeting of 3,000 people. 'Yes, I am a free lover,' she said, in reply to a heckler, 'I have an inalienable, constitutional and natural right to love whom I may, to love as long or as short a period as I can, to change that love every day if I please, and with that right neither you nor any law you can frame have any right to interfere.'[73]

Her remarks, widely reported in the newspapers, were too much for their landlord; the family was evicted from the 38th Street house, the landlord not wanting to be associated with the taint of free love, and Woodhull settled them all in a boarding house. Worse in terms of their long-term future, the brokerage firm was failing, a decline which had begun when Vanderbilt had begun to withdraw his favours. Woodhull was to be caricatured in a famous cartoon where a woman burdened with poverty, children, and a drunken husband declares that she would still rather tread her path than that of Free Love promoted by 'Mrs Satan': Victoria Woodhull with huge black wings.[74]

Showing their talent for dramatic scenes, in local elections in November 1871 Victoria and Tennie went to the polls accompanied by her lawyer, Judge Reymart. Having had their names listed with no particular difficulty, they went to the polls to exercise their right and were refused by the inspector. In front of a crowd they threatened legal action against the polling inspectors for preventing them from exercising their constitutional rights.

Woodhull was receiving more invitations to lecture across the country than ever before, so the fees kept her afloat. She was still welcomed by the leadership of the National Woman Suffrage Association, though a number of the members had asked for her to be expelled. She gave her usual brilliant performance at the annual conference, supported by Stanton and Anthony.

Woodhull took the advantage of her position and proposed a political party promoting women's suffrage. The announcement by leading suffrage supporters was made in the absence of Susan B. Anthony, who was on a lecture tour, but her name was added to the list of supporters in the announcement in *Woodhull and Claflin's Weekly*. Anthony distanced herself from the proposal and when the NWSA meeting was held and Woodhull declared from the platform it was a joint meeting between the Association and the People's Party, Anthony asserted herself and called on People's Party members to leave. Elizabeth Cady Stanton, in temporary disgrace, resigned as president of the Association and Anthony replaced her. This might have been the end of the matter but Victoria Woodhull was nothing if not convinced of her own rectitude and she re-entered the hall that afternoon, mounted the platform and began a speech calling for immediate political action. Anthony tried to call the meeting to order but Woodhull continued and the audience listened. Anthony, her leadership position and her control of the movement now challenged, left the platform to find the janitor, ordered him to turn off the gas lights in the hall and called the meeting to a close in darkness. 'Never did Mrs Stanton do so foolish a thing,' she wrote in her diary, 'all came near to being lost.'[75]

Woodhull's political organization, which decided to call itself the Equal Rights Party (thus joining with an existing group), met at Apollo Hall the next day, 10 May 1872. The gathering of 600 included Woodhull's radical friends and supporters, along with a large number of suffragists to hear her passionate appeal: 'A revolution shall sweep over the whole country, to purge it of political trickery, despotic assumption, and all industrial injustice.'[76] The new party nominated her for president (previously she had declared she would be running) and proposed the unwitting Frederick Douglass as a vice-presidential candidate, who when he heard about it, repudiated the honour.

The boarding house where the family was staying now asked her to leave because of her radical views; a hotel into which she booked while the manager was away evicted them, putting their belongings on the street and locking the door to their rooms. They stayed at their office in the brokerage firm but the owner now increased the rent by £1000 dollars a year, payable immediately. They were obliged to find another office. Their last treasure, *Woodhull and Claflin's Weekly*, suspended publication in June 1872. Woodhull was sued for debt later that summer.

Woodhull was convinced there was an organized conspiracy by her enemies and she threatened to expose the private lives of women's suffrage campaigners in retaliation. Finally, she simply gave the details to the annual meeting of the National Association of Spiritualists meeting in Boston in September 1872. She had attended the meeting of the organization that had cheered her the previous year, but found the audience now largely hostile to her. When it was her turn to speak, she later explained, 'Standing there before that audience I was seized by one of those overwhelming gusts of inspiration which sometimes come upon me, from I know not where; taken out of myself; hurried away from the immediate question of discussion, and made by some power stronger than I, to pour into the ears of that assembly...the whole story of the Beecher and Tilton scandal.'[77] She was said to have spoken as if inspired, and she certainly electrified a previously unfriendly audience for they unanimously re-elected her president of the Association.

Energized by the Spiritualists, Woodhull and her supporters, from a newly reopened office, produced a special edition of *Woodhull and Claflin's Weekly* in which the full sordid story of the Beecher–Tilton scandal and the squalid cover-up were revealed. Giving the intellectual underpinning of the decision to go public, she referred back to the battle over slavery and the work of the revered William Lloyd Garrison (who had supported the women's cause at the Anti-Slavery Convention of 1840): 'I went back and studied the history of other reforms,' she wrote in the editorial, 'I found that Garrison had not only denounced slavery in the abstract, but that he attacked it in the concrete' thus she must move to create a new public opinion, free of hypocrisy.[78] Another and more sexually explicit article attacked a stockbroker called Challis who was said by Tennie (ever eager with hands outstretched whenever there was attention to be grabbed) to seduce young women. The 2 November 1872 edition of the *Woodhull and Claflin Weekly* was a publishing sensation, with distributors refusing to handle it, so news vendors stormed Woodhull's office to obtain copies. Supply could not keep up with the massive demand and soon copies with a cover price of ten cents were changing hands at ten or twenty dollars.

The publication came to the attention of Anthony Comstock, a dry-goods salesman and self-appointed guardian of public morals, who sought a warrant for Victoria and Tennie's arrest for sending indecent material through the mail. Arrested in their carriage, they were taken to court where the assistant district attorney accused them of 'an atrocious, abominable and untrue libel on a gentleman whom the whole country reveres', already at this stage finding it impossible to justify a charge of obscenity.[79] Bail was set but the sisters, unwilling to call on friends to post bail and aware of the publicity value of going to jail, chose imprisonment. On the day of the election in 1872 the Equal Rights Party candidate Victoria Woodhull was in prison and there may not have been any ballot papers with her name on them (political parties were responsible for printing ballots at the time, and none have been preserved with Woodhull's name which may mean none were printed).

The sisters faced charges relating to the issue for two years, ultimately being found not guilty of obscenity in 1873 and also not guilty, the following year, of a libel charge brought by Luther B. Challis, the stockbroker that Tennie had wished to attack. An assault by both Challis and Comstock meant the sisters were assailed by an unlikely alliance of a puritan and a libertine. During their imprisonment and court appearances the government confiscated their printing press, brokerage firm documents, and personal papers; the court costs ruined the family. Woodhull continued touring and lecturing, when she was free, to publicize the persecution she was suffering. She once evaded the police presence around a lecture hall she was due to attend by wearing the costume of an old lady Quaker, flinging it off only when she reached the stage to speak. They were not without their friends; George Francis Train who had previously backed Susan B. Anthony and Elizabeth Cady Stanton, now came forward to support the sisters and he attacked Anthony Comstock in print. Comstock rose to the bait and had a warrant issued for Train's arrest, at which the millionaire refused to post bail so he went to prison from which place he issued frequent bulletins on national government. The supporters of women's suffrage were presenting a lively spectacle to the nation.

The leaders of the National Woman Suffrage Association were in an invidious position. Susan B. Antony refused to comment on the case; Elizabeth Cady Stanton deplored the publication of the Beecher–Tilton story but did not deny it and when she heard of Beecher's mendacious denial, she said privately that she would testify in Woodhull's favour (she did not in fact do so).[80] She had more loyalty than many of the erstwhile supporters of Woodhull, and a clearer vision of what the story meant for feminism. 'The true social code, whatever it is, must be the same for both sexes,' she wrote to Woodhull; and to Tilton she wrote, 'Victoria Woodhull has done a work for Women that none of us could have done. She has faced and dared men to call her names that make women shudder.'[81] The scandal around the presidents of the two national women's suffrage organizations continued, until Beecher was obliged to set up a commission, whose members were chosen by himself, to examine the rumours about his conduct, which loyally declared he was blameless of any wrongdoing. Tilton then brought a suit against Beecher for alienation of his wife's affections but after a six-month trial the jury was unable to decide. Beecher continued his distinguished career until his death in 1887; Tilton took himself off to exile in Paris. The blame for the scandalous morass was laid at the door of Victoria Woodhull. Stanton declared 'scandalum magnatum' had been 'rolled down on our suffrage movement' and the chance of emancipation had 'gone down in the smash'.[82]

Woodhull divorced Colonel Blood and the irrepressible sisters went to England, perhaps with help from the heir of their old friend Vanderbilt after his death in 1877 (to preclude their assistance in a challenge to the will). They both made brilliant marriages. Tennessee married Francis V. Cook, who later was made a baronet, thereby making her Lady Cook. Woodhull married a wealthy banker, John Biddulph Martin, and was feted in newspapers in her later years as 'The United States Mother of Women's Suffrage'.[83] She spent her English years in philanthropy and publishing a journal, *Humanitarian*, promoting planned parenthood and eugenics; she died in Worcestershire in 1927 at the age of 88.

The Anthony Amendment

Victoria Woodhull had shown the way to gain maximum publicity and polarize supporters on the issue of women's suffrage. On election day 1872, hundreds of women went to the polls to exercise the right to vote they claimed to have already, just as Victoria Woodhull had done in New York in 1871. Sojourner Truth tried to vote at her home in Battle Creek, Michigan, Susan B. Anthony and some other women registered at her local polling place in Rochester (in the male environs of a barber shop), and voted on 5 November 1872 (she voted Republican). Police came to her home on Thanksgiving Day and arrested her, they also arrested the inspectors who had allowed her to vote. Anthony used this persecution to launch an educational campaign, hoping to influence public opinion (and therefore the jury, drawn from the local male populace), and in retaliation the authorities moved the trial further upstate. The trial commenced on 18 June 1873; the judge refused to allow Anthony to testify as a witness, as she was 'incompetent' in law as a woman; and he ordered the jury to find her guilty, refusing to poll the jury or to allow Anthony's lawyer to address them. She was allowed to address the court before sentence, at which she declared that in her trial every principle of justice had been violated; that every right had been denied; that she had no trial by her peers; that the court and the jurors were her political superiors and not her peers; and she announced her determination 'to continue her labours until equality was obtained'.[84] She furthermore demanded the full rigour of the law but the judge was not foolish enough to increase her martyrdom, he imposed a fine of $100 and costs. 'May it please your honour,' she said, 'I shall never pay a dollar of your unjust penalty.' And she never did.[85] The cases of other women who had voted were not brought to trial, though the inspectors who had allowed them to vote were prosecuted.

The matter was finally settled by the Supreme Court decision in the case of Minor v. Happersett in 1875 when Virginia Minor, assisted by her lawyer husband Francis, failed in her challenge that the state of Missouri had acted unlawfully in obstructing her right to vote two years previously. Thus the fourteenth amendment clearly did not grant women the right to vote. They were still not, however, denied the right to stand for election, and in 1884 and 1888 Belva Lockwood, one of the first female lawyers in the US, stood as a presidential candidate in the Victoria Woodhull tradition.

These manoeuvres kept the issue of women in politics in the public mind, but for gaining the vote, a new strategy was called for. Women such as Susan B. Anthony were deeply influenced by the anti-slavery campaign and the subsequent civil war whose political mainspring was the right (or not, as the Confederacy had seen it) of central government to dictate to the states. Anthony wrote to Stanton, 'If only now—all the Woman Suffrage women would work to this end of enforcing the existing constitutional supremacy of national law over state law.'[86]

Anthony therefore drafted a federal amendment which was put forward by Senator Aaron Sargent of California in 1878. It declared 'The rights of the citizens of the United States to vote shall not be denied or abridged by the United States or by any state on account of sex.' Elizabeth Cady Stanton was to argue the case before the Senate Committee on Privileges and Elections, whose chairman, Senator Wadleigh of New Hampshire, treated her with what she called 'studied inattention and contempt', looking over newspapers or manuscripts, gazing at the ceiling, cutting his nails, and sharpening his pencil. 'It was with difficulty I restrained the impulse more than once to hurl my manuscript at his head,' she remarked.[87]

In 1882 both houses appointed select committees and both recommended a women's suffrage amendment. The Anthony amendment was introduced in the Senate for the first time on 25 January 1887. It was rejected by more than two to one: sixteen in favour, thirty-four against, with twenty-six not voting. All those in favour were Republicans, bolstering the belief that women's suffrage was more likely to be achieved with them.

After the departure of Victoria Woodhull from the scene and the furore of the Beecher–Tilton scandal, the women's movement took pains to distance itself from an association with free love and attacks on marriage and instead to identify only with pure and womanly actions in the public sphere (identifying with female virtues in the domestic sphere would have encouraged the response that women were so good at homemaking they should stick to it). The predominant argument by the end of the 1870s was that women should have the vote not because they were the equal of men but because they were his superior in moral matters. A 'Broadside: To The Women of New Jersey' opined: 'The cause of morality requires your presence at the polls, the cause of temperance needs your voice in the choice of public officials, the cause of home demands that women have some political control.'[88]

Urbanization increased prostitution and, as in Britain, some American feminists (including Susan B. Anthony who in 1876 lectured on 'Social Purity') were moved to campaign against the 'state regulation of vice' or 'white slavery'. The rise of the temperance movement also engaged women, particularly in the 1870s in a 'women's crusade' against alcohol involving the disruption of bars and sometimes the destruction of saloon property. The Woman's Christian Temperance Union was founded by Annie Wittenmeyer of Iowa in 1874; five years later she was ousted from the leadership by Frances Willard, who steered the organization to supporting women's suffrage, both in the US and in other nations where the WCTU sent 'missionaries', with notable success in New Zealand and Australia. Anthony pursued an alliance with the WCTU despite Stanton's misgivings. The 25,000 members of the Union were to grow to 200,000 by the end of the century, a formidable and dynamic force.[89] However, by allying themselves so closely with temperance campaigners, women's suffrage leaders risked alienating both men and women who were anti-prohibition but in favour of women's suffrage.[90]

Temperance and anti-prostitution were perfectly proper areas for political discourse; but the general absence of women in other areas of life suggested a narrowness of political outlook which did not win new friends, as they would have done if women were evenly distributed through a greater variety of pressure groups, such as anti-trust and fiscal and labour law campaigning. Stanton and Anthony had early flirted with the National Labour Union but, as Alexander Keyssar said, 'Middle-class suffragists such as Stanton, believing as they did in the reconciliation of capital and labour, never fully grasped the sense of class antagonism that informed the NLU's politics and programs.'[91]

The temperance issue, which had always been of some significance to activist women, as the century wore on began to impinge seriously on suffrage campaigning. Women were thought to be more likely to vote for prohibition, because of the role of alcohol in family poverty and marital violence, so a block on women's suffrage came to be seen as a defence of the liquor interest and the rights of people to drink alcohol if they chose. Liquor became the great enemy of women's suffrage; the *History of Woman Suffrage* declared, 'Each of the two dominant parties is controlled by what are known as the liquor interests... There are few legislators who do not owe their election in a greater or less degree to the influence wielded by these liquor interests, which are positively, unanimously, and unalterably opposed to woman suffrage.'[92]

Suffragists lost state suffrage battles in Nebraska and Indiana due to the liquor interest in 1882. Washington territory with its poor transportation had relied on local liquor production until the Northern Pacific Railroad allowed the big brewers with their improved technology to develop in the state. This galvanized the temperance forces and both prohibition and women's suffrage were endorsed by the executive in 1883, but the supreme court invalidated both measures as local options. Temperance and women's suffrage campaigners called for their causes to be embraced by the state constitution but both measures were voted down so neither made the constitution of the new state as recognized in 1889. Some women blamed the hated 'liquor interests' but others concluded that association with prohibition was detrimental to their cause.

Girded by their setbacks (and the diminishing importance of the difference between them) the divided American and National organizations came together as the National American Woman Suffrage Association in 1890, pledged to winning rights in the states. Once they were won, voters would have enough real political strength to recognize their demand for a constitutional amendment. Stanton–Anthony supporters were in the majority in the new organization; Stanton was the first president, succeeded in 1892 by Anthony.

Concentration on state-wide campaigns needed a new kind of organizer. Carrie Chapman Catt, an Iowa school principal and a newspaper reporter in San Francisco, was one of the new breed of suffragist activists. She first came to prominence in a referendum campaign in Colorado where she set up a state-wide organization with an adequate campaign fund, and support from all three major political parties. The temporary strength of the Populists or People's Party in balancing the other two was of importance; they supported women's suffrage in the belief that women voters would improve moral standards. In an intelligent campaign the suffragists supported economic recovery, linking the vote to the 'free silver' controversy rather than any social concern or specifically women's issue. In 1893 Colorado's men voted for women suffrage in a referendum, though a taste of the future was to be sampled by this state, more typical of the rest of the US than underpopulated Wyoming or Mormon Utah. The extension of the franchise for women made no difference, neither positive nor negative. As Federal Judge Moses Hallett said, 'the presence of women at the polls has only augmented the total votes, it has worked no radical changes. It has produced no special reforms, and it has had no particularly purifying effect on politics.'[93] A San Francisco Examiner investigation by a woman reporter of Colorado women's voting lamented, 'we women have found out that that our politics are just as corrupt as men's politics, they are just a little bit trickier if anything.'[94]

Idaho had a referendum in 1896, the vote influenced by the Mormon interest as there were many Mormons living in the south of the state. The Populists were again a factor in favour of women and it was also a benefit that a veteran suffrage campaigner, Abigail Scott Duniway, lived in Idaho. She had trekked west in 1852, burying her mother and infant brother on the journey; she later ran a millinery store and began publishing the New Northwest, a voice for 'we toiling and tax-paying, but reading and reasoning women.'[95] She had long opposed the linking of suffrage and prohibition; she felt the 'Women's Christian Temperance Union is spoiling everything' and she also rejected NAWSA advice and organizers. This was not without its friction but Carrie Chapman Catt sensibly decided to give Idaho suffragists help by organizing a series of meetings, but otherwise allowing the national organization with its eastern bias to stay at arm's length. Idaho voted two to one for women's suffrage.[96]

A campaign in 1896 in California where women's suffrage and temperance were historically linked failed disappointingly, despite an expensive campaign launched by the National Association that Susan Anthony considered so important she directed it herself. Carrie Chapman Catt felt the defeat had come about at the hands of the (very few) Chinese men voting against the amendment: 'Chinese voters... directed their votes to deny self-government to American women. It was the hour of the Chinese!'[97] In fact suffragist progress had been thwarted by their failure to balance and appeal individually to a range of political and interest groups, including the Catholics, who had hitherto not been a major factor in the equation; over the next fifteen years they were to learn how to operate politically to win the vote in a large, complex state and Californian women were enfranchised in 1911.[98]

The story of the enfranchisement of women in the American west was to continue after 1910 when in the next four years six states (plus Kansas) enfranchised women: Washington, California, Oregon, Arizona, Nevada, and Montana; and the new territory of Alaska with the exception of native American women unless they were married to white men or 'severed' from tribal relations.[99]

Women's suffrage had become part of what was presented as a forward-looking set of policies aimed at improving democracy. In accordance with what were seen as progressive racial policies, this included maintaining the supposed natural superiority of native-born white Americans, whose political strength could be increased with women's suffrage, respective to that of new immigrants who were flooding in to the west in the early years of the twentieth century. These were more western than eastern (or southern) notions of the Americanism that was being created in the post-civil war nation. The argument from equality had been decreasingly successful for women's suffrage at the end of the nineteenth and beginning of the twentieth centuries; elitism, nativism, and white supremacy were more attractive.[100] As an anonymous Wyoming legislator is reported to have said, 'Damn it, if you are going to let the niggers and pigtails vote, we will ring in the women, too.'[101]

The end of the century was the end of the rule of the old matriarchs. Elizabeth Cady Stanton died in New York in 1902 at 87, surviving her rival Lucy Stone by nine years. Susan B. Anthony died in 1906, also at 87, a month after delivering her final speech to the annual NAWSA convention at Baltimore, declaring 'Failure is impossible.'[102] The new century was going to have a new leadership.

7

Out of the doll's house in Scandinavia

'Much less worthy of this great success'

At a ball in Christiania, Norway's capital in the 1870s, men stood in their dinner jackets to make speeches to the guests. As was traditional, the usual sugary speech of flattery was made in favour of the glamorously dressed ladies present. Then, a young student rose and made a startling address: 'We have done with these phrases about women now,' he said, 'comparing her to stars and to flowers and to anything but human beings. We want companions in life, an equal in our own flesh and blood, an equal in our needs and wants and ideals.' Then he quoted from John Stuart Mill's *Subjection of Women* and ended with the cry 'Votes for Women.' There was an outcry. Some women fled frightened to the corners of the room, and some men were visibly angry. Ella Anker, the teenage daughter of the hosts, was shocked and bewildered, then she saw her mother 'walking up to the speaker and thanking him with tears in her eyes', and she said she knew everything was going to be all right.[1]

Literary feminism

In the middle of the nineteenth century Swedish culture dominated Finland; and Sweden politically dominated Norway. Iceland was under the Danish crown, so these nations had more of a cultural interchange than would be indicated by the fact that they all had different languages and parliaments. Additionally, the educated from these nations would usually speak English which became a medium for political communication.

What has come to be called 'literary feminism' based on the insights of literature, made more contribution to the women's movement in Scandinavia than in any other region. People such as the Swedish novelist Frederika Bremer travelled and brought back insights that would quickly permeate through the intellectual elites of the Scandinavian countries. Bremer, the daughter of an iron manufacturer, renounced the life of marriage and domestic incarceration which was her lot, and devoted herself to literature. She went on a tour of the US starting in 1849, specifically mentioning that she was looking at the situation of women in the new world, and she met Lucretia Mott and other early feminists. She wrote the influential book *The Homes of the New World* about her travels including remarks on the situation of women, and a classic novel, *Hertha*, published in 1856 about marriage and women's rights which was considered responsible (rightly or wrongly) for positive social legislation for women in Sweden in the 1850s.

Camilla Collett, a Norwegian novelist (also known by her married name of Wergeland) began a vigorous debate on marriage and morality with *The Governor's Daughters*, in 1854. The debate about women, society, and the law came to a head in the late 1870s and early 1880s with such plays as Ibsen's *A Doll's House* and Bjornson's *The Glove*, Strindberg's stories in *The Red Room*, and the Swedish translation of Mill's *Subjection of Women*. In a striking demonstration of the power of literature in Scandinavia, in 1883 the *Subjection of Women* was the reading matter for a discussion group for women in Helsinki who founded the Finnish Women's Association as soon as they finished it.[2] Ella Anker, the witness to the ballroom scene described earlier, was to tell an English audience in the early twentieth century of the effect of the *Subjection of Women* on her mother's generation: 'women at that time came together to discuss this book, how they cried over it, and dreamt over it, as if a new age was dawning.'[3]

The Danish Woman's Association had been formed in 1871 but did not become an assertive pressure group until 1883. The Norwegian Woman Suffrage Society was founded in 1885. The Swedish feminist group, the Fredrika Bremer Society, was founded the same year. Dedicated to social goals, its very name was a statement of the way in which it was informed by literature. Iceland proceeded at a different pace (though with, apparently more non-political equality between men and women). Though the Icelandic Women's Association was founded in 1895, it was calling only for equal rights for women in educational and economic matters; it was not until 1907 that the Women's Rights Association of Iceland was founded, arguing for political emancipation.

Much of the rhetoric of women's organizations mixed an attack on conventional marriage with the elevation of women as a morally and spiritually superior beings—a similar picture to that which was presented in Britain and the US. Not surprisingly, therefore, Scandinavian feminism borrowed from 'social purity' advocates abroad, so Camilla Collett translated into Danish Josephine Butler's work attacking the government regulation of prostitution.

The weight of opposition to women's suffrage in Scandinavia was literally a conservative opposition: a genuine reluctance to do anything differently from the way in which it had always been done. Ross Evans Paulson remarks that because Scandinavia has a custom-based political system the weight of tradition ensured continuity, and was not so subject to change by direct political means, 'Since changes in customs must ultimately flow from changes in public opinion, the novelist, playwright, and popular preacher-teacher were more important in Scandinavian feminism and the quest for women's rights than were such persons in more formally democratic political systems.'[4]

While women enjoyed comparative freedom, assumptions about men's and women's roles were deeply entrenched in a culture which put women under the guardianship of male relatives but, paradoxically, afforded women a great deal of freedom to work and manage affairs outside of the home.

Any appeal for political change had to be to a largely traditional population: in 1850 in Sweden 90 per cent of people lived off the land; by 1900 the figure was still as high as 75 per cent. In Finland 90 per cent of the population lived in the countryside just after 1900; Norway's most important export in 1850 was timber, followed by fish.[5] Another part of the mix for Scandinavian countries was nationalism; though Sweden and Denmark were independent in the nineteenth century, Norway, Finland, and Iceland were under foreign powers (Sweden, Russia and Denmark respectively) so nationalism became the dominant political movement, and the personal freedom of enfranchisement became associated with the national freedom of independence.

Nationalism triumphant in Finland

Finland had formed part of Sweden until 1809 when it came under Russian rule and was officially a Grand Duchy of Russia. The Tsar liberalized his rule in 1863 after a recent uprising in Poland had led him to fear the same in Finland; a communal administrative structure was established with a new parliament, the Diet, subject to regular convocation, though only 15 per cent of the population voted for them.[6] Property-owning women who paid taxes were granted the local franchise in the country in 1863 and the municipal franchise in 1872.

A complication of Finnish cultural life was that though only some 12 per cent of the population were Swedish-speaking, they predominated in the upper class and Swedish was the country's official language. A decree announcing a twenty-year programme for the achievement of full linguistic equality of the Finnish language with Swedish was promulgated in 1863. This 'linguistic nationalism' deeply involved women who were the instructors of children in their native tongue and who worked towards setting up schools. It was shortly after the completion of this Finnish language programme, in May 1884, that the group of women inspired by reading John Stuart Mill's book and by their own experiences set up the Finnish Women's Association. The Association called for the suffrage, equal rights in higher and professional education, and the right to hold political office as well as a range of social reforms and an equal sexual code 'in law and custom' for men and women.

This was standard fare for women's movements of the late nineteenth century but, as Richard J. Evans notes, the unusual feature was not just the involvement of women in the nationalist movement, but the politicization of the peasantry which was essential if a nationalist movement was to succeed in an overwhelmingly rural nation.[7] This mix of women's rights, nationalism, and the countryside saw the Finnish Women's Association taking the unusual step of expanding its activities into rural areas. By 1894, half of its branches were reading and lecture groups for peasant women; by 1900 the nation had almost complete adult literacy. The keys to advances in women's suffrage in Finland were the politicization of the nation through nationalism, and complete female literacy. The arguments which had been raised in Britain and the US about the poor education of women and their ignorance of political realities were not tenable in Finland. It may also have been a factor that co-education was widespread in Finland which was said to have 'abolished in a practical and natural way...feelings of supremacy and subjection' between young people.[8]

Baroness Alexandra Gripenberg, president of the Finnish Women's Association from 1889 to 1904, had attended the World's Congress of Women

Rekordet

längdhopp vid den internationella täflingen i demokratins stora utförsbacke sattes af den käcka jäntan Suomi. Utdrag ur prisdomarprotokollet:
Finland främst i ledet! Satsen barnsligt djärf, hållningen något osäker, språnget världsrekord i anseende till sin utomordentliga längd, hvarför nedslaget först kan bedömas en god bit bortom den 16 dennes.

Figure 6. The Finnish maiden soars ahead in the ski jump in the 'democratic world record', making Finland in 1906 the first European nation to enfranchise women, as part of adult suffrage. Other nations watch the sport in which Russia falls, including Britain as 'John Bull'.

in Chicago in 1893 and had become acquainted with Susan B. Anthony and other leading suffragists. She was of the Swedish-speaking nobility but she allied herself with Finnish nationalists who were more sympathetic to women's rights. She was, however, of the old guard who were prepared to compromise with the Russians. A new and more radical movement, the Union of Women's Societies, was set up in 1892 by Lucina Hagman, a teacher who had studied abroad. Her group, to which men could belong, shared the radicalism of the Young Finns, who wanted complete independence from Russia. Their enthusiasm was tempered by a programme of aggressive imperial rule in the late 1890s aimed at the Russification of education and administration, with the introduction of Russian postal, toll, and monetary systems which was the Russian government's attempt to standardize legislation in different parts of its massive empire. Men and women worked together in resistance, gathering signatures for a petition, printing illegal newspapers and pamphlets, holding secret meetings and sheltering men hiding from the recruiting officers of the Russian army.

Anna Furuhjelm, a delegate at the 1906 International Woman Suffrage Alliance conference in Copenhagen, explained, 'Hundreds, even thousands of women of all classes who perhaps up to this time had never given a thought to their rights, or rather their want of rights, enrolled in the ranks of the opposition, offering their help. And our men accepted the offer of the women with enthusiasm.'[9] In general, Finnish women did not grandstand suffrage, it was one objective among a number, and not the most important when national liberation was at stake. They were not active as feminists so much as nationalists. A bill giving women the right to stand in local elections was passed by the Diet (parliament) in 1897 but rejected by the Russian government, thus locking women's political rights and nationalism even more closely together. Aino Malmberg speaking in the early years of the twentieth century declared: 'the woman's question—and to some extent also the temperance question—were almost the only important expressions of intellectual life that had power enough to unite members of the different political parties.'[10] She added that the experience of repression by the Russians may have given men a taste of what it was like to have no rights, and to quicken their sympathy with women.

In 1898 the crisis deepened when Russia decided to integrate Finnish manpower into the Russian army, meaning all Finnish men could be conscripted. The Finnish Diet rejected the proposal unanimously, the Tsar abolished the Diet and suspended the constitution in April 1903. The assassination of the Russian Governor-General in 1904 intensified the conflict but Russia was a beleaguered nation and feared an escalation of dissent at a time of war with Japan. The Russians decided to conciliate the Finns and repealed the conscription law.

Women's suffrage was first introduced to the Diet in 1897 but political instability prevented normal business and the first debates did not take place until 1904 and 1905. The Bill before the Diet offered the franchise to some upper-class women, unmarried women and widows, and teachers. The peasants' section of the Diet, where Finnish speakers prevailed and which held a quarter of the seats, supported the measure but the other three (nobility, townspeople, and clergy) rejected it. It may be that the peasants were untainted with theories about how revolutionary women's suffrage would be, and recognized women's suffrage as a conservative measure. Women's suffrage continued to be more strongly supported in rural than urban parts of Finland, and among Finnish-speaking people rather than the Swedish-speaking upper class.

Russia's defeat in its war with Japan in 1905 and that year's revolution provided a further opportunity for Finns to press their demands for greater autonomy and for those Finns without the vote to argue for it—nationalism thus went hand in hand with the development of democracy as it did in India. Women were part of the national liberation movement at every level: raising funds, smuggling literature and serving on the central committee elected at a mass meeting to co-ordinate the national strike called to demand the restoration of Finnish autonomy. This started on 31 October 1905 when all factories schools, railways, and telegraphs stopped as the nation ground to a standstill. With the General Strike widely supported, and Russian forces needed at home, the Tsar gave way and charged the senate with drafting a new legislature. Jubilant meetings were held to discuss the new constitution and at a mass meeting in Helsingfors on 7 December a resolution was carried demanding full adult suffrage for all adults over 24. Even the conservative Women's Association had now come round to universal suffrage, moving away from its stance of enfranchising only the wealthy.

The Finnish nationalists, in a deal with the Social Democrats, agreed the terms of suffrage for both sexes on 28 May 1906, for a modernized parliament with the four chambers of the Diet to be replaced with a single chamber. The proclamation of general adult suffrage was made on 20 July 1906. Universal suffrage was thus forced by the revolutionary situation on the streets and the general strike. The Governor-General, Oblensky, skilfully pacified the striking masses by permitting them what appeared to be a large measure of democracy, in order to prevent the unrest from expanding into a full-scale revolution.[11]

The law the Tsar was sent in 1906 proposed simply, 'Every Finnish citizen, man as well as woman, who has reached the age of twenty-four before the election year is entitled to vote.'[12] One of the most conservative, estate-based parliaments in Europe was replaced at a stroke by the most democratic system on the continent.

Summing up the debate on women, historian Aura Korppi-Tommola said,

> Many trusted that women would be moderate in their views on political issues compared to radical socialist men. They imagined that women would want to handle the taxpayer's money in a way that a good housewife handles the domestic budget while the temperance movement had high hopes of renewed support of women...Men began to calculate how many women's votes could be collected from their particular social group rather than continuing the debate over whether women could be trusted to behave reasonably in the public sphere.[13]

She emphasized the high educational level and preponderance of women in the labour market in Finland, and their participation in the struggle against Russification. The Finnish historian Irma Sulkunen has stressed the influence of religious revivalist movements in which women were prominent, which reached their peak at the end of the nineteenth century, and which associated with the Old Finn Party with its ideals of an agrarian society.[14]

The Finns went on to elect Europe's first nineteen female deputies (forming 10 per cent of the total—a higher rate than most democracies 100 years later). One of the deputies was Alexandra Gripenberg, elected for the conservative Finnish Party with its roots in the countryside; Lucina Hagman, now a headmistress, was also elected. In terms of the party strengths, Aino Malmberg said all predictions of an overthrow of Socialists or Conservatives were wrong: 'It has caused no change whatever in the relative strength of each party, because the women voters, as well as the women members of the Diet, are divided among the different parties in the same proportions as men.'[15]

Finnish women were granted unrestricted rights both to vote and to stand for parliament, unlike in New Zealand where rights to stand were not conferred, while in Australia the right to vote in all state elections was not granted until 1908. It could be said, therefore, that Finland was in fact the first nation to enfranchise women fully, but Finland was still dominated by the Tsar, so women's suffrage was not the political liberation it could be claimed to be in an independent nation, though it was certainly complete equality with men. Alexandra Gripenberg wrote, 'The gratitude which we women feel is mingled with the knowledge that we are much less worthy of this great success than the women of England and America, who have struggled so long and so faithfully, with much more energy and persever-ance than we.'[16]

Finnish independence was declared on 6 December 1917, after the Bolshevik Revolution, and in 1919 there was a complete severance of con-nection with Russia, and Finland became an independent republic.

Temperance and social purity in Norway

Norway was transferred from Danish to Swedish control in a dual union under the Swedish king in 1814 as a result of the Napoleonic wars. The transfer was resented and Norwegians were urged to elect a parliament of resistance. The folk history of Norway tells of a woman who rode to the church which was used for polling to register her vote; it was resisted, but the point had been made.[17]

Anti-Swedish agitation took place in which women as well as men were radicalized in the nationalist cause and Norway eventually secured a measure of indigenous government. Norway was allowed a parliamentary govern-ment, though it was subject to checks by the Swedish crown and less than 8 per cent of the population had the right to vote.

Under a hard-fought constitutional amendment, manhood suffrage was extended in 1884. As a response, leading feminist Gina Krog founded the Women's Suffrage Society the following year, after reading the first volumes of *The History of Woman Suffrage* which had been sent by Susan B. Anthony to the university at Christiania. This grouping was small and, in keeping with Krog's conservative nature, limited to requesting the municipal fran-chise. The group did not endure but its existence indicated the rise of a politicized elite drawn from the class about whom Ibsen wrote: the families of ship owners and lawyers who were enjoying an expansion in their num-bers as Norway's merchant shipping fleet expanded to become the third largest in the world (after Britain and the US), thus drawing wealth into the country.

Krog was already leader of the Norwegian Association for Women's Rights, which she had founded in 1884 with Hagbart Berner, a lawyer and newspaper owner. The disparity between this movement, which went from strength to strength, and the specifically suffrage society, which was allowed to die, demonstrates the low importance placed on women's suffrage in Norway compared with issues of nationalism and women's place in marriage and the economic sphere. A new women's movement at the end of the 1880s was related to the rise of the Radical Liberals who wanted to hasten the break with Sweden and favoured temperance, 'social purity', and women's suffrage. Such campaigners as the writer and nationalist Bjornstjerne Bjornson toured the country denouncing the sexual double standard, promoting a strict code of sexual morality to apply to women and men equally.

Women's suffrage was thus borne forward on a tide of nationalist sentiment fuelled by temperance and social purity rhetoric, all of these being presented as progressive. Norwegian feminism was intermixed with these movements but the organized women's suffrage movement trailed behind the parliamentary efforts for women's suffrage. The Radical Liberals promoted a universal suffrage bill in 1890 that was defeated in the parliament, the Storting, by 44 votes to 114. Another attempt three years later secured a majority, but not the two-thirds majority necessary for a constitutional change, though it stimulated the creation of a new National Women's Suffrage Association by Gina Krog. In line with her generally conservative approach, Krog favoured a property-based franchise, even after 1898 when universal manhood suffrage was introduced. Even the Conservative Party now favoured a limited bill for better-off women, to offset the working-class vote, so Krog's position was anything but radical.

The Association persuaded the Storting to introduce women's suffrage in a municipal suffrage bill in 1901 but, while this legislation used only a residency and age qualification for men, women had to own property or be married to a man who did. It did not pass, though communal (regional administrative) suffrage was granted to all tax-paying women, married and unmarried, that year.

Norway unilaterally declared independence from Sweden on 7 June 1905 in a bloodless revolution when the Swedish king was deposed by the government and the Storting sitting in secret session. The Swedes responded that this was an arbitrary act of the parliament and was not supported by the Norwegian people, so parliament called a referendum. Women urged the Storting that they should be allowed to vote but were not permitted to do so, though women had been active in support of the nationalist movement. As evidence of their steadfastness, the Storting received an address of loyalty organized by the Women's Suffrage Association, signed by 300,000 women, practically all the adult women in the country. The constitutional crisis was settled in 1905 with concessions from both sides.

An important national factor in Norway was the capital pouring into the country from abroad, mainly Sweden and France, to fund industrial expansion. In 1906 three-quarters of all developed water power in Norway was owned by foreign concerns. In a battle for legislation to protect the natural resources of the country, the Radicals and the Socialists, who were in a majority in the Storting, were pushing for the Concession Laws for controlling new industrial development. They felt the more loyal Norwegians who were involved in the struggle the better. These two political groups also, in principle, favoured the women's vote. Limited women's suffrage was granted in 1907, after only two hours' debate, for all those tax-paying women who already possessed the municipal franchise, and the wives of men who were so qualified.

The Labour and Liberal parties had first voted for a universal suffrage bill enfranchising all women, but when that failed and the franchise for only the middle class was before them, the Labour delegates magnanimously voted in favour, opening the way for women's suffrage even though their natural supporters would not be enfranchised.

Most middle-class, property-owning women now abandoned the battle for votes for all women. The first election in which they voted, in 1909, returned a Conservative government opposed to further extension of women's suffrage, though universal communal suffrage was introduced in 1910. The Radicals were back in power in 1912 and the following year enfranchised all women on a mere residency qualification for those over 25.

In both Finland and Norway women's suffrage (much as it was in India later in the century) was seen as a recognition of loyalty in the independence campaign and as a consolidation of nationalism by the raising of more patriots to political strength. There was also clearly party advantage to be had by women's enfranchisement in Norway where support was sought for the Concession Laws. In Finland the women's movement was of prime importance in educating women nationally; in Norway the women's suffrage movement was of little consequence.

Radical victory in Denmark

The Danish Woman's Association was founded by Fredrik and Mathilde Bajer in 1871, influenced by the publication of a Danish version of Mill's

Subjection of Women in 1869. The Association was divided along the usual fault line of sexual morality when the ideas of Josephine Butler over the state regulation of prostitution were vigorously supported by a faction of the Association led by Elisabeth Grundtvig who felt men should aspire to the moral condition of women and embrace chastity. They were bitterly opposed to the ideas of writer and critic Georg Brandes, translator of *The Subjection of Women*, who believed that women should enjoy the same sexual freedom as men. Brandes, a principal voice bringing the liberal and political cultural trends of western Europe to Denmark, had met Mill and other major thinkers on European travels and conceived it as his personal mission to liberate Denmark from provincialism and cultural backwardness.

Fredrik Bajer withdrew from active participation in the Association when he entered parliament, though he supported the women's cause as a Liberal MP, and ensured married Danish women had legislative protection for economic independence in 1880. In 1886 he put forward a modest franchise bill, to give women taxpayers in Copenhagen the right to vote for the city council. It is some indication of the conservatism of Danish society that this was criticised for including married women, and it failed before its final reading. Bajer amended the bill and re-introduced it to apply only to widows and unmarried women. The lower house passed the bill with a healthy majority but the conservative upper house, elected on a privileged franchise, refused even to discuss it as the bill was 'neither in the interests of women nor of society.'[18] Bills for the local franchise, for the whole country, were repeatedly re-presented and repeatedly thrown out through the next decade. The argument was simply that it was not in society's interest to turn marriage into a 'political battlefield' and challenge the divisions of society by gender: that men should perform in the public arena and women in the domestic.

In support of Bajer's bill for local voting rights a woman called Line Luplau from remote West Jutland started a petition and gathered 20,000 signatures. This caused astonishment in parliament as it was believed that women's emancipation was a phenomenon of urban intellectuals. The notion that rural women in outlying areas were concerned about their political rights was a new concept to parliamentarians, and perhaps to 'modern' women in Copenhagen, too. Luplau founded the Danish Women's Suffrage Association in 1889. Members questioned politicians about women's suffrage and were generally courteously received at election meetings though in some towns they were refused permission to speak and in Frederica in Jutland they were refused admission to campaign meetings.

As had happened in Britain, a galvanizing effect was brought about by the contemptuous behaviour of parliamentarians who brought in an electoral bill with no mention of votes for women. The Danish Women's Suffrage Association was hesitant about protesting so a new organization was formed by the more radical members, the Danish Women's Associations' Suffrage Federation.[19]

Their aim was still too limited for the radicals who broke away in 1900 to form the left-leaning National League for Women's Suffrage that campaigned for full voting rights. Both of these organizations were to gain ground (as liberal politics also did on a national level) in the first decade of the twentieth century; by 1910 the two suffrage associations had 23,000 members. In 1908 they won the hard-fought battle for local franchise for women taxpayers and the wives of taxpayers, 'who have lived in the municipality for over a year, are twenty-five years of age and of untainted reputation'.[20] The negative influence of British militancy was apparent in Danish women's reluctance to engage in lobbying or demonstrations, lest these bring about their association with suffragette methods. From 1908 they had an annual Women's Suffrage Day on 20 June with meetings and speeches—but no marches or lobbies.

A bill was passed by the lower house in 1912 for universal suffrage for men and women over 28 years old, but it was stopped by the Conservatives who dominated the upper house. The Conservatives suffered a crushing defeat in the election of 1914 and a reforming government of the Radicals and the Social Democrats enfranchised women (equally with men, for those over 29) on 5 June 1915.

Conservative progress in Sweden

Sweden in the mid-nineteenth century has been described as 'sunk in backwardness, its government archaic, its economy rural'.[21] Paradoxically it was the first country in Europe to give women the municipal vote and among the last to grant the parliamentary franchise.

Married women's inheritance, trading, and other rights were gained in the twenty years from 1845 in Sweden, along with the municipal and provincial franchise in 1862 for widows and spinsters who had paid taxes (though twenty-five years later it was found that only 6.5 per cent actually voted).[22] The municipal franchise had a special significance in Sweden as it conferred an indirect vote for the upper house which was elected through nomination from the provincial and municipal councils.

The feminist movement in Sweden concentrated on educational and economic goals, reflecting the conservative nature of society which was dominated by aristocratic landowners. A familiar mix of economic liberalism, a vigorous temperance movement, and trade unions developed. The New Liberal Party proposed universal suffrage for men and women in 1868 but the Riksdag defeated the proposal without a debate. It was sixteen years before another bill to give women full voting rights was presented by Frederick Borg in 1884. Borg had founded Sweden's first labour association in 1850; he was a proponent of social legislation to provide schools, libraries, and poor relief, and was a voice in the Riksdag for democracy and republicanism. His proposal for women's franchise was rejected amid laughter from fellow parliamentarians.

Industrial unrest in the 1890s, concurrent with rapid industrialization, culminated in a general strike of 1902 to back the demand from opposition groups for a reform of the suffrage which was based on 'financial citizenship' of income or property; and 'civilian citizenship' of autonomy and authority. Property qualifications favoured the traditional rich, rather than the newly rich mercantile and professional classes, so working-class and middle-class unrest were combined as they had been in Britain prior to the 1832 Reform Bill. It was at this time of heated conflict over the extension of manhood suffrage, supported by the Liberal Union, that the Association for Women's Political Franchise was established in Stockholm and Gotenborg in 1902, to merge into the National Association for Women's Political Franchise the following year. A characteristic member of the inner circle of the Association was Frigga Carlberg who founded the Gotenborg branch. She was a journalist and social worker who was an expert on child care and was also one of the founders of an orphanage in Gotenborg. She wrote most of the material used by the Association for public presentations, including several plays on the theme of suffrage.

That the organization emerged at a time of agitation over manhood suffrage was in keeping with the history of other suffrage societies in other nations. It had a principle of promoting women's self-empowerment and a women-only membership policy. Historian Josafin Rönnbäck emphasizes that the Association 'did not only want to change the form of politics i.e. the rules and actors of the political performance, but also the content of politics'.[23] They thus had similarities with suffrage campaigners in Britain who felt women's franchise was desirable not merely as a right but because it was believed it would make a difference to national politics. To this end the Association urged women to use their existing rights to claim their place in party political organizations, city councils, and poor relief boards.

In Sweden there was no battle for national independence intertwined with women's suffrage, as there was in Norway, Finland, and Iceland, but Josafin Rönnbäck suggests nationalism played a part, since the argument for the franchise was about national identity on an individual as well as a collective level, for the franchise 'was regarded both as a symbol of individual woman's majority and national citizenship and as one showing national foresight and degree of civilisation'. So women's franchise was a recognition of social progress, with ethnocentric undertones: women's franchise came as part of a package establishing a superior nation.[24] The Association's arguments were those of traditional liberalism—that citizens should be equal before the law, without regard to gender, and (in contradiction) that women's traditional role as mother gave her attributes which should be brought to the political arena. This fed into the national symbols of the Good Mother and the Good Home, again suggesting nationalism.

Ellen Key, the leading Swedish writer of that time, was mistrustful of organized feminists who appeared to be hostile to the sex act itself; their preoccupation with prostitution offering a distorted view of their own natures. In their demand for a new single standard for both sexes, of an old model of chaste womanhood, she detected a failure of imagination. Feminists were 'that army of strong women who are to educate men to chastity by denying them their love'. Thus her first thought was to reject women's suffrage, as neglecting what women uniquely had to offer; but she later changed her mind and became a supporter.[25]

The National Association for Women's Franchise argued for the franchise on the same basis as it was given to men—thus, as in other countries, there was an immediate division between those who would be prepared to enfranchise only propertied women, and the Social Democrats who argued for universal franchise and encouraged members to oppose the prevailing class structure of society. Such women as the socialist agitator Kata Dalström queried whether there *was* a woman's question in the labour movement, and opposed separate women's sections and unions.[26]

Thus while the Association presented itself as a party-political neutral organization, its policy, of enfranchising better-off women, was in fact that of the Liberal Party.[27] This issue caused internal disagreements, as did the question of whether the Association should work for political rights only, or over other issues, and whether they should work with men or entirely independently. In general, it was the 'party women' in the Association, who had already done some political work within the existing system, who favoured co-operation with men and engagement with the political system.

Women's suffrage bills were defeated in the Riksdag in 1902, 1904, and 1905; four bills were introduced in 1906, and six in 1907, during which year the Labour Party then the Liberal Union adopted women's suffrage. The introduction of proportional representation in 1909 for the parliament was a key boost to the women's position as it contributed to the introduction of the Swedish multi-party system. This meant a proliferation of small parties who relied for their share in power on compromises with other parties. It became easier for the women's franchise issue to be introduced into the party-political trading that went into making up a coalition. The weakening of the parliamentary system also meant the weakening of the generally conservative influence of the monarchy.

In this atmosphere of heightened interest, a woman's suffrage bill passed the lower house in 1909, but a similar bill was rejected in the upper house by 104 votes to 25. Eventually, the Liberals, being unable to achieve even universal manhood suffrage, had to accept a compromise Conservative measure of giving only male taxpayers over the age of 24 the vote.

Swedish feminists had previously been mild, sending letters of gratitude to members of parliament when they had supported the cause, and had appealed to the King or to the Riksdag as a whole. Now they put their influence behind the defeat of the Conservative Party that had shown itself so hostile to their interests, though they sensibly (in contrast to the WSPU in Britain and the National Woman's Party in the US) declared they would not be involved in constituencies where both candidates were in favour of women's suffrage.

It was obviously against the interests of the Conservatives to oppose the women's franchise, for they were in need of conservative women's votes, but they tended to believe their opponents' propaganda, that votes for women meant drastic, radical change. They genuinely believed they would be witnessing the breakdown of family life if women voted in national elections. The leader of the Conservatives, Arvid Lindman, remarked in 1910 that 'nothing can be done until further light has been thrown upon the question of the effect woman's suffrage is likely to have on the marriage-rate and birth-rate'.[28]

Finally, with a Liberal and Social Democratic (left-wing) triumph at the polls in 1911 the Conservative cabinet resigned and a Liberal, Karl Staaff, a member of the Men's League for Women's Suffrage, became prime minister. The suffragists were rewarded with a bill that passed the second chamber in 1912 but fell in the first (which could be compared to opposition to women's suffrage in the British House of Lords and the US Senate). Unfortunately for women's suffrage, being bundled in with a package of radical and left-wing policies frightened off middle-class voters, who then abandoned the Liberal Party, allowing the Conservatives to take power again in 1914. The growth of the Social Democrats did not help the women's cause, even though they were formally committed to women's suffrage, as trade unionists dominated the Social Democrats and the trade unions concentrated on the interests of heavy industry. Women did light industrial work in tobacco, clothing, and food industries but were not well represented in the trade union movement; those who were members were marginalized, demonstrating that even the socialists and trade unionists were conservative in Sweden.

The breakthrough for women's suffrage came after the revolutions at the end of the First World War (in which Sweden was neutral). Economic unrest led to fears of a Bolshevik revolution in 1918. In response, all traditional parties agreed to strengthen parliamentary democracy by introducing women's suffrage among other reformist measures including the reduction of the voting age for the second chamber from 24 to 23, and the abolition of some property qualifications. This was agreed on 24 May 1919 but delayed for procedural reasons until it was passed by a new parliament on 26 January 1921. Almost half the women entitled to vote did so.[29]

This development, mirrored in other countries including Holland, was a significant event in the history of women's suffrage: it was so clearly not a revolutionary or even very radical act to enfranchise Swedish women but, on the contrary, the result of a collective realization that women's suffrage would be a conservative and restraining force; the consolidation of democracy against revolution.

Democracy returns to Iceland

Iceland at the end of the nineteenth century was a land of peasant farmers and fishermen under the Danish crown. The island had a tradition of women running farms, many of them widows, as might be expected in a society dependent on fishing, where men faced danger in the north Atlantic. The rural attitude was that a woman became almost the equivalent of a man if she took on a man's role. In 1881 the Icelandic general assembly, the Althing, unanimously passed a law to give the franchise in local elections to unmarried women and widows over 25 who ran farms or were householders or who maintained a family—but the Danish king held up the law. Another law, for women to be eligible to stand in local elections, was similarly held up in 1888 (though both were eventually passed).

Nationalism was thus mixed with women's rights as it was in Finland and Norway. Icelandic nationalists had been arguing through the second half of the nineteenth century first for internal self-government, then for complete independence. Iceland received a constitution that guaranteed home rule in 1874 but the Danes, through a minister in the Danish government, were still supervising the island, leading to continual conflicts in the 1880s and 1890s. National government with a separate ministry in Reykjavik was not established until 1903.

Feminist issues were becoming common currency at a time of change in the nation: modernization of the fishing industry; the development of Reykjavik; the supplanting of Norway in Icelandic trade; and nationalist conflict with Denmark. Temperance organizations also played a part as they did in the rest of Scandinavia and in other countries at the forefront of women's suffrage. The Icelandic Women's Alliance was founded in 1895, with the objective of the general improvement of women's condition.

Bríet Bjarnhédinsdóttir attended the International Woman Suffrage Alliance in Copenhagen in 1906. She had previously, at the age of 29 in 1885, written what was said to have been the first newspaper article ever published in Iceland by a woman and she later married the editor of the newspaper, the *Fjallkonan*, and began editing a magazine for women. In 1907 she organized the Women's Suffrage Association, touring the entire island on horseback for two months, going from place to place to speak and start branches. The municipal franchise was extended to married women and in 1908 a woman's list, with four names, stood for election to the town council in Reykjavik; it won the highest number of votes of all lists, almost 22 per cent, and all four candidates were elected to a council of fifteen.[30]

Nationalists had been pressing for full manhood suffrage and, as was common in these circumstances, feminists used the discourse about democracy to push their case, gaining the signatures of almost a quarter of the entire population in favour of women's suffrage.

Attempts to give women equal rights in education and appointment to the professions were successful in 1911, despite the protestations of one member of the Althing, who remarked that it would be 'inconvenient' if a woman sheriff 'were to give birth when she was called upon to investigate a criminal case or issue a sentence of imprisonment or if she went into labour while travelling between her annual communal meetings'.[31] At the same Althing session women and hitherto unenfranchised men were given the franchise, with the intention to enfranchise all in time for the 1913 elections. Such debate as took place was not about the admission of women to the franchise, but about the admission of domestic servants of both sexes. In a recurrence of debates elsewhere about extending the franchise, when hard decisions had to be made, gender was considered of secondary importance to class. Eventually servants were admitted, and only those who were in receipt of poor relief were excluded.

The reform was held up by the political relationship with Denmark where there was disagreement over the wording of other parts of the Act. When the issue was returned to the Althing, members had obviously rethought the issue as the franchise for women and servants was restricted to those of 40 and over. The age limit was to be reduced progressively over fifteen years until a universal age of 25 was reached. It was this amendment that was ratified by the King on 19 June 1915. In fact, as in other legislatures, the admission of women caused no great upset and the special age limits for women and servants were abolished in 1920. By the Act of Union of 1918, after a referendum, Iceland had been made almost completely independent, united to Denmark only by the monarchy and a common foreign policy.

The first woman elected to the Althing, in 1923, was Ingibjörg H. Bjarnason, headmistress of the women's school in Reykyavik; she was the only successful candidate from a woman's list—something common in the early years of women's franchise in Iceland. Bjarnason was, however, insufficiently convinced of the merits of an exclusively women's representation and she joined the Conservative Party, to the great disappointment of some of her voters who thought they were inaugurating a new period of electoral politics.

The Scandinavian enfranchisements, most specifically in Finland, were the penetration into Europe of developments which, as Markoff has asserted, happened early on the peripheries of power: island communities, the

Antipodes, the western United States.[32] The historian Rochelle Ruthchild has drawn attention to the central importance of the Russian empire to the early women's suffrage story, though Finland was an outpost of that empire, and not at its core.[33] Finland in 1906 led the way both in Scandinavia and Europe and, most importantly, set an example for revolutionary Russia to enfranchise women, making Russia the first of the major powers to do so.

The early Scandinavian enfranchisements showed nationalism, not feminism, as the most important motivating force. In each case women embodied national virtues and their political enfranchisement promoted a consolidation of nationalist ideals. It was a national, even a conservative, rather than a radical act to enfranchise women. Women's enfranchisement was later, after the example of Sweden, to be a specifically conservative act, aimed at expanding democracy to subvert revolution.

The disappointing outcome of women-only lists in Iceland was later experienced in Britain and the US in the failure of the pressure-group politics of women's suffrage to be translated into effective political strength. Merely being female clearly did not confer a sufficient unity of interests for continued political action.

8

Lobbyists to militants in Britain

'It is better to burn a house than to injure little children'

Emmeline Pankhurst was on her way from Geneva where she had taken her eldest daughter Christabel to stay with a family friend. She had been travelling unceasingly—from Switzerland to Paris, to the coast, across the channel, to London, until finally she took the train to Manchester. She was anxious because she had received a telegram the previous day, Monday 4 July 1898, which said her husband Richard was ill and she should return. The eldest family member at home was her 16-year-old daughter Sylvia, who must be caring for her sick father. The last letter from him to Emmeline had been a loving note showing that nineteen years of married life had not dimmed their affection, 'When you return, we will have a new honeymoon and reconsecrate each to the other in unity of heart.'

Finally, on the last leg of her journey, she boarded the train from London to Manchester. A man entered her compartment and opened an evening newspaper. She saw in it a black border and the announcement 'Death of Dr Pankhurst'. Emmeline cried out in shock, to the consternation of the other passengers. Richard Pankhurst's death was an event of tragic drama for the Pankhurst family, and a blow to the radical causes he had supported with such zeal, but it also had more far-reaching consequences. It led directly to the most bizarre sequence of events in the history of women's suffrage: the development of militancy.[1]

Cause first

Emmeline Goulden was born on (or near) 14 July 1858 to Sophie and Robert Goulden who lived in Moss Side, Manchester. Robert Goulden was a partner in a cotton printing firm. Emmeline's parents were vigorous anti-slavery campaigners; her earliest political memory was of collecting money in a bag at a bazaar to relieve the poverty of newly emancipated slaves. Sophie Goulden subscribed to *Women's Suffrage Journal* and Emmeline attended her first women's suffrage meeting when she was 14 in 1872. As a girl she was sent to school in Paris and was forever afterwards inspired by the romantic spirit of the French Revolution, and for this reason may well have chosen to celebrate her birthday on the revolutionary anniversary of 14 July. On the bourgeois side, her daughter Sylvia reports her as an advocate of the dowry and 'the French system of marriage by arrangement'.[2] She showed herself in later life to be as deeply rooted in conventional assumptions about sex and marriage as any average middle-class woman, which put her at odds with both her father and her daughter Sylvia.

Richard Pankhurst was a friend of her family, an inspiring local leader whom Emmeline instantly adored on seeing him cheered at a radical meeting. At 20 in 1878 Emmeline was small, slim, with violet-blue eyes, olive skin, and jet black hair. Pankhurst was a small, energetic man with a surprisingly high voice, red hair, and a pointed, red beard. Emmeline's mother accused her of throwing herself at this man, twenty-three years her senior, but the couple gave every impression of being made for each other. Their courtship took place against a backdrop of the agitation for the Married Women's Property Act (of 1884) and high-minded conversation about the higher education of women. She proposed they have a free union after the style of Mary Wollstonecraft, but Pankhurst told her it would be better for the cause if they didn't, as 'people who had displayed unconventionality in that direction, had usually been prevented from doing effective public work in any other.'[3] They were married on 18 December 1879.

The couple had five children, those who were influential in the suffrage movement were Christabel who was born in 1880, Sylvia in 1882; and Adele in 1885. Two boys died young, one an infant. Richard Pankhurst insisted that the children should be worth the trouble he had taken in having a family and exhorted them 'almost daily': 'If you do not work for other people, you will not have been worth the upbringing.'[4] Adela Pankhurst gave one of the most penetrating critiques of her family when she said, 'It was the family attitude—Cause First and human relations—nowhere.'[5]

Richard Pankhurst had delayed marriage because he wanted to devote himself to the cause (in fact, many causes) and he had probably made the correct decision as his high principles always seemed to lead him to take

the path which produced the least income. As he was unable to provide sufficiently for the family they moved into Emmeline's parents' household. In
a dispute over pacifism and imperialist expansion, Richard determined he
would resign from the Liberal Party and stand as an independent. He lost by
a large margin, and lost again when he stood as a radical in Rotherhithe in
the general election of 1885; and again when he stood for the Independent
Labour Party in Gorton in 1895.

The couple became increasingly socialist through the 1880s, and Richard
had become an agnostic, thus offending against both his father-in-law's
Liberalism and his Christianity. The atmosphere became so unbearable that
the young couple left the Goulden house in 1885. Emmeline had argued
with her father about an amount of property she supposed she had a right
to have settled on her (this was a recurrence of an earlier argument she had
had with him about a dowry). She never spoke to him again.

The Pankhurst family went to London where they opened a fancy goods
shop, one of three unsuccessful shop-running ventures that Emmeline
undertook in her life. At their home in Russell Square, Emmeline became a
hostess to gatherings of people including such radical women as Annie
Besant and Eleanor Marx. Emmeline was prominent in progressive causes
including the match girls' strike and the right to free assembly, and during
this period she left the Liberals (of whose promises for the enfranchisement
of women she had become deeply suspicious) and joined the Independent
Labour Party.

'Labour', both as represented by trade unions and the nascent political
parties (the Independent Labour Party then the Labour Party to which it
was affiliated) was a new and ever more powerful force in British politics
at the beginning of the twentieth century. The labour movement was not
necessarily in favour of votes for women; many working men were conservative by nature and assumed that an increase in the affluence of the working
class would strengthen the family set-up to which they aspired, that of the
middle class, with a man properly remunerated for his labour presiding over
a family in which his wife stayed at home and looked after the children. For
them women's political rights were at best a distraction from the real business of labour representation. Others simply looked at the parliamentary
arithmetic and judged that the enfranchisement of women on the same
basis as men would give greater power to property-owning women who
were most likely to vote Conservative, less likely to vote for the Liberals, but
hardly likely at all to vote for Labour candidates.

Against this was the contribution of women to trade union and political activity and the fact that, as women were members of trade unions such as those in the textile industry, their membership contributions would be used to support parliamentary activity, a situation which was obviously inequitable when women had no representation. The seemingly fair solution was to put forward a demand for full adult suffrage. At Trades Union Congresses in 1901 and 1902, adult suffrage amendments were put forward in order to sideline specifically women's suffrage. At the end of the nineteenth century, after the 1884 electoral reform, two in every three men were enfranchised, so making mere adulthood a qualification for voting would add proportionately few men to the register, and they would be almost entirely lower class. Adding women would, similarly, see the working class predominate as they were in the majority in society, so universal suffrage was unlikely to be welcomed by the middle class. There was also the persistent fear among those who contemplated the future that as women were in the majority in Britain, universal suffrage would be nothing short of a gender revolution, with women moving from a position of having no political power to having the majority share. This made universal suffrage unlikely in the short term— and therefore an easy idealistic demand to make. Within the ranks of organized labour, however, there were radical thinkers who genuinely believed in political equality such as Keir Hardie and George Lansbury, with Ramsay Macdonald and Philip Snowden rather more lukewarm. Supporting labour's political representation was a good bet for those supporting women's suffrage; the questioning of parliamentary candidates to ensure their support, and meetings in public halls, which was the staple of the National Union of Women's Suffrage Societies, could achieve only so much.

The birth of the WSPU

The Pankhurst family's poor financial plight meant they could no longer afford to live in London, so in early 1893 they returned to Manchester where Richard still had some work. His sudden death five years later at the age of 64 from a gastric ulcer was a shock to all; its effect on Emmeline was devastating, she was said never again to have shown the lightness of spirit she had when her husband was alive. The influence on her politics was the removal of his restraining influence over her tempestuous nature. It was not merely that no one could tell her what to do, either in her family or her political life, but that she respected no guiding influence save that of her eldest daughter, Christabel. Emmeline Pankhurst was a great, inspiring activist, but her political thinking was crude and unsophisticated, which led her to repeated strategic mistakes. The activism brought the grudging admiration of other suffrage campaigners, the mistakes brought their contempt.

Richard Pankhurst had left less than £500 but the funeral costs and his debts exceeded that, and the family was obliged to sell their furniture and paintings and move to a smaller house in Nelson Street, in a poorer neighbourhood. Emmeline took on a job as a Registrar of Births and Deaths which gave her an income and an official position and, she later commented, gave her a deeper understanding of the injustices in society which she believed would be addressed if women had the vote.

The long-term effect of Richard Pankhurst's death on the political scene was connected with efforts to help to provide for his family. Emmeline had a resistance to receiving charity and refused to take money from an appeal in her husband's name, saying instead that money collected should be used to finance a hall to be used for socialist meetings.

Sylvia, always closest to her father, was the artist of the family and had won a scholarship to the Manchester School of Art. She took on the task of painting murals in the hall which had been built in St James Road, Salford, to commemorate her father. While doing this Sylvia discovered that the Independent Labour Party branch that was to meet there would not admit women. The Pankhursts were outraged that Pankhurst Hall, decorated at no charge by Sylvia and dedicated to Richard's memory, was to embody an injustice against which Richard Pankhurst had always fought.

With the call to action that always characterized her, Emmeline Pankhurst told women friends, 'We must have an independent women's movement. Come to my house tomorrow and we will arrange it.'[6] Thus on 10 October 1903 a group of women socialists met at Nelson Street and voted to form what became called the Women's Social and Political Union. It was to be a women-only organization, thus embodying the paradox that confronted with a single-sex club, Emmeline formed a single-sex pressure group. Though the WSPU was a female membership organization, it was one to which men contributed. Keir Hardie, one of two Labour MPs, met WSPU women in Manchester and gave practical support from the beginning; and men were always needed to do the technical work of bringing forward and arguing parliamentary bills.[7]

The success of women in other areas of life had left suffrage as something of an anomaly. What did women want it *for*, if the most clearly unjust laws had been addressed by an all-male legislature and contributions in the professions and wider political life were actively being made by women? Emmeline Pankhurst addressed this question by saying the vote was wanted for three reasons, 'first of all, a symbol, secondly a safeguard, and thirdly an instrument'. It was a symbol of liberty, and 'a safeguard of all those liberties which it symbolises' and an instrument for redressing society's wrongs.[8]

The WSPU's objective was 'To secure for Women the Parliamentary Vote as it is or may be granted to men' which was the same as the objective of the National Union of Women's Suffrage Societies so there was no rift between them on that. 'Deeds not words was to be our permanent motto,' declared Emmeline about the founding of the Women's Social and Political Union, though the first two years of the organization found it involved in the same kind of activity as other suffrage societies: building membership and sending out visiting speakers to ILP and trade union functions and other gatherings that were likely to support them.[9]

Emmeline worked with the ILP until 1905, being re-elected to its National Administrative Council in spring of that year. She found it easy to obtain full approval for policies calling for women's suffrage on the same basis as men, but the same delegates also supported complete adult suffrage. She was still asking the working class to support a measure which, by giving women the vote on the same basis by which men currently held it, would increase the number of Conservative and Liberal voters at a time when the tiny ILP needed all the votes it could get. John Bruce Glasier, chairman of the ILP and formerly a good friend of the Pankhursts argued this point with her and expressed 'scorn of their miserable individualist sexism'.[10]

Hardie showed a longstanding dedication to 'the woman question' and, most importantly, to Emmeline's gender-based approach to suffrage that points to a deeper motivation than the cause alone, particularly as he had to countermand explicit instructions from his party in order to forward motions for the Pankhursts. Hardie's colleagues knew he was entranced by the Pankhursts but believed, as Glasier wrote, that Emmeline was 'the Delilah who had cut our Sampson's locks'.[11] In fact it was Sylvia. The second daughter of the Pankhurst family had completed her studies in Manchester, travelled to Venice and finally went to the Royal College of Art in Kensington. It was here, living in Chelsea, that she started having sex with Keir Hardie, twenty-six years older than herself, and whom she had known since she was a schoolgirl, though she was 22 in 1904 which is probably when the affair started. 'To me, he was a tremendous hero,' she wrote; they were to be intimate until his death in 1915.[12]

Emmeline was appalled when she found out; knowledge of the affair further irritated her already difficult relationship with Sylvia. The age difference between the lovers might have concerned some mothers, but as it was not much more than the difference between her own age and that of Richard Pankhurst when they married, she could hardly make a great deal of it. His adultery (he had a wife in Ayrshire) and the issue of extra-marital sex doubtless perturbed her. Probably the main problem was Emmeline's excessively fastidious attitude to sex. As the ghost-writer of her biography, Rheta Childe Dorr said, 'I never found her interested in the full freedom of women. I could never get her to talk about any phase of women's sexual nature. The subject repelled her...I sometimes suspected that Mrs Pankhurst believed celibacy for both men and women an ideal condition.'[13] This narrowness is not so remarkable for a Victorian woman (though it is for a radical one) and is only worth remarking on because of the direction taken by the WSPU in the final stages of 'militancy'.

The other main player in the Pankhurst family dynamic was Christabel, who studied law in Manchester for three years from 1903. At university she took more of an interest in women's suffrage than she had previously, falling under the influence of Eva Gore-Booth and Esther Roper. Her mother resented their influence over Christabel, 'her first-born had ever been the dearest of her children' according to Sylvia in her book *The Suffragette Movement*, which is both a history of the pressure group and a family memoir that gave her ample opportunity for the working out of sibling rivalry.[14]

Emmeline stayed with Sylvia in February 1905 while they worked with Kier Hardie to find a member who had drawn a high position in the ballot for private members' bills and whom they might persuade to bring in a Women's Enfranchisement Bill. This was the first women's bill for eight years and that it was even set down was entirely due to the lobbying efforts of Emmeline, and Keir Hardie's dedication and parliamentary skills.

At the reading of the Women's Enfranchisement Bill on 12 May Emmeline was one of some 300 women in the lobby; the Bill was a Second Order of the Day. The opponents of women's suffrage were able to extend the debate on a previous bill with parliamentary jocularities until the afternoon—a common parliamentary procedure but one which infuriated the women in the gallery. They went outside when the house rose and, with Hardie, held a meeting there—against the law that no demonstration must take place in the precincts of Westminster when the house was sitting. It was the WSPU's first militant act. The next time Hardie attempted to bring forward a parliamentary resolution, in April 1906, Emmeline Pankhurst and her supporters in the ladies' gallery, misunderstanding procedure and believing the resolution would be talked out, started shouting and throwing flags down into the chamber. The debate ended without a vote. Hardie was embarrassed before his colleagues, among whom he now had few friends (he had retained his party leadership by just one vote). Emmeline clearly had no skill in, or sympathy for, parliamentary activity: her talents lay in another direction.

True to its origins among Independent Labour Party activists, the Women's Social and Political Union took to engaging the working class in meetings at open-air fairs where their new recruit, cotton factory girl Annie Kenney, spoke to her own in their own language. Annie, whose mother had died in 1905, had been taken in by Emmeline as if she were another daughter. Another new recruit was Teresa Billington, a schoolteacher whose agnosticism had brought her into conflict with school authorities; Emmeline Pankhurst was then on the Manchester Education Committee and was able to arrange for Billington's transfer to a Jewish school where she would not be expected to give religious guidance.

Emmeline Pankhurst was convinced that women must get the vote before manhood suffrage or, she believed, they would never agree to enfranchise women. Time would tell that this prediction was wrong: in many countries in the next half century men's preceded women's suffrage, but in the first years of the twentieth century, with women enfranchised only in New Zealand, Australia, and some parts of the US, there was no pattern of women's suffrage for her to gauge the likely outcome: she was looking at uncharted political territory.

An election was imminent in 1905, which the Liberals were sure to win, so it was judged by the WSPU inner circle that the way forward was to press leading Liberals on the subject in the election campaign. To this end, Emmeline and some trusted supporters including Christabel, Annie Kenney, and Teresa Billington discussed making the leap into direct action. On 13 October 1905 Christabel left the house in Nelson Street with Annie, saying to Emmeline, 'We shall sleep in prison tonight.'[15]

The young women went to a meeting at the Free Trade Hall where the future Foreign Secretary Sir Edward Grey (incidentally, a consistent supporter of women's suffrage) was speaking. After he had spoken Annie stood up and shouted out, 'Will the Liberal government give women the vote?' There was no answer and Christabel unfolded a fabric 'Votes for Women' banner she had hidden in her blouse and shouted the question again. The chief constable of Manchester intervened to invite them to put their question in writing so it could be handed to the speaker. Sir Edward then responded to the vote of thanks but did not answer the question. Annie stood on her chair and shouted the question again as did Christabel and stewards roughly manhandled the two shouting women to an ante-room where police asked them to behave themselves and said they could leave. Christabel had anticipated this, and she spat in the faces of two policemen, thus committing a technical assault, and struck one of them in the mouth. The police took them downstairs to the street and asked them to leave. Outside, Christabel declared they must hold a meeting and addressed the crowds leaving the hall. Now they finally achieved their goal and were arrested.

The next day they were charged with disorderly behaviour, causing an obstruction, and assaulting the police. Christabel admitted the offences but said it was a result of the legal position of women that they should be obliged to commit acts of civil disobedience: 'We cannot make an orderly protest because we have not the means whereby citizens may do such a thing.'[16] The magistrates imposed small fines with an alternative of seven days in jail for Christabel and three for Annie. Refusing to pay, they were both driven off to prison, as the WSPU's first martyrs.

Teresa Billington had originally intended to form part of the protest but, with an early indication of the value the WSPU gave to publicity, she stayed away in order to promote press interest. This was a spectacular success, as Christabel wrote, 'The long, long newspaper silence as to woman suffrage was broken.'[17] It mattered not at all to her that the coverage was almost without exception hostile: women's suffrage was on the political map for this election. They had also pushed the barriers of the sort of political activity women might undertake: spitting, standing on chairs, shouting, and calling a meeting in the street were received with disdain by many, but for a new generation of women, tired of the patient and fruitless campaigning of the NUWSS, it spelled advance.

Emmeline had wished to pay the women's fines, and did not immediately realize the explosive effect of imprisoning women for political offences. Her quality as a leader was not strategic thinking, but her ability to seize the moment and act decisively before her opponents had time to know what was happening. The night of the sentencing, while Christabel and Annie were in prison, Emmeline called a meeting; a crowd of two thousand met Annie on her release on the 16 October; four days later on Christabel's release, there was a huge rally, symbolically held at the Free Trade Hall, at which the two women spoke and received bouquets, and Keir Hardie condemned the treatment they had received.

Christabel now had to retreat from the fray temporarily, under threat of being expelled from Owen's college. Emmeline's position as a Registrar was also threatened, so their commitment was not without personal cost. Emmeline made maximum use of the excitement generated by the election and her confrontational approach by herself travelling widely to address meetings on 'Women and Socialism' while calling on WSPU members to attend meetings conducted by the members of the Liberal cabinet, which was serving as a caretaker government following the resignation of the Conservatives. In a foretaste of the future, some previous supporters were put off by the barracking. Winston Churchill, who had voted for women's suffrage, declared himself against the proposition if militants were going to 'henpeck' him on a question of such importance.[18] The election resulted in a Liberal landslide, a respectable number of Labour MPs elected (twenty-nine including Keir Hardie), and the emergence of the WSPU as a political force. They even gained a distinguishing name, 'suffragettes', a supposedly insulting diminutive applied to them by the *Daily Mail* but which they embraced.

In a light on the usual process of women's suffrage advances taking place in peripheral areas, a remarkable event occurred in Wigan in Lancashire: textile workers ran a Women's Suffrage candidate. Thorley Smith, a stonemason and a local councillor who was well known locally in Labour and trade union circles, stood for women's suffrage in 1906. He was unsuccessful but he received 2,205 votes, beating the Liberal candidate but being defeated by the Conservative who received 3,575. This straw in the wind did not impress Emmeline, who always considered the centre of political activity was London. She sent Annie Kenney as an emissary to live with supporters (in fact she lived with Sylvia) and 'rouse London'. She first set out to contact women in the impoverished East End, showing again the left-wing radicalism of the WSPU at this time.

They planned a rally for the state opening of parliament on 19 February 1906, for which on Keir Hardie's advice they booked the Caxton Hall. Emmeline, when she arrived in London, was worried that the meeting might be an embarrassment, just a handful of supporters rattling in the enormous hall. Sylvia and Hardie called on East End MP George Lansbury, who with his daughters rounded up East End support. On the day, the hall was full to its 700 capacity with more women outside. The meeting was taking place when the news came through that no mention was made in the King's Speech of women's suffrage. Emmeline, as usual in command of the situation, immediately moved a resolution that the meeting should at once proceed to the House of Commons to lobby members. It was raining and bitterly cold but the gathering took up this adventure: 'they followed her to a woman,' wrote Sylvia, 'though many of them had never set eyes on her before.'[19] They found their way barred by the police with orders not to admit women. They waited in the cold and wet outside the House of Commons while relays of twenty were allowed in to lobby MPs. The press attention further publicized Emmeline's position and emphasized the WSPU as the primary force in the women's suffrage cause.

Despite its publicity successes, the WSPU was a poorly run pressure group with more enthusiasm than organization. Keir Hardie in 1906 introduced Emmeline Pankhurst to Emmeline Pethick-Lawrence, a wealthy activist, and her equally radical husband, Frederick. Emmeline Pankhurst wooed her unsuccessfully, and they were never to be friends; but Annie Kenney won her over with her unique charm. The wealthy couple also became devoted to Christabel, who lived with them once she had completed her law degree. The London WSPU committee now became the national committee with Emmeline Pethick-Lawrence putting the movement on a sound financial footing and Frederick becoming business manager. They first operated from a spare room in the Pethick-Lawrences' London flat in Clement's Inn, then took over the lower floor of Clement's Inn, from which they launched the newspaper with its name the same as their bold, modern slogan: *Votes for Women*.

This phase of WSPU activity involved activists in the harassment of government ministers, technical assaults on the police and subsequent imprisonment. On one occasion a deputation sat on the steps of 10 Downing Street insisting on seeing the prime minister; at another time Annie Kenney jumped on the prime minister's car and began to give a speech. The objective was to disrupt the government in any way possible until it acceded to their demands. Although this might have appeared an effective procedure, in fact it meant that supporters such as Lloyd George were under attack, while opponents of women's suffrage on the conservative side were not. There was, however, considerable publicity value.

With public success came the divisions of the Pankhurst family, with Sylvia under the influence of Keir Hardie staying on the left, while Christabel, never a natural socialist, was more at home entertaining fashionable ladies in Emmeline Pethick-Lawrence's rooms at Clements Inn. She and her mother's distancing from Labour was accelerated by the Labour Party conference early in 1907 that rejected a motion brought by Hardie for women's suffrage. By almost three to one the delegates voted instead for adult suffrage. Emmeline and Christabel soon resigned from the ILP.

The WSPU's principles were soon enunciated in a way which would not alienate the middle class by threatening to swamp their influence with working-class voters: 'The Women's Social and Political Union are NOT asking for a vote for every woman, but simply that sex shall cease to be a disqualification for the franchise.'[20]

Splits and militancy

When the organization was run from Emmeline Pankhurst's home, the dominance of Emmeline and her family members was unquestioned. With a national movement and the engagement of practical women such as Emmeline Pethick-Lawrence, Teresa Billington, and Charlotte Despard, it was thought time to give the movement a constitutional framework.

In the annual conference planned for 12 October 1907 several leading members intended to put the WSPU on a democratic footing; there had been extensive discussions regarding the form a democratic constitution would take. Teresa Billington described discussing differences with Emmeline Pankhurst: 'You might have offered some variation of agreement, some indication of a differing view. But this was ignored. You left her [Emmeline Pankhurst] feeling that without any definite committal on her part or agreement on yours, the line of action to be taken was settled.'[21] Emmeline Pankhurst was not keen on losing hold of her organization. Emmeline Pethick-Lawrence described Emmeline Pankhurst's response: 'I shall never forget the gesture with which she swept from the board all the "pros and cons" which had caused us sleepless nights. "I shall tear up the constitution" she declared.'[22] Assured of Mrs Pethick-Lawrence's support, Emmeline Pankhurst called an 'urgent' meeting of the WSPU, annulled the constitution, cancelled the annual conference and declared that a new committee could be elected from those present. Only London members had been invited, however, so the meeting could hardly be considered representative of a national organization.

Those who favoured democracy with their campaigning for the vote, including such notables as Teresa Billington (now Billington-Greig) and Charlotte Despard, left the WSPU, and continued with non-violent militant actions under the name Women's Freedom League. At its height the Women's Freedom League had sixty-one branches to the WSPU's ninety (though the WSPU was less interested in forming branches than in having individual agitators working in districts).[23] The net result of the split was the loss of many working-class members from the WSPU with the realignment of northern branches, and the almost complete loss of Scotland and Wales, which each had only three branches remaining. Despite its spirited interventions in public life, the Women's Freedom League was never to seize the public imagination as did the WSPU, which was also more emotionally satisfying for the activists.

The absurdity of calling for democracy by an organization that did not practise it was lost on Emmeline Pankhurst, who felt that she was a military leader of a volunteer army: no one had to join up but if they did they must be disciplined. Her supporters were fired by such an approach: 'our committee was replaced by a dictatorship. As a fighting unit this was immeasurably superior for a committee can never fight,' wrote one.[24] The suffragettes as they were now formed up after the 1907 split, with their brass bands and processions, open-air meetings and domination by one family, had more than a little of the Salvation Army about them. There was also something of revivalist religion about the promise of redemption when the vote was won, which would introduce an era of peace and social progress. The feting and parading of imprisoned women fed notions of 'martyrdom' and 'suffering for the cause' and some elements of Christianity were adopted wholesale such as 'self-denial week', a secular Lent in which activists abstained from using butter, sugar, meat, and sweets so the money saved by the sacrifice could be offered up to the movement.

The high point of spectacle was reached at a vast demonstration on 21 June 1908 following (and overshadowing) a similar demonstration by the NUWSS the previous week. Under colourful banners fluttering in the sun bands played stirring suffrage songs in processions under the direction of a chief marshal who had under her command group marshals, banner marshals, group captains, stewards, and sergeants. Women came to London from seventy provincial centres, forming a crowd of between a quarter and half a million. Seven processions converged on Hyde Park, for the first time marching in white with trimmings of green and purple, following Emmeline Pethick-Lawrence's colour scheme of white for purity, green for hope, and purple for dignity. In five years the WSPU had developed from a meeting of a handful of people in a Manchester sitting room to a demonstration of hundreds of thousands in the centre of the capital; but such dynamism needed an ever increasing level of excitement to sustain itself.

Representations from the great suffrage demonstrations were met with disdain by Prime Minister Asquith, which led to women throwing stones through the windows of 10 Downing Street—damage to property being an escalation of militancy from the technical assaults that had previously led to imprisonment. Emmeline Pankhurst visited the perpetrators in the police cells and assured them of her approval of their actions.

An organized 'rush' on the House of Commons at the resumption of another parliamentary term in October 1908 led to a charge of incitement to riot against Emmeline and Christabel Pankhurst, who refused to go to the police station, obliging the police to come to WSPU headquarters to arrest them in front of the waiting press cameras. Supporters arranged for beds and other comforts to be sent to the police station from the Savoy Hotel and a meal was served by three waiters.

In court, the case for the women was conducted by Christabel; she had passed her law degree but as women were forbidden from practising in Britain, she had never commenced the process of being called to the bar. She turned the proceedings into a legal spectacular by serving subpoenas on Home Secretary Herbert Gladstone and Chancellor of the Exchequer Lloyd George who were obliged to answer her questions, making the trial a fine performance for the newspapers. Emmeline finished her statement to the magistrate with the memorable line, 'We are here not because we are law-breakers, we are here in our efforts to become law-makers.'[25] Emmeline was sentenced to three months, Christabel to ten weeks. At the end of this Christabel had served eleven weeks of imprisonment in total; she did not react well to the experience and ensured that she would not be imprisoned again, though she posed in prison dress with her mother for promotional photographs.

The Home Secretary now made a major error that was taken to justify all the following acts of militancy by the suffragettes. He explained why the government was refusing to give time to a private member's bill brought by Liberal Henry Stanger that had received a second-reading majority of 273 to 94. Women had a fine argument for the vote, Herbert Gladstone acknowledged in the House of Commons, but

> experience shows that predominance of argument alone...is not enough to win the political day...Members of the House reflect the opinions of the country not only in regard to the numbers outside, but with regard to the intensity of feeling.... Men have learned their lesson, and know the necessity for establishing that force majeure which actuates and arms a Government for effective work. That is the task before the supporters of this great movement...Looking back at the great political crisis in the thirties, the sixties and the eighties [when reform bills enfranchised successive groups of men] it will be found that people did not go about in small groups, nor were they content with enthusiastic meetings in large halls; they assembled in their tens of thousands all over the country...of course it is not to be expected that women could assemble in such masses, but...power rests with the masses and through this power a government could be influenced into more effective action.[26]

If women would only behave as men had done, he was saying, they could win the vote. The Conservative leader Arthur Balfour had given similar unintentional encouragement to militancy when he told Christabel, in answer to her question why the Conservatives had not enfranchised women, 'Well, to tell you the truth, your cause is not in the swim.'[27] Obviously these men did not think women would (or could) threaten masculine levels of political violence. They were to be enlightened over the next six years.

Herbert Gladstone also foolishly refused demands for suffragettes to be treated as political prisoners, and remarked that they could not court a prison sentence and then, when they had received one, expect to be treated better than everyone else. This was a serious mistake: immediately making it publicly known how well the suffragettes were being treated in prison would have undermined admiration for such martyrdom. At a later stage when the suffragettes contrived to make their prison sentences as demeaning and brutal as possible they gained the greatest sympathy. Suffragettes worked hard to establish prison uniform as a badge of courage; they demonstrated outside Holloway prison, dressed in copies of prison uniform to show solidarity, loudly singing suffragette songs so Emmeline and her colleagues could hear them over the walls. A silver 'prison badge' was made up in Union colours to be awarded to those who had been imprisoned for the cause.

By the summer of 1909, however, the movement had stalled and was losing support, even though its ability to attract support from society women
meant funds were high; again no mention of women's suffrage was included
in the King's speech in February and again there was a protest and arrests.
Despite WSPU interventions, the government was not losing by-elections
and was in fact extremely popular, having introduced old age pensions in
1908, and was gearing up for a great constitutional battle against the House
of Lords. Millicent Fawcett and the NUWSS tended to side with the government, partly because there were so many Liberals in their ranks, but also
because the House of Lords would otherwise be an insuperable barrier to
women's suffrage, as the upper house in any parliament was almost invariably more conservative than the lower.

The WSPU needed to raise the stakes and, in a characteristic procedure,
it was the activists who led, with Emmeline Pankhurst and the headquarters
team supporting their spontaneous actions. The first hunger striker, an artist
called Marion Wallace Dunlop, refused food in a bid to be declared a political prisoner in July 1909 and was released after a few days. Other women
therefore followed the same tactic, and the government escalated by starting
forcible feeding in September. Emmeline Pankhurst said hunger striking
had, 'lifted the militant movement onto a new and more heroic plane'.[28]

Women were being forcibly stripped for refusing to wear prison regulation clothes and forcibly fed. Descriptions for the public emphasized the
physical brutality of such procedures, often carried out by male prison doctors, making the procedures seem like a rape, such as Sylvia's description:

> A man's hands were trying to force open my mouth; my breath was coming
> so fast that I felt as though I should suffocate. His fingers were striving to pull
> my lips apart—getting inside. I felt them and a steel instrument pressing round
> my gums, feeling for gaps in my teeth. I was trying to jerk my head away,
> trying to wrench it free. Two of them were holding it, two of them dragging
> at my mouth. I was panting and heaving, my breath quicker and louder,
> coming now with a low scream which was growing louder. 'Here is a gap,' one
> of them said 'No, here is a better one. This long gap here!' A steel instrument
> pressed my gums, cutting into the flesh. I braced myself to resist that terrible
> pain.[29]

Internationally, though attitudes were equivocal, the publicity was bene-
ficial. The leading Dutch women's suffragist, Aletta Jacobs said, 'From its
inception I had disliked this movement's militancy, but I had to admit that
it had brought us closer to achieving our goal. Millions of people who had

Femminismo eroicomico : lo sciopero della fame delle suffragiste inglesi interrotto con la loro nutrizione forzata in prigione.

(Disegno di A. Beltrame).

Figure 7. The force-feeding of imprisoned British suffragettes attracted inter-national attention. This 1909 picture from the Italian newspaper the *Sunday Courier* shows an imagined situation; in fact there would have been no policemen present in the prison and no audience of other women for the procedure, but the image of a woman being literally man-handled is compelling.

not heard or read of suffrage, and hence had never thought about it, were now being confronted with the subject almost every day.' Another benefit was that by comparison, Jacobs' group and other suffragists were praised for their calm and moderate behaviour.[30]

Another Dutch suffragist, Rosa Manus, described a rally at the Albert Hall in 1909:

> Mrs Pethick-Lawrence was in the chair and Mrs Pankhurst and Christabel Pankhurst spoke. On the platform were seated all the women and girls who had been in prison. They were dressed in white and wore the colours of the suffragettes, green, mauve and white. They held big banners and flags in their hands and every moment when one of these women said a word they approved of they *all* called out together—here here!! [*sic*] Or if they disapproved—shame—shame. It is a ridiculous way. They wanted to persuade everybody that the militant tactics are the best and that only the vote can be obtained through the militant tactics. Everybody who at first thought they like the work of the suffragettes changed their opinion after that evening.[31]

With little being achieved by government or suffragettes, both sides were happy when a truce in militant activities was declared in 1910 in the hope that the new Liberal government, elected in January with a reduced majority, would make concessions over suffrage. Discussions between Millicent Fawcett and other moderate suffragists resulted in the Conciliation Committee chaired by Lord Lytton, a Conservative peer and brother of a prominent suffragette. With representatives from all parties, it aimed to put forward a compromise bill. Though the objective was honestly intentioned, its provisions tended towards the Conservative Party's wish to enfranchise the propertied class: female heads of household and occupiers of property with a £10 rentable value. Liberals were more inclined to favour adult suffrage. All the suffrage societies supported it, though many without enthusiasm. The WSPU was able to generate publicity, but it was always a minority organization: historian Martin Pugh comments that the WSPU's branch membership represented only one in six of the total number of women's suffrage organizations in the country.[32]

Labour MP David Shackleton's Women's Franchise (Conciliation) Bill passed its second reading in the House of Commons with a majority of 110 but it was then sent to a 'committee of the whole house' which meant that unless the government would give it time, it must fail. Emmeline Pankhurst had been threatening a resumption of militancy, and true to her gift of timing, she was speaking to a meeting at the Caxton Hall on 18 November 1910 when the news came through that only government business would be dealt with in the near future, and nothing was said of the Conciliation Bill. The audience was immediately divided into contingents of twelve for a march on parliament. Emmeline Pankhurst and Elizabeth Garrett Anderson were allowed through, but others in the first group were refused and for hours police used force to beat the women back. Police had been instructed not to make arrests, which would only have resulted in a celebration of imprisonment and hunger striking, but to use all force necessary repel the women. This gave the men free rein—uniformed police officers, plain clothes officers, and members of the public who took advantage of the confusion to molest women. Accusations were made of sexual assaults consisting of wrenching breasts and lifting skirts, in an event that came to be called 'Black Friday'. The use of force when women protested in person was a direct cause of the next stage of militancy which concentrated on attacks on property.

Millicent Fawcett and the National Union of Women's Suffrage Societies were infuriated that the WSPU had broken their truce when there was still life in the Conciliation Bill. As Lord Lytton said to a meeting, 'Conciliation and militancy cannot go hand in hand. What is so humiliating in this fresh outbreak is that it implies that the committee has failed, and we have not failed. The committee has accepted on good faith the Prime Minister's statement as an undertaking to grant facilities to our bill in the next parliament.'[33] The bill was resurrected in the new parliament and in May 1911 passed its second reading with a larger majority than previously.

The bill now aimed to enfranchise only a small number of women householders, and many Liberals wanted a wider extension of the electorate. On 7 November 1911 Asquith announced the next session would include a government manhood suffrage bill. He added that the bill would be open to amendment and the government would not oppose a women's suffrage measure, but for the WSPU it was a betrayal.

The resumption of militancy had been planned: women with stones and hammers smashed the windows of government offices and the National Liberal Federation but for the first time also targeted private property: the *Daily Mail*, Swan and Edgar's, and other businesses. Emmeline Pankhurst announced ominously in February 1912 that, other arguments having failed to persuade, the next argument would be that of the stone, but: 'If the argument of the stone, that time-honoured official political argument, is sufficient, then we will never use any stronger argument.'[34] Throughout 1 March 1912 suffragettes were engaged in smashing plate glass windows in the West End. Well-dressed, harmless-looking groups of women with no obvious connection to the WSPU approached major department stores and produced hammers from muffs or bags which they used to smash windows. Almost 400 were smashed, for which 121 women were arrested.

The (revived) Conciliation Bill was rejected on its third reading by four-teen votes. The Irish nationalists, previous supporters, at this point voted against for fear that the bill's success would mean Asquith's resignation and they relied on him for their Home Rule plans. The Liberals could claim they had rejected it in favour of the government's recently announced man-hood suffrage Bill with the possibility of a women's suffrage amendment. However, more Conservatives had voted against it this time than previously, despite the fact that the alternative manhood suffrage Bill would do them no good electorally. The reason for their opposition had to be that they found the militant suffragette tactics repellent. The other suffrage societies felt there was the chance for real progress in 1912: an extended franchise was on the agenda and was being discussed, the last thing they wanted was van-dalism which discredited the cause.

The destruction of private property was too much for the authorities and warrants were issued for the arrest of the Pethick-Lawrences and Christabel Pankhurst (Emmeline Pankhurst was already in prison for her own window-breaking episode). Frederick Pethick-Lawrence was able to send a message to Christabel. She counter-signed a cheque to withdraw all the funds from the WSPU; they would be deposited in the bank account of a supporter. She took a cab to Victoria, entered the station to throw off police who might be pursuing her, and left to take a cab. She went to a nursing home run by supporters in West London where she was disguised as a nurse. Police called just after her recognizable, flamboyant hat had been destroyed in the drawing-room fire; Christabel had already gone to the flat of another sup-porter. The next day she took the train to Folkestone and a boat to France. She was to live out the rest of the period of militancy in Paris, regularly visited by supporters who took back her instructions on further militant actions.

Christabel was easily open to accusations of leading from the rear, par-ticularly as this was not the first time she had evaded danger: she had stayed behind in Caxton Hall when ranks of women had marched out to Parliament to be confronted by the police. On her side, the authorities clearly had the objective of destroying the leadership and so had to be frustrated in this aim by her preservation. Moreover, there was a real danger of Emmeline Pankhurst's dying as a result of her repeated imprisonments and hunger striking which she undertook for the first time the month after Christabel's departure. The movement needed a healthy leader. Christabel was also con-vinced of her own abilities: 'I was fortunately able to read the mind and discern the purpose of the government in general and in particular of Mr Lloyd George,' she wrote.[35] She invited comparisons between herself and such great political exiles as Sun Yat-sen and Mazzini.[36]

Emmeline Pankhurst and Emmeline and Frederick Pethick-Lawrence were tried for conspiracy, imprisoned, and began hunger strikes. Frederick Pethick-Lawrence's hunger strike was an action all the braver for his lack of supporting comrades; there were not many struggling for the women's cause in men's prisons. He had endured repeated forcible feeding, 'an unpleasant and painful process' as he described it.[37] He had lost four stones in weight when he was discharged three days after his wife and Emmeline Pankhurst.

The Pethick-Lawrences shared the feelings of many that increasing militancy was alienating support and not advancing the cause. After their release from imprisonment they went abroad to recuperate, stopping off at Boulogne to see Emmeline and Christabel to discuss the future direction of the movement. Mrs Pethick-Lawrence described it: 'Henceforward she [Emmeline Pankhurst] said there was to be a widespread attack upon public and private property, secretly carried out by suffragettes who would not offer themselves for arrest but wherever possible would make good their escape. As our minds had been moving in quite another direction, this project came as a shock to us both.'[38] Frederick later recalled that 'Mrs Pankhurst, as a born rebel, was even more emphatic than Christabel that the time had come to take sterner measures. She appeared to resent the fact that I had even ventured to question the wisdom of her daughter's policy.'[39]

The Home Office had its own plans for militancy, and made the first moves towards making individuals responsible for WSPU activities. The government claimed the costs of the conspiracy trial from Frederick Pethick-Lawrence and compensation for the shopkeepers whose windows were broken. The Treasury solicitors eventually sold his house and made him bankrupt.

After their recuperation, when the Pethick-Lawrences stepped off the boat back in England, they were met by a friend on the dock who told them: 'They are going to turn you out of the Women's Social and Political Union.'[40] The Union had moved to new headquarters at Lincoln's Inn House, the returning couple found they had no offices, and conversations ceased as they approached. Emmeline called them in to her office and told them they would be expelled, a statement they found literally unbelievable. In particular they could not accept that Christabel, who had lived as a member of their family for six years and was particularly adored by Frederick, could have acquiesced in this. Christabel therefore briefly flitted in from her exile, heavily disguised, on the South Coast of England, and took part in a meeting at which Annie Kenney, Emmeline Pethick-Lawrence's favourite, was also present to emphasize a united front against them.

The Pethick-Lawrences faced their fate with dignity, Frederick noting the irony that 'There was ... no appeal against our expulsion from the WSPU. Mrs Pankhurst was the acknowledged autocrat of the Union. We had ourselves supported her in acquiring this position several years previously; we could not dispute it now.'[41] The Pethick-Lawrences owned the newspaper *Votes for Women* that they maintained as a general women's suffrage newspaper. Emmeline and Christabel Pankhurst had already set up a successor newspaper, *The Suffragette*. Days after the expulsion, speaking at the Albert Hall, Emmeline made a renewed call for militancy: 'Be militant each in your own way ... Those of you who can break windows—break them. Those of you who can still further attack the sacred idol of property so as to make the Government realise that property is as greatly endangered by women's suffrage as it was by the Chartists of old days—do so.'[42]

Arson was an obvious strategy to adopt as an escalation of militancy once a decision had been taken to attack private property, though its first practitioners were rank and file members acting on their own initiative. Emily Wilding Davison had been the first to set fire to the mail in pillar boxes using a rag soaked in paraffin in December 1911; she had conceived and enacted her plans alone, but as with other militant actions, it was taken up an endorsed by the WSPU. Two suffragettes tried to burn down the Theatre Royal in Dublin by pouring petrol on the curtains of a box and setting fire to them, then throwing a flaming chair over the edge into the orchestra. Emmeline Pankhurst remarked: 'we love and honour them for their splendid courage.'[43] With the disintegration of focus suffered by the WSPU after the expulsion of the Pethick-Lawrences, the Union's members were tumbling into sporadic acts of violence. Keir Hardie considered that Emmeline Pankhurst had made 'a grave error of judgement' in the way she chose to fight the women's case, though this was in a private letter; in public he showed solidarity.[44]

From arson, the militants progressed to sabotage and bomb-making. More pillar boxes were set on fire or their contents damaged with acid; it was the first attack on the general public and a real problem at a time when many business affairs were conducted by mail; in addition, telegraph and telephone wires were cut. Public buildings were burned down and the turf was damaged on golf courses and acid used to cut 'Votes for Women' into the green; it was said that 'Golf green activity' aroused more hostility than any amount of window breaking.[45] As part of the disruption of a sporting event, Emily Wilding Davidson ran onto the course at the Derby and fell under the hooves of the King's racehorse. She died a few days later. The suffragettes had their martyr, who was accorded a grand funeral procession, a spectacle that touched a nerve in the national consciousness, feeding into a Christian concept that suffering *ought* to have a meaning, and sacrifice an object.

For more than two years, from March 1912, sabotage tore through the country with historic houses and churches burned and bombed; paintings slashed; water mains, telegraph cables, sporting venues, and letter boxes damaged. Hundreds of women were imprisoned for the cause, many undergoing hunger-strikes and forcible feeding. At the high point of destruction during this part of the campaign, on 19 February 1913 a bomb blew up a house being built for Lloyd George in Surrey, leading to Emmeline Pankhurst's declaration to a public meeting: 'We have blown up the Chancellor's house!'[46] She intended to be arrested for sedition, as she was.

Many people felt hunger-striking militants should be allowed to die but more thoughtful types feared the creation of suffragette martyrs. Protests over the 'torture' of force feeding had made the procedure counter-productive: it generated sympathy for the women's cause that they had forfeited by their acts of vandalism. The Home Office therefore rushed through a measure to release prisoners until they had recovered sufficiently to be reimprisoned to complete the sentence. It became notorious as the 'Cat and Mouse Act,' a name given it by Frederick Pethick-Lawrence who was still editing *Votes for Women*. As usual, Emmeline Pankhurst led by example: she was rearrested nine times between May 1913 and July 1914. Once again Emmeline pushed the government to the limits of absurd brutality by making it act out the provisions of the Cat and Mouse Act day by day with a food-and-water strike and by deliberately exhausting herself by walking about her cell. She attended a meeting to commemorate her 55th birthday on 14 July 1913 to give the defiant call, 'I mean to be a voter in the land that gave me birth or they shall kill me, and my challenge to the government is: Kill me or give me my freedom: I shall force you to make that choice.'[47]

The end of 1913 coincided with the culmination of two strands of thinking from Emmeline and Christabel, neither in any way likely to improve the Union's fortunes: they decided to expel Sylvia, and they became preoccupied with 'social purity'. Sylvia Pankhurst had restrained her criticism of the Union, instead arguing positively that the WSPU must be part of a mass movement which involved working-class women. She wrote that she regarded the new policy of militancy 'with grief and regret, believing it wholly mistaken and unnecessary, deeply deploring the life of furtive destruction it would impose on the participators, and the harsh punishment it was preparing for them'.[48] She continued with loyalty to the cause, once smuggling out of prison a letter to her mother describing her struggle against force feeding, which Emmeline released to the press. Sylvia also smuggled out a letter to Hardie, but Emmeline withheld it from him and later, when Sylvia was released, the letter was returned to her. Sylvia never forgave her mother for this low behaviour.

Sylvia had stayed in the East End and had developed the East London Federation of the WSPU. With the fragmentation of the national leadership, this developed in time into a virtually autonomous body, with its own militia, the 'citizen's army' that protected Sylvia from the police; its own wealthy funders devoted to Sylvia; and, most disturbingly for Emmeline and Christabel, its own policy of co-operating with men. Sylvia had her personal relationship with Keir Hardie but also a close political relationship with George Lansbury and with the Men's Federation for Women's Suffrage, and had been urging Lloyd George to promote an adult suffrage bill, against WSPU policy.

Sylvia was summoned to Paris early in 1914, when she slipped out of the country via Harwich and Holland, weak from hunger strikes and forcible feeding. At the Paris meeting in Sylvia's account (Christabel's narrative does not mention the event) Christabel said, 'You have a democratic constitution for your Federation; we do not agree with that' and complained that the Federation put the weakest and least educated women in the forefront by representing working women: 'We want picked women, the very strongest and most intelligent.'[49] Sylvia was expelled from the WSPU.

Both Asquith and Lloyd George were later prepared to see Sylvia's East End delegation (and Lloyd George saw Sylvia herself, with Lansbury). The working women were more to their liking than women who thought disrupting a church service was a route to political advancement. Ironically, the National Union of Women's Suffrage Societies was now supporting the Labour Party which had in 1912 agreed to support women's suffrage and to vote against any franchise Bill that did not include women: all that Emmeline had ever asked of it.

After 1910 the NUWSS, though still middle class, increased its popular support. Branches in Scotland and the north of England, where Labour women were prominent in the women's suffrage movement, urged an alliance with the Labour Party. Despite the longstanding Liberal relationships of the NUWSS leadership in London, it was clear the Liberal party was too weak on the suffrage issue. Millicent Fawcett was finally urged to call a meeting of the NUWSS council in May 1912 which agreed to an alliance: to raise funds for and support Labour candidates, particularly in constituencies represented by Liberals with an unsatisfactory record on suffrage.

Social purity and suffrage

The first feminist text devoted to venereal disease was commissioned by the NUWSS from Dr Louisa Martindale in 1908. *Under the Surface* linked prostitution and VD with the demand for the vote; copies of the pamphlet were sent to every member of both houses of parliament.[50]

Five years later, in April 1913, Christabel Pankhurst started writing in *The Suffragette* about venereal disease and 'white slavery'. She remarked, in a series of articles she later collected and published under the name *The Great Scourge and How to End It*, 'The sexual diseases are the great cause of physical, mental and moral degeneracy, and of race suicide. As they are very widespread (from 70 to 80 per cent of men being infected with gonorrhoea, and a considerable percentage, difficult to ascertain precisely, being infected with syphilis), the problem is one of appalling magnitude... The cure, briefly stated, is Votes for Women and Chastity for Men.'[51]

On Emmeline's American tour of 1913 the focus on the lively subject of sex was a gift. Her militant policy was not popular in the US and, though she did not repudiate the policy, it was wise to concentrate on other aspects of the movement. Sometimes she combined both, as she explained for a New York audience: 'A broken window is a small thing when one considers the broken lives of women, and it is better to burn a house than to injure little children. This is a holy war.'[52]

Sylvia found Christabel's dwelling on a newfound interest in sex both curious and revolting. Christabel was 33 in 1913 and may have never had a sexual relationship; her sister remarked, 'She who had deprecated and shunned every mention of her sex, now hinged the greater part of her propaganda upon the supposed greater prevalence of venereal disease and the sex excesses of men.'[53] Teresa Billington-Greig presented a less personal criticism of 'the Pankhurst domination' arguing that 'it set women on the rampage against evils they knew nothing of, for remedies they knew nothing about. It fed on flattery the silly notion of the perfection of woman and the dangerous fellow notion of the indescribable imperfection of man.'[54]

The focus on a political solution to the admitted problem of VD was backward-looking, applying the 'moral purity' rhetoric of the late nineteenth century. Progressive doctors and social reformers in the first decades of the twentieth century were moving from a guilt-centred anti-VD programme towards social hygiene programmes that stressed prevention. Research towards treatments had already borne fruit in the discovery by Paul Ehrlich's laboratory of Salvasan in 1908. Dora Marsden, formerly a paid organizer for the WSPU, in 1911 launched a magazine called *The Freewoman* with such contributors as Teresa Billington-Greig, H. G. Wells, and Rebecca West. The paper covered eugenics, birth control, and prostitution from a humanist perspective, condemned Christabel's preoccupation with VD as hysterical, and promoted sexual freedom, declaring they were 'not for the advancement of Woman, but for the empowering of individuals—men and women'.[55]

Why did Christabel in particular turn to sex at this time? The self-inflicted miseries of hunger striking and other prison treatment have a certain gruesome interest in this story, but the more important historical point is why people were prepared to subject themselves to such treatment. They had to trust their leaders, and their leaders had to give them something worth the pain as they were called upon to greater devotion to the cause. Now people could be dying, Christabel Pankhurst had to ratchet up the stakes to meet the scale of the sacrifice; the women's vote had to be a major force for social change (against the evidence from countries where women already voted). The vote had to be offered as a solution to VD and child abuse. Those with a more sophisticated view of society had long since fallen away from the WSPU, leaving only the zealots.

The end of militancy

Destruction continued on an escalated scale in the first months of 1914 with targets as random as churches, the Carnegie Library in Birmingham and paintings in galleries. The effect on the people of Britain was, as Emmeline remarked, 'Not yet did they show themselves ready to demand of the Government that the outrages be stopped in the only way they could be stopped—by giving votes to women.'[56]

The government was unmoved—indeed, the government, having attained victory in its constitutional crisis with the peers, now had trade union unrest and an Ulster revolt over Irish home rule to contend with. The paragraph he gave to the suffragettes in his two volumes of autobiography show Asquith's irritation and complete refusal to be affected by the suffragettes, who were 'women intoxicated by a genuine fanaticism. Not a few of them showed the temper of the confessors and martyrs of a persecuted faith.' It was not lost on Asquith that the suffragettes attacked Liberal supporters of their cause almost as much as opponents like himself.[57]

In a debate in the House of Commons on 11 June 1914, the Home Secretary discussed actions to be taken against the suffragettes, expressing a genuine fear of lawlessness: it was not that militants would gain their ends by their destructive tactics, but that outraged members of the public would attack suffragettes.

Even Christabel, out of touch as she was, realized their time was over and wrote what seems to be a valedictory leader in *The Suffragette* eight days after a march on Buckingham Palace on 21 May, 'The Militants will rejoice when victory comes in the shape of the vote, and yet, mixed with their joy will be regret that the most glorious chapter in women's history is closed and the militant fight over—over, while so many have not yet known the exultation, the rapture of battle.'[58]

The international crisis intervened to bring an end to the militant phase of suffrage history. Emmeline Pankhurst had slipped out of the country after another imprisonment and was in St Malo when Britain declared war on Germany after the attack on France in August 1914. Emmeline had always loved France as she had mistrusted Germany, and despite her disagreements with the British constitution, her first feelings were patriotic. She therefore ordered the WSPU membership to suspend all activity until the international crisis was over. The government declared the unconditional release of all suffrage prisoners on 10 August.

Emmeline returned to England with Christabel, who thus ended two and a half years of exile, and who wrote in *The Suffragette* that the war was 'God's vengeance upon the people who held women in subjection'.[59] She called on men to join up to fight on behalf of women: they must do men's work. Women must attend to their own task of building up the race, and

take on war work. *The Suffragette* was renamed in 1915 as *Britannia* and
edited by Christabel to promote war activities. At the suggestion of the
King, Lloyd George (now Minister of Munitions) sent for Emmeline and
offered her expenses for a demonstration in favour of war work, particularly
for munitions work for women. The Treasury eventually paid more than
£4,000 towards the costs of Emmeline and the WSPU office staff for organizing a 'Call to Women' demonstration with a procession through London
on 17 July 1915 behind a banner saying 'We Demand the Right to Serve'.
Similarly, the NUWSS became the Women's Active Service Movement.

Meanwhile constitutional political activity was working towards wom-
en's suffrage despite the suffragettes. Asquith was concerned that women's
suffrage was Labour Party policy and Labour was now allied with the
non-militant suffragists. The Conservatives were certain to make some
kind of statement on limited women's franchise before the next election,
and at that election a majority of Liberal members would probably insist
on the women's vote being party policy if for no other reason than because
the Women's Liberal Association would demand it as a price for their
electoral work.

The life of the parliament ran out in 1915, though it was extended by six
or seven months at a time as a war measure; as soon as possible an election
would have to be called. Suffrage became a burning constitutional issue because a new electoral register was therefore essential. The current franchise
was based on the occupation of property by men. Fewer than 20 per cent of
men were still in the same place by the second year of the war. Men had
changed their residence by going to fight abroad and had therefore become
disenfranchised. This was obviously anomalous, as was a suggestion that only
men at arms should be automatically enfranchised: should those who had
been ordered to stay at home for vital war work be discriminated against?
But if those men on war work were to be enfranchised, why not women on
war work? The war had thus created an impossible conundrum for legislators which, after considerable parliamentary discussion, Asquith dealt with
by creating a Speakers' Conference of backbench MPs from all parties in
August 1916. It was clearly time to make a concession or compromise his
leadership on a question he regarded without enthusiasm, so he bent to the
prevailing wind.

A joint committee of all the women's suffrage societies was called under
the National Union of Women's Suffrage Societies to present women's case
to the conference. Emmeline had sworn the WSPU would desist from cam-

paigning for women's suffrage until after the war and so refused to join the committee; the WSPU made no contribution to the grant of the vote to women as a technical measure.

Lloyd George, always more sympathetic to the women's cause than Asquith, replaced him as Prime Minister in December 1916. The Speaker's Conference reported the following year recommending the enfranchisement of all men on a residency qualification, all soldiers and sailors, and a women's suffrage measure for women householders and the wives of householders with an age limit—30 was eventually decided. Technically the measure was the opposite of everything Emmeline and the WSPU had argued for, they had always campaigned on an exactly equal franchise for women and men. The NUWSS held a similar position, though they had always been prepared to accept some measure of compromise. The period leading to the franchise being granted, however, as Martin Pugh says, was distinguished by 'the virtual disappearance of the women's campaign'; he cites the curious example of press magnate Lord Northcliffe writing to Millicent Fawcett and imploring her to seek publicity for the measure.[60]

It was not so much that war work was the winning argument, but that it disarmed the opposition. There had long been a body of goodwill supporting women's suffrage with frequent majorities since the 1890s (even in 1866 J. S. Mill was supported by a third of those voting in the House), the 1917 requirement was for the opposition to acquiesce, and women's war work gave them a justification for that. By the end of the war around a million women were in employment in jobs previously done by men. The sheer numbers involved demonstrated that all women were deserving of the franchise, not just a superior few. As Lloyd George said, 'the heroic patriotism of the women workers during the war had now made their claim irresistible.'[61] Even Asquith conceded this point and dramatically intervened in the debate to say that women's war service had changed his mind. Whether this was true or a gracious way of bending to the inevitable, women's war work was still part of the equation. The under-thirties had in fact borne the brunt of war work, and they were not enfranchised—war work was an excuse, not a reason.

The women's suffrage clause of the bill was passed on 19 June 1917 by 387 to 57; the whole bill was passed in the House of Common in December 1917 by 364 votes to 23. Royal assent was given for the Representation of the People Act on 6 February 1918, after which some eight million women had the vote and thirteen million men. The same year women were allowed to stand for election to the House of Commons. The House of Lords did not admit newly created peeresses until 1958.

The WSPU was relaunched as the Women's Party on 7 November 1917 with a programme of gender equality including equal pay and equality of opportunity of employment, but also a number of more questionable proposals such as raising the age of consent from 16, and the dismissal of government officials who had German family ('enemy blood') or pacifist connections. Emmeline was urged to stand but with characteristically poor judgement where her eldest daughter was concerned, she insisted the honour should go to Christabel: 'Mrs Pankhurst said that Miss Pankhurst was the founder of the movement which had resulted in the emancipation of the women of this country.'[62]

Christabel contested and failed to win Smethwick; her political career was now at an end as she converted to Adventism and devoted the rest of her life to preparation for the Second Coming. Sex-based warfare in the Pankhurst family continued with Sylvia having a child as a single mother; she insisted on giving her son the name Pankhurst, to her mother's dismay. His first names were Richard, after her father, Keir after her lover Hardie and Pethick after Frederick Pethick-Lawrence whom her mother had repudiated. He grew up to be a historian who did much to restore the position of William Thompson in the story of women's suffrage.

Exacerbated by her unhappiness at the 'disgrace' Sylvia had brought on the family, Emmeline's old gastric complaint flared up and she was unable to retain food. She died on 14 June 1928 at the age of 69 in a nursing home in Wimpole Street, a month after the final passage of the bill giving women over 21 the vote on equal terms with men. The measure, introduced after a question from Frederick Pethick-Lawrence who had become a Labour MP, was introduced by Stanley Baldwin's Conservative government.

John Bull's other island

Though Irish women were enfranchised at the same time as mainland British, they had their own battles over women's suffrage which became as in the Scandinavian countries, linked with national liberation. A somewhat genteel Dublin Women's Suffrage Association had been set up in 1876, though it fell into decline, with only forty-three members in 1908. In November that year, stimulated by the example of British suffragettes, the militant Irish Women's Franchise League was formed by Margaret Cousins, and Francis and Hannah Sheehy-Skeffington at the Skeffingtons' home. They were denounced as selfish and unpatriotic for not subordinating women's suffrage to the Irish home rule movement.[63] They argued that equal votes for women should be included in a Home Rule Bill to go through the British parliament, to the anger of other nationalists who felt that anything that complicated the issue of home rule should be omitted. Hanna Sheehy-Skeffington, 'the most significant of all Irish feminists' according to her biographer Margaret Ward, insisted that male politicians could no more be trusted with women's rights than the leprechaun with the crock of gold (as soon as you take your eyes off him he will slip away with it).[64] Mainstream nationalists in Ireland therefore took a different path from those in countries such as India and Finland, where part of the nationalist momentum involved engaging women in the political process. Sinn Féin, founded in 1905, was a colourful exception to this, promising to restore the ancient Celtic rights of women that the English occupation had obliterated—but only after the revolution.[65]

Sheehy-Skeffington was correct: Irish nationalists voted against the 'Conciliation Bill' to enfranchise women when it had a good chance of passing in 1912. They feared the Bill's success would mean resignation for Asquith, who had always opposed women's suffrage, and with him would go the immediate chance for Irish independence. A Home Rule Bill (with no women's suffrage provision) was then introduced. As historian Karen Offen remarks, 'they had sold out Irish women for Male Home Rule.'[66]

Sheehy-Skeffington was born Joanna Sheehy in 1877 to a mill-owning, Irish nationalist family and studied in Dublin, Paris, and Bonn. In 1903 she married another nationalist, Francis Skeffington, and as a gesture of their belief in gender equality, both changed their names, to Sheehy-Skeffington. The same year as their marriage, Francis was appointed the first lay registrar at University College, Dublin. He later lost the post as he had helped the Women Graduates Association to fight for the admission of women to the university on the same basis as men. Francis Sheehy-Skeffington and James Cousins (Margaret Cousins' husband) launched the suffrage newspaper *Irish Citizen* 1912 under the editorship of Francis. Its declared aim was 'To win for men and women equally the rights of citizenship and to claim from men and women equally the duties of citizenship'.

Following the 'torpedoing' of the Conciliation Bill, the Irish Women's Franchise League started a hostile campaign which involved demonstrations, window breaking, and imprisonment; both Margaret Cousins and Hannah Sheehy-Skeffington served terms in prison. Soon after the founding of the *Irish Citizen* the Cousins moved to Garston, near Liverpool, where James worked for a vegetarian food company. In 1915 the couple emigrated to India where James would work on a new newspaper set up by Annie Besant, and Margaret devoted herself to the cause of Indian women's suffrage.

Francis Sheehy-Skeffington was a fervent pacifist, consequently the *Irish Citizen* opposed the First World War. Its message was put succinctly in one poster: 'Votes for Women Now! Damn Your War!'[67] He was imprisoned for urging Irishmen not to enlist; and was released after hunger striking. His pacifism led him to oppose the Easter Rising in 1916 and he tried to recruit volunteers to stop the looting which was taking place. Walking home on the second day of the Rising, he was arrested and taken to Richmond Barracks, the following morning he was led to the barracks yard and executed without charge or trial. Hanna was not notified of her husband's death and was then refused information. The military made every effort to cover up the events until finally, at Hanna's insistence, a court martial was held and the Captain who had ordered Francis's killing was found guilty but insane and sent to Broadmoor. Hanna then put her efforts into Irish nationalism, raising money for Sinn Féin, and later serving as a councillor under the Irish Free State.

Women's equality among nationalists went so far as for Con Markiewicz to be indignant that she was not executed after the Easter Rising, being spared the fate of her comrades because of her sex. Markiewicz had been second in command of a troop of Irish Citizen Army combatants who held out for a week against the British Army. Markiewicz, born in an Irish landowning family in 1868, had been interested in women's suffrage as a young woman and presided over a meeting of the Sligo Women's Suffrage Society in 1896. She remained committed, but Irish nationalism was the more pressing cause. Her sister, Eva Gore-Booth, became known as a leading suffragist and had considerable influence on the young Christabel Pankhurst.

Markiewicz (who had married a Polish count) was sentenced to penal servitude for life for her part in the Easter Rising but was released under a general amnesty in 1917. She stood in the general election of 1918, as a Sinn Féin candidate for Dublin St Patrick's division and became the first woman elected to the British parliament though as she had again been imprisoned at the time, she could not take her seat.

Irish women got the same limited vote as British women in 1918 with the Representation of the People Act. When the Irish Free State was set up in 1922, women and men were given the vote equally.

Who won what?

Carrie Chapman Catt wrote to Aletta Jacobs 16 July 1910, 'When the suffrage is gained in England, the suffragists all over the world will fall to quarrelling over the question: Did the Suffragists or the Suffragettes do it?'[68] Another option, given that women's suffrage has been achieved in countries with no or no significant women's suffrage movement, is that neither can claim victory as theirs.

British feminism before the First World War was a paradox: it had more MPs supportive in the legislature, had a larger non-militant suffrage movement (proportionate to its population) than any other country, and yet it had failed repeatedly to secure anything further than a municipal franchise. Other English-speaking countries and other parts of English-speaking countries (such as the western states of the US) were far in advance of the Mother of Parliaments.

It was to break this log-jam that militancy was born, but the contribution of militancy to the suffrage panorama can be over-stated. To put it in terms of Emmeline Pankhurst's career: she attended her first suffrage campaign meeting as a girl in 1872. The WSPU was formed in 1903 but the first stone was not thrown until 1908. There was a truce for most of 1910 and 1911 and the policy of militancy was called off in August 1914. There was therefore some five years of militancy, two of them involving serious acts of destruction.

However, the end result was merely that Britain could add to its list of superlatives: now it was also home most the most militant women's suffrage movement in the world, but was no more successful in winning the franchise. Indeed, when looking at the history of world suffrage movements, it is obvious that, as Pankhurst-style levels of militancy were not necessary in any other country, they were not really necessary in Britain.

They were influential as far away as China where their exploits were eagerly read by Chinese women who invaded parliament and broke windows in pursuit of their aims. It is difficult to imagine Doria Shafik and her Egyptian women's hunger striking would have taken place, or Mexican women's hunger striking outside the president's palace, without the example of the suffragettes. However, suffragist women in such places as Latin America where the struggle for women even to be heard was incomparably harder than it was in Britain, struggled to distance themselves from violent painting-slashers and window-breakers.[69] In the Philippines suffragists made a point of dissociating themselves from the suffragettes, making their difference a point of national pride and their superiority: 'The character of our women forbids them to resort to the militant methods employed by British women.'[70] Later in the century Eva Peron showed disgust at the 'English suffragettes' who 'seemed to be dominated by indignation at not having been born men, more than by the pride of being women'.[71] In general, however, women in other countries viewed the suffragettes with awed respect; as historian Ray Strachey wrote, 'At the distance of thousands of miles the drawbacks were of no effect, and the courage stood out undimmed by undignified incidents or political unwisdom.'[72]

The outcome of women's suffrage being granted in 1918 was part of a pattern of enfranchisement in nineteen nations, between 1915 and 1920, some of them very populous. Britain was unlikely to delay for much longer when such comparable nations as the United States and Germany had women's suffrage. Unlike China and Russia, where conditions of repression and backwardness forced rebels into acts of violence, militancy was not an inevitable consequence of the British situation in the early twentieth century. If Asquith had been prepared to grant concessions (or Emmeline Pankhurst were a more level-headed leader) militancy could never have taken off. With or without militancy, a men-only parliament would not have survived the franchise revision that the war situation made inevitable.

The conservatism and the rigid class divisions of British politics meant suffrage could only be granted when democracy was widely acceptable. Universal manhood suffrage had long been an objective of the Liberal and Labour parties and with the experience of total war, engaging the entire population, the Conservatives would not be opposing it. The sophistication of class, conflicting ideologies, and party loyalties enabled the most informed and elevated debates on women's suffrage. These complexities, however, also impeded its achievement. The great simplicities of war and national survival made clear progress possible, and by this stage with minimal involvement from suffrage organizations.

9

Victory and disenfranchisement in the US

'A mother's advice is always safest'

Carrie Chapman Catt dominated the suffrage movement over a time of hiatus to its final, successful years. Catt, née Lane, was born in 1859 and grew up in Wisconsin and Iowa. She attended Iowa State College, graduating in 1880, and worked as a high-school principal and a superintendent of schools, one of the first women to hold such a position. Her first marriage in 1884 to Leo Chapman, a newspaper editor, ended with his death from typhoid just two years later. From 1887 to 1890 she devoted herself to organizing women's groups in Iowa, first the Women's Christian Temperance Union then the Iowa Woman Suffrage Association. Her intended marriage to George W. Catt, an engineer, in 1890, was preceded by a legal contract providing her with four months of free time each year to work exclusively for women's suffrage. Her first major success was in organizing the Colorado state referendum in 1893, the first state to win the vote for women by the popular vote. In 1900 she was elected to succeed Susan B. Anthony as president of the National American Woman Suffrage Association (NAWSA). George Catt encouraged and supported his wife's dedication and when he became seriously ill in 1904, she resigned her presidency of the NAWSA to care for him until his death the following year. He left her financially independent so she was able to devote all her time to campaigning. She founded the International Woman Suffrage Alliance in 1902 (it held its first full meeting in Berlin in 1904) and over the following years she attempted to assuage her grief following the death of her husband and other members of her family with travel in Europe, the East, and Africa, observing the conditions of women and setting up suffrage organizations.

Little progress was made by suffragists in the US in the twenty years after 1890 (and none east of the Mississippi). To begin with, for its first ten years, the leadership of the NAWSA, in the persons of Stanton and Anthony, was elderly, and then under Catt and her successor Dr Anna Shaw uninspiring. Moreover, Shaw, though a fine orator, had none of Catt's administrative abilities. The issue of women's suffrage was continually raised and continually rebuffed; these were 'the doldrums' where only some limited local franchises were extended, some with restrictions limiting voters to taxpayers or those who could pass a literacy test. The slackening pace was more than simply a success of the anti-suffragists: the hardening of party blocs led to the increased power of machine politicians, who opposed *any* new franchises that would upset their careful calculations of voter strength (indeed, in the South black and poor white men were being disenfranchised). In some cases the party bosses were blatantly manipulative: women in Illinois were given the presidential vote in 1913 but not the vote for the governor, congressmen or state representatives. Allowing women to vote for president was less important to the party machine than giving them votes for these positions. Plum local jobs had to be kept for the boys who were loyal to the party, and women suffragists' rhetoric that they would end corruption and vote for the best person for the job would hardly have been an attractive proposition.

Western successes with the complete franchise had taken place as territories developed into states, and the political fluidity of having to decide their constitutions concentrated minds on suffrage issues. The eastern and southern states with already established constitutions were harder to move. Southern white women joined the movement at the turn of the century and shifted the focus away from a federal amendment because of their adherence to states' rights; they were also to push the movement towards white supremacist arguments. Women's suffrage had lost its connection with racial equality which had from the late 1860s been shaky.

The extension of women's property rights and educational opportunities had also discouraged women from feeling that the vote was the all-important means of improving their condition; the indifference of many women to the campaign for the vote was a boon to anti-suffragists, as was the low turnout by women in areas where they had the vote.

The other major factor in the slackening pace of women's suffrage was that the movement had lost vigour; the middle-class suffrage activists had failed to appreciate the development of labour organizations and trade unionism among women workers who were rapidly becoming politicized. Historian Rebecca Mead argues that Catt and other conservatives in the leadership 'routinely underemphasized or denied working class and socialist support even though they were well aware of its importance' for fear of alienating middle-class supporters.[1]

Carrie Chapman Catt represented a more right-wing attitude than that of Stanton and Anthony, and was prepared to stir up resentment against the 'the votes possessed by the males in the slums of the cities, and the ignorant foreign vote', this nativist sentiment was gaining ground in the early twentieth century, with the influx of foreign immigrants.[2] Carrie Catt had begun her lecturing career with such titles as 'America for Americans' criticizing the morals and manners of new immigrants.[3] By 1903 only five of 150 delegates at the National American Woman Suffrage Association convention opposed an educational requirement for the ballot.[4]

Catt was appealing to elite groups who were necessarily more conservative, though they were not immune to social changes, and at the NAWSA convention in 1906 children's reformer Florence Kelley attacked the movement for its class and ethnic prejudice; she called for a renewed commitment to reform, particularly in compulsory education and child labour laws. As a result, the NAWSA became more inclusive of poor whites and attracted the new generation of educated, self-supporting women.

Unionists and militants

In 1902 Stanton's daughter Harriot Stanton Blatch returned from England after twenty years there and was appalled by the middle-class conservatism of the NAWSA. In response she formed the Equality League of Self-Supporting Women in January 1907 to work with the working class (later it became the Women's Political Union). They copied the tactics of labour activists with outdoor meetings, and from 1910 Blatch organized a series of massive, eye-catching parades in New York and Washington DC.

The Women's Trade Union League coordinated a strike of 20,000 women garment workers in New York in 1909. The strike created new links across previous ethnic and class divisions as Jewish and Italian women were prominent in the trade unions; middle-class women supported the garment workers with a purchasing boycott. Working-class suffragism in New York was stimulated by the Triangle Shirtwaist Fire in 1911 where 146 women were burnt to death or killed when they jumped from the upper floors. Of course, unsafe factory conditions affected enfranchised men as well as unenfranchised women, but a wave of sympathy for working women benefited the suffrage movement. It was now felt that the urgent need for women's enfranchisement came from the needs of working women, not the middle class, whose priorities regarding marriage, property ownership, education, and access to the professions had largely been addressed.

The American Federation of Labour had supported women's suffrage since 1892 as a matter of principle but it was not until suffrage campaigners began to appeal to working class organizations that support became enthusiastic. Sam Gompers the AFL president talked in 1915 of the labour movement and women's suffrage as 'two tremendous movements for freedom' and gave a familiar message of both solidarity and self interest. He wrote, 'Men must join the women in an effort to join their common problem, or else they will find women used against them as competitors.'[5]

Historian of democracy Alexander Keyssar remarks that the convergence of working-class interest in women's suffrage with the suffragists' interest in the working class meant the campaign for women's suffrage became a mass movement for the first time from 1910.[6]

A petition for a federal amendment signed by more than 400,000 women was presented to Congress in 1910, the same year in which President William H. Taft addressed the annual convention of the NAWSA. He was equivocal, but the mere fact that he had been prepared to speak meant the NAWSA was a player on the political scene. Women's suffrage was now a coming issue in which everyone wanted to be involved: the membership of the NAWSA stood at 100,000 in 1915; by 1917 it was two million.

The women's movement was reinvigorated from the Old World: the influence of Britain was apparent in literature; in Emmeline Pankhurst's lecture tours of the US in 1909, 1911, and 1913; but most potently in the activities of young women who had travelled to England and learned the lesson of militancy. Among them was Anne Martin, daughter of a state senator, who was arrested in London on Black Friday in 1910. She returned to the US to be the driving force of the Nevada movement for women's suffrage which was successful in 1914. Two other suffragists who had learned militant tactics were Alice Paul and Lucy Burns who had been in England between 1906 and 1912. Alice Paul was another east coast Quaker activist. She had studied at the New York School of Social Work then went to England to do settlement work between 1906 and 1909 where she became an active suffragette, was jailed and was force fed. Paul was joined in 1912 by Lucy Burns, who graduated from Vassar College then attended universities in Germany and England. She also won her spurs in Britain as a colleague of Emmeline and Christabel Pankhurst; she was awarded a special medal from the Women's Social and Political Union for her bravery in the course of several arrests and prison hunger strikes.

Back in the US, Paul organized marches, White House protests, rallies, and monumental parades. In March 1913 a demonstration of 8,000 suffragists paraded through Washington DC, organized by Alice Paul, with twenty-six floats, ten bands, and five squadrons of cavalry. It was watched by an estimated 500,000 people who had come to the capital to see the inauguration of the new president, Woodrow Wilson. Despite Paul's advance appeals for adequate police protection, none was forthcoming and the march was attacked by rowdies while the police stood by, the suffragists thereby gaining a great deal of national sympathy for the cause. The Fifteenth Cavalry finally had to be summoned to restore order.[7]

Paul was chairman of the congressional committee of the NAWSA, but soon asserted her independence, and in 1913 Paul, Burns, Anne Martin, and other like-minded radicals founded the Congressional Union for Woman Suffrage to support a federal amendment. Paul and her supporters believed in the possibility of a federal amendment in the short term, as against Catt's conviction that it would be a lifelong struggle as it had been for the previous generation of suffragists. The NAWSA tried to control the radicals, who were still working within the Association, concerned that there might be a spread of British-style militancy using methods 'which had clearly harmed the movement' in the US.[8] Catt charged members of the Congressional Union with insubordination and financial irregularities, though later she admitted that none of the officers believed the accusations of misappropriated funds. What really troubled them was 'a dark conspiracy to capture the entire National for the militant enterprise'.[9] She called Paul and Burns 'Pankhurst imitators' and feared their militant tactics would antagonize male allies.[10] There was also an underlying division in philosophy between Paul and the leaders of the American suffrage movement, who had come to promote suffrage as a benevolent form of moral welfare. For Stone the argument was one of 'natural rights': of the universal and inalienable right to political equality.

When the NAWSA ejected the Congressional Union in 1916 Paul worked independently, though with an Advisory Council that included such luminaries of the suffrage movement as Florence Kelley, Olympia Brown, Abigail Scott Duniway and Harriot Stanton Blatch. Inspired by the early Pankhurst model, Alice Paul orchestrated a series of publicity stunts including, in addition to pageants and conventions, a 'suffrage drive' across the nation in a car; a 'suffrage special' train; and the use of motion pictures to excite interest in the vote.

The suffrage trade between the US and Britain was not only west across the Atlantic: Alva Vanderbilt-Belmont, one of the wealthiest women in America, donated large sums to the British movement as well as supporting the NAWSA until she left it because of its conservatism. Her mansions provided meeting places and homes for suffrage workers; during the women's union strikes she sat in the court rooms and paid bail charges of arrested strikers. She believed she had a divine calling to support the women's cause, but at least one commentator has remarked it was to spite her ex-husband, William K. Vanderbilt, who opposed votes for women.[11] It was the second time the Vanderbilt name had become entwined in the story of women's enfranchisement in the US (the first being with Victoria Woodhull).

Again following the Pankhurst lead, in summer 1914 and in 1916, Alice Paul decided to attack the party in power, the Democrats, for not enfranchising women. President Woodrow Wilson's view (unsurprising for a southern Democrat) was that votes for women was a state issue and he would take no federal action. Paul founded the National Woman's Party in 1916 to contest elections in states where women had the vote. They sent organizers to the western suffrage states to urge women to vote against Democrat candidates to punish them and show women's political power. This meant voting against candidates even if they favoured women's suffrage and their opponents did not, thus introducing to the US the most absurd aspect of the Pankhurst campaign—encouraging voting on party lines against pro-suffrage candidates to the benefit of anti-suffrage candidates.

Anna Howard Shaw, the NAWSA president at the time, remarked: 'if there is any possible way of making a political blunder, the Congressional Union has a facility of finding how to do it.'[12] Paul's defence was that she considered any politicians in a women's suffrage state to be pro-women's suffrage in public (whatever their private views). In the US, as in Britain, the existence of a radical activist wing of the women's suffrage movement served to keep the issue before the public, and there were now two groups arguing the case, testing the political arena for weaknesses and seeking out alliances.

The strategy of mobilizing existing women voters was monumentally unsuccessful: Wilson was re-elected, carrying ten out of the eleven states in which women voted; there was no evidence that Democrats had suffered because of their party's stance on the voting rights of women.[13] This was a lesson that women could not be relied upon to vote along gender lines at the urging of self-appointed leaders; they would vote on the same issues as men. This benefited the women's suffrage movement, again showing the machine politicians that giving women votes would make no difference to the political landscape; women were not the reforming force they had been made out to be.

As has been noted, enfranchisement in western states proceeded from 1910 but the only non-western state before New York in 1917 was Kansas in 1912. From 1912 to 1914 there were twelve unsuccessful referendums (three of them in Ohio). Even holding a referendum, however, was some kind of success for the women's suffragists; in many southern states even proposals for a referendum on the issue were defeated.

There was slow movement: in 1916 the Republicans nationally supported women's suffrage, though without great enthusiasm. Their candidate for president that year, Charles E. Hughes, announced at the beginning of the campaign that he favoured a federal amendment to enfranchise women. Woodrow Wilson throughout the election reiterated his position that he supported votes for women but 'that the thing can best and most solidly be done by the action of the individual states, and that the time it will take to get it that way will not be longer than the time it would take to get it the other way...if I should change my personal attitude now, I should seem to the country like nothing less than an angler for votes.'[14] Times had certainly changed when women's suffrage was seen as a vote-winner. There was now a feeling that women's suffrage was imminent, at least state by state if not nationally, and any man in politics would be a fool to oppose it if he hoped still to be elected after enfranchisement. Thus every success carried the seeds of future success, and opposition was more muted. Between 1915 and 1920 the machine politicians turned round to favour women's suffrage and factor women's voting into their calculations.

An additional element on the political scene was the movement for prohibition, often engaging the same energies as the women's suffrage campaign. Prohibitionists were also making progressive gains, state by state: before 1910, the growth of women's suffrage movements in five southern states generally coincided with the passage of alcohol prohibition laws; and in the three years from 1914 to 1916, fourteen states adopted prohibition. Prohibition represented 'civilized' values: the control of the urban populations of new immigrants and blacks by the settled white, middle class. If anything, prohibition was the more popular cause than women's suffrage in the pre-war years. By January 1920 prohibition was already in force in thirty-three states; the eighteenth amendment to ban alcohol went into effect on 29 January 1920 with the state legislatures of only three states voting against.

The winning plan

The influence of the Congressional Union/Women's Party was pushing the NAWSA towards a federal campaign rather than state by state enfranchisement. In 1915 Carrie Chapman Catt returned to the presidency, replacing Anna Howard Shaw (who had served since Catt's departure from the post in 1904) because Shaw's conservatism had led to a loss of support. Buoyed by an almost $1 million bequest from a publisher, Miriam Leslie, Catt devised a 'winning plan' which was kept secret so it could not be sabotaged by antisuffragists, but which was known to the state leaders of the suffrage movement who signed an agreement to it in 1916. The plan prioritized the federal amendment while supporting key state campaigns in the thirty-six states most likely to ratify an amendment (as any amendment, however successful in Washington DC, would need three-quarters of states to ratify it). It also promoted the adoption by as many states as possible of the 'Illinois law' which had given presidential suffrage to women, consequently another six midwestern and northeastern states gave women the presidential vote in 1917. Catt personally conducted the referendum campaigns in New York, the most populous state in the Union, first unsuccessfully in 1915 then, following the influx of Leslie money for propaganda, successfully in 1917.

The symbol of the Winning Plan was the new NASWA headquarters 'Suffrage House' which opened in the capital in December 1916. The impressive twenty-six room mansion of dressed stone 'declared to the nation that the NAWSA was so solidly housed and so solidly financed that the women would stay until they got the federal amendment they wanted'.[15]

Alice Paul's National Woman's Party began picketing the White House in January 1917 with banners and their purple, white, and gold suffrage flag. They made no particular waves and were treated with respect (President

Wilson raised his hat to them) but when the US entered the war in April 1917 their activity increasingly seemed to be anti-American. They protested that America was fighting to make the world safe for democracy abroad while women did not have democracy at home; they went too far when they unfurled a banner attacking 'Kaiser Wilson' in August 1917 and they were assaulted by a hostile crowd and arrested. After this they courted arrest as the British suffragettes had done, went on hunger strikes, and were forcibly fed. Alice Paul was put in a ward for the insane.

Opinion is divided over whether this militancy helped or hindered the cause, probably it did both (with different interest groups). Certainly those used to the small successes of slow diplomacy were irritated by it. Anna Howard Shaw wrote to Aletta Jacobs that these Pankhurst-inspired women were 'hurting us fearfully. I think by their unwisdom they have put us back ten years in Congress. It is pretty hard to work for years and years to bring the cause up to a point where it has some chance of going through and then have a lot of young things who never did anything to build up the cause, attempt to run things their way without being responsible to anyone.'[16] The 'young things' did stimulate the NAWSA to greater efforts of demonstration and lobbying, and to make them look more reasonable by comparison with the militants. Militancy did not, at least, prevent the success of the referendum in New York State in November 1917.

In general, political activity was scaled down so work could be directed towards the war effort. As well as a general sense of patriotism, war work was eagerly sought out by suffrage women, who could thereby respond to the argument that women should not vote as they did not bear arms: in a modern war far more needed to be done to maintain forces in combat than bearing arms. Catt pledged that the NAWSA would stand by the government and both Catt and Shaw served on the Women's Committee of the Council on National Defence which went some way towards ameliorating the impression that women would undermine the war effort, though, as a lifetime pacifist, Catt had a dilemma in reconciling her personal feelings with her nationalism. Some had an even greater dilemma: Jeanette Rankin from Wyoming, the first woman Senator, felt obliged as a strong pacifist to vote against US entry into the war, which led to suggestions that women were unpatriotic.

Carrie Catt's support of President Wilson, though unpopular with her pacifist friends, was an astute move that effectively offered him her two million supporters at a time of national crisis, in return for his support for women's suffrage. The president was therefore able to announce in January

Figure 8. A graphic demonstration that it was the less developed western states of the US that enfranchised while the sophisticated east lagged behind: the enlightenment of women's suffrage is shown spreading west to east in 1915, a figure holds aloft the torch of enlightenment to the striving women in unenfranchised darkness.

1918 that he supported a federal suffrage amendment as a war measure. The next day the House of Representatives endorsed by one vote the nineteenth amendment. Later that year, on 30 September 1918, he urged the Senate (many of whose members resented his making this unprecedented direct appeal to them),

> I regard the concurrence of the Senate in the constitutional amendment proposing the extension of the suffrage to women as vitally essential to the prosecution of the great war of humanity in which we are engaged... We have made partners of the women in this war. Shall we admit them only to a partnership of suffering and sacrifice and toil and not to a partnership of privilege and right? This war could not have been fought, either by the other nations engaged or by America, if it had not been for the services of the women—services rendered in every sphere—not merely in the fields of efforts in which we have been accustomed to see them work but wherever men have worked and upon the very skirts and edges of the battle itself.[17]

Declaring the war could not have been fought without the services of women was undercutting the argument that women should not be full citizens because they did not fight. The amendment was defeated or, rather, failed to obtain the necessary two-thirds majority, obtaining 62 votes in favour against 34 opposing.

The Republicans won control of both houses of Congress in the election of November 1918. After the war militants continued their demonstrations, arrests, and hunger strikes; meanwhile the NAWSA got on with its lobbying, patiently trying to get a few more votes in the Senate to secure the necessary majority. Eventually, with at least a two-thirds majority in each of the Houses of Congress, a nineteenth or 'Susan B. Anthony' amendment on women's suffrage was on its way once more, but still needed to be ratified by states in their own state legislatures. The presidential election of 1920 was approaching, the women's vote was now worth courting, and Congress agreed to send the women's suffrage amendment to the states for ratification on 21 May 1919. The Senate approved it on 4 June—more by strategic abstentions than a rise in active support. With no more than usual hyperbole the *History of Woman Suffrage* declared the fifty-year campaign for a national amendment was ended, 'a struggle which has no parallel in history'.[18]

The amendment was passed in most of the northern, midwestern, and western states; but the battle continued in the South, where anti-suffragists held their last bastion, and where they were joined by others who opposed the amendment because it abrogated the principle of states' rights, and by those who feared for the future of white supremacy.

The South and race

In 1914 when the Senate voted on a Susan B. Anthony amendment which was lost by one vote, Anne Martin criticized Nevada senator Key Pitman for voting against, even though he was in favour of women's suffrage. He had done it because he opposed Negroes getting the vote and took a states' rights view of federal amendments. Martin told him he need not worry, 'Woman suffrage means the establishment of Anglo-Saxon supremacy.'[19]

The racial fault line running through the US women's suffrage movement was never more obvious than over the southern states in the early twentieth century. There was particular concern to stop black women from becoming enfranchised because they were thought to be better educated than black men, more likely to be assertive about their rights, and more difficult to bully into submission as this would offend the sense of gallantry of white southern gentlemen.

The National American Woman Suffrage Association meeting held in New Orleans in 1903 was racially segregated, so that Sylvanie Williams of the National Association of Coloured Women was delegated to attend the meeting in what was her own home city but was not allowed to attend.[20] Also in 1903 the NAWSA voted to allow state affiliates to determine their own entrance qualifications, obviously to accommodate the developing southern suffragist groups who would wish to be whites-only organizations fighting for a whites-only vote.

The executive board was forced to make a public statement about its attitude towards black women as potential voters. They endorsed a states' rights position on the question of giving black women the vote (so the southern states could write in an opt-out clause). At the following meeting, where black women were admitted, in the District of Columbia, a black woman, Mary Church Terrell, challenged a motion calling for federal protection for children and animals by adding that the Convention should stand up 'also for Negroes'.[21] At the beginning of the century black women had slipped so far down the agenda that they were no longer being considered as part of substantive motions; the process of exclusion, which was eventually going to disenfranchise them, had already begun.

As the suffrage battle continued state by state, white supremacy was an important factor in the strategy of the suffragists who needed to develop southern support for a woman suffrage amendment. The historian Rosalyn Terborg-Penn emphasizes that this was not only a southern prejudice; in 1915 a women's suffrage amendment to the state constitution was lost in New York when 'White voters were heard to have said that they changed their minds about supporting the amendment when they saw so many black women campaigning for it.'[22] The glaring political fact of life in the US was not a gender division, but white supremacy. The black male franchise had been clawed back in the southern states under the Jim Crow laws so it was possible for a senate committee to be told: 'eleven states have successfully defied the Federal Government in any effort to admit Negro men to the polls.'[23]

At the great parade of 1913 in front of the White House where white women said they would not march if black women participated, the NAWSA established a segregationist solution by having black women marching, but

Figure 9. Programme for the women's suffrage parade on the day before the inauguration of President Woodrow Wilson; it was led by Inez Milholland riding a white horse. Despite the imagery of heroic virtue, the march was segregated, with black women obliged to march at the back, even if they came from states where their suffrage organization was mixed.

in their own black section at the end of the parade. This obliged even integrated women's suffrage organizations to ask their black members to go to the back. Carrie Catt felt the South had to be placated with segregation though it was not necessarily to the exclusion of black women; she urged white southern women to stay away from the 1916 annual convention in Chicago because the Chicago delegates would be mainly black.

Anti-suffragists argued that women's suffrage would mean 'Negro rule', thus adding an anti-black to an anti-women argument. It was furthermore argued by Democrat supporters that black women would vote Republican, so black female voting would destroy the Democratic Party in the South. In response, it was said that poll taxes and literacy tests would ensure that black women would be easily disenfranchised, just as black men had been. It became expedient to argue that the white supremacist vote would be increased by women's voting. In 1913 Kate Gordon organized the Southern States Woman Suffrage Conference where suffragists planned to lobby state legislatures for laws that would enfranchise white women only. She was later to campaign against the nineteenth amendment out of a commitment to states' rights.

The Anthony Amendment

By 22 March 1920, thirty-five states had ratified the 'Anthony Amendment'—only one further state was necessary. Four states remained to decide: when Delaware voted against, only Tennessee, Connecticut, and Vermont were left.

Tennessee in the South seemed the best choice for a thirty-sixth state, but the Governor, Albert H. Roberts, did not want to see the matter discussed, despite appeals from President Wilson to do so, and delayed a meeting of the legislature until August, the hottest month of the year. Thus the final battle took place in sweltering conditions, the steam-bath heat of a humid Tennessee summer hardly alleviated by whirring fans. Prohibition was supposedly already in force but this was not apparent around the Nashville legislature—prohibition was already demonstrating its fatal flaw, its inability to stop people from drinking alcohol.

Carrie Chapman Catt visited with the intention of staying only for a few days, but seeing the size and force of the opposition, set up camp and remained there for six weeks. An army of lobbyists descended on Nashville to hold meetings, write letters, and lobby the legislators though they doubtless knew all the issues anyway. The suffragists wanted the vote to be decided as fast as possible. The main tactic of the anti-suffragists was to delay the proceedings in the hope that time would produce a break in the deadlock in their favour.

Anti-suffragists also gathered to influence the legislators with promised rewards and threats. Their tactics against the suffragists were such that Catt was moved to say, 'Never in the history of politics has there been such a nefarious lobby as laboured to block the ratification in Nashville. In the short time that I spent in the capital I was more maligned, more lied about, than in the thirty previous years I worked for suffrage.'[24] She accused the opposition of appropriating their telegrams, tapping their phones, and listening outside windows. The Tennessee Senate voted approval on 13 August 1920, now it was all down to the House. The representatives were evenly matched at 48 votes each and after weeks in the stifling heat, everyone was getting tired and wanted the business over with. The Speaker Seth M. Walker was said to have given the suffragists his word that he would lead the fight for ratification. In the event he reversed his position and fought against the amendment bitterly for the entire session, tabling the resolution in an effort to kill it on 18 August 1920, when key members were absent. He was openly lobbying after clearing the House of suffrage lobbyists and tried to stop one senator from voting. Meanwhile suffragists brought one member from his sick bed and reached another just as his train was pulling out of the station, persuading him to leap off and return to the chamber.

The youngest member of the House, 24-year-old Harry T. Burns had previously been voting with the opposition, as his constituency had indicated he should, though he believed in women's suffrage. He therefore had promised the suffragists that if his vote were needed, he would vote in favour. The vote was a tie, 49 to 49. Burns said, 'I know that a mother's advice is always safest for her boy to follow and my mother wanted me to vote for ratification.' However, he was not unaware either of the historic nature of the act he was about to perform: 'I appreciated the fact that an opportunity such as seldom comes to mortal man—to free 17,000,000 women from political slavery—was mine.' He voted for ratification.

Governor Roberts finally conceded and signed the amendment on 24 August. Anti-suffragists fought a rearguard action to have the decision annulled, but Connecticut soon followed in ratifying the amendment so the necessary number of states was achieved anyway. Tennessee became the 36th state to vote positively on the amendment and it was signed into law by the Secretary of State on 26 August 1920. Carrie Chapman Catt left Tennessee exhausted and returned to New York where she was met at Grand Central Station by crowds of supporters.

Disenfranchisement

The story of the enfranchisement of women in the US is not complete without mention of the disenfranchisement of black women less than a decade after the Nineteenth Amendment enfranchised them.[25] This was done by a variety of devious means, learned from the previous experience of disenfranchising black men. One recorded example was in Columbia, South Carolina, where black women were told to wait to register; they waited and waited until it was apparent some black women were prepared to wait for twelve hours to register their vote; the following day property tax requirements were declared mandatory and set at $300 worth of property. As *The Crisis* ('A record of the darker races') notes, for women who could fulfil this requirement, 'instead of being required to read the constitution, as the law provides, they were given sections from the civil and criminal codes of the state to read which they did read in an intelligent and orderly manner. They were then asked to explain these laws, a thing they refused to do since it was not required by law, and as they knew it was an attempt on the part of the board to disqualify them. The registrars thereupon refused to give the women registration certificates.'[26]

More honestly, for some white southerners the objective was just to get out the white women's vote. Congressman Thomas M. Bell of Georgia feared that as the constitution 'enfranchises the Negro women... I fear they will at the last moment, register and vote, as they have in Virginia', the only solution was to 'urge the ladies of the state to register and be prepared to vote. It may be obnoxious to many of them, but this is better than to suffer bitter humiliation when it is too late to remedy it.'[27]

By such means the majority of the black female population of the South was disenfranchised. When black women suffragists sought assistance from their erstwhile friends the white women suffragists in the National Woman's Party they were told that as black women were discriminated against in the same way as black men, this was a race issue not a women's rights issue, so they felt under no obligation to help.[28]

Individual suffragists were sympathetic to black women, Susan B. Anthony, for example, addressed black audiences and had no doubt about the immorality of racial discrimination, but felt she was justified in compromising on race to placate the white supremacists of the South because women were more moral than men and women would end racism when they got the vote, through the exercise of their higher morality.[29] In fact, by submitting on race, the suffragists proved in action a basic truth about politics: once a principle has been compromised, it cannot be uncompromised.

No change

Clearly the history of women's suffrage in the US is complex, and in some cases unique: no other place enfranchised women in order to defend polygamy, as did Utah, though it is an interesting coda to the Mormon

experience that with the 'serial monogamy' of multiple divorce and remarriage, the modern US has found itself with something resembling acceptance of polygamy.

Patient and determined activity with incremental advances were the
building blocks of success for women's suffrage, but additional injections of
militancy, organizational flair and the sense of mass progress given by the
labour movement were essential to invigorate what would otherwise have
been merely a worthy pressure group.

The story is complex because of the different territorial bodies of power
across the US: women's suffrage was a different issue in the West from that
which it was in the East and the South. It also meant opposing things at
different times: for some it meant free love, for others a more morally
restrictive society. The equal rights rhetoric of the pre- and immediately
post-civil war period shrivelled away to be replaced by nativist and even
white supremacist arguments for the women's vote.

The fact that the final phase took place during and after the First World
War is unremarkable, as women's suffrage was most often gained at or
immediately after times of national upheaval. The war did not 'bring
about' women's suffrage in the US, but it created the right atmosphere
and it gave additional arguments to suffragists while removing them from
anti-suffragists.

Historian Alan Grimes describes a 'puritan ethic' that was in the ascendant
in the period of the First World War. Legislation affected by puritan values
included the compulsory literacy test for immigrants, passed in 1917; prohibition of alcohol, and women's suffrage. These were measures which could be
described as progressive (or could be described as elitist, depending on one's
point of view); they demonstrated a yearning to engage with society and to
improve it, if necessary by the enforcement of a moral standard on others.

Richard J. Evans feels that these issues came to a head as a result of the
perceived threat to American values represented by the conflict with
Germany; but to a much greater extent from the fear of Bolshevik and allied
revolutions, when 'the fear of the subversion of the values represented by
the Protestant middle class reached panic proportions'.[30]

The key to the progress of the women's suffrage movement in the US is
a paradox: it was both mutable and unchanging. It was mutable in that in
each group of states it was offering something different: respect for hearth
and home, Anglo-Saxon ascendancy, justice for all; women's potential votes
could be promised to any power-broker in the ascendant if they backed

women's suffrage. But this could only take the movement so far, the key was that it changed nothing: the overwhelming success of the women's movement came after the experience of the western states showed that women would vote as their menfolk did and politics would not change by the addition of them to the electoral register.

10

Who won votes from the war?

'The work of generations had been swept away'

After four years of the most terrible war the world had ever seen, with the German army defeated, its rulers discredited, its people literally starving, the president of the nation's united women's suffrage societies Marie Stritt picked up her pen sadly to write her report to *International Suffrage News*. It was March 1918, and with measured understatement she commented: 'We German women have at present no reason to rejoice over the progress of our cause, but we have followed with all the greater joy the unexpected success of our sisters in other countries.'[1] Yet before the year was out German women had the vote on the same terms as men in a constitution that was a beacon of enlightened democracy.

How could a leading campaigner have read the situation quite so wrongly, have found widespread enfranchisement so 'unexpected?' Nor was she alone; *The History of Woman Suffrage* remarked that at the start of the war, 'The first thought of the suffrage leaders was that the work of generations had been swept away and after the War it would have to be commenced again.'[2] Their pessimism was understandable, for the war had fractured the suffrage movement, as some suffragists remained pacifists and others became zealous patriots. Suffragists had seen themselves as internationalist, part of a worldwide movement united in peace and co-operation. Their conception of what would bring victory was focused on these qualities. They had not connected winning the vote with nationalism and national identity but, rather as in early enfranchisements in the new world and Scandinavia, these turned out to be the winning factors.

Russia's revolutions

In common with many traditional societies, a number of women voted in Russia prior to any suffrage movement coming into play. As *The History of Woman Suffrage* explains:'In the villages and among the peasants women had long voted at the local elections either as proxies of the husband or by right of owning property, and among the nobility and wealthy classes they could vote through male proxies.'[3]

Women were involved both in intellectual life and revolutionary activity, though the restrictions placed on women's education meant that mere access to intellectual stimulation was the primary battle that women fought. Repression over education radicalized many of the country's most intelligent women. In the public sphere women's work was limited, but the experience of philanthropic and educational activity gave women invaluable experience in organization which enabled some of them to become leaders in the suffrage struggle of 1905–17.[4]

For the more extreme, such women as the nihilists of the 1860s with their short hair, plain dress, cigarette smoking, and 'free love' counterposed a new code of morality to the straitjacket of life for the middle-class female. This was a revolution of style and manners and was essentially personal, there was no intention to transmit it to others except by example. For many women this was not enough, and a more wide-reaching political activism was needed.

Questions of the franchise were not so important in a nation subject to rule by decree, where few men had the vote; women and men had an equality in their lack of rights. And women were highly active in resisting the oppression of the Tsarist state: of fifty radicals tried in 1878, sixteen were women; in another Great Trial of the left, thirty-seven of 193 were women.[5]

Ten of the twenty-eight member executive committee of the group The People's Will, who assassinated Alexander II in 1881, were women. One of them, Vera Figner, gained lasting celebrity. This assassination was the culmination of a campaign of terror which The People's Will offered to call off if the Tsar gave the Russian people a constitution guaranteeing free elections with universal suffrage and an end to censorship, under the (perfectly accurate as it turned out) threat of total revolution if democracy were not granted.[6]

Vera Figner was born in 1852, the eldest of four daughters and two sons of a wealthy and liberal-minded landowner in the Kazan province. She had what passed for an education for the daughters of the rich—in dancing, singing, drawing, and writing. She was fortunate in finding a serious young man from a family acceptable to hers, and she and Aleksei Victorovich married in 1870. He was a lawyer, working as an examining magistrate which she considered 'horrible' as she 'was already convinced that crime proceeds from poverty and ignorance' rather than immorality.[7] The two of them studied in preparation for going to Zurich; their intention was that both should study medicine, Aleksei should become a village doctor and Vera would run a hospital. Vera was 19 when she arrived Zurich in 1872, and became involved in the political life of a city swelled with young activists from all over Europe. They included her sister Lydia, who introduced her to revolutionary activism, as Vera's path diverged from that of her husband, who became more conservative. Also in 1872 the Russian Ministry of the Interior set up a special commission to discuss 'measures required to deal with the ever increasing flood of women leaving for Zurich, and the deplorable events taking place in their midst'.[8] Such events were political meetings, contact with agitators, the dissemination of propaganda, and the adoption of communist theories about love and marriage. The government therefore decreed that Russian women educated abroad could not take up state exams in Russia to confirm their diplomas. This effectively denied them the right of employment based on their studies and further education in the Russian universities which were now, as a conservative expedient, being opened to women. The successful objective was to ruin the Zurich colony.

Vera Figner went to Berne, along with the majority of the Zurich colony, and enrolled at the medical faculty. Some women moved to Paris, then returned to Russia where they worked for the revolutionary movement, some joining factories so they could mix with and influence women workers. When their work began to bear fruit in the form of strikes, the government acted and arrested the 'Moscow Group' including Vera's sister Lydia Figner, and threw them in prison for years to await trial. The remaining revolutionaries called on Vera Figner to bolster their spirits and she returned from Switzerland to give what help she could to the imprisoned women. The 'Moscow women' were eventually sentenced to vicious periods of imprisonment; sympathy for their appalling treatment in prison and admiration for their heroic speeches from the dock increased sympathy for their cause. Vera Figner organized a Red Cross group to visit prisoners and to work for their escape.

Figner followed in her friends' footsteps and went out among the peasants, giving medical assistance (she had not graduated as a doctor). Another
revolutionary, Leo Deutsch, described her engaging in debates about
whether to attack the existing representatives of the despotic state, or to
work among the people, educating them to demand their freedom. He described her as 'slender and beautiful' after her return from a village where

> she had been living as a peasant for purposes of propaganda. The impressions
> she had received there had stirred her deeply, and she described in graphic
> language the fathomless misery and poverty, the hopeless ignorance of the
> provincial working classes. The conclusion she drew from it all was that under
> existing conditions there was no way of helping these people. 'Show me any
> such way; show me how, under the present circumstances, I can serve the
> peasants, and I am ready to go back to the villages at once' she said.[9]

In this state of mind she determined that direct attack on the oppressors was
the only step, and to join with others to form The People's Will that was to
carry out its threat to assassinate the Tsar.

Several unsuccessful attempts were made on the Tsar's life including setting explosives under a railway track over which his train was due to cross,
and beneath a dining room where he was eating. Eventually the Tsar was
killed by bombs thrown at his carriage, by co-conspirators of Figner's. She
wrote that on hearing of it, 'I wept. And many of us wept... a heavy burden
was lifted from our shoulders; reaction must come to an end and give place
to a new Russia.'[10] This was when the executive committee of The People's
Will wrote to Tsar Alexander III reiterating the demand for free elections,
freedom of the press, and the release of political prisoners.

Vera Figner survived the retributions following the assassination, though
two other women who were involved in the plot did not—Gesya Helfman
died in prison and Sofia Perovskaya was hanged. Figner was betrayed and
arrested in South Russia where she was attempting to resuscitate the party
in 1883, and was put on trial the following year. She was sentenced to death
on 28 September 1884 but the sentence was commuted to penal servitude
in the 'living grave' of Schlüsselburg prison. She continued to cause trouble
to the authorities, once ensuring she was transferred to the punishment cells
so a comrade, who had already been taken there, should not be tortured
without a witness; once she went on hunger strike to improve conditions.
She served twenty years then was exiled; she went abroad in 1906 where she
worked to spread the incendiary message and collect money for Russian
revolutionaries.

Women in 1905

Before the first revolutionary year of 1905, women's issues had been regarded with disdain in the political arena; after then, 'Matters relating to sex
or suffrage were likely to evoke storms of controversy,' comments historian
Richard Stites.[11]

The debacle of the Russo-Japanese war of 1904–5 fed unrest at the autocratic system of rule under Nicholas II, who had refused to establish constitutional government and had not even delivered military efficiency. Disorder
began on 22 January 1905, 'Bloody Sunday,' with troops opening fire on a
procession of workers. There were strikes, agrarian unrest, assassinations, the
famed mutiny on the Battleship Potemkin, and a general strike organized by
the St Petersburg Soviet under Leon Trotsky.

A significant but passive distinction also appeared at this time between
women and men. Previously women and men had shared the political disability of having no rights. Now men were arguing for votes in an all-male
parliament. In common with other feminist movements, Russian feminists
became radicalized when a move towards male enfranchisement (however
slight, as in this case) took place with no regard to women. Despite their
years of oppression, by the early twentieth century Russian feminists had
developed organizational skills and self-confidence; a new generation
showed a growing dissatisfaction with mere philanthropy; and the stirring
example of Finland demonstrated the ability of women to demand political
rights through solidarity and agitation.[12]

In the political turbulence of 1905 a Russian Union of Defenders of
Women's Rights was established in Moscow a month after Bloody Sunday,
with the principal demand of a Constituent Assembly elected by universal
suffrage with a secret ballot. They declared 'that the struggle for women's
rights is inseparably connected with the struggle for the political liberation
of Russia'. They additionally demanded rights of habeas corpus and freedom
for political prisoners.[13] Other feminist groups called for women's suffrage
at the same time, and existing philanthropic organizations were radicalized,
but the Russian Union was the largest and most vigorous of them.

The trade unions were joining forces in the Union of Unions. The
Russian Union of Defenders of Women's Rights applied for membership on
paper and found it easy to be accepted on the basis of their radical programme, but when women actually started attending meetings, the men in

charge thought there was some kind of mistake. Women continued to attend, and to assail members with their propaganda until, in July 1905, the Union of Unions agreed to endorse the women's group and officially recognized equal rights for women. Many local councils, particularly urban ones, had accepted women's suffrage before the end of the year. The local government congress, however, was prepared to support the *principle* of women's suffrage, but not as a practical issue. Liberal delegates feared peasant women voters and female conservatism, and there were the usual fears that politics was an unnatural imposition on females. The Russian Union women warned that if the next congress of Liberals did not support women's suffrage, they would have to look for support among the extremist parties of the working class.[14] The local government congress finally gave in and approved a project for both sexes to vote and hold office.

Women's rights were included in the proposals for a new elective law for the whole nation in November 1905, but in a land in which there was no effective government. The revolution of October had forced the Tsar to yield and he finally granted Russia a constitution with a legislative Duma, an appointed prime minister, and a (less clear) promise of a wider franchise. When the new government announced this franchise, however, on 11 December 1905, women were specifically excluded, to the anger of suffragist campaigners.

The political scene was changing fast over the winter of 1905–6. The settlement with the Tsar split the revolutionaries, with some willing to accept the deal; but the Soviet held out, and fighting continued until the first days of 1906, when the Soviet was defeated. The Union of Unions was dissolved amid renewed repression but, concurrently, some semblance of democratic life began in Russia. The left-liberal Constitutional Democrats (Kadets) who were the foremost party in the Duma supported women— Ariadna Tyrkova, one of the leading members of the Russian Union of Defenders of Women's Rights, was on the party's central committee. The Marxist parties also supported women's suffrage, as a part of universal suffrage.

On election day in March 1906 the Moscow branch of the Russian Union of Defenders of Women's Rights issued a statement to say, 'We the women of Russia, who chance to be living in this great epoch of Russia's renewal, and who have more than once demonstrated our undying love for the Fatherland, feel at this moment with special intensity the bitterness of being without rights, and we warmly protest being excluded from taking part in decisions which concern us.'[15] Thus the appeal for women's suffrage was made at a time of national emergency and in recognition of previous loyalty to the nation—the same mixture of patriotism and deserving loyalty that has been a theme through other successful women's suffrage struggles.

The Duma discussed women's suffrage, and there was clear, if minority support: on 15 May 2006 a group of 111 deputies signed a declaration calling for the enfranchisement of all excluded groups: peasants, nationalities, and women. The right wing derided the women's claims in familiar terms: that women did not serve in the army and that the Bible decreed the divisions of gender. The suffrage project was referred back for more committee work, but the Duma was dissolved before it could be reintroduced.

As a conservative measure, the Tsar gave votes to a small number of women who owned considerable property, who could vote by proxy for their husband or son. The first Duma ended in deadlock over the Tsar's restriction of the assembly's rights, accompanied by renewed repression. A second Duma in 1907 introduced a new electoral law that increased the representation of the middle classes. Its successors introduced basic reforms but proposals for adult suffrage, including one by Social Democrat Paul Miliukov for enfranchising men and women over 21 died in committee. Anna Filosofova, whose position as the wife of a high-ranking official gave her some measure of protection, had set up a moderate women's club, the Mutual Benefit Society, with philanthropic ends. Mainly committed to charitable work, the organization had been radicalized during the events of 1905 and then set up an Electoral Department to campaign for women's suffrage. They now petitioned the second Duma calling for the vote but the second Duma was dissolved before the petition could even be discussed.

The suffrage movement was falling apart from its own disunity and lack of effective leadership, and under political assaults by the Social Democrats who wanted women to be active politically in their party's cause, rather than as radical feminists. Feminists threatened, as they had in Britain and the US, that they would withdraw support from the Social Democrats if they did not bring in a suffrage bill and the atmosphere became increasingly acrimonious.

The right wing also attacked suffragists, out of an ideological opposition to the very concept of rights for women. The suffragists were vocal in their opposition to the renewed repression of the Tsar's forces after 1906, and the authorities launched a crack-down against the weakened movement. Zinaida Morivich, a Moscow-based Russian Union leader and one of the truly international figures of Russian feminism, who had enthralled the delegates at the 1906 meeting of the International Woman Suffrage Alliance in Copenhagen, was forbidden from giving a lecture about English feminists in 1907. By the following year it was virtually impossible for suffragists to hold a legal meeting, and membership of the Russian Union of Defenders of Women's Rights dwindled away.

Alexandra Kollontai

It was the political left who were to make the running in delivering suffrage in Russia, rather than feminist groups. The most important left-wing thinker on women was Alexandra Kollontai who was born in St Petersburg in 1870, the daughter of a general who had married into a Finnish timber merchant's family. She married her cousin, Vladimir Kollontai, an army officer, but found her situation confining and left him in 1898 at the age of 26 to study politics in Zurich. She returned to Russia and started publishing work on Finland in Marxist journals. She took part in the demonstration that ended in the 'Bloody Sunday' massacre in 1905 and in following years met leading international socialists such as Vladimir Lenin and Rosa Luxemburg. She lived in exile after 1908, touring Europe and the US and making speeches, occasionally suffering imprisonment for revolutionary activities.

Kollontai's work of 1909, *The Social Basis of the Woman Question*, preached 'free love', considering bourgeois marriage part of the apparatus of the state which would wither away after socialism. She argued that marriage and divorce should be contracted within the heart, and divorced wives and children should be financially supported by the community from taxation revenue. Her enemies attempted to undermine her with accusations of licentiousness though her personal life seems to have been lived in the state of serial monogamy that was to become the common experience of western individuals towards the end of the twentieth century. She was inspired by Clara Zetkin's dismissal of bourgeois feminists and in the same vein she attacked feminists in Russia and abroad who were, she said, concerned with winning voting rights for privileged women rather than the emancipation of all women and the liberation of the poor.

After the 1917 Revolution she was able to write her own history of the women's movement in which she was scathing about the women's suffragists who 'approached the women workers with narrowly feminine causes and aspirations'. She described how middle-class feminists tried to enlist domestic servants in 1905, who 'eagerly responded to this call to "organise" and turned up at the early meetings in large numbers'. Servants had a clear list of demands: an eight-hour day, a minimum wage, better living conditions, and polite treatment by their employers. However, the vision of feminist organizers was 'to set up an idyllic, mixed alliance between lady employers and domestic employees', with the result that the domestic servants turned away from the suffragists, 'to the disappointment of the bourgeois ladies'.[16]

Such views were not calculated to ensure popularity in every quarter. At the founding of the All Russian Union in 1905 one irate feminist raised the less than fraternal cry, 'Strangling is too good for you' to Kollontai.[17] When she visited the moderate feminist Anna Filosofova's home the old lady had to make the sign of the cross to exorcise Kollontai's revolutionary spirit.

Kollontai returned to Russia in 1908 but had to stay underground for fear of arrest by the authorities. Despite the danger, she insisted on attending the First All Russia Women's Congress which had been called by Anna Filosofova. Filosofova's low-profile Mutual Benefit Society had been less of a target than the Russian Union of Defenders of Women's Rights and so had suffered less abuse and had quietly maintained restrained activity, and some former Russian Union leaders such as Zanaidia Mirovich helped organize the conference. More than a thousand participants attended the Alexandrovsky Hall in St Petersburg, including all the major feminists as well as male officials and politicians who were interested in women's questions. The agenda was heavily censored by the government: the organizers were forbidden to invite any foreigners and the police were in constant attendance.[18]

Feminists proposed equal rights for women but the meeting was disrupted by Alexandra Kollontai and her vociferous Social Democrats who offered a more extreme view of women's position in society, promoting separate socialist women's movements, not a common cause with the bourgeois feminists. These women from the 'labour delegation' tried to keep economic problems and class interests to the fore, while deriding the women's solidarity offered by feminism as useless, saying working women had nothing in common with bourgeois women.

In a weak motion that attempted to please all, the organizing committee finally endorsed the principle of female equality, while noting that full equality would come only with universal suffrage. Historian Rochelle Ruthchild remarks that 'it was on the rocks of the suffrage that the feminist ship foundered'.[19] It was reported that 'both sides resorted to grimacing, foot-stamping and interruptions'.[20] If the Congress sounds unnecessarily vituperative, it has to be seen in the context of Russian political life, a right-wing Duma deputy wrote to the organizer Anna Filosofova and compared her congress to an assembly of whores, a letter she contrived to get published in a newspaper, to shame him.[21]

Alexandra Kollontai had to flee from the police before the meeting was over. She went first to Germany and continued her journalistic and revolutionary activity, from 1914 working exclusively for the Bolsheviks. She acted as an intermediary when the Germans arranged for Lenin to return to Russia in 1917; she herself had returned shortly after the 'February' revolution.

War and two revolutions

The underlying trend over the turbulent years after 1905 was, first, for a vast and all-inclusive women's movement and, second, for more specialized and more moderate groupings, attempting to work within the limited democracy now permitted under the Tsar. The League for Women's Equality was the last of its kind to make any mark; it emerged as a regrouping of the right wing of the Russian Union in the wake of the Women's Congress. Its president was a St Petersburg doctor (many of the most active feminists were physicians), Poliksena Shishkina-Yavein. The League presented the third Duma in 1912 with a petition for women to be elected on the same basis as men, arguing that women had already shown their ability in other fields; that women would oppose militarism; and that some social problems, such as alcoholism, prostitution, and the protection of children, would be more amenable to solutions proposed by women. It was, therefore, a classic feminist argument such as might have been made by Fawcett in Britain or Shaw in the US.

It was fashioned into a bill that met the same fate as other bills: it was proposed by the left, opposed by the right, sent to committee and was still there when the third Duma came to an end a few months later. Some advances were made in this Duma, however, including the abolition of the passport system under which Russian women had no legal identity or freedom of mobility. A bill to enfranchise all women failed in the following year in the next Duma, by 206 to 106 votes.

The patriotic urge at the beginning of the First World War was supported by feminist women in Russia, as giving them a chance to prove their citizenship. As the League for Women's Equality said in 1915, 'This is our obligation to the fatherland, and this will give us the right to participate as the equals of men in the new life of a victorious Russia.'[22] The First World War hastened the demise of Tsarist rule with its appalling mismanagement of yet another war, this time a total war involving the entire population: in the first two and a half years of the war the Russians suffered 5.5 million casualties. At the beginning of 1917 the troops were not getting ammunition, the civilian population was not getting food. The government was divided, with four different prime ministers in the last year of Tsar Nicholas II's rule. The opposition consisted of the liberal intelligentsia, who believed democratic reform would transform Russia and enable the nation to win the war; and the left, including the Bolsheviks, who believed total revolution was imminent among all combatants in the war and gloried in the prospect.

The Tsar compounded his association with the disaster of the war by taking personal command late in 1916. Factories were closed through lack of coal; crowds gathering in bread queues took part in street demonstrations. International Women's Day on 8 March 1917 saw a demonstration with the theme 'Peace and Bread' calling for adequate food supplies and a return of husbands and sons from the front. An annual International Women's Day was a new innovation, proposed at the Second Conference of Socialist Women by Clara Zetkin in 1910; such a regular commemoration of women related to a New York demonstration of socialist women that had taken place on 8 March 1908. The Bolsheviks, while generally supportive of public expressions of discontent which they hoped would develop into revolutionary disorder, were not expecting a major event in March: they were preparing for a big day of demonstration and protest on 1 May.

The female crowds grew in the streets of Petrograd (formerly St Petersburg), calling on the factories still working and urging workers to come and join them for a demonstration that was officially prohibited. The crowd was bolstered by the appearance in their ranks of soldiers and young army officers amid the sea of red flags and demonstrators chanting and singing. Some of the crowd began looting shops, the police tried to take control but were beaten back. The Cossacks, the last line of defence for the Tsarist regime after it had lost the support of the people and the strength of the police, were reluctant to intervene.

Over the next few days, far from dying down, unrest grew, with the crowds swelled by more workers from munitions factories and others. The Cossacks were still mounted and guarding the bridges and other key points but, as a commentator remarked, 'the Cossacks had a softer side for the opposite sex. Ringed by female demonstrators during these difficult days, a new phenomenon had developed, as somewhat benign and sometimes frisky banter had broken out between the women and the Cossacks.' Women asked why the Cossacks didn't attack the hated police instead of the people; clearly the Cossacks were thinking about it.[23] Soldiers of the Petrograd garrison were turned out and, though some people were shot, after the troops returned to their barracks the revolutionary fervour took over and 170,000 mutinied, calling 'Down with the Romanovs' and 'Land and Freedom'. On 12 March the Duma, refusing the Tsar's orders to disperse, called for a provisional government under Prince Georgi Lvov. The Tsar, with insufficient loyal troops to command, was obliged to abdicate on 13 March. Alexander Kerensky, a socialist deputy, became war minister then replaced Lvov as prime minister, fatally damaging his government by urging continuance of the war.

Members of League for Women's Equality had, like women's movements in Britain and the US, spent the war in patriotic work in the national cause. Now politics was again centre stage, they wanted to take part and began to campaign again for the vote. As Rochelle Ruthchild has emphasized, the demand for the women's vote resonated among all levels of the population in these weeks after the 'February' revolution, it was not merely a demand of privileged women.[24] The League for Women's Equality held a large street demonstration at the beginning of April, in which the venerable Vera Figner, revered for her part in the revolutionary past and now returned to Russia, took part. She was doubtless uplifted to see the decades of struggle finally bearing fruit, though now she was marching with the feminists not the socialists.

The demonstration on 20 March of some 40,000, led by Shishkina-Yavein, protested that 'only we women, outcast of the outcasts, living as slaves of yesterday's slaves, are waiting for the government frankly and openly to put forward a declaration of our rights.'[25] It was guarded by a female militia on horseback and marchers carried banners such as 'War to Victory'. A few days after the demonstration Prince Lvov received a deputation which included Shishkina-Yavein and Vera Figner, and assured them that women would be granted the vote. Within days, on 15 April 1917, women over 20 were given full voting rights; the act was ratified on 20 July. This made

Russia the fourth European country, after Finland, Denmark, and Norway, to enfranchise women, in the usual state for enfranchisement of national upheaval and self-definition.

The war ground on for eight months with the government unable to assert control and the revolutionaries increasingly restive and swelled by the return of exiles including the leaders Lenin and Trotsky. They attempted a coup in July but finally succeeded in seizing power early in November (the 'October Revolution') and Kerensky fled to exile. After the Bolshevik seizure of power Alexandra Kollontai, who had been with the Bolshevik leaders at their headquarters at the Smolny Institute, was made Commissar of Public Welfare. She was the only woman member of the government and one of the first woman cabinet members in history. Vera Figner worked under her for a time.

In their first months in power the Bolsheviks proposed 'measures of the emancipation of women from servitude'; where women had been given the right to vote, they were now granted the right to stand for office.[26] During the revolutionary period of 1917 to 1920, with the active involvement of Kollontai, the new government granted women full equality before the law and established divorce by mutual consent, gave judicial recognition to free unions, permitted abortion, made marriage a civil rather than a religious act, and illegitimate children were given the same status as those born within marriage.

With enfranchisement, as was often the case, went disenfranchisement for some former voters. The first Soviet constitution of 1918 placed limitations on suffrage on the basis of class, in this case a reversal of the usual practice of excluding the poor, now it was the rich—people from the 'exploiting classes'—landowners, bourgeoisie, clergy, and white (Tsarist) army officers were excluded from the franchise without distinction as to gender.[27]

Kollontai had resigned as a Commissar in 1918 over disagreements in policy but maintained a high profile in the party, and in 1919 was one of the founders of the Zhenotdel or women's section of the party, and its leader from 1920. In order to carry the revolution into everyday life, the Bolsheviks (who were called Communists from March 1918) promoted newspapers and booklets for women, then realized the primary problem was illiteracy. Three-quarters of women workers and larger proportion of peasants were illiterate in 1920.[28] The solution was a network of women organizers who 'threaded their way through the vastness of Russia on agit-trains and agit-boats, propaganda vehicles fitted out with printing

Figure 10. Poster proclaiming 'Hail Equal Women of the USSR'. On the left a peasant woman puts a ballot in a box, on the right a woman is a deputy. The text in the box is article 137 of the Soviet Constitution of 1936 (known as the Stalin Constitution) which guaranteed political equality for men and women: an example of how the state could engage women's suffrage in its service.

presses, movie projectors and visual aids. They marched on foot the long miles from a district party centre to the sleepy villages, bringing news of female equality, and setting up "reading cabins", literacy classes, nurseries, and health points.'[29] Alexandra Kollontai brought some of the Eastern women to Moscow for conferences where they would tear off the veils covering their faces for the audience, as a dramatic demonstration of emancipation.

Soon it was officially considered that the position of women in Soviet Russia was 'resolved' and the Zhenotdel was abolished in 1930. In fact, despite having equal voting power with men, women had long disappeared from any positions of power in the party and government, so in the new Communist system women were learning the same lesson as in capitalist countries where the vote was won: it conferred the right to a small share in conferring power on someone chosen by a political party.

Russian feminism began as a demand for education, much as had feminism in Britain and other countries; the level of repression by the Tsarist authorities prevented the growth of liberalism in Russia and also the peaceful transition from philanthropic to political ends. Women who might have become constitutional feminists in other circumstances in Russia became the most violent of political militants. The revolution of 1905 radicalized women along with the rest of the politically aware population, so women played a significant part in the first revolution of 1917 of which universal suffrage was an obvious corollary.

Vera Figner died in 1942, Alexandra Kollontai in 1952, shortly before her 80th birthday, 'only partially assimilated into the mainstream of Soviet political life' as historian Cathy Porter has it.[30] She had been Soviet Ambassador to Norway from 1924 (the world's first woman ambassador) and continued a career in diplomatic work, conveniently far from the power and intrigue of Moscow.

Germany—unity without liberation

When Susan B. Anthony visited Berlin in 1883 she innocently posted letters in her own organization's envelopes bearing such slogans as 'No just government can be formed without the consent of the governed', but in a few days an official brought back the letters saying 'Such sentiments are not allowed to pass through the post office.'[31]

Germany was, as Richard J. Evans remarks, a place with many of the preconditions for the growth of a strong feminist movement. There was a Catholic minority but the dominant culture was Protestant, the population was highly literate, there was a large and well-established middle class.[32] Nationalism was, moreover, one of the most powerful forces in German politics and culture in the nineteenth century and women's suffrage movements went hand-in-hand with nationalist movements in Finland and Norway, and accompanied the creation of new national identity as in New Zealand, Australia, and the western United States. Modern Germany was created only in 1871 as the Germanic Federation, and the unification could reasonably be thought of as a nationalist struggle.

German Protestantism was not, however, progressive: it presented itself as a monolithic set of truths without the proliferation of reforming sects that characterized the British Protestant experience. German nationalism was focused not on freedom from an exterior force, but unity of many disparate political units within Germany: it was therefore not a movement towards liberation which tended towards the liberal, but towards national consolidation, which was authoritarian. Prussian militarism rather than bourgeois liberalism was in the ascendant.

In the revolution of 1848 novelist Louise Otto-Peters had promoted female equality including enfranchisement. She later became president of the General German Woman's Association which was founded in 1865. Though Otto-Peters always believed in women's suffrage, the Association was limited to educational and economic and not political ends in accordance with the increasingly illiberal nature of German society. At one time women had called for equality between girls and boys in education; by 1875 the request was for the proper education of women for motherhood. Hedwig Dohm called on the Association to support a female suffrage society in 1876 but the political impetus was weak, if it was there at all.

The united Germany was a nation in which, as contemporary suffrage commentator Alice Zimmern said, 'the status of woman as the home-maker and *Hausfrau* was so firmly established and the intellectual superiority and absolute predominance of man so much taken for granted' that nothing by way of political revolt could be expected of German womanhood.[33] Additionally the Combination Laws of 1851 made it illegal for women to take part in political meetings or join political associations in most parts of Germany, including Prussia and Bavaria, the two largest states.

August Bebel, one of the giants of European socialism, led the Social Democratic Party (SDP) from the 1870s until his death in 1913; early in his career he wrote *Woman and Socialism*, published in 1883. In this text (pre-Marxist, in that Bebel wrote it before he had read much Marx) Bebel described the evils of capitalism as visited on women, and the vision of a socialist utopia in which, separate but equal, women would have a right to work in any occupation but would mainly opt for a familial role. The way to work towards this happy state of affairs was to campaign for women's equality in education, before the law, at work and for women's suffrage. This was to become one of the founding texts of socialism as it related to women.

With a relaxing of Bismarckian restrictions on socialists organizing in 1890, and an increase in trade unionism following on the heels of massive industrialization, the German Social Democratic party began to assert itself. Some Social Democrats stayed revolutionary, but it became apparent to many that the parliamentary road could bring benefits. The Social Democrats at the Erfurt congress in 1891 set forth a programme clearly informed by Marxism, beginning 'The struggle of the working class against capitalistic exploitation is of necessity a political struggle' and offering as the fruit of the electoral struggle the common ownership of the means of production. As part of this move to popular control, in remarks owing their essence to

Bebel, the congress demanded 'Universal, equal and direct suffrage, with secret ballot, for all elections, of all citizens of the realm over twenty years of age, without distinction of sex' with proportional representation.[34] They introduced a bill for women's suffrage in the Reichstag in 1894, though without enthusiasm or success.

A new Federation of German Women's Associations was founded in 1894 and in the early twentieth century its moderate leaders were giving way to a more radical generation including Marie Stritt, president of the Federation from 1899. A suffrage society was founded in 1901 by Anita Augspurg and Lida Gustava Heymann in Hamburg (a 'free city' where the laws forbidding political association did not apply); Frankfurt and Bremen followed. These united with societies in the southern states in 1902 to form the German Association for Women's Suffrage with Anita Augspurg as president. As well as the practical possibilities of reform via women's suffrage, there was an element of national pride in the development of these organizations: Germany was not to be represented at the first international women's suffrage congress in Washington in 1902, something that caused embarrassment in radical circles.[35]

They asked for an audience with the Chancellor, Count von Bülow, who received a deputation of thirty-five women on 20 March 1902. They called for the repeal of the Combination Laws as they related to women (forbidding their political association) for the reform and extension of girls' schools and the right of women to matriculate from universities. The difficulties suffragists faced are obvious—they could not even ask for the vote, because then they would be an organization with a political aim and that was forbidden in the most populous states; they first had to ask for the right even to meet and discuss politics. All these demands were conceded within the next six years, culminating in the repeal of the Combination Laws in 1907.

The franchise demand was often represented in terms of the difference between women and men, and the specific female biological function: 'The German woman who has hitherto ceaselessly and with stern adherence to duty to promoted the prosperity of the nation, is beginning to realise that she who gives the State its citizens, may also lay claim to the rights of a citizen.'[36]

The Union for Women's Suffrage supported sympathetic electoral candidates; took arguments for the municipal vote through the courts; encouraged the few property-owning women who could vote (via a male proxy) to do so; argued for the ecclesiastical vote (for church councils) where they did not have it; and petitioned the Reichstag for the full suffrage, though its early years were cursed by divided aims with the usual *non sequiturs* of the women's suffrage movement, 'moral reform' and a commitment to end state-regulated prostitution. The range of panaceas on offer was impressive; a leaflet of 1908 claimed that: 'Women's suffrage encourages peace and harmony between different peoples. Women's suffrage effectively promotes abstinence and prevents the ruin of people through alcohol. Women's suffrage opposes the exploitation of the economically and physically weak, it takes pity on children and tortured animals...'[37]

In 1907 a group of women led by Helene Stöcker advocated the use of contraceptives, the legalization of abortion, and an end to the stigma on unmarried mothers and illegitimate children. As Evans notes, elsewhere other feminists had advocated sexual freedom, but they had never before gained a foothold in the organized feminist movement.[38] It may be that the repressive authoritarianism of German political culture pushed such fringe elements as the feminists to more daring extremes. This does not mean that they were 'left' (though many were) or that the left unequivocally supported the women's vote: when the left-liberal splinter groups joined together in 1910 the organization's non-acceptance of women's suffrage was a condition of the South German liberals' joining.

All men over 25 had the vote for the Reichstag, but universal manhood suffrage was not a tool of democracy in Germany but a means to reinforce militarism. The Reichstag's powers were limited and it was often ignored by the government which was appointed by the Kaiser and responsible only to him. The federal franchise for the twenty-two states of the federation was much less democratic than the franchise for the government; it was often held on a property franchise. The whole was dominated by the arrogant and militaristic Wilhelm II, who ruled from 1888, and allowed himself to be controlled by the German Officer Corps; thus, a nation which had the outward appearance of a democratic, constitutional monarchy was in fact a militaristic oligarchy with a pretence to democracy to lend itself legitimacy.

Nor was suffrage a great national cause as it was in Britain or the US; even compared to Germany's neighbours in Holland and Denmark, the suffrage movement was small, and was split into a number of hostile groups who argued over such issues as whether Social Democrats should co-operate with bourgeois feminists. The SDP were more effective in demanding a better measure of protection for women workers, which (as a paternalistic demand) fitted more easily into the male-dominated model of German society.

The SDP also supported equal pay and equality in education and in the professions. It did not always press for women's suffrage, however, relegating the issue when pressing for greater democracy in state legislatures. The Social Democrats in 1895 and on some other occasions attempted to amend government bills to permit votes for women but as a party they were half-hearted and the dominant parties were dismissive of the very idea.

Revolution in 1918

Rosa Luxemburg, the great woman socialist of the time, took no interest in women's emancipation, thinking the role of the true socialist was emancipation of the entire working class, after which such social questions would be resolved. She and Clara Zetkin, leader of the 'Women's Office' of the SDP, even opposed contraception and abortion as the proletariat needed all the people it could produce for the revolution.[39] Obviously this reinforced women's role as being primarily in the home, as did the constant emphasis on women helping their menfolk in proletarian striving. Reactionary attitudes were common among the socialists, who feared women would vote in large numbers for right-wing candidates.[40] They could be dismissive even of the most loyal women party members. An official, Ignaz Auer, told the Mainz Party Conference of 1900, 'The trouble is that there are too few women comrades in the Party. I wish there were many more. The few who we have to do all the work are overloaded and thus prone to become bad-tempered. So it comes about that they sometimes make life miserable for us, even though we are not to blame.'[41]

The Combination Laws were repealed in 1907 (the repeal going into effect on 15 May 1908) permitting women to attend political meetings of all types. The preamble to the bill specifically referred to its being brought 'in accordance with the desire expressed by large sections of the population, and in particularly by women'.[42] A Women's Suffrage Congress of 3,000 people was held in Frankfort in 1907. Emmeline Pethick-Lawrence and Annie Kenney visited from Britain to address them, but the mood was against militancy. The relaxation of control over politics resulted in an influx of conservative women who began to move the suffrage movement further to the right. The left-liberals were prepared, in the less repressive atmosphere that now prevailed in the Empire, to support a coalition with the right wing. This led more radical feminist leaders such as Augspurg and Heymann to consider the movement betrayed and they split from the left-liberals, thus losing a consistent source of support and the only party on which they had any influence. Augspurg and Heymann attempted to follow a path of independent militancy, though rejecting violence. This quickly descended into farce: a kind of militancy without militancy. Even a march through the streets of Munich in 1912 was considered too extreme, and was eventually held with the participants all in carriages, though sporting the militant suffragette colours of green, purple and white.

Clara Zetkin, the leading SDP theorist, argued against feminists (and had some of them expelled from the party) to promote a vision of women's position within the grander proletarian struggle for socialism and not as a separate movement. She attended the International Conference of Working Women in Copenhagen in 1910, along with women from seventeen countries, including the first three women elected to the Finnish parliament. There she successfully argued for an International Women's Day and joined forces with Alexandra Kollontai to speak for universal suffrage, linking the struggle for the political rights of working-class women with their economic rights. They opposed a partial franchise of propertied women, which had been put forward by moderates.

The German suffrage movement disintegrated between 1910 and 1914 by which time there were three mutually hostile female suffrage societies. Only one of them supported universal suffrage, the German Women's Suffrage League. The problems for women's suffrage in Germany lay in the nature of the German system rather than the women or their principles. What, as Richard Evans asks, were they even calling for in asking for 'Votes for women'? Was it a universal suffrage for the Reichstag, a property franchise in Prussia and fewer rights in states with even less democracy than Prussia?[43] As he points out, in countries with a liberal constitution the feminists acted to preserve middle-class privileges by enfranchising other middle-class women, normally on the basis of property ownership. Women could help to shore up the middle class against the increasing demands of the working class by adding more privileged women to the electoral mix. Germany's political atmosphere tended towards repression, however, and the notion of widening the franchise in response to a threat was not part of the nation's mental picture of itself; in terms of democracy, Germany was therefore moving in the opposite direction from that travelled by comparable industrialized nations. As the twentieth century progressed, individual states of the German Empire revised their franchise by introducing more stringent

Figure 11. German poster announcing Women's Day 8 March 1914 and calling for women's suffrage. The day was commemorated at the suggestion of socialist leader Clara Zetkin, who argued for women's position in the wider labour movement, not as a separate feminist group.

property qualifications; at the same time they increased the volume of imperialist rhetoric, as well as increasing spending, particularly on the navy. Women simply did not fit into this scenario except to emphasize their difference from it in their sphere as mothers and homemakers.

Rosa Luxemburg's approach demonstrates the divisions in German society over women and politics. Luxemburg had always been contemptuous of the women's rights movement and considered the question of suffrage within capitalism to be an irrelevant bourgeois distraction. 'Red Rosa' had been born in Russian Poland in 1870, the daughter of a Jewish timber merchant. At the age of 18 she had to escape the country in 1889 because of her revolutionary activity, and she left Poland for Zurich where she met other revolutionary exiles and studied for her doctorate. In 1898 she went to Berlin where she joined the Social Democratic Party and established herself as a socialist intellectual and orator arguing that class war was the only way forward. She applauded the Russian revolution of 1905 as a sign of hope for the future.

The SDP was already riven with dispute before the war over whether to choose peaceful or aggressive methods of changing society. There was only a semblance of unity in a party which remained theoretically true to the goal of revolution while in practice following the path of reform. This long-fomented division meant the coming of the war confronted German socialism with a crippling challenge: how to reconcile their class antagonism with the call to national unity? It was obvious that many leading Social Democrats were nationalists first and socialists second. Some on the left were arguing for a united front with their enemies for a German national victory; others for a peace conference; others for revolution which would, it was believed, be international.

Rosa Luxemburg worked against the war with Karl Liebknecht, an SDP deputy who had been so bold as to vote against a financial bill to support the war in the Reichstag; they formed the Spartacist League in summer 1915. Luxemburg spent three years of the First World War in prison. The collapse of the German offensive of spring and summer 1918 meant defeat was inevitable, and when in October Germany called for an armistice the militaristic state fell apart, first in Munich where a socialist government was set up in November. The Kaiser abdicated and left for Holland and the first German republic was declared on 9 November 1918. Those in control of the government were now indubitably the reformist wing of the socialist party. Soldiers, sailors, and workers who wanted a real revolution were in open revolt, waving red flags in the streets and tearing the insignia of rank from officers. Among the activists were Luxemburg and Liebknecht who founded the German Communist Party in December 1918; for them the Russian Revolution of the previous year was a harbinger of world revolution. Their enemies in the army high command shared this vision, and were determined it would not happen. With the SDP finally enjoying a taste of power, they used it to call on the army to put down the revolutionaries. Luxemburg and Liebknecht were arrested in Berlin on 15 January, killed and their bodies dumped in a river.

Weimar democracy

The National Assembly, having decamped from Berlin while the uprising was being put down, met at Weimar in February 1919 to work out a new constitution, which was named after the provincial town. The new constitution was the most democratic ever yet put into practice, with universal suffrage for all citizens at the age of 20 and proportional representation. Maria Stritt in 1920 (by which time she was a member of the city council in Dresden) wrote,

> Although throughout the more than four years of war the women worked eagerly for the suffrage, through their organisations, demanding it in public meetings and petitioning legislative bodies, they did not get it by their own efforts but by the Revolution in November, 1918, at the end of the war. In August 1919, their rights were confirmed unanimously by all parties in the new constitution. They received the suffrage and eligibility for the Reichstag, and for the parliaments of the states and local bodies—universal, equal, direct and secret and applied exactly on the same terms as to men. Women are by the constitution eligible to all state and government offices.[44]

Alice Salamon, the German secretary of the International Council of Women, wrote that women's suffrage 'was accepted as the most natural thing in the world. It was neither questioned nor opposed by any political or professional groups. All political parties resolutely accepted woman suffrage as a fact and issued electoral platforms in which they declared themselves for the full partnership of women in political life.'[45] The National Union for Woman Suffrage met in Erfurt in autumn 1919 and dissolved itself, considering its work accomplished, though in fact its sole contribution (though not a negligible one) had been to keep the issue of women's suffrage on the agenda, they had not been consulted by the legislators who had simply reached for the solution proposed in the SDP's Erfurt Congress of almost thirty years previously.

Germany had been defeated and humiliated, and the legislators had striven to move as far away as was possible from the undemocratic regime of the Kaiser. Yet with their own lack of knowledge of advanced democracy, and the absence of a base of liberalism in the nation, they had gone too far too fast. The introduction of unrestricted proportional representation allowed tiny extremist parties such as the Nazis to gain a foothold in local and national assemblies. The government had, moreover, at its outset given free licence to the far right to dominate the streets, leading to a regime of terror which was not to be stabilized until after the Beer Hall Putsch of 1923. An ultra-democratic constitution had been laid over an autocratic state. As the title of an influential book by Theodor Plivier had it, *The Kaiser Goes: The Generals Remain*. With no history of democracy or democratic thought, Germany was still bitterly divided between right and left, with the right claiming that military Germany had been betrayed by its new democratic politicians.

Germany did not therefore become a woman-friendly democracy, despite suffrage and equal rights being written into the constitution. The SDP promoted social work as a specifically female sphere of activity, even making it a women's monopoly, thus rendering it more apparently reasonable to have other sectors exclusively male. The transformation of the Social Democrats into a state-supporting reform party had its parallel in the metamorphosis of the proletarian women's movement into a training organization for social work. When the Nazis took power they rejected most of Social Democrat practice but found the notion of women being restricted to the social work sphere, or the home, very much fitting to their way of thinking.

Women were widely believed to be voting with the parties of the right; certainly the Social Democrats did not gain from an electoral roll containing women, and they lost power in the election of June 1920. The election of the unrepentant monarchist Hindenburg as the republic's second president was claimed by anti-suffragists as the inevitable result of votes for women, as was the later election of Hitler, but in fact women tended to vote for the Catholic Centre Party.[46]

The attitude of the Nazis towards political women was expressed by their leader: 'In 1924 we had a sudden upsurge of women who were attracted by politics: Frau von Treuenfels and Matilde von Kemnitz. They wanted to join the Reichstag, in order to raise the moral level of that body, so they said. I told them that 90 per cent of the matters that were dealt with by parliament were masculine affairs, on which they could not have opinions of any value. They rebelled against this point of view, but I shut their mouths by saying "You will not claim that you know men as I know women".'[47] Ideologically, he considered 'The phrase "emancipation of women" is the product of Jewish intellect and its content is stamped with that same intellect.'[48]

The emphasis on home and family found its dire apotheosis in 1933, the last free election in Germany, in which the Federation of German Women's Associations significantly supported the Nazis, looking forward to a Nazi government's 'biological policy' which would promote the pure German family. Women's suffrage had been widely promoted as a moral force in politics, socially sensitive and anti-militaristic. In Germany, at least, it failed to fulfil this promise.

Aletta Jacobs and the Dutch movement

The most important Dutch leader, who stamped her imprint on the suffrage campaign in her native land, was Aletta Jacobs, who was born on 9 February 1854 in Sappemeer, the eighth child of a Jewish doctor. She noted in her autobiography that she was her father's favourite child; her respect for her mother declined as Aletta had no interest in housework and her mother simply did not understand the bookish child.[49] After primary education, she found her 'ladies' school' intolerable and so was educated at home. At the age of 16 she took the admission examination to become a pharmacist and then faced an effective barrier to further studies as no woman had previously been educated at a university. The teenager wrote to the liberal prime minister, Rudolf Thorbecke, asking for permission to take up university studies which he granted (after asking her a series of questions) first for a period of a year, then, when she was obviously successful, to completion. She described herself as 'frail and sexually underdeveloped' and said she had no thought of female emancipation, being driven only by her own thirst for knowledge. She studied medicine first at Groningen then at Amsterdam Universities and in 1879 became the first fully qualified woman doctor in Holland. With a gift from a grateful patient she visited England where she met Dr Elizabeth Garrett Anderson, her sister Millicent Fawcett, and birth control pioneers Charles Bradlaugh and Annie Besant. She attended 'drawing room meetings' where lectures on women's suffrage would be held 'before an audience of forty or fifty well-to-do women'.[50]

She began to practise in Amsterdam where she met women reformers and the liberal trade union leader B. H. Heldt. He made available several rooms in the union's building so she could teach hygiene and infant care to poor women, then set up a free clinic from which she treated destitute women and promoted birth control. She became famous for adapting the 'Mensinga pessary' (the diaphragm) into an effective contraceptive device and was an active social reformer. She worked for shopgirls to have stools so their long hours of standing were ameliorated, and like other suffrage women she contributed to the 'moral purity' campaign to abolish the state regulation of prostitution.

Most importantly, Jacobs was in the forefront of campaigning for women's suffrage in the Netherlands; she had been committed since her teenage years when her father, who was in the habit of reading aloud to the family, read them a Dutch translation of Mill's *The Subjection of Women*.[51] When a new voters' list was published in 1883, Aletta Jacobs' name was not on it despite fulfilling the requirements for the franchise—of being a tax-paying Dutch citizen. She therefore wrote to the mayor and councillors in Amsterdam asking why her right to vote had been refused. Thus she was following the same path as women in Britain and the US, of considering gender as irrelevant to politics and using the loophole that the law did not specify male suffrage. She took her case all the way to the Supreme Court which judged against her. They said it was not in the spirit of the law to allow women to vote; women 'do not have full citizenship or civil rights' because 'they lack the right to vote' and they charged the costs of the case against her. The only change in legislation was in 1887 when 'male' was added to legislation by the Dutch parliament whenever enfranchisement was mentioned, just as had occurred in nineteenth-century Britain and the US.

The publicity Jacobs attracted brought her friends in the form of Alexandra Gripenberg from Finland and Gina Krog from Norway as well as reacquaintance with English campaigners. She was also becoming engaged with the political process through her work with Carel Victor Gerritsen, a radical politician who had long been her companion; they married in 1893 in expectation of having children. They did have a child, but a mistake by someone in attendance at the birth led to the baby's death; Jacobs does not give the name or sex of the child in her memoirs. Gerritsen died in 1905. The extensive collection of women's history books and periodicals that bears his name, that he began collecting in the 1870s, is publicly available.[52] Jacobs continued to work for suffrage but confessed to a painful loneliness: 'Most of all I missed the intellectual atmosphere I had enjoyed at home for so many years. Initially it was even difficult to send off articles without showing them to a kindred spirit, as had been my custom with Gerritsen.'[53]

The Woman Suffrage Association was established in 1894. Jacobs was president of the Amsterdam branch in 1895 and leader of the Association from 1903. She followed the policy of the American NAWSA and the British NUWSS to concentrate on winning the suffrage, regardless of members' other interests. Jacobs was keenly aware of the danger of associating women's suffrage with any kind of controversy. She wrote to Hungarian suffragist Rosika Schwimmer after she had been asked to speak on Malthusianism (birth control): 'Surely they don't want a lecture? If they do, it will have to be in private without press or any [suffrage] propaganda. It's not that I fear the publicity but it certainly would harm our cause. People are so stupid, they get the wrong end of the stick, and everything concerning sex may not be mentioned.'[54]

Early operations were conducted in a hostile environment, with the press against them and all political parties opposed except a small group of Constitutional Democrats. They did not have a single MP who would introduce the question. They started at the bottom, meeting and interviewing MPs who were interested in bills relating to women and children, hoping they could persuade these MPs to broaden their interests to encompass women's suffrage.[55] An account of the organization told of how groups of two or three women were deputized by a women's suffrage 'captain' to go to question electoral candidates: all would wear a white sash with Women's Suffrage in black letters; one would question the candidate, the others were there to give moral support. These tiny groups would also call on electors after first having sent a circular to the head of a family saying a visit would be paid unless there were an objection. If he preferred not to receive a women's suffrage delegation, he was asked to put in the window a little card on which was printed 'Visits in connection with the election not received'.[56]

After four years of a conservative government, in 1905 left-wing parties won the election and a liberal parliament was formed. Despite their request, no women were appointed to the government's commission to prepare a report on the constitution, so the Suffrage Association decided to prepare a report of their own. They sought an interview with the Queen and with the Prime Minister, presenting them with their constitutional amendment, and appealing that women's suffrage would be regarded favourably. The suffragists' proposed revision was to include women wherever it currently named men, but additionally argued over non-combative defence obligations: 'we are not only quite willing to perform these duties, but we wish to be obliged to do them, for Dutchwomen protest as much against unjust privileges as unjust discrimination.'[57]

The proposal for women's suffrage was recommended by six out of seven members of the commission in 1907, but the decision was left to the cabinet which did not recommend women's suffrage but showed some sympathy for the principle in their explanatory remarks, which gave an impetus for the press to take sides and enter into a debate where previously the press response had been a contemptuous silence. A ministerial crisis forced the resignation of the liberal cabinet, and it was succeeded by a conservative one, ending short-term hopes of reform.

A split occurred in 1907 when a number of women left Aletta Jacobs' organization to form the Dutch Women's Suffrage League. The new group allowed men to sit on the board, called themselves 'ethical feminists' and have been described as moderate. There was doubtless a considerable personality conflict as the new League 'did not refrain from public—and often very personal—criticism of Jacobs' and she considered suing for defamation.[58] Aletta Jacobs' friendship with Carrie Chapman Catt stood her in good stead over this split, when the 'ethical feminists' applied to join the International Woman Suffrage Alliance and Catt showed Jacobs their letters. She had previously voiced her support, 'My dear little doctor—I am grieved indeed to hear the news of the dissenting organisation. But let it trouble you as little as possible. Of course it cannot join the Alliance.'[59]

The following year, in 1908, Aletta Jacobs ensured that the International Woman Suffrage Alliance should be held in Amsterdam so as to concentrate the maximum amount of attention on the suffrage issue. It had positive results, with a generally favourable amount of coverage and an increase in membership for the Association from 2,500 to 6,000 in a year. A description of the gala dinner during the conference showed the distance between the everyday world of women and these international goddesses of the suffrage movement sitting around the table decorated with gold chrysanthemums and purple irises, the colours of the Alliance: 'the rule was that each person should dress in her best and wear her best jewellery. The English and American ladies were in full evening dress, low cut and with long sleeves. The Amsterdam ladies had brought out their jewels especially for the occasion—a very rare occurrence! A few English ladies wore tiaras.'[60]

When parliament reopened in September 1908 the Queen's speech contained no mention of the proposed changes in the constitution. All campaigners for a widened franchise were now equally disappointed and angry—women's suffrage was no longer a side issue but a part of the substantive demand for a new constitution. The socialists now moved from their demand of manhood suffrage and supported universal suffrage. In the budget debate in parliament the leaders of four of the seven political parties declared for the enfranchisement of women: the Free Liberals, Union Liberals, Radicals, and Socialists.

The Dutch Woman Suffrage Association adopted the usual paraphernalia of pressure groups, with posters, pamphlets, lobbies, petitions, and a specifically Dutch contribution: women's suffrage barges travelling around the canals to spread the message. Aletta Jacobs writes of gruelling speaking tours through remote regions, once speaking in a barn by the light of lanterns strung up on a rope, to an audience seated on a ladder resting on empty barrels. Suffrage activists managed to mobilize not just the urban elite, but also the large agrarian population in Holland with propaganda embracing pageantry that included regional dress, dialect language, the staging of clog dances, and peasant-related narration.[61]

In 1909 the re-election of a conservative government led to the postponement of the much-discussed constitutional revision. Dutch suffragists were facing the same kind of obstruction and teasing offers of advancement that suddenly disappeared as had enraged their British counterparts. The right-wing victory extinguished any hope of women's suffrage in the short term. The Prime Minister, Theo van Heemskerk, announced in parliament that 'The women of Holland simply do not want to vote!' This attitude led the Woman Suffrage Association to put their efforts into building up membership so they had greater power to influence a future government. Their growth shows the exponential interest in women's suffrage in Holland, from 62 branches with 6,500 members in 1909, to 108 branches with 14,000 members in 1913.[62] A Sunday in May, with elections coming up, saw the organization's first public event: a march which was routed through back-streets to a rally held in the zoological gardens.

During the First World War Jacobs, a pacifist, attempted to mobilize women from all nations to protest at the horrors of war and organized an International Congress of Women in Holland, which was neutral in the conflict. Many women from combatant nations were prevented for attending, however, and some—notably British, French, and German women—did not want to attend, as they put their nationalism first. For Aletta Jacobs and other Dutch women the congress was influenced by nationalist sentiment, as it was part of the Dutch national self-image that they should take on the role of inter-national peace intermediary.

Dutch suffragists were again roused in 1915 by an announcement that there would be a constitutional amendment giving the vote to all men but that women should only have the right to be elected (passive suffrage) with no right to vote (active suffrage). The Association held a mass demonstra-tion in Amsterdam in June 1916 with the bands, banners, stewards, and a Joan of Arc figure on a horse reminiscent of British suffrage marches. The Dutch suffragists put forward national themes, however, with a focus on folklore and regional dress, relying on the language and rhetoric of Dutch nationalism.[63]

For weeks members of parliament went to debate the constitution walking past picket lines of silent women wearing the sash of the Woman Suffrage Association, but the most progressive MPs were not willing to see an amendment granting manhood suffrage endangered by linking it with women's suffrage.

Eventually the so-called 'pacification' constitutional amendment was passed, providing for manhood suffrage. National unrest continued, how-ever, stimulated by mutiny in Germany and the Russian revolutions of 1917. A Dutch revolution was felt to be in the air. The response from the prime minister was to increase rations and promise reforms, one of which was government help to a women's suffrage bill that had been introduced by the Liberal Democrat leader H. P. Marchant. In Holland as in other countries, the spectre of revolution urged the consolidation of democratic regimes, and the obvious next step to bolster democracy was votes for women.

When the Marchant Bill for the complete enfranchisement of women came up, the government adopted it, securing its passage. The suffragists were again demonstrating, now going with the tide. On 9 May 1919 universal suffrage for women on the same terms as men was passed by 64 to 10 in the second chamber and was passed in the first chamber two months later. It became law on 8 September.

Aletta Jacobs had become a leading member of the International Woman Suffrage Alliance and a close confidante of Carrie Chapman Catt. They travelled though central Europe together in 1906, when both were newly widowed; Jacobs' command of languages was a winning asset. On another joint voyage, the two women travelled through Africa and Asia from 1911 to 1912. Jacobs' letters, addressed to the general Dutch public, stressed the internationalist mission the small nation believed it had, and the benevolence of Dutch colonial rule.[64] Jacobs died on 10 August 1929 at the age of 75.

An unpleasant device in Canada

Debates about women's suffrage fed into the national, religious, and language division in Canadian society. When it came, the enfranchisement of women in Canada took place specifically as a wartime measure, via what one historian has called 'an unpleasant device'.[65]

The women's suffrage movement in Canada began with Dr Emily Howard Stowe, the first woman doctor in Canada, who founded the Toronto Women's Literary Club in 1876. Despite its name, it was dedicated to women's suffrage but 'The time was not considered opportune for the bold use of the word "suffrage", the mere mention of that term producing violent reactions in many quarters.'[66] Within a decade there were women's suffrage movements in almost all the provinces of Canada with the exception of Quebec where the inhabitants showed the antipathy to women's suffrage that was common in Catholic Europe. The suffrage movement quickly expanded to encompass a range of social reform issues including public health, prohibition, anti-prostitution, and the 'Canadianization' of immigrants; it therefore closely resembled the suffrage movements in the western United States. In Quebec at the same time, moves were being taken to prohibit women from voting in local elections and render them legally 'incapable' of owning or inheriting property.

Bills were introduced in provincial legislatures to give women the vote in the thirty years after 1885 but they all failed, some by a small margin, some with insults and derision or with pious homilies like that of James P. Whitney, who opined that women's suffrage 'is a matter of evolution, and evolution is only a working out of God's laws. For this reason we must not attempt to hurry it on'.[67]

Robert Borden, a Conservative, who became prime minister of Canada in 1911, was harangued on a visit to Britain by a delegation of suffragettes who threatened to introduce 'militancy' on the Canadian scene. He replied, 'Any suggestions as to methods in your campaign which may be introduced into Canada will not have the slightest influence upon me. If I am to be subject to methods which are to make my life unpleasant or inconvenient or even shortened, I frankly tell you these considerations will not govern my actions in the least.'[68]

When war broke out in 1914 the English-speaking parts of the nation were notably more committed to the war than French-speaking Canada—perhaps surprisingly as France and Belgium were getting the worst of the war. However, French Canadians did not have the same feeling for France that British Canadians had for Britain. The war ate up Canadian manpower and voluntary service could no longer maintain the supply. Conscription was the only answer, and there was agreement from some members of the Liberal opposition who joined the Conservatives in the wartime Unionist government and supported conscription.

However, the opposition Liberals were strong in Quebec, where they looked ready to take every French-speaking seat. In order to be able to push through conscription, the coalition government had to win every possible seat outside Quebec. Another problem was the fact that in the west of the country there were large numbers of immigrants with no loyalty to the British Empire (or who even had loyalty to other belligerents) who would vote against conscription.

Women were an available electoral resource, and a tried and tested one: all female property owners had the municipal vote by 1900 and provincial assemblies gave women the vote in Manitoba, Saskatchewan, and Alberta in 1916. Ontario and British Columbia did so early the following year. There had been no great suffrage crusade in Canada, those who had granted these extensions of suffrage tended to believe, like 'progressive' activists in the US, that women would exert a morally uplifting influence on society, and help wipe out alcoholism and immorality. Their enfranchisement in the prov-inces effectively meant that constituencies in the west had vastly more electors than those east of the Ontario/Quebec border.[69] An election was fast approaching and Robert Borden faced a challenge to keep his Conservative-Unionist government in power to ensure that Canada would keep making a major contribution in the war.

Borden therefore sponsored the Wartime Election Act, passed in September 1917, which enfranchised all Canadian women who were the wives, mothers, sisters, or daughters of men in the forces (or who had been—the female relatives of dead servicemen were also enfranchised). At the same time, in 1917, the Military Voters Act was passed intending to enfranchise any otherwise unenfranchised soldier; it enfranchised all serving personnel, including some 2,000 military nurses known as 'bluebirds'.

The new voters supported conscription as their relatives were already abroad, so they wished to send more men in their support. No one was fooled that this was a measure motivated by concerns for women's democratic rights. The *Morning Chronicle* of Halifax said, 'No more partisan measure than this freak scheme to corral votes for a discredited government, has ever been presented to, much less passed by, the parliament of Canada.... It is, in effect, Prussianism and not the British sense of justice and fair play which is the guiding spirit.'[70]

The Conservative-Unionists were duly elected, though in fact by such a large margin that these late suffrage measures made no difference—they would have won anyway, particularly as Liberals in the western states had taken their provincial governments over to the Conservative-Unionist banner. In the long run the move backfired as it so alienated French-Canadians and recent immigrants that they would oppose the Conservatives for years to come.

As was often the case, enfranchisement for women meant disenfranchisement for others: immigrants from Germany and Austria-Hungary and the Ukraine lost their right to vote in the Wartime Election Act, as did conscientious objectors, and women in the provinces that had previously enfranchised them who were *not* the close relative of a serving soldier. As the *Canadian Annual Review* put it, the Act 'brought in a large electorate of women voters who would probably be friendly to the government, and disenfranchised a large western element which was undoubtedly hostile to both government and war policy'.[71]

All women got the vote in national elections in 1918, under the explicitly titled Act to Confer the Electoral Franchise on Women, urged by a women's suffrage movement which had been revitalized by the controversy over the Wartime Election Act, and promoted by the Liberal Party. Women were, in fact, enfranchised under the same requirements as applied to men, which made for another round of disenfranchisements: in provinces where the franchise was via a property qualification, propertied women got the vote and women who had previously had the franchise because of their relationship to a serving soldier, but who had no property, lost it. The property qualification was dropped in 1920.

The exceptions to women's enfranchisement in Canada were women excluded from the franchise (along with men) for racial reasons: British Columbia, for example, excluded people of Japanese and Chinese origin and 'Hindus' (which meant any person from the Indian sub-continent, whatever their religion). Such discrimination by race was eliminated in 1948; men and women described as 'Indians' (native Canadians) were given the unconditional right to vote in 1960. Provinces were left to make their own arrangements for local suffrage; Quebec did not enfranchise women locally until 1940, showing the same delay in local compared to national enfranchisement as Switzerland. The only other nation that took up a scheme of women's franchise based on the war service of male relatives was Belgium.

Votes from the war?

The war work that women did, while it was widely appreciated, was hardly a factor in enfranchisement in most countries. Women were enfranchised where there was considerable contribution to the war effort by suffragist women; but they were also enfranchised in counties which had not been in the war and where women's war work was minimal. Even active opposition to the war was not a hindrance: in Hungary the leading suffragist (and close colleague of Carrie Chapman Catt and Aletta Jacobs) Rosika Schwimmer was a pacifist who opposed the war yet women were enfranchised both in the revolution of 1918 and then (as if to confirm that this was no issue for the left or the right) they were first disenfranchised then re-enfranchised by the counter-revolutionary government in 1920. After 1921 the Hungarian franchise was restricted to women over 30 who fulfilled certain educational and economic qualifications; full suffrage was regained in 1945.[72]

Luxemburg, in a Constituent Assembly set up after the end of the German occupation adopted universal suffrage for all men and women over the age of 21. This was agreed on 8 May 1919 without any organized campaign, by a vote of thirty-nine to eleven. This was a pattern followed in many nations: from 1917 to 1920 inclusive, seventeen nations enfranchised women, many of them 'new' or ancient nations newly liberated from imperial control, where there was minimal discussion: Hungary, Latvia, Lithuania, Poland, Albania, and Czechoslovakia.

War was certainly a factor in women's suffrage. Though the point hardly needs emphasis, plotted on a graph the same bell-shaped curve exists for enfranchisements (even more dramatically) after the Second World War, peaking in 1946, as it had previously peaked in 1918. However, the First World War saw the great breakthrough in women's enfranchisement; by the end of 1920 there were only two major countries with a constitutional form of government where women did not have the vote: France and Italy.

Historian Trevor Lloyd commented 'it turned out that defeat in battle was what really helped the cause of votes for women' but this does not stand up to scrutiny: Britain and the US were on the side of the victors and enfranchised women, Italy and France were on the same side but did not; Belgium was a 'winner' but only partially enfranchised women. Holland and Sweden were neutral but they enfranchised.[73]

Germany, the former countries of the Hapsburg Empire, and Russia, however, do fit into the scheme of defeated nations enfranchising women under their new constitutions. But more important than military defeat was nationalism, and the consciousness that new nations would do things differently.

In the new Europe, having been made safe for democracy, in Woodrow Wilson's words, the guiding principles were to be national self-determination, peace, and prosperity. These aspirations of modernity encompassed the feminine ideal; women's values were those of peace and the home, an idealized woman often personified the nation. With a new constitution, new countries could show themselves fully equipped to deal with the modern world. Germany, the former Hapsburg Empire countries, and Russia needed to get as far as they possibly could from the old autocratic rule; women's suffrage was a reform relatively easily made which underlined the difference between autocracy and the new social order.

In contrast, nations such as France and Belgium primarily wanted to return to the way things were *ante bellum*, before their nations were invaded. This was not an option for countries such as the UK and US which had previously hosted large and vociferous women's suffrage movements: no future franchise alterations would be possible without considering women and until the final argument—of women doing work of equivalent value to that of man—had been addressed by war work. It was time for a change in the great democracies at the end of the war: a change that had been much discussed, and had been tested in foreign lands and found benign.

II

The Pope and the vote—Catholic Europe

'Not ballot boxes but kisses'

Two young women, Mary Kendall and Gabrielle Jeffrey, were standing outside Holloway Gaol on 8 December 1910, among a group gathered to welcome released suffragettes. Gabrielle Jeffrey was a WSPU organizer; the young women found in conversation that they were both Roman Catholics, and they clearly felt that their feelings about women and society were only partially answered by any current branch of the women's suffrage movement.

Their feelings were certainly not represented by the church hierarchy. By the start of the twentieth century the Catholic Church acknowledged the education of women and their acceptance into the professions, but suffrage was a step too far. 'Women electors, women deputies?' said Pope Pius X to an Austrian feminist, 'Oh no. That is all we need! The men there have already created enough confusion! Imagine what would happen if there were women there!'[1] The interview was picked up and widely circulated; subsequently its accuracy was disputed, and the leaders of the two most prominent Catholic women's organizations in France obtained their own papal audience. The Pope confirmed his opinion that it was an error for women to seek the same political rights as men.

The only positive thing about the Pope's position was that it was clearly personal and not doctrinal—holy writ was not cited to sanction the view, no papal pronouncements underlined it. The Pope's view reflected the conservatism of Catholic thinking: that the family was the centre of life for a woman, and any involvement in politics would divert her from service to husband and children.

Kendall and Jeffrey were not inhibited by the Pope's views from calling a meeting of other Catholics at Kensington Town Hall on 25 May 1911. The historian of the movement writes: 'they founded the first Catholic organization anywhere dedicated to obtaining the franchise for women.' Dedicated to 'converting Catholics from the position of indifference or outright negativeness towards women's suffrage', the Catholic Women's Suffrage Society commissioned a banner featuring Joan of Arc; wrote to the Archbishop of Westminster (who was unwilling to express an official position) and joined the Coronation Procession on 17 June 1911.[2] Though itself non-militant, the Society sent women to court to observe as fair witnesses when suffragettes were on trial.

The advantages of women's enfranchisement were presented from the Catholic point of view as: 'a fresh attitude in legislation dealing with social and domestic problems; the raising of the standard of sex purity; adequate protection for minors; increased attention to the health, comfort and spiritual wants of the growing child; stringent enforcement of the laws relative to parental responsibility; effective control of the iniquitous White Slave Traffickers, until the plague itself is abolished.'[3] None of these were likely to shake the foundations of the Holy Mother Church.

The sea-change for Catholic women and suffrage came with a new Pope, Benedict XV, who in 1919 was coming to terms with the post-war world. He granted an audience with Annie Christitch, a member of the Catholic Women's Suffrage Society. As she put it, she was among those who 'have the privilege of prostrating themselves before the successor of St Peter'. She was 'Graciously permitted to lay before His Holiness the projects and problems of the day on which light is needed, it was a great joy to be able to bring before the Head of Christendom the aims and strivings of a brave little group of Catholic women in England.' The Pope's willingness to hear of the (decidedly un-militant) activities of the British Catholics was evidence of change: in the nations of Europe new constitutions were being produced every month that gave women the vote in countries emerging from the wreck of war; in the east the godless Communists had taken control in the name of the people. With no revision of doctrine, the Pope had to use what room he had to interpret his message for a new world.

Asked about his response to the British women's activities Benedict XV said, 'Yes, we approve.' He emphasized, 'We should like to see women electors everywhere.'[4] Other papal pronouncements of 1919 on the woman question amplified his conservative social intentions. In a discourse in reply to the Italian Catholic Women's Union, Sono Avventurati, Benedict agreed that 'the conditions of the times have enlarged the field of woman's activity.' He stressed, however, that 'no change in the opinions of man, no novelty of circumstances and events, will ever remove woman, conscious of her mission, from her natural centre, which is the family.'[5]

The Habsburg Empire

In Habsburg Austria, male proxies could cast votes on behalf of women nobles then, following the 1848 revolutions, women property holders, tax payers and professionals could vote. One reason for the lack of interest in the vote among Austrian women before the twentieth century was, therefore, because a number of them had the vote already. Feminism, such as it was in the late nineteenth century, confined itself to questions of economics such as the right of women to work in such fields as the postal service, and education where the modest demand was for education to fit girls for motherhood.

The movement of liberalism then socialism took its usual course: first a spread of democratic ideas which was then supplemented by the strength of the labour movement as Vienna industrialized. Calls for universal manhood suffrage therefore fell on ground well prepared; it was an obvious development. Feminist women were involved in the agitation to open up staid Austrian institutions and gave support to the Progressive and Social Democrat parties. The Social Democrat leader Victor Adler had supported the principle of women's suffrage but his support stopped short of any practical steps. In alarm at the Russian revolution of 1905, the government was pushed towards granting universal manhood suffrage.

The Social Democrat women's section had been ordered by the party to suppress claims to women's suffrage until the men's suffrage bill had gone through. Liberal women were not prepared to abide by this prohibition and they founded a Women's Suffrage Committee in 1905. This was a more daring act than it would be in other countries as, in a similar situation to that which persisted in Germany, by a law of 1867 women were forbidden to attend political meetings or form political societies (a committee was legal, an association was not).

Aletta Jacobs writes of visiting Vienna and addressing a private meeting of invited guests after which the Viennese women 'asked me to help them set up a committee for woman suffrage'.[6] She dates this as 1903, so clearly the subject had been to some extent under discussion when the committee was formed in 1905. Thus, as in Britain and other countries, women were stimulated to protest their situation at a time of heightened political engagement when men were arguing for the franchise. The socialists (Social Democrats) were committed to universal suffrage, but were prepared to drop women from the demand, in pursuit of manhood suffrage which was felt to be a realistic goal.

In January 1907 universal male suffrage was granted for men over 24. The new constitution, however, took away the ancient voting rights and property voting rights that some women already enjoyed. Therefore in common with other nations, democracy for men brought limited women's suffrage to an end; and enfranchisement for some meant disenfranchisement for others. Limited women's suffrage had been dependent on existing social hierarchies; noble women had precedence because of their nobility, regardless of their sex. Democracy did away with those hierarchies while implanting a masculine model of political organisation.[7] It would require an appeal back to the roots of democratic thought in the 'rights of man' for women to be welcomed as part of the political ideal of democracy.

A concurrent battle, as in Germany, and also going to the heart of what was meant by democracy, was the right to organize. The Women's Suffrage Committee continued its activity and gathered signatures on a petition for the repeal of the Assemblies Law, forbidding political association. In 1910 they received a sympathetic hearing from the Prime Minister and the Minster of Internal Affairs who also gave support for the municipal franchise.

A motion for the repeal of the Assemblies Law went to the lower house where it received almost unanimous support. Parliament was dissolved before it could be sanctioned by the upper house but the law was obviously defunct and there was widespread defiance of it. A new Law of Assemblies was passed in 1913 where the section forbidding women the right of political association was omitted.

Now an unfettered national suffrage campaign was launched. The rhetoric of women's suffrage was in keeping with a conservative, Catholic country, as Gisela Urban, one of the founders of the Women's Suffrage Committee and author of such books as *The Diary of the Housewife* wrote: 'Woman shall stimulate politics with her fresh and unexpended strength, ennoble it with her higher morality and her stronger feelings for social responsibility, with the gifts which form the essence of her femininity, especially with her motherliness.' Formerly passive and home-based female qualities were therefore presented as active qualities, to fit them for the public arena. Urban further wrote that women wanted the franchise, 'to compliment the work of man'.[8] Though the Social Democrat women promoted the primacy of class over gender, the leader of their women's movement spoke in similar terms, demanding suffrage 'exactly because we are womanly and motherly'.[9] The images were therefore of women bringing their qualities as moral exemplars and mothers into the political sphere, it was an argument of separateness, not equality.

Other arguments included the image of the municipality as a big house-hold requiring female qualities for its management; that enfranchised women would impart civic values to their children; and that they would guarantee protection to the weak and freedom from war. The generally conservative and home-based nature of woman's suffrage arguments meant the Christian Social opposition to women's suffrage began to evaporate. As usual, the Liberals and Social Democrats were lukewarm about women's suffrage in the fear that women's votes would be too much under the con-trol of their priests, but ideologically these parties supported women's suf-frage. Their fears did not prevent their support for the principle, and their votes could therefore be counted on, but their trepidation tended to reinforce conservative views that votes for women could be good for conservatism. Thus both sides of the political divide were moving towards women's suf-frage, albeit in a half-hearted way.

Unfortunately for the suffragists, the First World War caused a cessation of activities. Ironically, Charles, who ascended to the imperial throne in 1916, wanted to reform the constitution of his empire and secure a separate peace with the allies, but Germany strengthened its hold over the Austrians to prevent further peace talks, and wartime conditions impeded further reform. A move against authoritarian rule was in the air but events overtook the emperor and the fall of the dynasty followed defeat in the war; the emperor abdicated in November 1918. Now the field was open for the cre-ation of a new republic with the Social Democrats in the lead. With their party pledge for women's suffrage and women party members arguing for it, votes for women had to be part of the new constitution that was intro-duced in December 1918. All women over 20 had full suffrage and the same eligibility for office as men. The one exception was prostitutes who were not enfranchised until 1923.

The suffrage was therefore granted in Austria after a time of national crisis as happened in other countries. It was also a bolstering of democracy at a time of fear for revolutions which had already spread from Russia to Germany and Hungary.

In order to maintain conservative strength, their representatives now argued, after some had questioned whether women should vote at all, that women must be *obliged* to vote. Their fear was that their supporters might be too timid and conservative to vote (though their preference could be relied upon if they did) while radical women would flock to the polls and vote out the conservatives.[10] The effect of women's votes was, as in other countries, slight: women tended to favour conservative candidates though there were regional differences so that Viennese women, for example, voted for the Social Democrats.[11]

The now crumbling Habsburg Dynasty ruled two kingdoms: Austria and Hungary and eleven peoples: German, Magyar, Polish, Czech, Slovak, Slovene, Serb, Croat, Ukranian, Italian, and Romanian. The conflicts within the empire were more nationalistic than class based; and gender conflicts were not to the fore. Aletta Jacobs on a visit to Austria-Hungary in 1906 described the less than fraternal relations between different ethnic groups in Prague: 'Our welcoming committee of Austro-Germans immediately launched unflattering descriptions of the Czech counterparts and urged us to speak only German. No sooner had they left than a group of Czech women arrived to pay their respects with the ulterior motive of suggesting that we should take absolutely no notice of the opposing camp.'[12] Suffragists in different regions of the Hapsburg Empire proceeded as best they could; Czech, Polish, Slovenian, and Hungarian women formed their own movements and conducted suffrage activities apart from the German-speaking organizations.

One of President Wilson's celebrated Fourteen Points demanded the reorganization of the Habsburg monarchy in accordance with the principles of national autonomy, though even before its publication the Czechs had demanded the establishment of independent constituent assemblies for national homelands. The movement was clearly towards disintegration of the empire, and in its constituent parts universal suffrage came as part of the reward for these national struggles; women were enfranchised in Hungary and Poland in 1918 and in Czechoslovakia in 1920.

Votes of the absent men in Belgium

Much of the fighting on the Western Front in the First World War had taken place on Belgian and French soil and, indeed, it was Germany's violation of Belgium's neutrality that made Britain's entry into the war inevitable. Belgium's losses in terms of population and property had been immense, both for the military and civilian populations; for Belgium more than most countries involved in the war, it had been a truly national struggle. If it followed that women's suffrage inevitably emerged from periods of struggle when the nation was endangered, Belgian women should have had the vote at the end of the war.

Manhood suffrage on a property franchise had been in place since a general strike in 1891 had forced the issue. Before the strike, only two men in a hundred were enfranchised; the constitutional revision of 1893 gave householders over 25 the vote, but to maintain social inequality, more than one vote was given to university graduates, property owners, heads of families, and those in professional or public service.[13] The new electorate caused the old two-party system of Catholics and Liberals to be joined by the Socialists; the Socialist Party included women's suffrage in its manifesto but dropped the proposal in 1902 from the usual fear that women would vote with the Catholic Church.

The League of Women's Rights was set up in 1905, chiefly to ameliorate some of the worst aspects of the Napoleonic Code, such as permitting women rights over their own savings and allowing them to give testimony in civil court. Belgian women were so far behind those in other European countries that constitutional advances were not under consideration, women's suffrage had not been a major issue; as Alice Zimmern lamented in 1909 in *Woman Suffrage in Many Lands*, 'the class of women who usually take up reforms of this nature is almost completely lacking.'[14] Zimmern was using 'class' to refer to the women of a reforming bent who formed the backbone of suffrage movements in English-speaking countries. Belgium did have an economic middle class, but its members were a mainstay of the church and associated charities and not committed to social action.

By 1918 women's suffrage was back on the Socialist agenda, with a programme of universal suffrage including women's suffrage, but the commitment was weak: they would not sacrifice universal manhood suffrage (on an equal basis, without plural voting for the privileged) for a women's suffrage measure.

Shortly after the armistice, the National Federation for Woman Suffrage in Belgium wrote an appeal to the new government and started a petition, but when parliament was opened, the King's speech recommended only universal manhood suffrage. The suffragists lobbied, held meetings and collected signatures (ultimately totalling 175,000) on a petition in an increasingly heated controversy among the parties about how far suffrage should be extended. Three parties were sharing power in 1919, representing the Socialists, Catholics and Liberals. In a reversal of the situation in Italy and France, the Catholic Party favoured women's suffrage, and the Liberals opposed it. The manhood suffrage bill that the Socialists wanted, to consolidate working-class representation, depended on the Liberals for its passage through parliament, and the Liberals were virulently anticlerical. They believed that women would bolster the reactionary, Catholic vote. This belief was doubtless behind the Catholic support for women's suffrage. The Socialists would have their comparative strength increased by universal manhood suffrage but weakened, they believed, if women voted. As a commentator said, 'when the Socialists include votes for women in their program they are less than half-hearted in urging it; Liberals, admitting the theoretical justice of equal suffrage, refuse to commit what they think would be political suicide by advocating it.'[15]

The one thing that they could all agree on was that they had all suffered in the war, so they made that the basis for suffrage: the parliamentary votes was given to men over 21 and 'all widows of soldiers and civilians killed by the enemy, or, when there is no widow, to the mother' and to 'all woman condemned or imprisoned for patriotic acts during the enemy occupation'.[16] Some women were, therefore, rewarded for their part in the war or the war was (as in Canada) used as a reason for enfranchising some women. It was not used as a reason, or pretext, for enfranchising all women as it was in the US or for a large number of women as in the UK.

By way of compensation for disappointed expectations, or as a measure of gradualism, the communal franchise (for regional administration) was granted in April 1920 for all women over 21. Suffrage was finally granted to all women in 1948 under the Socialist Paul-Henri Spaak heading a Socialist–Catholic coalition.

Why was Belgium so slow to enfranchise women when other Low Countries, Holland and Luxembourg, did so early, in 1919? Belgium's position regarding women's suffrage of course reflected the balance of party divisions in society, but may also have shown the low level of feminist activity in the kingdom. Holland had a strong organization, the Woman Suffrage Association, set up in 1894. By 1911 it had 100 branches with 10,000 members. By contrast, the Belgian Feminist Union for the Vote was founded only in 1907 and by 1910 had three branches with members counted in scores, not hundreds. Belgium also lacked charismatic leadership, not an essential prerequisite for women's suffrage but it certainly helped. Women consequently did not have a sufficiently powerful voice in Belgium for politicians to take notice of them, and an insufficiently argued case for their ideas to have been fully absorbed.

One reason for Holland's advanced position was its concentration on trade (rather than, as in Belgium, manufacturing); this led to fluency in foreign languages and an openness to foreign ideas. There was also a more heterogeneous political society in Holland; in Belgium Liberals, Socialists, and Catholics tussled for power between them in a three-way split which could easily lead to deadlock. Catholic parties did not think they would get enough from the women's vote to push for it, their opponents feared what they would lose.

By contrast, in Holland power was more fragmented; the Liberals, Protestants, and Catholics were joined by Socialists, Conservatives, and Communists, making the opportunities for power-broking more varied. The religious parties in Holland were prepared to back universal manhood suffrage immediately before the First World War, for example, in return for state funding of religious schools, which was their primary concern. This sidelined the Liberals who supported a more restrictive franchise and, though powerful, could be outvoted by a coalition of opposing parties.

France's long wait

Napoleon may have gone, but his code lived on. The French civil code of 1804, part of the Code Napoléon, literally codified French custom and Roman Law as it related to the family. It made the family a reflection of the nation over which Napoleon had presided: a little dictatorship with the husband as dictator. Women lost control over family property and children, and suffered stringent rules of marriage and divorce. The wife was legally under the guardianship of her husband: obliged to obey him and unable to enter into legal or official transactions without him.

Following the restoration of the monarchy Frenchmen were officially equal before the law, women had few rights as people, but the unit of the family was protected. For example, newlywed men were exempted from military service, the production of a family was thought to be sufficient service to the state in a nation that was perennially anxious about its low

Figure 12. French suffragists on the front page of a Parisian daily in 1908, invading a polling station and overturning the ballot box. Attacks on polling stations and other expressions of militancy did not take off in France.

birth rate. The idealization of the French family offered social sanctions against its disruption and corresponding comfort for its maintenance.

The ideals of the Revolution were not forgotten, however, and when the monarchy was toppled in 1848 the Provisional Government on 5 March declared 'universal suffrage' with no property qualifications. This was not thought to include women, though a group of Parisian women, the Committee for Women's Rights, immediately began to lobby for the vote and other rights. The left did not support them for reasons that would become familiar in Catholic countries with the passing years: women were not considered sufficiently educated to use the vote wisely, and they were too much under the control of priests who would incline them to conservatism.

Universal male suffrage being won so early was a curse for French suffragists for reasons that are obvious only from the international picture: in every other country an extension of an initially limited suffrage for men stimulated a demand for women's suffrage. In France, with men's suffrage already granted, there was no such stimulus and an agitation was harder to get off the ground.

Male voters in the first election of 23 April 1848 tended to vote for the moderate and conservative elements, and the new Assembly quickly passed a law barring women from participating in political clubs and associations. Two victims were Jeanne Deroin, co-founder of the Club de l'Emancipation des Femmes; and Pauline Roland, founder of an association of socialist schoolteachers. Both women were sentenced to six months in prison in 1850 for violating the law forbidding associations. From the prison of St Lazare they wrote to the woman's rights convention in Worcester, Massachusetts proclaiming socialist unity—rather inappropriately as the likes of Elizabeth Cady Stanton and Lucretia Mott had never pretended to socialism. The American women wanted not so much to change the system as to join it.[17]

The pattern of national crisis and revolution stimulating women's activism which had occurred in the French Revolution after 1789 and in the revolution of 1848 was repeated in 1870 after France's defeat by Prussia, the Commune, and the collapse of the Second Empire. The ground had been prepared for feminism, with the founding of the Society for Claiming Women's Rights (Société pour la Revendication des Droits de la Femme); and the publication of feminist works including a French translation of Mill's *The Subjection of Women* in 1869.

Echoes of the debates around the extension of the ballot in Britain and the enfranchisement of former slaves reached France but the response was muted, though Julie-Victoire Doubié argued in print for the vote for single adult women. In general, radical feminists were not agitating for the vote at this stage, feeling that enfranchised women would benefit conservatism and the Catholic Church at the expense of the republic. Such women as Maria Deraismes were arguing for better education for girls, economic independence and divorce law reform, fields in which progress was made in the last quarter of the nineteenth century. The reluctance to deal with the franchise caused dissension, not least when a women's rights conference in 1889 (to coincide with the hundredth anniversary of the French Revolution) did not discuss women's suffrage.

Disappointed at the moderation of feminists, a radical, Hubertine Auclert, founded the Société le suffrage des femmes in 1883; Susan B. Anthony attended a women's rights meeting in 1883 in the Rue de Rivoli Paris where Auclert was the leading speaker.[18] Auclert argued for the vote and for full equality before the law; she petitioned the Chamber of Deputies, attempted to have her name put down on the voters' list at her local town hall and started a protest in which women withheld taxes until they were politically represented, but all were ultimately failures. The Chamber of Deputies took merely a cursory look at her petition, but it was the occasion for a debate in 1885. The bailiffs were sent to requisition her furniture in response to her tax boycott, but at least it attracted the attention of newspapers. The police had long been aware of her feminist activities: a report of 1880 noted that she suffered 'from madness or hysterics which make her think of men as equals'.[19]

Progress was slow because of the conservatism of erstwhile supporters, both the general constituency of women and of male politicians, the latter of whom were unconvinced that women's suffrage would do them any good. It may be that Auclert's combative approach was not best calculated to appeal to a largely conservative nation; one of her tactics to draw attention to the wrongs of woman was to attend civil marriage ceremonies at town halls and then harangue brides on the iniquities of the marriage laws. From 1881 to 1891 her principal platform, and the voice of women's suffrage in France, was La Cityoenne (The Citizeness), a newspaper she set up and ran with financial assistance from four men friends, one of whom, Antonin Lévrier, she was to marry in 1888, though six years earlier she had refused his offer of marriage in order to devote herself to the cause.[20] Auclert was the moving spirit behind the campaign for six women to be candidates in the legislative election in 1884 but the government ordered that no count be taken of their votes.

Even municipal suffrage, usually the precursor of full suffrage for women, was granted in only a few councils in France. Bourgeois feminists had no better success than in other countries at drawing working-class women into the fold. A feminist congress in Paris in 1900 devoted time to the problems of working-class women, but when domestic service was discussed, middle-class delegates felt they had to say that giving servants a day off or regulating their employment would inevitably lead to an increase in prostitution. The working-class delegates were not impressed.[21] Socialists were committed to women's rights from the mid-1880s and paid the usual lip-service to women's political equality but considered it a minor issue compared to the great industrial struggle, after the success of which equality would reign supreme.

Two bills proposing principally municipal suffrage for women, in 1901 and 1906, were lost amid other parliamentary business. The seeming impossibility of making any progress led some French feminists to become more militant in the early twentieth century, and the influence of British suffragettes was apparent. Christabel Pankhurst was living in Paris from 1912 and many WSPU women visited. The French militants were constructing their own form of militancy; Hubertine Auclert led a group of supporters to disrupt the Chamber of Deputies; she tore up a copy of the Code Napoléon in a demonstration to mark its centenary; Madeleine Pelletier disrupted a banquet celebrating the Code; she also picketed elections, and both Auclert and Pelletier smashed polling stations in 1908. They never commanded widespread support and militancy as a tactic, even among other suffragists, did not take off.

Madeleine Pelletier was, if anything, even more radical than Auclert. She overcame a terrible childhood of poverty and sexual abuse to qualify as a doctor, specializing in mental illness. She set up a monthly journal, *La Suffragiste*, to promote the women's vote and her own brand of feminism. While other feminists argued for the vote to promote the values of the family, she felt the family should be subservient to the individual, but children were better brought up collectively anyway. She refused to accept society's rules for women, dressing as a man and going far beyond contemporary 'progressive' thought: she argued for sexual freedom, for pleasure aided by contraception and for abortion on demand.[22]

A more characteristic forerunner of future women's organizations in France was the group around the journal *Le Féminisme chrétien* founded by a wealthy heiress, Marie Maugeret. She was an ultra-Catholic anti-Semite who felt that it was not only republicans and free-thinkers who had a right to call themselves feminists. She and the other wealthy women grouped around her felt (in common with views Carrie Chapman Catt had about immigrants voting) that it was appalling that sophisticated, wealthy women should not have a vote when it was freely awarded to coalmen.[23] She held an annual congress to celebrate Joan of Arc and succeeded, in 1906, in pushing through a motion for women's suffrage, with a rousing speech calling for women to purify politics: 'In order to clean up a house, it is first necessary to enter it. Let us enter this house.'[24] The opposition of Pope Pius X to women's suffrage, widely publicized in France, thereafter tempered Maugeret's activities and she lost the vote in the session on suffrage at the 1910 Joan of Arc congress.

Finally, with the example before them of women's suffrage making progress in other nations, in 1909 a French Union for Women's Suffrage (Union français pour le suffrage des femmes) was formed with the assistance of the National Council of Women of France (which had been dedicated to municipal suffrage for women since 1900) and soon had 3,000 members, mostly professional women; there were 12,000 by 1914. They participated in a mock election in 1914, organized by a daily newspaper, *Le Journal*, collecting more than half a million female ballot forms; thus setting aside the notion that women were not interested in the franchise.

Anti-clericalism among the political 'Radicals' (republicans) cursed the French suffrage movement as Radicals would not give away votes that might be cast in favour of the right-wing Catholics. The obvious ploy of the suffragists should have been to woo the Catholic politicians, but the French feminist leaders were Protestants, and they too resented the influence of the church on women's lives. Clericalism therefore did not help and anti-clericalism actively hindered French suffragists.

A parliamentary committee headed by a woman suffrage sympathizer, Ferdinand Buisson, proposed a municipal women's suffrage measure, but the legislature refused to consider even this until proposed national changes were discussed in mid-1913. French women tended to abjure the mass rally, feeling they were more discreet and reserved than English or American women who flocked to such things, but a suffrage rally was held on 5 July 1914 to honour the memory of the father of women's suffrage, the Marquis de Condorcet, and in support of the Buisson proposal.

The war stopped all franchise activity but, in common with other nations, women's contribution was thought to be worthy of reward. However, the atmospheric change for French suffragists came with the new Pope, Benedict XV, who replaced Pius X in 1914, and in 1919 was coming to terms with the post-war world and relaxed the Catholic opposition to women's suffrage, so deputies could not hide behind the claim that they were being obedient by denying women the vote. Deputies voted for full enfranchisement on 20 May 1919 by 329 to 95 with 104 not voting. A proposal for a 'family' franchise failed.

By the end of 1919 this bill plus four other proposals for enfranchisement were waiting for Senatorial attention, which would begin with a committee discussion of the general principles. The bill was blocked by the Senate Commission of Adult Suffrage, which even refused a measure to give the franchise to women relatives of men who had been killed in the war, the so-called 'suffrage des morts'. The Commission did not call on feminists to testify, and asked a notorious anti-suffragist, Alexandre Bérard, to write their report. He came forward with 'fourteen points' why women should not have the vote, including such remarks as, 'While women did give immense service to France during the war, they did so for love of *patrie*, not in the expectation of a reward: it would be an insult to pay them for their patriotism. . . . women's suffrage would be "a formidable leap into the unknown" that might produce the election of a new Bonaparte' and 'Women are different creatures than men, filled with sentiment and tears rather than hard political reason: their hands are not for political pugilism or holding ballot boxes, but for kisses.'[25]

This set a pattern for the inter-war years when women's enfranchisement bills were repeatedly passed by the Chamber of Deputies but blocked by the Senate. In July 1927 the Chamber voted to give women the municipal vote by 396 to 24 and the Senate also blocked this. A Senate report of 1927 gave a Gallic twist to the argument that women were biologically inadequate to the franchise: 'The woman of the Latin race does not feel, has not developed, in the same way as the women of the Anglo-Saxon or German races.'[26]

In 1936 a bill for full political rights for women gained a majority of 409 votes to nil but the Senate still refused to budge. The Third Republic Senate, in fact, never debated a women's suffrage bill, they were always blocked at earlier stages or in discussion on general principles. There was doubtless a certain amount of cynicism about the votes in the Chamber as deputies who opposed women's suffrage could still vote for it and appear progressive, secure in the knowledge that the Senate would stop the bills. *Le Temps* remarked on finding 'in the bouquet of flowers offered to French women a few poisoned roses on which the reform will wither and die'.[27]

Historian James F. McMillan refers to the Senate's intransigence as an expression of the *immobilisme* from which the Third Republic had become infamous by the 1930s, the sclerosis in a political system dominated by Radical politicians who after the separation of church and state in 1905 were committed merely to defending the status quo which they saw as 'defending the Republic'. They genuinely feared that women would hand back power to the church. While the conservatives were opposed to women's suffrage, the left were markedly apathetic about the issue, despite its being part of their programme, answering the call for women's suffrage 'with varying degrees of hypocrisy, cynicism, apathy and boredom'.[28] French feminists were isolated and ineffectual, unwilling to agitate for a mass movement; or to take isolated radical actions as had Auclert and Pelletier; or to engage in mainstream politics to learn the craft and become familiar with its ways.

Karen Offen additionally remarks that the opponents of women's suffrage suffered from a heightened fear that, with the losses incurred by the male population in the First World War, women now vastly outnumbered men. Some men were alarmed at the promised 'social housekeeping' over alcoholism and legalized prostitution that suffragists proposed as a reason *for* the women's vote. Catholics did no favours for the cause of women's suffrage when they argued that the women's vote would defend Catholic liberties and challenged concepts of emancipation, individualism, and equality as false dogmas propagated by international freemasonry.[29] Ironically, considering its conservative influence in previous times, it was perhaps the very success of the widespread conversion of the Catholic Church to suffragism that now condemned the women's vote. As historians Steven Hause and Anne Keeney remark, 'The combination of its size, its potential for future political action, and its Catholicism alarmed those Radical politicians who feared the church.'[30]

In keeping with the trend that women were enfranchised during or after major national crises, it took invasion, occupation, and the demise of the Third Republic at the end of the Second World War to enfranchise women. The question of what sort of society they were fighting for preoccupied combatants in the war, producing the Nazi model of the greater Reich for Germany and the Beveridge Report on the 'welfare state' (the word was not used in the report) in Britain. Following the Allied landings in North Africa in 1942, the Free French set up their headquarters in Algiers and universal suffrage was agreed during their debates about the war aims. The Radicals had maintained their opposition to women's suffrage in these deliberations, which were not binding, but when France was retaken in 1944 and discussions continued on French soil, the Radicals were in a minority.

The objectives of the Free French were decided during debates chaired by Georges Bidault, a former history teacher who had been politically active before the war as one of a group of Catholic intellectual activists. In the 1930s he established a left-wing newspaper, *L'Aube*, that campaigned against

Figure 13. French poster for the French Union for Women's Suffrage, giving a non-militant message in 1909: women, including one holding a baby, want to vote 'against alcohol, slums and war'.

Fascism and anti-Semitism. During the war he had organized an underground press for the Resistance, including editing *Combat* where he worked with Albert Camus. Bidault became president of the Resistance Council from which position in 1944 he became the key figure behind the Resistance Charter, an extensive reform programme that was to be implemented after the war was over, calling for the re-establishment of the rights of man: freedom of thought, of religion, of speech and association and for 'true economic and social democracy'.[31]

A decision to enfranchise women was taken in principle in January 1944 and finally established in March, with the left and the Catholics in favour and in a majority over the Radicals. Later that year, by an overwhelming vote of 96 per cent the French rejected the idea of continuing the Republic that had so failed their nation in the 1930s. In the same month, October 1945, an Assembly was charged with the task of setting up a new constitution. As often happened, an enfranchisement for some went along with disenfranchisement for others; some 100,000 collaborators were disenfranchised by imprisonment or 'national degradation' which meant the loss of civic rights.[32]

At the same time as the referendum a new Assembly was introduced which was almost half left (Communists and Socialists); with the Radicals (conservative and anti-clerical) reduced to 10 per cent. Thus the enfranchisement of women did not mean the decline of the left, as they had so feared. The left, because of its association with the Resistance, was generally popular. The real surprise was the rise of a progressive Catholic party, the Mouvement Républicain Populaire group of Catholic intellectuals founded by Georges Bidault at the end of the war, which received 24 per cent of the vote.

Two vital factors had taken place to ease the costive temperament of French politics: the political representatives of Catholics become more liberal than previously, so that with enfranchisement, even if women did overwhelmingly vote for them, it would not be a political disaster. Additionally, the 'Radicals' who had so blocked any electoral progress for women, had to be discredited along with the notion that they stood for the defence of the Republic: invasion and occupation accomplished this. The action of Catholic activists is pointed as crucial by Hause and Kenney who say, 'the Catholic women's suffrage movement in France converted more women to suffragism than all other feminist groups combined. The militant feminists of Paris began the suffrage movement, created its ideology, fought its public battles, and captured the headlines, but Catholic suffragism conquered the provinces.'[33]

Votes delayed in Italy

In the usual procedure when 'modern' democratic constitutions were written, the new Italy that emerged from the Risorgimento after 1861 actually disenfranchised those noble and property-owning women in Lombardy, Venetia, and Tuscany who had previously enjoyed an Austrian franchise.[34] The new code would ignore class distinctions but impose gender distinctions: women were denied all political rights and rights to public office. This was despite the support radical women gave the patriotic cause and in contradiction of the beliefs of such leading patriots as Garibaldi, who had repeatedly pressed for female emancipation and the participation of women in public life.[35]

Women in the more advanced north of the country were therefore faced not only with promoting women's rights but with recovering losses they had suffered. It was in response to this challenge that Anna Maria Mozzoni wrote *Woman and her Social Relationships (on the occasion of the revision of the Italian Civil Code)* in 1864. Mozzoni had been born in 1837 in Rescaldina in Lombardy to a genteel, if impoverished liberal family. All her life was spent swimming against an undercurrent of conservatism that flowed with the nationalist tide. In her attack on the proposed new constitution she lambasted a family law that virtually equated women with minors and mental incompetents: 'A legal husband is, for a woman, intellectual castration, perpetual minority, the annihilation of her personality.'[36]

Mozzoni was the main contributor to a feminist newspaper, *La Donna*, from 1868. *La Donna*, published by Gualberta Alberta Beccari, the daughter of a leading patriot, referred to women's maternal role to emphasize their commonality of interests. It supported family law reform and opposition to licensed prostitution. In personal life Mozzoni regarded the church as morally corrupt and had no sympathy with marriage as a state for women, though she had sex with men and bore a daughter while unmarried (she married later). The fact that she was never made to suffer for her private life testified to a tacit Italian bargain, historian Donald Meyer remarks: 'so long as private lives were kept private, Italians privileged by class were excused from abiding by official standards.'[37]

Mozzoni's personal feminism was working through the stages followed by entire movements in other countries: from concern for women's education and women in the family, to agitation about their position in society, towards a political solution with women's suffrage. She translated John Stuart Mill's *The Subjection of Women* into Italian in 1869; by the end of the 1870s *La Donna* was supporting women's suffrage. Mozzoni presented a petition to parliament on the issue in 1877 and the following year she enhanced her international reputation when she represented Italy at the International Conference on Women's Rights in Paris.

Progressive thought, however, looked towards a model of free Italy, *La Donna* was condemned for its 'foreign' model of the women citizen; the nationalist image of Italian woman was as the angel of the hearth and mother of the family.[38] Mozzoni was soon joining with other radicals in arguing for universal suffrage and moved further towards socialism, away from her liberal roots, though she stayed an autonomous feminist. She formed the League for the Promotion of the Interests of Women in Milan in 1881 but progress was slow, she lamented: 'The Senate, the nobility, the clergy, the Queen—who is very devout, very aristocratic and not very intelligent—hesitate at every reform measure.'[39]

There was another problem this time with her supposed allies: the new industrial working-class Italian man who formed the mainstay of the Socialist Party did not favour women working; and in a situation common from other countries, while women's suffrage was given lip-service by the leaders as a principle, it was not felt practicable to pursue that goal at this particular time. Mozzoni grew old (she was 70 in 1907) without seeing even a suggestion of votes for women.

The National Committee for Women's Suffrage was founded in 1905 but it was small and unrepresentative, particularly when compared to the massive support the Catholic Church could attract for its women's initiatives.[40] The liberalization of politics culminating in the enfranchisement of all men in 1912 fomented a vigorous women's suffrage movement. The 1912 reform had swelled the electorate from 3.3 million to 8.7 million men. Many of them, particularly in the South, were illiterate, which removed the stigma of enfranchising illiterates, which would otherwise be used against women, and meant that many women who were educated did not have the vote while men who were clearly their intellectual inferiors did.

There was no appetite, however, for a further massive increase in the franchise. The liberal politician Giovanni Giolitti, the dominant force in Italian politics who was five times prime minister between 1892 and 1921, in response to a petition for women's suffrage, said that full civil rights must first be given to women. Giolitti was said to have had 'no ideological convictions on the matter one way or another. Had granting women the vote served his political ends, he would have pushed for women's suffrage.'[41] Giolitti was not anxious to antagonize the Catholics, when the Vatican was currently hostile to women's suffrage; the socialists were both divided on the issue (for the usual reason that women were thought to be too much under the influence of their priests) and were not in accord with bourgeois feminists so presented no united front of argument. A women's suffrage amendment was voted down by 209 votes to 48 in the lower house of parliament.

After 1914 the war disrupted the usual political processes; however, in 1917 a conference in Rome promised a reform bill. The 'Sacchi Bill' of 1919 went some way to relieving women of their disabilities in abolishing the absolute authority of the husband, giving women the right of guardianship of their children, the right to control their own property, to enter the professions, and to fill public offices. In the same spirit of feminist reform the lower house voted to enfranchise women in 1919 by 174 votes to 55, but in a manner characteristic of the usually more conservative upper houses, the Senate refused to endorse the measure.

Unrest bordering on civil war in 1921 led the King, fearing a Communist revolution, to put his confidence in Mussolini who was appointed prime minister in 1922 following the so-called 'March on Rome' by his Fascist supporters—in fact it was a ceremonial parade; Mussolini arrived in Rome by train. He assumed dictatorial powers and over the rest of the 1920s quashed the parliamentary opposition and established full Fascist government. The response to a perceived threat from the left in Italy, therefore, was to look to authoritarian solutions where in northern countries (Holland and Sweden for example) the response was to widen the franchise to women who were felt to be a conservative, balancing influence.

Why this was not a course more vigorously pursued in Italy is a question that will have to await further study. Disappointed by conventional politics, 'all the major feminist associations supported Fascism voluntarily in the early years of Mussolini's premiership' before a full Fascist regime was imposed.[42] This is less reprehensible than it might at first seem: the Fascists promised to control the socialists who were seen as responsible for the widespread unrest in Italian society; Fascists gave every impression of supporting the Catholic Church which was seen as the mainstay of Italian family life; and even liberals such as Giolitti supported Mussolini's government initially, sharing the widespread hope that the Fascists would become a more moderate and responsible party upon taking power. Mussolini was patron of the congress of the International Woman Suffrage Alliance held in Rome in 1923 and promised a progressive enfranchisement of Italian women so they could exercise their 'fundamental qualities of foresight, balance and wisdom'.[43]

The newly formed Fascist Party had joined in the protest at the refusal of the Senate to endorse the women's franchise, so suffragists had some reason to believe their cause would be supported by the new government. The Fascists were to disappoint in many ways, not least in the lack of social progress and their suppression even of the moderate feminist society, the Association for Women, in 1925. The Concordat with the Vatican in 1929 showed that Mussolini was more concerned to placate Catholic authority than defy it; increasingly close links with the Nazis in the early 1930s meant there was no going back to democracy.

Mussolini himself had appeared before parliament on 15 May 1925 to support a bill giving women the municipal vote, chiding opponents for being 'frightened at the thought that every four years a woman will be dropping her ballot in the ballot box', but later that year he abolished local elections altogether, disenfranchising everyone; in supporting the women's vote at that time Mussolini had merely been showing the regard for truth and integrity that characterized all his utterances.[44]

It took the disintegration of Fascism (from 1943 onwards) and the re-establishment of democracy in Italy for women to be enfranchised in 1945. During the war, after the German takeover in 1943, northern Italian women formed Women's Defence Groups for Aid to the Fighters for Liberty. Their stated aim was 'to organise women for the conquest of their rights as women, and as Italians in the context of the battle of all people for national liberation'.[45] The Union of Italian Women was formed in 1944 of all anti-Fascist women: Communist, Socialist, Catholic, and Radical, coming together out of the national crisis. Late that year they called upon all the political parties, now again functioning openly, to support women's suffrage.

A suffrage decree was proposed by the Christian Democrats and the Communist Party; all the other parties supported it and it was issued on 1 February 1945. The following year they voted with a heavy majority for abolishing the monarchy that had failed to protect Italian democracy against Mussolini. The feminist writer Gabriella Parca remarked, 'After so many battles and so many polemics, the right to vote arrived almost unexpectedly, as fighting continued in the North. The press gave it little notice.'[46]

In 1948 a crushing defeat for the combined Socialist and Communist ticket left the Communists asking if it had all been the work of women, if they were wrong to have given women the vote (though men also had voted overwhelmingly for the Christian Democrats). Later that year Communists won local victories, taking control of municipalities all over the north. The notion of women's suffrage condemning a country to perpetual right-wing government was false.

Not ready yet in Spain

Spanish political life was characterized by extremism at both ends of the spectrum, from far-right Catholics to violent anarchists and socialists. The so-called Tragic Week in Barcelona in 1909 started with an anarchist and socialist call for a general strike and culminated in the burning of convents.

The church through its control of education was widely seen as responsible for the backwardness of Spain compared to other European countries. The Catholic Church opposed enfranchising women in Spain though the monarchy was favourable, thinking it a liberal measure which would protect national institutions from the left.

In keeping with other nations in Europe, the franchise was much under discussion at the end of the First World War (though Spain was neutral, the international upheaval of the war affected the institutions of the nation, as in Sweden). A bill was proposed in 1919 that would give the vote to all women over the age of 23. It was unsuccessful but it became part of the Republicans' programme. The military dictatorship of General Primo de Rivera, following a coup of September 1923, placated the right wing. Growing discontent obliged the King to insist on the general's resignation, but it was too late to save the dynasty. King Alfonso XIII abdicated and a coalition provisional government founded a republic in 1931.

Spanish feminism tended to the social, in common with other feminist groupings in Catholic countries, and did not have suffrage as a basic demand. The key figure in women's suffrage was Clara Campoamor who was born in 1888 in Madrid in a liberal family; her father's death when she was 12 meant she had to leave school and work alongside her mother as a dressmaker. She continued to study as best she could, and was able to obtain a job as a secretary in a newspaper, from which position she was able to pursue her political interests in socialist and radical politics. Eventually, at the age of 32, she enrolled to take a high school diploma (baccalaureate) and went on to study law, becoming at 36 one of the very few female graduates in Spain. She became a lecturer at the Academy of Jurisprudence in 1928.

She stood for election (which she could do, though she could not vote) and Campoamor became one of only three women to win a seat in parliament, which afforded women full legal status, legalized abortion, abolished the crime of adultery, and ensured women's equal access to employment. Campoamor led the campaign for women's vote, making an impassioned speech on the new constitution arguing that the only way women could learn to be free was by exercising their rights. She was opposed both by reactionary men who claimed women were hysterics by nature and unfitted to political debate; but also by the two other women deputies, Victoria Kent and Margarita Nelken. They considered the time was inopportune, that women were not ready for political activity though the underlying fear was that women would vote for the candidates of the right, supported by the church. 'It is dangerous to concede the vote to women,' Kent said.[47] Clara Campoamor argued that the franchise was an inalienable right, regardless of how it was used.

A compromise position of restricting the vote to women over the age of 45 was rejected and the Spanish constitution of 1931 gave women and men over the age of 23 the vote. In the first elections under the new constitution, in 1933, the political right were victorious, and Clara Campoamor both lost her seat and had to suffer the reproaches of colleagues who believed that votes for women had condemned progressive elements in Spain to perpetual opposition through mobilizing such organizations as Catholic Action. Her response was a book published in 1936, *My Mortal Sin: Woman and the Vote*. The left won the next election, in 1936, demonstrating that a female electorate would not invariably deliver a right-wing government.

The same year General Francisco Franco began an extreme right-wing revolt against the government that developed into a civil war, after which democracy was extinguished in Spain for the next thirty-five years. Spain became a one-party state and democratic trends were reversed, including those affecting women: laws on civil marriage and divorce were abolished and abortion was re-criminalized. A form of parliament was set up in 1942 with (among representatives from the Falange Party and various national

Figure 14. Spanish clerics and a capitalist, standing on the bodies of workers, unsuccessfully try to restrain a woman from voting in 1936 for the Popular Front who promise to free political prisoners and put food into the homes of the unemployed and repressed.

organizations) 100 'family members elected by heads of families and married women' though the first were not elected until 1967.[48] While this experiment in a kind of family-friendly democracy was not imitated elsewhere, it is interesting from the point of view of arguments about women's suffrage, as it completely reverses arguments in Britain, France, and other nations that unmarried women and widows should be enfranchised as they had no representation via a husband.

Clara Campoamor fled to France when the civil war broke out, and spent the rest of her life abroad, writing, translating, and giving lectures. She died in Switzerland in 1972 at the age of 84, three years before the death of Franco, after which democracy was restored in Spain.[49] A constitution of 1978 re-established universal suffrage and declared there should be 'no distinction by birth, sex, religion, opinion or any other condition or circumstances, private or social'.[50]

Overall, it was the conservatism of Catholic societies, rather than papal opposition, that delayed women's enfranchisement in Catholic countries. Some Catholic women were organizing for the vote even when the Vatican was in opposition. Papal support for women's suffrage was not enough to bring it about in France and Italy where it took almost thirty years after the Pope accepted the principle to put it into effect. The delay was reinforced by radicals and the left, who in other countries were supporters of women's suffrage. In Catholic countries they feared the conservatism that the church cherished and therefore opposed women's suffrage, so suffragists were divided from their natural supporters.

The range of enfranchisements in primarily Catholic European counties shows unanimity of attitude. If Austria is separated from the picture (with her formerly subject nations) as being so closely associated with Germany that the same post-war model of women's franchise was followed, a picture emerges of the other Catholic countries enfranchising women tardily after the Second World War.

Portugal is a good example of tentative women's enfranchisement. The nation had a very limited franchise for highly educated women in 1931; a more effective franchise was introduced for married, taxpaying women in 1946; the marital status requirement was lifted in 1968 and the full franchise only awarded in 1976 with a new, democratic constitution. This is more closely comparable to Spain, successfully enfranchising in 1978, and France and Italy in 1944 and 1946, than it is to the women's enfranchisement of Protestant neighbours—or even to the story of Latin America, an almost completely Catholic continent.

12

Latin American mothers
of the nation

'I resigned myself to be a victim'

In the motorcade down the Avenida de Mayo for the inauguration of the
president of Argentina Eva Perón was next to her adored husband, receiving
the cheers of the crowd. She was, as always, glamorous: wrapped in a fur
coat, glittering with jewels and showered with the love of the poor.

Most of the four million newly enfranchised women had voted for Perón
or, in fact, had voted for Eva, though she was not a candidate and was
anyway in the last stages of terminal illness.

At the victory parade where she apparently stood in a car receiving the
applause of the people, she was sustained by a triple dose of pain killers and
weighed only eighty pounds. Her wasted body was covered with her
floor-length coat. The president's wife was so weak she could not stand but
was held up by a frame specially constructed from wire and plaster, hidden
under the coat.

Eva Perón had been fuelled by a burning sense of indignation at the
injustice done to her, and compelled forwards by identification with the
poor whose suffering she saw as representing herself. She pondered that
'the best women's movement in the world' might be that 'which gives itself
for love of the cause and of the doctrine of a man who has proved himself
to be one in every sense of the word'.[1] In releasing the political potential of
women the example of Eva Perón presents a strange and uniquely Latin
American chapter in the story of women's suffrage.

Latin America

Ethnically the Latin American population is made up of natives; the descendants of conquistadors and European colonists; and the descendants of African slaves. Concepts such as equal treatment before the law and respect for individual rights were alien to Latin American nations when they became independent from their colonial masters in the first half of the nineteenth century.

Culturally, despite obvious national differences there are marked similarities between countries on the South American continent: overwhelmingly the common language is Spanish (with the exception of Brazil where Portuguese is spoken); the common religion is Catholic; all nations were dominated by European countries until independence when they came to be overshadowed by the superpower to the north. Independence had followed Napoleon's invasion of Spain and Portugal in 1807–8 when they lost the military power and confidence to hold on to their overseas possessions.

Socially in Latin American culture there have traditionally been clear roles for men and women with an assertive masculinity, often referred to as 'machismo', that was unhelpful for such a joint political venture as winning women's suffrage. What has been called the Madonna/whore dichotomy, where women are socially conceived only as mothers or sexual partners has been prevalent, with unfortunate consequences for women who wished to be politically active, as neither of these stereotypical roles easily admits of a political dimension. Politically, self-government in Latin America has been cursed by *caudillismo*—the rule of a strong man whose will was dominant over any restraints proposed by law. This was not a forum in which an appeal for democratic rights for women was destined for easy success. Over the period of women's enfranchisement in Latin America, from 1932 to 1961, governments were generally volatile; the first solution to political problems was more often increased repression than an extension of democracy.[2]

Legally there were restrictive codes, normally written into law, enshrining the doctrine of coverture with different judicial standards for infractions of family law between men and women. As historian Asunción Lavrin says, 'for social reformers . . . the recognition of the rights of women as mothers, wives and wage-earners, female education and the solution of public health problems affecting women and children, were more pressing than female suffrage.'[3]

Suffrage was not a central concern for Latin American feminists because in most countries there was no legacy of effective male suffrage. Others felt that women should 'abstain from such a corrupt, masculine realm' as that of politics.[4]

In terms of outside influence, there were mixed messages: Spain and Portugal, the former colonial masters, were not politically progressive; but across the Mexican border women's suffrage was one of the great issues in the US, and looking west across the Pacific rather than east across the Atlantic, Latin Americans found a model and inspiration in New Zealand.[5]

Progressives believed inequality between the sexes was but one aspect, among many, of Latin American life that would have to be redressed if the continent were to achieve European levels of progress. However, progressives also feared women's traditionalist influence. The Catholic Church was unsympathetic to women's stepping out of their gender roles, but even radicals (with an attitude common in European Catholic countries) were reluctant to argue for women's political rights as they were feared to be too much under the control of their priests.

As sociologist John Markoff has remarked, the pattern of the enfranchisement of women taking place in smaller areas remote from the centres of power was followed in Latin America, in that it was tiny Ecuador that first enfranchised women, in 1929, not one of the larger nations such as Brazil or Mexico, or one of those most inclined to identify with European culture, such as Argentina or Chile.[6] Admittedly, Brazil was second in 1932, but small Uruguay was next, the same year.

'Inexplicable delays' in Mexico

The peripheral state of Yucatán in Mexico was the site of early, if short-lived experiments in voting for women. In the revolutionary upheaval of Mexico in 1910–20 a progressive general, Salvador Alvarado, was appointed governor in Yucatán. He may have been influenced by reading or by his trips to the United States, but for whatever reason he went further than any other leader of his time in Latin America in opening up jobs in public administration to women, reforming the Civil Code and promoting women's education. He called feminist congresses in 1916 and advocated that women should be allowed to vote, first in municipal and then in state and then national elections, the stages permitting their political education to take place.[7]

However, before he could make any further progress, as a true democrat Alvarado wished to be elected as constitutional governor. He formed a socialist party but found he could not stand: he was neither a native of the province nor had he the residency qualification of five years. In 1918 when he had to step down, his place was taken by Felipe Carrillo Puerto, a journalist and radical deputy. He became governor of Yucatán in 1922 and, among other revolutionary measures, accelerated Alvarado's programme for women. He proposed a law to the state legislature to give women the vote and promoted women as candidates for the election in November 1923. Puerto had built up enemies, however: his strident anti-clericalism alienated many and his promotion of free love and birth control appalled feminists at the Pan American Women's Congress of 1923. As historian Anna Macías comments, 'To the moderate feminists, Mexico's big problem was "paid love" not free love; and prostitution was as much in evidence in Yucatán, despite all the revolutionary rhetoric, as anywhere else.'[8]

Puerto's enemies staged a counter-revolutionary military coup in January 1924 and executed him. The election results of the previous November were set aside, and when socialists regained power a few months later they did not reinstate women candidates and there was no further reference to women in politics on socialist platforms for the rest of the decade. It may be that by championing women in such an assertive manner, Puerto had merely convinced conservatives of the dangers of feminism.

The leader of the 1910 revolution, Francisco Madero, had absorbed liberal sentiments in Europe and was generally a radical thinker; he was also influenced by his wife and by his personal secretary Soledad Gonzáles whom he had adopted as a girl. Madero's term as president was brief and insecure, however; he was imprisoned and shot in a coup in 1913. Subsequently the issue was raised by the National Revolutionary Party which had supporters of women's suffrage in its ranks, and women participated in the national election of 1934, some under the banner of the recently formed Feminist Revolutionary Party; the presidential candidate, Lárazo Cárdenas, agreed that in return for such assistance he would support women's suffrage.[9] Women were given the right to participate in party primaries in 1936 but proposals for full suffrage were not high up on an agenda dominated by revolutionary in-fighting.

Spain's descent into fascism had a knock-on effect in Mexico where fascist sympathizers fought with liberals and left wingers on the streets. Women did not gain politically from this conflict because of the fear that if given the

Figure 15. A French magazine illustrates armed Mexican women in their dresses and hats, having just derailed a government train, while fighting for the revolution in 1913. The revolutionary period in Mexico saw the first calls for women's suffrage in Latin America.

vote they might back the right wing and endanger the revolution. As a member of the Central Political Institute said in setting forth policy, 'the conquest of the vote—for which, with a tenacity worthy of a better cause, certain feminist groups have fought—is certainly undeniably important' but before women could be given full suffrage rights they must develop a 'revolutionary conscience'.[10] In other words, they could not be given the vote until they could be trusted to vote for the National Revolutionary Party. The president, Cárdenas, emphasized that as 'the Mexican woman is much more superstitious and fanatical than the man' it would be best not to enfranchise her but to allow her to become politically aware first through trade union activity.[11]

Angered at their being sidelined again, women of the United Front for Women's Rights held a dramatic hunger strike outside the president's home in Mexico City, after two weeks of which President Cárdenas committed himself to bringing women's suffrage before Congress the next full session. The resulting proposal went to Congress to give all Mexicans the vote equally if they had an 'honest' livelihood (thereby presumably excluding prostitutes, as Latin American suffrage proposals often did); and if they were 18 if married or 21 if not. It was supported, if without enthusiasm, and Congress adjourned with the proposal still pending but Cárdenas called for a special session at which it was discussed and passed on 6 July 1938, to be referred to the state legislatures for ratification.

The Eighth Pan American Conference met at Lima, Peru, in December 1938 and Mexico's revolutionary delegation successfully proposed a declaration of women's political and civil equality with men. At home more concrete equality was less easy to achieve: despite all the states ratifying the women's amendment, party in-fighting again prevented its passage—not through opposition, but through the pressure of other business and on account of Cárdenas' opponents' determination to stop his programme. Congress was adjourned with no declaration of constitutional change being made. A later report remarks, 'This reform, which lacked only the legal declaration, was left abandoned in the archives of the Chamber in an inexplicable form for almost ten years, possibly in fear of the undesirable results it might produce in the political life of the nation.'[12]

An election of 1940 installed a new president and the outbreak of World War Two redrew political boundaries; those feminists who had argued for the vote reacted with anger and frustration. One observer commented, 'Frequently Mexican husbands are Marxists outside and feudalists within their homes, and politicians fight tenaciously, with every weapon in their power, the efforts of organised women to secure the vote.'[13] This was all the more galling because of the number of nations that were enfranchising women before Mexico.

Women were finally given municipal voting rights in 1946. The next major campaign in which women's suffrage was involved was the presidential election in 1952. The favourite, Adolfo Ruiz Cortines, a former revolutionary army officer, had sincere views on women's rights about which he promised, 'Reform of feminine affairs so that women may enjoy the same civic rights as men and the termination of odious inequalities which are repudiated by science.'[14] Clearly he did not think women's suffrage was a vote-loser. Ruiz Cortines won the election and immediately made it clear he would submit women's suffrage proposals as soon as he took office, which he did. His opponents therefore sought the proclamation of the 1937 amendment, which had lain 'in an inexplicable form' for so many years, in order to steal a march on the new president. There was an unseemly row in various committees, where women suffragists were presented with the unusual spectacle of legislators fighting over who should enfranchise them. Eventually the proposals of the president were passed on 22 December 1952, by the Congress unanimously and by the Senate a few days later with one dissenting vote. They were ratified and pronounced the following year, on 6 October 1953, providing equal rights to vote and stand for office.

Ecuador—leading from the periphery

In 1929 Ecuador became the first Latin American state to enfranchise women; but in 1924 Ecuador also produced the continent's first woman voter. Mathilde Hidalgo de Procel was born in Loja in 1889 in a family of six children. Her father died when she was young and her mother was obliged to work as a seamstress to keep the family. Matilde attended a convent school, she was an academic child but her education was soon to stop as girls did not go to high school. She spoke to her older brother, who asked the director of the local secular high school for permission for her to attend. He did so, but the local community acted with outrage to the spectacle of a girl becoming educated—mothers stopped their daughters from associating with her and the priest made her stand outside the church at mass. She became the first woman in Ecuador to graduate from high school and then, in the tradition of suffragist women going into medicine, became a doctor in 1923, the first Ecuadorian woman to do so; she married a lawyer, Fernando Procel, in 1925.

She continued to lead by example, and announced (in common with European and American suffragist pioneers) that she was going to vote in the presidential elections as she judged that women were not specifically barred. The issue was referred to the State Council which deliberated on constitutional matters. They decided that as an early constitution had specified 'men', but the one under which they were working at the time, that of 1906, did not do so, the implication was that women were not excluded.[15] In 1924 Mathilde Hidalgo de Procel became the first women to vote.

The issue concentrated attention on the position of women in Ecuadorian society at a time when politicians were seeking stability. During the first century after it gained independence in 1830, Ecuador changed its constitution thirteen times, and few presidents served a full four-year term. A military coup of 1925 was brought by the League of Young Officers with a range of social reforms designed to end the stagnant, three-decade rule of the Liberal Party. The following year they installed Isidro Ayora as a reforming president, committed to social development and to the dominance of the Conservatives. A range of fiscal reforms were undertaken to secure the country's economic future at a time when world demand for cocoa had brought wealth to parts of the country; pensions and protective employment laws were brought in with the new constitution of 1929.[16]

Women were enfranchised in this constitution in the frank belief that they would be responsive to the views of Catholic clerics and support the Conservatives. The qualification for the ballot was literacy so, as fewer women than men were literate, women's participation was commensurately lessened. The enfranchisement was not only a cynical ploy to gain more political support, however; it was one measure in a generally progressive constitution that also gave representation to Indians.

Historian Nicola Foote has argued that the co-option of women's suffrage by conservatives 'occurred only because women had been so successful in normalising the radical idea of female suffrage by a strategy of gradualism and a focus on maternalist language and ideas'.[17] Feminists in Ecuador had realized, faster than in most Catholic countries, that progress would be made by working with a conservative culture rather than against it.

Ayora's measures did not bring stability because of the disastrous effect of the Wall Street Crash that year, and the 1930s were a decade of political chaos; but women's suffrage endured. Another constitution, in 1946, made voting obligatory for men but optional for women, and in 1967 it became obligatory for both men and women. Matilde Hidalgo de Procel became Ecuador's first woman deputy, for her home town of Loja, in 1941. Since her death in 1974, a museum has been established in Loja in her memory.

Brazil and the Pan American Conference

Slavery was abolished in Brazil only in 1888. As happened in Britain and the US, attention to the rights of slaves informed debates on reform elsewhere.[18] By the late 1880s some feminists in Brazil were calling for the vote, even when few men had it. As elsewhere, agitation for male political rights stimulated women to ask why they should not also be enfranchised. The declaration of a republic on 15 November 1889 moved Francisca Senhorinha da Motta Diniz the publisher of the women's magazine *The Female Sex* (*O Sexo Feminino*) to change its title to *The Fifteenth of November of the Female Sex* to emphasize the way in which she was determined to secure political rights for women. Suffragists followed the familiar route of trying to enter their names on the electoral lists and chided the nation's republican leaders that 'men who proclaim equality' should 'put it into practice'.[19]

There was some radical support in parliament for women's enfranchisement when the new constitution was discussed in 1891 but even a severely restricted proposal failed—it had proposed the enfranchisement of women with university degrees who owned property and were not under a husband or parent's authority. One of the deputies, César Zama, remarked that 'it will be sufficient that any important European country confer political rights on [women] and we will imitate this'.[20]

Brazil was the only South American country to declare war on Germany in the First World War so, though not overtly involved in the conflict, the war had a greater impact in Brazil than elsewhere on the continent. Unrest led to increasing middle-class calls for electoral reform in a state in which, in the 1920s, less than 3 per cent of the population participated in the presidential elections.[21] With a literacy test for the franchise for males over 21, lower class Brazilians both male and female were disenfranchised.

Unlike socialism and anarchism, the involvement of feminism in politics could be used to demonstrate national unity and patriotism in the precarious economic position following the First World War. Women's magazines supported this view, so the magazine *Nosso Jornal* opposed 'radical feminism' from other countries which subverted 'the classical moulds of women's existence'. Historian June Hahner says of this and similar magazines, 'The need to preserve family life and Christian morality provided the justification for women's entry into the political sphere... Women's role as wives and mothers remained paramount.'[22]

Bertha Lutz, the daughter of a Swiss-Brazilian doctor and an English nurse, returned from Europe at the end of the First World War after studying zoology at the Sorbonne. She dedicated herself to the study of amphibians, about which she became a world expert, and remarkably obtained a job at the National Museum of Brazil even though access to public posts was supposedly forbidden to women.

Based on her experiences in Europe, Lutz wrote a proposal for a Brazilian woman's movement which she described as not 'an association of "suffragettes" who would break windows along the street, but rather of Brazilians who understand that a woman ought not to live parasitically based on her sex, taking advantage of man's animal instincts, that she be useful, educate herself and her children, and become capable of performing those political responsibilities which the future cannot fail to allot her'.[23]

In 1922 she was the government-sponsored Brazilian representative to the Pan American Conference of Women in Baltimore, Maryland, which was a joint venture between Carrie Chapman Catt's League of Women Voters and the Pan American International Women's Committee. Invitations were issued through the US Department of State; US Secretary of State Charles Evans Hughes addressed the conference and there was a presidential reception for delegates at the White House.[24] This high-level involvement shows how seriously the US took the role it had assumed of leadership of the continent, and how women's suffrage had, only two years after it was ratified after a fiercely-fought campaign in the US, become part of the mission of spreading democracy.

Suffrage was a major objective of the conference, and a number of Latin American countries set up suffrage societies when delegates returned, but reports suggest delegates were most interested in education, marriage, the 'white slave trade', and protective employment legislation. As the Chilean ambassador said in his address to the delegates, 'Aspirations for active participation in political life have not as yet become vocal in our countries.'[25]

Bertha Lutz spent a weekend after the conference at the home of Carrie Chapman Catt and there wrote the constitution of the suffrage society she founded on her return, the Federação Brasileira pelo Progresso Feminino. Her choice to ally herself with Catt despite her European family and education showed how she was determined to follow the American and not the British model of the suffragettes. She encouraged the involvement of prominent men at a women's conference in Rio de Janeiro in 1922, feeling this would increase the conference's legitimacy.

Lutz's timing was excellent—Brazil was celebrating the centennial of its independence from Portugal and the nation was looking to the future; educated Brazilians wanted to be seen as progressive leaders of Latin America. Lutz played on such national pride, remarking, 'we find ourselves lagging far behind the peoples who dominate the world today.'[26]

Close ties with the political elite reassured them that the aim of the suffrage movement was not revolutionary. The movement was confined to urban upper-class and middle-class women, indeed, the novelist Alfonso Henriques de Lima Barreto satirized such organizations as the 'League for the Manumission of White Women'.[27] The radical Patricia Galvão (known as Pagú) expressed her own disgust for bourgeois feminists, 'bleating for sexual liberation, conscientious motherhood, the right to vote for cultured women'.[28]

The campaign made no effort to be radical. Many suffragists were practising Catholics and they did not attack the parts of church dogma that fostered women's subordination; the church did not oppose the suffrage campaign.[29] The Federação remained the major suffrage organization during the unsuccessful passage of bills thought parliament. As in Mexico, the reforming influence of a local governor was more important than national debates or feminist organizations in the next enfranchisement of women, which took place not in the national capital of the economically powerful state of São Paulo, but in the impoverished and thinly populated Rio Grande do Norte. A newly elected governor in 1927 had the voting laws altered to enfranchise women in a place that has been described as 'Brazil's Wyoming'.[30] When elections for federal offices were held in 1928, the women's votes were declared invalid, but women continued to vote for local and state elections. Other places started to register women, beginning with the politically marginal (in keeping with John Markoff's contention that democratic innovation takes place away from the centres of power) but soon encompassing Rio de Janeiro and other major political centres.

The Federação stepped up its campaign, citing Rio Grande do Norte and international precedents, and declaring the right to suffrage in terms of human rights. The world depression caused the collapse of the coffee market which weakened the power of the previously dominant states in Brazil and a revolution in October 1930 promised a reform agenda; a new president brought in a new constitution. When an electoral code was drawn up in 1932, it gave the same voting rights for women and men, with illiterates of both sexes denied the vote (which limited the electorate to 5 per cent of the population).[31]

Bertha Lutz was elected a federal representative in 1934, but this flowering of democracy had a short life: in 1937 the president assumed dictatorial powers and closed down both houses of parliament. No one, male or female, participated in open elections again until 1946. Bertha Lutz died in Rio in 1976 at the age of 82.

Social reform in Uruguay

Women enjoyed a positive political atmosphere in Uruguay in which some members of the dominant Colorado Party backed women's suffrage in an attempt to widen their appeal, and socialists also supported women's suffrage. A deputy introduced a bill to enfranchise women at national level, arguing that women's moral sense would elevate the national scene. The conservative and Catholic press seemed to accept this point but opposed the bill because women's energy was required for the supreme task of maternity.[32] A progressive government in 1916 promoted new legislation including a new constitution offering universal male suffrage; women's suffrage was mooted, but postponed until a two-thirds majority of legislators would agree to it.

The National Council of Women formed in 1916 under the direction of Paulina Luisi. She was born in 1875, to parents who were themselves of Polish and Italian descent. She shared the theme of primacy in education with many other suffrage leaders: she was the first woman in Uruguay to gain a bachelor's degree and the first to qualify as a doctor. Like many feminists of the period, 'Luisi believed that women's suffrage would be a weapon to cleanse the world morally and to prevent further wars.'[33]

Again in common with other suffragists, she was influenced by Josephine Butler and took particular interest in prostitution, venereal disease, and eugenics. As a teacher-trainer she promoted sex education emphasizing the need for will power and self-discipline, regular moderate physical exercise to burn up sexual energy, and the desirability of avoiding sexually stimulating entertainments. The intention was to 'emphasise the citizen's moral and social obligation to improve the mental and physical fibre of the nation through the practice of one sexual moral standard'.[34] While there was some opposition, with parents believing that sex education would encourage children to put their knowledge into practice, the underlying conservatism of her message convinced her opponents.

The political direction of the National Council of Women (if any) was unclear and dissipated; much of the organization's time was spent in support of a regional congress against alcoholism; it was also committed to child health and a campaign against tuberculosis. Luisi dominated the movement between 1916 and 1932, devoting herself to feminist and public health causes and steering the movement towards causes of current interest to her, such as pacifism or the working conditions of telephone operators. Her restless dominance led to squabbling within women's organizations, as Asunción Lavrin says, 'since she was surrounded by other capable women who were also strongly driven, it was to be expected that some friction would develop'.[35] In order to develop political direction, the Uruguayan Women's Alliance for Feminine Suffrage was founded in 1919 as an offshoot.

The Uruguayan Women's Alliance restated its programme in 1929 to place legal equality as the top goal, with women's suffrage ranked fifth. Philosophically, Uruguayan feminists were arguing for protection for women from violence, coercion, and industrial exploitation rather than equality with men. The suffrage was required to guarantee women's rights within the family and society generally.[36] They were therefore not promoting the women's vote because women were in some way superior to men, as in suffrage rhetoric in the US and Britain. Uruguayan women's generally unthreatening approach proved attractive to both socialists and conservatives, both groups feeling they would benefit from women's support, and a congressional committee on women's suffrage was set up in 1930. The discussion in the Chamber of Deputies in October 1932 'proved to be a contest among political leaders to demonstrate to each other and to the nation their long-standing belief in women's votes'.[37] The Senate approved women's suffrage without discussion: the feminists had been swimming with the tide of progressive movements of the right and left.

Soap-opera triumph in Argentina

A National Council of Women was set up in Argentina in 1900 but strove to distance itself from radicalism. It was decreed that a priest should be present at all general meetings and repeatedly announced that the National Council would never demand women's suffrage. When the parent body, the International Council of Women, called on them to take a position on suffrage, 'the Argentines responded, as they had before, that the civil status of women in Argentina was so primitive that any discussion of suffrage would be premature.'[38]

Their reluctance to commit politically was from fear of godless socialists, who were perceived as the overwhelming threat to Argentinian society. From its inception in 1896 the Argentine Socialist Party was an outspoken supporter of feminism, calling for universal suffrage and equality of the sexes in the Civil Code (it was not revised until 1926). Alfredo Palacios, Argentina's first socialist deputy, often spoke in favour of the Feminist Centre, an organization founded in 1905 to press for women's rights.[39] It had been founded by Elvira Rawson de Dellepiane (another leading woman who had trained as a doctor) but even the name Feminist Centre was too extreme for Argentine women and after three months Dellepiane changed its name to the Manuela Gorritti Centre after a nineteenth-century Argentinian writer.

The First International Feminine Congress met in 1910 in Buenos Aires with a delegate from the Socialist Feminine Centre, Raquel Messina, a teacher and social worker, calling for universal suffrage. She based her argument on the rights of man, referring back to the French Revolution, and pointed to the positive experience of Wyoming. A teacher, Ana Montalvo, also spoke, but delegates rejected the proposal to draft a women's suffrage bill for inclusion in pending manhood suffrage legislation. Suffrage was not a main theme of the conference, however, which was more focused on questions of maternity, the children of the poor, divorce, and the abolition of legalized prostitution. Universal male suffrage was passed two years later, and women's suffrage bills were unsuccessfully presented by the socialists in almost every session.

The National Feminist Union was founded in November 1918 by Dr Julieta Lanteri-Renshaw. She was born in Italy in 1873 but had become naturalized as a citizen of Argentina when she was appointed as a lecturer at the Faculty of Medicine at Buenos Aires, a position that only a citizen could occupy. Her marriage to a prominent Argentinian assisted in the decision to grant her citizenship. She applied to vote and was turned down, but the case was reviewed by a federal judge, who felt obliged to say that 'women have, in principle, the same political rights of male citizens' but added that such rights were qualified by cultural factors (which were subject to change). She attempted to register for military service to be able to qualify for the vote; and appealed unsuccessfully to the Supreme Court when she was refused. Dressed in lacy white to symbolize female purity, Dr Lanteri-Renshaw would project that the female was as good as the male: 'As a species, she might be superior. She has a more distinct and superior character.'[40]

Lanteri-Renshaw attracted attention to the cause by running for office and by holding a mock election in 1920 (an idea borrowed from French suffragists who had done the same in 1918) which brought women's suffrage into the public arena. She was able to prove that women could organize politically, which had been questioned by anti-suffragists, and attracted considerable international attention. She was disappointed at the indifference of women to calls for suffrage, however, saying that without the support of liberal men, she could not have waged a campaign.[41] In the end, despite all the effort, only 4,000 women voted. Lanteri-Renshaw died in a car crash in February 1932 at the age of 59.

Several bills for national suffrage were presented through the 1920s by radicals and socialists. And, although the 1930s did produce a mass movement for women, it was neither radical nor socialist. The Argentine Association for Women's Suffrage was founded by Carmela Horne de Burmeister, a teacher and social worker who stressed the nationalism of her cause rather than announcing the changes women would make if they had the vote. Her slogan was 'Fatherland Civic Pride and Humanity' which was likely to offend few. She could claim 100,000 members by 1934, doubtless with some exaggeration, this may mean only there were this number of signatories to a suffrage petition which called for the vote for native-born, literate Argentinian women over the age of 22.

A bill to give women over the age of 18 the vote (regardless of literacy) was passed in the lower house on 17 September 1932. The usual battle, familiar particularly from Catholic countries, of a conservative upper house refusing to pass a democratic measure, meant the bill was stalled and finally rejected by the Senate.

Women in Brazil and Uruguay got the vote in 1932; Chilean women got the municipal vote in 1934; Argentina seemed to be slipping behind other Latin American countries, to the disgust of the educated elite. Instead of widening the franchise, however, Argentina descended into a nationalist, military government which was pro-fascist, but in fact closer to National Socialism, with its harnessing of socialist language to a rhetoric of violent patriotism. It was not a place to have a debate about women's rights.

The stalemate over women's suffrage was broken by Juan Perón, aided by his politically astute partner Eva, often called by the diminutive Evita. Perón was born in 1895 and entered military school at the age of 16, thereafter rising through the army, a common profession for a young man of good family. Perón was obviously of superior intelligence; he published in the fields of history and political philosophy, and he served as a military attaché in Italy in the 1930s, observing fascism close at hand.

Perón joined a group of military officers plotting to overthrow the government in 1943, and after the coup he occupied the post of secretary of labour and social welfare in the new government. Early in the following year he set up a fund to help victims of a recent earthquake; to this end he promoted fund-raising activities by people in the arts. At a gala event as part of these activities on 22 January 1944, the 48-year-old Perón met a successful radio actress, Eva Duarte, who was 24 and was to become one of the most successful women in political history.

She was small, pale, and fragile but intensely driven. Juan Perón described her in her black dress, as he first met her: 'I looked at her and felt overcome by her words; I was quite subdued by the force of her voice and her look. Eva was pale but when she spoke, her face seemed to catch fire. Her hands were reddened with tension, her fingers knit tightly together, she was a mass of nerves.'[42]

Eva Duarte was born on 7 May 1919 in Los Toldos, a small town 150 miles from Buenos Aires. Her parents were unmarried, her father was a rancher from a nearby area where he had his own wife and family. He died when Eva was 6 or 7, and much has been made of the refusal of the 'legitimate' family to allow Eva's mother and her children entry to his funeral. This may have been the source of Eva's contempt for the middle class and their values, but she had ample further opportunity for resentment: 'From each year I kept the memory of some injustice that roused me to rebellion,' she wrote.[43] She explained her own personal appeal: 'I think that, just as some persons have a special tendency to feel beauty differently and more intensely than do people in general, and therefore become poets or painters or musicians, I have a special inherent tendency to feel injustice with unusual and painful intensity.'[44]

To get by, Eva's mother and sisters took in sewing, worked in the houses of the rich, and ran a boarding house. Eva was passionately attached to the theatre and radio drama, and by some means (it is said by hitching a lift with a touring tango singer) she arrived in Buenos Aires in 1935. She struggled for years as an actress, eventually taking leading roles in minor films and becoming a soap star on the nation's major radio station.

When she met the tall, handsome, intelligent, and powerful Perón at the charity gala, it was love at first sight. 'I will not leave your side until I faint,' she told him.[45] Eva and Perón talked together that evening and when the event ended at around two in the morning, they left the venue together. Very soon after their meeting at the charity gala performance she moved in with Perón—it was said that she moved in while he was away at his office, sending his current mistress packing. Much more remarkably, and against common practice, she started attending political meetings with him and his colleagues. Perón had realized that Eva had a natural political grasp with an instinctive understanding of the people of Argentina. Eva began promoting Perón in radio broadcasts, soon taking a position as president of the performers' union.

Perón had realized that women were an untapped political resource and in 1945 he sent a petition to the president asking for women's suffrage by presidential decree—as it was not specifically forbidden by the constitution the president could simply write a declaration to bring enfranchisement into effect. Feminists were outraged by this intervention from the nationalist right, believing that women's suffrage should come about as a result of the 'popular feminine will'.[46] A National Assembly of Women was formed that included most of the feminist organisations and traditional political groups favouring women's suffrage, in order to oppose Perón's measures and argue for a constitutional amendment. Out of a sense of doctrinal purism, Argentinian feminists found themselves opposing women's suffrage.

Perhaps alone among women leaders in Argentina, Carmela Horne de Burmeister supported Perón—not because she was a Perónist but she was sufficiently single-minded to go for suffrage and not allow other considerations to divert her.

Eva, being both a self-made woman from a poor family and also one who had made her way through glamour and presentation skills rather than intellect, had little in common with the intellectuals for whom moral purity was as important as suffrage. She was not a feminist, she wrote, 'everything I knew about feminism seemed to me ridiculous. For, not led by women but by those who aspired to be men, it ceased to be womanly and was nothing!'[47]

Perón had become minister of war and vice president by 1945 but his popularity among the workers and the poor (along with his continued authority in the army) was disconcerting to some within the government who feared he would displace the president. He was therefore arrested, which prompted Eva and their associates in the labour unions to call out their forces. On 17 October 1945 more than a quarter of a million people gathered in front of Argentina's government house to demand Peron's release.

Within days of being free, Perón married Eva and began to run for the presidency; by attacking him his enemies had therefore accelerated his political career—and that of Eva. The two campaigned heavily, travelling on the campaign trail throughout Argentina. Perón became president in February 1946 with 56 per cent of the popular vote. He did not in fact give women the vote by presidential decree, he gave his wife Eva the job of representing women's rights. Perón, with Eva's very public support, presented a bill to parliament to enfranchise all women. Eva organized suffrage rallies and spoke on the radio in support of the bill. She offered a vision not of assertive women taking over after the vote, but of women who would be feminine and attractive, a compliment to masculinity—just as she was to Juan. Evita had reconciled the Madonna/whore dichotomy: she was a woman who had risen by sex appeal and was now mother of the nation, a support and an inspiration to her man.

Some conservatives tried to block the women's suffrage bill, it 'seemed to linger in Congressional committees while other bills speeded through'.[48] Returning from a European tour to find the bill in the doldrums, Eva went to the Congress building with crowds of women supporters and made it known that she would not leave until the bill was passed. The bill went through, and on 27 September 1947 Argentinian women got the vote. Thousands filled the streets in celebration. But the feminists did not celebrate: as historian Marifran Carlson says, 'the feminists had not grasped the realities of the political situation in 1946, or possibly at any time.'[49] They utterly failed to see how Juan and Eva Perón represented the aspirations of working-class people, and women in particular.

It is easy to minimize the Peróns' part in achieving women's suffrage, by saying it was an idea whose time had come in Argentina.[50] The policy's time had come in Britain in the 1890s but it was not to be a fact for another twenty-five years. Another thirteen continental Latin American counties were still to enfranchise women when Argentina did, more than twice the number than had already done so. The people who were the proximate cause of the enfranchisement, the Peróns, must be considered responsible for it.

Eva continued to defy conventional morality—her illegitimacy and her many lovers before her marriage were no barrier to national pre-eminence, though her opponents used such crude ruses as printing postcards of her head superimposed on the body of a nude glamour model (in fact she had never done this kind of work).[51] Eva fought a class-based battle against the superior ladies of the venerable 'benevolent association' who snubbed her because of her lowly birth, creating her own charitable foundation, and taking over their organization. She had a deep, natural sense of hurt, which compelled her to identify with the poor and miserable: 'I resigned myself to be a victim' as she said in her autobiography, more in defiance than resignation, and with perfect sincerity.[52]

Argentina had emerged from the Second World War in a favourable economic situation; Perón could afford to put an ambitious political programme into effect. In return for support for his totalitarian regime, Perón's government delivered improvements in pensions, health care, housing, accident compensation, and a rise in real incomes. Legal equality in marriage was given to women, and equal control of their children in the case of separation. Eva and her Rama Femenina (Women's Branch) ensured limitations of working hours and minimum wages, funded hospitals and clinics, and increased the number of schools by a quarter.

There was a large popular movement of her supporters to have Eva accepted as a vice-presidential candidate, but opposition from the military, and her own increasing illness, prevented it. She had been suffering from uterine cancer since 1950, and it was probably because she knew her time was limited that Eva put herself through a cruel regime of ceaseless work; Perón complained that he had already lost her, he saw her

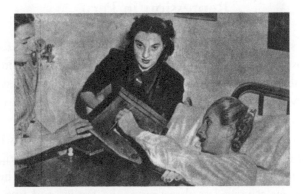

Figure 16. Eva Perón, stricken with cancer in 1951, summoning the strength to vote in a ballot box brought to her in the first Argentinean election where women could take part. The box became an object of veneration to her admirers.

so infrequently. She hid her symptoms for as long as possible and avoided her doctors: Perón suggested that she actually desired to destroy herself by overwork.[53]

Perón felt assured of women's votes and also relied for a great deal of his popularity on his charismatic wife. He even acceded to Eva's demands for a quota for female candidates to be reserved in the official Peronist Party lists. In July 1949 she brought into being the Women's Peronist Party, which at its height had half a million members. It was the most successful women's party ever founded, though of course its objective was the support of the main Peronist party. It was a winning strategy: in 1951 Perón won with two-thirds of the total vote, and more women were elected than at any other time in Argentina's history: twenty-three deputies and six senators.

Eva's vote had been cast in hospital, at the entrance of which women knelt in the rain, and reached up to try to touch the ballot box as it passed by, because Eva had touched it and it had, like the secondary relic of a saint, acquired mystical significance. Perón's inauguration took place on 4 June 1952, after the parade in which the heavily sedated Eva apparently stood beside Perón, receiving the applause of the people. It was her last public appearance. Eva Perón died on 26 July 1952 at the age of 33. Perón was overthrown in 1955, Eva's embalmed body was taken by the new military rulers, so great was their fear of her cult. So powerful was her legacy that Argentinians were forbidden to have mementoes or photographs of Eva, even in their own homes.

Repression in Peru

Many of the suffrage battles in Latin America were carried on by educated, women whose good families and proximity to the political elite protected them from the worst of government repression. A more typical women's life was that of María Jesús Alvarado Rivera, a largely self-taught teacher and journalist who was born in 1878 in Lima.

Alvarado started her activist career seeking justice for Peru's Indians and workers, and she succeeded in founding Peru's first women's rights organization, Evolución Femenina (Women's Evolution), in 1915. The organization was fiercely criticized as threatening the family, and was accused of being Protestant. Most of the administrative work fell on Alvarado, such support as she had was timorous; as late as 1924 when a newspaper carried a photograph of a meeting addressed by Alvarado, many of the audience shielded their faces so they could not be identified.[54] A significant advance, however, was the right of women to sit on public welfare committees which had considerable power over the distribution of benefits.

Alvarado took the opportunity of a visit to Lima by Carrie Chapman Catt to call together other women's groups with her own and to found a National Council of Women in 1923. The organization was at once torn with dissension: beyond the vote, the women could not agree on anything, even whether they should call for equality for women in law. Historian Elsa Chaney described Alvarado: 'No simple feminist, and strikingly beautiful in the bargain, Maria Alvarado with her advanced social ideas alienated many of the more cautious women of Lima who might have been willing to work simply for the vote.'[55]

Alvarado had too many enemies and not enough friends to survive the political climate that prevailed at the time, yet she felt constrained to print leaflets accusing the president of misconduct, including bloody assassinations of his opponents. Just before Christmas 1924 Alvarado was arrested, imprisoned in solitary confinement for three months, and was banished to Argentina. A newspaper commented philosophically on her punishment, 'When women meddle in men's affairs they expose themselves to the necessity of suffering the consequences of their masculine acts.'[56] She was allowed to return in 1936 but no unified, effective women's movement was formed in Peru.

Women in Peru got the vote in 1955, at the behest of General Manuel Odría who had ruled as dictator since 1948. He and his wife, Maria Delgado de Odría, wished to imitate the success of the Peróns, and the women's vote was an integral part of their strategy. But the plan backfired and the General lost the election of 1956: women's participation in elections was substantially lower than men's because of the high rate of illiteracy among women, which meant they could not qualify. Alvarado died at the age of 93 in 1971. Illiterate women (the majority of whom were female Amerinidians) were not enfranchised until the 1980s.[57]

Mothers of the nation

Trevor Lloyd considers wealth the key factor in the enfranchisement of women in Latin America: 'Countries like Brazil, Cuba, Uruguay and

Ecuador were reasonably prosperous and were willing to imitate the United States by giving votes to women.'[58] Wealth was not the only factor, however: Ecuador was not one of the wealthiest counties in the sub-continent yet was first to enfranchise women, even though it could be described as 'politically unstable and economically underdeveloped'.[59] Rich Uruguay and Brazil were among those which enfranchised early (before 1940), but large and relatively prosperous Argentina did not enfranchise women until 1947 and Mexican women had to wait until 1953.

A clue to the reason for Uruguay's enfranchisement is the strongly nationalist flavour: the constitution of 1934 said that all citizens were voters and entitled to hold office, but 'national citizens are all men and women born within the nation'.[60] In order to vote, foreigners had to be married, be professional or own property, and to have lived in Uruguay for fifteen years. Thus potentially disruptive and numerous immigrants were excluded from the vote: women's suffrage was established as a nationalist buttress to foreign radicalism in a labour market swelled with European immigrants.

Often women's suffrage came with a revolution, in keeping with the experience of Europe of great national events (wars or struggles for national independence) acting as a catalyst to women gaining suffrage. So, for example, the overthrow of the dictator Gerardo Machado in Cuba in 1934 led to that country becoming the fourth country in the region to enfranchise women.[61] Latin American countries were not strangers to national upheaval, however, and many violent political changes took place over the central years of the twentieth century without women's suffrage being part of the resulting settlements.

Nor did the progress of democracy as represented by an extension of suffrage generally follow an underlying pattern. Women's lagged behind male suffrage but not by a meaningful period that would form a pattern: men were enfranchised in 1912 in Argentina, 1916 in Uruguay, 1920 in Chile, and 1936 in Colombia. Women followed at intervals of, respectively, 35, 16, 29, and 21 years.

International agencies seem to have had a mixed effect. Carrie Chapman Catt's visits on behalf of the International Woman Suffrage Alliance stimulated enthusiasm but then left local organizations exposed. It was the year after Catt's visit to Peru, in 1923, that the leading campaigner was arrested (and more than thirty years before suffrage was attained).

The Pan American Union, a realization of the dream of the great liberator of Latin American, Simón Bolívar, was similarly disappointing as regards women's suffrage. They were able to make progressive declarations, but all too often these were aspirational, and reality fell far short. Thus the Union, meeting in Peru in 1938, announced its support for a political equality that the majority of member states were not to experience for periods of up to twenty-six years.

The key to women's suffrage in South America was for campaigners and legislators to advance on their opponents' own ground. The opponents of women's suffrage simply, and without embellishment, had adopted the 'separate spheres' argument, that women would be unsexed or masculinized by engaging in politics. While this contention was commonplace in all countries where women's suffrage was discussed, in Latin America there was a particularly strong strain of conservatism among women, the feeling they should keep to their sphere of the home and attendance at church; Asunción Lavrin remarked that the hardest task for South American feminists 'was not to convince men that they were prepared for suffrage, but to convince other women'.[62]

Independence movements in European countries, notably in Scandinavia, had radicalized women in the cause. In Latin America independence movements assumed nationality for women but not the rights of political citizenship. When they did, that citizenship was formulated as the franchise of the citizen mothers. Successful campaigns for women's suffrage in Latin America promoted voting women as those who could take the values of motherhood and family into politics. Pointing up the weakness and stupidity of men—their drinking, violence, and the mess they had made of the world—may not have been very sensible where it was adopted in Anglo-Saxon countries; it would have been an insanely losing strategy in Latin America.

In Argentina it was the populist appeal to femininity orchestrated by Eva Perón that won a mass following with her make-up, fur coats, and jewellery and her political skill—if Argentinian women ever aspired to be powerful in politics, she was the powerful woman they aspired to be—and that meant vocally supporting a strong man. It wasn't feminist but, then, neither were Latin American women, as the *International Encyclopaedia of Women's Suffrage* puts it, 'Argentinian feminists felt hurt and betrayed. Eva Perón's ability to attract and mobilise those women who had ignored or rejected feminist pleas and arguments for so many years was a bitter blow.'[63] It was in the end populist movements and progressive electoral systems that gained the vote for women, along with arguments that endorsed male values and strong gender roles. In Latin America women's suffrage was almost universally portrayed by its advocates with a platform that emphasized social motherhood issues and peace rather than gender equality.[64]

In international terms Latin America became a transitional region. Women's enfranchisement had been a bold experiment in the early years when Wyoming and Utah might have been out on their own with no one else taking the step; it had progressed through the struggle for representative democracy in great nations such as the US, Britain, Germany, and Russia. By the 1930s women's enfranchisement was a regular and unremarkable event internationally (though still of great national importance). By the time the thirties had ended and Ecuador, Chile, Brazil, Uruguay, Bolivia, and El Salvador enfranchised women, there was little sense of adventure about women's franchise, it was seen as a necessary part of modern nationhood: inevitable, if not to be rushed, in countries that were still defining themselves in the twentieth century. Democracy was, moreover, no longer the shining political objective it had been for progressives in the nineteenth century: fascism and communism now dominated the political scene and world attention was on militarism from right and left. Women's suffrage was being pushed down the agenda of national politics.

13

The enfranchisement
of the East

'Do you think the men of India will allow such a thing?'

Outside a government college in Allahabad in 1931 a small group of demonstrators gathered on the dusty road. They were led by a beautiful, pale-skinned, frail woman who addressed the indifferent students, urging them to boycott their studies in the national interest. Kamala Nehru was already showing signs of the tuberculosis that was to kill her within six years. Kamala's husband had been imprisoned by the British imperial authorities, along with many other men in the independence movement. Women therefore stepped forward to take their place, to call for a boycott of all things British. A ruddy-faced Parsi student, Feroze Gandhi with his laughing friends sat on a wall to watch this entertainment of a woman speaking in public, as they might watch a performing animal.

Suddenly, the heat and exertion overcoming her, Kamala fainted. Feroze was overwhelmed, rushed to get water and to tend to the fragile woman, and took her back to her home. The next day he left his college, enlisted as a Congress volunteer and became a permanent fixture in Kamala Nehru's home, attending to her every need personally and in her official capacity as president of the Allahabad District Congress committee. He would follow her as she travelled to the villages around Allahabad, walking just behind Kamala and carrying her lunch box as she spread her message of dissent and revolt.[1]

The emergence of such women on the political stage was a visible sign of the way in which the independence movement radicalized and brought women to the fore, ultimately leading to complete and equal female enfranchisement in the largest democracy in the world. As always, individual endeavour and sacrifice is inspiring, but the courageous women of India were moving at a time of tectonic shifts that were taking place in the political life of the nations of the East. These culminated in India, China, Japan and other populous nations, in the space of little more than a year in the middle of the twentieth century, in almost half the world's population of women being enfranchised.

Vassals to guardians

Prior to the independence movement the women who occur in histories of India are such anomalies as the occasional ruling woman: the Rani of Jhansi who fought the British in 1857–8; and the mothers of rulers acting as regent during the minority of an heir. J. S. Mill, who worked at the India Office, remarked that the evidence of these regencies gave him the impression that 'the natural capacity of women for government is very striking'.[2] However, for most women in India, up and into the twentieth century, the situation as observed by the British colonialists was described by Mill's father in his *History of British India*:

> A state of dependence more strict and humiliating than that which is ordained for the weaker sex among the Hindus cannot easily be conceived.... Nothing can exceed the habitual contempt which the Hindus entertain for their women. Hardly are they even mentioned in their laws, or other books, but as wretches of the most base and vicious inclinations, on whose nature no virtuous or useful qualities can be ingrafted.[3]

Obviously this speaks to the 'civilising mission' of imperialism but it was an image that Indian nationalists also used to justify their modernizing mission. Wealthy women, both Hindu and Muslim, were sequestered and the poor either accepted their lot or aspired to a condition in which the visibly active women of *their* families could be sequestered instead of working in the fields.

Electorally, few men voted in accordance with limited municipal franchises in the nineteenth century. Representation developed with the Morley–Minto reforms of 1909 allowing Indians to be elected to legislative councils; the Montagu–Chelmsford reforms of 1919 moving domestic policy (excepting finance and law and order) to elected representatives; and the Government of India Act of 1935 giving Indian provinces self-rule under state governors and parliaments. This was in line with a general trend towards colonial independence (the British had learned the lesson of the American Revolution) that was inscribed on the gateway to the Viceroy's Palace in Delhi: 'Liberty will not descend to a people, a people must raise themselves to liberty.' It was also a desire of the British to divest themselves of the burden of administering a nation of 353 million people (1931 census) with the hope that imperial links would be maintained, such as those with Canada, Australia, and New Zealand. These liberal aspirations were sabotaged by die-hard conservatives who predominated in Britain during the main decades of the independence movement, the 1920s to the early 1940s; and by impatient Indians frustrated at the slow rate of change; and by Indians who were using the independence movement for their own communal advantage. For none of them, the imperialists or any Indian faction, was female franchise an essential part of the programme.

The independence movement is best dated from the first meeting of the Congress Party of India in Bombay in 1885. Its prominent Indian leaders were to be western-educated lawyers such as Mohandas ('Mahatma') Gandhi, Jawaharlal ('Pandit') Nehru, Vallabhbhai ('Sardar') Patel, and Muhammad Ali Jinnah; though he was later to quit Congress. The initial aim of Congress was to pressure the British to give elite men in such professions as the law and civil service a say in the governance of the nation. As such, it had little to offer women excepting the benefit of enhanced status for women married to elite men. The independence movement was to bring women to the fore as part of the nationalist struggle.

Jawaharlal Nehru, who became the first prime minister of India, was educated at Harrow and at Trinity College, Cambridge, and was called to the bar by the Inner Temple. His two sisters were educated at home in Allahabad. However, during the independence campaign his sisters, his wife Kamala, his daughter Indira, and even at one point his deeply traditional (and completely uneducated) mother thrust themselves into the struggle. The image of the aged Swarup Nehru threatening to bare her breasts before the guns of her enemies is one of the compelling pictures of the independence movement.[4]

The independence movement first had a radicalizing effect on the middle class such as the Nehrus, then Gandhi's campaigning brilliance radicalized the poor. Concurrent with this was the effect on women of an atmosphere of challenge. Women were always involved in the tactics of the nationalist campaign—as both consumers and producers they were part of the 'swadeshi' movement to reject western imports and use home-grown products; and in the later 'khadi' movement to produce home-spun clothes. A change in the position of women was linked both to modernism and to nationalism. Modernism among Indians was influenced by advanced thinking in Britain and favoured education for women and a more public role outside the home. The involvement of such women as Annie Besant in the nationalist movement directly transplanted ideas and attitudes that had been honed on public platforms in London (where she advocated such issues as birth control) to the Indian stage. European reformers had claimed that the treatment of women was a marker of civilization; for example, James Mill wrote: 'The condition of the women is one of the most remarkable circumstances in the manners of nations. Among rude people, the women are generally degraded; among civilised people they are exalted.'[5] Such attitudes were widely held and ethnic Indian modernizers sought improvements along an agenda promoted by foreign critics: for widow remarriage, against sati and child-marriage (depending on which custom was prevalent in an area).

Nationalist thinkers looked for a better position in Indian society for the lawyers, civil servants, merchants, and others who were taking an increasing role but had little or no political power. To justify their intended status they built up a self-image of a glorious Hindu past in which the position of women had been high, as pure maidens or respectable mothers. Such a vision necessarily excluded the Muslim minority of India, whose leaders had been the previous conquerors of the country before the British. A comparatively small number of Muslims supported the nationalist movement, and some such as Jinnah were made to feel so uncomfortable they left Congress (ultimately to fight for a separate Muslim state). Hindu women were the traditional vehicles of spiritual values and were made in the nationalist conflict to represent the spiritual quality of national culture. This was therefore a Hindu version of the rise of the Victorian middle class and the domestic elevation of women to be unimpeachably pure. These two strains, the emancipation of women and the elevation of family life, came together in the nationalist movement with an emphasis on the education of the mother so she could raise children to serve the national cause. The nationalist ideal in this way served the cause of educating and therefore emancipating women.[6]

Part of the nationalist movement was still profoundly conservative. Bal Gangadhar Tilak, a leading nationalist and skilful journalist, bitterly opposed the Age of Consent Act which raised the age at which marriage could be consummated from 10 to 12, and which was introduced by the British after the death of a child bride from sexual injuries. Such interference with religion could not be tolerated; for championing such ancient Hindu practices, Tilak was given the title Lokamanya—Revered by the Nation.[7]

Effeminate men and strong women

By the early twentieth century women were breaking boundaries in the nationalist movement in the field of physical action. Bengali nationalist Sarala Devi Chaudhurani promoted a martial, heroic culture in opposition to the prevailing views of effeminate and weak Bengalis that associated all men from that culture with the supposed feminine characteristics of physical weakness and cowardice.

She was born Sarala Devi Ghosal in 1872, a member of the Tagore family which placed her among the Bengali literary and intellectual elite. Her father Janakinath Ghosal was one of the earliest secretaries of the Bengal Congress, her mother Swanakumari Devi was the first successful Bengali woman novelist, the elder sister of Nobel Prizewinner Rabindranath Tagore and daughter of 'Maharshi' Debendranath Tagore, a leader of the Hindu reforming society Brahmo Somaj. The Brahmo performed the same kind of networking and enabling function that the non-conformist church did for reforming movements in Britain. The Tagore family home at Jorasanko, where Sarala spent her childhood, became a place of intellectual pilgrimage for progressive Indians eager to discuss new social, scientific, and literary theories. Women's liberation, in terms of education and greater freedom from confinement in the home, had long been a theme of Brahmo thinking.

Sarala Devi had the rare privilege of education, graduating in English in 1890 from Bethune College and thus becoming one of only twenty-seven women in India who had degrees by the end of the nineteenth century. She had always been involved to some degree in the nationalist cause, and had led the chorus in a nationalist song she had composed at the Congress meeting in Calcutta in 1901. Her intense engagement in politics came with agitation over the partition of Bengal in 1905. This was clumsily handled by the British; the objective was administrative, but it was regarded as part of a political policy of 'divide and rule'. Sarala Devi's contribution was the formation of youth groups to stimulate heroism among Bengali youth. She promoted physical prowess through exercise, personal courage, and an attitude of self-respect that would brook no insult. To this end, she formed a club and a gymnasium linked to the nationalist cause. She would place a map of India before her new recruits and a red band around their wrists and call on them to promise they would serve India with their entire mind and body. In a symbolic binding of siblings, a sister would tie the band round her brother's wrist in an annual ceremony and he would promise always to protect her. Boys were taught boxing, sword fighting and games with knives and rods. Sarala Devi invented festivals in honour of Indian heroes in which muscular youths would compete; she was referred to as Bengal's Joan of Arc and likened to the goddess Durga who rode on a tiger to vanquish her enemies.

As only boys were members of the clubs she organized, she presents the image of a woman urging men to take up traditionally manly pursuits in the nationalist cause. As historian Bharati Ray says, 'at time when women were fighting for the right to vote in free England, a woman in colonial Bengal was struggling to initiate the men of her country into an ideology of courage and prowess.'[8] However, young women were to become highly active in Bengali terrorist acts such as the Chittagong Armoury Raid in 1930 and two schoolgirls shooting dead the District magistrate in 1932. Embracing violence was one way women could free themselves from the tyranny of their passive role, a route they would probably not have taken without Sarala's example.[9] Such an emergence is an interesting contrast to the supposedly feminine principle of non-violence promoted by Gandhi after 1916.[10]

Sarala Devi also founded the first women's organization in India, the Bharat Stree Mahamandal (Great Circle of Indian Woman) in Allahabad in 1910 dedicated to such practical rather than political objectives as women's education and access to medical facilities; soon there were eleven officers working for the organisation.[11] When her parents arranged a marriage for her in her absence when she was 33, she did not rebel; she was said to have accepted the marriage to please her dying mother. It does not appear to have been a bad marriage; she was to help her husband Rambhuj Dutta Chaudhury edit his nationalist Urdu weekly *Hindusthan*. In later life, under the influence of Gandhi, she was converted to non-violence (though her husband was not) and she later turned to religion.

Another Bengali, but on the other side of the communal divide, Rokeya Sakhawat Hossain, faced a far harder road to education and developed a more acute political sense. She was born in 1880 into an upper-class Muslim family in Pairaband, the second daughter of a rich landowner. The family practised not merely purdah, but a form of even more extreme sequestration, abarodh, where not only were men not allowed free entry into the

Figure 17. Nationalist agitation brought women to the fore in India. Here a woman addresses a meeting of Muslim men in 1927 in front of a banner saying 'All India Trade Union Congress'.

women's areas of the house, but girls had to conceal themselves even from women. 'From the age of five,' she wrote, 'I had to observe purdah even before ladies who were not family members.'[12] She was to write about the fear and misery of trying to remain concealed, as if her physical being were nothing at all.

She and her sister were probably taught some Arabic and Urdu at home so they could read the Koran and books of conduct literature respectively, but were not taught English or to read Bangla. Their brothers, however, were taught outside the home at St Xavier's, the premier English-speaking college. Rokeya's elder sister Karimunnessa learned Persian from her brothers and practised writing Bangla by scratching on the ground in the backyard of their house with a stick. When this transgression was discovered, she was quickly sent to her grandmother and then married off at the age of 14 before the dangerous process of education went too far in tainting her. The waste of potential in her sister's life became a prime motivating factor in Rokeya's career.

Rokeya's elder brother, Abdul Asad Ibrahim Saber, was a progressive who believed that Muslim women should be educated. After their father had gone to bed he and Rokeya would sit in candlelight with their books and he would instruct her in Bangla and English, despite the attempts of relatives to obstruct them. Later she was to dedicate her novel *Padmaraga* of 1924 to him: 'It is you who moulded me single-handedly . . . I know that you have been my only instructor.'[13] Abdul was to join the civil service and become a Deputy Magistrate. He performed another great service for Rokeya: he judged that an acquaintance of his, Syed Sakhawat Hossain, a London-educated district magistrate, was open-minded enough to make a good husband for his sister. He therefore arranged the marriage between 16-year-old Rokeya and Syed who was a widower in his late thirties. The couple settled in Bihar province and Syed encouraged Rokeya to write and to socialize with educated Christian and Hindu women. He taught her English and she taught him Bangla; they had two children but both of them died when only a few months old.

At the age of 22 Rokeya began to have articles about the condition of women published, with titles such as 'Jewellery, or Badge of Slavery'. Her most radical work, *Sultana's Dream*, was published in the *Ladies' Magazine* in 1905 (and as a book in 1908). Written in English, this utopian fantasy in the tradition of *Gulliver's Travels* describes the society in Ladyland where women rule and 'shy and timid' men are kept at home in the 'men's quarters'. Women roam about enjoying education and productive work while men perform menial tasks; women scientists ensure security through advanced weapons and travel by flying machines. Women's government is guided by the principles of truth, love, compassion, and welfare. As Bharati Ray says, it was a rebellion 'against the evils of a system that kept women subjugated, humiliated and subservient'.[14] She was to write other books distinguished by their biting sarcasm, such as *The Secluded Ones* of 1928, about the strict seclusion of women.

Syed died after eleven years of marriage and bequeathed a sum of money to fund a school for Muslim women. Rokeya opened the school in 1909, later moving it to Calcutta after property disputes with members of Syed's family. She was prepared to learn from other traditions and visited the Brahmo and Hindu schools to learn teaching methods. Rokeya resented purdah but had to accept it as a necessary evil in her school or Muslim families would not send their daughters there; as a result, she was obliged to collect pupils in a windowless 'purdah bus' though the heat was stifling.

In 1916 she founded the Anjuman-i-Khawatin-i-Islam, the Muslim Women's Association for the improvement of women's conditions. She argued that it was not Islam that had ordained the subjugation of women, but social customs and restrictions. Despite living at a time of revolt against the British, Rokeya was not a political activist in this field—Muslims generally judged that there was as much Hindu chauvinism as anti-imperialism in the nationalist movement. Rokeya was committed to the politics of gender: who ultimately was in charge of the country was less important than that women should have a share in that power. Consequently she was active in calling for women to have votes at whatever level the British were prepared to grant them, in sharp contrast to the nationalist women who subsumed a feminist objective under nationalist strategy. Rokeya died in December 1932; her last (unfinished) work was an essay called 'The Rights of Women'.

The Women's Indian Association

Also involved in lobbying the British for voting rights was Sarojini Naidu, a better-known champion of women whose experiences in England made her a rarity: an Indian woman who had travelled and met progressive thinkers abroad. She was born Sarojini Chattopadhyay in 1879 in Hyderabad where her father, a scientist and philosopher who had received his doctorate from Edinburgh University, was principal of Nizam's College. Sarojini's mother was a poet, musician, and dancer, and between them the couple made a cultured and happy home for their daughter who became a child prodigy: at the age of 12 she came first in the matriculation examination of Madras University. She had been groomed as a scientist but she became more interested in literature and began writing poetry, a volume of which was published in 1895 when she was 16. The previous year, however, she had fallen in love with Dr Muthyala Govindarajulu Naidu, the chief medical officer to the Nizam of Hyderabad, who was considered an unsuitable match for every reason: he was from a different region and linguistic tradition to herself and a different caste: she was a brahmin, he a sudra.

Caste should not have mattered as her family had progressive, Brahmo Samaj beliefs, but this match strained them. Her father could not countenance it and at the age of 16 she was sent to England on a scholarship, spending three years at Kings College, London, and Girton, Cambridge. While in England Sarojini became friends with some of the great literary figures of the day: W. B. Yeats; feminist writer Mathilde Blind; the critic and literary entrepreneur Edmund Gosse, who praised her work as India's most accomplished poet in English; and the decadent critic Arthur Symons. She wrote to Symons about her impossible love: 'I have spoilt his life for my sake . . . and it is this that makes my anguish intolerable—and I have hurt my father—I seem to bring nothing but pain to those for whom I would give my heart's blood.'[15] When she returned to India she must have prevailed upon her parents, as she married Dr Naidu in December 1898 in a civil ceremony. They had a happy and artistic home in which they brought up four children, one of whom, Padmaja, was to become governor of West Bengal.

In the early years of the twentieth century politics were to predominate in Sarojini's interests, and she mixed with such leading figures of the nationalist movement as Annie Besant, Nehru, and Gandhi, taking a prominent role in the 1906 Calcutta Congress. She took to the public stage on such issues as widow remarriage, the situation of dalits ('untouchables') and Hindu-Muslim unity.

When in 1917 the Secretary of State for India, Edwin Montagu, announced his intention to bring more Indians into the governing process, he and the Viceroy, Lord Chelmsford, toured India to listen to those who had views on a means of including more Indians in government. Sarala and the Bharat Srti Mahamandal applied to lobby on behalf of women's education, but were told the British government wanted to receive deputations only on political subjects.

Meanwhile other radical women were organizing in Indian politics. The Women's Indian Association was set up by merging the Tamil Women's Association with a women's improvement society. The latter had been started by Margaret Cousins who had experience of militant suffrage action, which had led to prison sentences in England and Ireland; and another Irish feminist, Dorothy Jinarajadasa (formerly Dorothy Graham), who married the Ceylonese-born chief international advocate of the Theosophical movement in 1916. Both women lived in Madras, the centre of the Theosophical Society to which they were attached. Theosophy was just one of a number of esoteric religious cults that have attracted westerners to India. Unusually, in this case its adherents wanted to make a positive contribution to Indian life and progress rather than merely work towards their own spiritual betterment.

The third Theosophist to take a leading role in women's suffrage in India was Annie Besant, a militant trade union organizer and birth control campaigner in England who had moved to India in 1893 and became president of the Theosophists in 1907. She set up the Home Rule League for Indian independence in 1916, feeling the Congress was being too soft on the British, and was imprisoned for three months shortly afterwards.

By 1917 the Women's Indian Association was active, with Annie Besant as president and Margaret Cousins as secretary. Dorothy Jinarajadasa toured south India to inspire women to set up local branches. Their original objective was to lobby the Secretary of State and the Viceroy on educational and other issues affecting women, but when it was clear only political representations would be heard, the deputation's draft was changed to address 'opportunities for political service' though Margaret Cousins herself was sceptical: 'I thought it would be a century before Indian women would understand, or be interested in political matters,' she wrote.[16]

Other members of the team which saw Montagu and Chelmsford in Madras on 15 December 1917, were Ramabai Ranade, Herabai Tata, and Uma Nehru (Jawaharlal's cousin-in-law); Lady Abala Bose sent a telegram. The team was led by Sarojini Naidu. They argued for the status of 'people' in a self-governing nation within the empire, that is: whatever rights were extended to men, should automatically include women also.

Montagu asked, 'Do you think that the men of India will allow such a thing?' Sarojini Naidu responded that far from objecting to the rights being granted to women, Indian men would support them.[17] Historian Geraldine Forbes has pointed out that women's enfranchisement became an issue which nationalist men could encourage. They did not want to hear about the evils of patriarchy, as they felt this was women being disloyal to Indian culture, but 'Franchise and civil rights were ideal issues for women to pursue since discussions of them could take place without reference to sensitive social or cultural matters.'[18] Thus the Indian women neatly side-stepped the morass into which English suffragists waded, of arguing about what social changes the vote would allow them to make; for the Indians it was right for women to have the vote, what they might do with it was a matter for another day and another place.

Sarojini Naidu caused a stir with her delegation to the Secretary of State, which came to be called the Votes for Women Delegation; now other franchise activists set about gaining support from established political bodies. In 1918 positive resolutions were passed by the provincial Congress conferences of Madras and Bombay, the India Home Rule League, and the Muslim League. The issue was presented to Congress in Bombay in August 1918 by

Sarojini Naidu who calmed the fears of those who felt the vote would erode femininity with, 'We ask for the vote, not that we might interfere with you in your official functions, your civic duties, your public place and power, but rather that we might lay the foundation of national character in the souls of the children that we hold upon our laps, and instil into them the ideas of nationality.'[19] This unusual argument—that women wanted political power not to exercise it but to act better in the domestic sphere—must have impressed the audience as the resolution to give the franchise to women on the same basis as to men was passed by a large majority.

Women were making considerable inroads, in December 1917 Annie Besant was elected president of the Indian National Congress, the first women to take the post (and one of only two Europeans, the other being Nellie Sengupta in 1931). Sarojini Naidu was elected president in 1925. At the same Congress session where Annie Besant was elected president, Sarala Devi Chaudhurani presented the resolution supporting the vote for women.

The Women's Indian Association had been careful to frame their objectives in nationalist terms. Their headed notepaper described their objects, starting with: 'To present to women their responsibility as daughters of India. To help them to realise that the future of India lies largely in their hands; for as wives and mothers they have the task of training and guiding and forming the character of the future rulers of India.' Local Congress committees in all parts of India had been approached to urge them to pass an equal rights resolution. All had with the exception of the Burma committee (Burma was an administrative part of the British Raj); Dorothy Jinarajadasa remarked that the Mandalay Committee had passed it but the Rangoon committee demurred.[20]

Montagu himself had told Millicent Fawcett that it was up to Indian women to make a strong case to the Southborough Franchise Committee that was deliberating on the details of franchise through 1918, and she knew him to be a suffragist who had given loyal support in the House of Commons, so she advised the Women's Indian Association which set about petitioning the committee.[21] Dorothy Jinarajadasa was able to tell the committee she represented forty-three branches of the Indian Women's Association with more than 1,400 members. She drew attention to the Indian National Congress motion saying sex should not be a reason for exclusion from the franchise, showing how important nationalist support was to the women's movement. In an optimistic address referring to the war that had ended less than two weeks previously she said, 'The era in the West of the rule of men alone has ended in chaos; now is the beginning of the era of nations ruled by *all* their people, men and women together, and the day of physical force is over, for women will bring the spiritual soul force into the affairs of state government, into economic and commercial life.'[22]

The results were disappointing: though the petitions were received, Lord Southborough concluded that Indian women did not want the vote and even if they did, social custom (purdah) would impede its implementation.[23] The response to women's franchise was therefore to sidetrack the issue, to the fury of Indian women who had been campaigning. The Women's Indian Association decided to send a delegation, consisting of Annie Besant and Sarojini Naidu, to London where the Joint Select Committee of the British parliament was refining proposals for Indian government reform. At the same time, Sir C. Sakaran Nair, a member of the Southborough Franchise Committee who had been in the minority in supporting women's franchise, met the Bombay Women's Committee for Women's Suffrage and advised them also to send a delegation to London. Consequently Herabai and Mithan Tata, wife and daughter of a Parsi businessman (not the great industrialist of the same name) travelled to London. This was a formidable, sophisticated delegation which was now at the centre of the empire and able to call on wider support. Millicent Fawcett, president of the National Union of Women's Suffrage Societies, and Carrie Chapman Catt, president of the International Woman Suffrage Alliance, lent their weight to the Indian women's cause. Representations were sent by the Indian National Congress, the Home Rule League, and the Muslim League.

The women's delegation argued for full electoral equality with men; women would be a powerful force for progress in India, argued Sarojini Naidu. Annie Besant, knowing that memories of suffragette activism were fresh in the minds of her listeners, suggested that if their demands were not met, Indian women might turn militant and provoke active police intervention, which would stimulate Indian men to act to defend their women. Whether this lurid scenario was actually believed (Indian women had shown no propensity to militancy in their own cause, only under the nationalist banner) the women's submissions probably swung the balance because, though Lord Montagu did not concede, he at least baulked at refusing a women's franchise when property–owning or taxpaying men over 21 were given the franchise.

The Joint Committee decided not to make a final decision on women, but to leave the responsibility for this to the Legislative Council for each province of India: women possessing the necessary qualifications 'might be admitted to registration as electors by resolution of the legislative body concerned'.[24] In a pattern familiar from other nations of concessions being granted first in local elections, Madras took the lead in removing the sex disqualification for legislative franchise in 1921.

In Bengal in 1921 a resolution to permit women to vote was defeated in the Legislative Council amid arguments about women's natural incapacity to be involved in politics and the neglect of husbands and children that would follow the granting of the vote; but women gained the right to vote in the Calcutta municipal election in 1923. Bolstered by this, a delegation including Rokeya Hossain went to the Viceroy Lord Lytton, unsuccessfully calling for women's right to vote in all elections. In 1925 after a political change on the Bengal Legislature resulting in a nationalist majority, they approved female suffrage, and in 1926 women exercised this right for the first time. By the end of 1930 all provinces had enfranchised women, often after local campaigning that mixed anti-colonialism with a nostalgia for a fabled ancient Hindu society; at a mass meeting in Bihar one of the resolutions claimed that the denial of women's political rights was a 'purely modern and Western importation' and the enfranchisement of women symbolized the restoration of ancient rights of Indian womanhood.[25] With the franchise on a property qualification, and many Indians being landless, relatively few men were enfranchised on the basis of these electoral reforms of 1919, and far fewer women, but there was clearly an advance in principle.

The Government of India Act and independence

Another round of reform began almost immediately, in keeping with the British government's intention to develop self-government in India. They set up the Simon Commission in 1927 to advise on a new India Act. Congress boycotted the commission because it did not have any Indians among its seven members—a petulant approach to an admittedly crass action by the British, and one that was self-defeating as they were merely excluded from a process that would happen with or without them. The Women's Indian Association had been willing to make representation to the Simon Commission as had other nationalist women's organizations. They went along with Congress, however, and were rewarded for their loyalty to nationalism with the Nehru Report of 1928, named from the Congress committee chaired by Jawaharlal Nehru's father Motilal. This demanded dominion status for India and formed the template for the political structure of future independent India, insisting on universal adult franchise and equal rights for women. It also enshrined the notion of a separate electorate with reserved seats for Muslims, to safeguard their rights in what would be a predominantly Hindu independent India. The report was, of course, nothing but the Congress movement's policy document and was binding on no one, but Congress had laid down a marker and it would be difficult to renege on this position when some measure of independence came.

After the Simon Commission, with a new Labour government in power, the British held a Round Table Conference in London, in November 1930. Again, the leading women's organizations were expected to boycott the meeting, in this case because Congress disagreed with the terms of the conference which was only prepared to commit to discussing giving India dominion status (Congress thought the principle of independence should be conceded in advance).

Boycotting the Simon Commission and the London conference that followed it was a difficult decision for the nationalist women who lost an opportunity to influence the next constitutional measure. Other women did attend, however, and for the first time put the case for reserved seats and a separate electorate for women, something that appealed to Muslim women who argued it would be impossible for them to campaign freely in a mixed electorate. This was against the principles of the Women's Indian Association and other activists who proposed universal adult franchise; they did not want a 5 per cent reservation for women, but equal rights; their absence from the conference table allowed the reservation idea to take hold.

The absence of a strong voice for Indian feminism also left the way open for British reformers to propose their own measures for Indian women's self-improvement. Independent MP Eleanor Rathbone, the successor to Millicent Fawcett as Britain's most prominent feminist activist, saw part of the imperial mission as the improvement of conditions for women and children in colonial properties. Profoundly influenced by the most negative portrayals of Indian women, she visited India in 1932 and wrote a book, *Child Marriage: An Indian Minotaur*, where she described the subjection of Indian women in a manner that did not endear her to progressive Indian feminists.

Rathbone decided that the solution for India's problems was the enfranchisement of women. She cultivated successive secretaries of state for India and set up the British Committee for Indian Women's Franchise with a press conference on 5 May 1933, representing eleven women's societies. This was largely a vehicle for Eleanor Rathbone who saw a progressive enlightenment of Indian women through education and public activity. She urged Indian women to drop their demand for universal franchise and argued for a literacy qualification, reserved seats, and special wives' qualifications. The inclusion of such provisions in the Government of India Act as eventually passed is a demonstration of the extent of her success in lobbying and introducing amendments in Westminster during the bill's final stages.[26]

Women were engaged with the intensification of the agitation for independence in the later 1920s and early 1930s, including Sarojini Naidu who went to the USA to plead the cause of Indian independence in a coast to coast lecture tour, claiming a common heritage with America in breaking free from the British; she accompanied Gandhi on the famous Salt Act march to Dandi; and she suffered imprisonment five times. Women were restive in Congress; male Congress leaders acknowledged that they had played their part in the civil disobedience movement but were unwilling to let them go further. Sarala Devi said in 1931 that Congress had 'assigned to women the position of law-breakers only and not law-makers'.[27] There were 4,859 women convicted for civil disobedience in 1932–3, less than 5 per cent of the total, but still a notable figure.[28] Geraldine Forbes comments that the Congress hierarchy 'Left women out of the major discussions, yet counted on complete solidarity'.[29] Gandhi, a profoundly conservative individual on most matters, resented women's petitioning the British government for the franchise; he felt the timing was wrong and the issue was divisive. He urged them to abandon the vote and instead work with men in the national interest.[30]

Gandhi engineered a peace pact with the Viceroy Lord Irwin and a second Round Table conference was held in London in 1931, with Indian women represented by Sarojini Naidu. The women called for universal suffrage with mixed general electorates and no special status, reserved seats, nomination, or cooption for women. They asked for 'equality and no privileges' and 'a fair field and no favour'.[31] A White Paper was finally produced recommending an increase in enfranchising women at a rate of one for every ten men, with details to be worked out by a Franchise Committee. The united women's organizations reiterated a demand for adult franchise but, as they had to make a positive recommendation, opted for the enfranchisement of literate and urban women.

The Franchise Committee accepted that women must have a role in Indian political life but fudged the proposals to increase the female electorate. In the legislation as enacted wives could vote in some provinces, literate women or the wives of military officers in others, and all these votes were to take place in special electorates for women. Male Congress leaders accepted this rag-bag of compromises without consulting the women's organizations.

Incorporating these changes (and a separate electorate for Muslims) the 1935 Government of India Act, coming into effect in 1937, gave Indian provinces self-government. Congress stood for election and formed governments in six provinces; women won fifty-six of the 1,500 seats in provincial legislatures. Vijaya Lakshmi Pandit, Jawaharlal Nehru's sister, became health minister in Uttar Pradesh, perhaps the most senior elected position yet held by a woman in any country.

Unsuccessful attempts were made at a reform of marriage legislation but national and international politics now took centre stage. Congress withdrew from government in 1939, in pique at not having been consulted over the involvement of India in the Second World War. After a period of unrest, the war ended with another Labour government in power in Britain, and independence was conceded. The Secretary of State for India was Frederick Pethick-Lawrence, now a Labour peer. India became independent on 15 August 1947 with Muslim majority areas seceding to form East and West Pakistan.

In India, women's participation in the independence movement, however galling some of the positions they had been expected to adopt, now paid off in goodwill and clarity of aims. Fate played a hand in giving Jawaharlal Nehru as prime minister the upper hand in faming the constitution, when the traditionalists Gandhi and Patel died shortly after independence (from assassination and heart attack respectively). Nehru was not just a western-educated modernizer, he was attracted to independent women, having close relationships with Lady Edwina Mountbatten and Padmaja Naidu. He appointed Vijaya Lakshmi Pandit as Indian ambassador to the UN, and (his wife Kamala having died at the age of 37 in 1936) had his formidable daughter Indira living with him to take up state duties as his consort from 1946 until his death in 1964. Building on her experiences, Indira later became a highly successful prime minister. She had married Feroze Gandhi, who had first met her mother when she fainted outside the government college; he became a radical member of parliament.

Added to the goodwill and sense of modernity about the new constitution, the all-powerful Congress, now the Congress Party, felt a genuine debt
to women. As Bharati Ray said, 'It was the willingness and spontaneous participation of women in the freedom struggle that finally tilted the balance
in favour of political equality between the two sexes in the Constituent
Assembly.'[32] Once again women were to win enfranchisement as a result of
their visible and active participation in a nationalist struggle, as they first had
in Europe in Finland.

The constitution Nehru's government introduced declared equality before
the law and equal opportunities in public employment between men and
women. It was a fundamental principle of modern India that all Indians were
equal and that the nation was secular. Reservations disappeared with universal
franchise in 1949 in the Constituent Assembly where women who themselves
had benefited from reserved seats argued against them. The dominion parliament constitution of 1950 came into effect on 26 January 1950.

Sarojini Naidu died in Lucknow as governor of the province in 1949; but
Margaret Cousins lived to see the 1951–2 election, the first in which women
voted on an equal basis with men—forming half of the vast electorate of
more than 173 million.

The Buddhist vote

India's story of development from colony to independent nation has been
often told, not least by its participants at the time it was happening, though
the women's suffrage element has received little attention. The influence of
Indian nationalist thought on the surrounding nations contributed to even
earlier enfranchisements than in India itself, in a sub-continental working
out of the theory that women's enfranchisement develops first in the more
remote and less politically sophisticated areas.

Ceylon (Sri Lanka after 1972) had a similar ethnic background to India
but enjoyed the considerable influence of Buddhism, which was prepared to
grant women a higher status than elsewhere. There was a comparatively high
estimation of women going back to the warrior queens. Women enjoyed a
respect for their spiritual capacities which was absent in Hinduism; Buddha
himself ordained women.[33] The Buddhist majority saved Ceylon from the
social evils that had cursed Indian women such as widow burning (sati),
purdah, child marriage, and a ban on widow remarriage.

This respect manifested itself in a high literacy rate among middle-class girls; as the *Buddhist Schools Magazine* put it in 1895, 'If they receive proper education, women of the East will no doubt become as prominent as those of the Western countries.'[34] In most eastern nations the idea of women aspiring to be prominent would have been abhorrent.

The island had been ruled in its entirety by the British from 1815, with the only semblance of democracy being the governor's consultation with Sinhalese aristocratic families. A native middle class and working class were developing at the end of the century; their public activities took the usual forms of industrial unrest among the working class and the demand for political rights among the middle class. Suffrage was granted to middle-class men in 1912 which, as in European nations, stimulated women to call for the franchise on the same terms.

A Women's Franchise Union was set up in 1927 enjoying the support of professional women, particularly those who had been involved in education. The meeting was chaired by Lady Dias Bandaranaike, mother of future prime minister Solomon Dias Bandaranaike, and mother-in-law of the world's first woman prime minister, Sirimavo Bandaranaike. Lady Dias' husband had been one of the most prominent allies of the British. Indeed, the family was referred to as 'lackeys of the British, and flunkeys at the governor's "court"'.[35] This did them no harm at all when they were promoting democratic values that the British could respect.

In keeping with this gradualist process that the Ceylonese practised, Lord Donoughmore was asked by the British to head a commission to determine means of future reform. Donoughmore was a Liberal peer best known for championing the rights of women in higher education. The Donoughmore Commission recommended a limited franchise to women over 30 (as Britain had under the 1918 Act). The Ceylon Legislative Council, however, was prepared to go even further and took up a proposal for universal suffrage for all over the age of 21. This went through in 1931, just three years after British women gained the vote on the same terms.

Burma was in a comparable position as a British colony with a Buddhist heritage. Margaret Cousins had been able to say in 1922 that 'Burmese women are possibly the freest women in the East, taken all round. They have the business of the country almost entirely in their own hands, and the standard of female education is also very high amongst them. They are fettered by neither caste system, purdah nor early marriage.'[36] This was a rather rosy picture of Burmese life but it is the case that, in 1923 when Burma was still a province of India and under British rule, men and women were given the franchise on equal terms on the basis of taxation. However, only men were obliged to pay a poll tax, so there were many more male taxpayers than female and this was hardly equality. This measure of democracy was introduced in order to head off a burgeoning home rule movement. It was to some extent a nationalist agitation on the Indian model, though with ethnic aspects as the Burmese rejected Indian settlers along with the British. Women were conspicuous; as the governor complained in 1923, 'the influence of women on politics in many countries has made for nationalism, and so far as I can gather it is making for it in Burma.'[37]

Women were still barred from standing for election to the legislature, however, and nationalists resented this influence on the rightful province of the Burmese legislators. A resolution was made to the legislative council to remove the prohibition on women in 1927, but it was opposed by the British, further fuelling resentment and a women's demonstration in Rangoon. The clause was eventually removed in 1929 and a new constitution in 1937 gave women the vote on the basis of a literacy test.

The constitution was dissolved when the Japanese invaded in 1942 but after British reoccupation and independence, women were fully enfranchised in 1948. It was, however, to a nation born in blood, in which non-Burmese minorities were threatened and where factional infighting destroyed what democracy was achieved.

Beauty queen suffrage in the Philippines

The US took up the 'white man's burden' of colonialism with the purchase of the Philippines from Spain after the Spanish–American war of 1898. The Filipinos conducted a guerrilla war for their independence and won a representative assembly in 1902, with full manhood suffrage in 1907.

During this time of agitation for democracy for men, and national upheaval, female suffrage became prominent, as was usual. Women's movements had concentrated on social welfare and charity work; until in 1905 the Asociación Feminista Filipina was founded by Concepción Felix. The association campaigned to appoint women to municipal and provincial posts and worked on social welfare, with suffrage as one of a number of goals. In 1906 the first organization to set women's suffrage as a main goal, the Asociación Feminista Ilonga was founded by Pura Villanueva, who saw no contradiction between her role as a feminist activist and that of beauty queen—she was Carnival Queen of Manilla in 1908. Her public appearances may have focused on clothes and make-up, but Villaneuva was no stranger to feminist rhetoric; in her memoir of the suffrage campaign Villaneuva remarks on the founding of a feminist magazine, *Filipina*, in 1909 with objectives including 'to revindicate the rights of women' in a reference to Wollstonecraft's work.[38]

The Philippine women's movement hosted a visit from Carrie Chapman Catt and Aletta Jacobs in 1912 which helped to motivate 'hesitant suffragists' and a new organization was formed, the Women's Club of Manila, that reinvigorated the suffrage movement, and between 1912 and 1918 four franchise bills were unsuccessfully introduced.

The most important hurdle to overcome in the Philippines was not the reluctance of men to grant suffrage to women, but of women to be concerned about it. Historian Mina Roces notes that during 1913–27 both of the incumbent American governor-generals supported women's suffrage, but the National Federation of Women's Clubs did not put the issue on their agenda until 1921.[39] The President of the National Federation was another former beauty queen, Trinidad Fernandez Legarda, who was editor of the Federation's magazine, *The Woman's Outlook*.

Women had been allowed into universities in 1908; the suffrage movement increased in success only when more women gained education and worked in the professions; and when suffragists started broadening the class and regional base of the movement by holding rallies and lobbying the press. A leading figure was, as was common in suffrage campaigns elsewhere, the first women to become a doctor, Maria Paz Mendoza-Guazon, who organized the Women Citizens League.

A bill to give women the vote was passed in 1933 and there were appropriate celebrations and medals struck, but a constitutional convention drafted the following year omitted women's suffrage. After concerted lobbying the convention decided on a plebiscite on women's suffrage, with voting only by women, who would be granted suffrage if 300,000 women voted for it. The requirement was so high that it 'practically guaranteed failure'.[40]

Urged by Concepción Felix and other feminists, and organized by the National Federation of Women's Clubs, more than half a million women registered to vote and 447,725 voted in favour in spring 1937, after which women finally were given the vote on the same basis as men.

The movement has been criticized as being led by the middle class and enjoying the blessing of the American colonial government, used as an instrument of political consolidation of American rule in the islands.[41] Certainly, the opposition to it did not come from the Americans, but from Filipino men and from women who were apathetic or opposed: even in 1937 more than 80,000 women who had registered to vote failed to turn out to support the franchise, and 44,307 went to the ballot to vote against.[42] Historian Kumari Jayawardena remarks how the women's movement was primarily orientated towards achieving legal equality, they do not appear to have questioned the subordinate position of women in the family and society.[43] The suffrage victory was celebrated by Pura Villanueva as 'the triumph of western dynamic civilisation over the traditional sheepish civilisation of the orient'.[44] Villanueva's daughter, Maria Kalaw, followed her mother's example to become carnival queen and a suffragist; she went to university, began a career as a journalist and in the 1950s became a senator.

Bombs and votes in China

Teenage revolutionary Tcheng Soumay sat with her suitcase full of explosives in an express train on the Mukden line between Tientsin and Peking. Tcheng had been brought up with dreams of Mulan, the girl-warrior who had dressed as a man to fight in battle; myths supplemented in adolescence by the vision of a modern China, a democracy with the strength to resist its foreign enemies. She wanted a land where girls would not be intentionally crippled and forced into marriages, where men and women would be equals.

For three months twice a week she had made the journey from Tientsin to Peking lugging heavy bags of explosives. Now the train boy came in and said the suitcase was too large to travel as hand luggage, it would have to be taken to the baggage car. If he picked it up, its weight would betray her. She had often tipped the boy and was now able to persuade him to leave the suitcase alone, she would speak to the conductor about it.

When one of the conductors came, Tcheng recognized him with relief as a man she knew well: 'as he entered the compartment, I greeted him with great cordiality and immediately plunged him into a lot of questions regarding the welfare of his family to distract his attention from the suitcase... how was his good wife? His bright little son?' They spoke at length, and eventually the conductor left without asking about the suitcase.[45] She told the boy the conductor had allowed her to keep it.

Relieved, Tcheng sat back, then became aware of another danger: from the direction of the suitcase at her feet came a series of hissing and sputtering noises. Tcheng Soumay knew nothing about dynamite, only that it would be used to destroy Yuan Shih-kai and the enemies of progress. 'Now I was convinced that my hour had come,' she wrote,

> the bombs were getting ready to go off, and there wasn't a thing I could do about it but sit there and wait: I was really frozen with fear, but in a few moments my chaotic thoughts began to resolve themselves in heroic form. I had wonderful, tragic visions of my friends and family grieving for me ('she was so young to die') and of the Koumintang in the South hearing the news of my sacrifice; in my mind there was a vivid picture of Dr Sun Yat-sen commemorating a memorial to Soumay Tcheng, Girl Patriot of Peking.

Tcheng survived this ordeal, but was so distraught when she arrived home that her mother was suspicious and Tcheng felt obliged to tell her about her revolutionary activities. The older woman was horrified, but Tcheng Soumay talked to her about the ideals of the new China, and far from betraying her to older members of the family, her mother agreed to help her daughter and her fellow revolutionaries in any way she could.

Chinese suffragettes

Women's political action in China was always connected with nationalism and the sense that the subjection of women was a hindrance to the progress of the nation. The bound feet of the middle and upper-class women were taken to symbolize the backwardness of Chinese society: China could not grow strong while boys spent their early years in the company of ignorant, footbound women; bound feet were both a literal crippling and a symbol of their limitations. As a reformer wrote, 'I look at the Europeans and Americans, so strong and vigorous because their mothers do not bind feet.'[46] This attitude to women can be contrasted with that of Britain or France where the maintenance of women in their unchanging traditional roles was considered by the establishment to be an integral part of the national and imperial mission.

Unlike the West, in China women's issues were not marginalized: as historian Roxane Witke said, 'issues of women's emancipation crossed sexual lines and evoked a depth of commitment in both sexes which might better be compared with . . . campaigns for racial equality than with the women's suffrage movement in the west.'[47] Women were therefore a part of the revolutionary equation in 1911 at the time of the overthrow of the Quing Dynasty and the founding of the Chinese Republic. There was, as often in revolutionary movements, a racial element: the Quings were Manchu, their defeat meant the restoration of Han Chinese rule; women were referred to as the slaves of men while men were enslaved by the foreign (Manchu) oppressors.[48] Women joined revolutionary movements and formed fighting corps, smuggling arms and planting explosives. Some fought at the front in all-women forces such as the Women's Murder Squad and the Amazon Corps of the Dare to Die Soldiers.[49] This latter group was sworn to eliminate people who were obstacles to democratic government; Tcheng Soumay in her dynamite smuggling operation was part of the Dare to Die unit.

Tcheng Soumay was born to a wealthy family in Canton in 1896. Her father was a government official, her mother was the daughter of a general. Always a rebellious child, she refused to have her feet bound, ripping off the bandages that would have crippled her. Her father encouraged her inquiring intellect and, wanting to take her around in public with him, dressed her as a boy.

She gave huge offence to her family and that of her fiancé (whom she had not met) when she wrote to this indolent young man telling him he should marry someone more to his taste, as she intended to go abroad to finish her studies. The family had to be rid of her after this disgrace, and her punishment was just what she wanted—to be sent to a boarding school run by American missionaries. She started to wear her hair and clothes in an imitation of western styles.

Hearing of the anti-Manchu and pro-democracy ideas of students who had studied abroad, in 1911 she persuaded her father to allow her to study in Tokyo which was the centre of radical expatriate Chinese activity. As she put it in her autobiography, 'I became an active revolutionary at the age of fifteen.'[50] She joined the nationalist Kuomintang, meeting Sun Yat-sen and swearing a revolutionary oath to establish a democratic regime in China or die fighting for it. Returning to China, she was able to use her inconspicuous appearance to good purpose, receiving mail for the rebels.

The revolution of 1911 led to the creation of two rival power bases; a provisional government was set up in Nanking on 1 January 1912 with Sun Yat-sen as president, but the north of the country was still in the hands of the Manchus, nominally under the five-year-old emperor, but in fact controlled by general Yuan Shih-kai, as imperial prime minister.

Tcheng Soumay volunteered to carry dynamite to be used to assassinate leading Manchu functionaries, including Yuan, who were based in Peking. An attempt on Yuan failed, but a leading general was killed with dynamite Tcheng had carried. When the 16-year-old heard the first of these explosions she said, 'In my jubilance I pulled out my gun and fired it in the air— just for the sheer fun of it'—then she got her hand stuck in the gun's mechanism.[51]

The boy-emperor was induced to abdicate February 1912 and a republic was declared. Yuan Shih-kai became president, side-stepping Sun Yat-sen who agreed to hand over authority in the interests of national unity. The political position of women became part of the debate about the form which a constitution should take in the new, republican China. Women's suffrage thus came to the fore at a time of national upheaval and constitutional change, a pattern seen also in women's enfranchisement in Europe and India.

Women's military organizations were disbanded, and many turned into associations arguing for the vote. One of the first suffrage associations in China was set up by Tang Qunying in Peking soon after the revolution of 1911. The Chinese Suffragette Society had the principal aim of gaining the right to vote, but additionally embraced the abolition of foot-binding, concubinage, child marriage, and prostitution and encouraged modesty in dress. Tang Qunying had been born in 1871, her father had been in the military but he retired from the army to devote himself to educating his children. In the revolution Tang Qunying organized a unit called the Women's Northern Attack Brigade and led the women in the battle to take Nanking. Like other revolutionaries, Tang Qunying studied in Japan, where she developed an international perspective on women and politics that led to her being influenced by the British suffragettes. Her organization published magazines with translations of foreign articles and stories about western suffrage activities, feeding what seemed an insatiable appetite for news of hunger strikes, demonstrations, and the firing of letter boxes. Chinese women learned the lesson of activism: Tang was said to have smashed up a newspaper office in her own province after they published a libel about her.[52]

Women's groups from eighteen provinces met in Nanking in 1912 to establish the Women's Suffrage Alliance that lobbied the National Assembly

Figure 18. A Chinese suffragist using her unbound foot to kick a policeman during a demonstration in Nanjing in 1912. The caption reads: 'If a woman can kick down a policeman, this woman must be extraordinarily brave and powerful. I have drawn a picture to show this.'

over three days while its members, under Sun Yat-sen's guidance, were constructing a democratic framework for China. Tang led a deputation to the building where the National Assembly was meeting: when they refused to consider giving women the vote and formally recognize the equality of the sexes, Tang Qunying and her Chinese Suffragettes joined with the Women's Suffrage Association to launch an assault which lasted three days in March 1912. The women forced themselves into the parliament building and remained there, insisting they would see the president of the Assembly. When they were refused and expelled they smashed windows and other property and attacked the police. The next day they were joined by another group, the Women's Suffragette Society, and the government was obliged to bring in troops to clear them out. Sun Yat-sen did write to Tang Qunying expressing his support for women's suffrage, but advising her that the goal was a long-term one.[53]

Aletta Jacobs met Chinese activists on her travels in 1912 and made some rather disparaging remarks:

> The Chinese women's movement, such as it was, lacked any form of organisation or unity of purpose, and it had appropriated the militant methods of the English suffragettes. When I asked these women why they had chosen

such a radical approach, I was surprised to hear that, instead of reporting on feminism throughout the world, the Chinese press had reported only on the campaign tactics of English suffragettes. No wonder that, when Chinese women began to demand their rights, their first action was to break all the windows of a parliament building.[54]

Jacobs often smartens up her anecdotes for her memoirs, but she is accurate that the Chinese were probably the only feminist movement to follow the Emmeline Pankhurst line and adopt the destruction of property as a tactic for women's enfranchisement. Several women's organizations added 'suffragette' to their names after reading of the WSPU's activities. Suffrage activists were drawn, as in other counties in the early stages of protest, from a narrow strata of urban, elite, educated women. As historian Elizabeth Croll says, their departure from tradition ensured maximum publicity, 'but their activities were more conspicuous than widespread'.[55]

The suffragists looked to the West for new ideas, and the West reciprocated the sentiment. In a suffrage parade in New York in 1912 a prominent banner read 'Catching Up With China', an allusion to reports that nationalists in one of China's provincial legislatures had declared women enfranchised.[56] This was, in fact, Canton (Guandong), where the provisional government had promised women the vote then went back on their pledge; women sent deputations, held protest meetings, and invaded the legislature, but to no avail. There were similar protests in Beijing where the provincial assembly was besieged.

President Yuan harboured dreams of grandeur, increasing his personal authority and having himself proclaimed emperor in 1915. Under Yuan's rule women's movements were crushed, magazines were banned, and laws were passed forbidding women to join political groups. A warrant was issued for Tang Qunying's arrest and she was thought to have been executed but in fact she went back to her home village. 'China had shown the world the way in dealing with the suffragettes,' a Chinese newspaper reported.[57] Activists in other countries were anxious about the fate of their Chinese colleagues, attempting to trace them for years afterwards; Mary Sheepshanks from the International Woman Suffrage Alliance wrote in 1919, 'Miss Sophie Chang in Shanghai was the secretary of the National Women's Suffrage Association but nowadays we get no reply to our letters from China, and we heard vaguely that Miss Chang had been beheaded or imprisoned for her progressive notions.'[58] Tcheng Soumay was warned by a policeman that Yuan's agents were coming to get her and left her home in Peking. She later went to study law in France with which she felt an empathy because of its revolutionary heritage.

After would-be emperor Yuan's death in 1916 the 'Nanking Constitution' was revived but there was no effective central government until 1927 when the Kuomintang was strong enough (now with Soviet aid, and with the involvement of the Chinese Communist Party) to move against the warlords and establish a government. Over this period of political turmoil from 1916 a cultural renaissance developed in which every aspect of Chinese traditional life was questioned. In 1900 some 400 new periodicals appeared, among them women's magazines of various stages of radicalism, influenced by visits by western feminists and reporting on such issues as birth control and motherhood.[59] Advanced writers such as Lu Xun played the part in China that Shaw and Ibsen did in Europe, presenting challenges to traditional notions of female inferiority and the sexual double standard. Women bobbed their hair, dressed in approximations of western women's dress, or adopted male dress and smoked pipes.

Western ideas had been at the centre of the women's suffrage movement and western liberalism was seen as the solution to China's problems. This approach fell into disfavour as a result of the Versailles peace settlement, the terms of which discredited the policies of arch liberal Woodrow Wilson. Chinese patriots were disgusted to be told that former German possessions in China were not to be subject to 'national self-determination' but they were allowed to be taken by Japan: western liberals were more interested in placating Japan than fairness to China. This began a distancing from western liberalism so that women's political participation and women's suffrage became not an extension of western ideas, but an assertion of Chinese nationalism—particularly in response to Japanese aggression.

As the international situation worsened, and the threat from Japan increased, the feminist argument became subsumed in nationalist rhetoric and the rise of the Chinese Communist Party. The issue of women and communist thinking was worked out by the young Mao Tse-tung who was born in 1893 in Hunan. Mao was from an upper peasant family, he resented his father's tyrannical manner and found refuge with his sympathetic mother, who was also persecuted. When Mao was 13 his father arranged a marriage for him; Mao ran away from home until his father retracted his threat to force him to consummate the marriage.

Mao studied in the provincial capital of Hunan, Changsha, where he was impressed by the vigour of the student movement and particularly the engagement of girl students who were active in resistance to the warlord government and to the menace of Japan. 'Even before Mao had become fully politicised, he had begun to take a strong stand on issues affecting women,' Jayawardena observed, who noted he was the first world leader who in early life put women's issues at the centre of his thought.[60]

Mao was involved in 1918 in organizing the New People's Study Society that engaged revolutionary students in discussion about change in China; and the Society for Work and Study in France that helped Chinese students, including women, to go to France to be exposed to western political influence. Mao, Tsai Chang (who was to become one of the leading women in Communist China), and her brother were to form a bond sealed with a vow: they so hated the tyrannies of the traditional marriage system that they swore never to marry. Mao later spoke of having no time for love and romance as a student; in the same spirit of revolutionary puritanism, he drafted the Society's manifesto which was to 'reform China and the world' and opposed prostitution, gambling, concubinage, and lewdness.[61] His was not an idiosyncratic view but was commonly expressed: 'down with love!' as 'Struggle', a revolutionary song of the period had it.[62]

It was in this spirit that Mao placed himself at the centre of radical action at the time of the May Fourth movement, which invigorated Chinese nationalism and anti-imperialism. Mao's passionate intervention in the situation of women was the result of what many would dismiss as a mere domestic tragedy. A woman of the city, Chao Wu-chieh was engaged to a man on 14 November 1919. The marriage had been arranged by her parents and a matchmaker. Chao detested her intended spouse and begged her parents to undo the match but they would not. On the day of the wedding, as Chao was being raised in the bridal chair to be delivered to the home of the groom, she drew a dagger she had previously concealed in the chair and slit her throat.

Mao used the subject to vent his outrage at society's treatment of women, the cruelly backward nature of Chinese society and his hatred of the marriage system. He wrote at least nine articles in thirteen days, blaming Chao's death on Chinese society, her family, and her intended husband's family. His work was exquisitely subversive of traditional literature, as biographies of famous women were traditionally part of the conduct literature for girls, in which martyrdom was celebrated as the ultimate sanctification of matrimony. The woman in these books would kill herself on the death of her fiancé or husband, to ensure her eternal devotion to her beloved; she could never be unchaste even after her husband's death. Mao subverted the genre to produce a biography of a heroine who did not sacrifice herself for divine love of her husband, but because she hated him so much.

Mao denounced 'the shameful system of arranged marriages, the darkness of the social system, the negation of the individual will', and he praised the revolutionary 'great wave of the freedom to love'.[63] His final article in the series known as 'Against Suicide' argued that society inclines people towards suicidal behaviour by its tyranny, but that people should resist suicide and rather choose to die in the struggle against oppression, 'It is so much better to be killed in fighting than to take one's own life.'[64]

Mao's literary executors, 'striving to keep afloat the myth that he was a born Marxist', later excluded these writings from his collected works.[65] Relating a political to a personal struggle put Mao in the company of the literary feminists of Scandinavia, which is not a leap of the imagination: Ellen Key visited China and translations of Ibsen were hugely influential.

The new wave of radicalism in China reignited calls for women's suffrage; in 1921 the press reported that in Canton more than 1,000 'militant suffragettes' met demanding 'Equality of the sexes! Give us the vote! Woman suffrage for China!' and 'equal rights'; several hundred women marched to the provincial assembly which was startled as at the time they were discussing the election of district magistrates. The assembly was apparently thrown into disorder 'and the women underwent some rough treatment' but it is a testament to the openness of the times that after the uproar subsided the women had an audience with the prime minister and later with the chief of the military government, both of whom promised to help them to attain the vote.[66]

The agitation, coupled with a genuine sense that change was necessary in China, led to women being granted the vote in the provinces of Hunan, Canton, and Zhejiang (influenced by the activist city of Shanghai). When a national constitutional congress met in Beijing in 1924 under Sun Yat-sen, however, women were denied permission to attend and suffrage was eventually limited to educated men over the age of 25. A women's demonstration against the proposal was broken up by troops, and public meetings were prohibited. In general, however, demands for the vote or the campaign against concubinage seemed of little relevance to the majority of women and the suffragettes complained of the lack of interest in their cause.[67]

Despite their anger over the suffrage issue, radical women supported the climate of change in China, and an increasing number of working-class women became involved in industrial unrest and accompanying agitation.

The Communist Party benefited from this radical mood, and from its own clear perspective: they had argued for equal rights and women's suffrage since the party's inception in 1921 (at a 'national congress' of twelve members in Shanghai). They gained from women's loyalty: the Communist Party depended upon the suffrage movement's networks of politically active women to expand the small party membership.[68]

One of the leading women, Xiang Jingyu, was born in 1895, the daughter of a Hunan merchant. She attended a progressive girls' school and was active in the May Fourth movement and organized an anti-footbinding campaign. She went to study in Paris in 1919 and joined a student discussion group where she studied socialism and anarchism. On her return to China she set up the women's section of the Communist Party in 1923.

She set out her views in a series of essays on women in China, where she contrasted the aims of socialists with those of 'bourgeois feminists,' a similar position to that taken in Europe by such left-wing leaders as Alexandra Kollontai in Russia and Rosa Luxemburg in Germany. Xiang saw no value in a movement that conceived of the struggle primarily as that of women versus men or that had for its platform the 'vote', 'individual liberty', and 'free love'.[69] Her argument was that the vote was irrelevant, a total social revolution was required, not a chance to participate in a flawed system. Her response to women's election to provincial legislatures in 1924 was uncompromising: 'If the suffrage movement is successful then it simply means that a whole bunch of women will enter the pigsties of the capital and the provinces where, together with the male pigs, they can preside over the nation's calamities and other people's misfortunes.'[70]

She married leading party activist Cai Hesen in a ceremony involving the two of them holding a copy of Das Kapital; they published a volume of poetry, The Upward Alliance, in which they vowed to fight for the revolution together. Revolutionary harmony was disturbed by Xiang's affair with another activist, and both she and Cai Hesen were sent away to Moscow in 1926:[71] her husband as a delegate to the Comintern, she to study at the Communist University of the Toilers of the East. Xiang returned to work in a Communist Party that was by now in alliance with the nationalists of the Kuomintang. Women students and propagandists followed the nationalist armies, forming independent women's unions and informing women of the footbinding ban, sheltering runaway slaves and prostitutes, and granting divorces on their own authority. They wore their hair short and wore trousers with military jackets and caps. One of them explained to a journalist how they approached peasant women: 'We first explain the difference between the northern troops and our revolutionary forces. We tell them we came to save them from oppression and to bring a new way to thinking. We explain that men and women are now equal.'[72]

Divided ways

Sun Yat-sen had allied with the Communists because that was the route to Soviet aid. The alliance broke down after Sun Yat-sen's death in 1925, when Chiang Kai-shek took over. In 1926 he moved against his former allies in a four-month-long campaign of slaughter. Among the massacres of Communists, women who could be identified as 'progressive' by their bobbed hair were killed; women found in the uniform of soldiers were stripped publicly and exhibited before being executed. The most common form of execution for female Communists was to be wrapped in blankets soaked in petrol and burned alive.[73] More than 1,000 women leaders were thus killed, many of them not Communists but simply active in the women's movement.[74] Xiang Jingyu, who had returned to China in March 1926, fell victim in these massacres, at the age of 33; Mao's wife was also executed by the Kuomintang, in 1930.

The story of women's suffrage in China now divides between the nationalists and Communists. The nationalist leader Chiang Kai-shek was able to form an effective government in 1928. Women were still active under the nationalist government, but their work tended towards social welfare and literacy classes. However, Tcheng Soumay, who had been working as a lawyer in Shanghai, was appointed President of the District Court in Shanghai, the first woman judge in China. She was involved in drafting the nationalist government's new Civil Code that permitted divorce for both men and women, and equality in civil and property rights. The commission on which she sat was charged with the delicate task of providing for the rights of women, while preserving the customs and traditions of China.[75] Elizabeth Croll notes that the nationalists did not stop talking about women's emancipation, they simply redefined the terms so that emancipation embraced the often contradictory demands for a return to the virtues of traditional femininity and domesticity, and new opportunities for professional employment.[76]

Though there were advances regarding marriage rights and equal pay, change was evident only in urban areas. There was some progress under the

Kuomintang in that a few women were represented in the People's Political Council, which was a move towards democratic government set up in 1939. Women had been proposed for enfranchisement nationally under a draft constitution in 1936. This declaration 'was to remain theoretical' until the constitution was promulgated in 1946. In the intervening period a change had occurred in suffragist thinking among the nationalists; whereas they had previously spoken of the similarities between men and women and their equal rights, now they stressed the differences and successfully lobbied for a quota of only 10 per cent of seats to be reserved for women.[77]

Women voted in the first elections held after this date in 1947–8. Historian Louise Edwards complains that, because of the success of the Communists, defeating the nationalists the following year, the work of women suffrage activists in winning the vote in China is routinely overlooked.[78]

However, during the 1930s and early 1940s, the Communist Party of China had continued to nurture women's aspirations and involved women in political work as part of the strategy of mobilizing the entire population of China. By 1946 between a quarter and a third of Communist Party members were women.[79] Women in the Communist Party regularly fought alongside men: a detachment of women had participated in the Long March of 1934-6, when the Party was relocated from South-East to North-West China in a 6,000-mile march under almost constant attack from the nationalists. Despite the ferocity with which they fought the civil war, the Communists and nationalists formed an alliance in 1937 to oppose the Japanese invaders. In areas that had been liberated, women's associations flourished and women often took leading administrative roles. In one village, when women were excluded from elections, the women's association refused to recognize the man who had been elected, and encouraged women to stage a sex strike to put pressure on their husbands until the decision to refuse them the vote was reversed.[80]

After World War Two ended with victory against Japan in 1945, civil war in China between the communists and nationalists resumed. The nationalists were defeated, and with the establishment of the People's Republic of China on 1 October 1949 the right to vote was guaranteed to all, and women were specifically given full political, economic, cultural, educational, and social rights under the Common Programme. China was defined by its constitution as a 'socialist state under the people's democratic dictatorship led by the working class and based on the alliance of workers and peasants'.[81] There was, supposedly, no distinction of sex. The All China Democratic Women's

Federation founded in 1949, six months before the People's Republic was proclaimed, absorbed all other women's organizations such as the Women's Christian Temperance Union. Supported by the Communist Party and operating at every level of government, the Federation's main function was 'to unite and educate the broad masses of women in carrying out the general party line'.[82] It is through the Federation that women helped to formulate laws and select candidates.

The official response to early suffrage campaigns is dismissive, as official historians write: 'Chinese women have no history of struggle to win the right to vote and to stand for election; rather, the victory of the Chinese revolution granted Chinese women the right to participate politically.'[83] The tradition of history in China has exaggerated the role of the Communist Party and minimized the non-Communist women's movement prior to the revolution of 1949.[84]

The nationalists had enfranchised women during the usual pattern of events: after a great national upheaval—civil war and foreign invasion in this case. The enfranchisement was for reasons that were apparent in other enfranchisements: following a modernizing agenda, a motif that was to come into its own in Africa; and as part of an attempt to consolidate the nation in the face of a communist threat, a motive that had been apparent in Scandinavia and Holland at the beginning of the century.

Chinese Communists enfranchised women as soon as they had power, just as German socialists declared as one of their aims at the Erfurt congress in 1891 (and which the British Labour Party declared it would), from a belief that universal suffrage was the correct path morally and politically. Morally, there had been a longstanding connection between revolutionary thought and the position of women in China, as evinced in Mao's early writings. Politically, it was rigid doctrine that 'the people' should have power. 'Equal rights' was part of the mix of liberal ideas that had been accepted into the socialist programme. It was not, however, a confidence in democracy that led to the Communist enfranchisement, but a belief in mass power.

Japan—'suffrage on the pillow'?

At one of the women's meetings called by the American occupying forces to encourage Japanese women to participate in politics, an American woman officer announced, 'I think you Japanese women are very lucky because one morning you woke up to find women's suffrage on the pillow.' An old woman stood up and insisted, 'We did not find women's suffrage on the pillow. I cannot remind myself of the services of Ichikawa Fusae without tears. She is suffering a hard life at Hachioji by raising ducks and cultivating potatoes because she was purged from public service by the American authorities. Let's send a telegram to thank her in the name of this meeting.' The old lady's speech was received with applause.[85]

The requirement that women had to walk three steps behind a man dramatically symbolized the inferior status of women; but their institutional inferiority was not something confined to the private realm, it pervaded every aspect of national life and even international affairs. During the period when nationalists stirred up the Japanese population to back an aggressive war against China, the neighbouring nation was represented as a woman while Japan was a man: it was not only the right but the obligation of the male to dominate the female.[86] The challenge Japanese feminists faced was exacerbated by the lack of support they received from politically motivated men. In contrast to northern countries where suffragists usually had the co-operation of supportive men, in Japan if a man assisted a woman, or joined her side, he became a laughing stock with other men, so even if men were sympathetic, they pretended to be otherwise.[87]

Before the beginning of the modernizing Meiji period in 1868, in common with other nations with a basically feudal structure, some women who were taxpayers were able to vote in local elections and hold office just as men did who fulfilled the same requirements. As in the northern democracies at the same level of development, such gender anomalies were quickly ironed out by 'modernizing' governments and by the end of the century adult males only were allowed to vote and women (and minors) were forbidden to attend political meetings under Article 5 of the Peace Preservation Law.

With the strictly political avenue blocked, the energies of middle-class women were limited to social organizations aimed at reforming morality over drinking and prostitution. Even this gave no protection if debate moved into politics—200 women were obliged to leave a meeting of the Purity Society (against licensed prostitution) in 1920 when male suffrage was discussed.[88] The first objective of politically motivated women was, therefore, as in Germany and Austria, merely obtaining the right to organize. With an expansion of women's education (there was a 98 per cent literacy rate for girls in 1912) and with women entering the workplace and the professions, the right to meet and discuss their situation became paramount.[89]

The most important feminist leader was Ichikawa Fusae who was born in 1893 in Aichi Prefecture into a farmers' family where she was influenced by her father's cruel treatment of her mother. She attended the local teacher training college with the intention of becoming a primary school teacher. When she moved to Tokyo in 1910, however, she encountered the literary feminist magazine *Bluestocking*, which argued for freedom from women's conventional roles, and she decided to change course.[90] She returned to Aichi and became a reporter with the daily newspaper for Nagoya, capital of the prefecture in 1917. Two years later, with Hiratsuka Raicho (who was earlier the founder of the 'Bluestocking Society'), she established the New Women's Association committed to gaining political rights for Japanese women. Their first objective, achieved in 1922, was to revise 'Article 5' that forbade political associations.

Ichikawa at her high point was described as a tall woman who wore western clothes, smoked and wore her hair short, all of which led the press to ridicule her. Like many strong women who played a part in women's suffrage (Aletta Jacobs and Emmeline Pankhurst, for example) Ichikawa was not easy for colleagues to work with and a breakdown in her relationship with Hiratsuka led her to leave the country in 1921.[91] There was also an ideological split, where Hiratsuka emphasized the position of women as wives and mothers, while Ichikawa devoted her energies to defending 'the principle of women's rights', comparing the lack of rights of all women to those possessed by all men.[92] Hiratsuka could not keep the Association going (an indication of the reliance of Japanese feminism on a few key women) and it was dissolved the following year. With discussions around male suffrage, however, there was renewed interest in women's suffrage, as commonly occurred, with several societies now taking an interest.

Ichikawa went to the US, where she was strongly influenced by the radical suffragist Alice Paul and to some extent by other suffrage leaders including Carrie Chapman Catt. She returned to Japan in 1924 and established the radical Women's Suffrage League of Japan. The following year, adult male suffrage was introduced and soon after, the lower house of parliament passed a petition for women's suffrage—it could not become law but it was an indication of progressive thinking. Parliamentarians were concerned to make Japan appear less backward in international comparisons.

They wanted to introduce feminine virtues into the body politic, and some were concerned to forestall suffrage militancy.[93]

The state was a more important entity in Japan than in northern countries, as its agents were representatives of the divine Emperor, therefore women's organizations were more inclined to co-operate with the state and enjoy official patronage in return for supporting a state view of women in terms of morality and prudence. While women's suffrage had been promoted as a right in the early part of the century, by the 1930s it was advantageous to present women's involvement in politics as of benefit to the national interest. With a habit of looking to and learning from the West, Japanese observers were already aware that women's suffrage had not brought radical social change or social upheaval in Britain or the US. By 1931 many legislators already viewed suffrage as a means to preserve the virtues of Japanese womanhood.[94]

The First Annual Convention of Women's Suffrage Organizations was held in April 1930, sponsored by the Women's Suffrage League which had been set up with the assistance of the Women's Christian Temperance Union in 1925. Thus, as in the US, New Zealand, and Australia, the WCTU played an important enabling role; in Japan its message of wishing to 'purify' society struck a chord with puritanical imperialists, who approved of the message despite suspicion over its alien origins. The idea of women's suffrage as a western import, however, counted against the suffragists at a time of anti-American and anti-European feelings. Later in 1930 Ichikawa became president of the Women's Suffrage League and was in a position to petition parliament for suffrage measures.

Politically, as was so often the case, the lower house was prepared to accept women's suffrage, at least at local and prefectorial level, but the upper house rejected the legislation in 1929 and 1930. Finally the government itself proposed a Suffrage Bill in 1931 which would have given women political rights at 25 (men had them at 20). The government was keen to introduce economy measures at a time of warfare and reasoned that, if women were more politically aware locally, they could become more effective advocates of economic restrictions. As historians Yukiko Matsuka and Kaoru Tachi note, the legislators 'were not so much admitting women into the public spheres as extending the definitions of the private sphere to embrace the community'.[95]

This measure also failed through conservative opposition. It was contended that engagement with politics would be bad for women's temperament, they were too ill-educated for it to be any use, and the home would suffer if women engaged themselves outside. There were also ideological debates within the women's movement, as to whether their organizations should be associated with a particular party, as left–wing women desired; and one rally in support of the government measure erupted in violence when a man from the audience attempted to drag Ichikawa from the stage. Not all women's organizations were progressive: in 1934 a women's primary school convention voted down women's suffrage by 800 votes to 3; the three-million-strong Patriotic Women's Society were cheerleaders for Japanese imperialism.[96]

Interest in women's suffrage faded as the political crisis in Japan developed, those advocating women's rights (and other reforms) were harassed and their publications censored; the Woman's Suffrage League magazine was closed down in 1941. The increasingly illiberal government in the 1930s was also focused on imperial expansion after the invasion of Manchuria in 1931. While both the authoritarian government and the aggressive imperialism were masculine enterprises, to a considerable extent they relied on support at the home front and this engaged active women.

Political parties were abolished in 1940, and in 1942 the government merged all women's groups into the Greater Japan Women's Association in 1942 for coordinating activity on the home front, including the mobilization of women and children. Ichikawa was made a director of it; she had previously opposed militarism, but with her country involved in a total war, she felt she should add her efforts to lessen the suffering caused by the conflict. She also felt she would help the suffrage movement by demonstrating the value of women in social action.[97]

After the Japanese defeat, Ichikawa went to the prime minister to urge that the Japanese government should voluntarily grant suffrage rather than having it imposed by occupying authorities, but she was given a frosty reception. A new liberal government, however, was more willing to grant women's suffrage and it may be that the change would have come about with or without the occupation. Ichikawa was 'purged' from public life for four years by the occupying forces for her support of government organizations during the war, particularly her membership of the government's propaganda organization.

It has been said that women were given political rights 'as an accident of military defeat... handed to Japanese women over the heads of their nation's defeated leadership by the American military occupation'.[98] The occupation functioned more like a revolutionary council effecting social change rather than a foreign occupying power. It reintroduced political parties and launched a far-reaching series of reforms to democratize Japan, including a series of women's rights measures with suffrage at the age of 20. The occupation even launched a media campaign to promote women's use of the ballot in the months prior to the April 1946 election. Japanese women who had been prominent in the suffrage campaign went on the radio and campaigned alongside occupation officials.

As frequently happened, enfranchisement for some meant disenfranchisement for others. Male Taiwanese and Korean residents of Japan, who had been entitled to vote since 1925, were excluded under the new constitution which enfranchised Japanese nationals only. Gender inequality had gone, but had been replaced by ethnic inequality as the shattered country sought to re-establish its national identity.

Japanese village men tended to view women's political participation with 'some amusement if not contempt' and village women mainly talked among themselves about politics to avoid criticism or belittlement from their husbands and other men who saw them overstepping the boundaries of appropriate female behaviour.[99]

Ichikawa feared that only 10 per cent of women would vote, so low was her expectation of their political sophistication, but in fact 67 per cent voted in 1946, and thirty-nine women were elected.[100] After being 'de-purged' Ichikawa Fusae served in the upper house of the Japanese parliament for the Tokyo district almost continuously from 1953 until 1981, sitting as an independent member, and becoming one of the few leading suffragists in the world to adapt their abilities to a successful parliamentary career. She died in office at the age of 87. 'She has not only survived longer than any other woman in Japanese politics,' it was said near the end of her life, 'but has become the symbol of an unfinished struggle for social equality.'[101]

Japan already had a tradition of democracy, albeit one that had been subverted during the war years; and the nation had known active suffragists even if only from the ridicule aimed at them in the press. This meant the extension of the franchise was within the boundaries of national culture. Enfranchising women was a step the new, liberal legislature might have taken itself. What was remarkable about Japanese enfranchisement was that it was imposed by the occupying authority. The fact of this, and its very success, set a disastrous precedent: policy makers in the US were led to believe that women's suffrage and other democratic apparatus could be imposed on a conquered country after an invasion. This notion was to have dire consequences in the twenty-first century.

Women's suffrage in Japan followed a pattern of being awarded after a time of national upheaval when women had been to the fore on the home front, comparably with the bulge of European enfranchisements of women during and after the First World War. It was also in keeping with other enfranchisements in formerly authoritarian states (such as Russia, Germany, and the former Habsburg Empire after the First World War and Italy and France after the Second), that the conservative administration that had blocked women's suffrage had to be defeated and humiliated before women's enfranchisement could be accomplished.

Overall, war and the making of new constitutions in the East resulted in women's enfranchisements whether the ideology of the state was a liberal democracy as in India, Communist as in China, or in a state of confusion and violence, as in Burma.

14

Africa and the Cold War

'I will reply "yes sir" to my husband'

The Women's Union meeting in the school compound in Nigeria listened to the story of the old woman, so infirm she had to be helped up. She had never been to a meeting before, but now this was the only place she could come. She was a widow whose son had died leaving thirteen children and four wives. The widow took over his farm and ran it to feed the family, and educate the children. Now the king's agents had imposed an exorbitant tax demand, so great the widow could never pay and would lose the farm and become destitute with her daughters-in-law and grandchildren.

The women of the Union looked at the tax demand and contemplated what to do in silence. Their leader Funmilayo Ransome-Kuti frowned; corrupt tax inspectors and unjust taxes were crippling the people. Then one woman rose and said they had heard enough, they must march on the palace and confront the king. The women stood, took off their head-ties and fastened them round their waists as sashes, they poured out of the compound and marched on the palace, gathering more supporters as they went.

The women's path to the king was not clear. Beside the royal palace with its arch bearing the insignia of a reclining elephant was the enclave of the Ogboni. This was the all-male secret society of kingmakers, protectors of the royal person. They held the real power of the king. 'We looked on them with a mixture of fear and fascination,' said Funmilayo's grand-nephew Wole Soyinka, who witnessed the demonstration as a child. The Ogboni were said to kidnap and sacrifice children for their rites.

The Ogboni were clearly identifiable in their proud uniform: they wore a broad cloth over one shoulder as a toga, a shawl, a broad brimmed hat of stiffened leather and an iron or brass staff of office that they carried themselves or was carried before them by a servant. When their bull-roarer let out a cry, that was a sign for women to run indoors for refuge. Their chants and the thumps of their staffs as they circled around in their rituals contained supernatural strength. They controlled the cult of *oro*, a ritual symbolized by a phallic stick. It was a length of wood about fourteen or fifteen inches long made of light wood with a hole at one end through which a piece of string was attached so it could be whirled above the head making a whining sound. The *oro* commanded obedience, only men could parade during the rite, women had to stay indoors.

As the women gathered, the Ogboni came out to see the crowd. One burly man, clearly important by the number of his retainers, made himself heard: 'The world is spoilt. The world is coming to an end when these women, these who urinate from behind can lay siege to the palace and disturb the peace.' He addressed the demonstrators directly: 'Go on, go home and mind your kitchens and feed your children. What do you know about the running of state affairs? Not pay tax indeed! What you need is a good kick on your idle rumps.'[1]

He aimed a kick in the general direction of the women and, unaccountably as he set his leg down, it gave way beneath him, as if the women had bewitched him. He quickly scrambled up, only to half-collapse again as he set his weight on the leg, and his retainers rushed in and bore him off.

The women had scented weakness, and they did not wait for more, they set upon the Ogboni. Any figure in Ogboni dress was assaulted, his shawl, was snatched, his wrapping cloth stripped off him. They were flogged with their garments and left only in their undershorts when finally let through the gauntlet of abuse of the women's demonstration. Soyinka recalled: 'I saw stocky, middle-aged and elderly, grizzled men, the fearsome Ogboni, abandoning their hats, shawls, staffs of office and run on the wind.'[2]

In a desperate attempt to reassert control, the *oro* was brought out to command the obeisance of the women and send them back, away from the palace. The sacred *oro* must be obeyed, it could not fail, it symbolized all the accumulated power of the Ogboni. Instead of relenting, Funmilayo Ransome-Kuti stepped forward and snatched the sacred male thing, and waved it aloft in triumph. It had become powerless: a woman had wielded the man stick.[3]

African society

There were obviously regional and cultural differences, but it is a fair generalization to say that in sub-Saharan Africa before colonial administration

African communities functioned with a tribal system. There are examples of female chiefs but women's roles were usually clearly defined in ritual, practical matters to do with courtship and with trading and agricultural production.

One observer has stressed how in agricultural societies of black Africa, where the majority of African women lived, women had a broad role in decision making; they derived their status from the role they played in production, where they had political control over some area of activity such as farming, marketing, trading, or household and family. They also had political institutions (usually councils) to decide how to rule their own affairs or to influence the affairs of men.[4]

A female anthropologist remarked that in Africa 'whatever the system may be, the position of women within it is neither superior nor inferior to that of men, but simply different and complementary'.[5] Colonial rule was to alter and subvert this relationship but the underlying tribal structure is a clue to the reason why there was no great debate about women's suffrage in sub-Saharan Africa—or why what debate there was, was restricted to the nations which were significantly Muslim.

The tribal political system prevailed despite European trading incursions which date back to the fifteenth century with the early Portuguese excursions down the west coast of Africa. Political changes came about with the age of 'new imperialism', often dated to the Belgian King Leopold II's claim to have founded a personal empire in the Congo in 1879. Thereafter British, French, German, Spanish, Portuguese, and Italian claims were made in the 'scramble for Africa' (or longstanding claims were consolidated with national boundaries being defined). Within twenty-five years almost all the continent excepting Ethiopia and Liberia was under European control.

The objectives of the imperialists were to obtain African raw materials, to seek new markets for manufactured goods, to prevent other nations from taking the territory, for the national aggrandizement of victory and conquest and, for some, to 'civilize' the dark continent. This last aim included ending slavery within Africa and spreading Christianity. One of the chief justifications for the 'civilizing mission' of empire was the supposedly downtrodden status of women in Africa, Asia, and the Islamic world.[6]

Western ideology was a potent factor in changing the position of women in sub-Saharan Africa: Christianity put forward a message of God's concern for both men and women; Christian missions encouraged faithful, monogamous marriages, and frowned on polygamy (if usually tacitly accepting it).

The western media of print, radio, and screen sent a message in songs and fiction of the overriding importance of love.[7] The female-only organizations the Girl Guides and the Young Women's Christian Association gave confidence to those fortunate enough to have a branch they could join.[8] Schools taught both boys and girls, even though there was often a disparity in numbers, so that in Ghana in 1918, for example, there was one girl for every six boys in government schools; and one girl for every three boys in Basel Mission schools.[9]

The small minority of wealthy, educated women in Freetown, Sierra Leone, received the right to vote in 1930 on the basis of ownership of property and taxation, but this was akin to the votes cast by noblewomen in old Europe, an enfranchisement on the basis of status. Women students did join militant organizations in London, however, often working with Sylvia Pankhurst who had turned her attention to Ethiopian issues.[10]

There was increased scrutiny of colonial rule by international organizations, including the League of Nations following the First World War. Consequently, failure to maintain a healthy population, measurable by such standards as infant and maternal mortality, became a source of political embarrassment for European powers.[11]

African resistance to colonial control was sporadic; in some cases Africans were prepared to co-operate, in others they had never accepted the newcomers. In some areas, notably those of long European settlement such as the Cape, resistance was recognizably that of a pressure group developing into a political party: the Native Education Association was formed in 1882, in 1912 it became the Native National Congress and later the African National Congress, which won the first fully democratic election in 1994.

Women frequently took an active role in nationalist movements: women were the majority of members of the Tanganyika African National Union during its first eighteen months; the Zulu ethnic movement drew more than half its members from women, and in Guinea activist women were said to have had success by refusing sex to their husbands unless they joined the nationalist movement.[12]

By the late 1950s and early 1960s the European powers were losing interest in sustaining settlers or ruling poor African communities, the taste for empire had gone, and all that was left was the expense. Hugh Dalton's attitude was scarcely unique, when he turned down the post of colonial secretary offered him by the prime minister in 1950, thinking of 'pullulating, poverty stricken, diseased nigger communities, for whom one can do nothing in the short run, and who, the more one tries to help them, are querulous and ungrateful'.[13] African nationalist movements pushed at the open door of imperial departure. There were exceptions to this. In the Portuguese territories of Angola and Mozambique the colonialists clung on until 1974 when a coup within the colonial power itself led the way for democracy there. In Rhodesia (later Zimbabwe) civil war, and in South Africa a condition approaching civil war, took place over the racial basis of government until the 1980s and 1990s respectively.

Pressure groups within Britain had long since argued about the absence of participatory democracy in the colonies. The Six Point Group, which argued for progressive legislation for women in a 1939 letter to the Colonial Office, noted 'now that democracy is challenged by other ideologies' they felt the matter was of greater urgency: 'we urge you to make democracy a reality throughout the territories under British rule.' They deplored the absence of votes for women in some colonies while in others, if women were not barred from voting, 'the various qualifications for voting keep the percentage of women voters down to under 1 per cent of the population.' The civil service response was that there were some twenty colonial dependencies and 'sympathetic concern would no doubt be given to any movement originating in a colonial dependency for the extension of its franchise'. Twenty years before the constitutions for the new African states were being written, there was no sense that such a move should be resisted.[14]

Some ten years after this statement, in 1948, the Universal Declaration of Human Rights was accepted by the new United Nations, including Article 21: 'The will of the people shall be the basis of the authority of government; this will shall be expressed in periodic and genuine elections which shall be by universal and equal suffrage and shall be held by secret vote or by equivalent free voting procedures.' By the 1950s voting rights for both men and women had emerged as a key demand and expectation of nationalist movements pushing for decolonization and independence.[15] Women's enfranchisement was part of the independence package, an aspect of modernity that a new country would have, like a parliament building and a national airline.

As the British left former colonial territories, the administrative objective became the need to hand over an efficient working structure. What could be seen as a humiliating defeat for a western nation became, in an exercise of good will (or self-delusion, depending on one's point of view) the culmination of its self-imposed imperial mission: conferring a democratic structure.

John Watson, Permanent Secretary to the Ministry of Internal Affairs in Sierra Leone, wrote in 1958 to the Colonial Office that the nation's prime minister wanted universal adult suffrage by the time of the next general election in 1962, but 'the chief difficulty appears to be the registration of the women who do not at present appear on any tax or rating lists'.[16] He was informed that East and Central Africa had voluntary registration and that Ghana had the longest experience of conducting elections under universal adult suffrage. The colonial administrators had moved quickly from controlling the native population, to seeing democracy among the natives as a challenge for advanced administrative brains. Women's franchise was a feature to be incorporated.

In the Western Region of Nigeria there were 1,009,716 female electors out of a total of 1,947,152 in the election of 1956.[17] This was something of a testament to the administrative ambition of the departing colonial authorities in ensuring that once a system was decided upon, it should be as successful as possible. The question of the popular vote was not in question. As Professor C. E. Carrington said to a Chatham House (Royal Institute of International Affairs) meeting in 1962, 'The cry of Africa is now "One man one vote", and rather less emphatically, "One woman one vote".'[18]

Staged suffrage in Kenya

Kenya in East Africa had been a British protectorate since 1895, white settlement had been encouraged. Women's roles did not do so badly as men's under colonialism, the colonial government's delineation of tribal boundaries and the abolition of inter-tribal fighting made the warrior obsolete, but the woman's role as maintainer of the domestic economy remained largely intact.[19] In the first decades of the twentieth century forced-labour policies on European farms for minimal pay removed men from their homes and traditional family and social networks were disrupted owing to massive male migration out of home farm areas. Hut and poll taxes further ensured the availability of labour for European farms by necessitating a cash income. As a consequence of these policies, many women became heads of households and developed a sense of empowerment that culminated in women's rebellions in the 1930s and 1950s over such things as refusal to pick coffee or undertake soil conservation measures as ordered by the Europeans.[20]

The largest outbreak of popular protest among the Kikuyu that the British faced in the first half of the twentieth century was over British and missionary attempts to outlaw clitorodectomy, which was seen as a cherished symbol of national identity.[21] When a martial conflict began, in the Mau Mau war of the 1950s, women were active, up to 5 per cent of the fighters were women and women also supported the rebels, some even rising to leadership positions.[22] Between 1952 and 1958, 35,000 women were arrested and sentenced to prison.[23]

Influenced by enfranchisement in Britain, white Kenyan women got the vote in 1919, to a legislative council that had been in operation only since 1907. The East African Women's League had submitted a petition bearing the signatures of 533 men and women, supporting representative government without sex disqualification 'in the case of white residents'.[24] Asian men and women were enfranchised in 1923. Most black Africans were enfranchised in 1957, with a property and educational qualification, but these qualifications were set so high that few women succeeded on getting their names on the electoral roles; less than 1 per cent of the electorate registered for the first African elections were women. Similarly in Sierra Leone a supposedly equal franchise on the basis of tax obscured the fact that few women paid tax so very few of them were enfranchised.[25] This was hardly an accidental consequence of the electoral mechanism, as a textbook for administrators noted in 1958: 'The effects of enfranchising women may be mitigated (if that is the object sought) by altering other qualifications; by the differentiation of age or by making the vote dependent on evidence of payment of tax, in countries where few women are liable to tax.'[26]

Those Muslims living in largely non-Muslim countries were in an anomalous position. The High Commissioner in Kenya Sir E. Baring sent a telegram to alert the Colonial Office: 'Majority of Arabs in Kenya have expressed themselves forcibly in opposition to the enfranchisement of women on the grounds of culture and religion.'[27] Arab women were omitted from the franchise, which led Arab women from Mombasa to petition the colonial government to protest; the petitions was successful and they were registered the following year.[28]

Kenya therefore contained elements of the women's suffrage deliberations on the African continent: a white, then Asian, then black suffrage. These voting rights were constrained by qualifications, but finally these were ironed out and universal suffrage at 18 was a reality by independence in 1963.

Vagina's head seeking vengeance in Nigeria

Professor Carrington at the talk at Chatham House referred to earlier was able to call on history to 'give credit to the British imperialists who put in ten years' hard labour at preparing the Nigerian Federation with such convincing integrity that the local politicians who in 1953 were crying for Independence Now, in 1958 were asking for a little more time to prepare their national freedom'.[29] Nigeria became an independent state in 1960.

The West African country was 'Federated' because of the disparate nature of its population: three principal peoples, the Hause, Ibo, and Yoruba, with hundreds of other ethnic groups, each with their own language and culture in a country also divided along religious lines, with half the population Muslim, 35 per cent Christian, and the rest practising traditional African religions.

The names and constitution of the regions or states changed several times during the 1960s, in this account geographical terms will be used for simplicity (and they often were the terms used for political delineations).

One of the most important women in African politics in the first half of the twentieth century was Funmilayo Ransome-Kuti, who was from the Yoruba people who had traditional structures allowing women to be involved in decision-making and administration. Yoruba areas had seen risings against the British-controlled administration in 1918 and 1919.[30]

Funmilayo Ransome-Kuti was born in 1900 in the British colonial protectorate of Southern Nigeria to Daniel Thomas and his wife Lucretia, who were Christian, English-speaking trading agents for British merchants.[31] Her parents believed, unusually for the time, that girls should be educated as well as boys so Funmilayo went to school where she showed academic promise. With the help of family and friends, at the age of 19 she was sent to England to continue her education. She boarded with a British family and stayed for three years, returning to Nigeria in 1923, when she became a teacher in her home region of Abeokuta.

Two years later she married the Revd Israel Ransome-Kuti, a grammar school headmaster. They had first met in 1912 but had both been engaged in studies that they wished to complete—Ransome-Kuti took a BA, a licentiate in theology, a teacher's certificate, and an MA. While Funmilayo was abroad her future husband had become, at 27, the youngest high school principal in Nigeria.

The early years of their marriage were spent in teaching and working in educational organizations; in their home life they were accused of having educational expectations for their four children that were almost unachievable.[32] As a mature woman Funmilayo was five feet four inches tall and of slender build, with high cheek bones and a piercing gaze; she had a strong voice which easily carried when she addressed a crowd.

Funmilayo and her husband were both founder members of the National Council of Nigeria and the Cameroons, set up in 1944 to represent native feeling against the British administrators; it grew out of student protests against the colonial government's educational policies. Funmilayo formed a 'Ladies Club' of women who were, like her, western-educated, Christian, and middle class; they concentrated on cultural and community-related projects. They saw their objectives in terms of Anglo-Saxon feminist movements: the right to vote and run for office.

In early 1944 Funmilayo was asked by a market woman to teach her to read; realizing there was a demand for education, she expanded the Ladies' Club to include these women, who had nothing in common with the earlier members: they were poor, uneducated, and not Christian. They in turn were able to educate Funmilayo, whom they radicalized with their stories of injustice and ill-treatment at the hands of Alake, the local king

Until women are fully represented in politics, laws will not reflect the realities of their lives.

Figure 19. The US-based Centre for Development and Population Activities working for improvement in the lives of women and girls in developing countries explicitly connects social progress in Nigeria with political participation.

whose role had been incorporated into the colonial hierarchy. Market women were subject to administrative control over what they could sell, and to frequent seizure without compensation of their goods, or forced sale at lower than the market price. The underlying impetus for this harassment was a gender-based objective: to have women stay at home and renounce the economic and social privileges they had previously enjoyed. To them the objective of paying tax was incomprehensible, but it became explicable when linked with the educated women's demand for the recognition of women's civil status.[33]

Funmilayo took the women's protests to the district officer, the Native Administrative Council, and to the press, achieving considerable success— the confiscation of rice stopped forthwith. She decided to abandon western clothing and instead wear traditional Yoruba dress. The women's demands expanded to include not merely the negative resistance to oppression, but positive benefits such as the establishment of health clinics, a safe water supply, and adult literacy.

The Abeokuta Women's Club became the Abeokuta Women's Union in March 1946, its new name indicating its more political purpose, and membership rose dramatically. Its membership cards were signed by Ransome-Kuti under the title Iya Egbe, 'Mother of the Society'. She was virtually worshipped by the market women, and she was accused by western-educated women of having an autocratic leadership style. As her biographers note, diplomacy was not her strong suit.[34]

Throughout the 1940s Funmilayo led the women in battles against the Alake and the British authorities, who usually supported him. She led up to 10,000 women in protest at unfair taxes in disciplined demonstrations that they called 'picnics' or 'festivals' as they could not obtain the necessary permit to hold demonstrations.

In one protest that became legendary in Nigeria, Funmilayo led a delegation of women to the District Officer, a young British man. He rudely told her to shut the women up and she stood up to him and answered him, 'You may have been born, you were not bred. Could you speak to your mother like that?'[35] There are different versions of this exchange but they agree that Funmilayo fearlessly upbraided a British official in public.

After the demonstration in which the women shamed the Ogboni and Funmilayo seized the *oro* stick, they camped out in a long demonstration outside the palace while leaders negotiated with a new District Officer (the insulting young one having been replaced). At the end of each meeting they returned to the demonstration which called curses on the head of the king: 'Alake for a long time you have used your penis as a mark of authority that you are our husband. Today we shall reverse the order and use our vaginas to play the role of husband on you...O you man, vagina's head will seek vengeance.'[36]

In another event in what became known as the Egba (tribal group) Women's War, when some protesting women were arrested and put into jail, hundreds of their supporters went to the British residency to maintain a vigil. They stayed, singing anti-government songs, until the arrested women were released. The colonial authorities would have used force against armed men, but to massacre unarmed women would have caused a scandal.

Funmilayo herself went to jail for refusing to pay her taxes. She was credited with being the primary force behind the abdication of the king on 3 January 1949; he had lost the support of the Ogboni (though they later engineered his return). The tax on women was abolished, Funmilayo became a character to be compared to those from African history and myth. She is said to have kept the *oro* stick on display in her home; presumably the Ogboni did not seize it back because, having been touched by a woman, it had lost its potency.

Funmilayo's protests were therefore against the British colonial adminis- tration, against the British-backed Nigerian administration, and against the traditional village power of men (who should not have been interfering in the women-dominated business of market regulation). She was involved in anti-colonialist agitation, but it was part of a wider rebellion. Funmilayo and the Abeokuta Women's Union began to articulate not only an anti-colonial position, but one that sought democracy in Nigeria and the establishment of women's equality, particularly in obtaining the franchise for women. She formulated the argument not on human rights principles, but economic justice: 'Inasmuch as Egba women pay taxes, we too desire to have a voice in the spending of the taxes.'[37]

The British were moving towards disengagement with the colonies, part of which was preparing new constitutions. The National Council for Nigeria and the Cameroons sent a delegation to Britain in 1947 to petition the sec- retary of state for the colonies, with Funmilayo Ransome-Kuti as one of seven members. She became a well known figure in the British press and was invited by the mayor of Manchester to speak on the condition of women in her country.

Funmilayo's fame had led women for other parts of Nigeria to call on her help to form branches of the Women's Union, and the Abeokuta Women's

Union became the Nigerian Women's Union in 1949, and at its height had around 80,000 members.[38] She was particularly pleased to be in contact with northern women who lagged behind the southern areas of the nation in enfranchisement, education and political representation.[39]

When the new governor Sir John Macpherson called for discussions on a new constitution in 1949, Funmilayo was the only woman representative at the Western Regional Conference. She was also the only woman candidate in the first direct federal elections in 1951, which had an all-male electorate. She denounced the corruption of the election and said, 'Women are earnestly praying for the day when there will be universal adult suffrage so that once again they can assist the men to do things properly.'[40]

She was subsequently to travel to the USSR, China, and other communist bloc countries, which led to her passport being seized. During the time of intensive work, travelling within Nigeria and abroad, her husband the Revd Israel Ransome-Kuti fell ill with prostate cancer. At one time in hospital, asked if his wife visited him daily, he replied, 'My wife is eaten up with her concern for women's affairs and I leave her to do it.'[41] When he died in 1955, Funmilayo described him as 'the most democratic man I have every known' in a remark showing how democracy was equated with decency for her— and perhaps for other Africans.[42]

The first native prime minister of the Eastern region, Nnamdi Azikiwe, was a colleague of Funmilayo from the National Party of Nigeria and the Cameroons and had argued for the franchise for women as far back as the 1940s, and in party constitutional conferences had called for universal adult suffrage.[43] There was universal suffrage for some municipal elections from 1949, in the usual process of local suffrage preceding national suffrage.

The National Party of Nigeria and the Cameroons sent a telegram in 1958 to the constitutional conference meeting in London to say 'We consider emancipation of women great factor in Nigeria's future development. Demand uniform electoral system based on right of franchise for all men and women of the federation.'[44] The Federation of Nigerian Women's Societies, an umbrella group of which Funmilayo was president, made determined representation to the Governor-General in 1959 that Northern Region women should be given the franchise, as women had been in the East since 1954 and were granted in the South that year, but to no avail. Universal suffrage, with a tax qualification (and few women paid taxes) was introduced in the Western region from 1955.[45] Even as late as 1962 when calls were made for the full franchise for Northern Region women, the president of the Northern People's Congress women's section said northern women did not want suffrage. The franchise for women in the north was finally imposed only by the Federal Military Government in 1976.[46]

Funmilayo left the National Council of Nigeria and the Cameroons over its refusal to accept her as an electoral candidate in 1959, and stood (unsuccessfully) as an independent. She said, 'Men do not want women to take part in our legislation; they want women as mere voters, ordinary election tools.'[47]

Her political disagreements were soon subsumed by national conflicts. Azikiwe became president of Nigeria in 1963, but the federation of Nigeria was not a success and there was an army coup in 1966. The attempted secession of the Ibo area of Biafra in the east, and the national government's use of starvation as a means of bringing the rebel region back into the federation, was a humanitarian disaster and a cause of great misery to Funmilayo. She was a true nationalist who had always fought for Nigerian people in general, regardless of tribal origin, and she had many political associates in the east. Funmilayo and her family were severe critics of the military governments that ruled Nigeria, after 1966; her grand-nephew Wole Soyinka was imprisoned for most of the Biafran war.

Funmilayo's son Fela was a leading musician who was often in conflict with the authorities. His songs poked fun at the government resulting in problems with the police and with the army. His personality and anti-government stance was formed particularly by the example of his mother, with her active contempt for arbitrary authority; and by the influence of 'black power' to which he was introduced in the 1960s by a girlfriend in the US. He founded a commune on property owned by the family on Agege Motor Road in Lagos. He called it the Kalakuta Republic, emphasizing his independence from the military rulers of Nigeria, and used the house as a base to entertain visiting foreign musicians and house his many wives.[48] Funmilayo adored her son, feeling he truly spoke for the people, and often lived at Kalakuta.

On 18 February 1977 Kalakuta was surrounded by soldiers armed with bayonets and clubs. Allegedly calling to arrest two young men who had committed a traffic violation, they broke down the door and began beating people. Fela and Bekolari, a doctor son of Funmilayo's, were badly beaten; clothes were torn off the young women in the house who were forced outside naked. The 76-year-old Funmilayo was pulled by the hair and thrown out of a window, badly injuring a foot. The property was then destroyed by fire.[49]

Funmilayo was said to have never recovered from the raid. She was treated for the foot injury but it did not heal well, and she was withdrawn and depressed, refusing to talk or eat; she died on 13 April 1978. Her body lay in state in the Ransome-Kuti Grammar School in her home town of Abeokuta, where the markets and shops closed on the day of her funeral.

Nationalism and self-reliance in Zanzibar

The coming of democracy to Zanzibar was a model of administrative order. It was announced in October 1955 that the island should have self-government within the Commonwealth. The all-male legislative council working out the details suggested the extension of the franchise to women and a committee was set up by the British Resident in May 1959 to consider the proposition. There was no suffrage movement and no direct demand from women for the vote.

The committee found that

> self-government, anti-colonialism, emotional nationalism, the dignity of man, feelings and thoughts about all these issues are involved and the franchise was part and parcel of the revolution of ideas. It was also said that the general proposition that women should be equal to men was incontestable: that the present was a time of change: that only the very strong emotional forces at present in motion would be able to alter the traditional position of women in this Islamic society: and that therefore the forces should be used to achieve this highly desirable aim.[50]

The committee's report addressed the issue that Zanzibar was predominantly Muslim: 'No evidence was received that the grant of the vote to women, or its exercise, was against the principles of Islam.' Leading Islamic countries such as Egypt and Pakistan already granted women the right to vote.[51]

Opposition to the vote was often covert, suggesting strong social pressures to accept the proposal but with private reservations: the Watumbatu people were given a special meeting in their area at which several hundred men and women were present, and none opposed the enfranchisement of women. A few days later a delegation of seventeen Watumbatu, some well known, appeared before the committee and strongly opposed the proposal; it was thought that people were afraid to oppose the political parties who were strongly in favour of votes for women.

The six-man committee heard from women who explained to them the dynamics of the household. One said, 'I will reply "yes sir" to my husband when he orders me to vote for a certain candidate: this will please him and keep harmony: but I will vote for my own choice, and as the vote is secret my husband will never know.'[52] It was discussed whether voters would hide their ballot papers and take them outside, to give them to their husbands, or sell them, but the committee was unconvinced that these were genuine threats and decided not to recommend searching women voters.

All independent Zanzibari women and married women over 21 got the vote—even if they were 'plural wives' of a registered elector; but not spinsters dependent on their families or women married to non-electors (foreign men). Thus nationalism and self-reliance were the principles enshrined in modern Zanzibari life. Zanzibar and Tanganyika united to form the republic of Tanzania in 1964.

In some predominantly Muslim countries the going was harder, such as in Sudan (though the southern part was black African). A mere fifteen women enrolled as voters in newly independent Sudan in 1958 where, having completed higher education, they fulfilled the requirements of having educational qualifications.[53]

Rhodesia and South Africa

By the early 1960s there was little interest in women as voters, the concentration of the administrators drafting constitutions was on preserving the interests of minorities—principally Europeans but also Africans or Arabs depending on the state—from oppression by the majorities in the new democracies.[54] In some cases, no solution could be found, as in Rhodesia where there was a small African electorate under a 1961 constitution (on a literacy and property or income qualification) who frequently did not bother to register to vote; and a European minority that controlled the state. An attempt to make the nation more democratic resulted in a constitution of 1961 under which 50,000 black men and women had the vote and some limited political power, with fifteen reserved parliamentary seats. The white Rhodesian Front party won the election of 1965 and unilaterally declared independence from Britain, because the mother country insisted on progress towards majority rule.

In terms of women's franchise, the significant fact is that it was not an issue; whether the constitution gave whites only the vote, or a selective franchise with reserved seats for blacks, or enfranchised the whole of the population (as was the case under the constitution of 1980 after a civil war). Whatever was to happen, the presence of women in the electorate of what became Zimbabwe was not questioned.

In common with other frontier people, Boer women in South Africa shared hardships with their husbands, the first recorded claim for political rights for women in South Africa was made in Natal in 1843, when a deputation of Voortrekker women went to the British High Commissioner and declared that: 'in consideration of the Battles in which they had been engaged with their husbands, they had obtained a promise that they would be entitled to a voice in all matters concerning the state of this country.' They pledged resistance to British authority, to 'walk out by the Drakensberg barefooted, to die in freedom, as death was dearer to them than the loss of liberty'.[55]

White women in South Africa settled into a position of racial superiority, dominating their servants and people involved in commerce, only suffering slight criticism such as that from Olive Schreiner in her novel *The Story of an African Farm*, who pointed up women's subordinate status in society. Schreiner was one of the founders of a Woman's Enfranchisement League in the Cape in 1907.

In 1892 an attempt in the Cape parliament to extend the franchise to women failed, though it introduced many of the elements that were later to play a part in women's politics in the Cape. J. M. Orpen, who proposed the women's suffrage amendment, argued the need to increase the 'civilized vote' by bringing in women of property and 'mental development'. Whiteness, civilization, and property therefore all formed part of the right of the franchise.[56]

The international movement for women's suffrage did not overlook South Africa, and the nation did not sneer at their representatives: Aletta Jacobs and Carrie Chapman Catt visited in 1911 and spent a day with the powerful government minister Jan Christiaan Smuts and his wife. Jacobs and Catt had intended to restrict their activity in South Africa to suffrage matters, but on arrival decided to campaign against prostitution also; as Jacobs wrote, 'many women in South Africa actually wanted the government to set up brothels in those places where they did not as yet exist!'[57]

The usual element of middle-class, reforming women came to the fore in South Africa with the white, English-speaking Women's Christian Temperance Union. In South African terms the 'social purity' principle beloved of feminists included the safeguarding of racial purity by preventing miscegenation.[58] Under the auspices of the WCTU suffrage societies were founded in centres of population throughout South Africa. They came together in 1911, the union stimulated by Catt and Jacobs' visit, in the Women's Enfranchisement Association of the Union which again comprised almost entirely women whose allegiance was to Britain and was led by women who were professionals or were married to professionals; of fourteen leaders whose biographies have been researched, only one was an Afrikaaner.[59]

The Anglo–Boer War and its related questions of nationhood had engrossed the political classes at the end of the nineteenth and beginning of the twentieth century: women's suffrage hardly featured. The National Convention, called to discuss the future Union of South Africa, was exercised about race and nationality, particularly the status of black voters in the Cape. Women's suffrage was mooted, but discussion was brief.

Ingenious arguments were brought to the fore by suffragist women such as 'The Homekeepers' Vote' where it was argued that women's maternal abilities must be used to civilize Africans who would be taking care of white children; so voting was an extension of other female roles, and just as she must care for children, the white woman must guide the child-like African.[60]

The Women's Enfranchisement Association petitioned parliament for suffrage for white women. Its objective was to secure the franchise on the same basis as that for men, which had the unintended but inevitable implication that where black and coloured men had the vote, under whatever kind of property franchise, black and coloured women would get it too ('coloured' was the universally used designation for people of mixed race). This proposal had virtually no support in parliament: in 1913 it was decided that a motion calling for the enfranchisement of women should not even be put to the vote.

The problem was that the British Cape Colony, prior to unification in 1910, had a franchise based on a property qualification: any man earning above £50 a year or owning a structure worth £25 could vote.[61] This was non-racial, though few Africans qualified in its early years. When the four independent states came together to form the Union of South Africa the non-racial Cape franchise remained; it was specifically protected when the Union constitution was discussed in 1909. The question of how to end this example of non-racial politics now came to dominate the political scene for the Afrikaaners and their parties.

Suffragist women were encouraged after the First World War by the number of countries that had enfranchised women and they resented having their vote held up by wrangling over the franchise for a few property-owning blacks and coloureds. It has been remarked that most members of the Women's Enfranchisement Association's understanding of the word 'woman' did not extend to women of other racial groups.[62] The only political group dedicated to women's suffrage was the South African Labour Party but it considered black people economic rivals in that they worked for lower wages than whites, and therefore the Labour Party fitted in with conservative opposition to black people's rights on spurious anthropological or religious grounds. The attitudes of other political parties moved towards women's suffrage in the early 1920s but without enthusiasm, so votes were not taken. A petition of more than 50,000 women in the various suffrage leagues was presented to parliament in 1921. Finally 1923 saw the first support of women's suffrage by the Afrikaaner women's associations, who were able to influence nationalist politicians as those who held allegiance to Britain could not.

Previously Afrikaaner women had not been welcoming to women's suffrage but conservative Afrikaaner organizations, particularly the Dutch Reformed Church, now encouraged a change. They were doubtless reflecting on the experience of other countries of women being seen as a politically stabilizing rather than a revolutionary influence.[63]

The support of Afrikaaner women pushed the matter up the nationalist agenda, and the obvious step for the nationalist James Hertzog, who became prime minister in 1924, was to combine this issue with the one paramount in his mind, the political segregation of Africans in the Cape. Hertzog was unable to raise the two-thirds majority necessary to change the constitution to eliminate the voting rights of Cape blacks, so he needed to find another way to achieve his object. A select committee was appointed to inquire into the enfranchisement of women but it ran up against the same difficulty: what to do about coloured and black women in the Cape who could meet the franchise qualification there if they were allowed to do so? Faced with what was to them an insoluble racial dilemma, the Women's Enfranchisement Association began to waver on its previous position of insisting on the franchise on the same basis as men.

Hertzog killed an opposition franchise bill but promised to introduce one himself. Now the English-speakers and the Afrikaaners at all levels supported votes for women. Hertzog had originally been prepared to enfranchise coloured women, the coloured population being treated as a racial buffer between black and white. In the end Hertzog decided he could do without the coloureds and in 1930 proceeded to carry through a government measure that enfranchised women 'of European descent' over the age of 18. Under the Women's Enfranchisement Act of 1930, for avoidance of any doubt, Clause 5 made it clear that under the Act ' "Woman" means a woman who is wholly of European parentage, extraction or descent'.[64]

Coloured and black men in the Cape were not thus disenfranchised, but their votes were worth commensurately less, as the white vote had doubled over the whole of the Union, allowing for a later, racially-based assault on their rights. The success of white women's suffrage was tied to the progressive disenfranchisement of black South Africans and to the construction of a more explicitly racist political and social order in the region from the 1930s.[65]

As historian Cherryl Walker remarks, what emerges from the history of the suffrage campaign in South Africa is the degree of unanimity within white society about basic principles of society: the suffrage campaign never represented a threat to the prevailing organization of racial or gender relations. Notions of white supremacy and women's place in the home were central to the suffragists' image of who they were and their place in society.[66] White women consoled themselves over their abandonment of coloured and black women with reassuring words emphasizing their socially benevolent role: 'enfranchised women will have far greater influence on matters affecting the interests of the non-European section of the population than they had when unenfranchised.'[67] With the passing of the 1930 Act, white women lost interest in further extensions of the vote to other women.

There was a protest meeting in Cape Town called by coloured organizations to protest against the discriminatory terms of the legislation, attended by 30-year-old Cissy Gool. Three years later she was to be the first coloured women to graduate from the University of Cape Town with a master's degree; in 1938 she founded the Non-European Women's Enfranchisement League.

The enfranchisement of white women was thought of as a particular rebuke to the elite Africans, who had believed that their improving education and social status would gradually result in their being incorporated into political life. To be denied this goal by the mechanism of the introduction of women into politics was considered humiliating.

The situation for black women was even worse, as they were not even represented in their own organization; the African National Congress constitution of 1919 did not grant full membership to women, they could only be auxiliary members without voting rights. This was the situation until the 1943 Conference where a resolution was passed to grant women full membership status and to set up the ANC Women's League

The ANC also committed itself to women's suffrage in 1943, while putting out progressive reform proposals in common with other liberation movements. They wished to reaffirm the democratic character of their proposed social structure to further throw into relief the undemocratic nature of the South African regime. Women's rights and the struggle for the vote were subsumed under a general struggle for basic human rights in a nation democratically in regression: 'coloured' men in the Cape lost the vote in 1956; the ANC was banned in 1960.

Women only gradually entered the political sphere. Black male activists concentrated on the encroaching racial discrimination; the perception that politics was a male preserve went unchallenged. International pressure and worsening economic conditions led to a new constitution and new parliament in 1984, which attempted to give a democratic structure to racial divisions, enshrining a racial divide in a democratic form, with two new chambers: one for coloureds and one for Indians. This was a theoretical advance as now all white, coloured, and Indian South Africans had the vote, male and female. The underlying idea was a reversion to the policy of creating a racial buffer between the blacks and whites, but the action was scorned; as few as 5 per cent of the coloured electorate voted in the 1984 elections.[68] With the fall of apartheid in 1990 a new constitution was put in place and black men and women were enfranchised to vote in the 1994 election.

The African path of enfranchisement

From Ghana in 1957 to Swaziland in 1968 (Rhodesia had declared independence unilaterally, but emerged as independent Zimbabwe in 1980), British territories in sub-Saharan Africa gained independence.

In formerly French colonies, the route to independence was in some cases startlingly different: in French West Africa a move towards increased self-government saw the very narrow suffrage measure in place expanded in

1952 to include mothers of two children. Most women at 21 were married mothers, so for a time there were more women voting than men. France's imperial objective then was for every subject country to follow the same path of constitutional development. Thus in 1956 the *loi-cadre* (framework law) granted virtually universal suffrage and significant self-government. Complete adult suffrage was conferred in 1960 with independence for almost all French sub-Saharan territories. Belgium departed central Africa in 1960 after hastily arranged elections, the former colonial masters having left the population with little or no preparation for self-government.[69]

Women's suffrage was granted throughout sub-Saharan Africa over the period of decolonization. It therefore fits into a pattern established from the time of such pioneers as Wyoming and Finland of women's suffrage being gained at a time of national upheaval and when new constitutions were being drafted.

Whether or not there was an armed struggle against colonialism (or whether women were involved in it) did not seem to make any difference. Where women had borne arms against the Europeans, in Zimbabwe and Mozambique, they were no further to the fore in terms of gaining suffrage than in Ghana where the transfer of power had been peaceful and Liberia which had not been under European control.

Equal suffrage was not related to what women had done in the nation, or even what men had done, but to a western idea of progress. The International Woman Suffrage Alliance (by now known as the International Alliance of Woman) in 1965 heard of 'the gradual awakening of African women from drudgery, slavery and apathy to modern times' which meant a widening of interests from family to nation and beyond.[70] That is: women were applauded when they appeared to be moving towards a model of what the West considered progress, with no notion of specific African conditions.

The West African nation of Ghana is a case in point. It was formerly named the Gold Coast, indicating not a geographical region or a people, but a commodity. Ghana became independent from Britain in 1957, the first Sub-Saharan country in colonial Africa to do so. The experience of women's suffrage in Ghana is representative of the African continent in that women played little part in the post-colonial political system. Women were not excluded from high positions in government, but women have had few significant political offices.[71] No women were elected in 1957; two women were elected to parliament in 1969, five in 1979. The Ghana National Council on Women and Development in the early 1970s wished to see more women in policy-making positions but it was remarked, 'at the time of its establishment, the country was under a military government, and it was explained that since there were no senior women army officers, it was not possible to have women in that government.'[72]

The main problem appeared to be not gender but class; as historian Audrey Chapman Smock commented, educated women exhibited little inclination to extend their horizons and organizations to include their uneducated sisters, 'the elite women, from whom the leadership of any women's movement would come, face little overt discrimination that would stimulate a sense of injustice and promote greater organisation.'[73]

In the majority of even the most advanced African countries, there was no significant women's movement. A historian of women in Kenya writes, 'During the early years of independence, a militant women's equal rights movement has developed in Kenya', that is, it had not existed prior to independence.[74] Western models of women's political activity were inappropriate. For example, Florence Abena Dolphyne, Chairman (sic) of the National Council on Women and Development in Ghana, did not consider herself a feminist, 'for the term evokes for me the image of an aggressive women who, in the same breath, speaks of a woman's right to education and professional training, her right to equal pay for work of equal value, her right to vote and to be voted for in elections at all levels, as well as a woman's right to practise prostitution and lesbianism'.[75] Some of what feminism had to offer was attractive, therefore, some simply culturally inappropriate, and some of it abhorrent. Overall, it failed to address the realities of women's lives in Africa, for many of whom there is no access to good drinking water, no hospital or clinic within easy reach, and where there is a constant threat of famine or drastically lowered standards of living because of fluctuations in the world price of cash crops. Rural women in South Africa argued, against more sophisticated town dwellers, that the right to accessible clean water was a 'women's issue' and should be included in the Women's Charter under discussion.[76] Rather than the ballot box, for most African women 'the emancipation of women and the status of women in society are closely linked with national development', wrote Dolphyne.[77]

Women's enfranchisement was one of a series of measures expected in a modern constitution which were not resisted by the departing colonial authority—or welcomed by the new political elite. In the decades following decolonization in Africa the disruptive effect of the rise of anti-social and authoritarian regimes destroyed hopes of democracy in many countries on the continent, and introduced such terms as 'kleptocracy' into the political lexicon. Ancient tribal conflicts resurfaced after the Europeans left, but with the antagonists better armed and able to use a corruption of the democratic process to secure their ascendancy. True democratization of Africa, argues political theorist Mahmood Mamdani, 'would have entailed the deracialisation of civil power and the detribalisation of customary power'.[78] In the event, the colonialists left, but the tribal hegemonies remained.

Women's rights and the Cold War

The overwhelmingly important political influence on the world from the end of the 1940s was the Cold War. This was not a conflict in which the enfranchisement of women was an issue: the Soviet Union inherited universal suffrage from the liberal government the Bolsheviks displaced; the Communist Party of China enfranchised women soon after the revolution in 1949 (though the nationalists had previously enfranchised women, it was in a country on which they were fast losing their grip).

A Communist front organization, the Women's International Democratic Federation was founded in Paris on 1 December 1945, indicating the intention of the Soviets to capitalize on women's involvement in politics. Linking the words 'democracy' and 'women' meant the Soviets were flowing with an existing political current. A Soviet Union's Central Committee resolution on 31 January 1977 claimed: 'a tremendously important task, that of guaranteeing women real equality in life—has been carried out in full in our country.'[79] Such equality did not display itself in political power, however; of seventy-five government posts none was filled by a woman.[80]

The United Nations subcommission on the status of women, reporting to the Economic and Social Council on 5 June 1946, recommended 'that all governments should be called upon to accord suffrage to women, since it was felt that little progress could be made in raising the status of women without the grant of political rights'.[81] With the United Nations, as mentioned earlier, explicitly presenting the women's franchise as a basic human right from 1948, there was no longer an ideological divide in the world between right and left or progressive and reactionary over this issue.

Political support for women's suffrage in the late years of the nineteenth and the early years of the twentieth century had been a measure of the difference between nations. Those that enfranchised were the pioneering,

Figure 20. Images of inclusive elections underpin a sense of nationhood: a woman votes in the independence referendum in South Sudan in 2011.

newly built nations; those that resisted were the old colonial powers. After 1920 the women's franchise was a measure of the difference between democracies and autocracies—or between an old and modern style of ordering relations between the state and people. By 1960 it was merely a mark of backwardness that a nation might not have a franchise for women; women's suffrage had largely lost its wider political meaning.

Why did so many otherwise dissimilar nation-states follow a similar path towards enfranchising women? By the late 1960s 100 counties had enacted women's suffrage, more than half of them since the end of the Second World War. The pattern which had been built up at the beginning of the twentieth century, from male suffrage to female suffrage, was not repeated after the Second World War. Nations moved directly to full enfranchisement of men and women, whether or not they had much representation previously. A sociological assessment at the end of the twentieth century, looking at women's suffrage in 133 countries from 1890 to 1990, referred to the rapid progress towards women's suffrage as a 'field pressure' from other nations, with women's enfranchisement as a predicate to authentic nation statehood. This was articulated by international organizations such as the United Nations and by women's suffrage movements. The authors remark on the decreasing importance of national political factors and the commensurate rise in the importance of international links and influences which take for granted an inclusive model of political citizenship. By the 1990s, 'the right of universal suffrage was already both an institutionalized feature of the nation-state and a core element of an incorporative model of political citizenship.'[82]

It assisted in the rapid progress towards women's enfranchisement that the women's vote did not presuppose any particular kind of government or even a style of government. By the 1950s at least half a century of female voting showed that it made no political difference: voting could as well take place in a one-party state as in any of a variety of republics or constitutional monarchies. Women's involvement had no profound influence on the structure of political systems, good or bad.

15

The veiled vote

'An untimely and inappropriate demand'

At Cairo Railway station one spring day in 1923 a crowd of women waited, their bodies covered in long, black traditional gowns. These were rich, secluded women with eunuchs to guard their honour. They had descended from their horse-drawn carriages to welcome travellers home, and were gathering to greet Huda Shaarawi who was returning from Rome where she had been representing Egypt at the International Woman Suffrage Alliance conference.

Alighting from the train, in a dramatic gesture, Huda drew back her veil and cast it aside.* Her companion Saiza Nabarawi did so too. Her biographer remarked that at this moment on the Cairo railway station, 'Huda stood between two halves of her life—one conducted within the confines of the harem system and the one she would lead at the head of a women's movement.'[1] The waiting women were shocked at first then broke into applause. Some also removed their veils while the eunuchs frowned with disapproval. Within a decade of this gesture, only a few women were still seen veiled in public.

This was the first public defiance of the restrictive tradition of veiling and is often mythologized as a key moment in Egyptian feminism, but there was both more, and less to the story than was obvious. Huda Shaarawi argued for a gradualist approach to removal of the veil and she had earlier encouraged Saiza Nabarawi to wear the garment while in Egypt, after her young companion and protégée returned from Paris, where she had been raised and educated.[2] Most Egyptian women veiled when in the street, but seclusion,

---

* The words for different forms of head covering have changed over time; in these pages 'veil' and 'unveiling' refers to the removal of any covering of the *face*—not to the headscarf which is now referred to as a hijab (a word which meant face covering in the early twentieth century).

symbolized by the veil, was only an issue for the wealthiest women in Egyptian society, since only affluent families could afford the elaborate measures necessary for purdah: architectural arrangements and eunuchs to guard women and act as go-between with the outer world. Veiling and the harem system were social conventions that connoted social standing; they were not dictated by Islam (Christian women of high social status also veiled in Egypt). Unveiling meant the emancipation of the rich—comparable to British ladies leaving their drawing rooms to address social causes at the time of Josephine Butler. Unveiling was also connected to western fashions, which were highly desired by women who had access to the fruits of Egypt's recent economic progress—a Parisian hat looked ridiculous on a veiled woman.[3]

Unlike many rich woman, Shaarawi had a great deal of freedom. Her husband (who was more than thirty years her elder) had died the previous year and there were no dominant male members of her family extant. She was in the unusual position of having a large fortune but no strong male authority figure to control her movements. She had also trained in the techniques of organization-building in nationalist campaigning, so she was able to pursue a personal goal: she was able to turn her attention away from the independence movement and towards the movement for women's equality. She had, therefore, a combination of personal freedom, the political experience of nationalism, and feminist ideas. It was a unique mix to bring forward in the fight for women's equality.

The emergent Muslim nations

At the beginning of the twentieth century almost the whole of the Middle East, North Africa, and the Asian countries with a Muslim majority were colonial dependencies and in most there was a national struggle for independence. Unlike in Europe and Asia, women's involvement in the national struggle did not result in women's political emancipation. If the European and Asian pattern had been followed, as outlined earlier in this book, there should have been women's political emancipation arising from their involvement in the national struggle. This did happen in some nations, notably Algeria and Indonesia, but it was not universal across the Muslim world.

If the African model for women's suffrage had been followed women's suffrage should have been part of the package left by the departing colonial administrators as they bestowed democracies on their former possessions. This happened, to a limited extent, in the French (or French and Spanish in the case of Morocco) dependencies of Tunisia, Morocco, and Mauritania. In Sudan, the British granted the vote to the small number of women with at least a secondary school education in 1953 at the time self-government was approved for the nation.

The colonialists wished, as they had in sub-Saharan Africa, to leave the best functioning democracy, but they were challenged by the relationship between the departing masters and their subjects, both men and women, in Muslim-majority nations. A telegram from Sir Harry Potter, governor of the island of Zanzibar, on 15 June 1959 reported that the 'chief difficulty lies in making satisfactory arrangements for purdah women', adding that even 'many of those out of purdah do not freely mix with men'.[4] How could the men of the British colonial service even approach women in these circumstances? In the northern region of the British Cameroons the United Nations insisted on votes for women, and the Muslim inhabitants resisted it. By this time, the departing colonialists were in no position to assert authority.[5]

Some parts of the Muslim world have been extraordinarily resistant to the message of women's emancipation. When the Muslim peoples of the Soviet East were visited by Bolshevik propagandists giving a message of equality after the 1917 revolution, these visits often resulted in the murder of Bolshevik feminists who were teaching local women to tear off their veils and assert their rights as human beings.[6] Such exotic and dangerous expeditions were an inspiration to feminists around the world. Elin Wägner in Sweden writes of her excitement in reading about 'women of Moslem Central Asia in the Soviet Unions who, awakened by Lenin's ukase and the Women's Department, had dropped their veils and learned to read, write and chair the village Soviets'.[7] Clearly these imperial excursions into Muslim culture, whether comparatively benign by the British or aggressive by the Soviets, were not likely to be crowned with success.

The nations of North Africa and the Middle East were more sophisticated than dependencies in sub-Saharan Africa or the Soviet East. Their ancient cultures, sustained by deeply held belief systems, meant that they considered themselves equal or superior to those in the West.

With the exception of Turkey, where in 1934 women were able to vote, enfranchisement in the Muslim-majority nations (the Middle East, the East and North Africa) took place in less than twenty years. Suffrage in Indonesia and Syria was followed by Lebanon, Egypt, Pakistan, Iraq, Morocco, and Tunisia in the 1950s and Mauritania, Algeria, Iran, Libya, Sudan, and (questionably) Afghanistan in the early 1960s.

The steady progress of enfranchisement in Muslim countries now stopped; Arabian and Gulf counties proved resistant to women's political emancipation into the twenty-first century. This left three routes for the path of women's enfranchisement in the remaining Muslim-majority countries: achievement through national struggle; a grant from departing colonialists; and a road-block because suffrage was seen as an un-Islamic practice to be resisted at all costs.

Islam is not monolithic and there is a diversity and specificity in women's experiences in different Islamic societies.[8] It is still true to say generally, however, that the supra-national hand of Islamic conservatism exerted control over and above national priorities and even revolutionary women were driven back to the household. Muslim feminists argue that in their societies there is a masculine view of female sexuality as dangerous and destructive in its power and in need of male supervision, and also that Islam has been distorted by male jurists who wished to attribute misogynist tendencies to Islam that the prophet Muhammad did not possess.[9] They argue that the fears awakened by the Westernization of the women can be interpreted as simply another instance of Muslim society believing that males are able to select what is good in Western civilization and discard bad elements, while women are unable to choose correctly.[10]

Pan-Islamists, arguing for Muslim unity above all, took the view that their people were best served by a rejection of modernism and a return to traditional ways. This train of thought maintained that women's position, dress code, behaviour, and roles were symbols of national authenticity and independence; sacrificing them was an imitation of the West or a concession to the colonizers. Against this weight of conservatism, the enfranchisement of women fed into a collective idea of what it was to be a complex, modern nation—something generally desired by nationalists.

Feminist thinkers fuelled this debate between nationalists and conservatives in the late nineteenth century: Fatma Aliye Hanim in Turkey wrote *The Women of Islam* in 1891 and the Egyptian judge Qasim Amin published *The Liberation of Women* in 1899 and *The New Woman* in 1901. The radicalism of these works was in merely acknowledging that there was a 'woman question'; for conservatives, it was all a matter of obedience to ancient texts. Intellectuals in Egypt, Iran, Turkey, and Syria debated the position of women in the context of the national need for 'modernity' which encompassed both technological progress and the western-style, monogamous family.

Modernizers in Turkey

Turkey did not directly experience any of the transforming movements that changed Europe, though the intellectual influence of such great events as the French Revolution was felt and resisted by the sultans of Turkey and their advisers. The western model which was adopted by the intellectual elite was, however, a French one, and France was notably unprogressive in terms of women's suffrage—France eventually enfranchised women ten years later than Turkey. Women in Turkey were long considered exemplars of involuntary idleness and ignorance. The Ottoman woman, wrote a Greek describing the Turkish upper class in the 1880s, 'has some good qualities which might make her a worthy member of society; but her ignorance, her humiliating position and her exclusive and sensual existence dwarf all development and destroy every hope of amelioration'.[11]

A movement for women's education preceded considerations of citizenship, as usually was the case, and girls' schools were established in the nineteenth century, though education was deeply religious and aimed mainly to produce good wives and mothers. Nevertheless, foreign schools and governesses began to influence upper-class women. In the early 1920s Turkish women had long been discussing their status and had been aware of moves in the West. More than forty magazines show them reflecting Victorian women's concerns with education, employment, marriage, and dress. Yet, despite the impression made by the women's suffrage movement they 'expressed the opinion that this was an untimely and inappropriate demand for themselves in the light of more immediate and pressing issues'.[12] Nevertheless, there were a number of Turkish women's organizations founded between 1908 and 1920, some of which encompassed militant action such as a sit-in to compel the telephone company to employ Muslim women.

Turkey had not been successfully invaded and colonized, so nationalist resistance was against the ingrained conservatism of society. Modernizing Turks looked to democracy as a solution to the problem of reinvigorating their nation. At the same time, subject people in Balkan counties were struggling in their own nationalist movements. A group of progressive thinkers called Young Turks were exiles living outside Turkey at the beginning of the twentieth century. From 1903 they formed relationships with dissident national minorities, particularly in Macedonia and Armenia.

For the Young Turks the position of women was undoubtedly part of progressive thought. The future Turkish president, Mustapha Kemal (later Atatürk—'Father of the Turks') was a member of the Young Turk group in Damascus. He hated the veil and examples of subservient behaviour from women. He said, 'I see women covering their faces with their headscarves or turning their backs when a man approaches. Do you really think that the mothers and daughters of a civilised nation would behave so oddly or be so backward?' He emphasized that religion was not an issue, saying 'nothing in our religion requires women to be inferior to men' and appealed to national pride, insisting that Turkish women could have the civic benefits of their northern sisters: 'I firmly believe that the women of our country are by no means inferior to European women.'[13]

Turkey's losses in the Balkan and the First World wars allowed republican, secular, and non-imperialist thought to flourish in Turkey as the Young Turks came to the fore. The education of women and further measures of emancipation were part of the reforming programme, but zeal for their implementation was tempered by the wars in which Turkey was involved. Then the internal crises that led to the foundation of the Turkish Republic occupied the ailing empire almost continuously from 1912 to 1923.

Modernization and secularization followed the collapse of the Ottoman Empire after its many centuries of decline. The Sultan's capitulation to the Allies led to the overthrow of the Sultanate and, soon after, came the abolition of the Caliphate which had maintained the supremacy of the Ottoman Empire in religious matters. Atatürk set up a revolutionary government in Ankara in April 1920 after being elected by the First Grand National Assembly; he and his modernizers set about transforming the Ottoman Empire into the secular republic of Turkey which was established in 1923.

Patriotic women's groups had been formed in the wake of the collapse of the Ottoman army in 1918 and the occupation of Turkish territory, so women were always part of the modernizing agenda which now, under Atatürk, included Latinizing the alphabet, adopting the Gregorian calendar, and promoting European dress. Women were requested, but not compelled, to abandon the veil and were given or promised rights in marriage, rights to succession, and an end to polygamy and harems. It is claimed, however, that 'activities by Turkish women demanding equality and rights were co-opted by the regime of Mustafa Kemal Atatürk'.[14]

Atatürk emphasized the necessity of giving women full citizenship status and women were encouraged to enter the workplace and public life. The first woman doctor, trained in Germany, started to practise in 1923. Women's positions were used to distinguish the newly established state from the Ottoman Empire as well as to prove to the West that Turkey was a democratic country, where 'women were treated as symbols and tools of modernisation and Westernisation, rather than equal partners of men'.[15] Significantly, Atatürk eschewed a pan-Islamic loyalty in favour of a more narrowly defined Turkish national pride. Atatürk's reforms can be seen as aiming to equip Turkish women with the education and skills to make them better wives in the national interest, similar to the 'state feminism' later seen in Egypt. 'Feminism' in Turkey became synonymous with a dependence on existing political systems and an interaction between women and the state.

Women's suffrage had a tough fight—supporters in the Turkish Grand Assembly were not even allowed to speak during debates on the electoral law bill of 1921–2 and fierce debate raged over the 1924 debate on women's role in the constitution.[16] Atatürk discouraged the Turkish Women's Federation, a feminist umbrella group, from nominating its own parliamentary candidates in the first elections of the new republic in 1927, and women's demand for membership of political parties was denied in the 1930s.[17] However, Atatürk was concerned about western impressions of his regime as a dictatorship and he wanted to push forward with 'democratization'; women's suffrage was a symbolic move towards this, 'a part of democratic image-building'.[18] Women won the right to vote and run in municipal elections in 1930 and in national elections in 1934.

Suffrage did not result in further politicization or independent political acts: women candidates acquired 4.5 per cent of the parliamentary seats in 1935 and all seventeen were handpicked by Atatürk. These women 'quietly performed duties that were assigned to them' and 'did not speak or question much'.[19] Though, as this could easily describe the behaviour of time-serving male politicians in the mature democracies of the West, it could reasonably be said that women therefore were performing just as well (or as badly) as men in the political domain. A civil code was adopted in Turkey in 1936 from one originating in Neuchâtel, Switzerland (one notes the provenance—Switzerland was to become a byword for tardiness in women's suffrage). The code was not markedly sympathetic to women, but was more so than the Shariat which it replaced, and it encouraged the recognition of women as individuals rather than the possession of husbands or male members of their family. It definitively abolished polygamy, set a minimum age for marriage and gave equal rights to women and men in divorce, child custody, and inheritance matters.[20] Once women had supposedly reached equality with men, by having an equal right to vote, the government banned the first women's party and put pressure on the Union of Turkish Women to dissolve.[21] Thus the nationalist state both granted rights and circumscribed their use, ensuring its own continued power.

Women in the Former Ottoman Empire

'The darkness of the Middle Ages has spread a thick cloud over Greece, and the tyrannical yoke which but just now we have thrown off has left ineffaceable scars. Nevertheless we advance, if only slowly,' Kallirroi Parren told the World's Congress of Representative Women in Chicago in May 1894:[22] Parren had pioneered a nationalist feminism, promoting women's education and their involvement in the arts, seeing women as a repository of Greek culture in opposition to the enemy Turkish culture surrounding them.[23] However, women's contribution to the nationalist struggle against the Turks (which extended from 1821 to 1913) did not bring them any measure of political emancipation. Women over 30 who were literate were supposedly enfranchised for local government elections in 1930. With up to two-thirds of women illiterate, this severely restricted access. A reluctant civil service was tardy in registering women and the exercise of civic rights was socially discouraged; in the end only 240 women voted.[24]

During the Second World War the resistance movement against the German invaders enfranchised women in liberated areas; a circular from resistance headquarters in 1944 urged men to stop having 'rusty' ideas and 'prejudices' and to send their mothers and sisters out to vote, and praised the roles (all of them traditionally 'feminine' such as cooking and social welfare) that women were fulfilling for the resistance.[25] Women's franchise was proffered as a gift and perhaps to some extent as a bribe, as active recruits to the resistance were badly needed. This therefore fits the model of women's suffrage being introduced at or after times of national crisis.

The civil war, however, from 1945 to 1949, threw democratic ideas into confusion: to allow women the vote might strengthen the left wing; such organizations as the Union of Greek Women Scientists opposed the women's vote 'due to reasons of high national interest'.[26] Women who had been involved in the resistance were (because of their engagement in the public sphere) denounced as 'prostitutes' and women were urged to return to 'traditional' values, in terms more reminiscent of the Middle East than Christian Europe.[27] A constitution of 1952 enfranchised the whole country, but women were enfranchised in a way that indicated another law was necessary to define the parameters of their vote, including the date when they could vote for the first time. They finally voted on the same terms as men on 19 February 1956.

It is evidence of the pervading influence of a dominant culture that countries of the former Ottoman Empire followed the Turkish (or Egyptian) model of the enfranchisement of women. Greece was established as a kingdom independent from Turkey in 1830 with universal manhood suffrage but Greek women did not get the vote until 1952 in the same decade as other former Ottoman dependencies Lebanon, Egypt, and Iraq. Clearly this was the effect of culture, not religion, as the Greeks had protected the Orthodox Church through centuries of Ottoman rule.

Bulgaria achieved independence from Turkey in 1878, and extended its borders in 1885. A limited women's suffrage encompassing married, widowed and divorced women was granted in 1937, universal suffrage was achieved in 1945; Romania and Yugoslavia enfranchised women in 1946, by this time under communist influence. The First World War and the defeat of Turkey led to the development of nationalist movements in the provinces that had been under Ottoman rule: Palestine, Iraq, Syria, and Lebanon; while Turkey forged a new form of national identity. For women, nationalism was now seen as an 'honourable door' to public life.[28]

Women called for the right to vote in Syria and Lebanon in the 1920s when the nations were under the French mandate and parliaments debated the question but without success. In Syria under the Electoral Law of 1949 every Syrian over 18 years old had the right of suffrage but women must have at least a certificate of primary education in order to be allowed to vote.[29] This was confirmed by the constitution of 1950 and full adult suffrage was introduced in 1953, but after a coup the following year the country reverted to the constitution of 1950. Finally, after years of political upheaval, universal adult suffrage was reached in 1973.[30]

Egyptian Militancy

Huda Shaarawi was born in Al Minya in Upper Egypt in 1879. Her father was the Speaker of the Legislative Assembly; she was married at the age of 13 to Ali Shaarawi who was a member of parliament prominent in the independence struggle, though it was not a happy marriage, because of his refusal to abandon his first wife for Huda, so they lived apart for the first years.

She had met Aletta Jacobs (and perhaps Carrie Chapman Catt) in Cairo in 1912 so was already taking an interest in women's political activity when the anti-colonialist movement began. Egypt was under Turkish sovereignty until 1914 when the British imposed a protectorate so it could form the main base for land operations against Turkey. After the war, the Egyptian revolt against British domination began in 1919 with the creation of the Egyptian Wafd organization, in which Huda's husband was a leading figure. Women participated in the 1919 revolution with strikes and protests against the British colonizers, including a demonstration of women, in which Huda Shaarawi participated, facing armed British soldiers. In 1920 Huda became president of the Wafdist Women's Central Committee. Men were, as in Finland and India, willing to see women take part in nationalist campaigns where they would not have supported purely political activities aimed at promoting women's rights.

When Wafdist leaders returned from negotiations in London in 1920 with an independence proposal, they discussed it with men's organizations but did not show it to the Wafdist Women's Central Committee. Huda Shaarawi and others made public their anger, writing, 'by disregarding us the Wafd has caused the foreigners to disparage the renaissance of women. They claim that our participation in the nationalist movement was merely a ploy to dupe civilised nations into believing in the advancement of Egypt and its ability to govern itself.'[31]

The British rescinded their protectorate in a formal recognition of Egyptian independence in 1922. The new constitution of March 1923, articles 74 and 82, granted universal suffrage, but when the electoral law was codified later that year, women were excluded.[32] In response Huda founded the Egyptian Feminist Union with other upper-class women, and became its president; they called for political rights for women, equal secondary education and university rights, and opportunities for professional work. In the domestic sphere they wanted controls on marriage laws such as those controlling polygamy and divorce. It was as leader of this organization that she attended the International Woman Suffrage Alliance meeting in Rome in 1923 with the dramatic gesture of unveiling on her return. She made two points to the conference: that women in ancient Egypt had equal status to men, and only under foreign domination had women lost those rights; and that Islam granted women equal rights to men, but that the Koran had been misinterpreted by those in power.

Excepting the wives of government ministers, Egyptian women were banned from the opening of the new parliament in 1924, though foreign women were admitted. Huda led a picket of the parliament, calling for the vote for educated women, and drawing attention to other issues of female disbarment. Previously they had every expectation of winning the vote; the leader of the Wafd, Saad Zaghlul, recorded in his diary that nationalist leaders had agreed to work for the liberation of women after independence, but they did not.[33] The Egyptian Feminist Union, disgusted at their betrayal by the Wafd Party, and at what they considered to be insufficient nationalist vigour of the Wafd in power, aligned themselves with the opposition Liberal Constitutional Party. This was a clumsy manoeuvre that lost them their grip on parliamentary politics. Between 1926 and 1934 they dropped the suffrage demand and concentrated on legal and educational work.[34] As in other 'bourgeois' movements, when they took to the streets it was in motor cars, one of which was seized by the police in a demonstration against the government (which had suspended the constitution) in Cairo in 1931. Other women protested at the police station and were arrested. Saiza Nabarawi, who had unveiled beside Huda at the Cairo railway station was at the demonstration and wrote, in terms reminiscent of the British suffragettes, 'For the first time in our history women were imprisoned for a political question. This inaugurates a glorious page in Egyptian feminism that henceforth will only develop.'[35]

But the movement lost its campaigning zeal, despite some high profile activity such as Huda Shaarawi's audience with Kemal Atatürk in 1935, the year after Turkish women got the vote, during the International Woman Suffrage Alliance conference in Istanbul. Egyptian women were granted municipal suffrage in 1935. Huda Shaarawi made a strong call for political rights for all Arab women at the Arab Feminist conference in Cairo in 1944. She died in 1947 after having been awarded the Nishan al-Kamal, the highest decoration of Egypt, for services to her country.

A younger generation of Egyptian women was now going to carry the movement forward. Chief among these was Doria Shafik, who was born in 1908 in the province of Tanta to a high class mother and a civil engineer. Her mother died when she was 13, and her father encouraged her education. She wrote to Huda Shaarawi who also encouraged the girl, supported her financially, and obtained a scholarship for her to study at the Sorbonne. In Paris she encountered her cousin, who was a fellow student there, and married him, making a point of doing so without parental approval or dowry. They had two daughters.

She obtained a doctorate in 1940 but was refused a post at the University of Cairo and so devoted herself to the women's movement and to literature—she produced seven books in French and Arabic.[36] In 1948 she founded a magazine, Bint al-Nil (Daughter of the Nile), with a group of women supporting its values in the Bint al-Nil Union. This organization of confident, middle-class women launched a programme with a primary campaign for women's political rights but also promoting cultural and social programmes. The symbolic title Daughter of the Nile was an assertion of Egyptian identity, excluding association with 'the Turko-Circassian elite' and declaring the importance of national origin: birth by the Nile whether rural or urban, Copt or Muslim.[37]

She unsuccessfully submitted electoral registration papers in an attempt to become a candidate. Taking a lesson from British suffragette militancy in taking the argument to the legislators, in 1951 she led an invasion by 1,500 women of the Egyptian parliament, demanding the right to vote. In response to claims that her organization was un-Islamic, and should be closed down, and the veil strictly imposed on suffragist women, Doria Shafik wrote that her critics had not faced realities: 'the education of girls at universities is a fact; the employment of women in public service is a fact; and women's constitutional rights is a problem that will be solved in spite of the opposition, the meetings, the insults and accusations because it is a logical and just cause supported by the merciful and generous religion of Islam.'[38]

Gamal Abdel Nasser's revolution of 1952 (making him prime minister in 1954) offered hope of change and, as commonly occurred, women's suffrage came to the fore at a time of national upheaval and the making of new constitutions—though one of Nasser's first actions was to ban political parties, including Doria Shafik's. The Egyptian Revolutionary Command Council set up a committee to advise on a new constitution, but included no women on it. When she read of this, Shafik determined that women's rights were in danger; she and eight other women staged a hunger strike on the steps of the Egyptian Press Syndicate to ensure maximum publicity. The hunger strike was ended when the president promised to give consideration to the hunger strikers' petition for women's rights.

The opposition was extreme: the Islamic scholars at Al Azhar, the mosque university, issued a fatwa (a ruling based on religious law) that women's unstable nature made them unfit to vote and so forbade the government from granting women's suffrage. Nasser's government found a place for the head of the Al Azhar as ambassador to Yemen, and continued with the modernizing programme.[39] Nasser was a politician in the mould of new populists, not a patrician like Asquith; faced with militant action, from Shafik and her supporters, he absorbed it into his political system. Women were granted the right to vote and run for political office in 1956, though women had to request to be registered while men were automatically registered. Now women's rights to employment and education were promoted in what has been called 'state feminism'. It was a process which has been described as bearing a strong resemblance to strategies employed by the Scandinavian welfare states.[40] Women were said to be economically independent of their families, but increasingly dependent on the state—women were still therefore dependent on a patriarchy.

Feminist activism receded during the time of Nasser's ascendancy as a result of the state's monitoring of political activism, banning autonomous organizations and monopolizing women's issues which were reformulated as social welfare issues. In a reversal of western attitudes about women's rights, there was an acceptance of women's public space, where women were not only permitted but expected to pursue public activities like education and work and to vote; while women's rights at home, in the private family sphere were ignored or considered outside the legitimate struggle for women's rights, making such subjects as abortion, reproductive issues, and domestic violence taboo.[41]

Doria Shafik's final act of protest was to stage a hunger strike in 1957 against the Israeli occupation of Egyptian land and 'the onset of dictatorship' in Egypt.[42] Her enemies in the women's movement denounced her. Her espousal of individual freedom and secular liberalism found no place in the new Egypt; she was placed under house arrest in 1957 and played no further part in politics. She committed suicide by jumping from her sixth-floor apartment in Cairo on 20 September 1975.

Nationalist Struggles and the Women's Vote

The most populous Muslim-majority nation is Indonesia; its interest in the current context is how little the specifically Muslim identity of the population affected its final political settlement. There were both secular and Muslim women's groups, but these came together at the Federation of Indonesian Women's Associations which in 1938 had suffrage as its main conference theme. Women's political emancipation became, as was common in anti-colonial struggles, a part and a symbol of national liberation. Thus when the Dutch colonial masters offered the municipal vote only to Dutch women in 1941, protests were so extreme that the proposal was withdrawn.[43]

Japan invaded in 1942; after the Japanese defeat the nationalist leader Sukarno declared independence in the name of the people on 17 August 1945. A constitution of that year enfranchised men and women but in a situation of upheaval in which no one clearly held power. The Dutch resisted and an armed conflict followed in which women came forward to support the guerrillas, organizing clinics and cooking centres. An independent government was finally established in 1948, and the constitution, framed the following year, gave equal voting rights to women in an effective democracy.

Looking at another populous Muslim nation, the provinces that became Pakistan went though the same independence struggle as India though with considerably less enthusiasm; the determination of the Muslim League to have a Muslim state led to the bloody partition of what had been India. The objective of Muhammad Ali Jinnah, father of the new state, and Liaquat Ali Khan, the first prime minister, was for a non-theocratic, liberal, democratic nation; they 'emphasised Islamic principles and not Islamic law'.[44]

Women of the provinces of the new Pakistan had, under British rule, enjoyed some measure of enfranchisement from arrangements made under the Government of India Act 1919 and expanded by the Government of India Act 1935. Independence in 1947 did not alter these local enfranchisements and the constitution finally adopted in 1956 enfranchised men and women equally. Pakistan underwent further difficulties (no election was held under this constitution) but these were related to the exercise of democracy and the relationship of civil to military power, women's suffrage was not an issue. The most extreme restriction (unsuccessfully) proposed, at the time of discussions about the constitution in the 1950s, was for all men but only educated women to be enfranchised. Attempts at Islamization by leaders such as the dictator Zia-ul-Haq extended to insisting women civil servants wear the chador (complete covering), not to disenfranchise them.

The emergence of Islamic societies from anti-imperialist struggles has caused problems for women, however, precisely because the cause of women's emancipation is one that has historically been identified with the West; thus, there is a tendency for nationalist movements to reject it in the name of their own 'national authenticity'. This was most evident in Algeria in the period after 1962 and in Iran after 1978 where, for example, those women arguing for women's right to choose whether to be veiled or not were castigated for being agents of foreign influence.[45]

Former French colonies Morocco (which also had Spanish influence) and Tunisia enfranchised women in 1956 and 1959 respectively, and Mauritania in 1961, as part of the creation of new constitutions while the colonial masters departed. There was a protracted battle for France to keep hold of Algeria, which had been annexed as an integral part of France, rendering the conflict effectively a civil war. The Statute of Algeria in 1947 created an Algerian assembly for European settlers (male and female) and 'meritorious' male Muslims, with a separate assembly for Muslim men, supposedly for elections in 1948, but most provisions were not brought in and the elections were manipulated by the French. Even benign efforts under this legislation would not have produced a realistic democracy: both the European college and the Muslim college had to pass any major legislation, the European minority could block any proposal they disagreed with.

The French administrators at a high level were concerned to block the access of Algerian women to the franchise in such a way as to deflect international criticism of the French regime.[46] The 1947 statute made provision for women to vote at some future time. One legal commentator wrote in 1953, 'as most Muslims are so strongly against it, the political equality of the Muslim women with the French women will probably not come into being for a long time.'[47] This was, recent research has revealed, just what the French wanted the world to think. The problem for the administrators was that the admission of Muslim women would double the Muslim vote, significantly reducing the European proportion of the electorate and altering the balance of power; the inequity of the dual assembly system would be glaring. The administration in 1957 therefore set itself to examining ways to restrict women's access to the vote—through literacy, age, and marital status requirements, or because the veil would prevent identification at polling stations.[48] After De Gaulle took power in June 1958 women were given voting rights, but in a nation on which France no longer had a firm hold (though it was these electoral provisions that were maintained when independence was eventually won).

Some Algerian women supported the French, seeing alliance with the European power as the means to a new equality. Many more supported the rebels, using the cover of traditional dress to transmit food, weapons and information during the armed struggle. Conversely, some women pretended to be westernized, and unveiled for the first time in their lives in order to plant bombs in French cafes and shops.[49] The French appealed to women to look to France as the means to lessen their oppression and take advantage of a new lifestyle. Thousands of Algerian women were 'unveiled' in a public ceremony on 17 May 1958 to show their support for French women who would lead them to modernity.[50]

With the achievement of independence, Algerian nationalists rejected that which had been French, and stressed a return to a subordinate role for women. Women activists had taken enormous personal risks to bring about the revolution but this was pushed aside in the fervour to restore the legitimacy of the new state.[51] Women won guarantees of equality in the political and educational spheres but liberal laws on personal status and the family drafted in 1966 were not passed: 'We want a free Algerian woman, not a free Frenchwoman,' said Colonel Houari Boumedienne who took over the leadership of Algeria after seizing power in a coup shortly after independence.[52]

Persian Protests

The nation known as Persia until 1935 had not been colonized but became divided into 'spheres of influence' by Britain and Russia. In the modern years of this ancient culture, women's position had been under discussion among members of the Bahai faith and Freemasons, but the Islamic majority resisted changes in the status of women until major national events forced the issues. The 1906 revolution brought the subject forward, with women now appearing among the protesters on the streets. Their role was specifically resisted, and even the new girls' schools were resented by conservatives; the sight of women teachers and girls walking to school aroused hostility manifested in insults, obscene gestures, and spitting. The mullahs declared women's education contrary to Islamic law and denounced them, but the education project continued.[53]

Women's engagement in the revolution was not sufficient to guarantee them the vote; the new 'democratic' constitution specifically excluded women along with minors and 'fraudulent bankrupts, beggars, murderers, thieves and other criminals punishable under Islamic law'.[54] The monarchy had been forced to make constitutional concessions, but had not conceded defeat and the Shah attacked parliament, leading to a national revolt. Women were again involved in demonstrations, particularly after the Russian invasion of northern Persia in 1911 when the defence of the nation became a defence against foreign aggression.

The national crisis and discussion of a constitution brought an entry point for women's rights to be discussed. A parliamentarian rose to call for women's suffrage in August 1911 during a debate on the bill enabling the next election. Hadji Vakil el-Roaya, the deputy for Hamandan, rose to oppose the clause declaring that no women should vote. From the rostrum he 'declared roundly that women possessed souls and rights and should possess votes'. He called upon the religious authorities to support him. The house listened in silence, unable to decide whether this was a joke. Another member rose and, according to a western account, 'solemnly declared that he had never in a life of misfortune had his ears assailed by such an impious utterance...he denied to women either souls or rights, and declared that such a doctrine would mean the downfall of Islam'. The official version, printed in a letter to *The Times* after the above account had been published, reported that the official response was:

> we must not discuss this question, for it is contrary to the etiquette of an Islamic parliament. But the reason for excluding women is that God has not given them the capacity needed for taking part in politics and electing the representatives of the nation. They are the weaker sex and have not the same power of judgement as men have. However, their rights must not be trampled upon, but must be safeguarded by men as ordained in the Koran by God Almighty.[55]

Some women did organize sporadic protests: a group of women were reported in a busy Tehran street, taking off their veils and shouting, 'Long live the constitution. Long live freedom.' The constitutionalist leaders of the revolution denied any connection with these sentiments, and declared that counter-revolutionaries had bribed these 'prostitutes' to discredit the revolution. Thus engagement with a political issue was disposed of by a sexual insult.[56] Women did take part in defending the constitution, in demonstrating in the streets and in giving refuge to threatened parliamentary deputies and volunteer revolutionary soldiers. Some women were armed and some were said to have dressed in men's clothes and taken part in fighting.[57] It was to no avail politically, the parliament was closed down in 1912.

Women's issues relating to reform of the law as it affected women and such matters as child marriage continued to be discussed in numerous women's magazines after the First World War, stimulated both by the women's suffrage advances in the UK, the US, and Russia and also by the example of Huda Shaarawi and the engagement of women in Egyptian nationalism.[58] A military officer, Reza Khan, took over the government in a military coup in 1921 and set about creating a centralized state along the Turkish model. Three years after taking power, he had himself proclaimed king and took the name Reza Shah Pahlavi. His regime was both authoritarian and western-looking in the style of Atatürk. He banned political parties, censored the press and cracked down on women's organizations; but he also abolished the veil in 1936 and reduced the power of the clerics. His son, Mohamed Reza Pahlavi, became king ('Shah') in 1941 and political parties were restored, many of which opened women's branches. A programme started in the 1960s, the White Revolution, aimed at land reform, improved literacy, and voting rights for women. The referendum over the White Revolution's reforms in 1963 excluded women, but they set up their own polling stations and created enough public interest for the Pahlavi regime to accept the situation and count women's votes. Women were expected to support the reforms, so the regime was boosting its strength by accepting them; a month after the vote, the Shah announced he was granting women the right to vote and stand for office.

The regime branded the religious movement as reactionary for opposing the enfranchisement of women, but the leading opposition figure, Ayatollah Khomeini, saw the White Revolution as an American ploy for western domination of the nation, supposedly imposed by Vice President Johnson on his state visit to Iran in 1961. Khomeini, leading the anti-Shah movement, described the proposed extension of suffrage to women as an instrument for moral corruption. The culture of the West was seen as a godless one in which women were primarily sexual objects; democracy was the freedom of the rich to exploit the poor and for superpowers to exploit the countries of the third world.[59] However, women played such an active part in the move to depose the Shah that the revolutionary regime of Shi'ite fundamentalists who took over in 1979 felt it would not be propitious to reverse the Shah's reforms and disenfranchise women. They had discovered as had so many before them that, though women's suffrage was often promoted by radicals, it could just as well be used to propel a conservative agenda.

The aggressive measures of modernization adopted by the Shah, such as ordering police to remove chadors forcibly and shred them with scissors, effectively countenanced the reaction after the revolution of 1979, of religious authorities enforcing a restrictive dress code with violence.

Revolutionary Women in Afghanistan

Afghanistan is a quarter of a million square miles of a mainly tribal nation that was fought over by the Russians and British in the nineteenth and twentieth centuries. After many years of bitter conflict a nationalist leader, Amanullah Khan, finally forced the British to recognize Afghan independence and in 1923 he proposed a new constitution with votes for women, claiming that 'the keystone of the future structure of the new Afghanistan will be the emancipation of women.'[60] He promoted the education of women and decreed that the veil should be abandoned, but his reforms offended against the tribal chiefs, whose power depended on rigid traditions of control; they deposed him in 1929 and reversed reforms: schools for girls were closed; the veil was made compulsory; and women were refused the vote.

The battle between traditional methods of control and 'modernization' continued through the twentieth century and into the twenty-first. A constitutional monarchy with a constitution supposedly enfranchising women was introduced in 1964, but after one election in 1965 in which women voted, the move towards democracy was in abeyance. The king was deposed and a republic proclaimed in 1973, with help from the Soviets who expanded their interests in Afghanistan. The absence of political parties prevented the effective functioning of parliament or everyday political life, and a traditional resistance to female participation in public life further restricted Afghan women. For some, the reaction to the godless materialism of the Soviets was a resort to what they saw as the fundamentals of Islam.

This was, however, a time when the political direction of the country was under discussion and feminists could organize. A leading activist, Meena 'Keshwar Kamel', was born in Kabul in 1957, the daughter of an architect who was often engaged on civic projects. As a child she suffered from typhoid, which left her with intermittent seizures; she went to a French-orientated school in Kabul where she was inspired, as so many women leaders have been, by the story of Joan of Arc.[61] Then, at Kabul University she became involved in political activity, marrying a doctor of medicine, Faiz Ahmed, who was also a socialist (but anti-Soviet) activist and who encouraged her in her work. Meena left university, aiming to dedicate herself to the education and political organization of women. She travelled to clandestine meetings in a burka because it allowed conceal-ment from the fundamentalists and the police; forbidden books and leaflets could also be carried under burkas. Women normally did not visit others outside the family (which was supposed to supply all their needs) so even a meeting of unrelated women was revolutionary; consequently Meena's organisation, founded in 1977, was called the Revolutionary Association of the Women of Afghanistan. It called for democracy, equal rights, and secu-larism—the separation of religion from the affairs of state.[62]

A communist-orientated 'People's Democratic' group with close links to the Soviet Union organized a coup, with the help of the army, and set about eliminating intellectuals and others thought to be enemies of the regime. Meena's husband had to flee to Pakistan, and Meena had a child while she was in hiding within Afghanistan. The Soviet Union invaded in December 1979, supposedly to restore order in a country that was in fact in chaos be-cause of the imposition of Marxist ideas on a feudal society, and women's emancipation again became an aspect of modernity imposed from outside. A number of nationalist and fundamentalist Islamic groups under the col-lective name Mujahideen began to resist the Soviet invasion, and were armed and supported by the US and various Arab countries.

Activists such as Meena were caught between their opposition to Islamic fundamentalism and their patriotic resistance to the Soviet invasion. She lived in hiding, sometimes wearing a burka, sometimes men's clothing. In 1981 Meena launched a feminist magazine, *Payam-e-Zan* (Women's Message), documenting the abuses of the regime, and argued internationally for a free and democratic Afghanistan. In 1982 she visited Europe, lobbying for the women of Afghanistan in France, Belgium, Holland, Germany, and Norway, where she was promoted as 'actively leading the underground Afghan wom-en's resistance against the Soviets and their puppet regime in Kabul'.[63] After almost being arrested in Afghanistan, Meena was told by other Revolutionary Association of the Women of Afghanistan members to leave. She settled in Quetta on the Pakistan border in 1982, a place that was to become home to

Figure 21. A roadside sign gives encouragement to women voters in Afghanistan in 2009, underlining women's equality as an allied war aim. The poster reassures women they will have a separate voting area from men, and will be protected by soldiers.

hundreds of thousands of refugees. She applied herself to the refugees pouring over the Afghan border into Pakistan, establishing schools and orphanages, a hospital, and handicrafts centres.

During this time support for the Mujahideen came from states who supported fighters against the Soviets whatever their character—including criminal warlords and Islamic extremists. These fundamentalists, with the support of the Pakistan government, set up hundreds of madrassas. This religious education for boys was the only schooling they received in a narrow, extremist form of Islam; girls were prohibited from attending. Meena's schools taught boys and girls equally. Because of their public presentation of women's rights and democracy, the women of Meena's organization were harassed and taunted as un-Islamic whores and lesbians. She was angry that western and Saudi aid bypassed her organization and went directly to the fundamentalists. 'If we had the money the fundamentalists have, we would be able to educate every Afghan child,' she said.[64]

Her husband, who was in hiding even in Pakistan, would visit her and they had two more children (twins). He was seized, tortured, and killed in 1986, probably by the fundamentalists who feared his influence. Meena's levels of security were understandably high, but after receiving a message whose contents are unknown at her headquarters in Quetta, on 4 February 1987, she set off in a car accompanied by a driver and a male escort. She and the two aides disappeared. Six months later two men were arrested for another crime and confessed that they had killed Meena and her two companions and hidden the bodies in the garden of a house in Quetta; she was 30 years old. She had probably been betrayed by a man she trusted, her translator, an educated man who had lived in Europe, and whose services she needed to speak in English with foreign supporters and donors. He had worked his way into her circle, and was even engaged to a member of her family. The Pakistani authorities hanged the two killers in a prison in Baluchistan without trying them for the murder of Meena. Her murderers are believed to have been agents of the Soviets or of fundamentalist leader Golboddin Hekatyar, both of whom had sufficient reason to fear her influence; Hekatyar was probably also her husband's murderer.

The Soviet withdrawal in 1989 led to warlords fighting over the nation, with the eventual victory of the Taliban in 1996. Now Afghanistan became a haven for Islamic extremists, including al-Quaeda. Following the 9/11 attack on the US in 2001, the United States and their allies invaded Afghanistan to attack al-Quaeda and ensure a friendly regime was in power. In terms of women's position in Afghanistan, these frequent changes of influence have led to the reiteration of a simple line of argument: outsiders have to be resisted, the fundamental values of traditional Afghanistan retained. One of the most visible symbols of outside influence had been the emancipation of women. The Taliban, in particular, expelled western aid organizations and enforced the veil. Unveiling and voting therefore continued to be seen as symbols of western incursion into Afghanistan.

From the start, the position of women in Afghanistan was presented as a principal reason for the invasion of the country; in November 2001 Colin Powell, the US secretary of state, said: 'The rights of women in Afghanistan will not be negotiable.'[65] The Afghan Women's Summit for Democracy held under the auspices of the United Nations in December 2001 called for equal rights for women including the right to vote, the 'Brussels Proclamation'. By Women's Equality Day of 2002 President George W. Bush was able to boast, 'In Afghanistan, the Taliban used violence and fear to deny Afghan women access to education, health care, mobility, and the right to vote. Our coalition has liberated Afghanistan and restored fundamental human rights and freedoms to Afghan women, and all the people of Afghanistan. Young girls in Afghanistan are able to attend schools for the first time.'[66]

Schools for girls were the key to women's civil rights, as Meena had realized. The fundamentalists realized this too, and took to attacking teachers, students, and schools across Afghanistan, with girls' schools being particularly hard hit. By the end of 2006 there were entire provinces where there was no girls' education, 300 schools had been shut or burnt down, the majority of them for girls. A Taliban threatening letter left at a still functioning school said: 'Respected Afghans: Leave the culture of the Christian and Jews. Do not send your girls to school.'[67]

The Revolutionary Association of the Women of Afghanistan continued to argue for a democratic and secular government: 'The oppression of Afghan women was used as a justification to overthrow the Taliban regime,' proclaimed Zoya, one of their speakers. 'No doubt the war on terror toppled the misogynist and barbaric regime of Taliban. But it did not remove Islamic fundamentalism, which is the root cause of misery for all Afghan people; it just replaced one fundamentalist regime with another.'[68] Activist women complained that fundamentalists were being invited back into Afghan government for the supposed restoration of order, though their values had not changed.

Tremendous efforts were made to register women to vote in the 2004 presidential election that was said to 'mark the advent of women's suffrage in a country steeped in conservative Islamic tradition' (though as noted earlier, women's suffrage had supposedly been established with a republic in 1964).[69] More than 4 million women registered for voting in the presidential election, 41 per cent of the 10.5 million people who signed up to vote. Four women were among the dozen election workers killed by anti-government militants during the months of voter registration. Most women were illiterate, their participation in the ballot was indicated by an ink mark on their thumbs; it was reported that men would threaten to cut off a woman's hand if she had this mark of participating with the forces of the West. As part of a public demonstration of commitment to equality, at the parliamentary election in 2005 women were given 25 per cent of reserved seats in the lower house. This was rather more than the 16 per cent of women in the US Congress or the almost 20 per cent in the British House of Commons.[70]

The Revolutionary Association of the Women of Afghanistan continued their work throughout the rule of the Taliban and learned to use new technology to publicize their message, setting up a website in 1997 with the initial message: 'Thank you for visiting the website of the most oppressed women in the world. If you are freedom-loving and antifundamentalist, you are with us.'[71] The attention of American television personality Oprah Winfrey has also attracted support to the project.

Iraq's troubled legacy

Iraq suffered a troubled history in the twentieth century, with foreign invasions, weak kings and military coups. The nation had been a sovereign state since 1932, and since the 1920s Iraqi women had been engaging in debate about their role in society. Women were supposedly given the vote in 1958 after a number of members of the royal family were assassinated and a republic was declared by military rulers who aimed at modernization; the women's vote was part of a programme of social and agrarian reforms aimed at making the nation more western, in a similar process to that which happened in Turkey, Egypt, and Iran, but without sufficient ideology or a strong leader to effect the national transformation.

It was not until the Baath party took control in 1968 that women were brought to active participation in politics; the Baathists were left-of-centre nationalists with some ideological connections to European fascism or national socialism. As in Turkey and Egypt, women's inclusion was a key component of the social revolution they offered. Women and men were to be equal in law, women were to receive an education, to work outside the home, they were encouraged to enter the professions and education was mandatory for boys and girls to the age of 16.

A series of coups was completed by Saddam Hussein who took over in 1979 and ruled for more than twenty years. The Baath Party outlawed the formerly influential League for the Defence of Women's Rights; only the Baath Party women's organization, the General Federation of Iraqi Women, was allowed to function openly. Baathists were secular, and therefore opposed by Islamic fundamentalists. Under their regime girls went to school; women worked outside the home, wore western clothes and make-up, and voted—in as much as a vote meant anything to either men or women in a one-party state. The regime was brutal to dissidents but no more so to females than males.

Saddam Hussein rapidly built up Iraq to be the strongest military power in the region; in this he was assisted by the US which wanted a counterweight to the growing power of neighbouring Iran. An eight-year war with Iran was fought to the point of stalemate, which had a profound impact on the position of women who took on the jobs of men who had been drafted into military service. Saddam Hussein's wish to dominate the region led to the invasion of Kuwait which was resisted by the United Nations and led to the first Gulf War in 1991. This ended in the Iraqis being driven out, but Saddam stayed in power. Sanctions subsequently imposed against Saddam's regime did not bring it down, but caused economic distress, unemployment, and a general retreat of women from the workplace to the home. A US-led invasion force attacked Iraq in 2003, with the swift overthrow of Saddam's regime but subsequent disorder.

The lack of a transparent justification for the invasion of Iraq resulted in a focus on democracy as a clear benefit to the end of Saddam's rule. Sovereignty was transferred to an interim government in 2004 and multi-party elections were held on 30 January 2005. The position of women was central to this equation; every third candidate on party lists for the 275-seat Transitional Assembly elections had to be a woman, with the objective of achieving at least 25 per cent women in the parliament (in fact women captured 31 per cent of the seats). However, Iraq is a nation divided along ethnic, religious and cultural lines. Its Sunni population (who had formerly been dominant, in the Baath Party) boycotted the elections. This left the majority Shi'ites, with their links to the fundamentalists of Iran, in a dominant position. Nearly half of the elected women ran on the list of the Shi'ite Alliance and had to toe the conservative line of the party. There were some radical women elected, but the political atmosphere of targeted assassinations made them maintain a low profile.

As an activist said, 'When we look at the Islamic women who are now in the parliament; they are not part of the Iraqi Women's Movement, they just repeat the programmes of their political parties. They do not see women's issues as their problem, because they are not politicians, they are not feminists.'[72]

Iraq's new constitution stated that Iraqis are equal before the law 'without discrimination because of sex' but it also stated that no law could be passed that contradicted the 'established rulings' of Islam which effectively handed the law over to religious interpretation. One of the eighty-seven women elected, Dr Jenan al-Ubaedy, explained her interpretation of Sharia law as it related to married women being beaten by their husbands: 'He can beat her when she is not obeying him in his rights.' She explained her colleagues' aspirations for a wife: 'We want her to be educated enough that she will not force him to beat her, and if he beats her with no right, we want her to be strong enough to go to the police.'[73]

Extremists in both Sunni and Shi'ite areas of the country imposed their own restrictions on women; forcing them to wear full covering, segregating the sexes in public, forbidding such activities as singing and dancing, and bombing hair salons. 'Misery gangs' patrolled the streets harassing women college students and others who did not dress or behave as approved. Forty-two women were reported to have been killed between July and September 2007 by militiamen for such offences as wearing make-up and being seen out unveiled.[74]

Figure 22. Iraqi women voters supporting a female candidate in parliamentary elections in 2010; a quota system ensured 25 per cent female representation.

The Arabian Peninsula

Women's suffrage was taken out of the conflict zone in the Cold War, as it was not disputed by capitalism or communism; countries under both spheres of influence enfranchised women, leading to the largest number of countries enfranchising women over the 1950s and 1960s when the Cold War was at its height.

In the post-Cold War world, particularly after the 9/11 attack and the announcement of a 'War on Terror', the world was again divided. One of the major distinctions that emerged between Islamic extremism and the liberal capitalist world was in the treatment of women. Countries in which fundamentalist hard-liners were in the ascendant were marked by the appearance (or, very often, the re-appearance) of veiled women. In western counties such as France and in westernized Turkey even the wearing of a headscarf became a point of conflict.

The division was not so simple, however: in the 1990s countries with varying levels of enmity to the West, Iran and Iraq, had functioning political systems incorporating women. However, countries friendly to the West, such as Kuwait, Saudi Arabia and the Gulf states, denied women a place in political life. The 1991 Gulf War was therefore fought to stop Iraq with an elected dictatorship in a one-party state, from taking control of the undemocratic kingdom of Kuwait or threatening the even more repressive kingdom of Saudi Arabia. There was considerable comment that service personnel, including servicewomen, were putting their lives at risk in the protection of states in which women had no voice and were subject to numerous petty restrictions such as a ban on women driving cars in Saudi Arabia.

This has led to pressure being put on countries which still deny votes to women in order that this tangible symbol of political equality could demonstrate progress. In 2000 none of the Arabian or Gulf states had enfranchised women for national elections excepting Yemen where a long national struggle and the presence of armed foreigners in the form of the British and the Egyptians had a strong influence. This meant universal suffrage in the finally united nation followed a model of the more western-influenced Middle Eastern counties. Women were enfranchised in the divided south and north of the country in 1967 and 1970, a position that was constitutionally reiterated after they joined together in 1990.

The other Arabian Peninsula countries where women had no political rights were Bahrain, Kuwait, Oman, Qatar, Saudi Arabia, and the United Arab Emirates, all of them maintaining friendly relations with the West. Within five years of the endorsement of a 'war on terrorism' by the US Congress on 18 September 2001, all these countries had taken steps towards some measure of democracy and all, except Saudi Arabia, had enfranchised women for national elections. The model here was of a grudging, arms-length enfranchisement where concessions were made in the teeth of conservative opposition.

Kuwait is a constitutional monarchy with an electorate of male nationals (on a strict nationality test) participating since 1961. In May 1999 the Emir Jabir al-Ahmad al-Sabah issued a decree granting women the vote but the National Assembly refused to ratify it, repealing the decree in November.

An active movement by women (who enjoyed considerable personal freedom compared to women in other Arabian peninsular countries) mobilized in favour of the enfranchisement, safe in the knowledge that as the Emir had expressed this view, their actions were not a rebellion but loyalty to the nation's leader. Technology came to their aid in 2005—as it had not when the subject was fought over previously; economist Rola Dashti organized protests of girls by using text messages to mobile telephones to call them into the streets.

Dashti, who had studied for a PhD in the United States, explained: 'Those who fought for suffrage were accused of ruining the social fabric of Kuwait, of being anti-religious and anti-nationalist. They were called traitors, agents of the west, and advocates of divorce. Despite such criticism, the women's movement prevailed. When 1,300 women staged a peaceful march recently, it was indicative of their refusal to allow extremists to control their lives.' The Kuwaiti parliament on 16 May 2005 granted women's suffrage by a 35 to 23 vote, with an ambiguous concession to the fundamentalists that women must 'abide by Islamic law' when voting and campaigning.

Dashti acknowledged the influence of outside powers, including the United States, for their 'tremendous influence on efforts to change the Middle East', adding that 'embracing liberal reformers would help foster economic openness, which would in turn contribute to a higher standard of living, foster a more vibrant society, and deter citizens from supporting despotic regimes'.[75] So liberalism plus capitalism would make people feel better and discourage extremism, in this benign presentation of what modernity had to offer.

No women were elected the following year, despite their being in a majority in the electorate; Rola Dashti received the highest number of votes.
The peculiar alchemy of electoral politics was already apparent when the
most extreme fundamentalists, who had opposed enfranchising women,
started campaigning for women to vote for them in the weeks leading up
to the election. Women's enfranchisement did not usher in a period of liberalism; laws were passed in the years 2005–6 to restrict freedom of speech
and the media's ability to criticize the government's performance. In 2009,
Dashti and two other women became the first to be elected to a Kuwaiti
parliament. She became minister of state planning and development affairs
in 2012.

Progress towards female enfranchisement in other Arab peninsular states
related to their own particular forms of public participation in politics.
Women went to the polls for the first time in Bahrain on 23 October 2002.
Bahrain was more motivated to improve the condition of women than
other nations, needing to replace imported labour with local workers because it is one of the poorest of the oil-producing countries, with its oil
expected to run out in the near future. Accordingly, girls' school enrolment
matched that of boys with almost no dropping out at puberty (where girls
were traditionally removed to be forced into marriage).[76] The general population of women showed no enthusiasm for politics: despite a numerical
majority of women in the electorate, no woman candidate was elected, and
a survey prior to the election found that 60 per cent of Bahraini women
were opposed to the participation of women in elections.[77]

Oman held its first parliamentary elections in October 2003 under a new
constitution giving suffrage to all Omanis over 21, and two women were
elected, though none were elected in the 2007 elections, and only one in
2012.

In Qatar, a constitution of 2003 granted universal suffrage in all elections.
This consolidated the municipal franchise for women which had been
granted in 1999. No national elections had taken place ten years later, but in
2003 Sheika Yousef Hassan al-Jufairi became the first woman in a Gulf state
to win elected office (though in an unopposed election) as a member of the
Central Municipal Council.

In the United Arab Emirates electors are selected by the rulers of the
states; in 2006 for the first time women formed a part of this select electorate which made up less than one per cent of the population; this went up
to around 12 per cent in 2011. In each election one woman was elected
among the twenty members of the advisory Federal National Council.

Saudi Arabia, the last and most powerful of the Arab peninsular nations, has been taking slow steps toward democracy, with the first municipal elections being held for a male-only electorate in 2005. Women were not specifically excluded under electoral laws, but were then said to have been excluded for administrative reasons, because there were not enough women electoral staff to run women-only registration centres and because women rarely had independent photo IDs. Such feeble excuses by a spokesman for the administration suggest that opposition to women's suffrage in the kingdom is bankrupt and will not be maintained.[78] In a move reminiscent of women's suffrage campaigns in the nineteenth century, some Saudi women insisted they did have the right to vote in the 2011 municipal elections and tried to register in Jeddah, Riyadh and Damman. In response King Abdullah announced that women would be able to participate as voters and candidates in the planned 2015 municipal elections.

The denial of political rights to women in some Islamic counties is not intrinsic to the faith but a social imposition in order to maintain existing power structures. The same arguments about home and family were used by Christians in Europe and the US in nineteenth-century societies. Muslim feminists point out that Islam is no more naturally repressive than Judaism or Christianity, but it appears so by the machinations of those who have vested interests in blocking women's rights. 'If women's rights are a problem for some modern Muslim men, it is neither because of the Koran nor the Prophet, nor the Islamic tradition, but simply because those rights conflict with the interests of a male elite.'[79]

Women in modern states such as Turkey, Egypt and Iran were exhorted to 'look like the civilised women of the world', meaning western women, so the states could be accepted in the international community of nations.[80] In those countries women could be said to have been enfranchised for symbolic reasons, since suffrage boosted their image as modern nations, but in each case the women were seen to be subject to the state, they were not given personal liberty but a 'right' to support the state. In the early twenty-first century a second wave of Muslim nations enfranchised women as part of social changes brought about in the War on Terror.

A move to women's suffrage makes best progress following a nationalist and conservative agenda. Therefore progress is likely to be made in Arab states which are 'threatened' by westernization by involving women in a conservative resistance. This will marginalize radicals and strengthen conservatism—for the family, the state, and for religion, in a defence against both western values and terrorist fundamentalism.

Conclusion

At the Time of the Making of Nations

Suffragists in their self-adulatory tomes have done women something of a disservice in pronouncing so clearly the priority of organized women's movements in gaining the vote. This edges women's suffrage off the main stage of world politics and makes it a pressure group issue; interesting enough in its way, but of no great consequence in the halls of power. The repositioning of women's suffrage in terms of national identity, nationalist movements, and war gives a perspective that puts gender at the heart of national and international politics.

The lobbying, demonstrating, rallying, letter writing, and perhaps even 'militancy' of women's suffragists and their allies helped to a greater or lesser degree; but the most important factor in women's gaining the right to vote was the re-evaluation of nationhood in terms of citizenship. That is: however peoples in a region had previously been described, with the granting of a women's franchise the new nation was going to be defined in terms of citizenship. Whatever its previous existence—tribal or ethnic, girded by political boundaries or natural features—after the constitution that awarded men and women the franchise equally, the nation was going to be known as the one in which citizens of that place voted on their leadership.

The great movements of women's suffrage, where tens of nations enfranchised in a few years, are associated with national solidarity and reorganization. This holds true from revolutionary Russia, through war-shocked Europe and North America, to the revolutions in India and China, to the emergent nations in Africa, up to the tentative democracies in Arabian states during the 'War on Terror.'

The forge for most of these enfranchisements was war, that most masculine of activities. Association is not cause, women's suffrage was not 'caused by' war, but it is right to say it is more closely associated with war than with any other events—it is not, for example, associated with prolonged periods of national peace in which enlightened legislators considered what helpful thing they could do for the betterment of their people. It was very rarely part of a forward programme of advancement that was projected to take place whatever the future circumstances, as, for example, pension policy usually was and progressive income taxation often was.

There were countries in which there was no association with war—notably the first enfranchisements in New Zealand and Australia, though these were still a matter of national self-definition. Enfranchisements between wars are seen to be slow and sporadic, mere dots on the graph of women's enfranchisements, compared with the solid blocks of nations that cluster round the periods of war.

After the Vote Was Won

Adelheid Popp in Austria argued that 'The vote is only a weapon with which the struggle for the complete transformation of society may be served.'[1] That such transformation should come about was not doubted by the first wave of suffragists in Europe and the US.

After the first major enfranchisements, with the obvious failure of society to be 'transformed', the call for the vote was reformulated. Now the benefits were proffered in terms of the supposedly ameliorative qualities of women on the body politic. Where they were described at all it was in terms of national motherhood—but by the second half of the twentieth century women's enfranchisement was usually taken into new constitutions as a matter of course and no justification was necessary.

Pioneers of women's emancipation did not imagine a future in which women might have the vote, and use it as a large percentage of the electorate, but have no significant involvement in active political life at national level. There were, however, even in the early days indications that women's involvement was not going to set the heath alight. Louise Creighton in giving arguments *against* women's suffrage was already arguing in 1889 that women were not making use of what political power they possessed, complaining that it was difficult to find women to stand for office on boards of guardians of the poor and on school boards.[2] Women's lack of political ambition continued to be evident, notwithstanding the sprinkling of outstanding women in most political gatherings. Exceptional women have triumphed even in the most masculist cultures: both Turkey and Pakistan have had women prime ministers, Tansu Çiller and Benazir Bhutto; but the average men sitting in national legislatures have not been accompanied by an equal number of average women.

The great feminist Ichikawa Fusae, one of few suffragists to go on to a parliamentary career, said 'getting the vote was a waste', she regretted the 'passive' use of the vote by women as a mirror of their husbands and male relatives.[3] If anything, women's votes have exerted a mildly conservative effect on politics in democracies. Women's tendency to be more politically conservative was noted from the early twentieth century: in 1922 some 75 per cent of Rhodesian women voted against union with South Africa in a referendum, a fact that led Jan Christiaan Smuts to argue that women were more politically cautious than men.[4]

The low numbers of women in the parliaments of most democracies has led to suggestions that there should be quotas on party lists for candidature, or quotas in the legislature as a whole. Such organizations as the International Institute for Democracy and Electoral Assistance have presented 'gender quotas as a measure for boosting women's access to decision-making bodies' on the basis that 'a critical mass of women is necessary to ensure women's representation'.[5] There has been no apparent grass-roots enthusiasm for the idea, and some evidence of voter resentment in the UK at least.[6] A number of Latin American countries have enacted laws establishing a minimum level of 20 to 40 per cent for women's participation as candidates in national elections.[7]

After more than a century of universal suffrage in some countries, the legislative impact of adding women to the voting rolls was slight, if it was felt at all. Those areas that particularly interested suffrage campaigners in the social sphere were not revolutionized by women's votes; prostitution, venereal disease, and child abuse have not been subject to the effective social control promised by suffrage campaigners. Definitions of sex crime and legislation over sexual experiences have continued to be a problem, and such issues as the legalization of prostitution are as controversial as ever. The civil rights of prostitutes about which Mill was concerned are still circumscribed in Britain; their behaviour is still criminalized and they are more likely to receive harassment than protection from the law. Opinion is still divided on whether to sanction or further criminalize the activities in which they are involved. The women's suffrage pioneer nation New Zealand, under Helen Clark as prime minister, decriminalized prostitution in 2003.

The control over alcohol, a long-standing goal of many suffragists, saw results in the early twentieth century with the ill-starred prohibition experiment and the more successful use of licensing. These were the fruit of the debates of the 'progressive' era that were concurrent with women's suffrage arguments in the late nineteenth century; they did not represent a new twentieth-century reform, or one brought in on the back of the women's vote.

The vote for women did not result in even the most basic level of workplace equality. It was not until the Equal Pay Act of 1970 (coming into effect in 1975) that UK women were entitled, for the first time, to equal pay for the same or equivalent work as that done by men. This elementary step of simple fairness was therefore not enacted until more than half a century after women first gained the vote in Britain. An even more glaring example of the failure of women to grasp political opportunities to redress gender-based wrongs is of marital rape. Although Elizabeth Wolstenholme Elmy had campaigned in the nineteenth century against the legal position of sex as a husband's absolute right, marital rape was not a crime in Britain until 1994.[8] Neither the first suffragists with their new-found power nor the 'second wave' feminists of the 1970s saw fit to end such a clearly gender-based abuse.

Women and Peace

One of the principal reasons for the opposition to women's suffrage was the presumed weak and pacific nature of women: a nation where women had political power would be at the mercy of more martial nations as women would not go to war. The peace-spreading effect of the women's ballot was also a profound belief of the suffragists themselves. Mary Stritt, president of the German Association for Women's Suffrage wrote from Dresden to the International Woman Suffrage Alliance in February 1918: 'When responsibility for the welfare of the people and humanity is in our hands, in the hands of the mothers, there can be no return to the horrors we have had to experience.'[9] It was a statement deficient in predictive power.

The first women leaders of democratic nations: Sirimavo Bandaranaika of Ceylon, Golda Meir of Israel, Indira Gandhi of India, and Margaret Thatcher of Britain were not notably pacific; their governments directed the armed forces as they felt necessary. Gandhi and Thatcher were markedly decisive war leaders.

Nor have women in politics been particularly prominent in opposing war even when there was a perfectly realistic prospect of doing so success-fully. On the crucial 'Declaration of War—Case Not Yet Established' vote in the UK parliament on the invasion of Iraq on 18 March 2003 women made up a respectable 15 out of 85 Labour rebels who voted against the war. However, this is 17½ per cent of the number of rebels, considerably less than the 23 per cent representation of women MPs in the Parliamentary Labour Party. On this crucial issue of war and peace, with a war already unpopular before it had even started, Labour women were under-represented in the anti-war lobby. They voted with their party whips. No Conservative women voted against the war.[10]

Women voters were no more likely to stand out as a gender. In the US, for example, after the passage of the Nineteenth Amendment in 1920, little changed. Conservative Republicans dominated political life which was not notable for reforming zeal. Voter turnout was low, even lower among women than men, until the twenty-first century. In recent years women who have troubled to register have been more likely to vote in the US: 65 per cent of women and 62 per cent of men voted in the presidential election of 2004.[11]

Women voted along class or race lines as men did, there was little division on gender lines, indicating the relative importance of class and race compared to gender: precisely the argument of socialist as compared to 'bourgeois feminists'. The socialists in power had nothing to feel proud about in terms of gender representation, however. When nominally socialist countries went to the polls, they reaffirmed markedly male power structures, and women were poorly represented at the tables of power. In communist countries voting levels were high (voting being a duty to the party) but female candi-dature and elevation was low: in 1976 the Eastern European bloc together with Albania and China had a total of 197 Politburo posts, of these 10 were filled by women. Of government posts in the same countries there were 557 positions, with 27 filled by women.[12]

Apart from a short period in which men had the vote and women did not, both males and females stood in the same relationship to political power: that of powerlessness. Now in almost all countries women have the vote as men do, and stand in the same relation to the elements that manipu-late democracy: business, political parties, established authority, the media, and pressure groups. These factors also manipulate the electorate in non-democratic societies—though political parties have more power in places such as China.

Women have, world-wide, now overcome the barrier of the diminished status of not having the national vote. However, as Ross Evans Paulson says of women facing political realities: 'they divide along roughly the same political lines as men; they respond to the same empty slogans, glib half-truths, and ideological fantasies as men.'[13] That women must have the vote was fair and just, but the notion that this might make politics a more fair and just business, or produce a realignment of morality along gender lines was fanciful. Politics is a profession where promise and betrayal are prominent, the gender of its practitioners is irrelevant.

The picture of voting in almost all parts of the world is that elections are an area where women see themselves as gender neutral. There is no apparent enthusiasm from women (or men, for that matter) to define political questions in terms of male and female. It appears that women might wish to see themselves as 'women' when they purchase clothes or a magazine or listen to a radio programme produced with them in mind, but as voters they are citizens with equal rights, and gender is not a factor. If it is less than the suffragists had promised, it is still not such a bad state of affairs as a final destination.

The strange case of Switzerland

Switzerland is a paradox; it has long been one of the most democratic nations in the world as regards manhood suffrage, but did not admit women to the franchise until late in the twentieth century.

Here was a peaceful, democratic nation, liberal enough to permit Russian revolutionaries to reside there, but women did not get the vote until the 1970s, and in some cantons (electoral districts) local powers were used to exclude women until the 1990s.

The Congress of Vienna in 1815 guaranteed Switzerland's 'perpetual neutrality,' but Swiss cantons had a high degree of autonomy even when Switzerland was a French puppet state. The Peace of Westphalia in 1848 followed by a new constitution in September 1848 provided for effective central government while retaining strong local administration. It stressed the principle of equality between various races and religious groups regardless of their numerical strength. Switzerland has made frequent use of plebiscites; in the smaller cantons citizens would gather in the open air to vote on local issues in scenes reminiscent of the Greek ekklesia or the Icelandic Althing.

The limited manhood franchise of 1848 was expanded to encompass all men in almost all cantons in 1874 and other basic reforms were carried out: Jews were given citizenship, mixed marriage between Catholics and Protestants was permitted. This left Switzerland a highly democratic country, at least as far as men were concerned.

In a similar way to France, it was difficult for any pro-democratic women's movement to sustain momentum as men were not fighting for their rights. There was never an agitation for manhood suffrage to push the issue of democracy up the political agenda, and leave an opening for women to assert themselves.

Women's education had often been considered the key to liberation and enfranchisement, but Switzerland was one of the first countries to open the doors of universities to women in the nineteenth century; with no effect on women's suffrage.

Low taxes and a well-ordered economy meant there was little unrest; Switzerland's neutrality and independence meant there were no national crises to precipitate women's suffrage.

There were many women's organizations, though suffrage was not a major issue for most of them. The socialist groups were concerned with the rights of working women, those influenced by Josephine Butler more interested in 'moral reform'. The conservatism of the men of Switzerland was shared by the women; when the Social Democrats introduced a motion for full enfranchisement of women in

St Gallen, the local suffrage association argued that it went too far, and they wanted a more selective franchise.[1] A National Association for women's suffrage was formed in 1909 and made slow progress with enfranchisements for some state church councils and school boards. The largest women's organization, the National Council of Women, only called for suffrage in 1919 when a revision of the constitution was expected in the wake of a general strike.

In the event, the only substantial change was proportional representation for the male electorate. The Federal Council held that women's suffrage should first be granted in the twenty-two cantons before it was submitted to the Federal plebiscite. As it was generally the case that municipal suffrage preceded national suffrage, this was not absurd, but given the conservatism of many of the agricultural cantons, it was unlikely suffrage would be granted locally in them. In the first vote in a canton, in Neuchâtel in June 1919, the proposition was defeated by 12,000 votes to 5,000, after, it was claimed, 'a dishonourable campaign' financed by the liquor trade.[2] In Zurich the following year the proposition was defeated by four to one.

In the late 1940s after the enfranchisement of women in France and Italy, the issue was again to the fore, but the Swiss parliament felt that as attempts on a cantonal level had failed, it was too early for a national franchise bill. The government changed tack in 1957 and said it would submit an amendment enfranchising women in two years' time; the change of heart was because a constitutional amendment obliging women to serve in civil defence (as men did) had been criticized by women's rights groups, who complained at being obliged to perform duties when they had no rights as citizens. Women's suffrage was, however, overwhelmingly rejected by the electorate, Swiss men used their franchise in a nation-wide referendum in 1959 to deny women the vote; though in 1959 Vaud and Neuchâtel became the first two cantons to accept women's suffrage.

The rise of the women's liberation movement from 1968 focused attention on the anomaly of Switzerland's unenfranchised women. Young women activists had little time for older suffragists, young women disrupted the 75th anniversary celebrations of the Zurich women's suffrage organization, shouting through a megaphone that '75 years of working for suffrage is no reason to celebrate'.[3]

Trevor Lloyd was able to write at a time when women had the vote in only a few Swiss cantons that the vote 'has not seemed very relevant; nobody would say that Swiss women are noticeably less free than French women or Italian women'.[4] To some extent, the passage of time meant suffrage was less, not more important for women. Switzerland's strategic situation at the centre of Europe meant ideas flowed freely through the nation, it was not a backward country; the advantages of women's emancipation were available without enfranchisement. A Swiss Minister of Justice, Ernst Brugger, told the Association suisse pour le suffrage féminin in 1965 that he would introduce a bill giving women the parliamentary franchise, but that they must encourage women to impress upon their voting menfolk that they wanted it. He quoted a woman as saying to him: 'Why do we want to make life more difficult, the men can manage without us: let them do it.'[5] By the 1960s voting was no longer seen as the key to liberty, it was just another civic duty.

Switzerland was suffering other pressures, however: by 1970 Switzerland was not merely alone among advanced countries in not having enfranchised women; it was one of a very small number of countries in the whole world that had not done so. Switzerland had to work within the community of nations; the Swiss wished to be signatories to the European Human Rights Convention but felt obliged to request a special proviso to exclude the sections giving political rights to women. This provoked the one demonstration of the women's suffrage movement in Switzerland, the so-called March on Bern in 1969.

By 1971 two-thirds of cantons had given women some voting rights. The question was put to the electorate again and women were admitted to the federal franchise after a referendum held on 7 February 1971 with 66 per cent in favour. However, the local franchise for the (still highly independent) cantons was left to the cantons themselves and not all approved the measure. Women in the recalcitrant cantons therefore had the reverse of the usual situation as women's suffrage developed—they could vote in national but not local elections.

The fiercely parochial Swiss who resisted women's suffrage often did so because they felt it was an outside intrusion on their age-old democracy; it was being forced on them by the national government, the press (who descended en masse when a women's suffrage vote was taking place), and foreign influences. Those who held out longest were from remote regions, separated from the rest of the nation by dialect and fiercely protective of their traditions. Activists could be counter-productive; some men were reported to be voting against women's suffrage, even though they supported it in principle, because they resented having groups of screaming protesters putting pressure on them.[6] The relationship of the cantons to national government was similar to that between the states and the federal government in the US: the *principle* of local independence was more important than any of the issues in which that principle was engaged.

The last women to gain full voting rights were in one of the smallest cantons, the mountainous Appenzell-Inner Rhoden with a Catholic population of around 13,000 and an area of 172 square kilometres, who obtained the right on 27 November 1990 and first voted in 1991. It had taken 56 cantonal referenda between 1919 and 1990 for this relatively simple change to take place. One factor in eventual victory was no doubt that the old men who had so opposed women suffrage were dying off and being replaced by younger men with a different outlook.

Historian Lee Ann Banaszak found that cantons with a women's suffrage association enfranchised women an average of only one and a half years earlier than cantons with no women's suffrage organization.[7] The suggestion is that women's suffrage organizations cannot deliver suffrage in the absence of other factors. Switzerland with its peace, beauty, prosperity, and the absence of national struggle, simply lacked the motivating factors for women's suffrage, while the inhibiting factor of conservatism was strongly apparent.

Chronology of Women's Suffrage

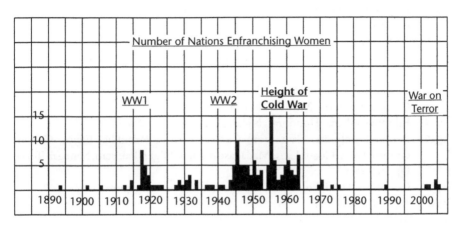

1893   New Zealand
1902   Australia
1906   Finland
1913   Norway
1915   Denmark, Iceland
1917   Russia
1918   Austria, Canada, Germany, Hungary, Latvia, Lithuania, Poland, UK
1919   Belgium, Kenya, Luxembourg, Netherlands, Rhodesia
1920   Albania, Czechoslovakia, US
1921   Sweden
1922   Ireland
1923   Burma
1924   Mongolia
1928   Guyana
1929   Ecuador, Puerto Rico
1930   South Africa
1931   Ceylon, Spain
1932   Brazil, Uruguay, Thailand
1934   Cuba, Turkey
1937   Philippines

1938   Bolivia
1939   El Salvador
1941   Panama
1942   Dominican Republic
1944   France, Jamaica
1945   Bulgaria, Guatemala, Italy, Japan, Panama, Senegal
1946   Cameroon, Djibouti, Democratic People's Republic of Korea, Liberia, Portugal, Romania, Trinidad and Tobago, Vietnam, Yugoslavia
1947   Argentina, Malta, Mauritius, Singapore, Venezuela
1948   Belgium, Israel, Republic of Korea, Seychelles, Suriname
1949   Chile, China, Costa Rica, India, Indonesia, Syria
1950   Barbados, Haiti
1951   Antigua and Barbuda, Dominica, Grenada, Nepal, Saint Lucia, St Vincent and the Grenadines
1952   Bolivia, Greece, St Kitts and Nevis
1953   Guyana, Lebanon, Mexico, Taiwan
1955   Ethiopia, Ghana, Honduras, Nicaragua, Peru
1956   Benin, Cambodia, Cameroon, Central African Republic, Egypt, Gabon, Guinea, Ivory Coast, Laos, Madagascar, Mali, Niger, Pakistan, Senegal, Togo, Upper Volta
1957   Colombia, Haiti, Honduras, Lebanon, Malaysia, Singapore
1958   Algeria, Iraq, Chad
1959   Morocco, Tunisia
1960   Congo, Cyprus, Gambia, San Marino, Swaziland
1961   Burundi, Mauritania, Paraguay, Rwanda, Sierra Leone
1962   Bahamas, Monaco, Uganda
1963   Iran, Mozambique, Somalia
1964   Afghanistan, Belize, Libya, Maldives, Sudan, Zambia, Tanzania
1967   Yemen (south; north enfranchised 1970)
1971   Bangladesh, Switzerland
1974   Jordan
1976   Nigeria
1990   Western Samoa
2002   Bahrain
2003   Oman, Qatar
2005   Kuwait
2006   United Arab Emirates

A list of national enfranchisements immediately throws up the question: what constitutes a nation? The Inter-Parliamentary Union lists countries which 'currently have a parliament or have had one at some point in their history'.[1] The question is then presented: when should enfranchisements be considered to have started, when national boundaries have often been fluid? Should all the countries of the former

Soviet Union be considered to have enfranchised women when Russia did so in 1917 (though the authorities had but a tenuous grip on power even in their own capital, let alone the provinces) or when they gained independence after the break-up of the Soviet Union? The Ukrainian Soviet Socialist Republic was proclaimed in the revolutionary year of 1917, and established in 1919 with a constitution enfranchising women. Independence from the Soviet Union was declared in 1991. Other Republics of the Soviet Union followed a similar path; in this list they are all considered to have been embraced by the 1917 declaration.

The large number of enfranchisements after 1950 represents the burst of new nations. The year 1956 in particular indicates the eagerness of France to relinquish her colonial possessions in a swift and uniform fashion with the *loi-cadre* (framework law) coming into effect in several countries at the same time. The number of sovereign states rose during the twentieth century from about 50 in 1900 to 180 in 1990; understandably as there are more nations there are more enfranchisements.[2]

With the populous countries of China, India, and Indonesia enfranchising women in or near 1949, the middle of the twentieth century is clearly the high point, accounting for almost half the world's population.

More problematic is the position of nations which were regions of another nation before becoming independent. Pakistani women enjoyed some measure of enfranchisement under the Government of India Acts of 1919 and 1935, and these were the electoral laws in place at independence in 1947, though national enfranchisement is taken as 1956. But should that part of Bengal that was later East Pakistan and then Bangladesh be considered to have been enfranchised under the British, the Pakistanis, or in 1971 when the new nation came into existence? By that time at least some women had been voting for the government of that part of the world for more than forty years; here enfranchisement in the new nation is taken as paramount.

Different lists often disagree because of questions about precisely when a new nation promulgated an electoral law. Three different dates in different sources are given for Tanzania, all of them earlier than 1964 when the nation came into existence as a union between Tanganyika, Zanzibar, and Pemba. That date therefore is taken for women's enfranchisement.

Regional franchises are problematic. Only national enfranchisement is considered here, not the United States' state-by-state enfranchisement nor (rather more anomalously) India's, where the states were more populous than some nations and were self-governing from the 1920s or '30s. Nigeria had a regional franchise for women in 1954 (east), 1955 (west), 1959 (south), and 1976 (north). Similarly, Somalia enfranchised in 1961 excepting the northern region where it took place in 1963. The final date, for the entire country, is taken as the date for women's enfranchisement in this list.

What is the franchise? is another conundrum. If only suffrage for women on the same basis as that for men were included, the UK's achievement would be dated 1928 not 1918, when six million women were enfranchised. If only complete adult suffrage were included, Canada would not be listed until the final racial distinctions

Figure 23. Spanish women voting in 1933, but enfranchisement could be followed by disenfranchisement. By the end of the decade Franco's regime would extinguish democracy; women with families were allowed to vote in 1967, but universal suffrage was not re-established until 1978.

were lifted in 1960, or Australia until 1962 when the last two states awarded Aboriginal women the vote.

On the other hand, Burmese women's suffrage in 1923 (when Burma was still a province of India and under British rule) was on a taxation basis, so fits the criteria of the vote 'as it is given to men'. However, only men were obliged to pay a poll tax, so there were many more male taxpayers than female and this was hardly equality. In Sudan in 1953 educated women were enfranchised but so few women had access to education, and such obstacles were placed in their path that they cannot be considered real enfranchisements. Afghan women could reflect that they were supposedly enfranchised in 1963.

When is enfranchisement? At the time the parliament passes the Bill, or at the royal (or presidential) assent? Here it is taken to be the final ratification of the law, so that women's suffrage was agreed in Sweden in 1919, for example, but not passed, for procedural reasons, until 1921.

The United Arab Emirates has an electorate hand-picked by the administration, for the election of half of an advisory council, but as those are the same conditions that relate to men, even though there were 6,595 male electors in 2006 and 1,163 women, that is still counted here as the enfranchisement of women.[3]

Disenfranchisement is another pitfall: Syrian women received limited suffrage in 1949 then full adult suffrage in 1953 but the following year a coup replaced the president who had granted adult suffrage and the new regime reverted to limited suffrage on an educational qualification. Women were fully enfranchised in Syria in 1973. Women were enfranchised in Spain in 1931, then disenfranchised under Franco and finally re-enfranchised in a constitution of 1978 after the dictator had died. The first date of enfranchisement is included here.

Finally, what constitutes a woman? In many places ethnic barriers cut across even such a seemingly straightforward factual matter. In at least South Africa, 'woman' was specifically defined as a white woman in an Act of 1930. Where only whites participated in government, white suffrage is taken as women's suffrage in this list, as the relationship of the voter to the government of the country is paramount. The question addressed is: when were women allowed a significant level of involvement in the election of those who ran the country? Therefore Kenya and Rhodesia are included for the enfranchisement of white women, because the countries were run by whites in 1919, and that was the date when white women had some relationship to power.

Endnotes

INTRODUCTION

1. John Markoff, 'Margins, Centres, and Democracy: The Paradigmatic History of Women's Suffrage', *Signs: Journal of Women in Culture and Society* 29/1 (2003), 109.

2. Ross Evans Paulson, *Women's Suffrage and Prohibition: A Comparative Study of Equality and Social Control* (Glenview, Ill.: Scott, Foresman and Co. 1973), 33, who remarks that Stanton 'was a better publicist than historian'.

3. Leila R. Brammer, *Excluded from Suffrage History: Matilda Joslyn Gage, Nineteenth-Century American Feminist* (Westport, Conn.: Greeenwood Press 2000), 109. The first three volumes of *The History of Woman Suffrage* (hereafter *HWS*) published in 1881, 1883, and 1887 were by Elizabeth Cady Stanton, Susan Brownell Anthony, and Matilda Joslyn Gage, the fourth, in 1902, by Anthony and Ida Husted Harper, the fifth and sixth, in 1922, by Harper alone. All published in New York by Fowler Wells.

4. Paulson, *Women's Suffrage and Prohibition*, 121. Rochelle Ruthchild's work, discussed in Chapter 7, qualifies this, noting that as Finland was part of the Russian Empire it was hardly on the edge of Europe—but it was hardly the Russian heartland, either.

5. Barbara Caine and Janet Howarth, Oxford *DNB* entries on respectively Ray Strachey and Millicent Fawcett.

6. Kathryn Dodd, *A Sylvia Pankhurst Reader* (Manchester: Manchester University Press 1993), 6 and 21.

7. Paula Bartley, *Votes for Woman 1860–1928* (London: Hodder & Stoughton 1998); Harold Smith, *The British Women's Suffrage Campaign 1866–1928* (Harlow: Pearson Longman 2007).

8. *HWS* 6: 789.

9. William Pember Reeves, *State Experiments in Australia and New Zealand*, vol. 1 (London: Grant Richards 1902), 112–13. Reawyn Dalziel analyses Reeves's position and possible reasons for it in 'Presenting the Enfranchisement of New Zealand Women Abroad', in Caroline Daley and Melanie Nolan (eds.), *Suffrage and Beyond: International Feminist Perspectives* (Auckland: Auckland University Press 1994), 48–50.

10. Richard J. Evans, *The Feminists: Women's Emancipation Movements in Europe, America and Australasia 1840–1920* (London: Croom Helm 1977); Trevor Lloyd,

Suffragettes International: The World-wide Campaign for Women's Rights (London: Library of the Twentieth Century 1971); Kumari Jayawardena, *Feminism and Nationalism in the Third World* (London: Zed Books 1986).

11. Daley and Nolan, *Suffrage and Beyond*, 346 and 252.

12. June Hannam, Mitzi Auchterlonie, and Katherine Holden, *International Encyclopaedia of Women's Suffrage* (Santa Barbara, Calif.: ABC-CLIO 2000).

13. Karen Offen, *European Feminisms 1700–1950: A Political History* (Stanford, Calif.: Stanford University Press 2000); Louise Edwards and Mina Roces, *Asia: Gender, Nationalism and Democracy* (London: Routledge 2004); Ian Fletcher and Laura E. Nym Mayhall, and Philippa Levine, *Women's Suffrage in the British Empire: Citizenship, Nation and Race* (London: Routledge 2000).

14. Markoff, 'Margins, Centres, and Democracy'; June Hannam, 'International Dimensions of Women's Suffrage: "at the crossroads of several interlocking identities"', *Women's History Review* 14/3 and 4 (2005), 543–60; Francisco O. Ramirez, Yasemin Soysal, and Suzanne Shanahan, 'The Changing Logic of Political Citizenship: Cross-national Acquisition of Women's Suffrage Rights, 1890–1990', *American Sociological Review* 62 (October 1997), 735–45.

15. China and India were the most populous nations in 1950, Indonesia the sixth most populous. Japan (where women were enfranchised in 1945) was just above Indonesia: US Census Bureau, International Data Base http://www.census.gov/population/interrnational/data/idb accessed Dec. 2013.

16. Eileen Janes Yeo (ed.), *Mary Wollstonecraft and 200 Years of Feminisms* (London, Rivers Oram 1997), 4 and *passim*.

17. Carrie Chapman Catt and Nettie Rogers Shuler, *Woman Suffrage and Politics: The Inner Story of the Suffrage Movement* (Seattle: University of Washington Press 1923), 130.

18. Offen, *European Feminisms 1700–1950*, 11.

19. Nina Boyle quoted in Leila Rupp, J. *Worlds of Women: The Making of an International Women's Movement* (Princeton NJ: Princeton University Press 1997), 24.

CHAPTER I: DEMOCRACY BEFORE DEMOCRACY

1. Sarah B. Pomeroy, *Goddesses, Whores, Wives and Slaves: Women in Classical Antiquity* (New York: Dorset Press 1975), 115. Pierre Vidal-Naquet, 'Esclavage et Gynécocratie dans la Tradition, et Mythe L'Utopie', in *Recherches sur les Structures Sociales dans l'Antiquité Classique* (Paris: Editions du Centre National de la Recherche Scientifique 1970), 77–8. Kallirroi Parren referred to this 'very old tradition' in Chicago in May 1894: May Wright Sewall, *The World's Congress of Representative Women*, vol. 1 (Chicago: Rand, McNally 1894), 28.

2. Robert Graves, *The Greek Myths*, Vol. 1 (London: Penguin 1966), 97.

3. Barbara Taylor, *Eve and the New Jerusalem* (London: Virago 1983); appendix includes a facsimile of Catherine Barmby's text. No page numbers.

4. Roger Just, *Women in Athenian Law and Life* (London: Routledge 1989), 4–7. H. D. F. Kitto, *The Greeks* (London: Penguin 1951) gives a mid-twentieth-century formulation of the question, 219–36.

5. Pomeroy, *Goddesses, Whores, Wives and Slaves*, 58.

6. Pomeroy, *Goddesses, Whores, Wives and Slaves*, 59.

7. Demosthenes, 'Against Neaira', from A. T. Murray, *Demosthenes' Private Orations*, vol. 3 (Cambridge, Mass.: Heinemann 1939), 122–3. Actually delivered by Apollodorus (Pseudo-Demosthenes).

8. Euripides, *Medea*, trans. David Kovacs (Cambridge, Mass. Harvard University Press, 317.

9. Just, *Women in Athenian Law and Life*, 41–2 and Demonsthenes, 'Against Neaira' (trans. Murray), 112–13.

10. An agreed date for its founding was needed as the thousand-year anniversary of the nation was approaching in the twentieth century. 1930 was chosen as the key date for both administrative and commemorative convenience.

11. *Laxdaela Saga*, trans. Magnus Magnusson and Herman Pálsson (London: Penguin 1969), 126.

12. Jesse Byock, *Viking Age Iceland* (London: Penguin 2001), 196.

13. Gunnar Karlsson, *Iceland's 1100 Years* (London: Hurst and Co. 2000), 26.

14. Judith Jesch, *Women in the Viking Age* (Woodbridge: Boydell Press 1991), 187.

15. Froissart, *Chronicles*, trans. Geoffrey Brereton (London: Penguin 1968), 212.

16. For a discussion of the religious 'construction' of women, see Olwen Hufton, *The Prospect Before Her: A History of Women in Western Europe, Volume One 1500–1800* (London: Fontana 1997), 25–58; and Jacques Dalarun, 'The Clerical Gaze', in Christiane Klapisch-Zuber, *A History of Women in the West, Volume Two: Silences of the Middle Ages* (Harvard, Mass.: Belknap Press 1992), 15–42.

17. Christopher Hill, *The World Turned Upside Down: Radical Ideas During the English Revolution* (London: Penguin 1972), 319.

18. Hill, *The World Turned Upside Down*, 322.

19. Hufton, *The Prospect Before Her*, 413.

20. Walter Brodie, *Pitcairn's Island and The Islanders in 1850* (London: Whittaker & Co. 1851), 82.

21. Brodie, *Pitcairn's Island*, 82.

22. Dick Scott, *Years of the Pooh-Bah: A History of the Cook Islands* (Rarotonga: CITC 1991), 43.

23. Scott, *Years of the Pooh-Bah*, 44.

24. Scott, *Years of the Pooh-Bah*, 58 but NB, 61—Moss's utopian island democracy would have involved the surrender of power by the chiefs if it were to work; but chiefs retained local power and were able to manipulate the elected commoners, particularly as Moss's plans for a secret ballot were frustrated.

25. These comments are based on observations made on travels in the South Seas in January–February 2004.

26. Markoff, 'Margins, Centres, and Democracy', 109.

CHAPTER 2: THE RIGHTS OF MAN

1. *True American*, 30 November 1807.
2. Jane Abray, 'Feminism in the French Revolution', *The American Historical Review* 80/1 (February 1975), 44. Abray remarks that French women and men had argued for equality of legal and political rights for the sexes since the Renaissance; I am concentrating specifically on voting rights not such issues as equality before the law. She lists French feminist publications since 1749.
3. Iain McLean and Fiona Hewitt, *Condorcet: Foundations of Social Choice and Political Theory* (Aldershot: Edward Elgar 1994), 4.
4. McLean and Hewitt, *Condorcet*, 6.
5. Marquis de Condorcet, 'Letters from a Freeman of New Haven to a Citizen of Virginia on the Futility of Dividing the Legislative Power among Several Bodies', in McLean and Hewitt, *Condorcet*, 297.
6. Condorcet, 'On Giving Women the Right of Citizenship', in McLean and Hewitt, 335 and *passim*.
7. Darline Gay Levy, Harriet Branson Applewhite, and Mary Durham Johnson, *Women in Revolutionary Paris 1789–1795* (Chicago: University of Illinois Press 1979), 90.
8. Joan Wallach Scott, 'French Feminists and the Rights of "Man" Olympe de Gouge's Declarations', *History Workshop Journal* 28 (1989), 2.
9. Scott, *Years of the Pooh-Bah*, 10.
10. Levy et al., *Women in Revolutionary Paris*, 89.
11. Reprinted in *Chronicle of the French Revolution* (London: Chronicle Communications 1989), 235.
12. Abray, 'Feminism in the French Revolution', 46.
13. Olwen Hufton, *The Prospect Before Her: A History of Women in Western Europe, Volume One 1500–1800* (London: Fontana 1997), 478.
14. Abray, 'Feminism in the French Revolution', 54, e.g. the right to vote and act as regents.
15. Hufton, *The Prospect Before Her*, 479.
16. Levy et al., *Women in Revolutionary Paris*, 214–16.
17. Scott, *Years of the Pooh-Bah*, 2. See also Markoff, 'Margins, Centres and Democracy', 85–7.
18. *Chronicle of the French Revolution*, 381.
19. Abray, 'Feminism in the French Revolution', 57.
20. Abray, 'Feminism in the French Revolution', 51; see also Elisabeth Roudinesco, *Théroigne de Mérincourt: Une femme mélancolique sous la révolution* (Paris: Seuil 1989).
21. Joseph Addison, *The Spectator* 57, 5 May 1711.
22. Mary Wollstonecraft, *Vindication of the Rights of Woman* (London: Penguin 1985), 107.
23. Mary Wollstonecraft, *A Historical and Moral View of the French Revolution*, ed. Janet Todd and Marilyn Butler (London: Pickering 1989), 128.

24. Wollstonecraft, *Vindication*, 260.

25. Claire Tomalin, *The Life and Death of Mary Wollstonecraft* (London: Weidenfeld and Nicolson, 1974).

26. Wollstonecraft, *Vindication*, 114.

27. Tomalin, *Life and Death of Mary Wollstonecraft*, 110.

28. Lyndall Gordon, *Vindication: A Life of Mary Wollstonecraft* (London: Little, Brown 2005), 283.

29. Tomalin, *Life and Death of Mary Wollstonecraft*, 226.

30. Wollstonecraft, *A Vindication* etc., introduction to anniversary edition by Millicent Garrett Fawcett (London: Fisher Unwin 1891), 22–3.

31. Miriam Brody, introduction to Mary Wollstonecraft, *Vindication of the Rights of Women* (London: Penguin 1982), 64.

32. Gordon, *Vindication*, 3.

33. Ray Strachey, *'The Cause': A Short History of the Women's Movement in Britain* (London: G. Bell 1928), 12.

34. L. H. Butterfield (ed.), The Adams Papers series II: *Adams Family Correspondence*, 1 (Cambridge, Mass.: Harvard University Press 1963), 329.

35. Butterfield, *Adams Family Correspondence*, 370.

36. Butterfield, *Adams Family Correspondence*, 382.

37. Butterfield, *Adams Family Correspondence*, 402.

38. Mary Philbrook, 'Woman's Suffrage in New Jersey Prior to 1807', *Proceedings of the New Jersey Historical Society* 57 (1939), 88.

39. Henry C. Shinn, 'An Early New Jersey Poll List', *Pennsylvania Magazine of History and Biography*, 44 (1920), 77–81.

40. Richard McCormick, *The History of Voting in New Jersey: A Study of the Development of Election Machinery 1664–1911* (New Brunswick: Rutgers University Press 1953), 78.

41. *Newark Sentinel of Freedom*, 19 October 1797.

42. Philbrook, 'Woman's Suffrage in New Jersey Prior to 1807', 94.

43. William A. Whitehead, 'A Brief Statement of the facts connected with the origin, practice and prohibition of female suffrage in New Jersey', *Proceedings of the New Jersey Historical Society* 8 (1858), 102.

44. Papers relating to women voting in Hunterdon County 1802, NJSA 1979AM. Petitions tended to follow the same formula.

45. William Griffith (anonymously), *Emenes: Being a Collection of Papers written for the purpose of exhibiting some of the more prominent errors and omissions of the constitution of New Jersey* (Trenton 1799), 33. Griffith was not an arch conservative, he was an early member of the society for promoting the abolition of slavery and freed his own father's slaves in 1806 after his father's death. *Biographical Encyclopaedia of New Jersey of the Nineteenth Century* (Philadelphia: Galaxy 1877).

46. *True American*, 18 October 1802, quoted in Philbrook, 'Woman's Suffrage in New Jersey Prior to 1807', 95.

47. Whitehead, 'A Brief Statement', 104.

48. J. R. Pole, 'The Suffrage in New Jersey 1790–1807', *Proceedings of the New Jersey Historical Society* 71 (1953), 56.

49. *Laws of New Jersey 1806–09*, Acts of the 32nd General Assembly, 14.

50. Pole, 'Suffrage in New Jersey', 55.

CHAPTER 3: EARLY BRITISH RADICALS

1. Samuel Bamford, *Passages in the Life of a Radical*, vol. 2 (London: T. Fisher Unwin 1893), 141–2.

2. E. P. Thompson, *The Making of the English Working Class* (London: Penguin 1978), 454–6.

3. Kathryn Gleadle, *Borderline Citizens: Women, Gender and Political Culture in Britain 1815–1867* (Oxford: Ouniversity Press 2009).

4. Charles Fox, *Hansard* 1792 col. 726.

5. Constance Rover, *Love, Morals and the Feminists* (London: Routledge 1969), 12.

6. Guy A. Aldred, *Richard Carlile Agitator: His Life and Times* (London: Pioneer Press 1923), 129.

7. Thompson, *Making of the English Working Class*, 791.

8. Aldred, *Richard Carlile Agitator*, 132.

9. Joel H. Wiener, *Radicalism and Freethought in Nineteenth-Century Britain* (London: Greenwood Press 1983), 128.

10. *Isis*, 14 April 1832, quoted in Barbara Taylor, *Eve and the New Jerusalem* (London: Virago 1983), 82.

11. *Isis*, 10 March 1832, quoted in Wiener, *Radicalism and Freethought*, 195.

12. *New Moral World*, 12 June 1841. In the same edition are translations of Charles Fourier's work by Goodwyn Barmby.

13. A Female Socialist, M. B. 'Female Improvement', *New Moral World* 27 April 1839.

14. *Encyclopaedia Britannica, Supplement*, 'Government', 500 reprinted on cover of 'Appeal'.

15. Richard A Pankhurst, 'Anna Wheeler: A Pioneer Socialist and Feminist', *The Political Quarterly* 25/2 (1954), 133.

16. *The British Co-operator*, April 1830, quoted in Taylor, *Eve and the New Jerusalem*, 60.

17. Michael Sadleir, *Bulwer and his Wife: A Panorama 1803–1836* (London: Constable 1933), 76 and 79.

18. Benjamin Disraeli, *Lord Beaconsfield's Correspondence with his Sister 1832–1852* (London: John Murray 1886), 15.

19. William Thompson, *'Appeal of one half of the human race, women etc,'* (Cork: Cork University Press 1997), 45.

20. Thompson, *'Appeal'*, 49.

21. Thompson, *'Appeal'*, 52.

22. Thompson, *'Appeal'*, 68.

23. Thompson, *'Appeal'*, 86.

24. Thompson, *'Appeal'*, 96.

25. Thompson, *'Appeal'*, 200.

26. Thompson, *'Appeal'*, 209.

27. Richard Pankhurst, Introduction to *'Appeal'* (London: Virago 1983), xvi.

28. Pankhurst, 'Anna Wheeler', 159.

29. Pankhurst 'Anna Wheeler', 138.

30. Dolores Dooley, *Wheeler* entry, Oxford *DNB* 2004–7.

31. Dolores Dooley, *Equality in Community: Sexual Equality in the Writings of William Thompson and Anna Doyle Wheeler* (Cork: Cork University Press 1996), 102.

32. John Stuart Mill, *Autobiography* (London: Oxford University Press 1969), 105.

33. John Wade, *The Extraordinary Black Book: An exposition etc* (London: Effingham Wilson 1831), 560.

34. Dooley, *Equality in Community*, 67.

35. Roger Fulford, *Votes for Women: The Story of a Struggle* (London: Faber 1958), 17.

36. House of Commons, *Journal*, 3 August 1832, 551; *Hansard*, 3 August 1832, col. 1086. She also 'expressed her indignation against those vile wretches who would not marry', suggesting a personal reason for her interest in the matter.

37. William Lovett, *The Life and Struggles of William Lovett in his pursuit of Bread, Knowledge and Freedom* (London: Trübner 1876), 95.

38. Lovett, *Life and Struggles*, 170.

39. Taylor, *Eve*, 271.

40. Lovett, *Life and Struggles*, 116.

41. Taylor, *Eve*, 175.

42. The complete document is reproduced in facsimile at the end of Barbara Taylor's *Eve and the New Jerusalem*. It is worth noting incidentally that ecclesiastical emancipation (the ordination of women as priests, which was agreed by the synod in 1992) did not occur in the Anglican church in fact until 1994, and the first woman bishop was not installed in the UK until 2013. The Catholic and Greek Orthodox churches show no signs of emancipating women.

43. Barbara Taylor, *Catherine Barmby* entry, Oxford *DNB* 2004–7.

44. Marion Ramelson, *The Petticoat Rebellion* (London: Lawrence and Wishart 1967), 71.

45. Lucretia Mott, *Slavery and 'the woman question': Lucretia Mott's diary of her visit to Great Britain to Attend the World's Anti-Slavery Convention of 1840*, ed. Frederick Tolles (Pennsylvania and London: Friends Historical Association and Friends Historical Society 1952), 25.

46. Mott, *Slavery and 'the woman question'*, 73.

47. Fulford, *Votes for Women*, 33.

48. Fulford, *Votes for Women*, 33.

CHAPTER 4: THE RISE OF THE MIDDLE-CLASS CAMPAIGNER

1. Eliza Lynn Linton, 'The Threatened Abdication of Man', *The National Review* 77 (July 1889), 578, 587.

2. Linton, 'The Threatened Abdication of Man', 579.

3. Carole Pateman, 'Three Questions About Womanhood Suffrage', in Caroline Daley and Melanie Nolan, *Suffrage and Beyond: International Feminist Perspectives* (Auckland: Auckland University Press 1994), 339. The question is discussed in Brian Harrison, *Separate Spheres: The Opposition to Women's Suffrage in Britain* (London: Croom Helm 1978).

4. William Lecky, *History of European Morals*, vol. 2 (London: Longmans 1869), 380–1.

5. J. S. Mill (prob. Harriet Taylor), 'The Enfranchisement of Women', *Westminster Review* (April–July 1851), 305.

6. Lord Salisbury, 30 November 1888 quoted in *Fortnightly Review* (April 1889), 568.

7. Carolyn Steedman, *Strange Dislocations: Childhood and the Idea of Human Interiority 1780–1930* (Cambridge, Mass.: Harvard University Press 1995), 6.

8. Ray Strachey, *'The Cause', A Short History of the Women's Movement in Britain* (London: G. Bell 1928), 71.

9. Barbara Caine, *English Feminism 1780–1980* (Oxford: Oxford University Press 1997), 96–100 discusses Wollstonecraft in correspondence between Parkes and Leigh Smith.

10. Caine, *English Feminism*, 111.

11. Constance Rover, *Love, Morals and the Feminists* (London: Routledge 1969), 65.

12. Frederick Pethick-Lawrence, *Fate Has Been Kind* (London: Hutchinson 1942), 68.

13. Ann Robson, Oxford *DNB* entry, Harriet Mill 2004–7.

14. Jose Harris, Oxford *DNB* entry, John Stuart Mill 2004–7.

15. John Stuart Mill, *Autobiography* (London: Oxford University Press 1969), 4.

16. Josephine Kamm, *John Stuart Mill in Love* (London: Gordon and Cremonosi 1977), 32.

17. Mill, *Autobiography*, 156.

18. Mill, *Autobiography*, 207.

19. Mill (Harriet Taylor), 'The Enfranchisement of Women', 289–308.

20. Harris, *DNB* entry J. S. Mill.

21. John Stuart Mill, *The Subjection of Women* (Ware, Herts.: Wordsworth 1996), xi.

22. Mill, *Subjection*, 117.

23. Mill, *Subjection*, 167.

24. Mill, *Subjection*, 172–3.

25. Mill, *Subjection*, 182.

26. Irene Clephane, *Towards Sex Freedom* (London: John Lane 1935), 89.

27. Clephane, *Towards Sex Freedom*, 90.

28. Mill, *Autobiography*, 244.

29. *Hansard* 20 May 1867, col. 822.

30. Strachey, *'The Cause'*, 109.

31. Patricia Hollis, *Women in Public: The Women's Movement 1850–1900* (London: Allen and Unwin, 1979), 314.

32. Millicent Fawcett, 'The Appeal Against Female Suffrage: A Reply', *Nineteenth Century* (July 1889), 95.
33. Strachey, *'The Cause'*, 205.
34. Alan Rushton, Oxford *DNB* entry, John Bright 2004–7.
35. Strachey, *'The Cause'*, 111.
36. Harris, *DNB* entry, J. S. Mill 2004–7.
37. S. Pankhurst, *The Suffragette Movement* (London: Virago 1977), 3.
38. Strachey, *'The Cause'*, 115.
39. S. Pankhurst, *Suffragette Movement*, 46.
40. Elizabeth Crawford, *The Women's Suiffrage Movement: A Reference Guide 1866–1928* (London: Routledge 1999), 328.
41. *Hansard* 12 May 1870, col. 619.
42. Constance Rover, *Women's Suffrage and Party Politics in Britain* (London: Routledge 1967), 211–23, details women's suffrage bills and major parliamentary events.
43. A Bill was introduced every year of the 1870s except 1874. In 1879 the majority against was 114.
44. S. Pankhurst, *Suffragette Movement*, 50.
45. Strachey, *'The Cause'*, 119.
46. Philip Magnus, *Gladstone: A Biography* (London: John Murray 1960), 383; letter of 11 April 1892 quoted in Hollis, *Women in Public*, 319–21.
47. W. F. Monypenny and G. E. Buckle, *The Life of Benjamin Disraeli*, vol. 1 (London: John Murray 1929), 915. Disraeli then gave himself a politician's let-out, in case his words were held against him, that 'All this proves that right has nothing to do with the matter.'
48. George Macaulay Trevelyan, *The Life of John Bright* (London: Constable 1913), 380.
49. Elizabeth Cady Stanton, *Eighty Years and More: Reminiscences* (London: T. Fisher Unwin, 1898), 364–5. She gives the date as 17 October 1882 and says 1,600 were present.
50. S. Pankhurst, *Suffragette Movement*, 69.
51. S. Pankhurst, *Suffragette Movement*, 69.
52. Quoted in *Fortnightly Review* (April 1889), 568.
53. This has been extensively researched by Laurel Brake in 'Writing Women's History: "The Sex" debates of 1889', in Ann Heilmann and Margaret Beetham (eds.), *New Women Hybridities* (London: Routledge 2004), 51–73.
54. 'An Appeal Against Female Suffrage', *The Nineteenth Century* 148 (June 1889), 781.
55. 'An Appeal Against Female Suffrage', 784.
56. Millicent Garrett Fawcett, in *The Nineteenth Century* 49 (July 1889), 89.
57. J. S. Stuart Glennie, 'The Proposed Subjection of Men', *Fortnightly Review* (April 1889), 569.
58. Balfour had also spoken in favour of women's suffrage in the debate on 27 April 1892.
59. Fawcett, in *The Nineteenth Century* (July 1889), 95.

60. Jad Adams, *Pankhurst* (London: Haus, 2003), 18–19 for a discussion of this.

61. S. Pankhurst, *Suffragette Movement*, 116.

62. S. Pankhurst, *Suffragette Movement*, 118.

63. Jane Howarth, Oxford *DNB* entry on Millicent Garrett Fawcett 2004–7.

64. David Rubinstein, *A Different World for Women: The Life of Millicent Garrett Fawcett* (London: Harvester Wheatsheaf 1991), 85.

65. Frances Balfour to Millicent Fawcett, undated but March 1895, Women's Library 7MGF/A/2/117. Her brother in law Arthur Balfour had been particularly pronounced in his efforts to have Cust marry Nina Welby and he raged at Fawcett, 'errors of a kind which, after marriage, are usually committed to a kindly oblivion, have been turned into subjects of party controversy; and worst of all, she has once again been made to feel that she is the chief obstacle in her husband's path. Perhaps you will say she deserved it. It may be so, but she must be wicked indeed if she has deserved all she has already suffered.' A. J. Balfour to Millicent Fawcett, 22 March 1894, 7MGF/A/2/123.

66. Sandra Holton sums up the divisions at the end of the century in *Feminism and Democracy: Women's Suffrage and Reform Politics in Britain 1900–1918* (Cambridge: Cambridge University Press 1986).

CHAPTER 5: NEW-FOUND RIGHTS IN NEW-FOUND LANDS

1. Reprinted in full in Margaret Lovell-Smith (ed.), *The Woman Question: Writings by the Women who Won the Vote* (Auckland: New Women's Press 1992), 59.

2. Lovell-Smith, *The Woman Question*, 248.

3. A. H. McLintock, *An Encyclopaedia of New Zealand* (Wellington: R. E. Owen 1966).

4. Richard J. Evans, *The Feminists: Women's Emancipation Movements in Europe, America and Australasia 1840–1920* (London: Croom Helm 1977), 61; Patricia Grimshaw, *Women's Suffrage in New Zealand* (Auckland: Auckland University Press 1987), 2–3.

5. Grimshaw, *Women's Suffrage in New Zealand*, 13.

6. Neill Atkinson, *Adventures in Democracy: A History of the Vote in New Zealand* (Dunedin: University of Otago Press 2003), 78.

7. Grimshaw, *Women's Suffrage in New Zealand*, 19.

8. Grimshaw, *Women's Suffrage in New Zealand*, 31 citing *The Leader*, 3 May 1889.

9. Kate Sheppard, 'Ten Reasons Why the Women of New Zealand Should Vote', in Lovell-Smith, *The Woman Question*, 66.

10. Grimshaw, *Women's Suffrage in New Zealand*, 41.

11. William Pember Reeves, *State Experiments in Australia and New Zealand*, vol. 1 (London: Grant Richards 1902), 107.

12. Grimshaw, *Women's Suffrage in New Zealand*, 47.

13. Grimshaw, *Women's Suffrage in New Zealand*, 48.

14. Judith Devaliant, *Kate Sheppard: The Fight for Women's Votes in New Zealand* (Auckland: Penguin 2000), 25.

15. Grimshaw, *Women's Suffrage in New Zealand*, 93.

16. Reeves, *State Experiments*, 112.

17. Grimshaw, *Women's Suffrage in New Zealand*, v.

18. Reeves, *State Experiments*, 112.

19. Daniel T. Rodgers, *Atlantic Crossings: Social Politics in a Progressive Age* (Cambridge MA: Harvard University Press 1998), 55.

20. Norwood Young, 'The Truth About Female Suffrage in New Zealand', *Westminster Review* (December 1894), 668.

21. Raewyn Dalziel, 'Presenting the Enfranchisement of New Zealand Women Abroad', in Caroline Daley and Melanie Nolan, *Suffrage and Beyond: International Feminist Perspectives* (Auckland: Auckland University Press 1994), 57. Incidentally, the two Maori members were decisive in voting against women's suffrage in the close vote in the legislative council in 1891.

22. Reeves, *State Experiments*, 114.

23. Devaliant, *Kate Sheppard*, 126.

24. Ross Evans Paulson, *Women's Suffrage and Prohibition: A Comparative Study of Equality and Social Control* (Glenview, Ill.: Scott, Foresman and Co. 1973), 129.

25. Evans, *The Feminists*, 60.

26. Christopher Nance, 'Paving the Way: The Women's Suffrage Movement in South Australia', *Journal of the Royal Australian Historical Society* 63/3 (December 1979), 192.

27. Audrey Oldfield, *Woman Suffrage in Australia: A Gift or a Struggle?* (Cambridge: Cambridge University Press 1992), 22.

28. Oldfield, *Woman Suffrage in Australia*, 24.

29. Elizabeth Mansutti, *Mary Lee 1821–1909* (Adelaide: Openbook *c.*1994), 17, 'No claim is put forward for women representatives.'

30. Mansutti, *Mary Lee*, 20.

31. Oldfield, *Woman Suffrage in Australia*, 36.

32. Oldfield, *Woman Suffrage in Australia*, 38.

33. Reeves, *State Experiments*, 130.

34. Mansutti, *Mary Lee*, 28.

35. Oldfield, *Woman Suffrage in Australia*, 46.

36. Oldfield, *Woman Suffrage in Australia*, 53.

37. Reeves, *State Experiments*, 132.

38. Reeves, *State Experiments*, 134.

39. Reeves, *State Experiments*, 143. Henry Parkes had moved the adoption of women's suffrage in 1891 in the New South Wales parliament and had been beaten on the issue. It was awarded in 1902 after Federation.

40. Oldfield, *Woman Suffrage in Australia*, 60.

41. Reeves, *State Experiments*, 135.

42. King O'Malley on 23 April 1902 in debate in House of Representatives, Commonwealth Franchise Bill parliamentary records, 11929.

43. Reproduced in Anne Summers, *Damned Whores and God's Police* (Camberwell, Victoria, Aus.: Penguin 2002). A Chinese man with an opium pipe, 'Ah Chew Fat' also remarks 'plenty savee vote.'

44. Summers, *Damned Whores*, 420.
45. Oldfield, *Woman Suffrage in Australia*, 141.
46. Reeves, *State Experiments*, 131–2.
47. *Census: General Report England and Wales*, vol. iv, 1891 (London: Eyre and Spottiswood 1993), 4.
48. Reeves, *State Experiments*, 137.

CHAPTER 6: 'IN WITH OUR WOMEN' IN THE WESTERN US

1. Lloyd C. M. Hare, *The Greatest American Woman: Lucretia Mott* (New York: American Historical Society 1937), 133.
2. Hare, *Lucretia Mott*, 190 and 123.
3. Lucretia Mott, *Slavery and 'the woman question': Lucretia Mott's diary of her visit to Great Britain to Attend the World's Anti-Slavery Convention of 1840*, ed. Frederick-Tolles (Pennsylvania: Friends Historical Association 1952), 29.
4. *HWS* 1: 55.
5. Mott, *Slavery*, 3.
6. Mott, *Slavery*, 9 (introduction by Tolles); 'almost' is presumably an act of gallantry on Garrison's part.
7. *HWS* 1: 62.
8. Report of the Woman's Rights Convention Held at Seneca Falls NY, 19 and 20 July 1848 (Rochester: John Dick n.d.), 5–6.
9. Ross Evans Paulson, *Women's Suffrage and Prohibition: A Comparative Study of Equality and Social Control* (Glenview, Ill.: Scott, Foresman 1973), 32.
10. Stanton's address to the Seneca Falls Convention 19 July 1848.
11. There have been, latterly, questions about how close this vote was; the official minutes refer to motions passed after debate by a 'large majority'. Paulson, *Women's Suffrage and Prohibition*, 38.
12. Paulson, *Women's Suffrage and Prohibition*, 41.
13. *HWS* 1: 803–4. Madeleine Meyers, *Forward into Light: The Struggle for Woman's Suffrage* (Carlisle, Mass.: Discovery Enterprises 1994), 8–9.
14. Elizabeth Cady Stanton, *Eighty Years and More—Reminiscences* (London: T. Fisher Unwin 1898), 166.
15. Paulson, *Women's Suffrage and Prohibition*, 1–4.
16. Paulson, *Women's Suffrage and Prohibition*, 7, contrast with 'liberation' as in 'women's liberation' drawn from the vocabulary of nationalism, anti-colonialism and revolution.
17. *HWS* 1: 13.
18. Delight D. Dodyk, *Education and Agitation: The Woman Suffrage Movement in New Jersey* (PhD, Rutgers University, NJ 1997), 21.
19. Frances D. Gage, 'Sojourner Truth', *National Anti-Slavery Standard*, 3 May 1863.
20. Meyers, *Forward into Light*, 25–6. This version renders into plain English the attempt of Gage to represent Truth's speech in Southern slave dialect (though she was born and raised in the North). Other accounts are in Suzanne Pullon

Fitch and Roseann M. Mandziuk, *Sojourner Truth as Orator: Wit, Song and Story* (Eastport, Conn.: Greenwood 1997), 103–7 and 141–3.

21. Fitch and Mandziuk, *Sojourner Truth as Orator*, 73–4, and see Carlton Mabee and Susan Mabee Newhouse, *Sojourner Truth: Slave, Prophet, Legend* (New York: New York University Press 1993), 67–82.

22. Lydia Sigourney, 'Woman's Patriotism', in *Ladies Wreath: A Magazine Devoted to Literature, Industry and Religion* (May 1846), 1–25.

23. Joanna L. Stratton, *Pioneer Women: Voices from the Kansas Frontier* (New York: Simon and Schuster 1981), 261.

24. Barbara Goldsmith, *Other Powers: The Age of Suffrage, Spiritualism and the Scandalous Victoria Woodhull* (London: Granta 1998), 137.

25. Stratton, *Pioneer Women*, 262.

26. *HWS* 2: 193.

27. *HWS* 2: 214, 216.

28. Nell Irwin Painter, *Sojourner Truth: A Life, A Symbol* (New York: Norton, 1996), 230. Painter convincingly demonstrates that the image the women's historian Frances Dana Gage gives to Truth in her telling of the 'ar'n't I a woman?' speech owes more to Gage's need to assert herself as a leading journalist of the movement than to Truth's actual behaviour (164–78).

29. *HWS* 2: 353–4.

30. *HWS* 2: 2, 383.

31. Rosalyn Terborg-Penn, *African American Women in the Struggle for the Vote, 1850–1920* (Bloomington: Indiana University Press 1998), 32. Terborg-Penn remarks that white women suffragists found it easier to quote illiterate Sojourner Truth than the educated black women in the suffrage movement.

32. Richard J. Evans, *The Feminists: Women's Emancipation Movements in Europe, America and Australasia 1840–1920* (London: Croom Helm 1977), 49.

33. While Wyoming deserves its accolades for priority, it was not alone in the field—suffrage bills in three western legislatures had been narrowly defeated previously: in Washington in 1854, Nebraska in 1856 and Dakota in 1869. Michael A. Massie, 'Reform is Where You Find It: The Roots of Woman Suffrage in Wyoming', *Annals of Wyoming* 62/1 (spring 1990), 7. One technical reason why women's suffrage succeeded in Wyoming was that it was a territory, where only a majority vote of the legislature and the governor's signature were required; amending a state's constitution was a considerably more difficult operation.

34. Sidney Howell Fleming, 'Solving the Jigsaw Puzzle: One Suffrage Story at a Time', *Annals of Wyoming* 62/1 (spring 1990), 36.

35. *HWS* 3: 730.

36. Grace Raymond Hebard, *How Woman Suffrage Came to Wyoming* (pamphlet, Laramie: University of Wyoming 1920), 8.

37. Mary Lee Stark, 'One of the First Women Voters Tells How the Franchise was Granted: Many Wrong Statements Are Corrected in Article', Typescript n.d. (but after 1916), Wyoming State Archives (hereafter: WySA), Woman Suffrage 3. Lee lost his place in history because he was removed from his position as

secretary after accusations from his enemies of drunkenness and his association with a prostitute, the 'Circassian Girl' (T. A. Larson, *History of Wyoming* (Lincoln: University of Nebraska Press 1978), 120–3). Subsequently his contribution to women's suffrage was ignored; his sister was attempting to redress the omission of his name from those responsible for the women's vote in Wyoming.

38. Anthony's 'fire and enthusiasm' were said to have aroused Morris: Grace Raymond Hebard, *How Woman Suffrage Came to Wyoming* (pamphlet, University of Wyoming 1920), 9. For Dickinson: T. A. Larson, 'Petticoats at the Polls: Woman Suffrage in Territorial Wyoming', *Pacific Northwest Quarterly* 44/2 (April 1953), 74. Governor Campbell is said to have heard Anthony speak in Ohio: Miriam Grant Chapman, 'The Story of Woman Suffrage in Wyoming 1869–1890' (unpublished MA Thesis, University of Wyoming 1952), 60 WySA.

39. *Chicago Tribune*, 17 June 1894.

40. *Acceptance of the Statue of Esther Hobart Morris Presented by the State of Wyoming* (Washington DC: US Government Printing Office 1961), 5–6.

41. Hebard, *How Woman Suffrage Came to Wyoming*, 10.

42. Fred D. Stratton, *Early History of South Pass City, Wyoming and How Women First Received the Right to Vote and Hold Public Office* (Cheyenne, Wyo.: 1950), 9.

43. *Acceptance of the Statue of Esther Hobart Morris*, 29.

44. Letter of Esther Morris to be read before Women Suffrage Conference, Washington DC 21 January 1871 (Hebard Collection, American Heritage Centre Box 40 file 20).

45. H. G. Nickerson, 'Historical Correction', in *The Wyoming State Journal*, 14 February 1919; typescript in Hebard collection, American Heritage Centre Box 40 file 32. Massie points out that this was the first mention of this event; that it is unlikely forty people could have been assembled to support women's suffrage in a gold mining town; and her log cabin was too small to accommodate them.

46. Massie, 'Reform is Where You Find It', 11.

47. Typescript document in WySA Woman Suffrage 2; author and date unknown. The uncertain provenance of such material accounts for the use of terms such as 'is said to have been', 'may have been'.

48. A. P. Grimes, *The Puritan Ethic and Woman Suffrage* (Oxford: Oxford University Press 1967), 63–5.

49. Amalia Post to Ann Simons, 4 April 1870, American Heritage Centre, Morton E. Post Papers, Accession 1362 Box 1 file 11. Bright cited 'Mrs M. E. Post' along with Esther Morris and another woman as being suffragists. Fleming, 'Solving the Jigsaw Puzzle', 61.

50. Paulson, *Women's Suffrage and Prohibition*, 135. This was not an official response to Congress but, it appears, a message to the Wyoming representative who was reporting the progress back home by telegram.

51. Massie, 'Reform is Where You Find It', 18.

52. This is the opinion of present-day archivists and of Professor T. A, Larson, author of the *History of Wyoming*. 'Dr Larson Questions Right to Single Out Esther Morris', *Laramie Republican-Boomerang*, 20 December 1954.

53. Hebard Collection, American Heritage Centre, Box 40 folder 32, 'Nickerson'. The file also contains Hebard's unsuccessful attempts, after Nickerson's death, to track down an affidavit she believed he made affirming the truth of the story. Nickerson presumably had not been prepared to swear an affidavit, but Hebard clearly believed he had done so (doubtless because he told her he had).

54. Hebard Collection, American Heritage Centre Box 21, folder 6, 'Politician or Diplomatist?', typescript May 1928.

55. Grace Raymond Hebard, *The History and Government of Wyoming* (San Francisco: C. F. Weber 1919), 55 'Mrs Esther Morris was the pioneer worker for Woman Suffrage in this State.'

56. Grimes, *The Puritan Ethic*, 30.

57. Grimes, *The Puritan Ethic*, 34, 38. There certainly did not appear to be a multiplicity of political views in Utah; when the state constitution was voted on in 1872 there were 25,000 voters in favour and 368 opposed.

58. Grimes, *The Puritan Ethic*, 28.

59. Grimes, *The Puritan Ethic*, 16.

60. Walter Prescott Webb, *The Great Plains* (Boston: Gin and Company 1931), 248.

61. Chapman, 'The Story of Woman Suffrage in Wyoming 1869–1890', 6. The total male: female ration was 7,219 males to 1,899 females.

62. Chapman, 'The Story of Woman Suffrage in Wyoming 1869–1890', 116.

63. Grimes, *The Puritan Ethic*, 76.

64. Johanna Johnston, *Mrs Satan: The Incredible Story of Victoria Woodhull* (London: Macmillan 1967), 13.

65. Johnston, *Mrs Satan*, 60.

66. Johnstone, *Mrs Satan*, 66.

67. Mary Gabriel, *Notorious Victoria: The Life of Victoria Woodhull, Uncensored* (Chapel Hill NC: Algonquin 1998), 80.

68. Johnstone, *Mrs Satan*, 89.

69. Johnstone, *Mrs Satan*, 92.

70. Goldsmith, *Other Powers*, 227.

71. Goldsmith, *Other Powers*, 274.

72. Robert Shaplen, *Free Love and Heavenly Sinners* (London: Andre Deutsch 1956), 124.

73. Gabriel, *Notorious Victoria*, 148.

74. *Harper's Weekly*, 17 February 1872.

75. Goldsmith, *Other Powers*, 319.

76. Johnston, *Mrs Satan*, 146.

77. Johnston, *Mrs Satan*, 154.

78. Johnston, *Mrs Satan*, 156.

79. Heywood Broun and Margaret Leech, *Anthony Comstock: Roundsman of the Lord* (London: Wishart 1928), 111.

80. Johnston, *Mrs Satan*, 172.

81. Johnson, *Mrs Satan*, 220 and 239.

82. Goldsmith, *Other Powers*, 427.

83. Johnston, *Mrs Satan*, 300.

84. *New York Times*, 20 June 1873.

85. Stanton, *Eighty Years*, 179.

86. Anthony to Stanton, 5 November 1872, in *Forward Into Light*, 33.

87. *HWS* 3: 93.

88. Theresa Walling Seabrook and Lillie Devereux Blake in 'Broadside: To The Women of New Jersey', 1887, quoted in Dodyk, *Education and Agitation*, 180.

89. Evans, *The Feminists*, 53.

90. When a gendered vote on continuing prohibition was taken in Finland in 1931 (men and women's votes were cast on different coloured ballot paper) the number of women favouring repeal was larger than the *total vote* in favour of prohibition. Paulson, *Women's Suffrage and Prohibition*, 172.

91. Alexander Keyssar, *The Right to Vote: The Contested History of Democracy in the United States* (New York: Basic Books 2000), 179.

92. *HWS* 4: xix.

93. William O'Neill, *Everyone Was Brave: The Rise and Fall of Feminism in America* (Chicago: Quadrangle 1969), 61.

94. Rebecca J. Mead, *How the West Was Won: Woman Suffrage in the Western United States 1869–1914* (New York: New York University Press 2004), 69.

95. Mead, *How the West Was Won*, 28.

96. Mead, *How the West Was Won*, 93–4.

97. Carrie Chapman Catt and Nettie Rogers Shuler, *Woman Suffrage and Politics: The Inner Story of the Suffrage Movement* (Seattle: University of Washington Press 1923), 123.

98. Mead, *How the West Was Won*, 119–20; Mead covers the state-by-state achievement of the vote in detail, emphasizing the influence of developing working class movements.

99. Mead, *How the West Was Won*, 52.

100. A statement of these ideas occurs in Aileen S. Kraditor, *The Ideas of the Woman Suffrage Movement 1890–1920* (New York: Columbia University Press 1965); and there is a questioning of them in Mead who emphasizes the involvement of working class women.

101. *Cheyenne Daily Leader*, 28 April 1870.

102. Carrie Chapman Catt, *The World Movement for Woman Suffrage 1904–1911* (London: IWSA 1915).

CHAPTER 7: OUT OF THE DOLL'S HOUSE IN SCANDINAVIA

1. Ella Anker, *Women's Suffrage in Norway* (London: NUWSS 1913), 4.

2. Richard J. Evans, *The Feminists: Women's Emancipation Movements in Europe, America and Australasia 1840–1920* (London: Croom Helm 1977), 19.

3. Ankeer, *Women's Suffrage in Norway*, 5.

4. Ross Evans Paulson, *Women's Suffrage and Prohibition: A Comparative Study of Equality and Social Control* (Glenview, Ill.: Scott, Foresman 1973), 98.

5. Irma Sulkunen, 'The Women's Movement', in M. Engman and D. Kirby, *Finland: People, Nation, State* (London: Hurst 1989), 189 and *Encyclopaedia Britannica* 2004, entries for appropriate countries.
6. Aura Korppi-Tommola, 'Fighting Together for Freedom: Nationalism, Socialism, Feminism and Women's Suffrage in Finland 1906', *Scandinavian Journal of History* 15/3 (1990), 181.
7. Evans, *The Feminists*, 87.
8. Aino Malmberg, *Woman Suffrage in Finland* (London: Women's Freedom League, n.d., prob. 1913), 3 Co-education had become widespread because of the expense for local authorities of building a school for each gender with few pupils because of the nation's scattered population.
9. Alice Zimmern, *Women's Suffrage in Many Lands* (London: Woman Citizen Publishing Society 1909), 63.
10. Malmberg, *Woman Suffrage in Finland*, 2.
11. Sulkunen, 'The Women's Movement', 179.
12. Paulson, *Women's Suffrage and Prohibition*, 147.
13. Korppi-Tommola, 'Fighting Together for Freedom', 188, 191.
14. Sulkunen, 'The Women's Movement', 183–7.
15. Malmberg, *Woman Suffrage in Finland*, 8.
16. Alexander Gripenberg, 'The Great Victory in Finland', *The Englishwoman's Review*, 16 July 1906.
17. Her great grand-daughter became the first woman member of parliament in Norway, Anna Rogstad.
18. Zimmern, *Women's Suffrage in Many Lands*, 50.
19. It concentrated on the municipal franchise for which petitions failed in parliament in 1904, 1905 and 1906.
20. Zimmern, *Women's Suffrage in Many Lands*, 53.
21. Donald Meyer, *Sex and Power: The Rise of Women in America, Russia, Sweden and Italy* (Middletown, Conn.: Wesleyan University Press 1987), 44.
22. Evans, *The Feminists*, 73.
23. Josefin Rönnbäck, 'The Struggle for Women's Franchise—a Menage à Trois of Women, Men and State', posted on the Women's History Collections site by Gothenburg University Library: <http://www.ub.gu.se/kvinn/portaler/rostratt/historik/>
24. Rönnbäck, 'The Struggle for Women's Franchise'; see also Josefin Rönnbäck, *The Gender of Politics: The National Association for Women's Suffrage and its Struggle for Women's Political Citizenship 1902–1921* (PhD thesis, University of Stockholm 2004).
25. Meyer, *Sex and Power*, 186–7, referring to Ellen Key's books *Woman's Power Misused* and *Woman's Psychology and Womanly Logic*, both of 1896.
26. Meyer, *Sex and Power*, 190.
27. Rönnbäck, 'The Struggle for Women's Franchise'.
28. Evans, *The Feminists*, 74.

29. This chapter is also indebted to Ingvar Anderrsson, *A History of Sweden* (London: Weidenfeld 1956).

30. Gunnar Karlsson, *Iceland's 1100 Years* (London: Hurst 2000), 277.

31. Karlsson, *Iceland's 1100 Years*, 278.

32. John Markoff, 'Margins, Centres, and Democracy: The Paradigmatic History of Women's Suffrage', *Signs: Journal of Women in Culture and Society* 29/1 (2003), 85–116.

33. Rochelle Goldberg Ruthchild, 'Women's Suffrage and Revolution in the Russian Empire, 1905–1917', *Aspasia: International Yearbook of Central, Eastern and Southeastern Women's and Gender History* 1 (March 2007), 2.

CHAPTER 8: LOBBYISTS TO MILITANTS IN BRITAIN

1. The Pankhurst story is best told collectively by Martin Pugh, *The Pankhursts* (London: Penguin 2001). This chapter has also benefited from June Purvis, *Emmeline Pankhurst* (London: Routledge 2002) and Jad Adams, *Pankhurst* (London: Haus 2003).

2. S. Pankhurst, *The Suffragette Movement* (London: Virago 1977), 55.

3. S. Pankhurst, *Suffragette Movement*, 56.

4. S. Pankhurst, *Suffragette Movement*, 4.

5. Pugh, *Pankhursts*, 312. The two elder children remembered a better time in their childhood home than Adela.

6. S. Pankhurst, *Suffragette Movement*, 168; Christabel Pankhurst, *Unshackled: The Story of How We Won the Vote* (London: Hutchinson 1959), 43.

7. Men continued to be active in the WSPU up to and involving acts of militancy; see Sandra Stanley Holton, *Suffrage Days: Stories from the Women's Suffrage Movement* (London: Routledge 1996), 183–204.

8. E. Pankhurst, *The Importance of the Vote* (London: Women's Press 1913), 1. Copy of a lecture delivered on 24 March 1908.

9. E. Pankhurst, *My Own Story* (London: Eveleigh Nash 1914), 38.

10. Caroline Benn, *Keir Hardie* (London: Hutchinson 1992), 198.

11. Benn, *Keir Hardie*, 225 and Patricia W. E. Romero, *Sylvia Pankhurst: Portrait of a Radical* (New Haven: Yale University Press 1990), 37. The sexual relationship continued until some time in 1912. They remained very close until his death three years later; their intimacy therefore extended over almost the entire period of activity of the WSPU.

12. S. Pankhurst, *Suffragette Movement*, 126.

13. Rheta Childe Dorr, *A Woman of Fifty* (New York: Funk and Wagnall 1924), 264.

14. S. Pankhurst, *Suffragette Movement*, 191. Sylvia even takes the trouble to tell readers that Christabel had a better bicycle than she had when they were children.

15. C. Pankhurst, *Unshackled*, 50.

16. Pugh, *Pankhursts*, 129.

17. C. Pankhurst, *Unshackled*, 52.

18. S. Pankhurst, *Suffragette Movement*, 193.

19. S. Pankhurst, *Suffragette Movement*, 199.

20. E. Pankhurst, *The Importance of the Vote*, inside front cover.

21. Teresa Billington-Greig, *The Non-Violent Militant: Selected Writings*, ed. Carol McPhee and Ann Fitzgerald (London: Routledge 1987), 90–1.

22. Emmeline Pethick-Lawrence, *My Part in a Changing World* (London: Victor Gollancz 1938), 176.

23. Pugh, *Pankhursts*, 167.

24. Clara Codd quoted in Elizabeth Crawford, *The Women's Suffrage Movement* (London: Routledge 1999), 738.

25. C. Pankhurst, *Unshackled*, 112; *Votes for Women*, 29 October 1908, 82.

26. *Hansard*, 28 February 1908, 242–4.

27. C. Pankhurst, *Unshackled*, 58.

28. E. Pankhust, *My Own*, 149.

29. S. Pankhurst, *Suffragette Movement*, 443.

30. Aletta Jacobs, *Memories: My Life as an International Leader in Health, Suffrage and Peace* (New York: Feminist Press 1996), 141.

31. Mineke Bosch, *Politics and Friendship: Letters from the International Woman Suffrage Alliance 1902–1942* (Columbus: Ohio State University Press 1990), 82.

32. Pugh, *Pankhursts*, 226.

33. Antonia Raeburn, *The Militant Suffragettes* (London: Michael Joseph 1973), 157.

34. E. Pankhurst, *My Own*, 212.

35. C. Pankhurst, *Unshackled*, 209.

36. *The Suffragette*, 30 May 1913, 539 which also contains reports of two anonymous attacks on Christabel's leadership.

37. Frederick Pethick-Lawrence, *Fate Has Been Kind* (London: Hutchinson 1943), 97.

38. E. Pethick-Lawrence, *My Part*, 277.

39. F. Pethick-Lawrence, *Fate*, 99.

40. E. Pethick-Lawrence, *My Part*, 280.

41. F. Pethick-Lawrence, *Fate*, 100.

42. *The Suffragette*, 25 October 1912, 16; *My Own*, 266.

43. *Votes for Women*, 16 August 1912, 749.

44. Benn, *Keir Hardie*, 315.

45. E. Pankhurst, *My Own*, 261.

46. Sylvia Pankhurst, *The Life of Emmeline Pankhurst* (London: T. Werner Laurie 1935), 125.

47. *The Suffragette*, 18 July 1913, 677.

48. S. Pankhurst, *Suffragette Movement*, 401.

49. S. Pankhurst, *Suffragette Movement*, 517.

50. Lucy Bland, *Banishing the Beast: Sexuality and the Early Feminists* (New York: New Press 1995), 244–5.

51. Christabel Pankhurst, *The Great Scourge and How To End It* (London: n.p. 1913), 188.
52. June Purvis, *Emmeline Pankhurst A Biography* (London: Routledge 2002), 237.
53. S. Pankhurst, *Suffragette Movement*, 521.
54. Teresa Billington-Greig, 'The Truth About White Slavery', in *Englishwoman's Review*, June 1913, 445.
55. Crawford, *The Women's Suffrage Movement*, 380 and Bland, 265–77.
56. E. Pankhurst, *My Own*, 307.
57. Herbert Asquith, *Fifty Years of Parliament*, vol. 2 (London: Cassell 1926), 126.
58. Raeburn, *The Militant Suffragettes*, 232; *The Suffragette*, 29 May 1914, 120.
59. *The Suffragette*, 7 August 1914, 301.
60. Martin Pugh, 'Politicians and the Women's Vote 1914–1918', *History* 59 (1977), 358 and 362.
61. D. Lloyd George, *War Memoirs*, vol. 2 (London: Odhams 1938), 1172.
62. *The Times*, 20 November 1920, 10. This statement (presuming it was correctly reported) is false: Christabel was not even at the founding meeting of the WSPU.
63. Margaret Ward, *Hannah Sheehy Skeffington: A Life* (Dublin: Attic 1997). Sybil Oldfield and Leah Levenson, Cousins and Sheehy-Skeffington entries respectively, Oxford *DNB* 2004–7.
64. Ward, *Hanna Sheehy Skeffington*, xii. Diarmaid Ferriter, *The Transformation of Ireland 1900–2000* (London: Profile 2004), 176.
65. Karen Offen, *European Feminisms 1700–1950* (Stanford, Calif.: Stanford University Press 2000), 225.
66. Offen, *European Feminisms*, 225. Constance Rover, *Women's Suffrage and Party Politics in Britain 1866–1914* (London: Routledge 1967), 130–1.
67. Levenson, Sheehy-Skeffington entry, *DNB* 2004–7.
68. Bosch, *Politics and Friendship*, 111.
69. June E. Hahner, *Emancipating the Female Sex: The Struggle for Women's Rights in Brazil 1850–1940* (Durham NC: Duke University Press 1990), 153.
70. Mina Roces, 'Is the Suffragist an American Colonial Construct: Defining "The Filipino Woman" in colonial Philippines', in Louise Edwards and Mina Roces (eds.), *Asia: Gender, Nationalism and Democracy* (London: Routledge 2004), 40.
71. Eva Peron, 'From the Sublime to the Ridiculous', in *Evita by Evita* (New York: Proteus 1953), 179.
72. Ray Strachey, *'The Cause', A Short History of the Women's Movement in Britain* (London: G. Bell 1928), 333.

CHAPTER 9: VICTORY AND DISENFRANCHISEMENT IN THE US

1. Rebecca J. Mead, *How the West Was Won: Woman Suffrage in the Western United States 1869–1914* (New York: New York University Press 2004), 172.
2. Aileen S. Kraditor, *The Ideas of the Woman Suffrage Movement 1890–1920* (New York: Columbia University Press 1965), 125.

3. Jacqueline Van Voris, *Carrie Chapman Catt: A Public Life* (New York: The Feminist Press 1987), 15.
4. Kraditor, *Carrie Chapman Catt*, 137.
5. Alexander Keyssar, *The Right to Vote: The Contested History of Democracy in the United States* (New York: Basic Books 2000), 205.
6. Keyssar, *The Right to Vote*, 206.
7. Christine A. Lunardini, *From Equal Suffrage to Equal Rights: Alice Paul and the National Woman's Party 1910–1928* (New York: New York University Press 1986), 28–30.
8. Carrie Chapman Catt and Nettie Rogers Shuler, *Woman Suffrage and Politics: The Inner Story of the Suffrage Movement* (Seattle: University of Washington Press 1923), 244.
9. Lunardini, *From Equal Suffrage to Equal Rights*, 42–8.
10. Linda Ford, 'Alice Paul and the Politics of Nonviolent Protest', in Jean H. Baker (ed.), *Votes for Women: The Struggle for Suffrage Revisited* (Oxford: Oxford University Press 2002), 177.
11. Trevor Lloyd, *Suffragettes International: The World-wide Campaign for Women's Rights* (London: Library of the 20th Century 1971), 81.
12. Mead, *How the West Was Won*, 167.
13. Keyssar, *The Right to Vote*, 213.
14. Ray Stannard Baker, *Woodrow Wilson: Life and Letters*, vol. 6 (London: Heinemann 1938), 277.
15. Van Voris, *Carrie Chapman Catt: A Public Life*, 142.
16. Mineke Bosch, *Politics and Friendship: Letters from the International Woman Suffrage Alliance 1902–1942* (Columbus: Ohio State University Press 1990), 133, letter dated 19 March 1914.
17. Keyssar, *The Right to Vote*, 216; Baker, *Woodrow Wilson*, 436; *HWS* 5: 761–2.
18. *HWS* 5: 646.
19. Mead, *How the West Was Won*, 167.
20. Rosalyn Terborg-Penn, *African-American Women in the Struggle for the Vote 1850–1920* (Bloomington, Ind.: Indiana University Press 1998), 91.
21. Terborg-Penn, *African-American Women*, 116.
22. Terborg-Penn, *African-American Women*, 121.
23. Terborg-Penn, *African-American Women*, 124.
24. *HWS* 6, 621.
25. These observations owe much to the work of Terborg-Penn.
26. *The Crisis* 21 (November 1920), 23.
27. Quoted in *Negro Year Book 1921–22* (Tuskagee Ala.: Negro Year Book Company 1922), 41.
28. William L. O'Neill, *Everyone Was Brave: The Rise and Fall of Feminism in America* (Chicago: Quadrangle 1969), 275.
29. Robert L. Allen and Pamela Allen, *Reluctant Reformers: Racism and Social Reform Movements in the United States* (Washington DC: Howard University Press 1974), 154.
30. J. Richard Evans, *The Feminists* (London: Croom Helm 1977), 227.

CHAPTER 10: WHO WON VOTES FROM THE WAR?

1. *HWS* 6: 791.
2. *HWS* 6: 789.
3. *HWS* 6: 788.
4. Richard Stites, 'Women's Liberation Movements in Russia 1900–1930', *Canadian-American Slavik Studies* 7/4 (winter 1973), 461.
5. Donald Meyer, *Sex and Power: The Rise of Women in America, Russia, Sweden and Italy* (Middletown, Conn.: Wesleyan University Press 1987), 84.
6. Vera Figner, *Memoirs of a Revolutionist* (London: Martin Lawrence n.d. (1927 or after)), 313.
7. Figner, *Memoirs*, 40.
8. Cathy Porter, *Fathers and Daughters: Russian Women in Revolution* (London: Virago 1976), 142.
9. Leo Deutsch, quoted in James Harvey Robinson and Charles Beard, *Readings in Modern European History*, vol. 2 (Boston: Ginn and Co. 1909), 360.
10. Figner, *Memoirs*, 103.
11. Richard Stites, *The Women's Liberation Movement in Russia: Feminism, Nihilism and Bolshevism 1860–1930* (Princeton NJ: Princeton University Press 1990), 158.
12. The influence of Finland is pointed up clearly in Rochelle Goldberg Ruthchild, 'Women's Suffrage and Revolution in the Russian Empire, 1905–1917', *Aspasia: International Yearbook of Central, Eastern and Southeastern European Women's and Gender History* 1 (March 2007), 1–35.
13. Alice Zimmern, *Woman Suffrage in Many Lands* (London: Woman Citizen Publishing Society 1909), 140, and J. Richard Evans, *The Feminists* (London: Croom Helm 1977), 121; see also Stites, *The Women's Liberation Movement in Russia*, 199–200, whose translation of this phrase is 'a change in women's status is impossible without the general political liberation of our country'.
14. Stites, *The Women's Liberation Movement in Russia*, 201.
15. Stites, *The Women's Liberation Movement in Russia*, 207.
16. Alexandra Kollontai, *Selected Articles and Speeches* (New York: International Publishers 1984), 148–9.
17. Stites, *The Women's Liberation Movement in Russia*, 213.
18. *International Woman Suffrage Alliance Report 1909* (London: Samuel Sidders), 64–5.
19. Ruthchild, 'Women's Suffrage and Revolution in the Russian Empire', 11.
20. Stites, *The Women's Liberation Movement in Russia*, 217.
21. Marianna Muravyeva, 'Anna Pavlovna Filosova', in Francesca De Haan et al., *A Biographical Dictionary of Women's Movements and Feminisms in Central, Eastern and South Eastern Europe, 19th and 20th Centuries* (Budapest: Central European University Press 2006), 138.
22. Stites, *The Women's Liberation Movement in Russia*, 282.
23. Roy Bainton, *1917: Russia's Year of Revolution* (London: Robinson 2005), 67–8.
24. Ruthchild, 'Women's Suffrage and Revolution in the Russian Empire', 17–18.

25. Evans, *The Feminists*, 220.
26. Natalia Pushkareva, *Women in Russian History: From the Tenth to the Twentieth Century* (Armonk NY: M. E. Sharp 1997), 257.
27. Pushkareva, *Women in Russian History*, 257.
28. Pushkareva, *Women in Russian History*, 259.
29. Stites, 'Women's Liberation Movements in Russia 1900–1930', 472.
30. Porter, *Fathers and Daughters*, 295.
31. Elizabeth Cady Stanton, *Eighty Years and More—Reminiscences* (London: T. Fisher Unwin 1898), 176.
32. Evans, *The Feminists*, 103.
33. Zimmern, *Woman Suffrage in Many Lands*, 79.
34. Bertrand Russell, *German Social Democracy* (London: Longmans 1896), 137.
35. Richard J. Evans, *The Feminist Movement in Germany 1894–1933* (London: Sage 1976), 72.
36. Zimmern, *Woman Suffrage in Many Lands*, 89, quoting Fräulein von Welczeck.
37. Evans, *The Feminist Movement in Germany*, 77. Evans points out how the poor ('economically weak') were put on a level with the physically disabled, children and animals, as if their disabilities were a matter of laws of nature and beyond rational redress, requiring merely pity and protection.
38. Evans, *The Feminists*, 107.
39. Evans, *The Feminists*, 163.
40. Werner Thönnessen, *The Emancipation of Women: The Rise and Decline of the Women's Movement in German Social Democracy 1863–1933* (Frankfurt am Main: Pluto 1969), 32.
41. Thönnessen, *The Emancipation of Women*, 66–7.
42. Zimmern, *Woman Suffrage in Many Lands*, 86.
43. Evans, *The Feminist Movement in Germany*, 99.
44. *HWS* 6: 791.
45. *HWS* 6: 791.
46. Paul Smith, *Feminism and the Third Republic: Women's Political and Civil Rights in France 1918–1945* (Oxford: Clarendon Press 1996), 121.
47. H. R. Trevor-Roper, *Hitler's Table-Talk 1941–1944: His Private Conversations* (London: Phoenix 2000), 251–2.
48. Adolf Hitler addressing National Socialist women in 1934, reprinted in Susan Groag Bell and Karen M. Offen, *Women, the Family and Freedom: The Debate in Documents*, vol. 2: *1880–1950* (Stanford, Calif.: Stanford University Press 1983), 229.
49. Aletta Jacobs, *Memories: My Life as an International Leader in Health, Suffrage and Peace* (New York: Feminist Press 1996), 8. Mineke Bosche in her biography of Jacobs, discusses how she shares this trait with many of her feminist contemporaries, but also stresses Jacobs' mother's contacts in the Jewish community as of great benefit to Jacobs' career (*Een onwrikbaar gevoel voor rechtvaardigheid. Aletta Jacobs, 1854–1929* (Amsterdam: Balans 2005)).

50. Jacobs, *Memories*, 35.

51. Jacobs, *Memories*, 54.

52. The Gerritsen Collection of Women's History is owned by the University of Kansas and accessible to libraries.

53. Jacobs, *Memories*, 143.

54. Mineke Bosch, *Politics and Friendship: Letters from the International Woman Suffrage Alliance 1902–1942* (Columbus: Ohio State University Press 1990), 69.

55. *HWS* 6: 784.

56. Zimmern, *Woman Suffrage in Many Lands*, 73.

57. Zimmern, *Woman Suffrage in Many Lands*, 75.

58. Bosch, *Politics and Friendship*, 44 and 73.

59. Carrie Chapman Catt to Aletta Jacobs, 17 March 1907 (Bosch, *Politics and Friendship*, 70). Similarly, the NUWSS prevented the Women's Social and Political Union from affiliating to the IWSA.

60. Bosch, *Politics and Friendship*, 47.

61. There is additionally a research project undertaken by Mineke Bosch at Maastricht University under the title: 'The Spectacle of Dutch Suffrage Women: Gender, Popular Culture and Politics During the Beginnings of Modernity'.

62. Evans, *The Feminists*, 134.

63. Mineke Bosch, ' "Das Stimmrecht als mächtigstes Mittel" Eine kurzgeschichte der frauenstimmrechtsbewegung in den Niederlanden (1883–1919)', in Bettina Bab (ed.), *Mit Macht zur Wahl: 100 Jahre Frauenwahlrecht in Europa* (Bonn: Frauenmuseum 2006), *passim*.

64. Mineke Bosch, 'Colonial Dimensions of Dutch Women's Suffrage: Aletta Jacobs' Letters from Africa and Asia 1911–12', *Journal of Women's History* 11/2 (Summer 1999), 8–34.

65. Trevor Lloyd, *Suffragettes International: The World-Wide Campaign for Women's Rights* (London: Library of the 20th Centrury 1971), 99. For information in this section: Hélène Papineau (ed.), *A History of the Vote in Canada* (Ottawa: Ministry of Public Works and Government Services 1997), ch. 3. There is an interesting section on disparate women's franchises in the nineteenth century, pp. 60–4.

66. Catherine Lyle Cleverdon, *The Woman Suffrage Movement in Canada* (Toronto: Toronto University Press 1950), 20.

67. Papineau, *History of the Vote in Canada*, 64.

68. Cleverdon, *The Woman Suffrage Movement in Canada*, 114.

69. It was widely believed that (outside of Alberta and Saskatchewan) the provincial vote conferred the federal vote. The issue would have to be tested in the courts—but the War-time Franchises Act was passed before the necessity of doing so. Cleverdon, *The Woman Suffrage Movement in Canada*, 115–19.

70. Cleverdon, *The Woman Suffrage Movement in Canada*, 129.

71. Cleverdon, *The Woman Suffrage Movement in Canada*, 130.

72. June, Hannam, Mitzi Auchterlonie, and Katherine Holden, *International Encyclopaedia of Women's Suffrage* (Santa Barbara, Calif.: ABC-CLIO 2000), 123. For a general discussion of suffrage and related issues during the war, see Alison S. Fell and Ingrid Sharp, *The Women's Movement in Wartime* (London: Palgrave 2007).

73. Lloyd, *Suffragettes International*, 99.

CHAPTER 11: THE POPE AND THE VOTE—CATHOLIC EUROPE

1. Steven C. Hause and Anne R. Kenney, 'The Development of the Catholic Women's Suffrage Movement in France, 1896–1922', *Catholic Historical Review* 67/1 (January 1981), 23.

2. Francis M. Mason, 'The Newer Eve: The Catholic Women's Suffrage Society in England, 1911–1923', *Catholic Historical Review* 72/4 (October 1986), 620. The remark about their precedence is not accurate as it ignores Marie Maugeret's contribution.

3. Annie Christitch, *A Word on Woman Suffrage* (London: Catholic Women's Suffrage Society n.d. (1912?)), 7.

4. Annie Christitch, 'Yes, we approve', *Catholic Citizen* 5/7 (15 July 1919), 51. Well aware of the importance of the event, Christitch quoted his exact words so there could be no suspicion of ambiguity in the translation: in fact he said 'Nous voudrions voir des femmes éléctrices partout.'

5. Steven C. Hause and Anne R. Kenney, *Women's Suffrage and Social Politics in the French Third Republic* (Princeton NJ: Princeton University Press 1984), 227.

6. Aletta Jacobs, *Memories: My Life as an International Leader in Health, Suffrage and Peace* (New York: Feminist Press, 1996), 59.

7. John Markoff, 'Margins, Centres, and Democracy: The Paradigmatic History of Women's Suffrage', *Signs: Journal of Women in Culture and Society* 29/11 (2003), 90. Liberal and Social Democrat representatives had in the late nineteenth century pressed the government to remove property qualification as a democratic step—but one which disenfranchised propertied women.

8. Birgitta Bader-Zaar, 'Women in Austrian Politics 1890–1934', in David F. Good, Margarete Grandner, and Mary Jo Maynes, *Austrian Women in the Nineteenth and Twentieth Centuries* (Providence RI: Berghahn 1996), 59 and 64.

9. Bader-Zaar, 'Women in Austrian Politics', 65.

10. Bader-Zaar, 'Women in Austrian Politics', 70.

11. Bader-Zaar, 'Women in Austrian Politics', 71.

12. Jacobs, *Memories*, 60.

13. Thomas Harrison Reed, *Government and Politics of Belgium* (London: George G. Harrap 1924), 39.

14. Alice Zimmern, *Woman Suffrage in Many Lands* (London: Woman Citizen Publishing Society 1909), 132.

15. Reed, *Government and Politics of Belgium*, 58.

16. *HWS* 6: 787.

17. Ross Evans Paulson, *Women's Suffrage and Prohibition: A Comparative Study of Equality and Social Control* (Glenview, Ill.: Scott, Foresman and Co. 1973), 54 and *HWS* 1: 234–6.

18. Elizabeth Cady Stanton, *Eighty Years and More—Reminiscences* (London: T. Fisher Unwin 1898), 177. Karen Offen notes that previous women's rights conferences had also avoided discussion of women's suffrage, despite the protests of Auclert (*European Feminisms 1700–1950* (Stanford, Calif.: Stanford University Press 2000), 151–3).

19. James F. McMillan, *France and Women 1789–1914: Gender, Society and Politics* (London: Routledge 2000), 191.

20. McMillan, *France and Women*, 189.

21. J. Richard Evans, *The Feminists* (London: Croom Helm 1977), 152.

22. McMillan, *France and Women*, 209.

23. McMillan, *France and Women*, 198.

24. Hause and Kenney, 'Development of the Catholic Women's Suffrage Movement', 21.

25. Hause and Kenney, *Women's Suffrage and Social Politics*, 238.

26. Paul Smith, *Feminism and the Third Republic: Women's Political and Civil Rights in France 1918–1945* (Oxford: Clarendon Press 1996), 124.

27. Hause and Kenney, *Women's Suffrage and Social Politics*, 229.

28. James F. McMillan, *Housewife or Harlot: The Place of Women in French Society 1870–1940* (Brighton: Harvester Press 1981), 182–5.

29. Karen Offen, 'Women, Citizenship and Suffrage with a French Twist 1789–1993', in Caroline Daley and Melanie Nolan, *Suffrage and Beyond: International Feminist Perspectives* (Auckland: Auckland University Press 1994), 163.

30. Hause and Kenney, 'Development of the Catholic Women's Suffrage Movement', 29.

31. C. A. Micaud, 'Launching the Fourth French Republic', *Journal of Politics* 8/3 (August 1946), 292.

32. Alfred Cobban, *A History of Modern France*, vol. 3: *1871–1962* (London: Penguin 1970), 203.

33. Hause and Kenney, 'Development of the Catholic Women's Suffrage Movement', 11.

34. Judith Jeffrey Howard, 'The Civil Code of 1865 and the Origins of the Feminist Movement in Italy', in Betty Boyd Caroli, Robert F. Harney and Lydio F. Tomasi, *The Italian Immigrant Woman in North America* (Toronto: Multicultural History Society of Ontario 1978), 16.

35. Lucy Riall, *Garibaldi: Invention of a Hero* (New Haven: Yale University Press 2007), 372. Mazzini has also been reassessed as a relative supporter of women's rights.

36. Howard, 'The Civil Code of 1865', 17.

37. Donald Meyer, *Sex and Power: The Rise of Women in America, Russia, Sweden and Italy* (Middletown, Conn.: Wesleyan University Press 1987), 449.

38. Meyer, *Sex and Power*, 222–3.

39. Theodore Stanton, *The Woman Question in Europe* (London: Sampson Low 1884), 317. Queen Margherita was an important example of a woman as public symbol of beauty and national pride but not social advance, see Stephen Gundle, *Bellissima: Feminine Beauty and the Idea of Italy* (New Haven: Yale University Press 2007), 31–57.
40. Evans, *The Feminists*, 36.
41. Meyer, *Sex and Power*, 17.
42. Evans, *The Feminists*, 199.
43. Arnold Whittick, *Woman into Citizen* (London: Athenaeum Publishing 1979), 82.
44. Meyer, *Sex and Power*, 28.
45. Meyer, *Sex and Power*, 136.
46. Meyer, *Sex and Power*, 643.
47. Karen Offen, *European Feminisms 1700–1950* (Stanford, Calif.: Stanford University Press 2000), 323.
48. Florence Elliott, *A Dictionary of Politics* (London: Penguin 1975), 431.
49. Concha Fagoaga and Paloma Saavenrda, *Clara Campoamor: La sufragista española* (Madrid: Ministerio de Cultura 1986).
50. Article 14, Constitution of Spain 1978.

CHAPTER 12: LATIN AMERICAN MOTHERS OF THE NATION

1. Eva Peron, *Evita by Evita* (London: Proteus 1978), 8.
2. Helpful guides to the history of Latin America are Claudio Veliz, *Latin America and the Caribbean: A Handbook* (London: Anthony Blond 1968) and Jose C. Moya, *The Oxford Handbook of Latin American History* (Oxford: Oxford University Press 2011).
3. Asunción Lavrin, 'Suffrage in Latin America: Arguing A Difficult Cause', in Caroline Daley and Melanie Nolan, *Suffrage and Beyond: International Feminist Perspectives* (Auckland: Pluto 1994), 185.
4. Francesca Miller, *Latin American Women and the Search for Social Justice* (Hanover: University Press of New England 1991), 86.
5. Lavrin, 'Suffrage in Latin America', 184.
6. John Markoff, 'Margins, Centres, and Democracy: The Paradigmatic History of Women's Suffrage', *Signs: Journal of Women in Culture and Society* 29/1 (2003), 92.
7. Anna Macías, 'Felipe Carillo Puerto and Women's Liberation in Mexico', in Asunción Lavrin, *Latin American Women* (Westport, Conn.: Greenwood Press 1978), 287–301.
8. Macías, 'Felipe Carillo Puerto', 297.
9. Ward M. Morton, *Woman Suffrage in Mexico* (Gainsville, Fla.: University of Florida Press 1962), 17.
10. Morton, *Woman Suffrage in Mexico*, 24.
11. Morton, *Woman Suffrage in Mexico*, 29.
12. Morton, *Woman Suffrage in Mexico*, 41.

13. Morton, *Woman Suffrage in Mexico*, 45.

14. Morton, *Woman Suffrage in Mexico*, 62.

15. Markoff, 'Margins, Centres, and Democracy', 98.

16. Osvaldo Hurtado, *Political Power in Ecuador* (Albuquerque NM: University of New Mexico Press 1977), 84–5, 255–6.

17. Nicola Foote, 'Between Motherism and Radicalism: The Struggle for Female Suffrage in Ecuador 1860–1929', abstract submitted to *Suffrage, Gender and Citizenship* conference at the university of Tampere, Finland, 16–17 October 2006.

18. June E. Hahner, *Emancipating the Female Sex: The Struggle for Women's Rights in Brazil 1850–1940* (Durham NC: Duke University Press 1990), 44.

19. June E. Hahner, 'The Nineteenth-Century Feminist Press and Women's Rights in Brazil', in Asunción Lavrin, *Latin American Women* (Westport, Conn.: Greenwood Press 1978), 275.

20. Hahner, 'Nineteenth-Century Feminist Press', 276.

21. Hahner, *Emancipating the Female Sex*, 126.

22. Hahner, *Emancipating the Female Sex*, 134.

23. Bertha Lutz, 'Women's Letters', in *Revosta da Semana*, 23 December 1918, repr. Hahner, *Emancipating the Female Sex*, 224.

24. Francesca Miller remarks that 'What was important to the United States government in the post-war period was the repair of inter-American relations' ('The International Relations of Women of the Americas 1890–1928', *The Americas* 43/2 (October 1986), 171).

25. Isabel Keith Macdermott, *A Significant Pan-American Conference* (Washington DC: GPO 1922), 17.

26. Hahner, *Emancipating the Female Sex*, 222.

27. Hahner, *Emancipating the Female Sex*, 153.

28. Miller, 'The International Relations of Women of the Americas', 103.

29. Hahner, *Emancipating the Female Sex*, 155.

30. Markoff, 'Margins, Centres, and Democracy', 99.

31. Miller, 'The International Relations of Women of the Americas', 101.

32. Asunción Lavrin, *Women, Feminism and Social Change in Argentina, Chile and Uruguay* (Lincoln: University of Nebraska Press 1995), 325.

33. Cynthia Jeffries Little, 'Moral Reform and Feminism: A Case Study', *Journal of Interamerican Studies and World Affairs* 17./4. (November 1975), 387.

34. Little, 'Moral Reform and Feminism', 395.

35. Lavrin, *Women, Feminism and Social Change*, 334.

36. Lavrin, 'Suffrage in Latin America', 188.

37. Lavrin, *Women, Feminism and Social Change*, 344.

38. Marifaran Carlson, *Feminismo! The Woman's Movement in Argentina from its Beginnings to Eva Peron* (Chicago: Academy 1988), 101.

39. Cynthia Jeffress Little, 'Education, Philanthropy and Feminism: Components of Argentine Womanhood, 1860–1926' in Lavrin, *Latin American Women*, 243.

The anarchists, the other bogeymen of the Argentine political scene, condemned feminism as a bourgeois irrelevance after 1910 and took no part in
debates.

40. Carlson, *Feminismo!*, 114. The *Buenos Aires Herald* called her 'the Pankhurst of
Argentina', 159.

41. Carlson, *Feminismo!*, 162.

42. Nicholas Fraser and Marysa Navarro, *Evita:The Real Lives of Eva Perón* (London:
Andre Deutsch 1996), 33.

43. John Barnes, *Evita First Lady:A Biography of Eva Perón* (New York: Grove Press
1978), 14.

44. Peron, *Evita by Evita*, 8.

45. Peron, *Evita by Evita*, 19.

46. Carlson, *Feminismo!*, 187.

47. Peron, *Evita by Evita*, 180.

48. Barnes, *Evita First Lady*, 113.

49. Carlson, *Feminismo!*, 190.

50. Miller minimizes the achievement of the Perons: 'The International Relations
of Women of the Americas', 122.

51. Fraser and Navarro, *Evita*, 88.

52. Peron, *Evita by Evita*, 17.

53. Fraser and Navarro, *Evita*, 135, 137, and 143.

54. Elsa M. Chaney, 'Old and New Feminists in Latin America: The Case of Peru
and Chile', *Journal of Marriage and the Family* 35/2 (May 1973), 335.

55. Chaney, 'Old and New Feminists in Latin America', 334.

56. Chaney, 'Old and New Feminists in Latin America', 336.

57. Maxine Molyneux, *Women's Movements in International Perspective: Latin America
and Beyond* (London: Palgrave 2001), 221.

58. Trevor Lloyd, *Suffragettes International: The World-Wide Campaign for Women's
Rights* (London: Library of the 20th Century 1971), 118.

59. *Encyclopaedia Britannica*, 'Latin America', 2004.

60. Miller, 'The International Relations of Women of the Americas', 98.

61. In this account 'Latin American' has been taken to mean countries of the continent of America south of the US (including Mexico). Caribbean nations, after
Cuba, enfranchised women from the 1940s to the 1960s.

62. Lavrin in Daley and Nolan, *Suffrage and Beyond*, 194.

63. June Hannam et al., *International Encylopaedia of Women's Suffrage* (Santa Barbara,
Calif.: ABC-CLIO 2000), 21.

64. Miller, 'The International Relations of Women of the Americas', 97.

CHAPTER 13: THE ENFRANCHISEMENT OF THE EAST

1. Jad Adams and Phillip Whitehead, *The Dynasty: The Nehru–Gandhi Story*
(London: Penguin 1997), 97–8 and *passim*.

2. John Stuart Mill, *The Subjection of Women* (London: Wordsworth 1996), 169.

3. James Mill, *The History of British India*, vol. 1 bk. 2 (London: James Madden 1840), 445 and 449.

4. Adams and Whitehead, *The Dynasty*, 92.

5. Mill, *History of British India*, 445.

6. Peter Robb, *A History of India* (Basingstoke: Palgrave 2002), 238–43 on the general issues. Bharati Ray, *Early Feminists of Colonial India* (Delhi: Oxford University Press 2002) on the nationalist construction of women, 38–42. See also Manmohan Kaur, *The Role of Women in the Freedom Movement 1857–1947* (New Delhi: Sterling 1968); and Nawaz B. Mody, *Women in India's Freedom Struggle* (Bombay: Allied Publishers 2000).

7. Anthony Read and David Fisher, *The Proudest Day: India's Long Road to Independence* (London: Cape 1997), 80.

8. Ray, *Early Feminists of Colonial India*, 38. This is an invaluable source for information on Sarala and other activist women of the early twentieth century.

9. Kalpana Dutta was sentenced to life imprisonment for her part in the Chittagong Armoury Raid; another member of the raid, Pritilata Waddedar, later led the attack on the European Club and committed suicide after the mission had been partially successful; Shanti Ghosh and Suniti Chowdhuri shot the district magistrate in 1932; Bina Das fired point blank at the Governor while receiving her degree at a ceremony.

10. Kathryn Tidrick, *Gandhi: A Political and Spiritual Life* (London: I.B. Tauris 2006), 112.

11. Ray, *Early Feminists of Colonial India*, 82, lists them.

12. Ray, *Early Feminists of Colonial India*, 19. Rokeya's biography is given here and in Roushan Jahan, 'Rokeya: An Introduction to Her Life', in Rokeya Sakhawat Hossain, *Sultana's Dream: A Feminist Utopia*, ed. Roushan Jahan (New York: Feminist Press 1988), 37–57.

13. Ray, *Early Feminists of Colonial India*, 20.

14. Ray, *Early Feminists of Colonial India*, 2.

15. Letter from Sarojini Naidu to Arthur Symons 19 March 1898, in Butler Library Rare Books and Manuscripts collection, Columbia University.

16. Padmini Sengupta, *Sarojini Naidu: A Biography* (London: Asia Publishing 1966).

17. Makarand Paranjape (ed.), *Sarojini Naidu: Selected Poetry and Prose* (Delhi: Harper Collins 1993), 158.

18. Geraldine Forbes, *Women in Modern India* (Cambridge: Cambridge University Press 2004), 93.

19. Paranjape, 'Resolution at the Bombay Special Congress 1918', *Sarojini Naidu*, 161.

20. Letter from Dorothy Jinarajadasa to Millicent Fawcett, 23 October 1918, Women's Library 7MGF/1/172 box FLO90.

21. Leaflet for association branches dated 14 November 1918, Women's Library 7MGF/1/172 box FLO90.

22. Letter from Dorothy Jinarajadasa and Meenakshi Amma to Chairman and Members of the Franchise Committee, 20 November 1918, Women's Library 7MGF/1/172 box FLO90.

23. Forbes, *Women in Modern India*, 95.

24. E. A. Horne, *The Political System of British India* (London: Oxford University Press 1922), 109.

25. Mrinalini Sinha, 'Suffragism and Internationalism: The Enfranchisement of British and Indian Women under an Imperial State', in Ian Fletcher, Laura E. Nym Mayhall, and Philippa Levine, *Women's Suffrage in the British Empire: Citizenship, Nation and Race* (London:Routledge 2000), 231.

26. Eleanor Rathbone India file 7ELR/20, Women's Library. Susan Pederson, *Eleanor Rathbone*, Oxford *DNB* online 2004–7. Six million women were enfranchised by the Government of India Act.

27. Geraldine Forbes, *Women in Colonial India* (Delhi: Chronicle Books 2005), 57.

28. Forbes, *Colonial India*, 62.

29. Forbes, *Modern India*, 108.

30. Forbes, *Modern India*, 100–1.

31. Aparna Basu and Bharati Ray, *Women's Struggle: A History of the All India Women's Conference 1927–2002* (Delhi: Manohar 2003), 71.

32. Bharati Ray, 'The Freedom Movement and Feminist Consciousness', in Bharati Ray (ed.), *From the Seams of History: Essays on Indian Women* (Delhi: Oxford University Press 1995), 203.

33. Daw Mya Sein, 'Towards Independence in Burma: The Role of Women', *Asian Affairs* 59/3 (1972), 289.

34. Kumari Jayawardena, *Feminism and Nationalism in the Third World* (London: Zed Books 1986), 124.

35. Piers Brendon, *The Decline and Fall of the British Empire 1781–1997* (London: Jonanthan Cape 2007), 443.

36. Margaret Cousins, *The Awakening of Asian Womanhood* (Madras: Ganesh & Co. 1922), 9.

37. Daw Mya Sein, 'Towards Independence in Burma', 295.

38. Pura Villanueva Kalaw, *How the Filipina Got the Vote* (Manila: n.p. 1952), 8.

39. Mina C. Roces, 'Women in Philippine Politics and Society', in Hazel M. McFerson, *Mixed Blessings: The Impact of the American Colonial Experience on Politics and Society in the Philippines* (Westport, Conn.: Greenwood Press 2002), 175.

40. Mina Roces, 'Is the Suffragist an American Colonial Construct: Defining "The Filipino Woman" in Colonial Philippines', in Louise Edwards and Mina Roces, *Asia: Gender, Nationalism and Democracy* (London: Routledge 2004), 32.

41. Lilia Quindoza Santiago, 'Rebirthing *Babaye*: The Women's Movement in the Philippines', in Amrita Basu, *The Challenge of Local Feminisms: Women's Movements in Global Perspective* (Boulder, Colo.: Westview Press 1995), 118–19.

42. Kalaw, *How the Filipina Got the Vote*, 44. In one precinct equal numbers voted yes and no.

43. Jayawardena, *Feminism and Nationalism in the Third World*, 166.

44. Kalaw, *How the Flipina Got the Vote*, 45.

45. Wei Tao-ming, *My Revolutionary Years* (New York: Scribners 1943), 59. Tcheng Soumay wrote the book under her married name.

46. Elizabeth Croll, *Feminism and Socialism in China* (London: Routledge 1978), 45.

47. Roxane Witke, 'Mao Tse-tung, Woman and Suicide in the May Fourth Era', *China Quarterly* 3/31 (1967), 128.

48. Louise Edwards, 'Chinese Women's Campaigns for Suffrage: Nationalism, Confucianism and political agency', in Louise Edwards and Mina Roces, *Asia: Gender, Nationalism and Democracy* (London: Routledge 2004), 61.

49. Robin Morgan (ed.), *Sisterhood is Global: International Women's Movement Anthology* (London: Penguin 1984), 148.

50. Wei Tao-ming, *My Revolutionary Years*, 6.

51. Wei Tao-ming, *My Revolutionary Years*, 66.

52. Croll, *Feminism and Socialism in China*, 70.

53. Louise Edwards, 'Tang Qunying', in *Biographical Dictionary of Chinese Women: The Twentieth Century* (Armonk NY: M. E. Sharpe 2003), 508.

54. Aletta Jacobs, *Memories: My Life as an International Leader in Health, Suffrage and Peace* (New York: Feminist Press 1996), 161.

55. Croll, *Feminism and Socialism in China*, 72.

56. Ellen Carol DuBois, 'The Next Generation: Harriot Stanton Blatch and Grassroots Politics', in Jean H. Baker (ed.), *Votes for Women: The Struggle for Suffrage Revisited* (Oxford: Oxford University Press 2002), 164.

57. Croll, *Feminism and Socialism in China*, 78.

58. IWSA/2/31 John Rylands University Library of Manchester.

59. Jayawardena, *Feminism and Nationalism in the Third World*, 184.

60. Jayawardena, *Feminism and Nationalism in the Third World*, 186.

61. Witke, 'Mao Tse-tung, Woman and Suicide', 131.

62. Croll, *Feminism and Socialism in China*, 132. Mao was married, in 1921, to Yang Kaihui who was executed by the Kuomintang.

63. Stuart Schram, *Mao Tse-Tung* (London: Penguin 1966), 55.

64. Stuart Schram, *The Political Thought of Mao Tse-tung* (London: Penguin 1969), 336.

65. Witke, 'Mao Tse-tung, Woman and Suicide', 128.

66. Cousins, *The Awakening of Asian Womanhood*, 9.

67. Croll, *Feminism and Socialism in China*, 102.

68. Louise Edwards and Mina Roces, 'Orienting the Global Women's Suffrage Movement', in Edwards and Roces, *Asia: Gender, Nationalism and Democracy* (London: Routledge 2004), 6.

69. Croll, *Feminism and Socialism in China*, 120.

70. Louise Edwards, 'Bourgeois Women and Communist Revolutionaries? De-Revolutionising the Chinese Women's Suffrage Movement', in Maja Mikula, *Women, Activism and Social Change* (Oxford: Routledge 2005), 3.

71. Andrea McElderry, 'Xiang Jingyu', in *Biographical Dictionary of Chinese Women: The Twentieth Century* (Armonk NY: M. E. Sharpe 2003), 579.

72. Croll, *Feminism and Socialism in China*, 128.

73. Morgan, *Sisterhood is Global*, 152.

74. Edwards, 'Chinese Women's Campaigns for Suffrage', 64.

75. Wei Tao-ming, *My Revolutionary Years*, 168.

76. Croll, *Feminism and Socialism in China*, 153.

77. Louise Edwards, 'Women's Suffrage in China: Challenging Scholarly Conventions', *Pacific Historical Review* 69/4 (November 2000), 627.

78. Edwards, 'Bourgeois Women and Communist Revolutionaries?', 32.

79. Croll, *Feminism and Socialism in China*, 210.

80. Croll, *Feminism and Socialism in China*, 220.

81. Yue Daiyun and Li Jin, 'Women's Life in New China', in Barbara J. Nelson and Najma Chowdhury, *Women and Politics Worldwide* (New Haven: Yale University Press 1994), 162.

82. Yue and Li, 'Women's Life in New China', 163.

83. Yue and Li, 'Women's Life in New China', 162.

84. Edwards, 'Bourgeois Women and Communist Revolutionaries?', *passim*. See also Louise Edwards, *Gender, Politics and Democracy: Women's Suffrage in China* (Stanford, Calif.: Stanford University Press 2008).

85. Yukiko Matsukawa and Kaoru Tachi, 'Women's Suffrage and Gender politics in Japan', in Caroline Daley and Melanie Nolan, *Suffrage and Beyond: International Feminist Perspectives* (Auckland: Auckland University Press 1994), 171. Barbara Molony, 'Women's Rights, Feminism and Suffragism in Japan 1870–1925', *Pacific Historical Review* 69/4 (November 2000), 23.

86. Piers Brendon, *The Dark Valley: A Panorama of the 1930s* (London: Jonathan Cape 2000), 180–1.

87. Dee Ann Vavich, 'The Japanese Woman's Movement: Ichikawa Fusae: A Pioneer in Woman's Suffrage', *Monumenta Nipponica* 22/3–4 (1967), 431.

88. June Hannam et al., *International Encyclopaedia of Women's Suffrage* (Santa Barbara, Calif.: ABC-CLIO 2000), 157.

89. W. R. Nester, 'Japanese Women: Still Three Steps Behind', *Women's Studies* 21 (1992), 460.

90. Miyamoto Ken Ito, 'Noe and the Bluestockings', *Japan Interpreter* 10 (Autumn 1975), 190–204.

91. Vavich, 'The Japanese Woman's Movement', 413; she said both women were becoming neurotic and her work had left her exhausted.

92. Barbara Molony, 'Citizenship and Suffrage in Interwar Japan', in Louise Edwards, *Gender, Politics and Democracy: Women's Suffrage in China* (Stanford, Calif.: Stanford University Press 2008), 132.

93. Molony, 'Citizenship and Suffrage in interwar Japan', 137.

94. Sharon H. Nolte, 'Women's Rights and Society's Needs: Japan's 1931 Suffrage Bill', in *Comparative Studies in Society and History* 28/4 (October 1986), 709.

95. Yukiko and Kaoru, 'Women's Suffrage and Gender politics in Japan', 180.
96. Nester, 'Japanese Women', 461.
97. Vavich, 'The Japanese Woman's Movement', 422. Based on the author's interview with Ichikawa in 1964.
98. Susan. J. Pharr, *Political Women in Japan: The Search for a Place in Political Life* (Berkeley: University of California Press 1981), 5. It has been suggested that the government was prepared to include women's suffrage in the new constitution and received the order from the Americans to do so pre-empting their decision: Vavich, 'The Japanese Woman's Movement', 426.
99. Pharr, *Political Women in Japan*, 27. It is contended by Pharr, however, that the dramatic extension of women's rights in Japan was the result of a policy alliance between a core group of Japanese leaders and a group of low-ranking American women serving in the Occupation. Susan J. Pharr, 'The Politics of Women's Rights', in Robert E. Ward and Sakamoto Yoshikazu, *Democratising Japan: The Allied Occupation* (Honolulu: University of Hawaii Press 1987), 222.
100. Pharr, *Political Women in Japan*, 24.
101. Patricia Murray, 'Ichikawa Fusae and the Lonely Red Carpet', *Japan Interpreter* 10 (Autumn 1975), 176.

CHAPTER 14: AFRICA AND THE COLD WAR

1. Wole Soyinka, *Aké: The Years of Childhood* (London: Rex Collings 1981), 201–12. The translation of the language is Soyinka's—presumably the man actually used more vulgar expressions, and likewise in later encounters referred to here, where the witnesses have used 'vagina' and 'penis'. The influence of other militant African women is described in Dorothy L. Hodgson and Sheryl A. McCurdy, *'Wicked' Women and the Reconfiguration of Gender in Africa* (Oxford: James Curry 2001).
2. Soyinka, *Aké*, 213.
3. Cheryl Johnson-Odim and Nina Emma Mba, *For Women and the Nation: Funmilayo Ransome-Kuti of Nigeria* (Chicago: University of Illinois Press 1997), 81–2. These authors' witnesses attest to the incident, but remark that none of those describing it would consent to be identified (p. 96).
4. Jean O'Barr, 'African Women in Politics', in Margaret Jean Hay and Sharon Stichter, *African Women South of the Sahara* (London: Longman 1984), 141.
5. Audrey Chapman Smock, 'Ghana: From Autonomy to Subordination', in Janet Zollinger Giele and Audrey Chapman Smock, *Women: Roles and Status in Eight Countries* (New York: John Wiley 1977), 180.
6. Ian Christopher Fletcher, *Sex and Gender: Manuscript Sources from the Public Record Office* (Marlborough: Adam Matthew 2002), 7.
7. Joseph Gugler, 'The Second Sex in Town', *Canadian Journal of African Studies* 6/2 (1972), 289–301.
8. Audrey Wipper, 'Equal Rights for Women in Kenya?', *Journal of Modern African Studies* 9/3 (1971), 439.

9. Smock, 'Ghana', 182. NB: the gap was closing and on the eve of independence the boy:girl ratio was 1:2.2.

10. Catherine Coquery-Vidrovitch, *African Women: A Modern History* (Boulder, Colo.: Westview Press 1997), 175.

11. Lynn M. Thomas, *Politics of the Womb: Women, Reproduction and the State in Kenya* (Berkeley: University of California Press 2003), 23.

12. John Iliffe, *Honour in African History* (Cambridge: Cambridge University Press 2005), 312.

13. Hugh Dalton, *The Political Diary of Hugh Dalton 1918–40, 1945–60* (London: Jonathan Cape 1986), 472.

14. Monica Whately of The Six Point Group, 2 November 1939 and reply, PRO CO 323/1694/2. The Group used an example from the Caribbean: 'To exclude from voting in Barbados, all employed in a domestic or other menial capacity savours of the discredited system of domestic slavery.'

15. Fletcher, *Sex and Gender*, 8.

16. Letter from John Watson to Colonial Office, 10 December 1958, PRO CO 554/1578.

17. T. E. Smith, *Elections in Developing Countries: A Study of electoral procedures used in tropical Africa, South-East Asia and the British Caribbean* (London: Macmillan 1960), 91.

18. C. E. Carrington, 'Decolonisation: The Last Stages', *International Affairs* 38/1 (1962), 32.

19. Wipper, 'Equal Rights for Women in Kenya?', 429.

20. For other women's rebellions see O'Barr, 'African Women in Politics', 145–7.

21. Susan Pederson, 'National Bodies, Uspeakable Acts: The Sexual Politics of Colonial Policy-making', *Journal of Modern History* 63/4 (1991), 647–80.

22. Wilhelmina Oduol and Wanjiku Mukabi Kabira, 'The Mother of Warriors and Her Daughters: The Women's Movement in Kenya', in Amrita Basu, *The Challenge of Local Feminisms: Women's Movements in Global Perspective* (Boulder, Colo.: Westview Press 1995), 194–5.

23. Coquery-Vidrovotch, *African Women*, 197.

24. IWSA/3/34 John Rylands University Library of Manchester.

25. T. E. Smith, *Elections in Developing Countries*, 91.

26. W. J. M. Mackenzie, *Free Elections: An Elementary Textbook* (London: George Allen and Unwin 1958), 22.

27. Sir E. Baring to Colonial Office, 14 July 1959, PRO CO 822/1472.

28. June Hannam et al., *International Encylcopaedia of Women's Suffrage* (Santa Barbara, Calif.: ABC-CLIO 2000), 7.

29. Carrington, 'Decolonisation', 32.

30. Raisa Simola, 'The Construction of a Nigerian Nationalist and Feminist, Funmilayo Ransome-Kuti', *Nordic Journal of African Studies* 8/1 (1999), 99.

31. Her name at birth was Frances Abigail Olefunmilayo Thomas; for simplicity here her married name is used throughout.

32. Johnson-Odim and Mba, *For Women and the Nation*, 54.
33. Coquery-Vidrovitch, *African Women*, 161.
34. Johnson-Odim and Mba, *For Women and the Nation*, 73 and 76.
35. Soyinka, *Aké*, 211. The event is also recounted in Coquery-Vidrovitch, *African Women*, 169–72.
36. Johnson-Odim and Mba, *For Women and the Nation*, 83. As previously, the language as reported is presumably euphemistic. This encounter is also covered in Folake Onayemi's paper in *Women's History Review*, 'Finding a place: women's struggle for political authority in classical and Nigerian societies', 16/3 (July 2007), 305.
37. Simola, 'The Construction of a Nigerian Nationalist and Feminist', 104, quoting Funmilayo Ransome-Kuti in the *Nigerian Daily Service*, 8 August 1946.
38. Jane I. Guyer, 'Women in the Rural Economy: Contemporary Variations', in Margaret Jean Hay and Sharon Stichter, *African Women South of the Sahara* (London: Longman 1984), 45.
39. Johnson-Odim and Mba, *For Women and the Nation*, 94.
40. Johnson-Odim and Mba, *For Women and the Nation*, 110.
41. Johnson-Odim and Mba, *For Women and the Nation*, 156.
42. Simola, 'The Construction of a Nigerian Nationalist and Feminist', 105.
43. Nina Emma Mba, *Nigerian Women Mobilised: Women's Political Activity in Southern Nigeria 1900–1965* (Berkeley, Calif.: Institute of International Studies 1982), 241.
44. Mba, *Nigerian Women Mobilised*, 247.
45. Mba, *Nigerian Women Mobilised*, 178 and 240.
46. Mba, *Nigerian Women Mobilised*, 247 and 298. Barbara J. Nelson and Najma Chowdhury (*Women and Politics Worldwide* (New Haven, Conn.: Yale University Press *c.*1994), 512) give 1978 as the date for enfranchisement in the north.
47. Johnson-Odim and Mba, *For Women and the Nation*, 117.
48. Fela Kuti had learned the revolutionary rhetoric of the Black Panthers but that of the concurrent women's liberation movement seems to have passed him by, e.g. 'Do I beat my wives? Not beat; not that... But sometimes it's necessary to give my wives some paf-paf-paf-paf-paf-paf... I slap 'em.' Carlos Moore, *Fela, Fela, This bitch of a life* (London: Alison and Busby 1982), 162.
49. Precise facts are difficult to determine (whether the women of the compound were raped, for example) except for the undisputed facts that the raid took place, people were injured and the building destroyed by fire—the government held a tribunal which blamed the raid on unknown 'overzealous' soldiers. Johnson-Odim and Mba, *For Women and the Nation*, 168–9.
50. Report of the Committee on the Extension of the Franchise to Women (Zanzibar), PRO CO 822/1472, 4.
51. Report... Women (Zanzibar), PRO CO 822/1472, 3.
52. Report... Women (Zanzibar), PRO CO 822/1472, 5.
53. T. E. Smith, *Elections in Developing Countries*, 91.
54. Details in 'Suffrage Arrangements in Colonial Territories 1960–62', PRO CO 1032/265.

55. Cherryl Walker, *The Women's Suffrage Movement in South Africa* (Cape Town: Centre for African Studies 1979), 318.

56. Walker, *Women's Suffrage Movement*, 324.

57. Aletta Jacobs, *Memories: My Life as an International Leader in Health, Suffrage and Peace* (New York: Feminist Press 1996), 154.

58. Pamela Scully, 'White Maternity and Black Infancy: The Rhetoric of Race in the South African Women's Suffrage Movement, 1895–1930', in Ian Christopher Fletcher, Laura E. Nym Mayhall, and Philippa Levine, *Women's Suffrage in the British Empire: Citizenship, Nation and Race* (London:Routledge 2000), 68. The fear of miscegenation may have been at the root of South African women's tolerance of brothels: perhaps it was thought that if men had enough commercial sex available, they would not have to have relationships with the natives.

59. Walker, *Women's Suffrage Movement*, 328.

60. Scully, 'White Maternity and Black Infancy', 78.

61. Scully, 'White Maternity and Black Infancy', 70.

62. Cherryl Walker, *Women and Gender in Southern Africa to 1945* (Cape Town: David Philip 1990), 314.

63. Walker, *Women's Suffrage Movement*, 104.

64. Walker, *Women's Suffrage Movement*, 111.

65. Scully, 'White Maternity and Black Infancy', 69.

66. Walker, *Women's Suffrage Movement*, 338.

67. Walker, *Women's Suffrage Movement*, 84, quoting *Flashlight*, July 1930, 1.

68. June Hannam et al., *International Encyclopaedia of Women's Suffrage* (Santa Barbara, Calif.: ABC-CLIO 2000), 277.

69. John Iliffe, *Africans: The History of a Continent* (Cambridge: Cambridge University Press 1995), 248.

70. Arnold Whittick, *Woman into Citizen: The Word Movement Towards the Emancipation of Women in the Twentieth Century* (London: Athenaeum 1979), 207.

71. Smock, 'Ghana', 205.

72. Florence Abena Dolphyne, *The Emancipation of Women: An African Perspective* (Accra: Ghana Unversities Press 1991), 46.

73. Smock, 'Ghana', 208.

74. Wipper, 'Equal Rights for Women in Kenya?', 429. Some women were successful in political life, however; see LaRay Denzer, 'Gender and Decolonisation: A Study of Three Women in West African Public Life', in Andrea Cornwall, *Readings in Gender in Africa* (Bloomington. Ind.: Indiana University Press 2005).

75. Dolphyne, *The Emancipation of Women*, xiii. She refers to the 'hostile reception given the lesbian women's group attending the Forum' in Nairobi in 1985.

76. Amanda Kemp, Nozizwe Madlala, Asha Moodley, and Elaine Salo, 'The Dawn of a New Day: Redefining South African Feminism', in Amrita Basu (ed.), *The Challenge of Local Feminisms: Women's Movements in Global Perspective* (Boulder, Colo.: Westview Press 1995), 143.

77. Dolphyne, *The Emancipation of Women*, xiv.

78. Mahmood Mamdani, *Citizen and Subject: Contemporary Africa and the Legacy of Late Colonialism* (Kampala: Fountain Publishers 1996), 24.

79. Genia K. Browning, *Women and Politics in the USSR* (Brighton, Sussex: Wheatsheaf 1987), 4.

80. Maxine Molyneux, *Women's Emancipation Under Socialism: A Model for the Third World?* (Brighton, Sussex: IDS Publications 1981), 32.

81. *Journal of the Economic and Social Council* (New York: United Nations 1946), 305.

82. Francisco O. Ramirez et al., 'The Changing Logic of Political Citizenship: Cross-National Acquisition of Women's Suffrage Rights 1890 to 1990', *American Sociological Review* 62 (October 1997), 735.

CHAPTER 15: THE VEILED VOTE

1. Huda Shaarawi, *Harem Years: The Memoirs of an Egyptian Feminist* (London: Virago 1986), 7.

2. Margot Badran, 'The Feminist Vision in the Writings of Three Turn-of-the-Century Egyptian Women', *British Society for Middle Eastern Studies Bulletin* 15/1–2 (1988), 14.

3. Beth Baron, 'Unveiling in Early Twentieth Century Egypt: Practical and Symbolic Considerations', *Middle Eastern Studies* 25/3 (July 1989), 370–86. Baron reports that *veiled* women going into the public domain of the Egyptian streets were assaulted but *unveiled* women were not—their unveiled state presumably indicating that they could look after themselves, 377.

4. PRO: CO 822/1472.

5. C. E. Carrington, 'Decolonisation: The Last Stages', *International Affairs* 38/1 (1962), 32.

6. Richard Stites, 'Women's Liberation Movements in Russia 1900–1930', *Canadian-American Slavik Studies* 7/4 (Winter 1973), 472.

7. In Donald Meyer, *Sex and Power: The Rise of Women in America, Russia, Sweden and Italy* (Middletown, Conn.: Wesleyan University Press 1987), 195.

8. This is discussed in Diane Rothbard Margolis, 'Women's Movements around the World: Cross-Cultural Comparisons', *Gender and Society* 7/3 (September 1993), 383 ff.

9. Fatima Mernissi, *Women in the Muslim Unconscious* (New York: Pergamon 1984).

10. Fatima Mernissi, *Beyond the Veil: Male–Female Dynamics in a Modern Muslim Society* (New York: John Wiley and Sons 1975), 101.

11. Kalliope A. Kehaya, 'The Orient', in Theodore Stanton, *The Woman Question in Europe* (London: Samson Low 1884), 458.

12. Nadje S. Al-Ali, *The Women's Movement in Egypt, with Selected References to Turkey* (Geneva: United Nations Research Institute for Social Development 2002), 21.

13. Naila Minai, *Women in Islam: Tradition and Transition in the Middle East* (London: John Murray 1981), 64–5. See also Patrick Kinross, *Atatürk: The Rebirth of a Nation* (London: Phoenix Press 2003).

14. Al-Ali, *The Women's Movement in Egypt*, 22.
15. Al-Ali, *The Women's Movement in Egypt*, 23.
16. June Hannam et al., *International Encyclopaedia of Women's Suffrage* (Santa Barbara, Calif.: ABC-CLIO 2000), 297.
17. Zehra F. Arat, 'Turkish Women and the Republican Reconstruction of Tradition', in Fatma Muge Gocek and Shiva Balaghi (eds.), *Reconstructing Gender in the Middle East: Tradition, Identity and Power* (New York: Columbia University Press 1994), 66.
18. Arat, 'Turkish Women and the Republican Reconstruction of Tradition', 66.
19. Arat, 'Turkish Women and the Republican Reconstruction of Tradition', 67.
20. Minai, *Women in Islam*, 64.
21. Al-Ali, *The Women's Movement in Egypt*, 22.
22. May Wright Sewall, *The World's Congress of Representative Women*, vol. 1 (Chicago: Rand, McNally 1894), 28.
23. Efi Evdela and Angelika Psarra, 'Engendering "Greekness": Women's Emancipation and Irridentist Politics in Nineteenth-Century Greece', *Mediterranean Historical Review* 20/1 (June 2005), 67–79. See also article on Parren in *Biographical Dictionary of Women's Movements and Feminisms*.
24. Fotini Sianou, 'Women in Decision-making: Country Report Greece', European Database: <http://www.db.decision.de/CoRe/Greece.htm>
25. Tasoula Vervenioti, 'The Adventure of Women's Suffrage in Greece', in Claire Duchen and Irene Bandhauer-Schöffmann, *When the War Was Over: Women, War and Peace in Europe 1940–1956* (London: Continuum 2000), 104 and *passim*.
26. Vervenioti, 'The Adventure of Women's Suffrage in Greece', 109.
27. Vervenioti, 'The Adventure of Women's Suffrage in Greece', 112.
28. Ellen L. Fleischmann, 'The Other "Awakening": The Emergence of Women's Movements in the Modern Middle East, 1900–1940', in Margaret L. Meriwether and Judith E. Tucker (eds.), *Social History of Women and Gender in the Modern Middle East* (Boulder, Colo.: Westview Press 1999), 108.
29. T. E. Smith, *Elections in Developing Countries: A Study of electoral procedures used in tropical Africa, South-East Asia and the British Caribbean* (London: Macmillan 1960), 91.
30. Hannam et al., *International Encyclopaedia of Women's Suffrage*, 188.
31. Shaarawi, *Harem Years*, 122.
32. Margot Badran, *Feminists, Islam and Nation: Gender and the Making of Modern Egypt* (Princeton NJ: Princeton University Press 1994), 207.
33. Shaarawi, *Harem Years*, 130.
34. Hannam et al., *International Encyclopaedia of Women's Suffrage*, 93.
35. Badran, *Feminists*, 211.
36. Cynthia Nelson, 'Biography and Women's History: On Interpreting Doria Shafik', in Nikki R. Keddie and Beth Baron, *Women in Middle Eastern History: Shifting Boundaries in Sex and Gender* (New Haven, Conn.: Yale University Press 1991), 312.
37. Nelson, 'Biography and Women's History', 322.

38. Nelson, 'Biography and Women's History', 324.

39. Audrey Chapman Smock and Nadia Haggag Youssef, 'Egypt: From Seclusion to Limited Participation', in Janet Zollinger Giele and Audrey Chapman Smock, *Women: Roles and Status in Eight Countries* (New York: John Wiley 1977), 67.

40. Mervat Hatem, 'Modernisation, the State and the Family in Middle East Women's Studies', in Margaret L. Meriwether and Judith Tucker (eds.), *Social History of Women and Gender in the Modern Middle East* (Boulder, Colo.: Westview Press 1999), 77.

41. Al-Ali, *The Women's Movement in Egypt*, 11.

42. Nelson, 'Biography and Women's History', 325.

43. Cora Vreede-De Stuers, *The Indonesian Woman: Struggles and Achievements* (The Hague, Holland: Mouton and Co. 1960), 96–7. See also Susan Blackburn, 'Women's Suffrage and Democracy in Indonesia', in Louise Edwards and Mina Roces, *Asia: Gender, Nationalism and Democracy* (London: Routledge 2004), 79–105.

44. Khawar Mumtaz and Farida Shaheed, *Women of Pakistan: Two Steps Forward, One Step Back?* (London: Zed Books 1987), 7–8.

45. Maxine Molyneux, *Women's Emancipation Under Socialism: A Model for the Third World?* (Brighton, Sussex: IDS Publications 1981), 7.

46. Neil MacMaster, *Burning the Veil: The Algerian War and the 'Emancipation' of Muslim Women 1954–1962* (Manchester: Manchester University Press, 2012).

47. G. H. Bousquet, 'How the Natives of Algeria Became French Citizens', *International and Comparative Law Quarterly* 2/4 (October 1953), 604.

48. MacMaster, *Burning the Veil*.

49. Minai, *Women in Islam*, 63.

50. Todd Shepard, *The Invention of Decolonisation: The Algerian War and the Remaking of France* (Ithaca NY: Cornell University Press 2006), 187–8.

51. Jean O'Barr, 'African Women in Politics', in Margaret Jean Hay and Sharon Stichter, *African Women South of the Sahara* (London: Longman 1984), 150.

52. Minai, *Women in Islam*, 76.

53. Mangol Bayat-Philipp, 'Women and Revolution in Iran 1905–1911', in Lois Beck and Nikki Keddie (eds.) *Women in the Muslim World* (Cambridge, Mass.: Harvard University Press 1978), 300.

54. Kumari Jayawardena, *Feminism and Nationalism in the Third World* (London: Zed Books 1986), 64.

55. 'Women's Rights in Persia', *The Times*, 22 August 1911 and (same title) 28 August 1911. Readers of *The Times* could not, of course, be so superior: at this time the only European country where women had the vote was Finland.

56. Bayat-Philipp, 'Women and Revolution in Iran, 301.

57. Bayat-Philipp, 'Women and Revolution in Iran, 302–3.

58. Eliz Sanasarian, 'Characteristics of Women's Movement in Iran', in Asghar Fathi (ed.), *Women and the Family in Iran* (Leiden: E. J. Brill 1985), 86–106.

59. Gholam-Reza Vatandoust, 'The Status of Iranian Women During the Pahlavi Revolution', in Asghar Fathi (ed.), *Women and the Family in Iran* (Leiden: E. J. Brill 1985), 113.

60. Jayawardena, *Feminism and Nationalism*, 71.

61. Melody Ermachild Chavis, *Meena: Heroine of Afghanistan* (London: Bantam 2004), 56. Keshwar Kamel was not Meena's name but one chosen during clandestine operations to allow her to pass easily through India.

62. 'Sixty Years of Asian Heroes', *Time Magazine*, 13 November 2006. Revolutionary Association for the Women of Afghanistan website: <http://www.rawa.org>

63. Chavis, *Meena*, 158.

64. Chavis, *Meena*, 184.

65. 'The Rule of the Rapists', *Guardian*, 12 February 2006.

66. White House Press release, Office of the Press Secretary, 24 August 2002.

67. 'The small advances women have made are now being wiped out', *Independent*, 26 September 2006.

68. 'Breaking the Propaganda of Silence': speech at fundraising meeting organized by the Afghan Women's Mission on 7 October 2006, Hollywood, USA. The speaker 'Zoya' goes by only her first name; RAWA women do not use their full names, in order to protect their families from recriminations.

69. 'Afghan Women having their say in landmark presidential election', *San Diego Union-Tribune* (but Associated Press copy), 10 October 2004.

70. 'Center for American Women and Politics' and 'Women in the House of Commons' websites.

71. Revolutionary Association for the Women of Afghanistan website: <http://www.rawa.org>

72. Sundass Abass, 'Campaigning for Women's Rights in Iraq Today', in *Iraq: Women's Rights Under Threat*. Women Living Under Muslim Laws occasional paper, 15 December 2006, 15: <http://www.wluml.org/english/index.shtml>

73. 'Iraqi Women Eye Islamic Law', *Christian Science Monitor*, 25 February 2005.

74. BBC Radio 4 'Today' programme report, 15 November 2007.

75. Abstract of speech at Symposium, 'Assessing the Winds of Change', Washington Institute for Near East Policy, 20 May 2005.

76. Minai, *Women in Islam*, 79.

77. 'In the Gulf, Women are not Women's Best Friend', *Daily Star* (Lebanon), 20 June 2005.

78. 'Saudi Women Get the Vote', *Guardian*, 10 March 2004; 'Saudi Women Barred from Voting', *BBC News*, 11 October 2004: <www.news.bbc.co.uk>

79. Fatima Mernissi, *Women and Islam: An Historical and Theological Enquiry* (Oxford: Basil Blackwell 1991), vii and ix.

80. Fleischmann, 'The Other "Awakening"', 119.

CONCLUSION

1. Karen Offen, *European Feminisms 1700–1950: A Political History* (Stanford, Calif.: Stanford University Press 2000), 289. Popp spent the final years of her professional life as a member of parliament.

2. Louise Creighton, 'The Appeal Against Female Suffrage: A Rejoinder', *The Nineteenth Century* (August 1889), 350.

3. Patricia Murray, 'Ichikawa Fusae and the Lonely Red Carpet', *Japan Interpreter* 10 (autumn 1975), 186.

4. Donal Lowry, 'Making Fresh Britains across the Seas', in Ian Fletcher, Laura E. Nym Mayhall, and Philippa Levine, *Women's Suffrage in the British Empire: Citizenship, Nation and Race* (London: Routledge 2000), 175–90.

5. Vidar Helgessen, 'It's not all about numbers', on International Institute for Democracy and Electoral Assistance website: <http://www.%20idea.int/news/editorial_gender.cfm>. The 'critical mass' theory is disputed, see D. T. Studlar, and I. McAllister, 'Does a Critical Mass Exist? A Comparative Analysis of Women's Legislative Representation since 1950', *European Journal of Political Research* 4/2 (March 2002), 233–53.

6. Peter Law resigned from the Labour Party in protest at the imposition of an all-woman shortlist and was supported by voters in Blaenau Gwent in Wales; he won, overturning a 19,000 Labour majority at the 2005 general election.

7. Mala N. Htun and Mark Jones, 'Engendering the Right to Participate in Decision-Making: Electoral Quotas and Women's Leadership in Latin America', in Nikki Craske and Maxine Molyneux, *Gender and the Politics of Rights and Democracy in Latin America* (London: Palgrave 2002), 32–56.

8. Michael Fielding, 'Ignota, the Unknown Woman: Elizabeth Clarke Wolstenholme Elmy 1833–1918', in Eileen Janes Yeo (ed.), *Mary Wollstonecraft and 200 Years of Feminisms* (London: Rivers Oram 1997). The Law Lords ruled against marital rape in 1991, it was legislated against in the Criminal Justice and Public Order Act in 1994.

9. IWSA/2/18 John Rylands University Library of Manchester. The Executive Committee of the Lyceum Club (where this letter was read out at a meeting) considered 'the reading of this letter from an enemy alien was a deliberate insult to British women present'.

10. 'Declaration of War—Case Not Established': <http://www.publicwhip.org.uk>. See also Philip Cowley and Sarah Childs, 'Too Spineless to Rebel? New Labour's Women MPs', *British Journal of Political Science* 33 (2003), 345–65.

11. Kelly Holder, *Voting and Registration in the Election of November 2004* (Washington DC: US Census Bureau 2006), 2.

12. Maxine Molyneux, *Women's Emancipation Under Socialism: A Model for the Third World?* (Brighton, Sussex: IDS Publications 1981), 32.

13. Ross Evans Paulson, *Women's Suffrage and Prohibition: A Comparative Study of Equality and Social Control* (Glenview, Ill.: Scott, Foresman and Co. 1973), 187.

APPENDIX I: THE STRANGE CASE OF SWITZERLAND

1. Lee Ann Banaszak, *Why Movements Succeed or Fail: Opportunity, Culture and the Struggle for Woman Suffrage* (Princeton NJ: Princeton University Press 1996), 13, 15.

2. *HWS* 6: 797.
3. Banaszak, *Why Movements Succeed or Fail*, 18.
4. Trevor Lloyd, *Suffragettes International: The World-Wide Campaign for Women's Rights* (London: Library of the Twentieth Century 1971), 119.
5. Arnold Whittick, *Woman into Citizen* (London: Athenaeum 1979), 212.
6. Banaszak, *Why Movements Succeed or Fail*, 211.
7. Banaszak, *Why Movements Succeed or Fail*, 119.

APPENDIX 2: CHRONOLOGY OF WOMEN'S SUFFRAGE

1. Inter-Parliamentary Union website: <http://www.ipu.org>. Other material from: June Hannam et al., *International Encyclopaedia of Women's Suffrage* (Santa Barbara, Calif.: ABC-CLIO 2000), 339–40; Caroline Daley and Melanie Nolan, *Suffrage and Beyond: International Feminist Perspestives* (Auckland: Auckland University Press 1994), 349–52; Elise Boulding et al., *Handbook of International Data on Women* (New York: John Wiley and Sons, 1976). For South American figures: *A Century of Struggle for Women's Rights in the Americas* (Washington DC: Inter-American Commission of Women 1995), 7.
2. *National Geographic Visual History of the World* (Washington DC: National Geographic Society 2005), 534.
3. 'Woman wins seat in first-ever UAE election', 17 December 2006: <http://www.mena-electionguide.org>

Bibliography

There is a vast literature on such matters as militancy and the relationship of the suffrage movement to political parties in some countries but hardly any works on women's suffrage in others. This book attempts to avoid contributing to that disparity, so there is little discussion of secondary material in this text, and few secondary sources cited in this bibliography. Works on suffrage in little-studied areas of the world have been favoured. The emphasis on sources cited has also been on what people did rather than what they thought they were doing, or how later commentators interpreted it.

Abass, Sundass, 'Campaigning for Women's Rights in Iraq Today', in *Iraq: Women's Rights Under Threat*. Women Living Under Muslim Laws, occasional paper 15, December 2006

Abray, Jane, 'Feminism in the French Revolution', *The American Historical Review* 80/1 (February 1975), 43–62

Adams, Jad, *Pankhurst* (London: Haus 2003)

Adams, Jad, and Whitehead, Phillip, *The Dynasty: The Nehru–Gandhi Story* (London: Penguin 1997)

Al-Ali, Nadje S., *The Women's Movement in Egypt, with Selected References to Turkey* (Geneva: United Nations Research Institute for Social Development 2002)

Aldred, Guy A., *Richard Carlile Agitator: His Life and Times* (London: Pioneer Press 1923)

Allen, Robert L., and Allen, Pamela, *Reluctant Reformers: Racism and Social Reform Movements in the United States* (Washington DC: Howard University Press 1974)

Anderrsson, Ingvar, *A History of Sweden* (London: Weidenfeld 1956)

Anker, Ella, *Women's Suffrage in Norway* (London: NUWSS 1913)

Anthony, Susan B., Stanton, Elizabeth Cady, and Harper, Ida Husted, *The History of Woman Suffrage*, 6 vols. (New York: Fowler Wells 1881–1922)

Arat, Zehra F., 'Turkish Women and the Republican Reconstruction of Tradition', in Fatma Muge Gocek and Shiva Balaghi (eds.), *Reconstructing Gender in the Middle East: Tradition, Identity and Power* (New York: Columbia University Press 1994)

Asquith, Herbert, *Fifty Years of Parliament*, vol. 2 (London: Cassell 1926)

Atkinson, Neill, *Adventures in Democracy: A History of the Vote in New Zealand* (Dunedin: University of Otago Press 2003)

Bader-Zaar, Birgitta, 'Women in Austrian Politics 1890–1934', in David F. Good, Margarete Grandner, and Mary Jo Maynes, *Austrian Women in the Nineteenth and Twentieth Centuries* (Providence RI: Berghahn 1996)

Badran, Margot, 'The Feminist Vision in the Writings of Three Turn-of-the-Century Egyptian Women', *British Society for Middle Eastern Studies Bulletin* 15/1–2 (1988), 11–20

Badran, Margot, *Feminists, Islam and Nation: Gender and the Making of Modern Egypt* (Princeton NJ: Princeton University Press 1994)

Bainton, Roy, *1917: Russia's Year of Revolution* (London: Robinson 2005)

Baker, Ray Stannard, *Woodrow Wilson: Life and Letters*, vol. 6 (London: Heinemann 1938)

Bamford, Samuel, *Passages in the Life of a Radical*, vol. 2 (London: T. Fisher Unwin 1893)

Banaszak, Lee Ann, *Why Movements Succeed or Fail: Opportunity, Culture and the Struggle for Woman Suffrage* (Princeton NJ: Princeton University Press 1996)

Barnes, John, *Evita First Lady: A Biography of Eva Perón* (New York: Grove Press 1978)

Baron, Beth, 'Unveiling in Early Twentieth Century Egypt: Practical and Symbolic Considerations', *Middle Eastern Studies* 25/3 (July 1989), 370–86

Bartley, Paula, *Votes for Woman 1860–1928* (London: Hodder & Stoughton 1998)

Basu, Amrita (ed.), *The Challenge of Local Feminisms: Women's Movements in Global Perspective* (Boulder, Colo.: Westview Press 1995)

Basu, Aparna, and Ray, Bharati, *Women's Struggle: A History of the All India Women's Conference 1927–2002* (Delhi: Manohar 2003)

Bayat-Philipp, Mangol, 'Women and Revolution in Iran 1905–1911', in Lois Beck and Nikki Keddie (eds.), *Women in the Muslim World* (Cambridge Mass.: Harvard University Press 1978)

Bell, Susan Groag, and Offen, Karen M., *Women, the Family and Freedom: The Debate in Documents*, vol. 2: *1880–1950* (Stanford, Stanford University Press 1983)

Benn, Caroline, *Keir Hardie* (London: Hutchinson 1992)

Billington-Greig, Teresa, 'The Truth About White Slavery', in *Englishwoman's Review* 14 (June 1913), 428–46

Billington-Greig, Teresa, *The Non-Violent Militant: Selected Writings*, ed. Carol McPhee and Ann Fitzgerald (London: Routledge 1987)

Blackburn, Susan, 'Women's suffrage and democracy in Indonesia', in Louise Edwards and Mina Roces, *Asia: Gender, Nationalism and Democracy* (London: Routledge 2004), 79–105

Bland, Lucy, *Banishing the Beast: Sexuality and the Early Feminists* (New York: New Press 1995)

Bosch, Mineke, *Politics and Friendship: Letters from the International Woman Suffrage Alliance 1902–1942* (Columbus: Ohio State University Press 1990)

Bosch, Mineke, 'Colonial Dimensions of Dutch Women's Suffrage: Aletta Jacobs' Letters from Africa and Asia 1911–12', *Journal of Women's History* 11/2 (Summer 1999), 8–34

Bosch, Mineke, *Een onwrikbaar gevoel voor rechtvaardigheid. Aletta Jacobs, 1854–1929* (Amsterdam: Balans 2005)

Bosch, Mineke, '"Das Stimmrecht als mächtigstes Mittel" Eine kurzgeschichte der frauenstimmrechtsbewegung in den Niederlanden (1883–1919)', in Bettina Bab (ed.), *Mit Macht zur Wahl: 100 Jahre Frauenwahlrecht in Europa* (Bonn: Frauenmuseum 2006), 134–45

Boulding, Elise et al., *Handbook of International Data on Women* (New York: John Wiley and Sons 1976)

Bousquet, G. H., 'How the Natives of Algeria Became French Citizens', *International and Comparative Law and Quarterly* 2/4 (October 1953), 596–605

Brake, Laurel, 'Writing Women's History: "The Sex" debates of 1889', in Ann Heilmann and Margaret Beetham (eds.), *New Women Hybridities* (London: Routledge 2004)

Brammer, Leila R., *Excluded from Suffrage History: Matilda Joslyn Gage, Nineteenth-Century American Feminist* (Westport, Conn.: Greenwood Press 2000)

Brendon, Piers, *The Dark Valley: A Panorama of the 1930s* (London: Jonathan Cape 2000)

Brendon, Piers, *The Decline and Fall of the British Empire 1781–1997* (London: Jonanthan Cape 2007)

Brodie, Walter, *Pitcairn's Island and the Islanders in 1850* (London: Whittaker & Co. 1851)

Brody, Miriam, Introduction to Mary Wollstonecraft, *Vindication of the Rights of Women* (London: Penguin 1982)

Broun, Heywood, and Leech, Margaret, *Anthony Comstock: Roundsman of the Lord* (London: Wishart, 1928)

Browning, Genia K., *Women and Politics in the USSR* (Brighton, Sussex: Wheatsheaf 1987)

Butterfield, L. H. (ed.), The Adams Papers series II: *Adams Family Correspondence*, vol 1 (Cambridge, Mass.: Harvard University Press 1963)

Byock, Jesse, *Viking Age Iceland* (London: Penguin 2001)

Caine, Barbara, *English Feminism 1780–1980* (Oxford: Oxford University Press 1997)

Carlson, Marifaran, *Feminismo! The Woman's Movement in Argentina from its Beginnings to Eva Peron* (Chicago: Academy 1988)

Carrington, C. E., 'Decolonisation: The Last Stages', *International Affairs* 38/1 (1962), 29–40

Catt, Carrie Chapman, *The World Movement for Woman Suffrage 1904–1911* (London: IWSA 1915)

Catt, Carrie Chapman, and Shuler, Nettie Rogers, *Woman Suffrage and Politics: The Inner Story of the Suffrage Movement* (Seattle: University of Washington Press 1923)

Chaney, Elsa M., 'Old and New Feminists in Latin America: The Case of Peru and Chile', *Journal of Marriage and the Family* 35/2 (May 1973), 332–6

Chavis, Melody Ermachild, *Meena: Heroine of Afghanistan* (London: Bantam 2004)

Christitch, Annie, *A Word on Woman Suffrage* (London: Catholic Women's Suffrage Society n.d. (1912?))

Clark, Anna, *The Struggle for the Breeches: Gender and the Making of the British Working Class* (London: Rivers Oram 1995)

Clephane, Irene, *Towards Sex Freedom* (London: John Lane 1935)

Cleverdon, Catherine Lyle, *The Woman Suffrage Movement in Canada* (Toronto: Toronto University Press 1950)

Cobban, Alfred, *A History of Modern France*, vol. 3: *1871–1962* (London: Penguin 1970)

Condorcet, Marquis de, 'Letters from a Freeman of New Haven to a Citizen of Virginia on the Futility of Dividing the Legislative Power among Several Bodies', in Iain McLean and Fiona Hewitt, *Condorcet: Foundations of Social Choice and Political Theory* (Aldershot: Edward Elgar 1994), 292–334

Condorcet, Marquis de, 'On Giving Women the Right of Citizenship', in Iain McLean and Fiona Hewitt, *Condorcet: Foundations of Social Choice and Political Theory* (Aldershot: Edward Elgar 1994), 335–40

Coquery-Vidrovitch, Catherine, *African Women: A Modern History* (Boulder, Colo.: Westview Press 1997)

Cousins, Margaret, *The Awakening of Asian Womanhood* (Madras: Ganesh & Co. 1922)

Cowley, Philip, and Childs, Sarah, 'Too Spineless to Rebel? New Labour's Women MPs', *British Journal of Political Science* 33 (2003), 345–65

Crawford, Elizabeth, *The Women's Suffrage Movement: A Reference Guide 1866–1928* (London: Routledge 1999)

Croll, Elizabeth, *Feminism and Socialism in China* (London: Routledge 1978)

Dalarun, Jacques, 'The Clerical Gaze', in Christiane Klapisch-Zuber, *A History of Women in the West Volume Two: Silences of the Middle Ages* (Harvard, Mass.: Belknap Press 1992)

Daley, Caroline, and Nolan, Melanie, *Suffrage and Beyond: International Feminist Perspectives* (Auckland: Auckland University Press 1994)

Dalton, Hugh, *The Political Diary of Hugh Dalton 1918–40, 1945–60* (London: Jonathan Cape 1986)

Dalziel, Reawyn, 'Presenting the Enfranchisement of New Zealand Women Abroad', in Caroline Daley and Melanie Nolan (eds.), *Suffrage and Beyond: International Feminist Perspectives* (Auckland: Auckland University Press 1994), 42–64

Daw Mya Sein, 'Towards Independence in Burma: The Role of Women', *Asian Affairs* 59/3 (1972), 288–99

Denzer, LaRay, 'Gender and Decolonisation: A Study of Three Women in West African Public Life', in Andrea Cornwall, *Readings in Gender in Africa* (Indiana: Indiana University Press 2005)

Deutsch, Leo, quoted in James Harvey Robinson and Charles Beard, *Readings in Modern European History*, vol. 2 (Boston: Ginn and Co. 1909)

Devaliant, Judith, *Kate Sheppard: The Fight for Women's Votes in New Zealand* (Auckland: Penguin 2000)

Disraeli, Benjamin, *Lord Beaconsfield's Correspondence with his Sister 1832–1852* (London: John Murray 1886)

Dodd, Kathryn, *A Sylvia Pankhurst Reader* (Manchester: Manchester University Press 1993)

Dodyk, Delight D., *Education and Agitation: The Woman Suffrage Movement in New Jersey* (PhD, Rutgers University NJ 1997)

Dolphyne, Florence Abena, *The Emancipation of Women: An African Perspective* (Accra: Ghana Unversities Press 1991)

Dooley, Dolores, *Equality in Community: Sexual Equality in the Writings of William Thompson and Anna Doyle Wheeler* (Cork: Cork University Press 1996)

Dorr, Rheta Childe, *A Woman of Fifty* (New York: Funk and Wagnall 1924)

DuBois, Ellen Carol, 'The Next Generation: Harriot Stanton Blatch and Grassroots Politics', in Jean H. Baker (ed.), *Votes for Women: The Struggle for Suffrage Revisited* (Oxford: Oxford University Press 2002), 159–73

Edwards, Louise, 'Women's Suffrage in China: Challenging Scholarly Conventions', *Pacific Historical Review* 69/4 (November 2000), 617–38

Edwards, Louise, 'Tang Qunying', in *Biographical Dictionary of Chinese Women: The Twentieth Century* (Armonk, New York: M. E. Sharpe 2003)

Edwards, Louise, 'Bourgeois Women and Communist Revolutionaries? De-revolutionising the Chinese Women's Suffrage Movement', in Maja Mikula, *Women, Activism and Social Change* (Oxford: Routledge 2005)

Edwards, Louise, 'Chinese Women's Campaigns for Suffrage: Nationalism, Confucianism and political agency', in Louise Edwards and Mina Roces, *Asia: Gender, Nationalism and Democracy* (London: Routledge 2004), 59–78

Edwards, Louise, and Roces, Mina, 'Orienting the Global Women's Suffrage Movement', in Louise Edwards and Mina Roces, *Asia: Gender, Nationalism and Democracy* (London: Routledge 2004), 5–24

Elliott, Florence, *A Dictionary of Politics* (London: Penguin 1975)

Euripides, *Medea*, trans. David Kovacs (Cambridge, Mass: Harvard University Press 1994)

Evans, Richard J., *The Feminists: Women's Emancipation Movements in Europe, America and Australasia 1840–1920* (London: Croom Helm 1977)

Evdela, Efi, and Psarra, Angelika, 'Engendering "Greekness": Women's Emancipation and Irredentist Politics in Nineteenth-Century Greece', *Mediterranean Historical Review* 20/1 (June 2005), 67–99

Fagoaga, Concha, and Saavenrda, Paloma, *Clara Campoamor: La sufragista española* (Madrid: Ministerio de Cultura 1986)

Fathi, Asghar (ed.), *Women and the Family in Iran* (Lieden: E. J. Brill 1985)

Fawcett, Millicent, 'The Appeal Against Female Suffrage: A Reply', *The Nineteenth Century* 48 (July 1889), 86–96

Ferriter, Diarmaid, *The Transformation of Ireland 1900–2000* (London: Profile 2004)

Figner, Vera, *Memoirs of a Revolutionist* (London: Martin Lawrence n.d. (1927 or after))

Fitch, Suzanne Pullon, and Mandziuk, Roseann M., *Sojourner Truth as Orator: Wit, Song and Story* (Eastport, Conn.: Greenwood 1997)

Fleischmann, Ellen L., 'The Other "Awakening": The Emergence of Women's Movements in the Modern Middle East, 1900–1940', in Margaret L. Meriwether and Judith E. Tucker (eds.), *Social History of Women and Gender in the Modern Middle East* (Boulder, Colo.: Westview Press 1999), 89–134

Fleming, Sidney Howell, 'Solving the Jigsaw Puzzle: One Suffrage Story at a Time', *Annals of Wyoming* 62/1 (spring 1990), 23–72

Fletcher, Ian Christopher, *Sex and Gender: Manuscript Sources from the Public Record Office* (Marlborough: Adam Matthew 2002)

Fletcher, Ian, Mayhall, Laura E. Nym, and Levine, Philippa, *Women's Suffrage in the British Empire: Citizenship, Nation and Race* (London: Routledge 2000)

Forbes, Geraldine, *Women in Modern India* (Cambridge: Cambridge University Press 2004)

Ford, Linda, 'Alice Paul and the Politics of Nonviolent Protest', in Jean H. Baker (ed.), *Votes for Women: The Struggle for Suffrage Revisited* (Oxford: Oxford University Press 2002), 174–88

Fraser, Nicholas, and Navarro, Marysa, *Evita: The Real Lives of Eva Perón* (London: Andre Deutsch 1996)

Froissart, *Chronicles*, trans. Geoffrey Brereton (London: Penguin 1968)

Fulford, Roger, *Votes for Women: The Story of a Struggle* (London: Faber 1958)

Gabriel, Mary, *Notorious Victoria: The Life of Victoria Woodhull, Uncensored* (Chapel Hill, NC: Algonquin 1998)

Gage, Frances D., 'Sojourner Truth', *National Anti-Slavery Standard* (2 May 1863), 4

Giele, Janet Zollinger, and Smock, Audrey Chapman, *Women: Roles Status in Eight Countries* (New York: John Wiley 1977)

Gleadle, Kathryn, *Borderline Citizens: Women, Gender and Political Culture in Britain 1815–1867* (Oxford: Oxford University Press 2009)

Glennie, J. S. Stuart, 'The Proposed Subjection of Men', *Fortnightly Review* 45 (April 1889), 567–78

Goldsmith, Barbara, *Other Powers: The Age of Suffrage, Spiritualism and the Scadalous Victoria Woodhull* (London: Granta 1998)

Gordon, Lyndall, *Vindication: A Life of Mary Wollstonecraft.* (London: Little, Brown 2005)

Graves, Robert, *The Greek Myths*, vol. 1. (London: Penguin 1966)

Griffith, William (anonymously), *Emenes: Being a Collection of Papers written for the purpose of exhibiting some of the more prominent errors and omissions of the constitution of New Jersey* (Trenton 1799)

Grimes, A. P., *The Puritan Ethic and Woman Suffrage* (Oxford: Oxford University Press 1967)

Grimshaw, Patricia, *Women's Suffrage in New Zealand* (Auckland: Auckland University Press 1987)

Gripenberg, Alexander, 'The Great Victory in Finland', *The Englishwoman's Review* (16 July 1906), 155–7

Gugler, Joseph, 'The Second Sex in Town', *Canadian Journal of African Studies* 6/2 (1972), 289–301

Gundle, Stephen, *Bellissima: Feminine Beauty and the Idea of Italy* (New Haven: Yale University Press 2007)

Guyer, Jane I., 'Women in the Rural Economy: Contemporary Variations', in Margaret Jean Hay and Sharon Stichter, *African Women South of the Sahara* (London: Longman 1984)

Hahner, June E., 'The Nineteenth-Century Feminist Press and Women's Rights in Brazil', in Asunción Lavrin, *Latin American Women* (Westport, Conn.: Greenwood Press 1978)

Hahner, June E., *Emancipating the Female Sex: The Struggle for Women's Rights in Brazil 1850–1940* (Durham NC: Duke University Press 1990)

Hannam, June, 'International Dimensions of Women's Suffrage: "at the crossroads of several interlocking identities"', *Women's History Review* 14/3–4 (2005), 543–60

Hannam, June, Auchterlonie, Mitzi, and Holden, Katherine, *International Encyclopaedia of Women's Suffrage* (Santa Barbara, Calif.: ABC-CLIO 2000)

Hare, Lloyd C. M., *The Greatest American Woman: Lucretia Mott* (New York: American Historical Society 1937)

Harrison, Brian, *Separate Spheres: The Opposition to Women's Suffrage in Britain* (London: Croom Helm 1978)

Hatem, Mervat, 'Modernisation, the State and the Family in Middle East Women's Studies', in Margaret L. Meriwether and Judith E. Tucker (eds.), *Social History of Women and Gender in the Modern Middle East* (Boulder, Colo.: Westview Press 1999), 63–84

Hause, Steven C., and Kenney, Anne R., 'The Development of the Catholic Women's Suffrage Movement in France, 1896–1922', *Catholic Historical Review* 67/1 (January 1981), 11–30

Hebard, Grace Raymond, *The History and Government of Wyoming* (San Francisco: C. F. Weber 1919)

Hebard, Grace Raymond, *How Woman Suffrage Came to Wyoming* (pamphlet, Laramie: University of Wyoming 1920)

Hill, Christopher, *The World Turned Upside Down: Radical Ideas During the English Revolution* (London: Penguin 1972)

Hodgson, Dorothy L., and McCurdy, Sheryl A., *'Wicked', Women and the Reconfiguration of Gender in Africa* (Oxford: James Curry 2001)

Hollis, Patricia, *Women in Public: The Women's Movement 1850–1900* (London: Allen and Unwin, 1979)

Holton, Sandra, *Feminism and Democracy: Women's Suffrage and Reform Politics in Britain 1900–1918* (Cambridge: Cambridge University Press 1986)

Holton, Sandra Stanley, *Suffrage Days: Stories from the Women's Suffrage Movement* (London: Routledge 1996)

Horne, E. A., *The Political System of British India* (London: Oxford University Press 1922)

Hossain, Rokeya Sakhawat, *Sultana's Dream: A Feminist Utopia*, ed. Roushan Jahan (New York: Feminist Press 1988)

Howard, Judith Jeffrey, 'The Civil Code of 1865 and the Origins of the Feminist Movement in Italy', in Betty Boyd Caroli, Robert F. Harney, and Lydio F. Tomasi, *The Italian Immigrant Woman in North America* (Toronto: Multicultural History Society of Ontario 1978), 14–20

Htun, Mala N., and Jones, Mark P., 'Engendering the Right to Participate in Decision-Making: Electoral Quotas and Women's Leadership in Latin America', in Nikki Craske and Maxine Molyneux, *Gender and the Politics of Rights and Democracy in Latin America* (London: Palgrave 2002)

Hufton, Olwen, *The Prospect Before Her: A History of Women in Western Europe, Volume One 1500–1800* (London: Fontana 1997)

Hurtado, Osvaldo, *Political Power in Ecuador* (Albuquerque NM: University of New Mexico Press 1977)

Iliffe, John, *Africans: The History of a Continent* (Cambridge: Cambridge University Press 1995)

Iliffe, John, *Honour in African History* (Cambridge: Cambridge University Press 2005)

Jacobs, Aletta, *Memories: My Life as an International Leader in Health, Suffrage and Peace* (New York: Feminist Press 1996)

Jahan, Roushan, 'Rokeya: An Introduction to Her Life', in Rokeya Sakhawat Hossain, *Sultana's Dream: A Feminist Utopia*, ed. Roushan Jahan (New York: Feminist Press 1988), 37–57

Jayawardena, Kumari, *Feminism and Nationalism in the Third World* (London: Zed Books 1986)

Jesch, Judith, *Women in the Viking Age* (Woodbridge: Boydell Press 1991)

Johnson-Odim, Cheryl, and Mba, Nina Emma, *For Women and the Nation: Funmilayo Ransome-Kuti of Nigeria* (Chicago: University of Illinois Press 1997)

Johnston, Johanna, *Mrs Satan: The Incredible Story of Victoria Woodhull* (London: Macmillan 1967)

Just, Roger, *Women in Athenian Law and Life* (London: Routledge, 1989)

Kalaw, Pura Villanueva, *How the Filipina Got the Vote* (Manila: n.p. 1952)

Kamm, Josephine, *John Stuart Mill in Love* (London: Gordon and Cremonosi 1977)

Karlsson, Gunnar, *Iceland's 1100 Years* (London: Hurst 2000)

Kaur, Manmohan, *The Role of Women in the Freedom Movement 1857–1947* (New Delhi: Sterling 1968)

Kehaya, Kalliope A., 'The Orient', in Theodore Stanton, *The Woman Question in Europe* (London: Samson Low 1884)

Kemp, Amanda, Madlala, Nozizwe, Moodley, Asha, and Salo, Elaine, 'The Dawn of a New Day: Redefining South African Feminism', in Amrita Basu (ed.), *The Challenge of Local Feminisms: Women's Movements in Global Perspective* (Boulder, Colo.: Westview Press 1995), 131–62

Keyssar, Alexander, *The Right to Vote: The Contested History of Democracy in the United States* (New York: Basic Books 2000)

Kinross, Patrick, *Atatürk: The Rebirth of a Nation* (London: Phoenix Press 2003)

Kitto, H. D. F., *The Greeks* (London: Penguin, 1951)

Kollontai, Alexandra, *Selected Articles and Speeches* (New York: International Publishers 1984)

Korppi-Tommola, Aura, 'Fighting Together for Freedom: Nationalism, Socialism, Feminism and Women's Suffrage in Finland 1906', *Scandinavian Journal of History* 15/3 (1990), 181–91

Kraditor, Aileen S., *The Ideas of the Woman Suffrage Movement 1890–1920* (New York: Columbia University Press 1965)

Larson, T. A., 'Petticoats at the Polls: Woman Suffrage in Territorial Wyoming', *Pacific Northwest Quarterly* 44/2 (April 1953), 74–9

Larson, T. A., *History of Wyoming* (Lincoln: University of Nebraska Press 1978)

Lavrin, Asunción, *Latin American Women* (Westport, Conn.: Greenwood Press 1978)

Lavrin, Asunción, *Women, Feminism and Social Change in Argentina, Chile and Uruguay* (Lincoln: University of Nebraska Press 1995)

Lavrin, Asunción, 'Suffrage in Latin America: Arguing A Difficult Cause', in Caroline Daley and Melanie Nolan, *Suffrage and Beyond: International Feminist Perspectives* (Auckland: Auckland University Press 1994), 184–209

Lecky, William, *History of European Morals*, vol. 2 (London: Longmans 1869)

Levy, Darline Gay, Applewhite, Harriet Branson, and Johnson, Mary Durham, *Women in Revolutionary Paris 1789–1795* (Chicago: University of Illinois Press 1979)

Linton, Eliza Lynn, 'The Threatened Abdication of Man', *The National Review* 77 (July 1889), 577–92

Little, Cynthia Jeffries, 'Moral Reform and Feminism: A Case Study', *Journal of Interamerican Studies and World Affairs* 17/4 (November 1975), 386–97

Little, Cynthia Jeffries, 'Education, philanthropy and feminism: components of Argentine womanhood, 1860–1926', in Asunción Lavrin, *Latin American Women* (Westport, Conn.: Greenwood Press 1978), 235–53

Lloyd George, D., *War Memoirs*, vol. 2 (London: Odhams 1938)

Lloyd, Trevor, *Suffragettes International: The World-wide Campaign for Women's Rights* (London: Library of the Twentieth Century 1971)

Lovell-Smith, Margaret (ed.), *The Woman Question: Writings by the Women who Won the Vote* (Auckland: New Women's Press 1992)

Lovett, William, *The Life and Struggles of William Lovett in his pursuit of Bread, Knowledge and Freedom* (London: Trübner 1876)

Lowry, Donal, 'Making fresh Britains across the seas', in Ian Fletcher, Laura E. Nym Mayhall, and Philippa Levine, *Women's Suffrage in the British Empire: Citizenship, Nation and Race* (London: Routledge 2000), 175–90

Lunardini, Christine A., *From Equal Suffrage to Equal Rights: Alice Paul and the National Woman's Party 1910–1928* (New York: New York University Press 1986)

Mabee, Carlton, and Newhouse, Susan Mabee, *Sojourner Truth: Slave, Prophet, Legend* (New York: New York University Press 1993)

Macdermott, Isabel Keith, *A Significant Pan-American Conference* (Washington DC: GPO 1922)

Macías, Anna, 'Felipe Carillo Puerto and women's liberation in Mexico', in Asunción Lavrin, *Latin American Women* (Westport, Conn.: Greenwood Press 1978), 287–301

Mackenzie, W. J. M., *Free Elections: An Elementary Textbook* (London: George Allen and Unwin 1958)

MacMaster, Neil, *Burning the Veil: The Algerian War and the 'Emancipation' of Muslim Women 1954–1962* (Manchester: Manchester University Press, 2012)

Magnus, Philip, *Gladstone: A Biography* (London: John Murray 1960)

Magnusson, Magnus, and Pálsson, Herman, *Laxdaela Saga* (London: Penguin 1969)

Malmberg, Aino, *Woman Suffrage in Finland* (London: Women's Freedom League, n.d., prob. 1913)

Mamdani, Mahmood, *Citizen and Subject: Contemporary Africa and the Legacy of Late Colonialism* (Kampala: Fountain Publishers 1996), 24

Mansutti, Elizabeth, *Mary Lee 1821–1909* (Adelaide: Openbook *c*.1994)

Margolis, Diane Rothbard, 'Women's Movements Around the World: Cross-Cultural Comparisons', *Gender and Society* 7/3 (September 1993), 379–99

Markoff, John, 'Margins, Centres, and Democracy: The Paradigmatic History of Women's Suffrage', *Signs: Journal of Women in Culture and Society* 29/1 (2003), 109

Mason, Francis M., 'The Newer Eve: The Catholic Women's Suffrage Society in England, 1911–1923', *Catholic Historical Review* 72/4 (October 1986), 620–38

Massie, Michael A., 'Reform is Where You Find It: The Roots of Woman Suffrage in Wyoming', *Annals of Wyoming* 62/1 (Spring 1990), 2–21

Mba, Nina Emma, *Nigerian Women Mobilised: Women's Political Activity in Southern Nigeria 1900–1965* (Berkeley, Calif.: Institute of International Studies 1982)

McCormick, Richard P., *The History of Voting in New Jersey: A Study of the Development of Election Machinery 1664–1911* (New Brunswick: Rutgers University Press 1953)

McLean, Iain, and Hewitt, Fiona, *Condorcet: Foundations of Social Choice and Political Theory* (Aldershot: Edward Elgar 1994)

McLintock, A. H., *An Encyclopaedia of New Zealand* (Wellington: R. E. Owen 1966)

McMillan, James F., *Housewife or Harlot: The Place of Women in French Society 1870–1940* (Brighton: Harvester Press 1981)

McMillan, James F., *France and Women 1789–1914: Gender, Society and Politics* (London: Routledge 2000)

Mead, Rebecca J., *How the West Was Won: Woman Suffrage in the Western United States 1869–1914* (New York: New York University Press 2004)

Meriwether, Margaret L., and Tucker, Judith E. (eds.), *Social History of Women and Gender in the Modern Middle East* (Boulder, Colo.: Westview Press 1999)

Mernissi, Fatima, *Beyond the Veil: Male–Female Dynamics in a Modern Muslim Society* (New York: John Wiley and Sons 1975)

Mernissi, Fatima, *Women and Islam: An Historical and Theological Enquiry* (Oxford: Basil Blackwell 1991)

Mernissi, Fatima, *Women in the Muslim Unconscious* (New York: Pergamon 1984)

Meyer, Donald, *Sex and Power: The Rise of Women in America, Russia, Sweden and Italy* (Middletown, Conn.: Wesleyan University Press 1987)

Meyers, Madeleine, *Forward into Light: The Struggle for Woman's Suffrage* (Carlisle, Mass.: Discovery Enterprises 1994)

Micaud, C. A., 'Launching the Fourth French Republic', *Journal of Politics* 8/3 (August 1946), 292–307

Mill, James, *The History of British India*, vol. 1 bk. 2 (London: James Madden 1840)

Mill, John Stuart (but prob. Harriet Taylor), 'The Enfranchisement of Women', *Westminster Review* 55 (April–July 1851), 289–311

Mill, John Stuart, *Autobiography* (London: Oxford University Press 1969)

Mill, John Stuart, *The Subjection of Women* (Ware, Herts.: Wordsworth 1996)

Miller, Francesca, 'The International Relations of Women of the Americas 1890–1928', *The Americas* 43/2 (October 1986), 171–82

Miller, Francesca, *Latin American Women and the Search for Social Justice* (Hanover: University Press of New England 1991)

Minai, Naila, *Women in Islam: Tradition and Transition in the Middle East* (London: John Murray 1981)

Miyamoto Ken Ito, 'Noe and the Bluestockings', *Japan Interpreter* 10 (Autumn 1975), 192–204

Mody, Nawaz B., *Women in India's Freedom Struggle* (Bombay: Allied Publishers 2000)

Molony, Barbara, 'Women's Rights, Feminism and Suffragism in Japan 1870–1925', *Pacific Historical Review* 69/4 (November 2000), 639–61

Molony, Barbara, 'Citizenship and Suffrage in Interwar Japan', in Louise Edwards and Mina Roces, *Asia: Gender, Nationalism and Democracy* (London: Routledge 2004), 127–51

Molyneux, Maxine, *Women's Emancipation under Socialism: A Model for the Third World?* (Brighton, Sussex: IDS Puiblications 1981)

Molyneux, Maxine, *Women's Movements in International Perspective: Latin America and Beyond* (London: Palgrave 2001)

Monypenny, W. F., and Buckle, G. E., *The Life of Benjamin Disraeli*, vol. 1 (London: John Murray 1929)

Moore, Carlos, *Fela, Fela, This bitch of a life* (London: Alison and Busby 1982)

Morgan, Robin (ed.), *Sisterhood is Global: International Women's Movement Anthology* (London: Penguin 1984)

Morton, Ward M., *Woman Suffrage in Mexico* (Gainsville Fla.: University of Florida Press 1962)

Mott, Lucretia, *Slavery and 'the woman question': Lucretia Mott's diary of her visit to Great Britain to Attend the World's Anti-Slavery Convention of 1840*, ed. Frederick Tolles (Pennsylvania and London: Friends Historical Association and Friends Historical Society 1952)

Mumtaz, Khawar, and Shaheed, Farida, *Women of Pakistan: Two Steps Forward, One Step Back?* (London: Zed Books 1987)

Muravyeva, Marianna, 'Anna Pavlovna Filosova', in Francisca De Haan et al., *A Biographical Dictionary of Women's Movements and Feminisms: Central, Eastern and South Eastern Europe, 19th and 20th Centuries* (Budapest: Central European University Press 2006)

Murray, A. T., *Demosthenes' Private Orations*, vol. 3 (Cambridge, Mass.: Heinemann 1939)

Murray, Patricia, 'Ichikawa Fusae and the Lonely Red Carpet', *Japan Interpreter* 10 (autumn 1975), 171–89

Nance, Christopher, 'Paving the Way: The Women's Suffrage Movement in South Australia', *Journal of the Royal Australian Historical Society* 63/3 (December 1979), 188–200

Nelson, Cynthia, 'Biography and Women's History: On Interpreting Doria Shafik', in Nikki R. Keddie and Beth Baron, *Women in Middle Eastern History: Shifting Boundaries in Sex and Gender* (New Haven, Conn.: Yale University Press 1991)

Nester, W. R., 'Japanese Women: Still Three Steps Behind', *Women's Studies* 21 (1992), 457–79

Nolte, Sharon H., 'Women's Rights and Society's Needs: Japan's 1931 Suffrage Bill', *Comparative Studies in Society and History* 28/4 (October 1986), 690–714

O'Barr, Jean, 'African Women in Politics', in Margaret Jean Hay and Sharon Stichter, *African Women South of the Sahara* (London: Longman 1984), 140–54

O'Neill, William, *Everyone Was Brave: The Rise and Fall of Feminism in America* (Chicago: Quadrangle 1969)

Oduol, Wilhelmina, and Kabira, Wanjiku Mukabi, 'The Mother of Warriors and Her Daughters: The Women's Movement in Kenya', in Amrita Basu (ed.), *The Challenge of Local Feminisms: Women's Movements in Global Perspective* (Boulder, Colo.: Westview Press 1995), 187–208

Offen, Karen, *European Feminisms 1700–1950: A Political History* (Stanford, Calif.: Stanford University Press 2000)

Offen, Karen, 'Women, Citizenship and Suffrage with a French Twist 1789–1993', in Caroline Daley and Melanie Nolan, *Suffrage and Beyond: International Feminist Perspectives* (Auckland: Auckland University Press 1994), 157–70

Oldfield, Audrey, *Woman Suffrage in Australia: A Gift or a Struggle?* (Cambridge: Cambridge University Press 1992)

Onayemi, Folake, 'Finding a Place: Women's Struggle for Political Authority in Classical and Nigerian Societies', *Women's History Review*, 16/3 (July 2007), 297–309

Painter, Nell Irwin, *Sojourner Truth: A Life, A Symbol* (New York: Norton, 1996)

Pankhurst, Christabel, *The Great Scourge and How To End It* (London n.p. 1913)

Pankhurst, Christabel, *Unshackled: The Story of How We Won the Vote* (London: Hutchinson 1959)

Pankhurst, Emmeline, *The Importance of the Vote* (London: Women's Press 1913)

Pankhurst, Emmeline, *My Own Story* (London: Eveleigh Nash 1914)

Pankhurst, Richard A., 'Anna Wheeler: A Pioneer Socialist and Feminist', *The Political Quarterly* 25/2 (1954), 132–43

Pankhurst, Richard, Introduction to William Thompson, *Appeal of One Half of the Human Race* (London: Virago 1983), xvi

Pankhurst, Sylvia, *The Life of Emmeline Pankhurst* (London: T. Werner Laurie 1935)

Pankhurst, Sylvia, *The Suffragette Movement* (London: Virago 1977)

Papineau, Hélène (ed.), *A History of the Vote in Canada* (Ottawa: Ministry of Public Works and Government Services 1997)

Paranjape, Makarand (ed.), *Sarojini Naidu: Selected Poetry and Prose* (Delhi: Harper Collins 1993)

Pateman, Carole, 'Three Questions About Womanhood Suffrage', in Caroline Daley and Melanie Nolan, *Suffrage and Beyond: International Feminist Perspectives* (Auckland: Auckland University Press 1994), 331–48

Paulson, Ross Evans, *Women's Suffrage and Prohibition: A Comparative Study of Equality and Social Control* (Glenview, Ill.: Scott, Foresman and Co. 1973)

Pederson, Susan, 'National Bodies, Unspeakable Acts: The Sexual Politics of Colonial Policy-making', *Journal of Modern History* 63/4 (1991), 647–80

Peron, Eva, 'From the Sublime to the Ridiculous', in *Evita by Evita* (New York: Proteus 1953)

Pethick-Lawrence, Emmeline, *My Part in a Changing World* (London: Victor Gollancz 1938)

Pethick-Lawrence, Frederick, *Fate Has Been Kind* (London: Hutchinson 1942)

Pharr, Susan J., *Political Women in Japan: The Search for a Place in Political Life* (Berkeley: University of California Press 1981)

Pharr Susan J., 'The Politics of Women's Rights', in Robert E. Ward and Sakamoto Yoshikazu, *Democratising Japan: The Allied Occupation* (Honolulu: University of Hawaii Press 1987), 221–52

Philbrook, Mary, 'Woman's Suffrage in New Jersey Prior to 1807', *Proceedings of the New Jersey Historical Society*, 57 (1939), 870–98

Pole, J. R., 'The Suffrage in New Jersey 1790–1807', *Proceedings of the New Jersey Historical Society* 71 (1953), 39–61

Pomeroy, Sarah B., *Goddesses, Whores, Wives and Slaves: Women in Classical Antiquity* (New York: Dorset Press 1975)

Porter, Cathy, *Fathers and Daughters: Russian Women in Revolution* (London: Virago 1976)

Pugh, Martin, 'Politicians and the Women's Vote 1914–1918', *History* 59 (1977), 358–74

Pugh, Martin, *The Pankhursts* (London: Penguin 2001)

Purvis, June, *Emmeline Pankhurst* (London: Routledge 2002)

Pushkareva, Natalia, *Women in Russian History: From the Tenth to the Twentieth Century* (Armonk NY: M. E. Sharp 1997)

Raeburn, Antonia, *The Militant Suffragettes* (London: Michael Joseph 1973)

Ramelson, Marion, *The Petticoat Rebellion* (London: Lawrence and Wishart 1967)

Ramirez, Francisco O., Soysal, Yasemin, and Shanahan, Suzanne, 'The Changing Logic of Political Citizenship: Cross-national Acquisition of Women's Suffrage Rights, 1890–1990', *American Sociological Review*, 62 (October 1997), 735–45

Ray, Bharati, 'The Freedom Movement and Feminist Consciousness', in Bharati Ray (ed.), *From the Seams of History: Essays on Indian Women* (Delhi: Oxford University Press, 1995)

Ray, Bharati, *Early Feminists of Colonial India* (Delhi: Oxford University Press 2002)

Read, Anthony, and Fisher, David, *The Proudest Day: India's Long Road to Independence* (London: Cape 1997)

Reed, Thomas Harrison, *Government and Politics of Belgium* (London: George G. Harrap 1924)

Reeves, William Pember, *State Experiments in Australia and New Zealand*, vol. 1 (London: Grant Richards 1902)

Riall, Lucy, *Garibaldi: Invention of a Hero* (New Haven: Yale University Press 2007)

Robb, Peter, *A History of India* (Basingstoke: Palgrave 2002)

Robinson, James Harvey, and Beard, Charles, *Readings in Modern European History*, vol. 2 (Boston: Ginn and Co. 1909)

Roces, Mina, 'Is the Suffragist an American Colonial Construct: Defining "The Filipino Woman" in Colonial Philippines', in Louise Edwards and Mina Roces (eds.), *Asia: Gender, Nationalism and Democracy* (London: Routledge 2004), 24–59

Roces, Mina C., 'Women in Philippine Politics and Society', in Hazel M. McFerson, *Mixed Blessings: The Impact of the American Colonial Experience on Politics and Society in the Philippines* (Westport, Conn.: Greenwood Press 2002), 159–90

Rodgers, Daniel T., *Atlantic Crossings: Social Politics in a Progressive Age* (Cambridge Mass.: Harvard University Press 1998)

Romero, Patricia W. E., *Sylvia Pankhurst: Portrait of a Radical* (New Haven: Yale University Press 1990)

Rönnbäck, Josefin, 'The Struggle for Women's Franchise—a Menage à Trois of Women, Men and State', posted on the Women's History Collections site by Gothenburg University Library: <http://www.ub.gu.se/kvinn/portaler/rostratt/historik/>

Roudinesco, Elisabeth, *Théroigne de Méricourt: Une femme mélancolique sous la révolution* (Paris: Seuil 1989)

Rover, Constance, *Women's Suffrage and Party Politics in Britain* (London: Routledge 1967)

Rover, Constance, *Love, Morals and the Feminists* (London: Routledge 1969)

Rubinstein, David, *A Different World for Women: The Life of Millicent Garrett Fawcett* (London: Harvester Wheatsheaf 1991)

Rupp, Leila J., *Worlds of Women: The Making of an International Women's Movement* (Princeton NJ: Princeton University Press 1997)

Russell, Bertrand, *German Social Democracy* (London: Longmans 1896)

Ruthchild, Rochelle Goldberg, 'Women's Suffrage and Revolution in the Russian Empire, 1905–1917', *Aspasia: International Yearbook of Central, Eastern and Southeastern European Women's and Gender History* 1 (March 2007), 1–35

Sadleir, Michael, *Bulwer and his Wife: A Panorama 1803–1836* (London: Constable 1933)

Sanasarian, Eliz, 'Characteristics of Women's Movement in Iran', in Asghar Fathi (ed.), *Women and the Family in Iran* (Lieden: E. J. Brill 1985), 86–106

Santiago, Lilia Quindoza, 'Rebirthing *Babaye*: The Women's Movement in the Philippines', in Amrita Basu (ed.), *The Challenge of Local Feminisms: Women's Movements in Global Perspective* (Boulder, Colo.: Westview Press 1995), 110–28

Schram, Stuart, *Mao Tse-Tung* (London: Penguin 1966)

Schram, Stuart, *The Political Thought of Mao Tse-tung* (London: Penguin 1969)

Scott, Dick, *Years of the Pooh-Bah: A History of the Cook Islands* (Rarotonga: CITC 1991)

Scott, Joan Wallach, 'French Feminists and the Rights of "Man", Olympe de Gouge's Declarations', *History Workshop Journal* 28 (1989), 1–21

Scully, Pamela, 'White Maternity and Black Infancy: The rhetoric of race in the South African Women's Suffrage Movement, 1895–1930', in Ian Fletcher, Laura E. Nym Mayhall, and Philippa Levine, *Women's Suffrage in the British Empire: Citizenship, Nation and Race* (London: Routledge 2000), 68–84

Sengupta, Padmini, *Sarojini Naidu: A Biography* (London: Asia Publishing 1966)

Sewall, May Wright, *The World's Congress of Representative Women*, vol. 1 (Chicago: Rand, McNally 1894)

Shaarawi, Huda, *Harem Years: The Memoirs of an Egyptian Feminist* (London: Virago 1986)

Shaplen, Robert, *Free Love and Heavenly Sinners* (London: Andre Deutsch 1956)

Shephard, Todd, *The Invention of Decolonisation: The Algerian War and the Remaking of France* (Ithaca NY: Cornell University Press 2006)

Shinn, Henry C., 'An Early New Jersey Poll List', *Pennsylvania Magazine of History and Biography* 44 (1920), 77–81

Sigourney, Lydia, 'Woman's Patriotism', in *Ladies Wreath: A Magazine Devoted to Literature, Industry and Religion* (May 1846)

Simola, Raisa, 'The Construction of a Nigerian Nationalist and Feminist, Funmilayo Ransome-Kuti', *Nordic Journal of African Studies* 8/1 (1999), 94–116

Sinha, Mrinalini, 'Suffragism and Internationalism: The Enfranchisement of British and Indian Women under an Imperial State', in Ian Fletcher, Laura E. Nym Mayhall, and Philippa Levine, *Women's Suffrage in the British Empire: Citizenship, Nation and Race* (London: Routledge 2000), 224–40

Smith, Harold, *The British Women's Suffrage Campaign 1866–1928* (Harlow: Pearson Longman 2007)

Smith, Paul, *Feminism and the Third Republic: Women's Political and Civil Rights in France 1918–1945* (Oxford: Clarendon Press 1996)

Smith, T. E., *Elections in Developing Countries: A Study of electoral procedures used in tropical Africa, South-East Asia and the British Caribbean* (London: Macmillan 1960)

Smock, Audrey Chapman, 'Ghana: From Autonomy to Subordination', in Janet Zollinger Giele and Audrey Chapman Smock, *Women: Roles and Status in Eight Countries* (New York: John Wiley 1977), 173–216

Smock, Audrey Chapman and Youssef, Nadia Haggag, 'Egypt: From Seclusion to Limited Participation', in Janet Zollinger Giele and Audrey Chapman Smock, *Women: Roles Status in Eight Countries* (New York: John Wiley 1977), 34–79

Soyinka, Wole, *Aké: The Years of Childhood* (London: Rex Collings 1981)

Stanton, Elizabeth Cady, *Eighty Years and More: Reminiscences* (London: T. Fisher Unwin 1898)

Stanton, Theodore, *The Woman Question in Europe* (London: Sampson Low 1884)

Steedman, Carolyn, *Strange Dislocations: Childhood and the Idea of Human Interiority 1780–1930* (Cambridge, Mass.: Harvard University Press 1995)

Stites, Richard, 'Women's Liberation Movements in Russia 1900–1930', *Canadian-American Slavik Studies* 7/4 (winter 1973), 460–74

Stites, Richard, *The Women's Liberation Movement in Russia: Feminism, Nihilism and Bolshevism 1860–1930* (Princeton NJ: Princeton University Press 1990)

Strachey, Ray, *'The Cause', A Short History of the Women's Movement in Britain* (London: G. Bell 1928)

Stratton, Fred D., *Early History of South Pass City, Wyoming and How Women First Received the Right to Vote and Hold Public Office* (Cheyenne, Wyo.: 1950)

Stratton, Joanna L., *Pioneer Women: Voices from the Kansas Frontier* (New York: Simon and Schuster 1981)

Studlar, D.T., and McAllister, I., 'Does a Critical Mass Exist? A Comparative Analysis of Women's Legislative Representation since 1950', *European Journal of Political Research* 4/2 (March 2002), 233–53

Sulkunen, Irma, 'The Women's Movement', in M. Engman and D. Kirby, *Finland: People, Nation, State* (London: Hurst 1989), 178–91

Summers, Anne, *Damned Whores and God's Police* (Camberwell, Victoria, Aus.: Penguin 2002)

Taylor, Barbara, *Eve and the New Jerusalem* (London: Virago 1983)

Terborg-Penn, Rosalyn, *African American Women in the Struggle for the Vote, 1850–1920* (Bloomington: Indiana University Press 1998)

Thomas, Lynn M., *Politics of the Womb: Women, Reproduction and the State in Kenya* (Berkeley: University of California Press 2003)

Thompson, E. P., *The Making of the English Working Class* (London: Penguin 1978)

Thompson, William, *'Appeal of one half of the human race, women etc,'* (Cork: Cork University Press 1997)

Thönnessen, Werner, *The Emancipation of Women: The Rise and Decline of the Women's Movement in German Social Democracy 1863–1933* (Frankfurt am Main: Pluto 1969)

Tidrick, Kathryn, *Gandhi: A Political and Spiritual Life* (London: I.B. Tauris 2006)

Tomalin, Claire, *The Life and Death of Mary Wollstonecraft.* (London: Weidenfeld and Nicolson 1974)

Trevelyan, George Macaulay, *The Life of John Bright* (London: Constable 1913)

Trevor-Roper, H. R., *Hitler's Table-Talk 1941–1944: His Private Conversations* (London: Phoenix 2000)

Vatandoust, Gholam-Reza, 'The Status of Iranian Women During the Pahlavi Revolution', in Asghar Fathi (ed.), *Women and the Family in Iran* (Lieden: E. J. Brill 1985), 107–30

Vavich, Dee Ann, 'The Japanese Woman's Movement: Ichikawa Fusae: A Pioneer in Woman's Suffrage', *Monumenta Nipponica* 22/3–4 (1967), 401–36

Vervenioti, Tasoula, 'The Adventure of Women's Suffrage in Greece', in Claire Duchen and Irene Bandhauer-Schöffmann, *When the War Was Over: Women, War and Peace in Europe 1940–1956* (London: Continuum 2000)

Vidal-Naquet, Pierre, 'Esclavage et Gynécocratie dans la Tradition, et Mythe L'Utopie', in *Recherches sur les Structures Sociales dans l'Antiquité Classique* (Paris: Editions du Centre National de la Recherche Scientifique 1970)

Voris, Jacqueline Van, *Carrie Chapman Catt: A Public Life* (New York: The Feminist Press 1987)

Vreede-De Stuers, Cora, *The Indonesian Woman: Struggles and Achievements* (The Hague, Holland: Mouton and Co. 1960)

Wade, John, *The Extraordinary Black Book: An exposition etc* (London: Effingham Wilson 1831)

Walker, Cherryl, *The Women's Suffrage Movement in South Africa* (Cape Town: Centre for African Studies 1979)

Walker, Cherryl, *Women and Gender in Southern Africa to 1945* (Cape Town: David Philip 1990)

Ward, Margaret, *Hannah Sheehy Skeffington: A Life* (Dublin: Attic 1997)

Webb, Walter Prescott, *The Great Plains* (Boston: Gin and Company 1931)

Wei Tao-ming (Soumay Tcheng), *My Revolutionary Years* (New York: Scribners 1943)

Whitehead, William A., 'A Brief Statement of the Facts Connected with the Origin, Practice and Prohibition of Female Suffrage in New Jersey', *Proceedings of the New Jersey Historical Society* 8 (1858), 101–5

Whittick, Arnold, *Woman into Citizen: The Word Movement Towards the Emancipation of Women in the Twentieth Century* (London: Athenaeum 1979)

Wiener, Joel H., *Radicalism and Freethought in Nineteenth-Century Britain* (London: Greenwood Press 1983)

Wipper, Audrey, 'Equal Rights for Women in Kenya?', *Journal of Modern African Studies* 9/3 (1971), 429–42

Witke, Roxane, 'Mao Tse-tung, Woman and Suicide in the May Fourth Era', *China Quarterly* 3/31 (1967), 128–47

Wollstonecraft, Mary, *Vindication of the Rights of Woman* (London: Penguin 1985)

Wollstonecraft, Mary, *A Historical and Moral View of the French Revolution*, ed. Janet Todd and Marilyn Butler (London: Pickering 1989)

Yeo, Eileen Janes (ed.), *Mary Wollstonecraft and 200 Years of Feminisms* (London: Rivers Oram 1997)

Young, Norwood, 'The Truth About Female Suffrage in New Zealand', *Westminster Review* 42/6 (December 1894), 666–72

Yue Daiyun and Li Jin, 'Women's Life in New China', in Barbara J. Nelson and Najma Chowdhury, *Women and Politics Worldwide* (New Haven: Yale University Press 1994)

Yukiko Matsukawa and Kaoru Tachi, 'Women's Suffrage and Gender politics in Japan', in Caroline Daley and Melanie Nolan, *Suffrage and Beyond: International Feminist Perspectives* (Auckland: Auckland University Press 1994), 171–83

Zimmern, Alice, *Women's Suffrage in Many Lands* (London: Woman Citizen Publishing Society 1909)

Index